W9-BZX-960

Interaction Design for
3D User Interfaces

The World of Modern Input Devices for Research,
Applications, and Game Development

Interaction Design for
3D User Interfaces
The World of Modern Input Devices for Research, Applications, and Game Development

Francisco R. Ortega
Florida International University
Miami, Florida, USA

Naphtali Rishe
Florida International University
Miami, Florida, USA

Fatemeh Abyarjoo
Florida International University
Miami, Florida, USA

Malek Adjouadi
Florida International University
Miami, Florida, USA

Armando Barreto
Florida International University
Miami, Florida, USA

CRC Press
Taylor & Francis Group
Boca Raton London New York

CRC Press is an imprint of the
Taylor & Francis Group, an **informa** business
AN A K PETERS BOOK

MIX
Paper from
responsible sources
FSC
www.fsc.org   FSC® C014174

CRC Press
Taylor & Francis Group
6000 Broken Sound Parkway NW, Suite 300
Boca Raton, FL 33487-2742

© 2016 by Taylor & Francis Group, LLC
CRC Press is an imprint of Taylor & Francis Group, an Informa business

No claim to original U.S. Government works

Printed on acid-free paper
Version Date: 20151207

International Standard Book Number-13: 978-1-4822-1694-3 (Hardback)

Dedication

To my wife Luz and my baby daughter Sofia Alejandra. This is also dedicated to my mom and dad, sisters, brothers-in-law, nieces, and nephews. Y para la mejor Abuela, mama Aida.
–Francisco

To my parents, my grandparents, and my sisters.
–Fatemeh

To my parents and siblings.
–Armando

To my spouse Tajana with love.
–Naphtali

To my family.
–Malek

Contents

Author Biographies   xix

List of Contributors   xxiii

Foreword   xxv

Preface   xxvii
  Why This Book? xxviii
  What Is in the Book? xxix
  Conferences and Journals xxxii
  Natural User Interfaces? xxxiii
  Other Books xxxiv
  Looking Forward xxxv
  Acknowledgment of Support xxxv
  About the Images xxxvi
  Personal Acknowledgment xxxvi

Abbreviations   xxxix

I   Theory   1

1   Introduction   3
  1.1   The Vision   4
  1.2   Human–Computer Interaction   5
      1.2.1   Usability   6
      1.2.2   The Sketchpad   8
      1.2.3   The Mouse   8
      1.2.4   The Light Pen and the Computer Mouse 10
      1.2.5   Graphical User Interfaces and WIMP 12
      1.2.6   3D User Interfaces 13
  1.3   Definitions 15
  Further Reading 17

2 Input: Interfaces and Devices   **19**
  2.1   Introduction 19
  2.2   Input Technologies 19
       2.2.1   Transfer Function 22
       2.2.2   Direct-Input Devices 23
       2.2.3   Input Device States 24
       2.2.4   Input Considerations 25
  2.3   User Interfaces: Input 26
       2.3.1   3D User Interfaces: Input Devices 26
  2.4   Input Devices 27
       2.4.1   Keyboard 27
       2.4.2   The Mouse and Its Descendants 29
       2.4.3   Joystick and the GamePad 31
       2.4.4   3D Mouse and 3D User-Worn Mice 40
       2.4.5   Audio 42
       2.4.6   Inertial Sensing 43
       2.4.7   Vision-Based Devices 44
       2.4.8   Data Gloves 44
       2.4.9   Psychophysiological Sensing 45
       2.4.10 Tracking Devices 45
       2.4.11 Treadmills as Input Devices 45
  2.5   Input Recognition 47
  2.6   Virtual Devices 47
  2.7   Input Taxonomies 49
  Further Reading 58

3 Output: Interfaces and Displays   **61**
  3.1   3D Output: Interfaces 61
       3.1.1   Human Visual System 61
       3.1.2   Visual Display Characteristics 63
       3.1.3   Understanding Depth 63
  3.2   Displays 67
       3.2.1   Near-Eye Displays 69
       3.2.2   Three-Dimensional Displays 70
  Further Reading 74

4 Computer Graphics   **75**
  4.1   Computer Graphics 75
       4.1.1   Camera Space 75
       4.1.2   3D Translation and Rotations 77
       4.1.3   Geometric Modeling 82
       4.1.4   Scene Managers 82
       4.1.5   Collision Detection 84

Further Reading 85

5 3D Interaction   87
  5.1 Introduction 87
  5.2 3D Manipulation 87
      5.2.1 Classification of Manipulation Techniques 91
      5.2.2 Muscle Groups: Precision Grasp 93
      5.2.3 Isomorphic Manipulations 94
      5.2.4 Pointing Techniques 94
      5.2.5 Direct and Hybrid Manipulations 101
      5.2.6 Non-Isomorphic Rotations 108
  Further Reading 109

6 3D Navigation   111
  6.1 3D Travel 111
      6.1.1 3D Travel Tasks 112
      6.1.2 Travel Techniques 114
  6.2 Wayfinding 122
      6.2.1 Training versus Transfer 123
      6.2.2 Spatial Knowledge 124
      6.2.3 Navigation Model 126
      6.2.4 Wayfinding Strategies 126
  6.3 3D Navigation: User Studies 128
      6.3.1 Search during Navigation 130
      6.3.2 Additional User Studies for Navigation 131
  Further Reading 134

7 Descriptive and Predictive Models   137
  7.1 Introduction 137
  7.2 Predictive Models 138
      7.2.1 Fitts' law 138
      7.2.2 Choice Reaction Time: Hick–Hyman Law 146
      7.2.3 Keystroke-Level Model (KLM) 148
      7.2.4 Other Models 152
  7.3 Descriptive Models 154
      7.3.1 Bi-Manual Interaction 154
      7.3.2 Three-State Model for Graphical Input 156
  Further Reading 160

8 Multi-Touch   161
  8.1 Introduction 161
  8.2 Hardware 164
      8.2.1 Projective Capacitive Technology 165

| | 8.2.2 | Optical Touch Surfaces | 172 |

8.2.2   Optical Touch Surfaces   172
8.2.3   Vision-Based Optical   173
8.3   Multi-Touch and Its Applications   175
8.3.1   Basics of Multi-Touch   175
8.3.2   Multi-Touch Gestures and Design   176
8.3.3   Touch Properties   177
8.3.4   Multi-Touch Taxonomy   180
8.3.5   Are Multi-Touch Gestures Natural?   182
8.3.6   Touch: Multi-Modality   189
8.3.7   More about Touch   197
8.3.8   Multi-Touch Techniques   197
8.4   Figures of Large Tabletop Displays   199
Further Reading   203

9   Multi-Touch for Stereoscopic Displays   205
Dimitar Valkov

9.1   Understanding 3D Touch   205
9.1.1   Problems with Stereoscopic Touch Interfaces . . .   206
9.1.2   Parallax Problem   207
9.1.3   Design Paradigms for Stereoscopic Touch Interaction   210
9.2   Touching Parallaxes   212
9.3   Multi-Touch above the Tabletop   216
9.3.1   Triangle Cursor   216
9.3.2   Balloon Selection   218
9.3.3   Triangle Cursor vs. Balloon Selection   219
9.3.4   Design Considerations   221
9.4   Interaction with Virtual Shadows   223
9.4.1   Shadow Hand   226
9.4.2   Shadow Hand vs. Void Shadows   227
9.5   Perceptual Illusions for 3D Touch Interaction   229
9.5.1   User Interaction States   231
9.5.2   Manipulation Techniques   233
9.5.3   Scene Shifts while Moving toward the Surface . . .   236
9.5.4   Object Shifts during Touch   240
9.5.5   Application Space   241
9.5.6   Manipulation of Stereoscopic Objects   241
9.5.7   Generalized Scaled Shift Technique   242
9.5.8   Discrimination of Stereoscopic Depth   246
9.5.9   Object Attracting Shift   248
Further Reading   252

10 Pen and Multi-Touch Modeling and Recognition   **255**
  10.1 Introduction   255
  10.2 The Dollar Family   256
       10.2.1 $1 Recognizer   258
       10.2.2 $1 Recognizer with Protractor   262
       10.2.3 $N Recognizer   262
       10.2.4 $ Family: $P and Beyond   264
  10.3 Proton++ and More   265
  10.4 FETOUCH   267
       10.4.1 FETOUCH+   270
       10.4.2 Implementation: FETOUCH++   274
  Further Reading   277

11 Using Multi-Touch with Petri Nets   **279**
  11.1 Background   280
       11.1.1 Graphical Representation   281
       11.1.2 Formal Definition   281
  11.2 PeNTa: Petri Nets   282
       11.2.1 Motivation and Differences   283
       11.2.2 HLPN: High-Level Petri Nets and IRML   285
       11.2.3 PeNTa and Multi-Touch   286
       11.2.4 Arc Expressions   287
       11.2.5 A Tour of PeNTa   289
       11.2.6 Simulation and Execution   290
  Further Reading   292

12 Eye Gaze Tracking as Input in Human–Computer Interaction   **293**
  12.1 Principle of Operation   293
  12.2 Post-Processing of POG Data: Fixation Identification   298
  12.3 Emerging Uses of EGT in HCI: Affective Sensing   300
  Further Reading   310

**13 Brain–Computer Interfaces: Considerations for the Next Frontier
in Interactive Graphics and Games**   **313**
Frances Lucretia Van Scoy

  13.1 Introduction   313
  13.2 Neuroscience Research   314
       13.2.1 Invasive Research   314
       13.2.2 EEG Research   315
       13.2.3 fMRI Research   315
  13.3 Implications of EEG- and fMRI-Based Research for the Brain–
Computer Interface   318

13.3.1 Implications of Constructing Text or Images from
Brain Scan Data 318
13.3.2 Implications of Personality Models for Digital Games 319
13.4 Neuroheadsets 321
13.4.1 Some Available Devices 321
13.4.2 An Example: Controlling Google Glass with MindRDR 323
13.5 A Simple Approach to Recognizing Specific Brain Activities
Using Low-End Neuroheadsets and Simple Clustering Techniques 323
13.6 Using EEG Data to Recognize Active Brain Regions 325
13.7 Conclusion 325
Further Reading 325

II Advanced Topics   327

14 Introduction to 3D Math for Input Devices   329
Steven P. Landers & David Rieksts

14.1 Introduction 329
14.2 Axis Conventions 329
14.3 Vectors 330
14.3.1 Equality 332
14.3.2 Addition 332
14.3.3 Scalar Multiplication 333
14.3.4 Negation and Subtraction 333
14.3.5 Basis Vectors 333
14.3.6 Magnitude 334
14.3.7 Unit Vector and Normalization 334
14.3.8 Dot Product 334
14.3.9 Cross Product in $\mathbb{R}^3$ 335
14.4 Matrices 335
14.4.1 Transposition 335
14.4.2 Trace 336
14.4.3 Addition 336
14.4.4 Scalar Multiplication 336
14.4.5 Matrix Multiplication 337
14.4.6 Identity Matrix 338
14.4.7 Determinant 338
14.4.8 Transformation Matrices 339
14.4.9 Reflection Matrices 340
14.4.10 Eigenvalues, Eigenvectors 340
14.5 Axis Angle Rotations 341
14.6 Two-Vector Orientation 342

14.7   Calibration of Three-Axis Sensors   342
    14.7.1   Bias   343
    14.7.2   Scale   343
    14.7.3   Cross-Axis Effect and Rotation   344
14.8   Smoothing   344
    14.8.1   Low-Pass Filter   345
    14.8.2   Oversampling   345
Further Reading   346

15 Introduction to Digital Signal Processing   347
15.1   Introduction   347
15.2   What Is a Signal?   347
15.3   Classification of Signals   349
15.4   Applications of Digital Signal Processing   350
15.5   Noise   351
15.6   Signal Energy and Power   352
15.7   Mathematical Representation of Elementary Signals   353
    15.7.1   The Impulse Function   353
    15.7.2   The Unit Step Function   353
    15.7.3   The Cosine Function   354
    15.7.4   Exponential Function   355
    15.7.5   Ramp Function   355
    15.7.6   Gaussian Function   357
15.8   Sampling Theorem   357
15.9   Nyquist–Shannon Theorem   360
15.10   Aliasing   361
15.11   Quantization   361
15.12   Fourier Analysis   362
    15.12.1 Discrete Fourier Transform   363
    15.12.2 Inverse Discrete Fourier Transform   365
15.13   Fast Fourier Transform   365
15.14   z-Transform   365
    15.14.1 Definitions   366
    15.14.2 z-Plane   368
    15.14.3 Region of Convergence   368
15.15   Convolution   368
Further Reading   371

16 Three-Dimensional Rotations   373
16.1   Introduction   373
16.2   Three-Dimensional Rotation   373
16.3   Coordinate Systems   374
    16.3.1   Inertial Frame   375

16.3.2 Body-Fixed Frame 376
16.4 Euler Angles 376
16.4.1 Rotation Matrices 376
16.4.2 Gimbal Lock 378
16.5 Quaternions 379
16.5.1 What Are Quaternions? 379
16.5.2 Quaternion Rotation 384
Further Reading 384

17 MEMS Inertial Sensors and Magnetic Sensors   **387**
17.1 Introduction 387
17.2 Inertial Sensors 387
17.2.1 Accelerometers 388
17.2.2 Gyroscopes 389
17.3 MEMS Inertial Sensor Errors 390
17.3.1 Angle Random Walk 391
17.3.2 Rate Random Walk 391
17.3.3 Flicker Noise 392
17.3.4 Quantization Noise 392
17.3.5 Sinusoidal Noise 392
17.3.6 Bias Error 392
17.3.7 Scale Factor Error 392
17.3.8 Scale Factor Sign Asymmetry Error 392
17.3.9 Misalignment (Cross-Coupling) Error 393
17.3.10 Non-Linearity Error 393
17.3.11 Dead Zone Error 394
17.3.12 Temperature Effect 394
17.4 Magnetometers 395
17.5 MEMS Magnetometer Errors 397
Further Reading 401

18 Kalman Filters   **403**
18.1 Introduction 403
18.2 Least Squares Estimator 403
18.3 Kalman Filters 405
18.4 Discrete Kalman Filters 405
18.5 Extended Kalman Filters 410
Further Reading 412

19 Quaternions and Sensor Fusion   **413**
19.1 Introduction 413
19.2 Quaternion-Based Kalman Filter 414
19.2.1 Prediction Step 415

	19.2.2	Correction Step	417
	19.2.3	Observation Vector Using Gradient Descent Optimization	418
	19.2.4	Observation Vector Determination Using Gauss–Newton Method	420
19.3		Quaternion-Based Extended Kalman Filter	422
	19.3.1	Measurement Process	424
19.4		Conversion between Euler and Quaternion	425
		Further Reading	425

III Hands-On   427

20 Hands-On: Inertial Sensors for 3D Input   429
Paul W. Yost

20.1	Introduction	429
20.2	Motion Sensing and Motion Capture	430
	20.2.1 Motion Sensing	430
	20.2.2 Motion Capture	431
20.3	Types of Motion Sensing Technology	431
	20.3.1 Marker-Based Optical Systems	431
	20.3.2 Marker-Less Optical Systems	432
	20.3.3 Mechanical Systems	433
	20.3.4 Magnetic Systems	434
	20.3.5 Inertial Systems	434
20.4	Inertial Sensor Configurations for Input	436
	20.4.1 Single Sensor Configurations	436
	20.4.2 Multiple Sensor Configurations	437
	20.4.3 Full-Body Sensor Configurations	437
20.5	Hands-On: YEI 3-Space Sensors	437
	20.5.1 Overview	437
	20.5.2 Using a Single YEI 3-Space Sensor	438
	20.5.3 Installing a Sensor	439
	20.5.4 Communicating with a Sensor Using Command and Response	441
	20.5.5 Communicating with a Sensor Using Streaming Mode	445
	20.5.6 Using the 3-Space Sensor API	447
	20.5.7 Hands-On: Single 3-Space Sensor Applications	448
	20.5.8 Hands-On: Multiple 3-Space Sensor Applications	461
20.6	Hands-On: YEI Prio for Whole-Body Input	466
	20.6.1 Using the Prio API	467
	20.6.2 Hands-On: Prio for Full-Body Immersion in Unity	471
	20.6.3 Hands-On: Prio for Full-Body Motion Capture	478

Further Reading   480

21 Simple Hands-On Project with Unity3D and Oculus Rift   483
Nonnarit O-larnnithipong

21.1   Installation and System Requirements   483
21.2   Getting Started   484
        21.2.1   Creating a New Project   486
21.3   Creating Game Scene   486
21.4   Lighting, Camera, and Skybox   493
21.5   GameObject and Basic Action Script   495
21.6   Graphic User Interface (GUI)   501
21.7   Oculus Rift Integration for Unity   503
        21.7.1   Installation and Package Import   504
        21.7.2   Oculus Rift Prefab   505
Further Reading   509

22 Hands-On Approach with Leap Motion   511
Frank E. Hernandez

22.1   What Is Leap Motion?   511
22.2   Installation   512
22.3   Hands-On Mini-Project   513
Further Reading   519

23 Hands-On Approach with Kinect Sensor v2   521
Frank E. Hernandez

23.1   What Is the Kinect Sensor?   521
23.2   Installation   523
23.3   Hands-On Mini-Project   523
Further Reading   533

24 Creating Home-Brew Devices with Arduino Microcontrollers   535
Sudarat Tangnimitchok

24.1   Microcontroller   536
24.2   Analog Sensor   538
24.3   Serial Communication   539
        24.3.1   Universal Synchronous Receiver/Transmitter   539
24.4   Hands-On Project: Ultrasonic Proximity Sensor   540
        24.4.1   Introduction to Arduino   540
        24.4.2   Ultrasonic Sensor   541
        24.4.3   Connecting Circuit   543
        24.4.4   Coding (Sketch)   545
        24.4.5   Testing the Project   551

Further Reading   552

25 Autonomous Bicycle with Gyroscope Sensor   555
    Panuwat Janwattanapong & Mercedes Cabrerizo

    25.1   Introduction   555
    25.2   AU Self-Balancing Bicycle (AUSB)   557
           25.2.1   Mechanical Structure   557
           25.2.2   Controller: dsPIC30F4011   557
           25.2.3   Gyroscope Sensor: MicroStrain 3DM-GX1   557
    25.3   Data Processing   558
           25.3.1   Structure of Data Processing   559
           25.3.2   Analog to Digital Converter   560
    25.4   System Implementation and Results   561
           25.4.1   Control System of AU Self-Balancing Bicycle (AUSB)   561
           25.4.2   Analysis of AU self-balancing bicycle (AUSB) System   563
           25.4.3   Result   564
    25.5   Conclusion   564
    Further Reading   564

26 Input Implementation Details   567
    26.1   Input Devices   567
           26.1.1   Device Listeners and Common Interfaces   567
           26.1.2   3D Mouse   570
           26.1.3   Inertial Navigation System   575
           26.1.4   Microsoft Kinect   575
           26.1.5   Keyboard and Mouse   578
           26.1.6   GamePad   580
    26.2   Multi-Touch Implementation   586
    26.3   Working with a 3D Graphics Engine: OGRE   592
    26.4   ECHoSS: Experiment Module   600
    Further Reading   604

IV   Case Study: Speech as Input   605

27 Multimodal Human-Like Conversational Interfaces   607
    Ugan Yasavur & Christine Lisetti

    27.1   Dialog Management Overview   608
           27.1.1   Dialog Management Based on Machine Learning .   610
           27.1.2   Dialog Management and Reinforcement Learning .   611
    27.2   Dialog Management in Health Dialog Systems   613
    27.3   Task-Based Spoken Dialog Systems   615

27.4   Embodied Conversational Agents   616
27.5   Brief Interventions for Alcohol Problems   618
27.6   Conclusion   625
Further Reading   625

28 Adaptive Dialog Systems for Health   627
Ugan Yasavur & Christine Lisetti

28.1   Approach   627
28.2   Reinforcement Learning Background   629
28.3   Markov Decision Processes   629
28.4   Modeling World with Interconnected MDPs   634
28.5   Agent and Dialog Strategy Learning   635
28.6   Reward Function Design   637
28.7   Speech Recognition and Language Model   638
28.8   Dialog Corpus   640
28.9   Conclusion   640
Further reading   640

V   Appendices   641

A   Displays   643
Jorge H. dos S. Chernicharo

A.1   Fixed Displays   643
       A.1.1   Single Display   643
       A.1.2   Multiple Displays   644
A.2   Portable Displays   647
       A.2.1   Tablets and Smartphones   647
       A.2.2   Portable Projectors   647
A.3   Hybrid Systems   649
       A.3.1   Fixed Displays + Smartphones or Tablets   649
       A.3.2   Fixed Displays + Portable Projectors   649

B   Creating Your Own Virtual Reality HeadSet   651
Karell Muller

B.1   Introduction   651
B.2   Google Cardboard   652

Bibliography   661

Index   729

Author Biographies

Francisco Raúl Ortega, Ph.D. Dr. Ortega is a postdoctoral research fellow at Florida International University. Dr. Ortega earned his Ph.D. in computer science from Florida International University (FIU) in 2014, co-advised by Dr. Naphtali Rishe and Dr. Armando Barreto. His dissertation, which dealt with 3D navigation using multi-touch, was nominated for an outstanding dissertation award in the College of Engineering. He was also named Outstanding Graduate Student for the year 2014 in the School of Computer Science and Information at FIU. Dr. Ortega earned  his bachelor's degree in computer science, cum laude, in December 2008 from FIU and a master's degree in computer science from FIU in December 2009. He was a member of the Digital Signal Processing (DSP) Laboratory at FIU. He has over 17 years of experience in software development and systems integration. His interests are in 3D user interfaces, input interfaces, human–computer interaction, 3D navigation, and input modeling. Dr. Ortega has written multiple publications in journals, lecture notes, and conference proceedings. Dr. Ortega was awarded a 3-year fellowship by the Department of Education of the United States. This fellowship, named GAANN (Graduate Assistance in Areas of National Need), was renewed for a fourth year. He was also awarded the McKnight dissertation fellowship for the academic year 2013–2014 with the Florida Education Fund. The McKnight fellowship was awarded for an additional semester. Additionally, Dr. Ortega has received small grants during his time as a student and is currently pursuing grants as a postdoc.

Fatemeh Sara Abyarjoo, Ph.D. Fatemeh earned a bachelor of science degree in computer engineering from the Azad University, Qazvin, Iran, and a master of science degree in mechatronic engineering from Azad University, Qazvin, Iran in 2002 and 2005, respectively. She earned a Ph.D. in 2013 from the Electrical and Computer Engineering Department at Florida International University. Since 2012,

she has been working as a research assistant in the Digital Signal Processing Laboratory. Dr. Abyarjoo's research work is on sensor fusion for human motion tracking. Her research interests are sensor fusion, data analysis, and Kalman filters. She is a former Open Science Data Cloud (OSDC) PIRE National Science Foundation (NSF) fellow.

Armando Bennett Barreto, Ph.D. Dr. Barreto earned the Licenciatura en Ingenieria Mecanica y Electrica (BS EE equivalent) from the National Autonomous University of Mexico (UNAM) in 1987, with a concentration in electronics and instrumentation. In 1989 he earned a master of science in electrical engineering from Florida International University (FIU) in Miami, Florida, and the Doctor of Philosophy in electrical engineering from the University of Florida, Gainesville, in 1993. His doctoral research focused  on digital signal processing (DSP), with application to epileptic focus localization from processing of multi-channel electrocorticogram signals. Since 1994, Dr. Barreto has been a faculty member of the Electrical and Computer Engineering Department at FIU and the director of FIU's Digital Signal Processing Laboratory. At FIU, Dr. Barreto has focused on applying DSP techniques to the facilitation of human–computer interactions, particularly for the benefit of individuals with disabilities. He has developed human–computer interfaces based on the processing of signals such as the electroencephalogram, the electromyogram, eye gaze tracking, etc. Dr. Barreto has also developed a system that adds spatialized sounds to the icons in a computer interface to facilitate access by individuals with "low vision." He is a senior member of the Institute of Electrical and Electronics Engineers (IEEE) and the Association for Computing Machinery (ACM).

Naphtali David Rishe, Ph.D. Dr. Rishe has authored three books on database design and geography and edited five books on database management and high-performance computing. He holds four U.S. patents on database querying, semantic database performance, Internet data extraction, and computer medicine. Dr. Rishe has authored 300  papers in journals and proceedings on databases, software engineering, geographic information systems, the Internet, and life sciences. He has been awarded over $55 million in research grants by government and industry, including NASA, NSF, IBM, DoI, USGS. Dr. Rishe is the founder and director of the High Performance Database Research Center at FIU (HPDRC); director of the NSF Center for Research Excellence in Science and Technology at FIU (CREST) and the NSF International FIU-FAU-Dubna Industry-University Cooperative Research Center for Advanced Knowledge Enablement (I/UCRC). Dr. Rishe is the inaugural FIU

Outstanding University Professor and Eminent Chair Professor of Computer Science. Dr. Rishe's TerraFly project has been extensively covered by the worldwide press, including The *New York Times*, *USA Today*, NPR, *Science Journal* and *Nature Journal*, and FOX TV News. Dr. Rishe's principal projects are TerraFly (a 50 TB database of aerial imagery and Web-based GIS) and medical informatics.

Malek Adjouadi Dr. Adjouadi is a professor with the Department of Electrical and Computer Engineering at Florida International University. He is the founding director of the Center for Advanced Technology and Education funded by the National Science Foundation since 1993. He earned his B.S. degree from Oklahoma State University and his M.S. and Ph.D. degrees all in electrical engineering from the University of Florida. Dr. Adjouadi's earlier work on  computer vision to help persons with blindness led to his testimony before the U.S. Senate Committee for Veterans Affairs on the subject of technology to help persons with disabilities. His research interests are in image and signal processing with applications to neuroscience and assistive technology research.

List of Contributors

Mercedes Cabrerizo
Assistant Professor
Florida International University
Miami, Florida

Jorge H. dos S. Chernicharo
Researcher
Tohoku University
Sendai, Japan

Frank E. Hernandez
Researcher
Game Developer Guild
Miami, Florida

Panuwat Janwattanapong
Ph.D. Student
Florida International University
Miami, Florida

Stephen P. Landers
Senior Research Engineer
YEI Technology
Portsmouth, Ohio

Christine Lisetti
Associate Professor and Director of the
   Affective Social Computing
   Laboratory
Florida International University
Miami, Florida

Karell Muller
Computer Support Analyst
Florida International University
Miami, Florida

Nonnarit O-larnnithipong
Ph.D. Student in Electrical Engineering
Florida International University
Miami, Florida

David Rieksts
Research Mathematician
YEI Technology
Portsmouth, Ohio

Sudarat Tangnimitchok
Ph.D. Student
Florida International University
Miami, Florida

Dimitar Valkov
Researcher
Visualization & Computer Graphics
   Research Group
Department of Computer Science
University of Münster
Münster, Germany

Frances Lucretia Van Scoy
Associate Professor
West Virginia University
Morgantown, West Virginia

Ugan Yasavur, Ph.D.
Research Engineer
IPsoft
New York, New York

Paul W. Yost
Chief of Research and Development
YEI Technology
Portsmouth, Ohio

Foreword

I have no doubt you are aware of the amazing technology that companies are working on and delivering to the consumer: Microsoft HoloLens, Oculus Rift, Google Glass (wearable technologies related to virtual and augmented reality), and Leap Motion (3D motion controller), among others. Many companies have attempted such technologies over the last couple of decades, but attaining a reliable and consumer-affordable product has been difficult. Certainly the advancements in low-power hardware with the capability to support compute-intensive applications have been necessary for success. However, the complexity of the science (computer vision, image processing) and the necessity for high-performance hardware (CPU, GPU, FPGA, ASIC) have been equally challenging.

One might think that providing a convincing mixed-reality world—and the ability to interact with that world in a natural manner—is not too difficult to achieve in a commercial engineering environment; as it turns out, this is not the case. Recognizing hand gestures as input, for example, and translating them to some desired output in a mixed-reality application is not trivial. Rather than trying various *ad hoc* approaches (as engineers are fond of doing) and hoping to find a simple solution to a complex problem, it is better to rely on the expertise of those who have studied this field extensively and have a solid grasp on the approaches that work—and on those that do not. *Interaction Design for 3D User Interfaces: The World of Modern Input Devices for Research, Applications, and Game Development* is exactly the book that you want to read. It is a collaborative effort by a group of experienced researchers who have distilled the literature to the most relevant references and presented the material in an easy-to-read discussion with a historical perspective that helps to understand why input devices and user interfaces have evolved to their current state.

Part I of the book is about the theory and has a well-written presentation on the history of input devices. Several chapters are about multi-touch, which is supported on nearly all devices we have come to rely on. A couple of chapters are about eye-gaze tracking and brain-computer interfaces. Part II is about advanced topics including a review of digital signal processing. The chapters on inertial and magnetic sensors and on Kalman filters are particularly of interest for understanding how to deal with the noise inherent in hardware measurements of position and orientation. For the practical-minded developers and researchers, Part

III is a collection of chapters about projects for specific hardware including Oculus Rift, Leap Motion, Kinect V2, gyroscopes, and Arduino microcontrollers. Part IV has a couple of case studies that are interesting to see how speech is a useful input for various applications. A new feature of the book is that the authors have provided additional chapters via online access, including information on gestures, multitouch for Windows 8, and multitouch for Windows 10.

Finally, one of my favorite features of the book is the extensive list of references: over 60 pages of papers and books that the authors have taken the time to identify as the important results for us to study. The time a single person would spend trying to read and identify the relevant research will make the book a worthwhile purchase. The authors have already done that work for you and saved you a lot of valuable time.

The information in this book is invaluable for the 3D input devices and user interface projects I work on, both software and hardware. I plan on having a copy of the book by my side at work. Others on my team will probably try to borrow it, but I will chain it to my desk and insist they purchase their own copy!

–David Eberly, CTO of Geometric Tools LLC.

Preface

> However bad life may seem, there is always something
> you can do, and succeed at. While there's life, there is
> hope.
>
> —Stephen Hawking

I started coding when I was 11 years old on a scientific calculator given to my sister, who was preparing to enter college. I remember my parents' intrigue at why I didn't want to go play football[1] with my friends. I spent weekends and weeknights playing with this calculator that had a single one-line display but could output text and symbols with its alphanumeric keyboard. Later, I received an Atari 65-XE computer that came equipped with a whopping 64 kilobytes of RAM memory. This also came with a tape-drive that meant waiting for games for a half-hour (if it loaded correctly) and an Atari joystick. I was 12 years old and I was amazed by the power of computing. Early on I was very intrigued with the Atari joystick but I never knew I would end up researching three-dimensional user interface (3DUI) or learning human–computer interaction (HCI). However, I knew that I loved programming. I knew that I loved computers. The movie *WAR Games* circa 1983 was the initial motivation for me to become a computer scientist. Just to be able to change your grade from your house was a reason enough to like it. I could have used a grade booster in my Castellano[2] class when I was a kid. I knew I loved programming, and later in life, computer science was my north. While computer graphics was a field that looked interesting to me, it was a project offered to me by my Ph.D. advisor, that led me to this field. I'm forever grateful.

While reading the user manual of this new Atari 65-XE computer, I learned how to code Basic and to code the joystick to create lines and shapes using Basic language. The Atari joystick and the Atari paddles allowed for some very interesting interaction in a computer that didn't have a mouse. The Atari computer 8-bit, simple yet marvelous graphics for the time (at least that one could afford), provided imagination for many kids my age. I believe that modern input devices will let many kids wonder about the possibility of user interaction.

---

[1] Also known as soccer.
[2] What native Spanish is called in some Spanish-speaking countries.

My journey, described in the previous paragraphs, is what led me to lead the efforts for this book. This book came about with initial help from David Eberly, who is one of my favorite technical authors. Not only did he help me but he also reviewed some of the chapters of this book. This book would have not been possible without the additional writing and support of my co-authors: Fatemeh (Sara), Armando, Naphtali, and Malek. I decided to look for authors who were close to me and had a different take (and expertise) on input devices and user interaction. This book is also made possible by collaborators who contributed different chapters that were needed to complement the book. While working on this book, it was clear that many topics important to user input interfaces were not able to be covered. This is why I with some of my co-authors, in collaboration with CRC Press, have decided to compile a *Handbook of Input and 3D User Interaction: Theory and Practice*, probably to be completed during 2016.

Why This Book?

While working on my Ph.D., the best book that I found for my work was *3D User Interfaces: Theory and Practice* [Bowman et al. 04]. It aligned with my topic, which was user interfaces and user interaction by using input devices. However, I noticed that user interfaces with the lenses of input devices had not been covered in depth. *3D User Interfaces: Theory and Practice* is a fantastic book and we have learned that they are working on a new edition. However, our objective was to provide additional information about input, in particular multi-touch (because of how pervasive it has become), and provide some hands-on chapters. In addition, we wanted to provide chapters about Kalman filters, which are extremely useful for input. There are excellent books that cover different topics in *3D User Interfaces*, an amazing chapter title "Input Technologies" [Hinckley and Widgor 12],[3] and *Human Computer Interaction: An Empirical Research Perspective* [MacKenzie 12], among others ([Dix et al. 04]).

This book talks about user interfaces with an emphasis on the input component of them. This includes physical devices, virtual devices, the theory behind the interaction and navigation, which those devices are used for, past and current techniques, practical topics about input devices, and some advanced topics such as Kalman filters.

About the Title of This Book

This book's title evolved over time. The original title included the word "Natural User Interaction", and as you read the book, you will notice why I have stayed away from this term. At a later time, the book was called "3D User Input Interfaces" because I wanted to give emphasis to input devices while working with user

---

[3]Previous editions of this chapter were written by Hinckley [Hinckley 08].

interfaces. With the help of the 3DUI community and in particular, Dr. Bowman, from Virgina Tech, I was able to find the title that best fit this book, in my opinion. The title finally became *Interaction Design for 3D User Interfaces: The World of Modern Input Devices for Research, Applications, and Game Development*, since interaction design describes techniques triggered by user input with its proper feedback. The subtitle included makes mention of modern input devices because of the perspective used for this book. In my mind, when I think about an interface, I think about the input and output of an interface, and this is why, the wording input user interfaces (or user input interfaces) made sense. However, keeping consistent with definitions is very important (as one may claim that is only semantics). Therefore, the input and output components are parts that make the interface.

What Is in the Book?

This book is divided into four parts: theory about user interfaces with a large emphasis on input devices and the input component of interfaces, advanced topics including Kalman filters and three-dimensional (3D) rotations in the context of input, hands-on approach to get someone started with a device, and a case study divided into two chapters.

Part I: Theory

Chapter 1 provides a brief overview of the vision and other topics related to HCI including 3DUI and some definitions. Chapter 2 provides information about the input component of user interfaces as well as information about input devices. Chapters 3 and 4 cover the output components of user interfaces, displays, and, computer graphics. Output is needed for input interaction to work. While the input may work without output, the lack of feedback would provide little use to most users. Chapters 5 and 6 cover 3D interaction and 3D navigation, respectively. These chapters provide an understanding of user interaction when using input interfaces. Both of these chapters, in particular Chapter 6, provide additional state-of-the-art information. For Chapter 6 (navigation), both topics of travel and wayfinding are covered. Chapter 7 covers some descriptive and predictive models related to input. The next four chapters deal with different aspects of multi-touch. Chapter 8 provides an overview of hardware and important multi-touch techniques and studies. This chapter also provides a look at multi-modal interaction, in particular touch and pen. Chapter 9 provides an overview of 3D touch. Chapter 10 provides a brief overview of some pen and multi-touch techniques. The last chapter that covers multi-touch is Chapter 11. This chapter provides a look at multi-touch modeling using high-level Petri Nets (HLPNs). While, in theory, this can be applied to other types of input devices, it is done in the context of multi-touch. This chapter provides an overview of Petri Nets (PN), which has remained a very niche topic in computer science. However, we believe that it is time for PNs to have their place. Chapter 12 deals with Eye Gaze Tracking (EGT), which provides another dimension for input. Finally, Chapter 13 in this part of the book is a look at brain–computer interface (BCI) and electroencephalogram (EEG) in the context of interactive application, providing a look at some recent publications.

Part II: Advanced Topics

The second part of this book requires a level of knowledge in statistics, digital signal processing (DSP), and mathematics in general. While not all of these topics could be covered in this book, we do provide a brief 3D mathematical overview in Chapter 14. This chapter is also provided with inertial navigation system (INS) sensors in mind. Some readers may feel that this chapter fits better in the appendix. However, there are important topics that are useful for this part. Chapter 14 was originally larger but due to space, we removed some concepts that we felt were already part of other chapters. Nevertheless, the missing part will be available on the book's website. Next, Chapter 15 deals with a basic introduction to DSP. Chapter 16 describes 3D rotations using quaternions and Euler angles. Then, Chapter 17 covers topics concerning inertial measurement unit (IMU) sensors, such as gyroscopes and accelerometers. This is followed by Chapter 18 dealing with Kalman filters. Chapter 19 provides a look at quaternions and sensor fusion in more detail, including topics of Kalman filters. It is worth mentioning that the original idea was to make the topic of Kalman filters and sensors as accessible as possible. However, after working with Fatemeh (Sara), who has led all the chapters in this part (except the math chapter), it is very apparent that additional information is needed to close the gap. One option is a book only about this topic, which should include background topics, implementation details, and additional information for dealing with Kalman filters with input devices. While having a dedicated book looks like the perfect solution and we will attempt to work on it in the future, the topics provided in this book are useful for people needing to use Kalman filters, micro-electro-mechanical systems (MEMS) sensors for motion, and work with complex 3D rotations (e.g., for 3D navigation). The best suggestion that I have is to read the Kalman filter chapters ignoring the equations at first, if it is the first time reading them.

Part III: Hands-on

The third part of the book deals with basic hands-on approach projects. The objective of this section is to get someone up and running with a project that may lead them to enhance an application or do research. In most cases, the chapter will detail a basic project or at least provide hints to help with the implementation. All the projects will be available in our book's website. Chapter 20 provides a detailed explanation about IMU sensors and how to implement them. This information is meant to be used with the YEI Technology sensor but some concepts are useful for other Imus. Next, Chapter 21 provides a look at unity and oculus rift. Chapter 22 provides a look at Leap Motion. The Leap Motion does provide a different set of data and gestures that makes it a very useful device. Chapter 23 covers the new Microsoft Kinect v2 for the Microsoft Xbox One and Microsoft Windows. There are times that the current devices do not satisfy our needs. The simplest way to create an input device is to use a micro-controller or small form-factor personal computer (PC) board (e.g., Raspberry Pi). For this book, we provide a chapter that covers the popular Arduino micro-controller device, which is explained in Chapter 24. While most of our chapters deal with devices for the desktop (or mobile) devices, we also wanted to provide a hands-on approach for input devices using an outdoor automated bicycle in Chapter 25. This provides a look at micro-controllers and gyroscopes. However, this gyroscope is analog, which makes less noise than one in a MEMS. Finally, Chapter 26 covers different input devices, including Microsoft Kinect v1, 3D mouse, and many other considerations that I have taken during my own input device development. We wanted to provide additional devices in this section. For example, one device we were hoping to test was Nimble[4] VR. During their Kickstarter funding campaign, they decided to sell their company to Oculus Rift (a division of Facebook). Maybe in the future, it will become available, unless it becomes bundled with Oculus Rift. Another device, which we purchased via Kickstarter in late 2013, was the Stem System by SixSense[5]. Unfortunately, at the time of this writing (2015), we still have not received the product but are still hopefull. Finally, we understand that some readers may want to understand the concepts from the ground up. We are in the process of creating an input device framework, which we hope in time will provide a unified input framework.[6] Therefore, if you want to understand input device development, we hope to provide a book in the future that covers that. We plan to update the book's website with more hands-on projects whenever posssible.

Part IV: Case Study

The last part of the book, which is divided into Chapters 27 and 28 is meant to cover one case study. The idea of this part of the book is to provide a look at a case study for a complete system, where natural language processing is a complete input/output solution.

Appendix

The appendix contains additional information that is relevant to the topic. The first appendix contains additional information about displays, provided by my good

---

[4]http://nimblevr.com
[5]http://sixense.com/
[6]See an existing one called VRPN. https://github.com/vrpn/vrpn/wiki

friend Jorge H. dos S. Chernicharo[7]. The next appendix covers considerations when building your own head-mounted display (HMD), which proves very useful for the Unity chapter for those that don't have Oculus Rift. While many online websites have instructions, this appendix covers the experience of building our own headset and the problems one may face if you have access to a 3D printer.

Exercises

A note about exercises. The book contains a few exercises in most chapters. Most of them provide a way to extend the knowledge of a given chapter. They are not (for the most part) meant as a review of the chapter. Most chapters have two to three questions.

Online Content

Our book's website, located at http://3DInputBook.com, will serve as a complement to this book. We plan to model this website as http://www.realtimerendering. com website, which will provide additional chapters, errata, and new content as it appears. We also hope to include book recommendations and general news about input user interfaces. We also invite you to visit our lab's (OpenHID Lab) website at http://www.openhid.com.

The online chapters of this book will be provided at no cost to you. The chapters will be written to complement topics of the book, including theory (e.g., gestures), and hands-on project, among others. We know that there are many additional topics that the reader may be interested in, and we hope to cover the rest in the *3D User Input Interfaces/Interaction Handbook*.

I also recommend the 3DUI mailing list (http://people.cs.vt.edu/~bowman/ 3dui-g@vt.edu). This mailing list has helped me to reach the 3DUI community. The amount of help given by the members of this mailing list has been without equal.

Finally, I would like to mention that we have plans to prepare power points and material to make this book ready for classroom.

Conferences and Journals

There are many conferences and journals that cover the topics related to this book. In the book's website, I will list the conferences and journals as they become available. Two conferences from IEEE that are very popular are the 3DUI symposium and VR. ACM has a few great conferences as well—for multi-touch, ITS (interactive tabletop surfaces). In addition, UIST (user interfaces software and technology) and SUI (spatial user interfaces) contain lots of material. Of course,

---

[7]I'm still waiting for Jorge to purchase an Xbox One in order to play a match of FIFA.

the flagship conference of HCI is CHI. For ubiquitous computing (not covered in this book), UbiComp contains very useful publications that can be applied in this area. HCI International, which may be considered to be a flagship conference, contains useful information as well. A conference that used to take more user interface (UI) work is SigGraph[8], by far it is the most popular conference from ACM and an amazing one to attend. SigGraph Asia is its counterpart in the other part of the world. For journals, *IEEE Transactions in Sensors* provides cutting edge information. Another journal found at IEEE, which has lots of virtual reality (VR) and UI publications is *IEEE TVCG* (*Transactions in Visualization and Computer Graphics*). Finally, the flagship journal in HCI is *ACM TOCHI*.

Natural User Interfaces?

The original title of this book was *Natural Input User Interfaces*. The title was changed. The world "natural" has become a hype term, and I'm not sure it belongs next to user interfaces. In Chapter 8, the question of whether gestures are natural is explored. While I'm not against anyone using the phrase "natural user interfaces," various factors tell me that what we are calling natural gestures today may not be. One of the definitions of natural is "existing in or caused by nature; not made or caused by humankind" [Stevenson and Lindberg 10]. I, in my experience as a multi-touch researcher, and most importantly, the literature by well-known researchers [Wobbrock et al. 09], have shown that users differ in the type of gesture for a given action. However, it is true that with learned behavior, people will tend to produce similar gestures. By now, most of us who have used a smartphone know that we can enlarge or shrink an image with a pinch gesture. Regardless of whether the input interaction is natural or learned behavior, the understanding of input user interfaces is what is important. Therefore, I decided to remove the word natural from the title, as I'm not convinced that many of the "natural" input devices are natural at all and the literature supports this. Sometimes, there are references to "natural" user interfaces but what they are actually referring to is direct interaction. There are times that mid-air interaction is referred to as "natural" but the lack of tactile feedback makes me doubt how natural they are. More than creating a debate about it, it is important to follow the work of researchers in this area and continue their work. Finally, as I have stated in this book, I prefer to use the word "intuitive" user interfaces or "modern" user intefaces rather than the word "natural".

---

[8]SigGraph 2016 contained a large amount of Virtual Reality demos.

Other Books

There are other books that have some overlaps with this one. The most important one is the seminal book *3D User Interfaces: Theory and Practice* by [Bowman et al. 04]. While their book covers different aspects of 3DUI and our book covers specific topics about input, there is a natural overlap in some of the chapters. We tried to make sure that this book provided additional information while keeping some topics for completeness. Our book needed to be self-contained whenever possible. Furthermore, the topics that may overlap have a different perspective because this book is input-centric.

Another book that has some overlap with our book is *Human-Computer Interaction: An Empirical and Research Perspective* [MacKenzie 12], a wonderful book about topics very close to many of us doing research in HCI. This is particularly true when this book describes predictive and descriptive models in HCI. A third book that was used for part of Chapter 3 is *Displays: Fundamentals and Applications* [Hainich and Bimber 11], among many others.

Book Recommendations

In the book's website, I will maintain a list of book recommendations for related topics. There are a few books that I must have near my desk at all times (whenever possible) and it is not *A Song of Ice and Fire* (Game of Thrones), which I keep in my Kindle. The following list of books, book chapters, and articles has been extremely useful to me for HCI, 3DUI, input user interfaces, computer graphics, software development, and computer science:

- *3D User Interfaces: Theory and Practice* [Bowman et al. 04].

- *Human-Computer Interaction: An Empirical Research Perspective* [MacKenzie 12].

- *Displays: Fundamentals and Applications* [Hainich and Bimber 11].

- *3D Game Engine Design* [Eberly 07].

  – Other books by David Eberly which have been very useful include *GPGPU: Programming for Games and Science, 3D Game Engine Architecture, Game Physics*, and *Geometric Tools for Computer Graphics*.

- *Human-Computer Interaction* [Dix et al. 04]

- *Discovering Statistics Using SPSS* [Field 09].

  – Also available for R.

- *Brave NUI World* by Wigdor and Wixon.

- *Sketching User Experiences: Getting the Design Right and the Right Design* by Bill Buxton.

- *Design Patterns* [Gamma et al. 94].

- *3D Math Primer for Graphics and Game Development* [Dunn and Parberry 11].

Looking Forward

Closer to the finish line, before the publication of this book, one always wonders if there is anything that could have been included but there was either no time or no space to do so. The answer is always yes and it is the hope of this author that others may fill the gaps in other books or publications. One particular gap that it was not filled, was the one of gestures. While I did cover gestures for multi-touch and pen, there is so much to cover, that may deserve its own book. One late example that comes to mind is by Dr. LaViola's team, that has been working with gestures succesfully. For example, Tarante and colleagues in *Exploring the Benefits of Context in 3D Gesture Recognition for Game-Based Virtual Environments* [Taranta II et al. 15]. Another example is **BenDesk**, which shows the potential of working with a curve display and multi-touch [Weiss et al. 10], and the *Interactive Slice WIM* [Coffey et al. 12b], among many other great work that was not able to be included in this book. We ask readers to send us research and important topics that did not make it into our book. We hope to add them in our next book and to our book's website.

There are many developments going on right now as we close this book. The Microsoft HoloLens, the HP Sprout, among many others. Most of these have come from the amazing research from the scientific community.

Acknowledgment of Support

We acknowledge the following sponsors, who made it possible in part to write this book and collect the information.

This material is based in part upon work supported by the National Science Foundation under Grant Nos. I/UCRC IIP-1338922, AIR IIP-1237818, SBIR IIP-1330943, III-Large IIS-1213026, MRI CNS-1429345, MRI CNS-0821345, MRI CNS-1126619, CREST HRD-0833093, I/UCRC IIP-0829576, MRI CNS-0959985, and U.S. DOT Grant ARI73. Additional sponsors will be mentioned in our website.

We would also like to acknowledge the grant provided by Taylor & Francis during the initial development of this book.

In addition, Francisco R. Ortega acknowledges the support from GAANN during his Ph.D. studies and the Florida Education Fund (McKnight fellowship). The support of Florida International University (FIU) has been amazing for the production of this book. It is specially true for the School of Computing and Information Sciences and the department of Electrical and Computer Engineering at FIU.

My current lab (OpenHID) inside of our HPDRC center has been great with the support by Martha Gutierrez, Scott Graham, Karell Muller, and the students in the OpenHID lab, Alain Galvan, Jason-Lee Thomas, and Ruben Balcazar.

Finally, this would have not been possible without CRC press and everyone working in this amazing publishing company (see my personal acknowledgements for more details).

About the Images

Most of the images for chapters in Part II (except Chapter 14) were created by Bahareh Abyarjoo (abyar.ba@gmail.com). The cover was created by a very talented student, named Alain Galvan (alaingalvan.com). Figure 7.7 was drawn by Patty Melo. Original (or adapted) in Chapters 1—8 and 10, were drawn by Luz Aguilar. All the images are property of their respective copyright holders and permissions were obtained for all images, either with direct copyright holder's permission or using the Copyright Clearance Center.

Personal Acknowledgment

This book would not have been possible without the guidance and support of my co-authors, Dr. Abyarjoo, Dr. Barreto, Dr. Rishe, and Dr. Adjouadi. Their insight into their own areas of expertise has made it possible to finish this book. I also thank my collaborators, without whom certain topics would not have been included in this book. It is because of the collaborators that this book is more well-rounded.

While all my co-authors and collaborators worked extremely hard and provided great help, two of them I want to give a special thanks, since they were both my former Ph.D. co-advisors: Dr. Barreto and Dr. Rishe. Dr. Barreto showed me how to be a good and integral researcher and has always provided me with help. Dr. Rishe, who has shown me how to always push further, to be the best version of me that I can be, has always support me and has provided funding to freely research and work way beyond my Ph.D.

Another important player in the making of this book is the 3DUI community. The many emails I sent asking for support were always answered with insight and support. I thank the research and practitioner community of 3DUI for their help and ask for their continued support to improve this book.

There are some friends and colleagues who have made it possible to get to the finish line: Daisy Lu, Frank Hernandez, Tessa Verhoef, Nacho Mora, Aaron Lebos, Sergio J. Ceron, Eddie Garcia, and Jose Ignacio (Nacho) Mora. My former lab mates, who have always supported me, are always present in my thoughts: Daisy, Raymond, Ong, Amy, Jarr, Jonathan, and Sara.

I'm grateful for people who helped from a distance: Dr. MacKenzie, Dr. Hinckley, Dr. Bowman, and Dr. Eberly, who have taken time to reply to my questions, though most of them have never met me in person. In particular, the exchanges between Dr. Eberly and me have been extremely rich.

CRC Press (Taylor & Francis) has been of great help. In particular, Rick Adams, who was always understanding with the delays that this book presented. I also have to thank Kari Budyk for her help, in particular when dealing with permissions. Also, Charlotte Byrnes, provided amazing editing help and sent many emails and was always willing to help. Karen Simon also provided lots of guidance in the final editing and lots of patience. Finally, I want to thank everyone at CRC Press for their continued support and amazing help. I chose them because of the quality of content they currently have. Many of their books in computer science (in particular computer graphics and HCI), I own and have enjoyed.

Without my family none of this would matter. Their support and understanding have been priceless. Their love has proven to be the best motivation to continue the research when there were difficult times. My dad Francisco, mom Patricia, my grandparents Aida and Pedro, my sisters Marcela, Cecilia, Jimena, for their continued love and care for my entire life. For my brothers-in-law Roberto, Kenneth, Eddie, for the love of my sisters and my nephews. For all my nieces and nephews Fernanda, Francisca, Felipe A., Sebastian, Roberto, Felipe, Nicholas.

I will always be in debt to my father and mother, for their love and support. For the Atari 65XE and disk drive 1050 that were given to me, and gave me the gift of coding. Because they let me dream, they let me be, they supported me in good and bad times, because they believed in me, when I couldn't do it myself.

I will also be in debt to every person who has helped me in the United States of America, which I call my own today, but was foreign when I came. Living as an immigrant at a young age was not always easy but many people have helped along the way.

Finally, my wife Luz Adriana and my daughter Sofia Alejandra are my north star, who guide me along this path called life. It is because of them that I keep striving to be a better person, better professional, and better husband and father. It is for you and our new family that I continue to move along this path. I love you, always and forever.

– Francisco R. Ortega

Abbreviations

1D	One-Dimensional.
2D	Two-Dimensional.
3D	Three-Dimensional.
3DUI	Three-Dimensional User Interface.
AC	Alternating Current.
ADC	Analog-to-Digital Converter.
AHRS	Attitude and Heading Reference System.
AI	Artificial Intelligence.
AIC	Adaptive Interference Canceller.
ANS	Autonomic Nervous System.
API	Application Programming Interface.
AR	Augmented Reality.
ARW	Angle Random Walk.
ASCII	American Standard Code for Information Interchange.
ATF	Adaptive Transversal Filter.
AUSB	AU Self-Balancing Bicycle.
BCI	Brain–Computer Interface.
BSP	Binary Space Partitioning.
CG	Computer Graphics.
CMOS	Complementary Metal-Oxide-Semiconductor.
CPN	Colored Petri Nets.
CPU	Central Processing Unit.
CR	Corneal Reflection.
CRT	Cathode Ray Tube.
CUBE	Computer-Driven Upper Body Environment.
D-Pad	Digital Pad.
DC	Direct Current.
DFT	Discrete Fourier Transform.
DI	Diffuse Illumination.
DIY	Do It Yourself.
DLP	Digital Light Processing.

DOF	Degrees of Freedom.
DPI	Dots per Inch.
DSI	Diffuse Surface Illumination.
DSP	Digital Signal Processing.
DTFT	Discrete-Time Fourier Transform.
DTMF	Dual Tone Multi-Frequency.
ECHoSS	Experiment Controller Human Subject System.
EEG	Electroencephalograph.
EEPROM	Electrically Erasable Programmable Read-Only Memory.
EGT	Eye Gaze Tracking.
EM	Electromagnetic.
F-LCoS	Ferroeletric Liquid Crystal on Silicon.
FETOUCH	Feature Extraction Multi-Touch System.
FFT	Fast Fourier Transform.
fMRI	Functional Magnetic Resonance Imaging.
FOR	Field of Regard.
FOV	Field of View.
FPS	First-Person Shooter.
fps	Frames-Per-Second.
FS	Fourier Series.
FSM	Finite-State Machine.
FT	Fourier Transform.
FTIR	Frustrated Total Internal Reflection.
GamePad	Video GamePad Controller.
GHz	Giga-Hertz.
GML	Gesture Markup Language.
GOMS	Goals, Operators, Methods, and Selection.
GPS	Global Positioning System.
GPU	Graphics Processing Unit.
GSR	Galvanic Skin Response.
GUI	Graphical User Interface.
GWC	GestureWorks Core.
HCI	Human–Computer Interaction.
HDTV	High-Definition Television.
HID	Human Interface Devices.
HLPN	High-Level Petri Net.
HMD	Head-Mounted Display.
HMM	Hidden Markov Models.
HP	Hewlett-Packard.
Hz	Hertz.
IDE	Integrated Development Environment.
IMU	Inertial Measurement Unit.

INS	Inertial Navigation System.
IO port	Input and Output Port.
IR	Infrared.
ITO	Indium Tin Oxide.
KHz	Kilo-Hertz.
KLM	Keystroke-Level Model.
LCD	Liquid-Crystal Display.
LCoS	Liquid Crystal on Silicon.
LED	Light-Emitting Diode.
LED	Organic Light-Emitting Diodes.
LLP	Laser Light Plane.
LRS	Landmark, Route, Survey.
LSQ	Least Squares.
MEMS	Micro-Electro-Mechanical Systems.
MIDI	Musical Instrument Digital Interface.
MLM	Moving Liquid Mirror.
MRI	Magnetic Resonance Imaging.
NES	Nintendo Entertainment System.
NLS	oN-Line System.
NUI	Natural User Interface.
OAE	Optical Axis of the Eye.
OCA	Optically Clear Adhesive.
OGRE	Object-Oriented Graphics Rendering Engine.
OIS	Object-Oriented Input System.
OS	Operating System.
p-cap	Projected Capacitive.
PARC	Palo Alto Research Center.
PC	Personal Computer.
PCB	Printed Circuit Board.
PD	Pupil Diameter.
PD controller	Proportional-Derivative Controller.
PeNTa	Petri Net Touch.
PET	Polyethylene Terephthalate Film.
PMPD	Processed Modified Pupil Diameter.
PN	Petri Net.
POG	Point-of-Gaze.
POS	Point of Sale.
Prt Net	Predicate Transition Net.
PWM	Pulse Width Modulation.
RAM	Random-Access Memory.
RBG	Red Green Blue.
RBI	Reality Based Interactions.
RegEx	Regular Expression.

RLS	Recursive Least Squares.
ROC	Region of Convergence (ROC).
ROM	Read-Only Memory.
RRW	Rate Random Walk.
RX	Receiver.
SDK	Software Development Kit.
SNR	Signal-to-Noise Ratio.
SONAR	Sound Navigation and Ranging.
STL	STereoLithography.
TFT	Thin-Film Transistor.
TUI	Tangible User Interface.
TUIO	Tangible User Interface Object.
TV	Television.
TX	Transmitter.
UART	Universal Asynchronous Receiver and Transmitter.
UbiComp	Ubiquitous Computing.
UI	User Interface.
USB	Universal Serial Bus.
VE	Virtual Environment.
VR	Virtual Reality.
VRD	Virtual Retina Display.
WiiMote	Nintendo Wii Controller.
WIM	World-in-Miniature.
WIMP	Windows-Icon-Menu-Pointer.
WINAPI	Windows API.
WinRT	Windows Run-Time.
XML	Extensible Markup Language.

Part I

Theory

1

Introduction

The most profound technologies are those that disappear. They weave themselves into the fabric of everyday life until they are indistinguishable from it.

—Mark Weiser

The seminal work known as Sketchpad [Sutherland 63] by Ivan Sutherland has inspired many researchers in the field of human–computer interaction (HCI) and three-dimensional user interface (3DUI). Sutherland created an elegant and sophisticated system, which is considered by some as the birth of computer user interface studies. The invention of the mouse by Douglas Engelbart in 1963 [English et al. 67] and the invention of the Graphical User Interface (GUI) at the Palo Alto Research Center (PARC) gave way to one of the most successful paradigms in HCI: Windows-Icon-Menu-Pointer (WIMP), which has allowed users to interact easily with computers. The seminal work known as Sketchpad [Sutherland 63] by Ivan Sutherland has inspired many researchers in the field of HCI and 3DUI. Sutherland created an elegant and sophisticated system, which is considered by some as the birth of computer user interface studies. The invention of the mouse by Douglas Engelbart in 1963 [English et al. 67] and the invention of the GUI at the PARC gave way to one of the most successful paradigms in HCI: WIMP, which has allowed users to interact easily with computers.

Today, with the introduction of new input devices, such as multi-touch surface displays, the Nintendo Wii Controller (WiiMote), the Microsoft Kinect, the Leap Motion sensor, and Inertial Navigation Systems (INS), the field of HCI finds itself at an important crossroads that requires solving new challenges.

Humans interact with computers, relying on different input-output channels. This may include vision (and visual perception), auditory, tactile (touch), movement, speech, and others [Dix et al. 04]. In addition, humans use their (long- and short-term) memory, cognition, and problem-solving skills to interact with computer systems [Dix et al. 04]. This computer interaction has a set of challenges that needs to be addressed. This book covers user input interfaces, the input for users when working with computer systems.

The areas of HCI and 3DUIs are broad fields, making it difficult for most books to cover details in depth about a specific topic. This book concentrates on input technology while other books may focus on other areas. There are some seminal books that covered more general topics that any developer or researcher must have. These are the seminal book titled *The Psychology of Human Computer Interaction* [Card et al. 83]; *User Interfaces: Theory and Practice*[1] [Bowman et al. 04]; *Human-Computer Interaction* [Dix et al. 04]; and *Human Computer Interaction: An Empirical Research Perspective* [MacKenzie 12]. The challenge for this book to be at par with the ones mentioned is great, the opportunity is welcome, and the journey is uphill.

This book deals with user interaction with a perspective on input technologies. The book is divided into three parts: theory, advanced topics, and hands-on approach. The book concentrates on concepts; however, whenever possible, complete source code will be made available on the book's website. Additional material will also be found on the website, which includes the online chapters we have provided with the book. Finally, it is important to note that while the objective is to cover input devices and user interaction, output devices are critical when using input. Therefore, this book will cover basic details about output.

The book covers input technology, which in most cases are commodity[2] devices. However, it is hard to avoid the topic of virtual reality with the introduction of the oculus rift or even the Google Cardboard. Many of the topics covered in this book may be used in different types of environments. This book covers basic concepts of virtual reality (VR) headset. However, it is important to keep in mind that VR is outside the scope of this book in its current form.

This chapters offers a brief introduction to HCI and input technologies.

1.1   The Vision

Vannevar Bush was the director of the Office of Scientific Research and Development, USA [Packer and Jordan 02] when he wrote "*As We May Think*" [Bush 45],[3] which was the inspiration for scientists to come, including Ivan Sutherland. His vision was prophetic for many scientists that have cited him over 4000 times [MacKenzie 12]. Bush envisioned the personal workstation (which he called Memex) as an essential tool for researchers and everyday users. He was ahead of his time saying that "a record if it's to be useful to science, must be continuously extended, it must be stored, and above all it must be consulted"(p.37).[4] He went on to write that "the human mind does not work that way. It operates by association"(p.43), which is important for 3D input user interfaces. This article

---

[1]The authors are working a newer edition.
[2]Off-the-shelf devices. We prefer affordable devices whenever possible.
[3]A reprint of this article is found in [Bush 96].
[4]The quotes were taking from [Bush 96]. For additional comments, see [Simpson et al. 96].

has proven an inspiration for many scientists because of the vision that was laid and the reminder that collaboration and thinking outside of the box is imperative. Ahead of his time, Bush wrote:

> A touch brings up the code book. Tapping a few keys projects the head of the trail. A lever runs through it at will, stopping at interesting items, going off on side excursions. It is an interesting trail, pertinent to the discussion. So he sets a reproducer in action, photographs the whole trail out, and passes it to his friends for insertion in his own memex, there to be linked into the more general trail.

1.2 Human–Computer Interaction

HCI is the field that studies the exchange of information between computers and their users. The field emerged in the decade of the 1980s, with influences from many other fields, such as psychology, computer science, human factors, and others. An alternate definition of HCI is the communication between computer systems and computer users. How the communication enables the use of the technology is a central part of the study of HCI.

A field closely related to HCI is human factors, which is concerned with the capabilities, limitations, and performance by people when using any type of systems.[5] Also, from the perspective of the system design, human factors studies the efficiency, safety, comfort, and enjoyability when people use a given system. This seems quite close to HCI if you think of systems as computer systems [MacKenzie 12]. The HCI field also draws knowledge from psychology. Some examples are cognitive psychology, experimental psychology, and others. This is very useful, as it helps us to understand users and tests how they interact with different types of computer systems. HCI is a very broad field. In HCI, you can find VR, 3DUI, affective computing (which draws as much as from psychology as it does from Artificial Intelligence (AI)), and others.

Major events in the HCI community [MacKenzie 12] started with the vision of Vannevar Bush with "As We May Think," the development of the Sketchpad by Ivan Sutherland, the development of the computer mouse by Douglas Engelbart, and the launch of the Xerox Star system. Then, the first interest group formed (SIGCHI[6]) in 1982, followed by the release of the seminal book, *The Psychology of Human-Computer Interaction*, and the release of the Apple Macintosh, starting a new era for computer systems.

---

[5]It doesn't have to be a computer system.
[6]See http://www.sigchi.org.

Side Note 1.1: The Mother of All Demos

The seminal talk by Engelbart and colleagues became to be known as "The Mother of all Demos." This presentation set the stage for what was to come. It prepared the way for later innovations at Xerox Parc (see Figure 1.1), the commercial success of the Macintosh, and Microsoft Windows. It presented collaborated editor, word processing, and video conferencing, among others. Most importantly, it showcased the use of the mouse in conjunction with the keyboard to perform cut, copy, and paste, among other operations.

Wendy Hu, reflected about Engelbart's demo and said: "Engerlbart was not wholly prophetic; his obsession with viewing the human as an information processor, for example, keeps him even today from appreciating the mouse's value for its ease of use" [Ju 08].

Figure 1.1: Xerox PARC System. With permission.

1.2.1   Usability

Usability is defined as the user acceptability of a system, where the system satisfies the user's needs [Nielsen 94]. Furthermore, usability is an engineering process that is used to understand the effects of a given system on the user, in other words, how the system communicates with the user and vice versa. Usefulness "is the issue of whether the system can be used to achieve some desired goal" [Nielsen 94]. This breaks down into utility and usability. Utility addresses the question of the functionality of the system, which means if the system can accomplish what it was intended for [Nielsen 94]. Usability in this case refers to "how well users can use that functionality" [Nielsen 94]. Finally, it is important to understand that usability applies to all aspects of a given system that a user might interact with [Nielsen 94]. The following list briefly describes the five traditional usability attributes (adapted from [Nielsen 94]):

- **Learnability**: The system must have a very small learning curve, where the user can quickly become adapted to the system to perform the work required.

- **Efficiency**: Once the user has learned the system, the productivity level achieved must be high in order to demonstrate a high efficiency.

- **Memorability**: The system is considered to have a high memorability if when the user returns after some time of usage, the interaction is the same or better than it was the first time.

- **Errors**: The system is considered to have a low error rate if the user makes few errors during the interaction. Furthermore, if users make an error, they can recover quickly and maintain productivity.

- **Satisfaction**: The interaction with the user must be pleasant.

To Test or Not Test

It is common in HCI to experiment on different prototypes and techniques. This is very important in HCI. However, there are a few pointers that are important to have in mind. One of them is the bias toward objective, quantifiable measurements, treated as facts, without the incentive of retesting by others [Greenberg and Buxton 08]. Also, Greenberg and Buxton provided compelling arguments about one myth held by some people in the community. Some researchers may think that to have a successful experiment, the new device must outperform the old one. A counter example offered by the authors in [Greenberg and Buxton 08] is Marconi's wireless radio (1901). This radio would not have passed any usability test and it was severely criticized at the time. This leads to the question whether a device is usable or useful (or both)? It is the opinion of this author (and the authors in [Greenberg and Buxton 08]) that the usefulness at early stages is far more important. Usability comes later in the process, as has been the experience in the field [Greenberg and Buxton 08, Buxton 10].

Figure 1.2: Sutherland's Sketchpad [English et al. 67]. (With permission from MIT.)

1.2.2 The Sketchpad

In 1962, during Sutherland's PhD studies,[7] he published *SKETCHPAD. A Man-Machine Graphical Communication System*. The Sketchpad was an amazing invention at the time and it has proven to have given birth to modern user interfaces. This was a new concept, where users were not typing commands in a terminal but interacting with a light pen. Sutherland's Sketchpad was able to create circles, arcs and lines. In addition, the interface could zoom in, zoom out, create instances of shapes. Furthermore, the user could make lines parallel or perpendicular.[8] Another important aspect of Sketchpad was the use of a pen to do the drawings. Figure 1.2 shows Sutherland working with the Sketchpad.

1.2.3 The Mouse

In 1963, Douglas Engelbart invented the mouse (see Figures 1.3 and 1.4). While the impact of the mouse is evident today, it was not obvious back in the 1970s. The patent was filed in 1967[9] with the title *X-Y POSITION INDICATOR FOR A DISPLAY SYSTEM* and approved November 17,1970, with US Patent ID 3541541. In 1968, before Engelbart could even show his invention, a German company

---

[7] At Massachusetts Institute of Technology (MIT).
[8] Search in youtube for Ivan Sutherland's Sketchpad to view the demo.
[9] In Google Patents search for: engelbart 1967 position pot

Figure 1.3: Engelbart's mouse. (With permission from SRI.)

Figure 1.4: Engelbart with original mouse and three button mouse. (With permission from SRI.)

(Telefunken) released a variation of the mouse. This mouse had a ball inside as the typical mouses used during the 1980s and 1990s before the optical mouse. While Engelbart created the mouse, there was another effort never patented and a

Figure 1.5: Engelbart's workstation, circa 1965. (With permission from SRI.)

Canadian secret by Cranston, Logstaff, and Taylor in 1952[10] [Ball and Vardalas 94]. This was a trackball for their Datar System. In 1981, a mouse was released commercially with the Xerox Star workstation. In 1983, Microsoft released their first mouse to be used with Microsoft Word (DOS version). The next year, in 1984, along with the Big Brother ad during the Super Bowl, with the era of the Apple Macintosh, came the Lisa Mouse. Additional pictures of the first workstation used with a mouse (Figure 1.5), a later modification of the workstation using a three button mouse (Figure 1.6), and Engelbart holding the original mouse and the modified three button mouse (Figure 1.4) are included in this chapter. For additional images, see http://Digibarn.com, http://www.dougengelbart.org/, and Bill Buxton's collection [Buxton 14], among many other sources on the web.

1.2.4 The Light Pen and the Computer Mouse

There are two major events that are critical moments in HCI for people who study input user interfaces: the Sketchpad by Ivan Sutherland[11] and the invention of the mouse by Douglas Engelbart. This all happened before the explosion of the field in the 1980s.

Having more than one device prompted English, Engelbart, and Berman [English et al. 67] to ask: Which device is better to control a cursor on a screen? This

---

[10]This was a secret project for the Royal Canadian Navy's Datar system.
[11]He also introduced the VR head-mounted display (HMD).

Figure 1.6: 1968 workstation with three-button mouse, keyboard, and chord keyboard. (With permission from SRI.)

Side Note 1.2: Predicting The Future

Bill Buxton said: "Innovation is not about alchemy. In fact, innovation is not about invention. An idea may well start with an invention, but the bulk of the work and creativity is in that idea's augmentation and refinement." [Buxton 08]. In TechFest 2013, he later said: "Any new ideas by the time that it reaches maturity, takes 20 years," adding that if we can't see past fifteen years of history leading up to a particular technology, either we haven't done our homework or the time predicted for this technology to become mainstream has been miscalculated. Appreciation of the work that has come before us it is really important to understand where we are heading.

---

was the first user study dealing with input devices for computing systems that may have marked a "before and after" in HCI [English et al. 67].

In this study ("Display-Selection Techniques for Text Manipulation"), the subjects were presented with a computer mouse, a light pen, a joystick with two modes (absolute and rate), Grafacon,[12] and a user's knee lever (also referred to as the knee controller). The study used repeated-measures, meaning that all devices were tested for each subject. The dependent variables that were measured were: **time** to acquire target and the **error rate** when trying to acquire the target. The combination of both measurements led researchers to the conclusion that the

---

[12]Graphical input device for curve tracing, manufactured by Data Equipment Company.

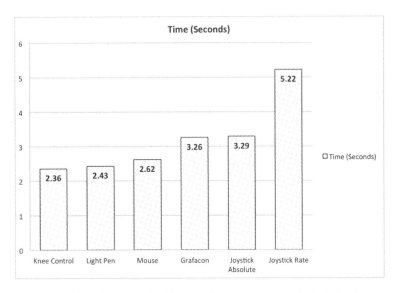

Figure 1.7: Mouse study: Time. Adapted from [English et al. 67].

computer mouse was a better device based on the study. This was great news, because a knee lever doesn't seem quite exciting to use. Figure 1.7 shows how the knee controller was faster than the rest of the devices. However, looking at Figure 1.8, it is clear that the mouse has the lowest error rate compared to the other devices tested. Another interesting part of the study is that while the light pen was faster than the computer mouse, it was known to cause discomfort[13] after prolonged use.[14]

1.2.5 Graphical User Interfaces and WIMP

GUI is a type of interface that allows the user to interact with windows or icons, as opposed to a text interface. The GUI was first seen in the Xerox Star system, developed at PARC [Hiltzik 09]. The GUI has allowed systems like Microsoft Windows and Apple Macintosh to become pervasive for day-to-day use in desktop computers and mobile devices.

The WIMP paradigm[15] emerged with the availability of Apple and IBM desktop computers. This paradigm refers to the interaction of users with the GUI, which includes WIMP [Rogers et al. 11]. The **windows**, which can be scrolled, overlapped, moved, stretched, opened, closed, minimized, and maximized, among

---

[13]Which was probably known from the times of the sketchpad [Sutherland 63].

[14]Using a pen while resting a hand on the surface may be more comfortable [Hülsmann and Maicher 14].

[15]Referred to as interface [Dix et al. 04].

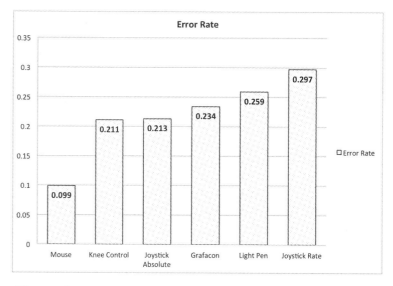

Figure 1.8: Mouse study: Error rate. Adapted from [English et al. 67].

other operations, were designed to be the core of the visual feedback and inter-action with the user. The **menus** allow the user to select different options that augmented the use of the Window. The menu can be activated by clicking on it. Once selected, the menu expands down (or in a different direction), which allows the user to select an option. The **icons** allow a representation of applications, objects, commands, or tools that, if clicked, become active. Icons are commonly found in a desktop area of the display or in a menu. Finally, the central part of WIMP is the **pointing**. This allows the user to interact with any of the interface elements already mentioned, using a mouse with a click button [Rogers et al. 11]. The paradigm, along with the GUI interface, has evolved to allow many new types of interactions. However, the basic principle remains the same.

1.2.6 3D User Interfaces

A user interface (UI) is the medium of communication between a user and a computer system. The UI receives the input (actions) from the users, it delegates the computation to a designated process, and then it represents the computer's output into a representation that the user can understand [Bowman et al. 04]. A 3DUI is the medium of communication between a user performing three-dimensional (3D) interaction with a computer. These are tasks "performed directly in a 3D spatial context" [Bowman et al. 04]. The fact that someone is working in a 3D environment does not mean that they are doing 3D interaction. For example, if the user is navigating a 3D landscape of Miami by using commands or menu-driven actions, they do not constitute 3D interaction. Conversely, 3D interaction does not have to involve 3D input devices. For example, by using a two-dimensional (2D) non-stereo display with multi-touch capability, the user performs a 2D gesture to move along the Z axis. This means that the 2D action has been mapped (or translated) to a 3D action. There are several reasons why 3DUIs are important to study. Bowman et al. provided five reasons in their seminal book [Bowman et al. 04]:

1. Real-world tasks are performed in 3D.

2. 3DUI are becoming mature.

3. 3D interaction is difficult to solve; hence, it provides a challenge to many researchers. This also means that there are many problems that need to be solved.

4. 3DUIs require better usability.

5. 3DUIs still have many open questions, leaving space to study and to innovate as much in academia as in industry.

Directions for 3D User Interfaces

Bowman and colleagues provided a way forward for 3DUI based on the research that had been accomplished at the time of this publication [Bowman et al. 06]. They proposed four general research directions, based on the observation that lots of research had concentrated in general methods, such as application-generality, domain-generality, task-generality, device-generality, and user-generality [Bowman et al. 06]. The alternative is to concentrate in specificity [Bowman et al. 06]. In other words, "explicit considerations of specific domains, tasks, and devices." Take for example task-specificity: If the researcher looks at scaling as a special case of manipulation, then it is generalizing the task; however, if the researcher looks at the unique properties of resizing, it allows to dig deeper into this task, making it more specialized. A counter example for task-generality is providing a ray-casting technique for any type of object without considering specific attributes about the environment. Similar examples can be found for application-specificity, domain-specificity, device-specificity, and user-specificity in their publication [Bowman et al. 06]. They also suggested to look into "flavors," which means adding complexity, features, tweaking to an existing technique [Bowman et al. 06]. Another recommendation is that 3DUI research should spawn into emerging technologies. Finally, implementation issues of 3DUI still need to be addressed.

Side Note 1.3: Desktops

Desktops are still important today. Computer graphics cards keep pushing the boundaries. Even more important, some of us use our laptops as desktops. To dismiss the desktop, in our opinion is wrong. To dismiss WIMP and the use of the keyboard or mouse is also wrong. Hinckley and Wigdor wrote: "Rumors regarding the death of the desktop computer are greatly exaggerated. After 40 years of iterative design, the personal computer, driven by a mouse and keyboard and controlling a WIMP GUI, continues to evolve" [Hinckley and Widgor 12]. They also state that pointing continues to be the main tool for selection as pointed out by [Balakrishnan et al. 97]. This is not say that other emerging paradigms and technologies may surpass WIMP and the keyboard and mouse devices, but to just overlook them is wrong based on the number of years of research. Furthermore, the research for WIMP and keyboard and mouse always serves as a foundation for other emerging technologies.

1.3 Definitions

It is important to cover some definitions that will be used throughout the book. It is possible that some definitions may differ from other people's definitions but we have to try to make it as standard as possible, while making sure we cover the definition that is used throughout the book. Some more specialized definitions will be either described or expanded in later chapters. The following are the basic definitions:

- **Virtual environments (VE)**: This is a synthetic world, usually created for 3D applications and games. The spatial space is used as a first-person camera. However, this term could be loosely used by some to refer to any synthetic world regardless of the point of view of the user. This is done in real-time.

- **Virtual reality (VR)**: Bowman and colleagues state that virtual reality is a synonym of virtual environments [Bowman et al. 04]. However, it is commonly viewed as the immersion of the user in a virtual environment.

- **Augmented reality (AR)**: Real-world environments with synthetic information form the world.

- **Mixed reality (MR)**: This refers to the combination of virtual reality and augmented reality.

- **Input device**: This is a physical device (hardware) that can sense physical properties (people, places, or things) [Hinckley and Widgor 12].

- **Output device**: This is the primary way for computers to communicate feedback to their users (physical device).

- **User interface**: This is the representation that allows the communications between users and computers. The user interface is "the summation of all its input devices, conceptual models, and interaction techniques" [Hinckley and Widgor 12].

- **User experience**: This is the perception of the user interface from the user's cognitive states, emotional states, and social interactions, among others.

- **Interaction technique**: This is the merging of input and output (including hardware and software) that allows the user to complete a task using the user interface. The interaction technique is delegated the task of mapping input to an action of the system, and the output action to the output device.

- **Conceptual model**: This is "coherent model that users visualize about the function of a system" [Hinckley and Widgor 12]. In other words, this helps users to visualize a system with metaphors such as the graphical user interface. These models are meant to be refined over time by the user's interaction with the system.

- **3D interaction technique**: User's interaction in 3D spatial context. Interaction techniques involve selection and manipulation. It is important to note that using 3D virtual environment (VE) or using 3D input does not constitute 3D interaction [Bowman et al. 04]. It is the action mapping that creates the 3D interaction. For example, a user that manipulates a multi-touch surface (which is 2D) to navigate in a 3D environment will constitute 3D interaction because of the mapping from the 2D input to the 3D world.

- **Ubiquitous computing (UbiComp)**: This term was coined by visionary Mark Weiser [Weiser 91]. He talked about technology being pervasive, everywhere, anytime, where the more we didn't notice the technology, the more efficient it would become [Weiser 91].

Further Reading

This book does not cover ubiquitous computing (UbiComp) but it is mentioned in this chapter. UbiComp is the target for many researchers working in 3D interfaces. The most important paper is the one by [Weiser 91]. Two books that cover this topics are also very useful, such as the ones written by [Poslad 11, Krumm 09]. The UbiComp conference is one of the major places to find the current research in this field.

Exercises

1. Watch "The Mother of all Demos." The video will show how advanced was Engelbart for his time.

2. Watch The Sketchpad by Ivan Sutherland on YouTube or similar Internet video repository. The video will show you a visual object-oriented language way ahead of its time.

2

Input: Interfaces and Devices

> The barometer has fallen and a brisk wind blows. Input and interaction are not what they used to be. Gusts drift over the line in the sand that separates input from output.
>
> —Ken Hinckley and Daniel Wigdor

2.1 Introduction

This chapter deals with input, which is the primary objective of this book. Some of the best advice for input devices was given by Hinckley and Wigdor in "Input Technologies and Techniques" [Hinckley and Widgor 12] by stating that to look at the complete picture of input devices one must go beyond the typical strengths and weaknesses. This means that "any property of an input device can be turned to one's advantage when used appropriately in an interface design" [Hinckley and Widgor 12].

2.2 Input Technologies

Input devices are the primary tool for providing information to a computer system, which is essential for the communication between a user and a computer. In general, input devices can sense different physical properties, such as "people, places, or things" [Hinckley 08]. When working with input devices, feedback is necessary. For example, using a brush to paint in mid-air without proper feedback will be as useless as using the pen without paper, or using a car alarm system without some feedback from the device or the car. This is why input devices are tied to output feedback from a computer system when immediate feedback is required.

While each device has unique features and it is important to know the limitations and advantages of a given device, there are some common properties that may apply to most devices. The following is a list of input device properties (adapted from [Hinckley 08, Hinckley and Widgor 12]):

- **Property Sensed:** Devices can sense linear position and motion. Some devices will measure force and others change in angle. The property that is used will determine the transfer function that maps the input to the output. Position-sensing devices are *absolute input devices*, such as multi-touch. *Motion-sensing devices* can be relative input devices, with the example of the mouse as one of them. There is room for ambiguity depending on the actual design of the transfer function. For example, a multi-touch device can be used as a relative input device if desired, even though it is a direct-input system.

- **Number of Dimensions:** The number of dimensions sensed by the device can determine some of its use. For example, the mouse senses two dimensions of motion for X and Y coordinates, while a vision-input system may sense three dimensions of motion for X, Y, and Z axes. While the mouse does sense two dimensions, the transfer function may be mapped to a higher degree of dimensions with some additional input, to provide a richer set of interaction (e.g., 3D navigation). Some other devices have different types of 3D sensors (e.g., gyroscope, accelerometer, etc.). Understanding the dimensions of the device can provide a designer with the correct mapping for the transfer function.

- **Indirect versus Direct Devices:** *Indirect devices* provide a relative measurement to be used with the computer system. For example, the motion of the mouse is relative to the position of the cursor and the movement of the user. In other words, while the cursor may traverse the complete screen from left to right, the movements by the user with the mouse may be confined to a smaller space than the screen. A mouse may even be picked up and moved to a different location without causing any movement on the display, using the transfer function to map the movements. *Direct devices* provide a different interaction for users. In general, they lack buttons for state transitions and allow the user to work directly on the display. One example is the use of a digital pen with a tablet. The user can paint directly on the screen, having a 1:1 relationship with the surface display. There are typical problems with direct devices, such as occlusion, i.e., the user may occlude a part of the display with his/her hand. Direct-input devices are expanded in Section 2.2.2.

• **Device Acquisition Time:** "The average time to move one's hand to a device is known as *acquisition time*" [Hinckley 08]. *Homing time* is defined as the time that a user takes to go from one device to another. One example is the time that it takes to return from a multi-touch desktop to a keyboard.

• **Gain:** The control-to-display (C:D) gain or ratio is defined as the distance an input device moved (C) divided by the actual distance moved on the display (D). This is useful to map indirect devices, such as the computer mouse. For a more detailed explanation, see Side Note 2.3.

• **Sampling Rate:** Sampling rate is given by how many samples are processed each second. For example, if the WiiMote Motion Plus has a sampling rate of 100 hertz (Hz), this means that for every one second, there are 100 digital samples from the device. In some devices, the sampling rate will be fixed, and in others, it may vary. The difference may be due to an actual delay on the computer system and not to the input device. Understanding the sampling rate by a designer can provide additional features for the user's interactions. For additional information about sampling rate and digital signal processing (DSP), see [Zölzer 08, Ifeachor and Jervis 02].

• **Performance Metrics:** Performance metrics are useful to study in order to understand the interaction of an input device, its user, and the computer system. One example is seen in the classic study of the mouse versus other devices [English et al. 67], where the error-rate was a significant factor in why the mouse was the device found to be most effective. Other metrics include pointing speed and accuracy, learning time, and selection time, among others.

• **State Sensed:** Device events are becoming more important with the current direct input devices (e.g., multi-touch). While indirect devices have events, such as out-of-range, tracking, and dragging states, direct input devices offer different types of states that are important to keep in mind while designing. The implications of touch-down, touch-move, and touch-up have implications "in the design of interactions" [Hinckley and Widgor 12].

• **Additional Metrics:** There are several other metrics, including some that may be unique to a specific input device. One example is the pressure size in multi-touch displays.[1] Understanding all the possible metrics is important. The recommendation by Bowman et al. is to know the capabilities and limitations of each device [Bowman et al. 04].

---

[1] If this is available to the device.

Side Note 2.1: The Loss of a Closely Held Abstraction

Hinckley and Wigdor talk about the loss of abstraction due to direct interaction [Hinckley and Widgor 12]. The WIMP paradigm has allow a very useful abstraction for users, where the cursor represents the user's center of attention, which separates the input from the output [Hinckley and Widgor 12]. In the world of direct interaction, either a device needs its own design or we may need to find a new paradigm post-WIMP. It is important to remember that WIMP paradigm with the use of GUI is highly optimized for the keyboard and mouse. However, many modern devices make use of the WIMP paradigm without the use a keyboard and mouse.

2.2.1   Transfer Function

The transformation of the input device data is called **transfer function**. The idea is to provide a function that allows for a smooth and stable interaction with the goal of delivering adequate performance. Adequate understanding and use of transfer functions requires control theory [Ogata 09] knowledge. An example of a video gamepad controller (GamePad) input data transformation is shown later in this chapter (see Section 2.4.3). There are many types of transfer function, including the control-display gain (see Side Note 2.3) [Hinckley and Widgor 12]:

- **Appropriate Mappings**: It is important to find mappings that matches "the properties of the input device" [Hinckley and Widgor 12]. One of them is force-sensing, where the force produces the velocity. Another one is position-to-position or velocity-to-velocity functions. One example of inappropriate mapping, provided by Hinckley and Wigdor is the mapping given by the "velocity based on the position mouse cursor" [Hinckley and Widgor 12].

- **Self-Centering Devices**: Devices that return to center (see Section 2.4.3) allow users to stop quickly. To optimize this movement, a non-linear function can be used, as shown in Equation 2.1, where the rate (d_x) is given by the gain factor (K) multiplied by the input signal (x) with its non-linear exponent (a). The values for gain (K) and the non-linear parameter (a) are found via experimentation [Zhai and Milgram 93].

$$d_x = Kx^a \tag{2.1}$$

- **Other Mappings**: Other transfer function mappings include motion-sensing devices (e.g., "exponential transformation of mouse velocity, known as an acceleration function" [Hinckley and Widgor 12]), absolute devices (one-to-one mapping), and relative mappings (e.g., temporarily violate one-to-one).

2.2.2 Direct-Input Devices

Direct input has become pervasive in technology with devices like multi-touch and digital pen, among others. The light-pen was used with the Sketchpad by Ivan Sutherland as mentioned in Chapter 1. Multi-touch has been around for a long time (see Chapter 8). However, as described in Side Note 1.2, technology takes time to be adopted by the majority of users (with the exception of early adopters and researchers). It was the introduction of the iPhone that may have marked the day before and after of the adoption of multi-touch devices. With this event, direct-input devices have become a major player for input researchers and developers. While direct-input devices may perform better in some scenarios, they are not "necessarily easier to use than indirect devices" [Hinckley and Widgor 12]. For example, direct-input devices may lack buttons or other common properties of indirect-input devices.

Direct-input has become very active in the research community as well as among developers. It does provide a way to unify input and output (e.g., multi-touch) with immediate feedback for users. With the pervasive use of multi-touch nowadays, sometimes it is forgotten that there is still a need to find a model that works for multi-touch (or for all direct-input devices). While this is not the case as of now, Hinckley and Wigdor provide some important questions for everyone working with direct-input devices [Hinckley and Widgor 12] (and a question about tangible objects added by us):

- Can the display sense touch? If it does sense touch, is it capacitive ("soft-touch") or pressure sensing ("hard-touch")? If it is "soft-touch," the interaction requires bare fingers. The fact that pressure is not needed, means that the interaction will have less fatigue. If it is "hard-touch," then fatigue will increase but it allows a different environment, where operators of the device may use gloves. It is important to note that the scale of "soft-touch" and "hard-touch" is not bound to a particular technology but to the sensitivy of the device.

- How many points of contact can the display sense? Some of the laptops may be limited to few contact points (two, three, or four) while other more specialized devices will have ten or more contact points. However, this trend may be shifting. For example, the Hewlett-Packard (HP) multi-touch notebook (HP Envy 360 Touchsmart) comes with ten contact points. It is true that not all capacitive multi-touch (or any other type of multi-touch) devices are made equal. Each device may report the contact points differently. For example, if a palm or thumb is use to touch the display, the contact point may be reported differently depending on the hardware. This may be reported as multiple contact points. The difficulties may come from the hardware itself, the driver, or the actual application.

- Can the area of the contact point be sensed? Is this reported as a bounding ellipse or is the image of the contact available to the developer? For example, in Windows Application Programming Interface (API) (WINAPI), the touch contact area is reported for X and Y axes measured "in hundredths of a pixel in physical screen coordinates" [Microsoft 09].

- Is a special digital pen needed for the interaction or can any hard object perform the same function? Does it need batteries (active pen) or does it just work by inductive coupling?

- Can pen contacts be distinguished from touch-contacts?

- Can pen contacts be sensed while one is touching the display? For example, The Microsoft PixelSense display can utilize multi-touch and pen at the same time very efficiently. If the pen is near the display, can the multi-touch display still sense the contact points? Some devices may disable the contact points if the pen is near the display to avoid false contact points.

- Can tangible objects be used with capacitive displays? What type of tangible objects can be utilized? For example, an approach presented by [Voelker et al. 13a, Voelker et al. 13b] allows the use of tangibles in capacitive displays like the iPad.

Hinckley and Wigdor made the point that data sheets leave most of this information out [Hinckley and Widgor 12]. Not only, do some of them leave this information out, but even contact points are not reported correctly (or at all), or additional information about hardware. Large vendors like 3M and Microsoft PixelSense do provide more information, but this is not always true with all devices. It is also pointed out by them [Hinckley and Widgor 12] that this can be an advantage, as it has been for us when developing multi-touch solutions. The reason that this can be an advantage is that without knowing what is supported, one can design for more universal usage and build from there. For example, it is likely that most devices will at least provide an identification field for each finger trace with the x and y coordinates. It can be assumed that at least most devices will support at least two contact points, with some others supporting four. However, the number of contact points should be determined at run-time to change the behavior of the gestures if needed.

2.2.3 Input Device States

Defining the states for modern input devices has proven not to be an easy task. In the seminal work by Bill Buxton [Buxton 90], he defined that almost any input device to be used with WIMP could be expressed in three states. His model was able to model devices, such as personal computer (PC) mouses, digital pens, or single-touch displays. However, even his model could fail in some instances. One example is in the work by Hinckley and colleagues, which demonstrated that a digital pen required a five-state model [Hinckley et al. 10a].

With the explosion of many new input devices, such as multi-touch, Microsoft Kinect, and Leap-Motion, among others, the three-state model needs to be expanded. Multiple attempts to define a new model have been made, as will be described in other chapters. Some of the attempts for modeling multi-touch have included Regular Expressions (RegEx), Finite-State Machines (FSMs), and high-level Petri Nets (HLPNs).

2.2.4 Input Considerations

Six-degrees of freedom (DOF) for input devices have been studied in full detail by Zhai in his doctoral dissertation [Zhai 95]. The dissertation goes in-depth into how subjects deal with 6-DOF. The study provided great insight for 3D navigation [Zhai 95]: The muscle groups involved in a 6-DOF vary depending on the device used. This in itself helps to design better interfaces. The study also talks about the transfer function (see Section 2.2.1), which must be compatible with the characteristics of the actual device. This was also stated by Bowman and colleagues in their guidelines suggesting to "match the interaction technique to the device" [Bowman et al. 04, p. 179]. Hinckley and Wigdor also looked at input technologies in [Hinckley and Widgor 12], as already described in this chapter. The recommendations by Zhai [Zhai 95] help to emphasize the 3D interaction design guidelines offered in [Bowman et al. 04] :

1. Use existing manipulation techniques unless an application will benefit greatly from creating new ones.

2. Match the interaction to the device.

3. Reduce wasted motion (clutching).

4. Use non-isomorphic techniques whenever possible.

5. Reduce the number of degrees of freedom (DOF) whenever possible.

From the previous list, item 4 reminds the designer that it is difficult to model isomorphic rotation techniques (see Chapter 5), as shown in [Poupyrev et al. 00]. Additional guidelines have been proposed. For example, Jacob and colleagues proposed interfaces within a post-WIMP framework [Jacob et al. 08]. In this framework, they tried to find a balance between reality based interactions (RBI) and artificial features. RBI includes naïve physics, body awareness and skills, environment awareness and skills, and social awareness and skills. Also, Hancock and colleagues proposed some specific guidelines when dealing with multi-touch rotations and translation [Hancock et al. 07]. These included the ability to rotate and scale independently or together by providing more DOF than WIMP. In addition, they suggested that a constant connection between the visual feedback and the interaction would prevent cognitive disconnect by avoiding actions that the user may not be expecting [Hancock et al. 07] . In other words, the system needed to provide a realistic 3D visual feedback to match the interaction. For additional discussion, see [Bowman et al. 99b, Bowman et al. 06, Hinckley 08, Bowman et al. 04].

2.3   User Interfaces: Input

This sections deals with the input aspect of a user interface. This is always achievable by some type of input device. This is a physical or virtual device working as a unit. For example, a virtual keyboard on a smartphone is the interface that allows the user to type (using the touch display) any number of characters. The UI allows the communication to happen between the human and the computer. The user input interface allows the human to communicate with the computer while the output user interface allows the opposite. At first, an input device and the input components of user interfaces may seem similar but an input device is only the hardware which for a given action sends an appropriate signal to the computer.

2.3.1   3D User Interfaces: Input Devices

3D input devices provide data, direction, or commands to a 3DUI, using different types of input devices. An input device does not require the user to have 6-DOF (but some are true 3D input devices with 6 or more DOF) to be considered a 3D input device. This means that an input device, to be a 3D input device, has to operate in such a manner that the input is mapped to a 3D action. The distinction here between the interaction technique and input device is critical when designing a system. The input device makes reference to a physical system (e.g., computer mouse) that allows some measurement from the user (or by the user), which is then forwarded to the computer system. The interaction technique is defined as how this input device is mapped into the 3DUI system [Bowman et al. 04].

Section 2.2 described characteristics for input technologies which can be applied to 3D input devices. In addition, there are specific characteristics for 3D input interfaces. The following attributes are important to consider when working with 3D input devices [Bowman et al. 04]:

- **Degrees of Freedom:** The degrees of freedom (DOF) are the most critical characteristics for a 3DUI interaction. For example, a 6-DOF device can give you a direct mapping between translations for X, Y, Z axes and rotations about X, Y, Z axes. A *degree of freedom* is "simply a particular, independent way that a body moves in space" [Bowman et al. 04].

- **Frequency of Data:** The frequency of the data determines how the data is sent to the computer system. The frequency of data may be continuous components, discrete components, or both [Bowman et al. 04]. For example, the button in a GamePad will only return pressed or not pressed. The thumb-stick found in the GamePad produces continuous values for a given range.

- **Active Devices:** Devices are said to be active (or purely active) if they require the user to perform a physical action with the device. One example is the multi-touch display, which requires the user to touch the screen before any action can be taken [Bowman et al. 04].

- **Purely Passive:** Devices Devices are said to be passive (or purely passive) if they do not require any physical action from the user to generate data. This could be a vision-based input system that is reading information from the environment, without the user input. Nevertheless, the user may work with this device as an active input system. For example, the device becomes an active system when the user performs hand gestures in the vision-based system to issue a command [Bowman et al. 04].

2.4 Input Devices

The vast number of computer input devices is not a new phenomenon but the adoption of new devices into everyday use has seen a shift from previous decades. It is the explosion of modern input devices that is giving way to a set of new interactions and possibilities.

The first person that comes to mind when dealing with input has to be Doug Engelbart because of the invention of the mouse, which is still the most pervasive and useful tool for everyday computing. Many inventors, researchers, and practioners have contributed to input. Two names that come to mind are Bill Buxton and Ken Hinckley (and their contributions are far beyond input). Bill Buxton has created an amazing collection of input devices on the web[2] and has provided a timeline for early input devices.[3] Many other great researchers and practitioners have also contributed to input devices, and some of them are cited in this book.

2.4.1 Keyboard

The computer keyboard originated from its ancestor the typewriter, which allowed users to type alphanumeric characters and perform special functions on their

---

[2]http://research.microsoft.com/en-us/um/people/bibuxton/buxtoncollection/
[3]http://www.billbuxton.com/inputTimeline.html

Figure 2.1: QWERTY keyboard.

computer. The most popular keyboard is the one derived from QWERTY Sholes–Glidden typewriter, as shown in Figure 2.1.

Besides entering commands or typing text with the keyboard, the keyboard has many other uses. In 3D environments, the keyboard plays an important role in navigation and control of the system by pressing different keys. For example, in a game or navigation environment, the arrows (up, down, left, right) or the AWSD key combinations (A=left, W=up, S=down, D=left), are very common. Other keys like the *space bar* are used to trigger certain actions (e.g., shoot a missile). The keyboard does provide a way to interact with 3D applications.

Chord Keyboard

A chord keyboard is a specialized keyboard that is meant to play keys in combinations as if the user were playing musical chords. We can think of the regular keyboard as a chord keyboard since there are some combinations of keys used. For example, the combination of **shift a** will produced A, or **control c** (**command c**) will be used to copy text or an image into a buffer for later retrieval.

Very early on Engelbart and English in 1968 presented a bi-manual system named oN-Line System (NLS), which included a chord keyboard [Engelbart and English 68b]. This came to be known as the "Mother of All Demos" (see Side Note 1.1) [Engelbart and English 68a]. A very interesting case study is found in Buxton's *Human Input to Computer Systems: Theory, Techniques and Technology* [Buxton 68].

There are many examples of chord keyboard, including specialized gaming

Side Note 2.2: The World of Watches

Bill Buxton showed his 1976's watch in a conference talk. It had been manufactured by Orient and was called the Touchtron watch. This is very likely the first watch with capacitive touch. This watch introduced single tap for time and double tap for date [Warren 13, Buxton 13] way before it was used with a PC mouse. Buxton showed different watches in this talk, finalizing with the 2009 LG smart watch. Buxton, during the talk, finished the topic of watches by saying: "I'm not trying to say what's going on today isn't interesting, but it becomes actually more interesting if you drop the hype and view it in context in the history of things and see it as a continuum. Then you start to see how we're doing and not get dazzled" [Buxton 13]. Understanding previous research and inventions, helps us not only to avoid reinventing the wheel, but it allows us to refine the technology, look at it with different eyes, and understand where it came from. Maybe the most interesting quote in this talk was: "If you are working in this space and you don't know the history, why are you doing this?" [Buxton 13].

For a look at how to perform gestures for smart watches, see the work by [Perrault et al. 13]. For a collection of digital watches, see http://www.digital-watch.com and Buxton's own collection http://research.microsoft.com/en-us/um/people/bibuxton/buxtoncollection/.

keyset (or keypad). One early example is the first portable word processor (1978), the Microwriter, as shown in Figure 2.2. Another example of a chord keyboard is the design by NewO Company, called Writehander (Figure 2.3). This one-handed chord keyboard had 12 buttons, which represented the ASCII code table [Buxton 14].

2.4.2 The Mouse and Its Descendants

The computer mouse (see Figures 2.4 and 2.5), invented for the computer era, signified a milestone in HCI. The mouse, together with the GUI gave way to one of the most important paradigms in UI: WIMP. Selecting a target with a joystick is not a fun endeavor. One of the authors of this book (Francisco) can attest to the difficulty of using the joystick in his Atari 8-bit computer when selecting menus and objects. The study conducted by English, Engelbart, and Berman showed why Francisco was frustrated (see 1.2.4). The mouse was superior in many aspects.

The basic mouse has the moving functionality to operate a cursor and a button to perform an action. The pervasive mouse of the 1980s operated using a weighted ball held inside of a small palm-sized box [Dix et al. 04]. The ball is in contact with rollers which were used to adjust values of potentiometers [Dix et al. 04]. The

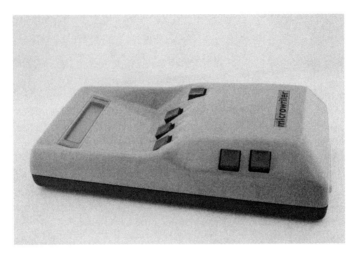

Figure 2.2: Microwriter. With permission from Bill Buxton. See [Buxton 14].

Figure 2.3: NewO Writehander. With permission from Bill Buxton. See [Buxton 14].

mouse has evolved over time giving additional features. It is very pervasive today to have a mouse that has two or three buttons, a scroll wheel (which may allow for pressing it as a button), and many other features. The ball has been replaced either with an optical tracking mechanism (with a light source and light detector) or a touch (or multi-touch) track pad.

The trackball (Figures 2.6 and 2.7) is an alternative to the regular mouse. While it has never been as popular as the mouse, it has its niche. Instead of moving the mouse with the hand across a region (e.g., mouse pad), the user moves the embedded ball with a finger. Depending on the design of the trackball, the user will either use the thumb to control the ball or the index finger. While the design of the ball is similar to the mouse, it does provide a different ergonomic feel. It also allows the user to spin the ball, which is a feature that the regular mouse cannot do because of the position of the ball. Some new computer mouses do come with touch surfaces that mimic the spinning of the ball. The trackball does offer some interesting applications. This is why smaller trackballs are still popular (e.g., Blackberry phone) when designing new user input interfaces.

The Apple Magic Mouse, as shown in Figure 2.8, is an example of the evolution of the original mice, which provides a multi-touch surface to press and perform gestures, laser tracking for pointing, and uses Bluetooth communication protocol to connect wirelessly with the system.

While the mouse and the trackball were not designed for 3D user interaction, they are commonly used for applications and games that required 4-DOF or greater. In many instances, the keyboard is used in combination with the mouse (or the trackball). As stated before, the trackball does provide a better interaction for immerse environments because (depending on the actual design of the device) it can be held with one hand [Bowman et al. 04].

2.4.3 Joystick and the GamePad

Joysticks, originally created for airplanes [Mirick 24], have been a very common device for computer systems, in particular video game systems. The first pervasive

Figure 2.4: Macintosh Model M0100 [Buxton 14] . With permission from Bill Buxton. See [Buxton 14].

Figure 2.5: Microsoft Arc mouse, circa 2010 [Buxton 14] . With permission from
Bill Buxton. See [Buxton 14].

Figure 2.6: Kensington Turbo Mouse 4.0, circa 1983 [Buxton 14] . With permission
from Bill Buxton.

joystick for video games was the Atari joystick, as shown in Figure 2.9. The
joystick, in its original form, was meant to be used for the X and Y axes of a
system. In other words, it was originally designed to work in 2D dimensions.
Joysticks have evolved into different forms. For example, a typical plane simulator
joystick may have an extra DOF already built in (by twisting the joystick from side
to side). Even more interesting is the evolution of the joystick into the thumbstick.

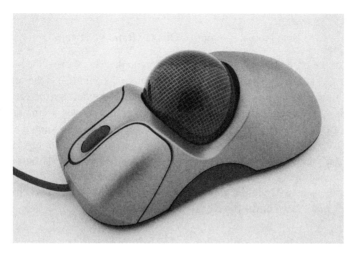

Figure 2.7: Dimentor - Inspector 6DOF trackball mouse, circa 2008 [Buxton 14] . (With permission from Bill Buxton).

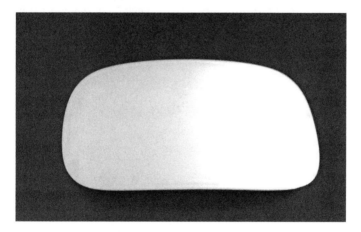

Figure 2.8: Apple Magic Mouse.

The thumbsticks found in most video game controllers (GamePads) are found in pairs, allowing at least 4-DOF, as shown in Figure 2.10.

Joysticks and GamePad sticks and buttons are either analog or digital. If they are analog, they provide a range value. For example, the left trigger of the Microsoft Xbox 360 controller provides a value between 0 to 255. The Y axis of the left thumbstick of the Xbox 360 controller provides a value between -32768 and 32767.

The GamePad originally was made famous by the Nintendo Entertainment

Side Note 2.3: Control-Display Ratio - CD gain

One of the properties used for relative-mapping devices, such as the mouse, is the CD gain, as shown in Equation 2.2, where the gain (G) is the inverse relation between the control (physical device) C divided by the (cursor) display movement (D). For example, if the mouse moves 4 cm and the cursor moves 8 cm, then the gain is 2. The CD gain is also known as the C:D ratio, where $G = 2$ is equivalent to the 1 : 2 ratio. This represents that each unit of displacement by the physical device yields two units of displacement for the display cursor. Another example is a one-to-one mapping that will yield a ratio of 1 : 1 (e.g., mouse moves two cm and cursor moves two cm) [MacKenzie 12].

$$\frac{1}{G} = \frac{C}{D} \tag{2.2}$$

This setting is available to users. The slower the setting is, the lower the gain is and vice versa. MacKenzie points out that the trade-off between getting to a target faster versus a finer acquisition of the target is harder to optimize given other factors that are available for optimization such as display size and scale (independent of C:D ratio) bringing the possibility of confounding factors [MacKenzie 12]. Below is the optimization option for the Mac OS X:

System, and contains a couple of buttons and a digital pad (D-Pad) (Figure 2.11), which is a digital up, down, left, right controller, without any intermediate values as is common in joysticks (and thumbstick). As time has progressed, the GamePad has been the perfected for over 40 years. Today, the Xbox One controllers shows the evolution, with two analog thumbsticks (each with the option to press for an additional action), a D-Pad, two back analog buttons providing a value from 0 to 255 (left and right triggers), two back digital buttons (left and right shoulder pads), four fire buttons (A,B,X,Y), two digital function buttons (start and menu), and a central function button that can be used for turning the GamePad on or off, or using it as an "interrupt" action button on any game, as shown in the Xbox One GamePad control (Figure 2.12).

Figure 2.9: Atari joystick.

Figure 2.10: Xbox 360 GamePad.

The Dead Zone

The GamePad or the joystick has a dead zone, like most other input devices with analog controllers. This means that if the device is at idle position (e.g., center position) it may report a moving value. This also means that after moving the

Figure 2.11: Nintendo GamePad.

Figure 2.12: Xbox One GamePad.

thumbstick (or joystick), and the device returns to center, it may keep reporting a moving position. There are different strategies to solve this problem. The most obvious way is to set any value within the dead zone to zero. However, this creates a strange behavior if the incremental value is used as a multiplier of some action.

The best approach is to normalizethe data. Normalization will transform the data into a range of -1.0 to 1.0, as shown in Equation 2.3. The value (val) is the original number which will be transformed into a new value (newval) using the minimum (minv) and maximum (maxv) values. To have a proper normalization, it is best to know the minimum and the maximum values (as opposed to guessing them). There are cases where the desired range may not be between -1.0 to 1.0. For example, it is common to set the values of the input between 0.0 and 1.0. If that is the case, then Equation 2.4 is used to obtain *newval*. Listing 2.1 shows the normalization function and the scaling function , among other useful functions.

$$newval = \frac{val - min}{maxv - minv} \qquad (2.3)$$

$$newval = \frac{-1.0 + 2.0 * (val - minv)}{maxv - minv} \qquad (2.4)$$

Listing 2.1: Common Math Operations

```
1   #ifndef COMMONMATHOPERATIONS_H
2   #define COMMONMATHOPERATIONS_H
3   template <typename T, typename R=T>
4   class NMath
5   {
6   public:
7     /// This function assumes data is
8     /// already normalized.
9     /// sets value from a normalized set
10    /// from 0 to 1.0
11    static inline R scaledNormalizedData(R val)
12    {
13      return static_cast<R>(-1.0 + 2.0 * val);
14    }
15    /// sets value between 0.0 to 1.0
16    static inline R scaledData(T min, T max, T val)
17    {
18      string s = "Hello";
19      return static_cast<R>(-1.0 + 2.0 * (val - min) / ( max - min));
20    }
21    static inline R normalizedData(T min, T max, T val)
22    {
23      return static_cast<R>((1.0 * val - min) / ( 1.0 * max - min));
24    }
25    /// returns -1 if negative, 1 if positive
26    /// or 0 if is neither negative or positive.
27    static inline int sgn(T val)
28    {
29      return static_cast<int>((T(0) < val) - (val < T(0)));
30    }
31    /// rounds value
32    static inline int round(T val)
```

```
33   {
34      return floor(val + 0.5);
35   }
36  };
37  #endif
```

A common way to deal with the dead zone, once the data has been normalized, is to apply a function that provides a smooth value for each input that is not in the dead zone [McShaffry 13]. Pat Wilson provided a very simple approach [Wilson 11] shown in Equation 2.5. This formula takes the linear input μ, with the dead zone value (λ) and the sign of μ ($sgn(\mu)$). This yields zero if it is within the dead zone ($|\mu| < \lambda$) or an incremental value if it is not. Remember that this assumes that data has been normalized (-1.0 to 1.0) already.

$$\mu' = \frac{sgn(\mu) * (|\mu| - \lambda)}{1 - \lambda} \tag{2.5}$$

Game development provides a great insight into input. In the same article, Pat Wilson provides additional tips for dealing with input. One of them is squaring the circle. if you look inside of the Xbox 360 GamePad, the thumbstick sits in a square component with a circle opening, as shown in Figures 2.13, 2.14, and 2.15. The objective of squaring the circle is to prevent someone who opens the controller from gaining an unfair advantage. Note, that $|\mu| = 1$ when is either at the top, left, right, or down positions. Equation 2.6 shows how to square the circle.

$$\vec{d}' = \vec{d} * \frac{min\left(|\vec{d}| * 1.25, 1.0\right)}{max\left(0.01, max\left(|\vec{d}.x|, |\vec{d}.y|\right)\right)} \tag{2.6}$$

If the output desired is non-linear, different functions may be tried depending on the need of the interface. Using the value (μ') obtained in Equation 2.5, we can obtain a new non-linear output using Equation 2.7, where $f(x)$ is continuous over interval $[0, 1]$, $f(0) = 0$, and $f(1) = 1$. For example, for the Marble Blast Ultra game, Pat used fine movements when the stick was slightly pushed and drastic movement when pushed to the edges by using $f(x) = e^x$. Different functions can be tried as $f(x) = x^c$ or $f(x) = max(0, ln(x) + 1$, among others. For additional information about transfer functions see Section 2.2.1.

$$\mu'' = f\left(|\mu'|\right) * sgn(\mu) \tag{2.7}$$

Isometric and Isotonic Devices

Isometric devices are pressure (force) sensing. This means that the user must apply force to move the device (e.g., joystick). Given this force, the movement

Figure 2.13: Thumbstick.

Figure 2.14: Thumbstick without top.

could be precise (e.g., isometric joystick). Isotonic devices are those with "vary-ing resistance" [Zhai 95]. In other words, as the "device's resistive force in-creases with displacement" [Zhai 95], the device becomes sticky, "elastic, or spring loaded" [Zhai 95]. For example isotonic joysticks "sense the angle of deflection" [Hinckley 08], with most isotonic joysticks moving from their center position [Hinckley 08]. There are also designs of joysticks that are hybrid [Hinck-ley 08]. An isometric joystick is shown in Figure 2.16 and an isotonic joystick is

Figure 2.15: Thumbstick top only.

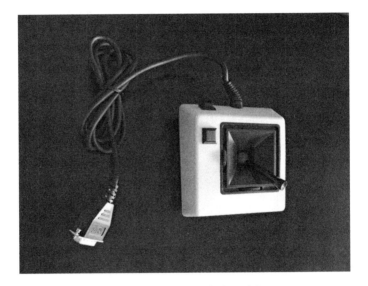

Figure 2.16: Isometric joystick.

shown in Figure 2.17.

2.4.4   3D Mouse and 3D User-Worn Mice

The 3D mouse was designed to use the popularity of an existing device while adding a 6-DOF. The 3D Connexion SpaceNavigator, as shown in Figure 2.18, is the core component of the 3D mouse. This serves as an additional device to perform bi-manual tasks with a standard mouse or use it to perform 6-DOF. Another version

Figure 2.17: Isotonic joystick.

Figure 2.18: SpaceNavigator.

of the 3D mouse is the SpaceMouse Pro (Figure 2.19), with additional features. A 6-DOF trackball was shown already (see Figure 2.7). Another approach is to use user-worn 3D mice. This is a device attached to the finger, which includes two buttons and tracker on the back of the sleeve, as shown in Figure 2.20 [Zeleznik

Figure 2.19: SpaceMouse Pro (With permission - 3D Connexion).

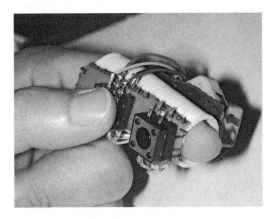

Figure 2.20: Finger Sleeve [Zeleznik et al. 02].

et al. 02]. A similar device is the Finger Sleeve Mouse, as shown in Figure 2.21. This device uses its 6-DOF tracking sensor to provide a 1 : 1 3D mapping if needed. The button serves as activation and the device is secured with Velcro. A similar device, called the Ring Mouse uses acoustic tracking to provide 6-DOF [Bowman et al. 04].

2.4.5 Audio

The most well-known method for an input interface that uses audio is speech recognition. Speech recognition can be used either for systems commands, dictation of text, or advanced speech recognition fused with natural language processing to create an advanced input mechanism.

LaViola's master's thesis described practical issues when using speech recogni-

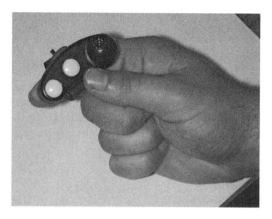

Figure 2.21: The Ring Mouse. Courtesy of Joseph J. LaViola, Jr.

tion with Virtual Environment [LaViola Jr. 99, pp. 17-22]. Those issues include the placing of the microphone(s), external noise, speaker awareness, and recognition latency. The latter problem is the most critical one for a real-time interactive system. The recognition must meet the demands of the interactive system that is being used. Latency is solved by having a faster recognition method and a smaller set of recognizable words.

Ultrasound Devices

Ultrasound has been around for a long time in our daily lives in the forms of ultrasound imaging. Currently, companies like Chirp Microsystems and Elliptic Lab have begun the commercialization of gesture-based ultrasound devices with work derived from Berkeley Sensor and Actuator Center (BSAC) and other scholarly work, such as [Kalgaonkar and Raj 09, Przybyla et al. 15]. The frequencies that ultrasound devices operate are from 20 kilo-hertz (KHz) up to several giga-hertz (GHz) [Wikipedia 14]. Gesture devices based on ultrasound can deliver 6-DOF just like vision-based systems but with less power consumption and less resources in general. As of this writing, it is too early to tell how the devices will compare to vision-based systems.

2.4.6   Inertial Sensing

INS has been around for a long time for aerospace, naval ships, and other systems that require navigational information. However, it has been only recently that the continued work on micro-electro-mechanical systems (MEMS) has allowed very small accelerometers, gyroscopes, and magnetometers. During the introduction of the Nintedo Wii System, the controller (called WiiMote) contained a 3-axis accelerometer that allowed a new type of game interaction. Later, with the addition of the Nintendo WiiMote MotionPlus add-on device, Nintendo added a 3-axis gyroscope.[4] Many smartphones and tablets today also incorporate a 9-axis INS MEMS. This means that they have a 3-axis accelerometer, 3-axis gyroscope, and a 3-axis compass.

The major limitation for INS is the error accumulation. An error within a kilometer may be acceptable for a vessel navigating in a large area but when dealing with user interfaces a large error produces inaccurate measurements, which will lead to an unsatisfactory experience by the user. This has been discussed by [Foxlin 02]. A few chapters in this book are dedicated to this technology and some solutions are provided.

2.4.7   Vision-Based Devices

Vision-based systems have exploded with the release of Microsoft Xbox 360 Kinect. With the maturity of computer vision field, the popularity of this depth-sensing vision device, and its affordable price by many developers, are among the reasons for the increased interest to use them. The Kinect includes a microphone array, an Infrared (IR) emitter, an infrared receiver, a color camera (red green blue (RGB) color system), and a DSP chip. The Leap Motion is another type of vision-based device. It works by emitting IR light (with three light-emitting diode (LED)s) and monochromatic IR cameras). Even the WiiMote is a vision-based system because it has an IR camera, which shows the potential of combining different devices.

2.4.8   Data Gloves

Data gloves provides tracking data about certain actions performed by the user. Data gloves can be active (using sensors) or passive (using markers). The book by Bowman and colleagues provides a few pages of detailed information for bend-sensing gloves, pinch gloves, and the combination of both [Bowman et al. 04]. The bend-sending feature usually provides joint angle measurements to detect a set of gestures. Pinch gloves provide information on how many fingertips are touching together.

Active data glove technology has evolved over time. One of the first data gloves that emerged was called Sayre Glove. This was developed back in 1977 using flexible tubes with a light source. Later, in 1983, the Digital Entry Data Glove was the first to use multiple sensors. By 1987 fiber optic was used for a data glove. Resistive ink printed on boards has also been used. With MEMS, additional sensors can be used with data gloves today. The Fifth Dimension Sensor Glove Ultra (5DT) uses a very high-precision flexor resolution. This advanced data glove provides a 10-bit flexor resolution, which is aimed for the movie industry [5DT 14]. A

---

[4]The new version of the WiiMote has the accelerometer and gyroscope incorporated in the control without the need for an additional add-on.

complete look at data gloves can be found in [Premaratne 14, Ch. 2] and [Dipietro et al. 08].

2.4.9 Psychophysiological Sensing

Psychophysiology is a field that emerged during the 1950s led by R.C. Davis and a group of psychologists but this topic had been studied by many philosophers, physicists, physicians, and physiologists, even as early as the ancient Greeks [Stern et al. 01]. Probably one of the major breakthroughs was the understanding of skin conductivity by the end of eighteenth century. This discovery was led by Luigi Galvani in Italy and demonstrated that "animals produce electricity that originates within the organism itself" [Stern et al. 01]. It is important to define the action potential. This is an event where the electrical membrane potential of a given cell rises and falls in a consistent trajectory [WIKI 14].

The equipment used can be divided into electrodes and transducers. The electrodes once attached to the subject's skin measure electrical activity. Electrodes help the conversion of ionic potential generated by the nerve, muscle, and gland cells. Transducers are "used to convert physiological events to electrical potentials" [Stern et al. 01]. In general, it is preferable to record an action derived by the muscle or nerve than the action potential. For example, by using light reflected from the pupil, one can measure the pupil diameter. A great book titled *Psychophysiological Recording* provides detailed information that is extremely useful for this type of input [Stern et al. 01].

These types of devices will gain greater acceptance as they become easier to wear and more affordable. For example, Emotiv produces two great products that utilize electroencephalogram (EEG) technology and are easier to wear.[5] The most common devices used are galvanic skin response (GSR), EEG, and pupillography (e.g., pupil size measurement), among others.

2.4.10 Tracking Devices

In many instances, it is important to track the user or objects in real-time 3D environments. For example, a user enters a room and an optical camera detects the user, detects the movements of the hands, and it finally detects when the user exits. There are different types of tracking, which includes motion tracking, eye tracking, and data gloves. Motion tracking includes: mechanical tracking, acoustic tracking, inertial tracking, and optical tracking.

2.4.11 Treadmills as Input Devices[6]

Travel (controlling the position and orientation of the viewpoint) is a core component of interaction in virtual environment [Bowman et al. 04, pp.183-226]. It

---

[5]http://emotiv.com
[6]Wendy Powell provided the information for this subsection.

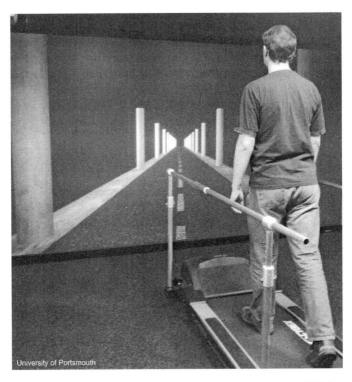

Figure 2.22: Customized treadmill input device. Courtesy of University of Portsmouth (UK).

can be achieved without physical translation of the user (e.g., joystick) or by direct user motion. To overcome the space limitations of tracked free walking, treadmills can be coupled to the interface to allow infinite forward motion. While there are a number of different types of input treadmill (e.g., self-driven, motorized fixed speed, motorized self-paced), the underlying principle requires that the walking motion of the user is translated into digital input (Figure 2.22). This can either be direct input (sensors record belt motion) or indirect (tracking the motion of the user). Treadmills are linear input devices with limited dimensions of direct control (speed, acceleration, distance). Heading changes can be achieved by either automating the heading direction along a fixed path, or combining the treadmill with additional input device(s) in order to directly control changes in direction.

2.5 Input Recognition

This section provides a basic overview of input recognition. This topic is expanded in other chapters found in this book. Input signals are not always straightforward. For example, recognizing gestures from a serious of points requires some additional work. This is one factor that makes input user interfaces very interesting to work with. Andrew Wilson from Microsoft Research provided a great chapter about sensor- and recognition-method [Wilson 12]. While each input has its own strengths and weaknesses, some common issues and considerations can be described based on the author's experience (and an example of a frustration detection device in [Wilson 12]):

- No trivial initial mapping exists with some input technologies.

- Some sensors (e.g., gyroscopes) output noise and create a high level of errors.

- In cases where one sensor fails to perform the desired task, a combination of sensors (or devices) may deliver the desired outcome.

- Users with previous experience expect the input interaction to be the same as in previous devices. For example, a user accustomed to the iPad tablet may want to have the same experience when using the multi-touch surface on a desktop or tabletop display.

- Depending on the interaction, the recognition processed must be performed in a critical window of time.

- The interaction by the user for a given device may be related to the application that is being used more than the device.

2.6 Virtual Devices

Virtual devices allow for software to emulate physical devices (e.g., keyboard). In addition, as will be discussed in Section 2.7, virtual devices can be used to separate the functionality of a device from the actual physical device. This allows not only to create input taxonomies but enables developers to look at the functionality separate from the actual device, hence allowing the developer to better choose the correct physical input device because of the interaction that he/she is after, or to change a device that has similar properties. This section talks about some "soft" devices, which are commonly referred as to virtual devices.

Nielsen and Olsen used a triad mouse to emulate a 3D mouse [Nielson and Olsen Jr 87]. In this study, they performed 3D rotations, translations, and scaling (independently of each other). For 3D rotations, they used point P_1 as the axis

Side Note 2.4: Buxton's Corollary: Cracker Jack

This corollary used the slogan of the Cracker Jack commercial: "The more you eat, the more you want." Buxton provides a path forward to input devices to continue to be successful without over saturating the industry. You may want to eat more Cracker Jack, but at some point, you will just be full. Buxton argues that with input devices, the same phenomenon applies. He provides two rules for a product to be released: (1) It must work and flow. In other words, the interaction must be smooth for the user, which means that not only is a functional device important but it must be pleasant to the user. He calls this phase 1 (it works), phase 2 (it flows). (2) It is also required for the product to reduce the complexity and increase the value of all of the other devices. They must work together. It is becoming more important to think about the eco-system of input devices and how they work in tandem. His vision is that we can't care only about one single device but the collection of devices as a whole. The reason is that a single device may not cause frustration but the collection of devices may create dissatisfaction among users [Buxton 13].

reference, and points P_2 and P_3 to define the line forming the rotation angle to be applied to the object. In more recent work [Hancock et al. 07], one can find subtle similarities with [Nielson and Olsen Jr 87], in the proposition of defining a point of reference to allow seamless rotation and translation.

The virtual sphere [Chen et al. 88] was an important development for 3D rotation methods previously proposed. This study tested the virtual sphere against other virtual devices. It was found that the Virtual Sphere and the continuous XY+Z device behaved best for complex rotations (both devices behaved similarly with the exception that the XY+Z device does not allow for continuous rotations about all X, Y, Z axes). The virtual sphere simulated a real 3D trackball with the user moving left-right (X axis), top-down (Y axis), and in a circular fashion (Z axis) to control the rotation of the device. Related work included the rolling ball [Glassner 93], The virtual trackball [Arvo 94], and the ARCBALL [Heckbert 94]. The ARCBALL "is based on the observation that there is a close connection between 3D rotations and spherical geometry" [Bowman et al. 04].

2.7 Input Taxonomies

Input taxonomies (or classification) provide a very useful way to find out which device is useful for a given task or how to replace one existing device for a similar one. Simply stated, this provides input device classification.

Early work was developed by [Foley and Wallace 74] to create a set of virtual devices (or user interfaces) that helped to separate the physical device with the actual interaction. They created four virtual devices: pick, locator, button, and valuator. A **pick** represents user-defined objects, like a line, resistor, window, or curve. They used the light pen as the prototype pick. A **button** is used to select system defined objects to trigger a given action by the system or to generate a character. A **locator** indicates the location and/or orientation in the user's viewable space. This is most commonly viewed as the cursor controlled by a mouse or joystick. A **valuator** helps the user to provide a single value in a real number space. "A potentiometer is the classical valuator" [Foley et al. 84]. With the introduction of the first computer graphics standard (GKS), two additional devices were added: a **stringvaluator** is a sequence of characters and a **strokevaluator** is a sequence of points [Bono et al. 82, Bowman et al. 04]. A third virtual device called **choice** was also added but it is very similar to Foley's button [Bono et al. 82]. While this approach helps the designer to choose from a smaller set of choices and then look for the correct physical device, the mapping between the actual device and the virtual device is not always accurate [Bowman et al. 04]. Furthermore, this is even more apparent when you compare two physical devices that match a category in the virtual device section with their physical properties. An example given by [Bowman et al. 04] is a mouse and trackball, which both are in the same category of virtual device but they are physically different. An improved version was later published by [Foley et al. 84]. This version mapped specific tasks: select, position, orient, path, quantify, text. Due to the type of mapping (task-oriented), devices can appear more than once in each classification. This taxonomy works better when the design is task-oriented. The taxonomy is designed to be in a tree graph, where each of the tasks divides into sub-tasks, and each of those sub-tasks divides into multiple devices. Note that the tablet device mentioned in this taxonomy is different from what we think of a tablet today (e.g., iPad) This is why in some places, the tablet is described as "Data Tablet Overlay." This was a tablet pad that contained different keys and shortcuts. The original image is found in the article by [Foley et al. 84]. Tables 2.1, 2.2, 2.3, 2.4, and 2.5 contained the taxonomy provided by Foley and colleagues.

Buxton's "Lexical and Pragmatic Consideration of Input Structures" [Buxton 83] also contributed to the taxonomy of input. Matching a logical device to many physical devices is not practical. Take a logical device that requires to move an object left, right, down, and up with the joystick. However, the experience is not the same when the user is giving the keyboard arrows to move the object, or a virtual pad on a touch screen. In *3D User Interfaces: Theory and Practice*

Table 2.1: Selection Techniques. Adapted from [Foley et al. 84].

Technique	ID	Devices
From Screen with Direct Pick	$S_{1,1}$	Light Pen
Device	$S_{1,2}$	Touch Panel
	$S_{2,1}$	Data Tablet Overlay
	$S_{2,2}$	Mouse
Indirect with Cursor Match	$S_{2,3}$	Joystick (Absolute)
	$S_{2,4}$	Joystick (Velocity)
	$S_{2,5}$	Trackball
	$S_{2,6}$	Cursor Control Keys
With Character String Name		(See Text Input)
Time Scan	$S_{4,1}$	Programmed Function Keyboard
	$S_{4,2}$	Alpha Numeric Keyboard
Button Push	$S_{5,1}$	Programmed Function Keyboard
	$S_{5,2}$	SOFT Keys
Sketch Recognition	$S_{6,1}$	Tablet and Stylus
	$S_{6,2}$	Light Pen
Voice Input	$S_{7,1}$	Voice Recognizer

by [Bowman et al. 04] points out two major flows. The first one is that this taxonomy does not handle discrete input devices. The second one is that while it is possible to know that a substitution for one device for another is incorrect, the taxonomy does not provide a reason why this is incorrect. With this said, we believe that this taxonomy is very helpful to aid developers or designers when choosing the right input device. Buxton's taxonomy is shown in Table 2.6.

Buxton's work was expanded in "A Semantic Analysis of the Design Space of Input Devices" [Mackinlay et al. 90]. The elegance in this approach is the way that input devices are described. The input device is defined as a 6-tuple, as shown in Equation 2.8. The tuple is described by [Mackinlay et al. 90] as follows: **M** is a *manipulator operator*, which corresponds to a physical property vector in Table 2.7 that the input device senses. **In** is an *input domain set*. In other words, the range sensing for a given device. **S** is a *current state* of the device. This is broken into the external state (input and output) and internal state of the device. **R** is a *resolution function* that maps from the input domain set to the output domain set. **Out** is an *output domain set*, which describes the range of the resolution function. Finally, **W** is a general purpose set with a list of production rules, which includes triggers, internal states, external states, and others. The production list of **W** offers different ways to deal with the input device, for example: if (*release* $==$ *true*) then *In* $= 0$ for a joystick that has been released by the user. This taxonomy provides interesting ways on how to define an input device. Take for example a trigger button, similar to the one in the Xbox controller. This trigger at idle has a value of zero and when

Table 2.2: Position Techniques. Adapted from [Foley et al. 84].

Technique	ID	Devices
Direct with Locator Device	$P_{1,1}$	Touch Panel
	$P_{2,1}$	Data Tablet Overlay
	$P_{2,2}$	Mouse
Indirect with Locator Device	$P_{2,3}$	Joystick (Absolute)
	$P_{2,4}$	Joystick (Velocity)
	$P_{2,5}$	Trackball
	$P_{2,6}$	Cursor Control Keys with Auto Repeat
Indirect with Directional Commands	$P_{3,1}$	Up-Down-Left-Right Arrows (See Selection)
With Numerical Coordinates		(See Text Input)
Direct with Pick Device	$P_{5,1}$	Light Pen Tracking
	$P_{6,2}$	Search for Light Pen

Table 2.3: Quantify Techniques.Adapted from [Foley et al. 84].

Technique	ID	Devices
Direct with Valuator Device	$Q_{1,1}$	Rotary Potentiometer
	$Q_{1,2}$	Linear Potentiometer
With Character String Values		(See Text Input)
	$Q_{3,1}$	Data Tablet Overlay
Scale Drive (One axis) with Locator Device	$Q_{3,2}$	Mouse
	$Q_{3,3}$	Joystick (Absolute)
	$Q_{3,4}$	Joystick (Velocity)
	$Q_{3,5}$	Trackball
Light Handle	$Q_{4,1}$	Light-Pen
	$Q_{4,2}$	Tablet with Stylus
Up-Down Count Controller by Commands	$Q_{5,1}$	Programmed Function Keyboard
	$Q_{5,2}$	Alphanumeric Keyboard

it is completely pressed, it has a value of 255. This can be defined as shown in Equation 2.9, where I is defined by Equation 2.10. In other words, I maps one to one with its input and its output. It is possible to create a different mapping. For example, say that to fire a missile, the button has to pass a certain threshold. In this case, the mapping could be defined 0 to 99 (input) to 0 (output). Otherwise, if it is 100 to 255, then the output value is 1. Any mapping is possible from the input to the output, depending on the function. This mapping just described is shown in Equation 2.11.

Table 2.4: Text-Entry Input. Adapted from [Foley et al. 84].

Technique	ID	Devices
Keyboard	$T_{1,1}$	Alphanumeric
	$T_{1,2}$	Chord
Stroke Character Recognition	$T_{2,1}$	Tablet with Stylus
Voice Recognition	$T_{3,1}$	Voice Recognizer
Direct Pick from Menu with	$T_{4,1}$	Light Pen
Locator Device	$T_{5,1}$	Touch Panel
Indirect Pick from Menu with		(See Positioning)
Locator Device		

Table 2.5: Orienting Techniques. Adapted from [Foley et al. 84].

Technique	ID	Devices
Indirect with Locator Device	$O_{1,1}$	Joystick (Absolute)
	$O_{1,2}$	Joystick (Velocity-Controlled)
With Numerical Value		(See Text Input)

$$< M, In, S, R, Out, W > \qquad (2.8)$$

$$T =$$

$$
\begin{aligned}
&<Manipulation: &&T_z, \\
&InputDomain: &&[0, 255], \\
&State: &&Z, \\
&ResolutionFN: &&I, \\
&OutputDomain: &&[0, 255], \\
&Works: &&\{\} >
\end{aligned}
\qquad (2.9)
$$

$$I =$$

$$T_z : \quad [0, 255] \rightarrow [0, 255] \qquad (2.10)$$

$$f(In) =$$

$$
\begin{aligned}
&T_z : [0, 100) \rightarrow < 0 >, \\
&T_z : [100, 255] \rightarrow < 1 >
\end{aligned}
\qquad (2.11)
$$

Table 2.6: Buxton's Taxonomy [Buxton 83].

Property Sensed		Number of Dimensions 1		2				3	
		rotary	linear	puck	stylus finger horz.	stylus finger vertical	small fixed location	small fixed with twist	
Position		Rotary Pot	Sliding Pot	Tablet & Puck	Tablet & Stylus	Light Pen	Isotonic Joystick	3D Joystick	M
					Touch Tablet	Touch Screen			T
Motion		Continuous Rotary Pot	Treadmill	Mouse			Sprung Joystick Trackball	3D Trackball	M
			Ferinstat				X/Y Pad		T
Pressure		Torque Sensor					Isometric Joystick		T

Table 2.7: Physical Property [Mackinlay et al. 90]

	Linear	Rotary
Position		
Absolute	Position **P**	Rotation **R**
Relative	Movement **dP**	Delta Rotation **dR**
Force		
Absolute	Force **F**	Torque **T**
Relative	Delta Force **dF**	Delta Torque **dT**

The next step in Mackinlay and colleagues's approach is to connect the devices with the application. To create the connection, they provided a generic device [Mackinlay et al. 90]. Therefore, the generic keyword **device** is used for a general case and the **input device** is used for physical devices in this particular context. Along with physical devices, they also provide definitions for virtual and composite devices [Mackinlay et al. 90]. It is possible to describe connections and applications parameters using the complete 6-tuple (in Equation 2.8.) as before. However, it is convenient to omit some of the tuples for some of the devices. One example is a device that provides a volume control. This example also shows how the device is connected using their approach, as shown in 2.12, 2.13, and Equations 2.14. The connected device can also be defined using the notation shown in Figure 2.15, where C_v is a constant gain.

Having the concept of generic *devices*, it helps the developer or designer to treat them as interfaces.[7] For example, a *GenericKnob$_z$* $= R_z : In - I \rightarrow Out$ provides a prototype. With this, one can initiate the device using *Instantiate(GenericDevice, DeviceArguments)*. With this in mind, a new device can be declared as shown in Equations 2.16 and 2.17.

---

[7]Meaning a prototype.

$$Volume =$$
$$<InputDomain: \quad [0,25] \; decibels > \qquad (2.12)$$
$$VolumeKnob =$$

$$
\begin{aligned}
<Manipulation: &\quad R_z, \\
InputDomain: &\quad [0°,270°], \\
State: &\quad \theta, \\
ResolutionFN: &\quad I, \\
OutputDomain: &\quad [0°,270°], \\
Works: &\quad \{\} >
\end{aligned}
\qquad (2.13)
$$

$$VolumeConnect =$$

$$
\begin{aligned}
InputDomain: &\quad [0°,270°], \\
ResolutionFN: &\quad f, \\
OutputDomain: &\quad [0,25] \; decibels >
\end{aligned}
\qquad (2.14)
$$

$$VolumeConnect =$$

$$
\begin{aligned}
(VolumeKnob, &\quad Volume, \\
f(\theta \; degrees) = &\quad C_v \times \theta \; decibels)
\end{aligned}
\qquad (2.15)
$$

$$GenericBoundedKnob_z =$$
$$Rz{:}[Min_z, Max_z] \quad -f \rightarrow [f(Min_z), f(Max_z)] \qquad (2.16)$$
$$VolumeKnob =$$
$$Instantiate(GenericBoundedKnob_z, \; In: \; [0°,270°]) \qquad (2.17)$$

There are some considerations that must be made for some more complex devices, such as a multi-touch device or a tablet. The first one is **component acquisition**: This is the need for a device to move to a specific location. The next consideration is **persistent state feedback**: This is the need for continued update and feedback of its state. Finally, **sensitivity over input domain**: This is the ability to specify a given value for a device.

There are different ways to compose high-dimensional devices. For example, a multi-touch display has two dimensions as well as a feedback state. Using formal set theory, one can compose more complex devices. Three important properties are **connection composition, layout**, and **merge composition**. Connection composition allows devices to cascade their output into their next device, as shown in Equation 2.18 (or *StationKnob* → *StationSlider* for short). The layout composition allows devices "on a panel to be described with a mapping of the local

coordinates of a device to the coordinates of the panel, usually involving translations and rotations" [Mackinlay et al. 90]. The formal symbol used is $\oplus$ to indicate
the composition. For example, $LMouseButtonT_1 \otimes LMouseButtonT_2 \otimes LMouse$-
$ButtonT_2$, where T_1, T_2, T_3 are transform functions. Finally, merge composition
uses standard set theory to classify the device. In our particular opinion, this is
the best option for complex devices and it is compatible with any other modeling
input technique that may use set theory as its foundation. This uses the cross
product $\times$ and $\cup$. We can now define a single tablet using a pen, as described in
Equation 2.19. In this particular case, the pen has a RestState, which is when the
pen is not touching the surface.

Expanding on the digital pen example, one can begin to formulate a single touch
display. A touch has move, down, and up states, This is shown in Equation 2.20.
The manipulation is for one finger (T_{xy}) with the input domain going from 0 to
X_{max} and 0 to Y_{max}. The output domain could use a function f that normalizes the
input if needed.

Given that it is possible to define different devices, as already explained,
[Mackinlay et al. 90] were able to provide a taxonomy of input devices and expand
the previous work by [Foley et al. 84] and [Buxton 83]. This taxonomy is shown in
Table 2.8. The linear movements are represented with tX, tY, tZ[8] , and the rotation
movements represented by rX, rY, rZ. This is the first part of this taxonomy which
refers to six degrees of freedom. The bottom part of this table shows the input
domain set measurement, which is the second part of this taxonomy. Finally, on
the left (for translation) and on the right (for rotations), represents the physical
property of the device. A device is represented by a circle, and the lines between
circles indicate a type of device composition. The merge composition is shown in
Figure 2.23a, the layout composition is shown in Figure 2.23b, and the connection
composition is shown in Figure 2.23c.

The taxonomies presented here allows designers and practitioners to find the
correct device and replace it with another one if needed. In general, we find that the
work by Bill Buxton [Buxton 83], and the extension of this work by [Mackinlay
et al. 90] provides a starting point for modern input devices. We have left some
interesting exercises to be solved about taxonomies in this chapter. Furthermore, we
invite the reader to read the cited paper in this section to find additional examples
and usage. In particular, [Mackinlay et al. 90] offers detailed information about
their taxonomy.

$$
\begin{aligned}
VolumeConnect = \\
(StationKnob, \qquad StationSlider, \\
f(\theta\ degrees) = \quad C_v \times \theta\ decibels)
\end{aligned}
\tag{2.18}
$$

---

[8]They labeled X,Y, Z in their paper.

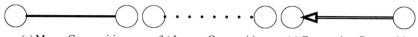

(a) Merge Composition   (b) Layout Composition   (c) Connection Composition

Figure 2.23: Device connectors and devices.

$Touch =$

$$
\begin{aligned}
&<Manipulation: & P_{xy}, \\
&InputDomain: & [Min_x, Max_x] \times [Min_y, Max_y] \cup \\
& & < RestState_x, RestState_y >, \\
&State: & < x, y, >, \\
&ResolutionFN: & f, \\
&OutputDomain: & [f(Min_x), f(Max_x)] \times [f(Min_y), f(Max_y)] \\
& & \cup < Null_x, Null_y >, \\
&Works: & \{\} >
\end{aligned}
\qquad (2.19)
$$

$Touch =$

$$
\begin{aligned}
&<Manipulation: & T_{xy}, \\
&InputDomain: & [0, X_{max}] \times [0, Y_{max}] \cup \\
& & < tState_{down}, tState_{move}, tState_{up} >, \\
&State: & \{X, Y, tState\}, \\
&ResolutionFN: & f, \\
&OutputDomain: & [f(0, X_{max})] \times [f(0, Y_{max})] \cup \\
& & < Null_{down}, Null_{move}, Null_{up} >, \\
&Works: & \{\} >
\end{aligned}
\qquad (2.20)
$$

Table 2.8: MCR's Taxonomy of Input Devices [Mackinlay et al. 90]

		Linear			Rotary			
		tX	tY	tZ	rX	rY	rZ	
Position	P							R Angle
Movement	dP							dR Delta Angle
Force	F							T Torque
Delta Force	dF							dT Delta Torque
		1 10 100 inf	1 10 100 inf	1 10 100 inf	1 10 100 inf	1 10 100 inf	1 10 100 inf	
		Measure	Measure	Measure	Measure	Measure	Measure	

Further Reading

For input taxonomies and considerations, A very interesting article by Jacob et al. titled "Integrality and Separability of Input Devices" is an essential read [Jacob et al. 94]. Another article by the same first author talks about language and modeling for post-WIMP devices [Jacob et al. 99].

An updated chapter by Hinckley and Wigdor in the current edition (third) of *Handbook of Human-Computer Interaction* talks about input technology [Hinckley and Widgor 12].

For additional information about unconventional devices for 3D interaction, see [Kruijff 06]. An example is using one-hand pressure-sensitive strips [Blaskó and Feiner 04].

Exercises

1. Implement the dead-zone for a GamePad on your preferred development environment.

2. Use the dead-zone concept for a different device.

3. Create a taxonomy for a multi-touch surface using the touch surface example provided in this chapter.

3

Output: Interfaces and Displays

A display connected to a digital computer gives us a
chance to gain familiarity with concepts not realizable
in the physical world. It is a looking glass into a
mathematical wonderland
—Ivan Sutherland

In this chapter we describe the output components of interfaces, which allows the
computer to communicate with the user. In Chapter 27, we describe its counterpart
performing the opposite action. While this book concentrates on input technology,
output is an interconnected piece of the puzzle.

3.1   3D Output: Interfaces

Required components of a 3DUI are the hardware and software that allow the
graphical representation of the output. The hardware devices, which are often
referred to as display devices, surface displays, or just plain displays, are the
focus of this chapter. In addition to displays, it is also important to describe the
perception of the output from the point of view of the user.

3.1.1   Human Visual System

The human eye optical schema, as shown in Figure 3.1, has some similarities with
a camera but rather a more complex optical system [Hainich and Bimber 11]. It is
important to understand the basic principles of human vision when dealing with
the output components of interfaces. The following properties are important about
the human eye and human vision system [Hainich and Bimber 11]:

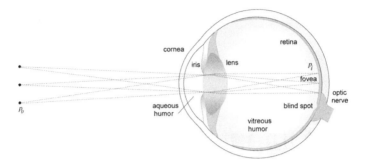

Figure 3.1: Optical schematic of the human eye [Hainich and Bimber 11]. With permission from CRC Press.

- The diameter of the eye is about 25 mm.

- The eye is filled with two fluids, which have a refraction index of approximately 1.336.

- The iris regulates the amount of incident light. This is done by either expanding or shrinking the aperture of the eye.

- The cornea and the elastic biconvex has a refraction index of approximately 1.4.

- The process of the lens to adjust its shape to different focal lengths is called accommodation.

  - The focal length accommodation is between infinity and < 100 mm.

  - The near accommodation degrades with age.

- Since the eye is a biconvex lens, the image is upside down.

- The vision is sharpened only at the center of the retina.

  - To perceive a large scene, the eye will move toward it. These quick movements are called saccades.

- Flickering can be seen at low frequencies. While flickering is not always detected with 70 Hz, there are exceptions for high-speed motion of the object or the eye.

3.1.2 Visual Display Characteristics

There are a few characteristics that visual displays have in common. Some of the characteristics are field of regard (FOR), field of view (FOV), refresh rate (in hertz), and spatial resolution.

Field of regard is the measurement of the physical space surrounding the user, measured in visual angle (in degrees). In other words, it contains all the available points from the user's perspective. **Field of view** is the measurement of the maximum visual angle observed by the user. The FOV must be less than 200 degrees, which is approximately the maximum for the human visual system [Bowman et al. 04]. **Refresh rate** is the speed of the next rendering cycle. Simply, it is how fast the screen is redrawn. In other words, each rendering cycle produces new output. **Spatial resolution** is a measurement of quality given by the pixel size. The unit for this measurement is dots per inch (DPI). Spatial resolution is also affected by the distance between the display and the user. There is a proportional connection between pixels and resolution. As pixels increase, the resolution also increases, and vice versa. Two different sizes of monitors with the same number of pixels do not have the same resolution. In other words, the number of pixels is not equivalent to the resolution [Bowman et al. 04].

Some other important aspects are the different type of screen geometries (e.g., spheres) and how they are drawn. **Light transfer** is a characteristic that is important for the design of user interfaces. How the transfer of light happens is determined by the type of projection (e.g., front, rear). Finally, how comfortable the display device is in respect to the user (**ergonomics**) is very important to consider when designing 3DUIs.

3.1.3 Understanding Depth

When using a 3DUI, depth plays an important role for human perception [Bowman et al. 04, Hainich and Bimber 11]. In a regular display, the drawing canvas is still 2D. It is easy to tell that the moon is far away when looking at it. It appears small and distant. However, when looking at two far away objects in space, it is harder to tell the difference in distance from one's point of view. At near distances, multiple cues allow users to easily process depth [Bowman et al. 04, Hainich and Bimber 11]. There are four visual depth cue categories that we will cover here:

- Monocular, static cues.

- Oculomotor cues.

- Binocular disparity and stereopsis.

- Motion parallax.

Monocular Cues

Monocular cues are present in static images viewed with only one eye. This type of cue is also called a **pictorial cue**. These techniques have been employed by artists for a long time (they were well known before computers) [Hughes et al. 13]. The following techniques are used to convey depth (list adapted from [Hale and Stanney 02, Bowman et al. 04]):

1. **Relative Size**: The user can be influenced by apparent sizes. One example is if you have a set of objects in decreasing size order, this will give an apparent distance effect.

2. **Interposition or Occlusion**: Conveys a sense of depth by opaquing and occluding parts that are farther away.

3. **Height Relative to the Horizon** For objects above the horizon, the higher the object is located, the further it appears. For objects below the horizon, the lower the object is drawn, the closer it seems.

4. **Texture Gradients**: It is a technique that includes density, perspective, and distortion. As the density of the surfaces increases, so does the depth understanding for the user, making the denser objects appear farther away.

5. **Linear Perspective**: As parallel (or equally spaced) lines are seen farther away, it appears that the two lines are converging. It is important to note that lines do not have to be straight but equally spaced. For example, a long train track.

6. **Shadows and Shading**: The user can determine depth information based on lighting. Light will hit the nearest parts of an object, allowing someone to deduce this information. Any object that has illumination will also produce shadows on the closer surface.

7. **Aerial Perspective**: This effect (also called atmospheric attenuation) gives closer objects the appearance of being brighter, sharper, and more saturated in color than objects far away.

Binocular Cues

The world is experienced by humans using both eyes but vision is a single unified perspective. By viewing a scene first with one eye only, and then with the other eye only, a significant difference can be perceived. This difference between those two images is called **binocular disparity**. A clear way to understand this phenomenon is to hold a pen close to the face and alternate each eye to view this object.

The fusion of these two images with accommodation and convergence can provide a single **stereoscopic** image. This phenomenon (**stereopsis**) provides a strong depth cue. If the two images cannot be fused, then **binocular rivalry** will cause the user to experience just one image or part of both images.

Oculomotor Cues

When dealing with binocular viewing, both eyes diverge with far-away objects and converge with near objects. This superficial muscle tension is thought to have an additional depth cue [Hale and Stanney 02] called **oculomotor cues**. This muscle tension, in the visual system, is called accommodation and convergence. The focus of the eye to a given image causes the eye muscle to stretch and relax while obtaining the target image. This physical stage is called **accommodation**. The rotations of the eyes is needed to fuse the image. This muscular feedback is called **convergence**.

Motion Parallax

Motion parallax is the change of perspective of the view. This can happen if the viewer is moving in respect to the target object. The target object moves in respect to the user, or both [Hainich and Bimber 11]. This phenomenon will make far-away objects appear to be moving slowly, and near objects will appear to be moving faster [Bowman et al. 04]. For example, take a race where two cars are traveling at 200 kilometers per hour. The first car is passing in front of the viewer and the second car is far away on the opposite side of the track. The second car will appear to move slower, while the first car will seem to be moving faster. Another example is a car traveling on the highway, with lights and trees that seem to be moving faster, and far-away buildings appear to be moving slower.

More about Depth Cues

There are more depth cues than the ones described above. For example, color is also used as a depth cue. The color blue appears far away because the atmosphere has a higher absorption for warm colors, giving the horizon a more accentuated blue color [Hainich and Bimber 11]. Adding blur to blue objects can give the illusion than an object is farther away. For additional references, see [Hainich and Bimber 11, Bowman et al. 04]. In particular, Section 4.4 found in the book *Displays — Fundamentals and Applications* [Hainich and Bimber 11] provides very detailed information about depth perception and depth cues.

Side Note 3.1: History of Display Technologies

Hainich and Bimber provide a rich history of display technology in their book [Hainich and Bimber 11]. After the optical era (early 1400s to late 1800s) provided the building blocks to what we have today. This included projected drawing, light reflection, and the *magic lantern* [Hainich and Bimber 11]. There are quite a few debates who invented what during this era. For example, was it Leonardo Da Vinci, sometime after 1515 who created the first perspective drawing (proposed by others before him)? However, it was Albrecht Dürer who demonstrated how to create perspective drawing for any shape in 1525, which is the basis for computer rendering today [Hughes et al. 13, p. 61]. Other debates included whether Kirchner (1659) invented what he called the *magic lantern* (device that passed light from a lamp) or was it Huygens (1671) that presented a similar device [Hainich and Bimber 11]? It is not clear who the inventor was. Later, in this era, Gurney demonstrated the limelight effect, which was an "oxyhydrogen flame heating a cylinder of quicklime (calcium oxide), emitting a bright and brilliant light" [Hainich and Bimber 11]. Later, the electromechanical era (late 1800s to early 1900s) provided the groundwork for the early projects that would lead to the television. This was first described by Paul Gottlieb Nipkow in 1884, scanning disks (known as the *Nipkow disk*). The next era, is called electromechanical. This Nipkow disk "is basically a spinning disk with holes at varying lengths from the the disk center" [Hainich and Bimber 11]. The spinning on the disk caused every hole to "slice through an individual line of the project image, leading to a pattern of bright and dark intensities behind the holes that can be picked up by a sensor" [Hainich and Bimber 11]. Various improvements were made in the first half of the 20th century. The electronic era (early and mid-1900s) was marked by the cathode ray tube (CRT) invented by Ferdinand Braun. The CRT was first used by Boris Rosing to receive a video signal. The CRT became a commercial product in 1922, replacing the Nipkow disk. The first color picture tube was invented by John Logie Baird in 1944. Finally, the digital era replaced many of our CRTs in our homes and desks in the late 1900s and early 2000s. It is remarkable that a discovery made by Friedrich Reinitzer in 1888 revolutionized display technology. Of course, the cholesteric liquid crystal was not the only componenet needed to make the displays we have enjoyed in the last few years. Semiconductors also played a role, which enabled advanced signal processing starting in the 1970s, which led to the development of the flat-panel displays. We went from plasma displays to liquid crystal displays (LCD). In the coming years, organic light emitting diodes (OLED) are expected to dominate the market. Hainich and Bimber provided a more detailed history of technology displays [Hainich and Bimber 11, ch. 1].

3.2 Displays

There are multiple types of displays, such as conventional monitors, HMD, virtual retina display (VRD), and optical HMD, among many others. Near-eye displays and three-dimensional displays are expanded a bit further later in this chapter. Multi-touch displays are mentioned in Chapter 8. The following is a partial list of output interfaces:

- **Conventional Monitor** is the most pervasive display found today in desktop computers, notebooks, tablets, and phones. Before the liquid-crystal display (LCD), the common form was the cathode ray tube (CRT). With the right equipment, a conventional monitor can achieve stereopsis with a pair of glasses and refresh rate of at least 100 hertz. A few years ago, most monitors did not fit the specifications mentioned, except for a few high-end displays. However, today, there are some affordable options available in the market, with 100 hertz or greater [Bowman et al. 04].

- **Head-Mounted Display** or Helmet-Mounted Display is a user-attached visual display commonly used in VR environments. The most recent and well-known example to consumers is the Oculus Rift, recently acquired by Facebook. There is a variety of HMDs with distinct designs; some of them may include 3D audio and other functionalities. HMD have become very accessible to the point that Google created a project using a cardboard[1] to create one using a smartphone. Appendix B provides guidelines that should be taken into account when creating your own HMD (with your current smartphone).

- **Virtual Retina Display** was invented by the Human Interface Technology Lab in 1991 [Bowman et al. 04, p. 54]. The first patent was granted to Thomas A. Furness III and Joel S. Kolin, filed in 1992 [Furness III and Kolin 92]. Today, with the Google glasses, this technology promises to become pervasive among users but it faces challenges which will be covered in Section 3.2.1. VRD works by generating coherent beams of light from photon sources, which allows the display to render images onto the retina.

- **Optical Head-Mounted Display** allows the user to see through the device while still looking at the computer's graphical-generated images. The most recent example is Google glasses.

- **Surround-Screen Display** is an output device with at least three large projection display screens, which surround the user. The screens are typically between 8 to 12 feet. The projectors are installed near the screens to avoid shadows. Front projectors can be used as long as their position avoids the user's shadows [Bowman et al. 04].

---

[1] https://www.google.com/get/cardboard/

- **Autostereoscopic Displays** generate 3D images without the need for glasses or other specialized devices (e.g., 3D glasses).

- **Hemispherical Displays** allow to display images in a 180° by 180° FOV using projection-based technology. Spherical mapping techniques are used in conjunction with a wide-angle lens to distort the output. This allows the image to be fitted in a curved display.

- **Workbenches** are designed to bring the interaction into displays on a table (tabletop), desks, or workbenches. They can provide an intuitive display and high spatial resolution. Some examples include Microsoft Surface TableTop and Diamond Touch by Circle Twelve.

- **Surround Screen Display** is a visual display system with "three or more large projection-based display screens" [Bowman et al. 04]. A very common surround display is known as a CAVE, introduced by [Cruz-Neira et al. 93]. The CAVE consist of four screens, the floor, and three walls, which surrounds the user. Another version of the surround display is called computer-driven upper body environment (CUBE). The CUBE is a complete 360° display environment [Bowman et al. 04].

Additional output display devices exist, such as the arm-mounted displays. For a presentation in detail about the devices and further references, consult [Hainich and Bimber 11, Bowman et al. 04]. Additional display information is provided in Appendix A.

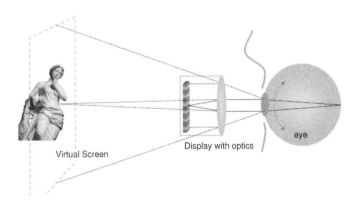

Figure 3.2: Basic principle of a near-display [Hainich and Bimber 11].

3.2.1 Near-Eye Displays

The introduction of near-eye display technology allows for new types of applications. The basic principle, as explained by Hainich and Bimber, is a miniature display and optics, which is projected onto a virtual screen [Hainich and Bimber 11], as shown in Figure 3.2. VRD was mentioned already as one of the types of displays which uses near-eye display technology. While the Google glasses (see Figures 3.3 and 3.4) and other similar devices have still not become pervasive among users, it may be a matter of time until it happens. Fighter-jet pilots currently utilize some type of augmented reality (AR) display, which is a very logical application for near-eye display technology. For users, this device can also be an input device. For example, eye steering and eye blinking provide a great input interface. An important characteristic mentioned by Hainich and Bimber was the need for a light near-eye display (before the Google glasses came out) [Hainich and Bimber 11]. "A near-eye display for everyday applications will have to work without any fixtures to the head exceeding that of simple eyeglasses" [Hainich and Bimber 11]. The current version of the Google glasses weighs around 43 grams. Therefore, while it is still not the perfect solution, it is a matter of time before the technology will improve while its pricing will go down. Other important characteristics are to have a high-resolution display and support for large FOV.[2] The near-eye display system must also compensate light intensity, since humans can see between "$\frac{1}{1000}$ lux (starlight) up to 1000000 lux (sunlight)" [Hainich and Bimber 11].

In a perfect world of displays, a resolution of 3600×3600 pixels for a $60° \times 60°$ of FOV would create a sharp display [Hainich and Bimber 11]. This sharpness will only concentrate in the center of the view while the outer sides become blurry. For near-eye displays, the clarity of an image only needs to be in the center of the display. Assuming that the display could adjust itself as the user changes focus, the actual display sharpness will only need to be in the center of where the user is looking. In order to create a dynamic system with near-eye displays (for focus adaptation and geometric correction), a very fast eye tracker is needed (with frame rates of 200 Hz to 1000 Hz) to be able to keep track of the eye position. Different types of display technology can be used for near-eye vision, including LCD, laser, and LED, among others. Table 3.4 shows the different options [Hainich and Bimber 11].

Some examples of near-eye display technology include view-covering displays, semicovering displays, and optical see-through displays (e.g., Google glasses). **View-covering displays** provide a simple vision technology that covers most of the FOV even up to the point of blocking any outside view. These are very common in VR and for personal video experiences (e.g., watching a movie). If video see-through (capture video from real-world) is integrated into the virtual experience, it is possible to use it for AR. **Semicovering display** is a type of near-display system

---

[2]Human eye FOV is over 180° horizontally.

Figure 3.3: User wearing Google glasses. Courtesy of Eric Johnson.

that covers only a portion of the natural FOV. The display can be configured in two forms: (1) mounted in front of the eye or (2) as a fixed (see Figure 3.5a), non-transparent mirror into the FOV (see Figure 3.5b). Because the user is able to tilt or turn to look at the real world, this can be used outdoors, finding many types of applications. Finally, **Optical see-through displays** is an ideal choice for general purpose applications, providing great value to AR and other types of domains. This technology works by mirroring the "image of micro-displays into the FOV, without occluding the view" [Hainich and Bimber 11, p. 449]. A recent announcement by Microsoft placed great importance on this technology: the HoloLens will allow a new type of interaction. For more information, including optical design, laser display, and holographic image generation dealing with near-eye technology, the reader is invited to see [Hainich and Bimber 11, ch. 10].

3.2.2   Three-Dimensional Displays

Three-dimensional displays are a highly desired commodity but they have many difficulties. In a regular display pictures that do not appear to be of the right size or correct perspective, still appear fine to the viewer because our brain is a lot more tolerant with flat images. However, this is not true with stereoscopic pictures.

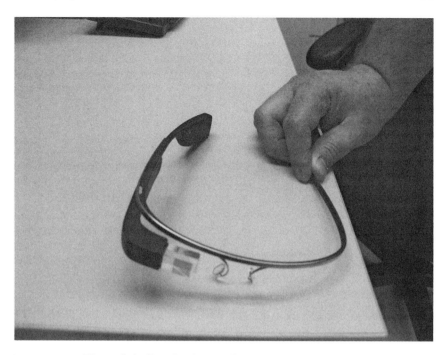

Figure 3.4: Google glasses. Courtesy of Eric Johnson.

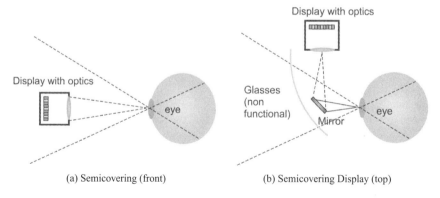

(a) Semicovering (front)   (b) Semicovering Display (top)

Figure 3.5: Semicovering displays [Hainich and Bimber 11].

The following basic considerations for three-dimensional displays are important to keep in mind [Hainich and Bimber 11]:

- Orientation: Classic stereoscopic displays use two cameras separated by a distance equivalent to the distance of the left and right eye. However, if the

Table 3.1: Near-Eye Display Technologies (Adapted from [Hainich and Bimber 11]).

Display Type	Comments
LCD	Contain small pixels, making it a challenge to use.
liquid crystal on silicon (LCoS)	It allows for smaller pixels because they use reflective basis.
Ferroeletric Liquid Crystal on Silicon (F-LCoS)	Similar to LCoS but have a fast switching speed.
Micromechanical	This technology allows holographic applications, and it could perform better with smaller pixels.
digital light processing (DLP)	Uses LED or laser illumination and it behaves similar to normal displays.
moving liquid mirror (MLM)	It may be useful for holographic applications. It is able to modulate light.
Holographic	This application display uses either F-LCoS or DLP to display holograms.
LED on complementary metal-oxide-semiconductor (CMOS)	It allows very small pixels but difficult to produce.
Organic Light-Emitting Diode (LED)	This can be use for miniature displays. A very interesting property is that LED can be designed as convex or concave displays. This is a very popular choice.
LED on CMOS	This may contain a retina tracker, a light sensitive structure with a camera built into the display.
Laser	This is a technology that presents challenges but seems to show potential for retinal displays.

user moves, the user can experience dizziness and headaches because the brain is trying to compensate for the double image that it is looking at.

- Distance: If the viewer's distance diverges considerably from the original camera distance, the 3D effect may become useless as images appear unrealistic. It is possible to generate different synthetic perspectives to correct this problem. The strategy is to "enlarge the stereo basis and to increase the focal length" [Hainich and Bimber 11]. Viewers have shown a tolerance for enlarged scenes while downscaled depiction is perceived as less realistic.

- Depth perception: This is based on retinal disparity and convergence. For example, if two projected images are received in two retinas, this creates a perceptual difference called stereopsis. If two images (belonging to the same object) are relatively displaced in 2D to the vision system, this is called retinal display. If this disparity becomes too large, the object appears twice (called diplopia or double vision). Finally, if the eyes rotate around their vertical axis, this is called vergence. If this is inward, it is called convergence and if it is outward, it is called divergence [Hainich and Bimber 11]. It turns out that depth perception for 3D content is easier for objects behind the screen plane compared to objects in front of the screen plane (see work about disparity constraint by [Lang et al. 10]). A lengthy discussion about depth perception is found in [Hainich and Bimber 11, pp. 372–377].

• Perspective: This is another basic problem with 3D displays. The reason for the perspective problem is due to viewers that do not sit within the "center of the line of the screen" [Hainich and Bimber 11]. This will cause the 3D object to appear distorted and tilted, making the scene unrealistic.

Viewing in 3D seems to be a desirable feature that users would want but only recently have 3D movies become popular and 3D displays (e.g., computer displays or television (TV)) have only been used in very specific applications. Is it that users prefer 2D for working on their computers? First we know that cinema has a predictable environment and bigger budgets. Therefore, it is easier to adjust the different parameters needed to have a better 3D experience. Maybe 3D TVs make some of the problems described more apparent, such as false perspective. It is also possible that smaller displays produce the *puppet-theater* effect and a "strong disparity between eye convergence and accommodation" [Hainich and Bimber 11, p. 378]. (Glasses with corrective lenses could provide a better focus distance.) Classic cinema has used either two individual projectors or a split image recorded on the film. In general, movie theaters have to accommodate expensive technology to display 3D movies. However, to make 3D pervasive, costs have to come down while the technology improves. Two examples provided by Hainich and Bimber are the color TV and high-definition television (HDTV) [Hainich and Bimber 11]. Color was very attractive and its initial adoption was still not affordable. Nevertheless, it was still popular because of how differently the image was perceived. HDTV did not provide the same difference as the black and white to color transition for most viewers (while some may disagree). It wasn't until HDTV became affordable that it was adopted, becoming a pervasive device in today's homes. Therefore, we ,may tend to believe that 3D displays will become pervasive when they become affordable and the typical problems have been addressed further. Only time will tell.

There are different technologies and different techniques for 3D vision systems. [Hainich and Bimber 11, pp. 381–431] provide a lengthy description (with further references). Some of the 3D systems include stereoscopic displays, autostereoscopic displays, light-field displays, and computer-generated holograms.

Further Reading

An excellent source is found in *Displays. Fundamentals and Applications* [Hainich and Bimber 11]. *Volumetric Three Dimensional Displays Systems* provides additional information [Blundell and Schwarz 00]. Of course, [Bowman et al. 04] provides a very detailed chapter about 3D user output interfaces. A very interesting book is *Visual Perception from a Computer Graphics Perspective* [Thompson et al. 13].

4

Computer Graphics

> Any treatment of input devices without considering
> corresponding visual feedback is like trying to use a
> pencil without a paper.
> —Ken Hinckley and Daniel Wigdor

4.1 Computer Graphics

Computer graphics (CG) is the primary reason that PCs and mobile devices have become pervasive in today's society. Furthermore, interactive computer graphics allows for non-static 2D and 3D images to be displayed on the computer with a redraw rate higher than humans can perceive. Interactive graphics provides one of the most "natural means of communicating with a computer" [Foley et al. 96] and a user. The primary reason is the ability to recognize 2D and 3D patterns, making graphical representation a rapid way to understand knowledge [Foley et al. 96].

The following chapter covers the essential parts of CG to help understand other chapters in this book. For example, how CG relates to 3D navigation. There are additional details, such as global illumination, programmable shaders, and other advanced features, that are beyond the scope of this book; the reader is referred to [Hughes et al. 13, Luna 11, Shreiner and Group 13]. For an introduction to various topics about real-time rendering, see [Akenine-Möller et al. 08].

4.1.1 Camera Space

There are various types of cameras. Two popular types of cameras are first-person and third-person. A first-person camera[1] is like viewing the outer space of the universe from the inside of a spaceship. This has been used in First-Person Shooter

---

[1] Popularized by the game Doom and later Quake.

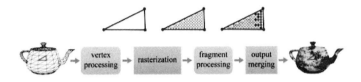

Figure 4.1: Graphics pipeline [Han 11].

Figure 4.2: GPU implementation of graphics pipeline [Akenine-Möller et al. 08].

(FPS) games. A third-person camera[2] is like viewing a spaceship as it interacts with the universe. For the purpose of this discussion, the camera plays a central role in 3D navigation.

In CG, a pipeline refers to a "sequence of data processing elements, where the output of one element is used as the input of the next one" [Han 11]. In other words, it is a sequential process that adds, modifies, and removes from the previous input until it creates the desired graphical output. The main steps in a pipeline include vertex processing, rasterization, fragment processing, and output merging, as shown in Figure 4.1 The pipeline has kept evolving over time. In *Real-Time Rendering* the pipeline shows fully programmable stages (vertex shader, geometry shader, and pixel shader), configurable but not programmable (clipping and merger), and fixed stages (screen mapping, triangle setup, and triangle traversal) [Akenine-Möller et al. 08], as shown in Figure 4.2. To read more about the current pipeline, see [Shreiner and Group 13, Luna 11].

The pipeline (see Figure 4.1) starts with the vertex process, which operates on "every input vertex stored in the vertex buffer" [Han 11]. During this process, transformations such as rotations and scaling are applied. Later, the rasterization "assembles polygons from the vertices and converts each polygon to a set of fragments" [Han 11]. Then, the fragment process works on each fragment and finds the color needed to be applied, as well as applying texture operations. A fragment is a pixel with its updated color. Finally, the output merging completes the process and outputs the graphical representation to the user. In general, the vertex and fragment processes are programmable[3] and the rasterization and output merging is fixed (hard-wired) into the software or hardware.

Before covering the space camera, it is important to have the local space and the world space in context. The local space is the coordinate system used to create

---

[2]The famous Nintendo game, Mario Bros, used a third-person camera.
[3]In older OpenGL, the entire pipeline was fixed.

a model, for example, a single mesh in 3DS Max.[4] The local space is also called object space or model space. The world space is the coordinate system used for the entire virtual scene, as shown in Figure 4.4. A simple example is for the world to remain static while the camera moves. However, there are many instances where local objects may need to have transformations applied that are not applied to the entire world. For additional information about transformations, see [Han 11]. The local, world, and camera spaces are right-hand systems (see Figure 4.6) in most instances. However, there are cases in which the system may use a different system (left-hand system) or axis orientation. For example, 3ds Max and OpenGL are both right-handed systems; however, Direct3D is a left-handed system. The orientation is also different between 3ds Max and OpenGL, as shown in Figure 4.7. The camera space is shown in Figure 4.3. The following list describes the camera components (adapted from [Han 11]):

- **EYE** is the current position of the camera, denoted by a 3D point, in reference to the world space.

- **AT** is a 3D point, where the camera is looking toward AT.

- **UP** is a vector that describes where the top of the camera is pointing. A common usage is to have this vector set to $[0, 1, 0]$. This indicates that the top of the camera is pointing to the positive Y axis.

The camera has a view frustum that defines the viewable space. This also helps the rendering system to clip anything found outside the frustum (see Figure 4.5). The parameters found in this view volume are (adapted from [Han 11]):

- **fovy** defines the vertical FOV, which is the visual angle of the camera.

- **aspect** is the ratio between the height and width of the view volume.

- **n** is the near plane for the view volume.

- **f** is the far plane for the view volume.

4.1.2   3D Translation and Rotations

In an interactive computer graphics system, the movements of a camera are accomplished using transformations (e.g., affine transformation). There are additional transformations such as scale and reflection, among others (see [Dunn and Parberry 11]). The most common transformations are translations and rotations.

Translations are the simplest to work with. Translation is the linear movement on X, Y, and Z axes. To perform a translation, simple addition and multiplication

---

[4]Other popular 3D modeling tools are Maya and Blender.

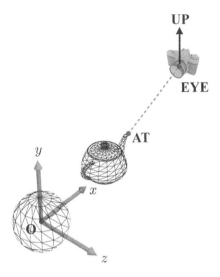

Figure 4.3: Camera space [Han 11].

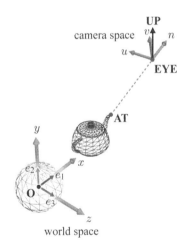

Figure 4.4: World space [Han 11].

done to each individual axis is enough. For example, to move the object 30 units to the left, the translation vector will simply be $T.x = T.x + 30$. The origin is set to be at $[0,0,0]$.

Orientation is closely related to direction, angular displacement, and rotations. **Direction** is usually denoted by a vector and indicates where the vector is pointing; however, the direction vector has no orientation. If you twist a vector along

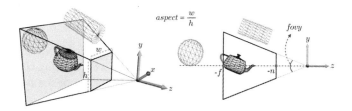

Figure 4.5: View frustum [Han 11].

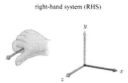

Figure 4.6: Right-hand system [Han 11].

the arrow, there is no real change. Orientation "cannot be described in absolute terms" [Dunn and Parberry 11]. An **orientation** describes a given rotation based on a reference frame. **Angular displacement** is the "amount of rotation" [Dunn and Parberry 11]. Orientation may be described as "standing upright and facing east" [Dunn and Parberry 11] or by adding angular displacement as "standing upright, facing north" [Dunn and Parberry 11] and then rotating "90° about the z-axis" [Dunn and Parberry 11]. There are several ways to describe orientation and angular displacement such as matrix form, Euler angles, and quaternions. Only Euler angles and quaternions are covered in this chapter.

Euler Angles

Euler angles are defined as the angular displacements of a "sequence of three rotations about three perpendicular axes" [Dunn and Parberry 11]. The order of application of the rotations makes a difference in the final result. This means that

Figure 4.7: Left- and right-hand systems [Han 11].

Side Note 4.1: GPU and GPGPU

With the current video cards that we have in the market, the graphics processing unit (GPU) has become more capable of producing better 3D graphics. For most 3DUI developers, working with Unity or similar frameworks may be sufficient to achieve a goal. However, there are times that understanding the graphics rendering system will provide an additional benefit (e.g., using geometry shaders). The graphics pipeline has become programmable (for quite a while now) and it provides ways to utilize the GPU that were not possible or practical. In addition to graphics, the GPU has been used for general purpose applications. In particular, those that are computationally complex. This is called GPGPU. A book that covers GPGPU in detail, from a low-level programming perspective and theory, is the *GPGPU: Programming for Games and Science* [Eberly 14]. Chapter 4 provides a great background about GPU computing and Chapter 7 provides interesting sample applications for GPGPU. Furthermore, this book has some chapters that are essential for people who would like to write more efficient and parallel code. For example, Chapter 3 covers single-instructions-multiple-data (SIMD) computing, which provides 3D mathematics. This book contains many gems which are indispensable for computer graphics and input device developers.

if a rotation about the X axis is applied before the rotation about the Y axis, the result can be different than the one obtained if the rotation about the Y axis is applied first. The fact that this method to describe orientation uses three individual operations for each type makes it very easy to use by humans.

With Euler angles, the definition of pitch, roll, and yaw are quite intuitive. The easiest way to think about these types of rotations is to think about an airplane, as shown in Figure 4.8. **Yaw** is defined as the rotation about the Y axis (also called heading). **Pitch** is defined as the measurement of rotation about the X axis (also called elevation). **Roll** is defined as the rotation about the Z axis (also called bank). These are called the principal axes.

There are a few important considerations that must be taken into account when using Euler angles. First, rotations applied in a given sequence will yield a result that may be different if the rotations are applied in a different order. For example, a pitch of 45 degrees followed by a yaw of 135 degrees may yield a different result if the yaw is applied before the pitch. Second, the three rotations in Euler angles are not independent of each other. For example, the transformation applied for a pitch of $135°$ is equivalent to a yaw of $180°$, followed by pitch of $45°$, and concluded by a roll of $180°$. A common technique is to limit the roll to $\pm180°$ and the pitch to

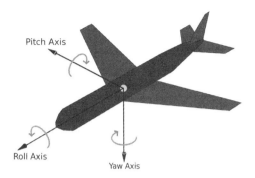

Figure 4.8: Principal axes. Drawn by Auawise.[5]

±90° [Dunn and Parberry 11].

An additional problem with Euler angles is known as **Gimbal lock**. This phenomenon happens when the second rotation angle is ±90°, which causes the first and third rotations to be performed about the same axis. To correct this problem, one can set the roll to 0° if the pitch is ±90° [Dunn and Parberry 11].

Quaternions

Quaternion is a number system used to represent orientation, which is very popular in CG. A quaternion is represented by a scalar value (w) and a vector (v) with x, y, and z components, as shown in Equation 4.1. Its popularity is due to some of its advantages. First, quaternions using the slerp function (see [Dunn and Parberry 11]) provide smooth interpolation. Second, quaternions use only four numbers. This makes it fairly easy to convert them from and to matrix form. It is very easy to find the inverse of a given angular displacement. Finally, it provides fast concatenation using the quaternion cross product. Nevertheless, they have some disadvantages as well. While four numbers is less than nine numbers in a matrix, quaternions are larger than Euler angle representation. Also, if the values provided to the quaternion are invalid, the quaternion may become invalid. This can be overcome by normalizing the quaternion. Finally, quaternions are not as easy to visualize as Euler angles. Regardless of the disadvantages mentioned, quaternions are the preferred method in graphics and game engines (e.g., OGRE [Junker 06]).

$$[w \quad (x \quad y \quad z)] = [cos(\theta/2) \quad (sin(\theta/2)n_x \quad sin(\theta/2)n_y \quad sin(\theta/2)n_z)] \quad (4.1)$$

---

[5]http://commons.wikimedia.org/wiki/File:Yaw_Axis_Corrected.svg.

4.1.3   Geometric Modeling

This use of various polygon meshes[6] is quite common in 3D games and applications. The polygon mesh represent a 3D model to be used in a rendering application [Watt and Policarpo 03]. The polygon representation is not the only way to model objects. Alternative methods include bi-cubic parametric patches, constructive solid geometry, and implicit surface representation, among others. In particular, object-oriented graphics rendering engine (OGRE) uses its own mesh binary format (and an available Extensible Markup Language (XML) version) to load 3D models. It is important to note that GPUs have been highly optimized to use polygon representations [Han 11]. In addition, polygon models can use hierarchical and spatial representation to define a group of objects working as a unit (e.g., person with legs and arms).

Polygon models are represented using vertices, faces, and edges. A very common approach is to use the half-edge data structure [Botsch et al. 10]. For more information about data structures for polygon meshes, see [Botsch et al. 10, Chapter 2]. A mesh also contains vertex normal and texture coordinates, among other properties. Sometimes, the mesh may also contain data related to the animation for the object. A very typical technique is called skeletal animation, where specific parts of the mesh are defined for movement. The animation topic is beyond the scope of this book. For more information about animation, see [Parent 08, Pipho 03].

The topic of geometric modeling is quite large. The reader is referred to [Botsch et al. 10, Mortenson 06, Watt and Policarpo 01].

4.1.4   Scene Managers

Scene managers are useful to handle large virtual worlds . While there are different ways to approach the design of a scene manager, the "common practice is to build scenes as ontological hierarchies with spatial-coherency priority" [Theoharis et al. 08]. Different types of scene managers are available to graphics engines, such as binary space partitioning (BSP), quadtree, and octree, among others. These types of hierarchies are called scene graphs. For example, Theoharis et al. define a scene graph as the set of nodes that "represents aggregations of geometric elements (2D or 3D), transformations, conditional selections, other renderable entities, (e.g., sound)," operations and additional scene graphs [Theoharis et al. 08]. A more compact definition is that a scene graph is a spatial representation of rendering objects in a virtual world where operations can be applied to parents or children of this graph. Mukundan defines a scene graph as a data structure that "represents hierarchical relationships between transformations applied to a set of objects in three-dimensional scene" [Mukundan 12]. The general type of graph used in a scene manager is directed, non-cyclic graphs or trees of nodes [Theoharis et al. 08].

---

[6]Commonly referred to as mesh.

The definition of a scene graph may vary depending on the actual type. The list below details some of the items that a scene graph includes in a node [El Oraiby 04]:

- Rendering elements:
  - Static meshes.
  - Moving meshes.
  - Skeletal meshes.
  - Materials.

- Collision elements:
  - Bounding volumes.
  - Trigger actions.
  - Bullets.

- Other elements:
  - AI path.
  - Game data.
  - Sounds.

Three very useful functionalities of a scene manager are instancing, operations, and culling. Instancing allows the use of existing objects (e.g., meshes) to create nodes. This means that instead of duplicating all the geometric information, a node can be created that points to the primary object. For example, this could mean that a car with certain material and geometric representation could be referenced 100 times, without having to duplicate this information. Later, using different transformation operations or changing basic details, some of those cars may look different and be placed in different locations. This is the importance of being able to perform different types of operations in the node. The most common operation is to perform geometric transformations to the object. The usefulness of the scene node is that the operation can be local to the node, without affecting the parents. Finally, culling allows the scene manager to make a decision about which objects to render. While this is done by the GPU as well, the scene manager can be highly optimized to minimize work. An extended study about culling is found in [Foley et al. 96, Chapter 15].

One implementation of scene manager can be found in the OGRE system [Junker 06]. This scene graph (**ST_GENERIC**) is a basic representation of a hierarchical tree with parent/child relationships. Another common scene graph used for large virtual worlds is the spatial hierarchical representation (partitioning the space), such as octree. For a detailed study on spatial representations, see [Samet 06]. For additional information, the reader is suggested to consult [Foley

Figure 4.9: AABB bounding box [Han 11].

et al. 96, Eberly 05, Eberly 07]. For a specific formal study about BSP see [Berg et al. 00, Chapter 12], quadtrees see [Berg et al. 00, Chapter 13], and octrees see [Langetepe and Zachmann 06, Chapter 1]. Without getting in depth, the important part to understand about spatial partitioning is how it works. First of all, the spatial representation can be static or dynamic. If static, it is expected for the world not to change; otherwise, it is dynamic. One common implementation is the BSP works by dividing the space in regions, which are represented by a binary tree. The quadtree recursively divides each region in four, forming a tree with a root followed by four leaves, and then each of those leaves with an additional four more, and so forth.

4.1.5 Collision Detection

Collision detection deals with the problem of how to find two objects occupying the same space at a given time [van den Bergen 04]. For 3D real-time environments (e.g., games, simulators), this topic defines how to detect the intersection (collision), and what to do when it happens [Ericson 05]. The latter part, which deals with the action following the intersection, is up to the designer. A common approach is to use physics engines (e.g., Bullet) to perform some type of reaction to the collision (e.g., bounce) [Eberly 10]. Another simpler type is to use bounding boxes to detect the collision, for example, the built-in simple collision detection functions provided by OGRE. This collision type is referred to as a bounding volume, where you can set spheres, boxes, and other 3D shapes that can help with the collision algorithms [Ericson 05], as shown in Figure 4.9. In systems like Unity or game engines, this functionality is already-built in.

> Side Note 4.2: Game Engine Design
>
> Game engine design can help input designers to understand the behind the
> scene that goes on in a real-time 3D application. An excellent resource
> about the development of game engine design are the books by David H.
> Eberly, *3D Game Engine Design* and *3D Game Engine Architecture*. The
> collection of books by David H. Eberly is full of insightful information
> hard to find in other books.

Further Reading

The books by David Eberly (see Side Notes 4.1 and 4.2) provide in-depth information about game engine design and advanced topics. The Red Book by
OpenGL [Shreiner and Group 13] and the OpenGL Super Bible [Sellers et al. 13]
are very useful. Note that the last three editions of the Super Bible are different.
The fourth edition talks about the fixed pipeline. The fifth edition covers the
programmable pipeline, and the sixth edition removes the intermediate code that
aided users to work with programmable shaders. The classical book by Foley and
colleagues on computer graphics still provides very valuable information [Foley
et al. 96]. A newer edition has been published [Hughes et al. 13]. Real-time
rendering provided a look at various components of computer graphics [Akenine-
Möller et al. 08]. For 3D mathematics used in computer graphics, see [Dunn and
Parberry 11]. Finally, a very unique book that talks about 3D graphics with a
perspective on games provides excellent information [Han 11].

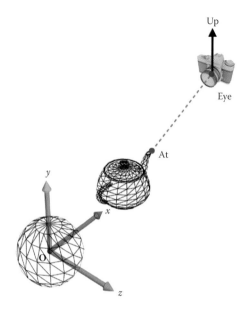

Figure 4.3. Camera space [Han 11].

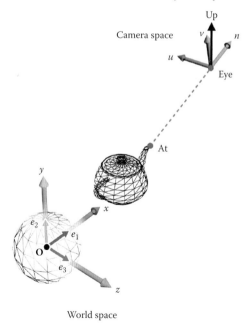

Figure 4.4. World space [Han 11].

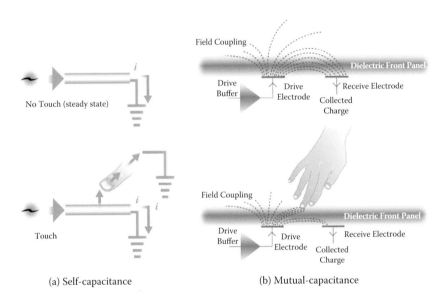

Field Coupling

Dielectric Front Panel

Drive
Buffer

Drive
Electrode

Receive Electrode

Collected
Charge

No Touch (steady state)

Touch

Field Coupling

Dielectric Front Panel

Drive
Buffer

Drive
Electrode

Receive Electrode

Collected
Charge

(a) Self-capacitance

(b) Mutual-capacitance

Figure 8.3. Multi-touch capacitance technology.

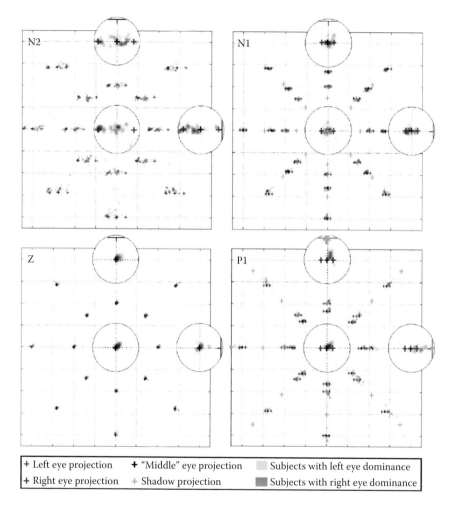

| + Left eye projection | + "Middle" eye projection | Subjects with left eye dominance |
| + Right eye projection | + Shadow projection | Subjects with right eye dominance |

Figure 9.4. Typical touch results from a 3D touch precision experiment: (top left) shows the touch locations for strong negative parallax, (top right) for negative parallax, (bottom left) for condition zero and (bottom right) for condition positive parallax.

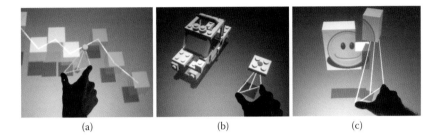

(a)   (b)   (c)

Figure 9.5. Three typical tasks with the triangle cursor metaphor: (a) following a predefined path; (b, c) completing a small 3D model.

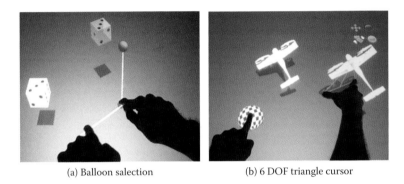

(a) Balloon salection   (b) 6 DOF triangle cursor

Figure 9.6. The two "move the touches" techniques: (a) balloon selection and (b) the extended version of the triangle cursor.

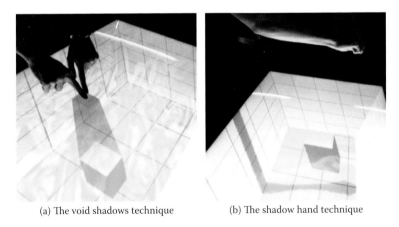

(a) The void shadows technique   (b) The shadow hand technique

Figure 9.8. Illustration of the two shadows interaction techniques: (a) the void shadows technique and (b) the shadow hand technique.

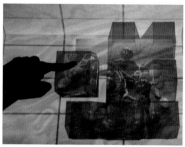

(a) Occlusion in void shadows   (b) Object penetrating the shadow

Figure 9.10. Illustration of some typical design problems with the void shadows and shadow hand techniques: (a) occlusion due to too many void shadows and (b) an object higher than the cursor penetrates the shadow hand.

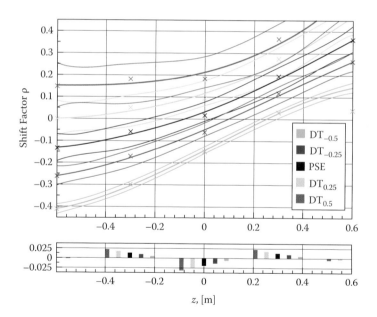

Figure 9.15. Fitted polynomial functions for $DT_{\pm 0.50}(z)$, $DT_{\pm 0.25}(z)$ and $PSE(z)$ (top) and the fitting residuals (bottom). The x-axis shows the objects' start position z, the y-axis shows shift factors ρ. The light curves show the 75% confidence intervals.

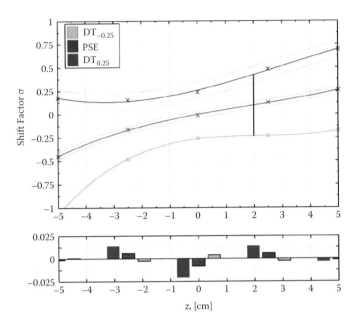

Figure 9.19. Fitted polynomial functions for $\sigma_{max}(z)$, $DT_{\pm 0.25}(z)$ and $PSE(z)$ (top) and the fitting residuals (bottom) for the generalized scaled shift technique. The x-axis shows the object's depth position z, the y-axis shows shift factors σ. The solid curves show fitted polynomial functions and the dotted curves show the 75% confidence intervals.

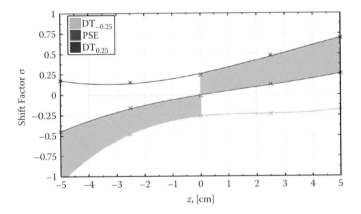

Figure 9.22. Illustration of the available shift factor space $\sigma_{max}(z)$. The solid lines show the fitted polynomial functions for $DT_{\pm 0.25}(z)$ and $PSE(z)$ for the generalized scaled shift technique. The shaded area represents the available shift factors, which could be applied to imperceptibly manipulate an object.

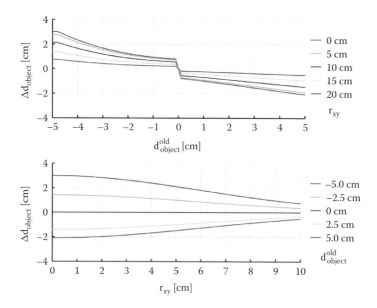

Figure 9.23. Illustration of the absolute object motion for finger motion $\Delta d_{finger} = 3cm$ as a function of object's start parallax (top) or distance to the attractor (bottom).

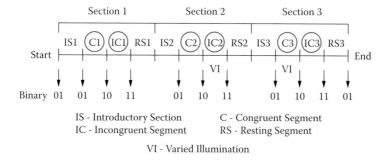

Figure 12.8. Timeline of the stress elicitation experimental protocol [Gao et al. 10].

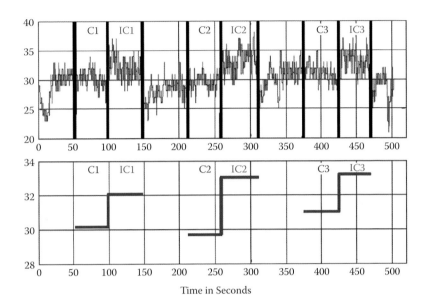

Figure 12.9. Pupil diameter variations (above) and mean values (below) originally observed during the protocol [Barreto et al. 07b].

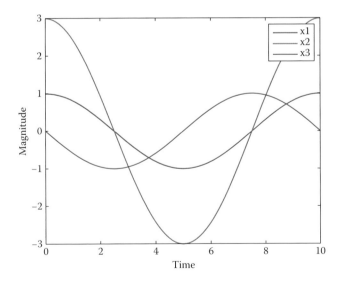

Figure 15.7. Cosine signal.

Figure 16.6. Three gimbals.

Figure 16.7. Gimbal lock effect.

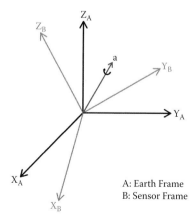

Figure 19.2. Hand and inertial reference frames.

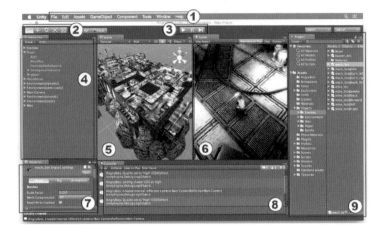

Figure 21.3. Layout of unity user interface.

Figure 21.8. Painting textures on terrain.

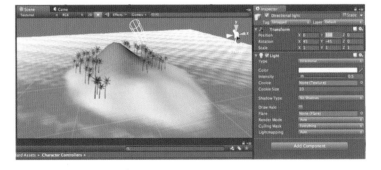

Figure 21.13. Directional light affects the direction of light and shadow for the entire game scene.

Figure 21.15. Game scene rendering in play mode without skybox.

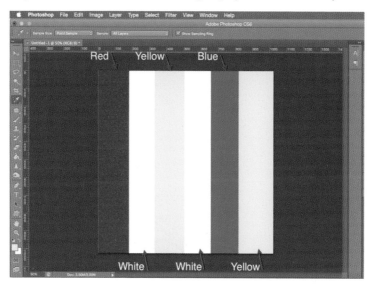

Figure 21.21. Create new texture image using Adobe Photoshop.

Figure 21.25. Game scene with multiple collectible objects.

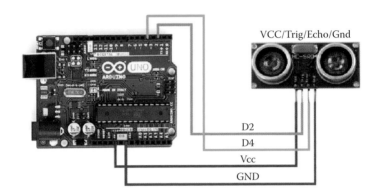

D2
D4
Vcc
GND

Figure 24.6. Circuit diagram.

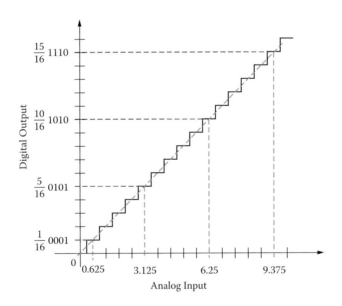

Figure 25.6. Example of ADC scaling.

5

3D Interaction

> If you want to compute in the future, you have to
> compute with the power of the future.
>
> —Alan Kay

5.1 Introduction

Computer interaction provides the communication channel that allows the user
to provide feedback to the computer system. This chapter deals with selection,
translation, and rotation of interactive systems, in particular 3D interaction. this
chapter deals (in most cases) with the selection and manipulation of an object or
group of objects. With this said, there are places where 3D navigation and 3D
interaction may overlap because of the interaction required in a navigational system.
Additional user interaction is found in Chapters 6 and 7. Interaction techniques and
design considerations are broad. Additional resources include MacKenzie's book,
which covers some very important interaction techniques for menus and buttons
(including some 3D techniques) [MacKenzie 12, Ch. 3]. Other important references
include *3D User Interfaces: Theory and Practice* [Bowman et al. 04, Ch. 5], and
Computer Graphics - Principles and Practice [Foley et al. 96, Ch. 8], among others
([Foley et al. 84, Dix et al. 04, Rogers et al. 11]).

5.2 3D Manipulation

Manipulation allows the user to interact with an object or multiple objects on the
display. Manipulation includes selection and transformations (e.g., rotations). If
the manipulation "preserves the shape of the object," then it is said to be *spatial
rigid object manipulation* [Bowman et al. 04]. Foley and colleagues provided
a guide to interaction techniques applicable to 2D interfaces [Foley et al. 84].
Some of their recommendations and definitions are valid for 3DUI. For example,

manipulation is defined by them as: "operations performed on a displayed object whereby the form of the object remains unchanged" [Foley et al. 84]. There are interaction techniques that modified an object (e.g., changing the size of a cube with a pinch gesture — scaling) [Mine 95b].

One of the options to work with manipulation tasks is to use application-specific methods. These types of methods are very specific to an application and while useful, they do not provide a general form to classify manipulation techniques (but generalization may not be the aim for the designer). The other option is to generalize the manipulations. If so, then we can decompose the task in a subset of accepted manipulation tasks, also referred to as *canonical manipulation tasks*. This subtask allows evaluation to be specific to each of them.

A 3D manipulation task simulates "acquisition and positioning movements that we perform in the real world" [Bowman et al. 04]. In other words, the ability to reach, grab, and move, among other manipulations to objects. The break down of these canonical tasks, described by [Foley et al. 84, Bowman et al. 97, Poupyrev et al. 97] are selection, positioning, and orientation. These tasks are described next.

Selection is the task that provides target acquisition from a set of targets [Zhai et al. 94]. This allows the user to select a target or possible group of targets among a universe of them. Zhai and colleagues offered the cubic silk cursor to acquired targets in 3D VE. One of the advantages of the silk cursor is that it does not "block completely the view of any object which it occludes" [Zhai et al. 94] because of its semi-transparency property. The progression of this 3D cursor is shown in Figures 5.1, 5.2a, 5.2b, 5.3a, and 5.3b. Another type of cursor is the bubble cursor. This cursor has been used for 2D target acquisition [Grossman and Balakrishnan 05]. It is possible to use a regular 2D cursor to pick items in a 3D environment. A tutorial is available [3D 14], which uses the concept of a ray query (see [Akenine-Möller et al. 08, pp. 738–756], object picking in [Eberly 07, pp 472–481], and ray intersection with a cylinder [Heckbert 94, pp. 356–365], among other [Kirk 92, pp. 275–283]) concepts. Selection provides a metaphor for someone picking an object in the real world [Bowman et al. 04]. Selection includes the following properties [Poupyrev et al. 97, Bowman et al. 04]: distance to target, direction to target, target size, selection count, target occlusion. In addition to the properties just mentioned, other properties about the objects or method of selection are important. For example, what type of bounding volume is the target using (e.g., AABB, see Chapter 4), density of objectsManipulation!selection!density of objects around the target(s), and method of selection (e.g., ray query).

Positioning is the task that allows the user to position the target in a different location; in other words, the translation of object (or objects) in the coordinate systems of a VE. In 3D space, this is translation on X, Y, and Z axes. Positioning includes the following properties [Poupyrev et al. 97, Bowman et al. 04]: distance to initial target position and final target position, direction to initial target position and final target position, distance for target to be translated in space, precision for the positioning (in particular, the final position), visibility, occlusion of target

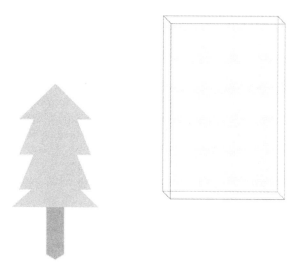

Figure 5.1: Cursor and tree object before selection. Note that the silk cursor is semi-transparent. Adapted from [Zhai et al. 94].

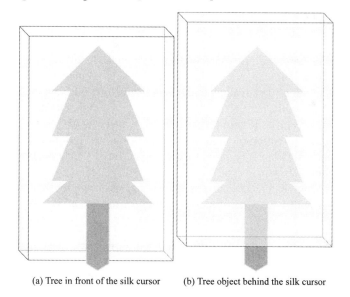

(a) Tree in front of the silk cursor   (b) Tree object behind the silk cursor

Figure 5.2: Silk cursor. Adapted from [Zhai et al. 94].

size, and size of the manipulated objects, among others. Positioning provides a metaphor for someone moving an object from A to B in the real world [Bowman et al. 04].

Orientation is the task that allows the user to rotate the target object. Orienta-

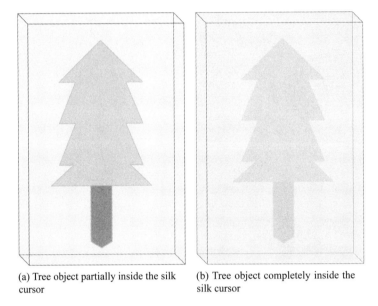

(a) Tree object partially inside the silk   (b) Tree object completely inside the
cursor   silk cursor

Figure 5.3: Silk cursor. Adapted from [Zhai et al. 94].

tion, as explained in this book (see Chapter 4), may have different outcomes. In positioning (translation), regardless of the order of steps taken to get to a final target destination, rotations do not allow that luxury. Therefore, different considerations must be taken from the perspective of user and system design. Orientation includes the following properties [Poupyrev et al. 97, Bowman et al. 04]: rotation amount, rotation matrix, initial orientation, final orientation, and required precision for target orientation. Orientation provides a metaphor for someone rotating an object in the real world [Bowman et al. 04].

In addition to the three canonical manipulation tasks mentioned, Poupyrev and colleagues provided a few performance metrics for manipulation tasks [Poupyrev et al. 97] (see also [Foley et al. 84]):

- Completion time: The time duration from start to finish of a given task.

- Accuracy: The actual position versus the desired position (precision).

- Error rate: How many times did the user failed to successfully complete the task?

- Ease of use: Cognitive load for the user.

- Ease of learning: The improvement over time by the user.

- Sense of presence: The immersion and spatial awareness.

Foley and colleagues, back in 1984, provided very useful guidelines for 2D interaction [Foley et al. 84]. As stated before, some of their recommendation are very important as of now. Some of them are aligned with the performance metric provided by [Poupyrev et al. 97]. The first criteria of performance are time, accuracy, and pleasure (similar to [Poupyrev et al. 97]). Additional criteria include learning time, recall time, short-term memory load, long-term memory load, and fatigue susceptibility, among others [Foley et al. 84]. This shows that similar criteria applied to both 2D and 3D.

5.2.1 Classification of Manipulation Techniques

Bowman and colleagues described a testbed evaluation for virtual environments. This included selection, manipulation, and travel experiments [Bowman et al. 99b]. The travel part of this work is described in Section 6.3.1. The taxonomies provided by Bowman and colleagues offered a way to classify the interaction by decomposition of tasks [Bowman et al. 97]. Another type of technique is described by exocentric and egocentric techniques [Poupyrev et al. 98]. Bowman and colleagues provide additional information about the taxonomies described here [Bowman et al. 04]. We now describe selection and manipulation taxonomies [Bowman et al. 99b]:

- **Selection**

    - **Feedback**:
        * Graphical
        * Force/Tactile
        * Audio
    - **Indication of Object**:
        * Object Touching
        * Pointing
            · 2D
            · 3D Hand
            · 3D Gaze
        * Occlusion/Framing
        * Indirect Selection
            · From List
            · Voice Selection
            · Iconic Objects
    - **Indication to Select**:
        * Gesture

   * Button
   * Voice Command
   * No Explicit

- **Manipulation**

  – **Object Attachment**:

   * Attach to Hand
   * Attach to Gaze
   * Hand Moves to Object
   * Object Moves to Hand
   * User/Object Scaling

  – **Object Position**:

   * No Control
   * 1-to-N Hand to Object Motion
   * Maintain Body-Hand Relation
   * Other Hand Mappings
   * Indirect Control

  – **Object Orientation**:

   * No Control
   * 1-to-N Hand to Object Motion
   * Other Hand Mappings
   * Indirect Control

  – **Feedback**:

   * Graphical
   * Force/Tactile
   * Audio

The other taxonomy offered by Poupyrev and colleagues provides a way to break down classification by points-of-view: egocentric versus exocentric. The VE manipulation techniques classification is described below [Poupyrev et al. 98]:

- **Exocentric metaphors**

  – **World-in-miniature**

  – **Automatic scaling**

- **Egocentric metaphors**

Side Note 5.1: Device Clutching

When a device is not able to provide an atomic manipulation, it is known as "clutching." In other words, a given manipulation can't be performed in a single motion [Bowman et al. 04]. The metaphor comes from the real-world example of using a wrench, which requires multiple motions to tighten a bolt; placing it in the bolt, rotating it, and placing it back in the bolt [Bowman et al. 04].

- **Virtual hand metaphors**:
  * "Classical" virtual hand
  * Go-Go
  * Indirect Go-Go

- **Virtual pointer metaphors**:
  * Ray-casting
  * Aperture
  * Flashlight
  * Image Plane

5.2.2   Muscle Groups: Precision Grasp

Zhai study 6-DOF in depth [Zhai 95] (see also 2.2.4). Devices use different muscle groups. For example, a hand-glove will use the larger muscle groups as opposed to a device attached to a finger that uses the smaller muscle groups [Zhai 95, Zhai et al. 96]. The latter type is referred to as **precision grasp** . Fine movements provide better results in certain task, such as rotation [Bowman et al. 04], decreasing device clutching (see 5.1). Zhai found some very interesting results about 6-DOF manipulation [Zhai 95]:

1. The physical 6-DOF input device "should provide a rich proprioceptive[1,2] feedback" [Zhai 95]. The proper feedback to an action will help the user to learn the task faster.

2. The transfer function (see Section 2.2.1) must match the capabilities of the physical input device.

---

[1]Proprioceptor: "Sensory receptor that receives stimuli from within the body" [Stevenson and Lindberg 10].

[2]Proprioceptive: "Relating to stimuli that are produced and perceived within an organism" [Stevenson and Lindberg 10].

3. Precise movements of smaller muscles (e.g., fingers) must be part of the interaction whenever possible.

4. The output (visual display) of the user actions should:

   (a) provide "immediate exteroceptive[3,4] feedback" [Zhai 95].

   (b) provide semi-transparency objects (e.g., silk cursor), which helps to provide a better relationship of depth between the cursor and the target.

5.2.3   Isomorphic Manipulations

An isomorphic manipulation is defined by a geometrical one-to-one relationship between the motion in the real world with the motion in the virtual environment [Bowman et al. 04]. An isomorphic manipulation provides a more natural interaction. However, this type of manipulation has some deficiencies [Knight 87, Bowman et al. 04]:

1. Given the constraints that physical input devices may have, the mapping may be impractical.

2. Given our own limitations, isomorphic manipulation may be limited.

3. It is possible to provide better interaction using 3D interfaces, like the **WIM** (world in miniature) [Stoakley et al. 95].

Deciding between isomorphic and non-isomorphic manipulation techniques depends on the application. Non-isomorphic techniques provide a "magic effect" in a VE [Bowman et al. 04]. It is important than non-isomorphic rotations require special attention. This will be covered later (see Section 5.2.6).

5.2.4   Pointing Techniques

Pointing is the fundamental operation in 3DUI that allows users to select and later manipulate objects. In a 2D VE, a very common way to select an object is by using the mouse cursor and pressing the mouse's button. One of the earliest works in this area was published by Bolt, titled "Put-That-There" (with emphasis on "that" object) [Bolt 80]. This allowed users to select objects by pointing. Once the object was selected, the user will command the object via voice command (e.g., "move that to the right of the green square" [Bolt 80]). There are several pointing techniques, some of them described in [Bowman et al. 04], which provide the UI designer with different options.

---

[3]Exteroceptor: "Sensory receptor that receives external stimuli" [Stevenson and Lindberg 10].
[4]Exteroceptive: "Relating to stimuli that are external to an organism" [Stevenson and Lindberg 10].

Ray-casting allows the user to point at an object using a virtual ray [Bolt 80, Poupyrev et al. 98]. Poupyrev and colleagues used a virtual hand to define the position and the orientation [Poupyrev et al. 98]. One option to attach the virtual hand is to use a one-to-one mapping to a direct 6-DOF input device. The other option is to use an indirect input device (e.g., mouse) to move the virtual hand and to select an object.[5] Attaching an infinite ray to the hand provides better visual feedback for the user to discern if the ray is intersecting an object or not [Bowman and Hodges 97]. This technique, while useful, has problems when selecting objects that are small (which require high-precision) or far away [Poupyrev et al. 98, Bowman et al. 99b]. One of the problems is the delay measurement, which is the "lag between the actual sensor position and the position reported" [Liang et al. 91] by the device. The noise and delay causes a lag that is perceived by the user [Liang et al. 91]. The increased distance causes the tracker to jitter. Bowman and colleagues summarized this problem by stating: "ray-casting selection performance erodes significantly because of the high angular accuracy required and the amplification of hand and tracker jitter with increased distance" [Bowman et al. 04]. For additional information about jitter, see [Liang et al. 91, Forsberg et al. 96, Poupyrev et al. 98]. A study compared ray-casting selection, 2D-plane technique, and 3D volume for air pointing (e.g., WiiMote) [Cockburn et al. 11]. This study showed that ray-casting selection technique was "rapid but inaccurate" [Cockburn et al. 11]. This further demonstrated some of the problems with ray-casting selection technique, as it was also shown in [Poupyrev et al. 98]. A possible solution is to use the approach by Argelaguet and Andujar, which developed a solution for dense VEs which combines image-plane technique and hand-rotation for ray control, showing their technique outperforms ray-casting selection [Argelaguet and Andujar 09a]. A similar approach for 3D games uses different techniques with improved selection techniques [Cashion et al. 12].

Ray-casting selection technique works by the intersection of the ray with the object (see Chapter 4). This is estimated by Equation 5.1, where the pointing direction is given by the virtual ray ($\vec{p}$), the 3D position of the virtual hand **h**, and the parameter α is between 0 to $+\infty$. The object selected should be the closest to the user. Andujar and Argelaguet developed a similar approach to the one just described using ray-casting (with the flexibility of virtual pointing technique [Olwal and Feiner 03]) for 2D GUIs embedded in 3D environments [Andujar and Argelaguet 06]. Riege and colleagues demonstrated the use of a **bent pick ray** for multi-users, which allowed users to select and move objects, bending the ray without locking the objects [Riege et al. 06]. For additional information about ray-casting methods, see [Bowman and Hodges 97, Poupyrev et al. 98, Bowman et al. 99b, Bowman et al. 04].

---

[5] "clicking with the mouse directly on 3D objects is an easier and more effective method" [Bowman et al. 04].

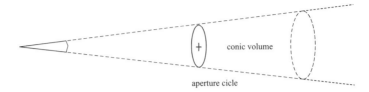

Figure 5.4: Aperture technique: selection cone. Adapted from [Forsberg et al. 96].

$$\mathbf{p}(\alpha) = \mathbf{h} + \alpha \vec{p} \tag{5.1}$$

Two-handed pointing is a variation of the ray-casting technique just described. This approach uses two virtual hands [Mine et al. 97]: one of the hands determines the orientation of the virtual ray and the other hand determines the direction of the ray (where it is pointing). This is described by Equation 5.2, showing the 3D coordinates for the right hand ($\mathbf{h}_{right}$) and the left hand ($\mathbf{h}_{left}$) and where the α parameter should point away from the user [Bowman et al. 04]. An alternate approach to the two-hand technique described in [Mine et al. 97] is the **virtual pointing technique** [Olwal and Feiner 03]. One hand may provide the length of the ray and the other hand the curvature of it, which allows us to move around objects [Olwal and Feiner 03].

$$\mathbf{p}(\alpha) = \mathbf{h}_{left} + \alpha \left(\mathbf{h}_{right} - \mathbf{h}_{left} \right) \tag{5.2}$$

Bi-manual input is described in detail in Chapters 7 and 8 (see Sections 7.3.1 and 8.3.6). However, there is specific literature about the performance of bi-manual input for selection. Ulinski and colleagues evaluated four classes of bi-manual techniques [Ulinski et al. 09] (see [Guiard 87] to read about the different classes.) They showed that no significant difference was found that would induce fatigue in experienced users [Ulinski et al. 09]. They also provided some important findings [Ulinski et al. 09]: (1) Symmetric and synchronous selection provided faster task completion; (2) asynchronous selection increased cognitive load, in particular when it was combined with asymmetric interaction; (3) usability significantly decreased when symmetric-asynchronous actions were taken. Ulinski and colleagues also looked at two-handed selection for volumetric data [Ulinski et al. 07]. Another technique that uses both-hands, is **balloon selection** [Benko and Feiner 07]. This technique uses a multi-finger approach (with both-hands) to use the real-world metaphor of controlling a helium balloon [Benko and Feiner 07]. Benko and Feiner found that the balloon selection technique provided "the user with fast and slightly indirect interaction, while simultaneously reducing hand fatigue and lowering selection error-rate" [Benko and Feiner 07] (see Chapter 9).

Another technique is the **flashlight** or **spotlight**. This metaphor of a real-life flashlight [Liang and Green 94] provides selection of an object via illumination, when the selection requires less precision [Bowman et al. 04]. This approach replaces the ray with a conic volume with the narrow end of the cone (apex) attached to the input device. If an object is within the selection cone, then the object can be selected. It is clear that the most immediate problem for this technique is to discern between multiple objects (e.g., dense environment) in the selection cone. Liang and Green offered two rules to select an object in the selection cone [Liang and Green 94, Bowman et al. 04]: (1) The object closer to the center of the line of the cone is selected. (2) If the objects shared the same angle between the center of the selection cone, then the object selected is the closest to the device. It is important to note that the object is not required to be entirely in the selection cone. A related technique, called **aperture**, allows the user to change the spread of the selection cone in real time [Forsberg et al. 96], as shown in Figure 5.4. This helps the user to adapt when the environment is dense or contains small objects [Bowman et al. 04]. The user's viewpoint is provided by head-tracking and the virtual hand-position by the input device (e.g., hand-glove), which for this aperture is represented by a cursor (e.g., a cube). This leads to the Equation 5.3, where **e** is the 3D coordinate of the virtual viewpoint, **h** is the 3D coordinate of the hand, and α is between 0 to $+\infty$.

$$\mathbf{p}(\alpha) = \mathbf{e} + \alpha(\mathbf{h} - \mathbf{e}) \qquad (5.3)$$

The **aperture** technique offers some advantages [Forsberg et al. 96]: (1) It mimics how people point to objects. (2) It offers similar desktop metaphor of placing a cursor on top of a target. (3) Visual feedback is not required other "than the aperture cursor itself" [Forsberg et al. 96]. (4) It reduces the noise of the tracker and the user by using volume selection (used in the spotlight technique). To select the object, the orientation of the aperture is used. Just like in a real environment, the orientation of the hands provides the intent of the object to manipulate. In the particular case of Forsberg's technique, two plates are used as visual feedback to select the object. Figure 5.5 shows the entire object being selected because of the orientation of the plates. Figure 5.6 shows the selection of the middle disk object because of the orientation of the plates.

Another approach that simplifies selection by requiring the user to control only 2-DOF is called **image-plane technique** [Pierce et al. 97]. This approach, inspired by "The id in the Hall"[6] show, where a character would pretend to "crush people's heads using his index finger and thumb" [Pierce et al. 97], provided an alternative interaction technique. The idea of this approach is to have the user work with 3D objects using their 2D projection. Pierce and colleagues created four ways for users to interact with objects [Pierce et al. 97]:

- **Head Crusher**: The user would use one hand to select the object between his/her index finger and thumb. The user's point of view is also taken into consideration to select the object.

---

[6]Canadian Broadcasting Corporation (CBC) 1988–1994.

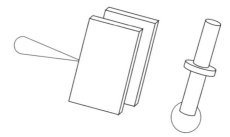

Figure 5.5: Aperture technique: entire object is selected. Adapted from [Forsberg et al. 96].

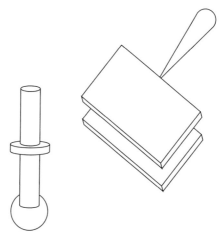

Figure 5.6: Aperture technique: partial object is selected (middle disc). Adapted from [Forsberg et al. 96].

- **Sticky Finger**: This approach uses one stretched finger to select the object. This technique is very useful for large objects and objects close to the user.

- **Lifting Palm**: This approach uses one of the user's palms, facing up and below the object. The way the object is selected is by finding where the palm is located plus an offset.

- **Framing Hands**: This uses both hands to select an object. The user finds opposite corners of the object to select it. This is similar to the head crusher technique. This technique also allows the user to select a group of objects.

Pierce and colleagues provided some guidelines when dealing with image-plane techniques [Pierce et al. 97]: (a) The system should provide feedback for the object to be selected. (b) Using the feedback, the user will choose the correct object. Also, while the head-crusher is similar to the aperture technique, it offers a disambiguation method inherent in the gesture but the object must fall within the index finger and thumb as opposed to the aperture technique that does not require the entire object to be in the selection cone [Bowman et al. 04]. This technique has a few problems [Pierce et al. 97]:

- **Arm Fatigue**: This may be caused by users constantly needing to move the arm to the level of their eyes. A solution to this problem, which causes fatigue, is allowing the users to move the object (once selected) to a more natural position.

- **Occlusion**: The hand may occlude the object, in particular if the object is small or far from the user's point of view. A possible way to correct this problem is to render the hands semi-transparent.

- **Stereo Rendering**: Selecting the left or right image plane will change how the image looks. A possible way to correct this problem is to choose the default plane view. Pierce and colleagues decided to render the scene monocularly [Pierce et al. 97].

A more recent technique in selection is called **SQUAD** [Kopper et al. 11], designed with cluttered environments in mind. This is a type of selection by progressive refinement, which means that the user reduces the number of objects until only the desired target remains. This refinement is done in discrete steps for SQUAD but it can also be done in continuous steps like cone-casting [Steed and Parker 05]. This technique was designed to overcome problems with ray-casting methods, such as hand and tracker jitter. The method uses a modified "ray-casting that casts a sphere onto the nearest intersecting surface to determine which objects will be selectable" [Kopper et al. 11]. This is called by the authors of this technique **sphere-casting**. The objects found within the sphere will become selectable. The sphere has a dynamic mode, where the sphere's radius increases if the user is farther "from the nearest intersecting surface" [Kopper et al. 11], allowing a larger set of objects to be selected. The sphere-casting allows selection of occluded objects while avoiding the typical ray-casting precision issues. Figure 5.7 shows the sphere with the selected objects. Once this phase is completed, a quad-menu is provided (see Figure 5.8), where the objects are "evenly distributed among four quadrants on the screen" [Kopper et al. 11]. The quad-menu reduces the number of objects to select by pointing each time where the desired object is found. The number of selections needed is $\log_4(n)$, where n is the initial number of objects [Kopper et al. 11]. While there is a trade-off between immediate selection and progressive refining selection, SQUAD offers some advantages. This technique was found to be significantly faster for selection in low-density environments and for smaller objects [Kopper et al. 11]. Another advantage is in the time that it takes to complete a task, the number of refinements grows linear in comparison to the exponential

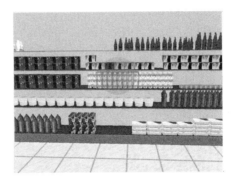

Figure 5.7: SQUAD selection technique: Sphere casting at the market. [Kopper et al. 11].

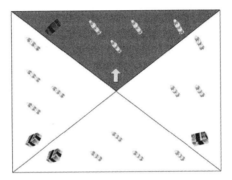

Figure 5.8: Quad-menu. Note that the target object needs to be visually distinct for the selection to be feasible. [Kopper et al. 11].

growth of ray-casting method [Kopper et al. 11]. However, it also suffers from some shortcomings. For example, SQUAD cannot performed well, if the selection is based on object location [Kopper et al. 11].

Jota and colleagues looked at the effects of ray-casting for *very large displays* [Jota et al. 10]. The purpose of this study was to understand the control type and parallax under large displays. The study looked at four variants: technique for laser pointing, arrow-pointing, image-planing pointing, and fixed-origin pointing [Jota et al. 10]. Their study showed that arrow and laser, which are rotational techniques, performed better than positional techniques, including vertical targeting, suggesting "that parallax is not important for targeting tasks" [Jota et al. 10]. In general, they recommend that if targeting is important, laser-style ray-casting technique is most appropriate [Jota et al. 10]. The study also talks about tracing, which showed that image-plane and arrow-pointing performed best compared to the other variants tested [Jota et al. 10].

Additional selection literature is available. For a general classification about 3D mobile interaction, see [Balaa et al. 14]. For 3D selection (see Chapter 9) [Argelaguet and Andújar 09b, Teather and Stuerzlinger 11, Strothoff et al. 11, Stuerzlinger and Teather 14], selection techniques for volumetric displays [Grossman and Balakrishnan 06], in-air pointing technique [Banerjee et al. 11], domain-specific design techniques [Chen and Bowman 09], selection and realism [Gunasekara and Wimalaratne 13], progressive refinement using cone-casting [Steed and Parker 05], and Steed's selection model for VEs [Steed 06], among others [Hernoux and Christmann 15, Otsuki et al. 13]. Some other techniques, such as the triangle cursor [Strothoff et al. 11], are described in Chapter 9. Some additional techniques are described in the book (e.g., Chapters 6 and 8). Also, direct and hybrid manipulation techniques are described in Section 5.2.5. A survey of 3D interaction while dated, is still useful [Hand 97]. Finally, a very detailed recent survey for 3D object selection contains a list of techniques and further explanation about the state-of-the-art [Argelaguet and Andujar 13].

5.2.5 Direct and Hybrid Manipulations

Direct manipulation provides a close relationship with the user's action. This mapping takes the forms of transfer functions (see Section 2.2.1) or control-display gain functions (see Side Note 2.3). One of the techniques for direct-manipulation is called **virtual hand**.

The **simple virtual hand**, an isomorphic interaction, allows direct mapping between the user's real hand and the virtual hand, which is described linearly scaled as in Equations 5.4 and 5.5 [Bowman et al. 04], where $\mathbf{p}_r$ is the 3D position and $\mathbf{R}_r$ is the 3D orientation of the real hand, while $\mathbf{p}_v$ is the 3D position, $\mathbf{R}_v$ is the 3D orientation of the virtual hand. The scaling factor (α) is the ratio between the real hand and the virtual hand. While Equation 5.5 does not include the scaling factor included in the position equation, in some cases, it may be useful to use it, yielding $\mathbf{R}_v = \alpha \mathbf{R}_r$.

$$\mathbf{p}_v = \alpha \mathbf{p}_r \qquad (5.4)$$

$$\mathbf{R}_v = \mathbf{R}_r \qquad (5.5)$$

One technique that improves on the virtual hand approach is called the **go-go** technique [Poupyrev et al. 96]. The motivation of Poupyrev and colleagues was to create a virtual arm that changes its length. This imposed several challenges: (1) How users would specify the desired length. (2) How users would control their virtual hand. (3) How to make this metaphor intuitive. The solution was to provide a non-linear mapping between the virtual hand and the user's hand.

The implementation of the go-go technique included the polar coordinate [Wikipedia 15k] r_r, ϕ, θ in a user-centered coordinate system [Poupyrev et al. 96].

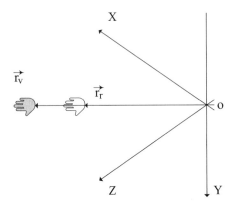

Figure 5.9: Go-go technique. Adapted from [Poupyrev et al. 96].

This non-linear mapping function ($F(r_r)$) is shown in Figure 5.9 and Equation 5.6, where r_r is the length of the vector $\vec{r}_r$ pointing from the origin (o) (drawn at the user's position) to the user's hand, and the direction of vector $\vec{r}_r$ provided by the angles ϕ and θ. The virtual hand is located in the environment in position r_v, ϕ, θ, where r_v is the length of ($\vec{r}_v$) the virtual hand from the origin. $\vec{r}_v$

$$r_v = F(r_r) = \begin{cases} r_r & \text{if } r_r < D \\ r_r + \alpha(r_r - D)^2 & \text{if otherwise} \end{cases} \tag{5.6}$$

This mapping provides two different transfer functions. One of them is linear when r_r is less than D. This provides the user a one-to-one mapping that corresponds to the movements of the user's hand reflected in the environment's virtual hand. The constant D is a threshold, which is $\frac{2}{3}$ the user's arm length[7] [Poupyrev et al. 96]. Once the value of r_r becomes larger that the threshold (D), then the mapping becomes non-linear. It is important to know that the transition between linear to non-linear is smooth because of the C^1 continuity [Poupyrev et al. 96]. The non-linear transfer function means that "as the user moves the hand, r_v increases or decreases faster than r_r" [Poupyrev et al. 96], making the virtual hand appear to increase or decrease as the user move its hands past the D threshold.

This technique is an improvement over the simple virtual hand approach providing a 6-DOF. Additional studies have shown that this technique is intuitive [Bowman and Hodges 97, Poupyrev et al. 98]. Bowman and Hodges found that, while it is a useful technique, the fact that the arm length coefficient must be adapted to different types of VEs "may lead to imprecision in the user's ability to position the virtual arm, so that for quite distant objects, the arm may extend and retract too quickly to allow easy grabbing and manipulation of objects" [Bowman

---

[7]This was the value chosen in their study [Poupyrev et al. 96] because it was found to be the optimal value for users to work with comfortably.

and Hodges 97]. Like in most 3DUI solutions it is hard to find a one size fits-all approach. This was noted by Poupyrev and colleagues [Poupyrev et al. 98]. In their well-documented study, they found that the go-go technique "allows for effective selection of objects at-a-distance" [Poupyrev et al. 98] yielding better performance whenever accurate selection is needed. However, ray-casting technique was found better for larger objects, when accuracy was not important [Poupyrev et al. 98].

A different approach is to provide a miniature view of the VE "within the user's reach" [Bowman et al. 04]. This technique is called **World-in-Miniature** (WIM) [Stoakley et al. 95]. This approach works well for small and medium VEs. However, it does not scale well for large environments. Nevertheless, WIM works well for different types of 3DUIs, such as augmented reality (see [Bowman et al. 04, Ch. 12]). For actual implementation considerations, see [Stoakley et al. 95].

A different technique is to combine direct (e.g., simple virtual hand) and indirect manipulations (e.g., ray-casting technique). We called this approach **hybrid** or **combination** technique, providing the best of both direct and indirect worlds. The simplest way to combined techniques is by *aggregation*. This allows the user to select the type of interactions to use based on a set of possible interactions. A more advanced form of creating a hybrid technique is to combine both based on task context. This approach is called *integration* technique. The system, based on different stages of manipulation (e.g., select and then manipulate), provides a way for the application to select the appropriate technique to be used.

One of these hybrid techniques, is called HOMER (**H**and-centered **O**bject **M**anipulation **E**xtending **R**ay-casting) [Bowman and Hodges 97]. This approach allows the user to select an object in the VE using a ray-casting technique by attaching the virtual hand to an object once it is selected [Bowman et al. 04]; this in contrast to the ray-casting, which attaches the object to the ray. Once the object is selected, HOMER allows the user to move and rotate the object (manipulation mode).

HOMER is based on previous hybrid techniques [Wloka and Greenfield 95, Mine 95a]. However those techniques use a one-to-S mapping (S is a scale factor) not allowing to specify object position and rotation. Bowman and Hodges provides two extensions to add the feature that was lacking in the previous techniques [Bowman and Hodges 97]: (1) The object manipulation is relative to the user's body. (2) The user may specify the distance of the object using an input device action, such as mouse button or hand motion. Equation 5.7 shows that this technique linearly scales, where r_r is scaled by constant α_h, yielding r_v [Bowman et al. 04]. The constant α_h is defined by Equation 5.8, where D_o is the distance from the user to the object when selected, and D_h is the distance between the user and user's hand when selected [Bowman et al. 04]. How far the user can reposition an object is limited by Equation 5.8. Please note that the rotation for the selected object is controlled using "an isomorphic mapping between the real and virtual hand" [Bowman et al. 04].

$$r_v = \alpha_h r_r \tag{5.7}$$

$$\alpha_h = \frac{D_o}{D_h} \tag{5.8}$$

Some of the advantages of HOMER over other arm-extension techniques are [Bowman and Hodges 97]: (1) Grabbing an object is easier for users because precise position of the virtual hand is not required. (2) No additional physical effort is needed to select objects regardless of their position in the VE. (3) Manipulation also requires less physical effort. The one problem refers back to Equation 5.8. Bowman and colleagues provide an example of the limitation of the equation [Bowman et al. 04]: Assume that an object is far away and a user decides to grab it, bring it close to him/her, and then release it. When the user decides to bring the object back to its original position, this becomes a challenge. The reason is that the scaling coefficient will become very small because "the object is located within the user's reach" [Bowman et al. 04]. There have been newer approaches to HOMER, for example, HOMER-S for hand-held devices (where 3DTouch and HOMER-S techniques are compared) [Mossel et al. 13].

A similar approach to HOMER is the **scale-world grab** technique [Mine et al. 97]. Instead of using the ray-casting technique, the scale-world grab uses the image-plane technique for selection. Once the object is selected, the manipulation mode is activated. The manipulation mode scales down the VE based on the user's virtual viewpoint using a scaling factor (α). The scaling factor is derived between the distance from the virtual viewpoint to the virtual hand (D_v) divided by the distance between the same virtual viewpoint and the selected object [Mine et al. 97, Bowman et al. 04]. This technique has the same problem as HOMER does, which is that the scaling coefficient will become very small when the object is at arm's reach and the user decides to move it further away.

$$\alpha_h = \frac{D_v}{D_o} \tag{5.9}$$

One of the problems with some of the scaling techniques, such as HOMER and scale-world grab, is that the scale factor works only in one direction [Bowman et al. 04]. The **Voodoo Dolls** technique tries to solve this problem, among other limitations found in some other techniques, providing additional features [Pierce et al. 99]: Users can work in multiple scales, visible and occluded objects can be manipulated, and the "user's dominant hand works in the reference frame defined by his non-dominant hand" [Pierce et al. 99], among others. Voodoo Dolls is a bimanual technique, which uses pinch gloves combining the image-plane technique for selection and WIM technique for manipulation. During the manipulation, the world is miniaturized and placed into objects named "dolls." For example, say that you have a football (soccer) ball that the user may want to modify in size and color. Once the object is selected, the user will have a copy of this ball in one of his/her virtual hands to operate with. Maybe a magic brush is found in the environment that allows the other hand to also place it in a "doll" and use their other hand to manipulate this brush with the ball already placed in the opposite hand. The technique is very powerful but it does require additional hardware, which is two 6-DOF degrees of freedom. Nevertheless, the technique itself is very useful to be duplicated with other hardware or by enhancing the technique. Additional information is found in the original publication [Pierce et al. 99] and study that compares this technique versus HOMER [Pierce and Pausch 02], among others [Bowman et al. 04].

Direct 3D interaction offers an intuitive way for users to work with a VE. However, as we have described, there are several challenges, such as accuracy. Frees and colleagues introduced a 3D interaction technique called **PRISM**: Precise and Rapid Interaction through Scaled Manipulation [Frees et al. 07]. Their goal was to increase the control/display ratio (see Side Note 2.3). In other words, improve accuracy and control. Using the notion derived from Fitts' law, "as the target gets smaller" [Frees et al. 07] the user must slow down the movement of his/her hand. Conversely, as the target gets larger, the user must increase the movement of his/her hand. This implies that it is quite likely that the goal is to have a "precise position or orientation in mind" [Frees et al. 07]. Using this notion, PRISM adjusts the control-display gain, in real time. As the speed decreases, the control-display gain increases to "filter out hand instability" [Frees et al. 07] and as the speed increases, the control-gain decreases, providing a direct interaction (C:D = 1).

To select an object in PRISM, the user touches the virtual object with a digital stylus and presses down on the stylus button. While the button is pressed, the position and direction can be modified. Once the button is released, the virtual object is also released. One of the interesting aspects of PRISM is how it uses the speed of the user's hand to alter the control-display gain.

PRISM uses different thresholds based on speed, as shown in Figure 5.10, which determines the control-display gain. There are three control-display ratio modes, which depend on three constants: (a) minimum-speed (MinS), which is the least speed needed to be considered valid (otherwise it is noise) (b) scaling-constant (SC), which is the maximum speed that a user may have while the goal is precision. (c) MaxS constant is used to trigger offset recovery.

The way that PRISM switches modes provides a better interaction for users. For example, assume a user is moving his/her hand close to the constant MinS. The control-display gain becomes larger with the virtual object moving very slowly [Frees et al. 07]. In the other hand, if the hand is moving closer to the constant SC, the C:D ratio approaches one. Once it passes SC, the relationship between the interaction and the user becomes a one-to-one relationship. The third-constant triggers the offset recovery. "The offset is automatically reduced, causing the object to catch up to the hand" [Frees et al. 07]. In most cases, MaxS is larger than SC. It is important to note the relationship that exists between SC and the user's sensitivity and precision. The lower SC becomes, the selected object will become more sensitive to the hand movement and it will scale less. The larger SC becomes, the selected object will become more resistant to hand motion, providing more scaling, and the ability to be more precise by the user [Frees et al. 07]. It

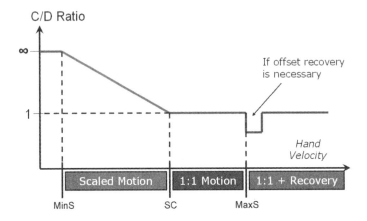

Figure 5.10: PRISM hand-speed adjustment.

is important to note that each user has his/her own preferences and abilities, for which the constant values may need to be adjusted. This adjustment is also useful for the same user that may require different requirements for different types of applications.

PRISM treats translations and rotations separately. The translation is controlled by the C:D ratio. To determine the speed of the user's hand, PRISM takes a sample of the hand position before each frame, and calculates the speed using the current location and the location from the sample taken 500 ms before [Frees et al. 07]. Any values in between those samples are ignored. The time was derived based on observation and the lack of user complaints. However, there are other ways to lower (or remove) noise [Liang et al. 91, Welch and Bishop 97]. Equation 5.10 shows the constant movement as long as the value is greater than SC and speed is smoothed out when the value is between MinS and SC.

$$K = \frac{1}{CD} = \begin{cases} 1 & \text{if } S_{\text{hand}} \geq SC \\ \frac{S_{\text{hand}}}{SC} & \text{if } MinS < S_{\text{hand}} < SC \\ 0 & \text{if } S_{\text{hand}} \leq MinS \end{cases} \qquad (5.10)$$

$$D_{\text{object}} = K \cdot D_{\text{hand}} \qquad (5.11)$$

A very interesting approach in PRISM is the offset recovery. During scale mode (see Figure 5.10), an "offset accumulates between the hand and the controlled object" [Frees et al. 07]. For the case of translation, there are two sub-cases [Frees et al. 07]: (a) User is in any mode and it has accumulated offset "in a particular direction, and then changes direction moving their hand back toward the object." When this happens, the "object is not moved until the hand crosses back through

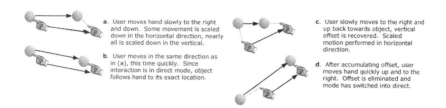

a. User moves hand slowly to the right and down. Some movement is scaled down in the horizontal direction, nearly all is scaled down in the vertical.

b. User moves in the same direction as in (a), this time quickly. Since interaction is in direct mode, object follows hand to its exact location.

c. User slowly moves to the right and up back towards object, vertical offset is recovered. Scaled motion performed in horizontal direction.

d. After accumulating offset, user moves hand quickly up and to the right. Offset is eliminated and mode has switched into direct.

Figure 5.11: Examples of typical interactions when using the PRISM translation technique.

the object" bringing the offset to zero. (b) When the speed exceeds MaxS, it is very likely that the user is not concerned with accuracy and the user is trying to move an object to a general location. In this case, the speed of the object is increased, so the object catches to the hand. For the algorithm, see [Frees et al. 07, Table I]. Another aspect that pertains to translation is the *axis independent scaling*. This means that PRISM works on each axis independently. For example, the speed in the X direction affects only the scaling mode for the X direction. This helps the user move the hand rapidly avoiding drift, helping users move an object in a straight line. Figure 5.11 shows some typical PRISM translation interactions.

PRISM rotation technique works differently than translation. It uses the hand's angular velocity and three constants to find the control-display gain (C:D) needed. Just like in translation, this works differently depending on the speed of the hand. If it is below MinS, the object will not rotate. If it is between MinS and SC, the object is rotated "by an angle proportional to the distance the hand has rotated in the most recent sampling interval" [Frees et al. 07]. As the value approaches SC, the "object rotates directly with the hand" [Frees et al. 07], with MaxS triggering automatic offset recovery. It is important to note that PRISM, instead of using Euler angles, uses quaternions to represent the orientation of the hand. The rotation is calculated between the current orientation and the orientation of the previous 200 ms, similar to the translation approach. The rotation is calculated by Equation 5.12, where the rotational difference is given by current frame (Q_t) and the previous frame (Q_{t-1}), yielding Q_{diff}. Equation 5.13 converts Q_{diff} from radians to degrees, which is later divided by 200 ms, as shown in Equation 5.14. This aids Equation 5.15 to calculate C:D. For the scale rotation, the inverse of C:D is used. Note that k is a real number between 0 and 1 [Frees et al. 07]. Finally, the difference in the offset recovery with translation is that the rotation removes the offset at once (as opposed to gradually over one second). For additional information, see [Frees et al. 07].

$$Q_{\text{diff}} = \frac{Q_t}{Q_{t-1}} = Q_t \, Q_{t-1}^{-1} \qquad (5.12)$$

$$A = (2 * \arccos(Q_{\text{diff} \to w})) \cdot \frac{180}{\pi} \qquad (5.13)$$

$$RS = \frac{A}{0.20 \, sec} \qquad (5.14)$$

$$k = \frac{1}{CD} = \begin{cases} 1 & \text{if } RS \geq SC \\ \frac{RS}{SC} & \text{if } MinS < RS < SC \\ 0 & \text{if } RS \leq MinS \end{cases} \qquad (5.15)$$

$$Q_{\text{new}} = Q_{\text{diff}}^{k} \, Q_{\text{Object}} \qquad (5.16)$$

5.2.6 Non-Isomorphic Rotations

The reasons to create non-isomorphic rotations may vary from hardware limitations to constraints of the human body [Poupyrev et al. 00]. For example, the joints have certain constraints that may not allow a full 360°rotation effect. The most basic form of non-isomorphic mapping is adding a scale factor, as shown in Equation 5.17, where k is the scale factor, D_d is the displacement of the device, and D_c is the displacement of the visual element [Poupyrev et al. 00]. Note that k could be a non-linear transformation.

$$D_d = k \times D_c \qquad (5.17)$$

Using quaternions (represented by q), a series of operations can be done for non-isomorphic operations (*linear zero-order control-display*). One of the options is to amplify the rotation while maintaining the direction of rotation, which is given by Equation 5.18 where $\hat{u}_c$ is the axis of rotation with angle v_c.

$$q_c = \left(\sin\left(\frac{v_c}{2} \right) \hat{u}_c, \cos\left(\frac{v_c}{2} \right) \right) = e^{\left(\frac{v_c}{2} \hat{u}_c \right)} \qquad (5.18)$$

The zero-order control-display "gain should amplify the angle rotation" v_c by k, independent of $\hat{u}_c$ [Poupyrev et al. 00], yielding Equation 5.19. In other words, the zero-order linear control-display "gain for spatial rotations is a *power function*" [Poupyrev et al. 00], as shown in Equation 5.20.

$$q_d = \left(\sin\left(\frac{kv_c}{2} \right) \hat{u}_c, \cos(kv_c2) \right) = e^{\left(k\frac{v_c}{2} \hat{u}_c \right)} = q_c^{k} \qquad (5.19)$$

$$q_d = q_c^{k} \qquad (5.20)$$

There are cases where the rotation is relative to an orientation q_0. This is accomplished by "calculating the rotation q_0 and q_c, amplifying it, and combining it with reference orientation q_0," as shown by Equation [Poupyrev et al. 00], which is similar to the *slerp* function [Shoemake 85], with Equation 5.22 as an equivalent formula. To obtain Ω, see Equation 5.23.

$$q_d = \left(q_c q_0^{-1}\right)^k q_0 \tag{5.21}$$

$$q_d = q_0 \frac{\sin\left((1-k)\,\Omega\right)}{\sin\left(\Omega\right)} + q_c \frac{\sin\left(k\Omega\right)}{\sin\left(\Omega\right)} \tag{5.22}$$

$$\cos\left(\Omega\right) = q_c \cdot q_d \tag{5.23}$$

It is possible to define non-linear non-isomorphic rotations. In order to accomplish this, the following definitions are needed [Poupyrev et al. 99]:

- Distance rotation between q_c and q_0. This is the smallest rotation connecting q_c and q_0.

- $\omega = 2\arccos\left(q_c \cdot q_0\right)$.

- Replace coefficient k with non-linear function $F(\omega)$.

$$k = F(\omega) = \begin{cases} 1 & \text{if } \omega < \omega_0 \\ f(\omega) = 1 + c(\omega - \omega_0)^2 & \text{otherwise} \end{cases} \tag{5.24}$$

  – Where ω_0 is "the threshold angle and c is a coefficient" [Poupyrev et al. 99].

Equation 5.24 shows that there is a one-to-one mapping if ω is less than ω_0. However, when ω_0 exceeds the rotation, the control-display ratio becomes larger. Poupyrev and colleagues recommended that to have a smooth transition between the cases in Equation 5.24, c should be "continuous in ω_0 and $f(\omega_0) = 1$" [Poupyrev et al. 99].

Non-isomorphic rotations provide the "magic" needed to improve the rotation experience. This was shown by the findings of Poupyrev and colleagues, which demonstrated that for a larger range of rotations, non-isomorphic techniques were 13% faster [Poupyrev et al. 00]. For a small range of rotations, the results were the same. In addition, subjects showed a strong preference for non-isomorphic rotations. Another interesting finding was that the mapping had no effect on the accuracy of rotation [Poupyrev et al. 00]. Additional information can be found in [Poupyrev et al. 99, Poupyrev et al. 00, Bowman et al. 04].

Further Reading

There is a large set of publications on the topic of selection and manipulation. In addition to the one described in this chapter, the reader is referred to an example of augmented reality (for object manipulation) [Kato et al. 00], multi-finger cursor [Moscovich and Hughes 06], and volumetric 3D interaction [Gallo et al. 08] using the WiiMote controller, among others.

Also, A very interesting chapter in Mine's Ph.D. dissertation [Mine 98, Chapter 2] describes manipulations using 2D input. A technical report by the same author provides information about manipulation and selection [Mine 95b].

Wolfgang Stuerzlinger, a professor in the School of Interactive Arts and Technology at Simon Fraser University, has a rich publication history in the field of 3DUI. In particular to this chapter, he has published about 3D pointing and 3D manipulation [Stuerzlinger and Teather 14, Teather and Stuerzlinger 14, Teather and Stuerzlinger 11, Liang et al. 13, Pfeiffer and Stuerzlinger 15]. His publication site is located at http://ws.iat.sfu.ca/publications.html.

As you can see from the citations in this chapter and their 3D user interfaces book [Bowman et al. 04], Bowman and colleagues are very active in similar topics. Visiting their site to see their publications can be very helpful.

Finally, for a brief look at 3D interactions (up to 1996), see [Hand 97].

Exercises

1. Implement the precise and rapid interaction though scaled manipulation (PRISM) described in this chapter. Use the text and equations as guides. Perform a small pilot study to compare PRISM (or your modified version of PRISM) with regular control-display ratio (see Side Note 2.3). Field provides excellent examples for different types of statistical analyses [Field 09].

2. Implement two pointing techniques described in Section 5.2.4. Perform a small pilot study to compare the different techniques. A t-test should be enough to make the comparison. See [Field 09].

3. Implement three pointing techniques, with at least one described in Section 5.2.4. Perform a small pilot study to compare the different techniques. Use ANOVA to see if there is any significant difference. See [Field 09].

6

3D Navigation

The voyage of discovery is not in seeking new landscapes but in having new eyes.

—Marcel Proust

This chapter covers 3D navigation, which includes travel (motion) and wayfinding. It is important to make certain distinctions about navigation, travel, and wayfinding. **Travel** is the engine component of navigation, which is the motion from one location to another. Darken and Peterson call this component of the navigational system **motion** [Darken and Peterson 15]. **Wayfinding** is the "cognitive process of defining a path through an environment" [Bowman et al. 04]. This cognitive process is aided by different cues, which allow the user to utilize the cues to create a path (or mental map) as well as acquire new cues. Some of these cues were discussed in Chapter 3. Therefore, **navigation** is composed of travel and wayfinding components. **3D navigation** concentrates on the actions of a 3D VE. Both components of navigation are important when dealing with input devices. It is a driving force for many of the types of interaction needed. Finally, it is important to note that while travel and wayfinding are part of navigation, if someone is working on the travel engine, the user will still be performing both tasks. The difference is that the objective of the researcher or practitioner may have been one of the two components of navigation but the line between both becomes blurry once they are being used. This chapter will expand on travel and wayfinding. In particular, the definition just offered for wayfinding is not complete without expanding it.

6.1   3D Travel

The action of moving around in a virtual environment is called travel (or motion), which is a component of 3D navigation. It is possible to find reference to 3D navigation when the primary objective was travel. While it is reasonable to call it navigation, it is best to use the correct term for this component of navigation. Of course, travel goes with wayfinding in many instances.

3D travel is critical for 3DUI, given that it is a common interaction task [Bowman et al. 04]. Travel is also important because it usually supports a primary task. An example is when a user is searching for objects in a game. The travel allows the user to search for the object (primary task). For this reason, 3D travel must be designed correctly. If the user needs to think how to navigate for too long, then he or she will be distracted from the primary task, which may be to find objects in a virtual world. There are different types of travel tasks. For the purposes of this chapter, it is important to understand exploration, search, maneuvering tasks, and travel characteristics.

6.1.1 3D Travel Tasks

The most common travel task is **exploration**. In this type of task, the user has no specified or required goal to complete. The user will only travel through the environment while building knowledge of the objects around and the locations of those objects. The most common example is navigating around a new city that the user has not known yet, to build knowledge of places and monuments, for a future visit. It is important in the **exploration** task that users are allowed to travel without constraint (other than outer limits or object collisions) around the virtual world [Bowman et al. 04].

Another type of task is called **search**. This type of task has a goal or target location within the virtual world. The user knows the final location of the required task. The user may or may not know how to get to the location, but he or she knows the objective. The search task can be divided into sub-categories. The first one is called **naïve search**, where the "user does not know the position of the target or path to it in advance" [Bowman et al. 04]. This type of search starts out as a basic exploration. The number of clues given to the user to complete the goal are limited and focused on the exploration. The second sub-category of a **search** task is called **primed search**. In the **primed search** task, the user "has visited the target before or has some other knowledge of its position" [Bowman et al. 04]. In this type of task, the user may know the final location; however, the user may still need to explore the virtual world, or the user may know the path to the target. In other words, the **primed search** provides more information to the user about the environment, in order to complete the assigned task. While there are clear differences between **naïve search** and **primed search**, the line dividing these two categories of search tasks can become blurred, depending on the design of the 3DUI and the user.

One task, often overlooked in the discussion of travel, is called **maneuvering**. This task is meant to take place "in a local area and involves small, precise movements" [Bowman et al. 04]. One example of this type of task is a user who may need to read a sign. In this scenario, the user moves slightly down and rotates

10° on the Y axis. The small-scale movements are critical for certain applications. A possible approach to facilitate **maneuvering** is to use vision-based systems that provide fine reading of the face (as it turns) or devices that provide physical motion with little or no error in the readings.

Another task to travel, quite useful in maps or large sets of data, is **travel-by-scaling** [Bowman et al. 04]. This technique allows intuitive zoom-in or zoom-out of a given portion of the virtual world. However, it is important to note that there are several challenges with this technique. For example, does the user understand their current position when they scaled the world? The view may be closer but the user is probably at the same location (before the zoom). Does the user understand the visual feedback when the virtual world has scaled in or scaled out? There are different solutions to these challenges, such as using a virtual body to understand the dimensions of the scale. Another major issue is that users may have trouble performing finer movements because when scaling the virtual world, the movements are larger.

3D Travel Task Characteristics

3D travel tasks have characteristics that may be used to classify them. It is also a good idea to have these characteristics in mind when designing a system. The following list contains a few important characteristics (adapted from [Bowman et al. 04]):

- **Distance to be traveled**: This is the distance that it takes to go from location A to location B. This may require velocity control in some instances.

- **Turns**: A travel task can also look into the number of turns taken (or the number of turns required) in a given task.

- **Required DOF**: The number of DOF required for the travel task. It is important to only use the required DOF for a given task. It also important to constrain some of the movements. For example, some rotations may be constrained to 90°. For example, if the system emulates a person walking in a real environment, it is common to restrict some of the rotations to 90° or 180°. This is very common in many games.

- **Accuracy of movements**: Travel task may need a very accurate movement (e.g., maneuvering) or use realistic physics.

- **Easy to use**: Given that 3D navigation in most cases is a secondary task, the user's interaction must be intuitive.

- **Visibility**: Some environments required objects to be visible. An example is gaze-directed tracking.

6.1.2   Travel Techniques

There are different travel techniques [Bowman et al. 04]. The most important techniques that must be taken into consideration when designing a system are: active versus passive, and physical versus virtual. The **active** technique is where the user has complete control of the movement of the scene. **Passive** technique is where the system has control of the movements. A middle ground is a **semi-automated** system, where the user has some level of control while the system automates the rest. The **physical** technique refers to the actual body of the user involved in performing the movements in the virtual scene (e.g., walking). The **virtual** technique allows the user to utilize a virtual device to control the movements.

Task Decomposition

Task decomposition for travel was offered by [Bowman et al. 97] providing a taxonomy for travel sub-tasks, which included direction or target selection, velocity/acceleration, and conditions of input. The following list expands the descriptions of those sub-tasks [Bowman et al. 97, Bowman et al. 04]:

- Direction target selection: This is how the user steers or moves around VE. This includes the following types:

  - Gaze-direction steering.
  - Pointing/Gesture steering.
  - Discrete selection.
    * Lists (e.g., menus).
    * Direct targets.

- Velocity/acceleration selection: Describes how users control their speed.

  - Constant velocity/acceleration.
  - Gesture-based.
  - Explicit selection.
    * Discreet.
    * Continuous range.
  - User/environment scaling.
  - Automatic/adaptive.

- Input conditions: The events which marked the initial and final times, yielding the duration time.

  - Constant travel/no input.
  - Continuous input.

- Start and stop inputs.
- Automatic start and stop.

This taxonomy provides a way to break down travel for navigation. Some of these sub-tasks can be combined. For example, a gesture-based technique can be adaptive and have selection tasks based on velocity or acceleration [Bowman et al. 97] while others may not be feasible to combine. Bowman and colleagues also identified quality factors for the effectiveness of travel, which include speed, accuracy (to target), spatial awareness, ease of learning, ease of use, information gathering (user's ability to continuously obtain information from the VE), and presence (immersion or having a feeling of being within the VE) [Bowman et al. 97].

Bowman and colleagues provided another taxonomy a few years later [Bowman et al. 99a]. This taxonomy subdivides the travel tasks in order: start moving, indicate position, indicate orientation, and stop moving. Each taxonomy provides its own advantages and it is up to the practitioner or researcher to pick the one that fits best on a case-by-case scenario. This taxonomy offers the advantage of classifying the sub-task by order of occurrence, while the actual events may not be in the order expected. For example, it may be possible to specify orientation and position before moving. Bowman and colleagues provided the following taxonomy [Bowman et al. 99a]:

- Start travel.
- Indicate position.
    - Specify position.
        * Discrete target specification: The user provides destination target and the system proceeds to move to this target.
        * One-time route specification: The user defines a path and the system moves along the path.
        * Continuous specification: The user is constantly steering.
    - Specify velocity.
    - Specify acceleration.
- Indicate orientation.
- Stop travel.

While classifications that breaks down the interaction in sub-tasks are very useful, it is also possible to make classification by metaphor. This type of classification does not allow to break the task into a sub-task but they are easier to understand [Bowman et al. 04]. For example, one could think of metaphors like "flying carpet" and "spaceship travel," among others.

Figure 6.1: Omni (by Virtuix) immersive system. With permission from Virtuix.

Physical Techniques

Physical locomotion provides users in immersive environments a more realistic feeling. These techniques try to mimic locomotion of our daily activities, such as walking. Some of the physical movements can be constrained, as with Omni (by Virtuix) immersive system, as shown in Figure 6.1.

The most common action for physical locomotion is walking. It is an activity that is intrinsic in our daily lives. The most important attribute to this modality is the spacial understanding as we walk because of the vestibular cues [Bowman et al. 04]. The **vestibular** cues provide understanding about the size of the environment. Walking can be challenging for the user. In immersive environments the space where the user walks should have no obstacles. It is true that more and more devices are wireless but not all devices are. For example, the Oculus Rift (version one and two) has a video cable and a Universal Serial Bus (USB) cable that connects to the computer, which makes walking a challenge. Also, in the case of devices like the Oculus Rift, the user is not able to see the real world, making walking a very difficult task. This could be alleviated by having either external cameras that capture the outside world and then render it back in the Oculus Rift. However, this still can pose problems for the users. The HoloLens from Microsoft allows the user to see-through, where walking may be easier than

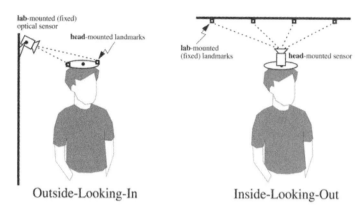

Outside-Looking-In   Inside-Looking-Out

Figure 6.2: Wide-area tracking [Welch et al. 01].

using Oculus Rift.[1] Having said this, Google glasses is the only device that we have tested that allows the user to walk and get augmented information about the environment. The University of North Carolina (UNC) has been working on large-area tracking for a while now. One of their milestones is the HiBall [Welch et al. 99, Welch et al. 01], currently marketed by UNC and 3rdTech. HiBall provides two different ways of tracking: *outside-in* and *inside-out* [Welch et al. 01], as shown in Figure 6.2. The idea of the *outside-in* technique is to provide fixed optical (or ultrasound) sensors and the tracking markers in the user's head. The other technique, *inside-out* fixes the camera in the user's head, while providing the markers around the world. For additional information about tracking research by UNC see their website (see [UNC 14]). Meyer and colleagues provided a survey with additional information about tracking [Meyer et al. 92].

Walking in place is another alternative, as has been demonstrated by Omni immersive system (see Figure 6.1). Walking in place does not produce any translation, removing any problems that you have with free walking. The Nintendo Entertainment System (NES) Wii Balanced Board is another example. While it does not constrain users, it does provide a way to walk in a smaller space using the board, and providing a smaller translation among X, Y, and Z axes. Of course, this can also be seen as a virtual technique. Of course, the NES Wii Balanced Board will be very difficult to use if the user is wearing a HMD (like the Oculus Rift). Usoh and colleagues showed that there is a correlation between the virtual body and the degree that the users associate presence [Usoh et al. 99]. In addition, walking in place was higher than virtual travel, but walking was higher than any of those [Usoh et al. 99]. Additional devices have been used, which includes treadmills and cycling devices to emulate immersion. Bowman and colleagues provide a larger discussion about these techniques, including additional references [Bowman et al. 04].

---

[1]At the time of this writing, we have not been able to acquired a HoloLens to test it.

Virtual Techniques

While physical techniques provide a more "realistic" feeling for users, the majority of users still rely virtual locomotion techniques. It is true that prices are coming down, whereas before there were only affordable by big research labs, government, and industry. For example, the price of the Omni is around $US 500 for an in-place walking system, the Oculus Rift for under $US 400, and the new Samsung for under $US 200 (plus a Samsung phone). This is helping to make these types of devices and systems more accessible. Prices will keep going down while the technology will keep improving. However, there are still instances where physical locomotion is not the ideal solution, either because of environment space, budget, or domain-specific requirements, among other reasons. This is why virtual locomotion techniques are still very important. An example of this is navigating in a 3D VE using a multi-touch surface (or other common devices, such as GamePad and wiiMote Motion Controllers, among others), which are pervasive in today's technological landscape. In addition to this book, *3D User Interfaces: Theory and Practice* [Bowman et al. 04, pp. 199–222] outlines various techniques. A direction of motion overview is found in [Mine 95b]. For completeness, we cover some of those techniques in this chapter (adapted from [Bowman et al. 04, pp. 199–222]).

A common virtual locomotion approach is the **steering technique**. One of those techniques is called **gaze-directed steering**. This technique works by moving the VE's view into the direction $\vec{g}$, which is the user's viewing direction. There are different ways to obtain the user's viewing direction. The ideal one is to use eye-gazed tracking (see Chapter 12) but in the absence of this tracking device, other computer vision techniques can be used. For example, using a head tracker. The eye-gazed tracking can be used by calculating a ray from the current position of the camera to the center of the viewing window. Bowman and colleagues provided a gaze-equation (Equation 6.1), which represents the current user's position (s) plus a translation along normalized gaze-direction ($\frac{\vec{g}}{||\vec{g}||}$) multiplied by a constant velocity (ψ) [Bowman et al. 04]. Another option is to modify the **up** vector from the camera coordinate system (see Chapter 4). The gaze-directed steering technique can also used specific triggers (e.g., GamePad buttons) to start and stop the desired tracking. With this technique it is possible to add *strafe*, which is the ability to translate in all three X, Y, and Z axes (up, down, left, right, in, out). Bowman and colleagues point out two difficulties with this technique: (1) It is difficult to travel in the horizontal plane because it is difficult to know if the user's head is upright. (2) It is also uncomfortable to travel up or down, in particular when using a HMD [Bowman et al. 04]. In addition, in a user study, it was found that pointing significantly outperforms gaze-directed steering for relative motion ("travel to a target located relative to a reference object" [Bowman et al. 97]). One primary explanation for this is that it is difficult for users to travel to a location while looking a different target when using gaze-directed steering.

$$S_{new} = s + \psi \frac{\vec{g}}{||\vec{g}||} \qquad (6.1)$$

Pointing is another technique that allows the user to direct the navigation. A common practice is to have a tracker in the user's hand to obtain the vector $\vec{p}$. This vector is transformed into the world's coordinates (see Chapter 4) and then normalized. Equation 6.2 for pointing is very similar to the gaze-directed equation. A common practice is to combine the keyboard for the travel direction and the mouse for the gaze direction. Mine offered an extension for pointing by using two hands [Mine 97]. This method was implemented using a pinch glove, which allowed to select the forward hand by knowing the left from the right hand [Bowman et al. 01] (a user has a left and right glove at all times). In addition, the distance between the hand can be calculated into δ, providing an additional factor for the velocity factor ψ. Equation 6.3 shows a general equation for the pinching hand h_p and the other hand h_{np}. If the pinch is performed with the right hand, then the difference is $h_R - h_L$. With multi-touch displays, we can see similarities to the pointing and pinch, as both operations are commonly available in touch systems.

$$S_{new} = s + \psi \frac{\vec{p}}{||\vec{p}||} \qquad (6.2)$$

$$S_{new} = s + \psi \delta \frac{(\vec{h}_p - \vec{h}_{np})}{||\vec{h}_p - \vec{h}_{np}||} \qquad (6.3)$$

There are additional steering techniques described in [Bowman et al. 04]: (1) **Torso-directed steering** where a tracker is attached to the user's torso (e.g., in the user's belt). This technique allows the user to have his/her hands free to perform another action. It also frees the eyes since the gaze-direction technique is not being used. (2) **Camera-in-hand** technique uses a tracker in the hand providing an absolute position and orientation. The tracker becomes the camera. This can be calculated with $c = Tp$, where T is the transformation between the tracking coordinate system and the world coordinates system, providing a mapping between the camera position (c) and tracking position (p). This technique provides a third-person perspective of the VE for the user. Additional steering devices can also help with navigation, like a video game steering wheel with an accelerator and brake (buttons or pedals). An example is the Virtual Motion Controller (VMC), which allows a user to move around its region (see additional examples in [Bowman et al. 04]. Finally, **semiautomated steering** allows the application to take some control of the navigation while leaving some up to the user.

Another virtual technique is **route planning technique**. This technique provides a path (or route) for the user to navigate. For a given path, the navigation may allow interruptions (e.g., start/stop). In general, this technique is based on

Figure 6.3: Blue button widget.

previous planning (the path) and execution (the navigation along the path). Maps can be used for route planning. 3D maps are useful because of the direct access to the complete VE but some users may find working with this type of map harder to visualize. 2D maps are simpler but certain assumptions must be made to create the mapping to the 3D environment. Maps can be used if needed in certain route-planning techniques. The following list provides a brief look at some path planning strategies:

- **Drawing a path**: Allows users to draw the path in the VE. Different techniques of drawing in a 3D environment can be used for this approach. One option is for the user to draw a free 2D stroke directly into the VE to create a path [Igarashi et al. 98]. The user can either create a long or short stroke depending on the route they try to create. Long strokes are useful "in how to get to the target position" [Igarashi et al. 98]. The short strokes are useful to specify camera direction or to specify a goal position. Other sketching techniques can serve to extend this type of route-planning, such as [Cohen et al. 99]. This technique can also use 2D or 3D maps.

- **Points along a path:** This technique allows the user to mark points in the VE. One option is to use 2D or 3D maps. Another option is to use keyboard and a mouse to mark the points. How the points are connected depends on the implementation (e.g., straight lines, curves, etc.).

- **User representation:** This technique allows the user to use some type of representation to create a path. For example, a spaceship or a person could be used in third person to represent the navigation direction desired. For example, a small creature was used in World-in-Miniature (WIM) to provide the user with position and orientation [Stoakley et al. 95]. A map can also be used with this technique.

Steering and route-planing techniques offer interesting options on how to navigate in a VE. In addition to those techniques, **target-based techniques** offer a different approach to navigation. Once the user has selected the target, one option is for the system to jump immediately to the object selected, which is called teleportation. However, this method was shown to "reduce the user's spatial awareness" [Bowman et al. 97]. Therefore, moving toward the object in a continuous way may improve the user's spatial awareness. Some of the types of target-based techniques are (described in more detail in [Bowman et al. 04, pp. 210–214]:

- **WIM-based:** This technique allows the user to use a 3D object (e.g., miniature figure). The user manipulates the object toward the desired target. The system must create a valid path for the navigation to move toward this target. The difference with the latter technique (placing target object) is that a path is created here and the other one provides only the final coordinates. However, one can see blurry lines between both of these methods.

- **Map-based:** Similar to the previous technique described, the map-based technique allows the user to manipulate an icon to create a path. For example, Bowman et al. used a stylus (pen) to create the path needed in the map shown in Figure 6.4 [Bowman et al. 98]. It is assumed that the point $o = (X_o, Y_o, Z_o)$ is known, the $h(x,z)$ function is implemented, which provides a way to calculate y_{target} since the map input is 2D (see Equation 6.6), and the scale factor σ. Equations 6.4 and 6.5 provide a very straightforward way to calculate the target for both of theses axes. For y_{target} the h function is needed. Finally, to calculate the movement vector, the target point is subtracted by the user's position. In addition, the velocity scalar ψ multiplies the vector and the factor δ is used to normalized the move vector, as shown in Equation 6.7.

$$x_{target} = \frac{x_{pointer} - x_o}{\sigma} \tag{6.4}$$

$$z_{target} = \frac{z_{pointer} - z_o}{\sigma} \tag{6.5}$$

$$y_{target} = h(x_{target}, z_{target}) \tag{6.6}$$

$$\vec{m} = \frac{\psi}{\delta}[x_{target} - x, y_{target} - y, z_{target} - z] \tag{6.7}$$

- **ZoomBack:** This technique, introduced by Zeleznik and colleagues, "allows the user to select a target point on the surface of an object in a virtual environment" [Zeleznik et al. 02]. Ray-casting is a common selection technique (see Chapter 5) that can be used with ZoomBack. The interesting fact about this technique is that it retains previously visited locations to allow the user to return to those. One possible implementation for ZoomBack is to use a user-worn 3D mouse (see Section 2.4.4). It is also possible to use a regular mouse to implement this technique but it may not be as convenient. This technique was used to look at paintings by selecting them, looking at them up close and then returning to a previous location.

- **Object Selection:** This technique allows the user to select a target using any type of selection technique, for example, selecting the object with the mouse or by touching the object on a multi-touch surface display.

- **Placing Target Object:** This technique allows the user to place an object in the desired target using manipulation to set the target's position.

- **Menu-based:** This technique allows the user to select a target based on a menu or a list (e.g., dropdown). Besides a typical one-dimensional menu (e.g., radial menu), other options include 2D menus and 2D or 3D widgets. An approach we have taken is to use visual widgets to return to a specific location (e.g., start point of navigation). This widget can be a simple push button that can be pressed with a multi-touch interface or the mouse, as shown in Figure 6.3.

- **Manual Entry:** This technique allows the user to enter the coordinates of the VE that he/she wants to travel to. It is also possible to have pre-defined keys to travel to specific places. A common-approach we have used is to provide an external keypad to travel to desired objects by pressing the correct key.

There are many more techniques that can be used for travel, such as non-isomorphic rotations (see Section 5.2.6) and the virtual sphere (see Section 2.6), among others found in this book (see Section 6.3). Bowman and colleagues provide additional techniques [Bowman et al. 04], such as grabbing the air technique ([Ware and Osborne 90, Mapes and Moshell 95]), which allows the user to make the grab gesture and move the world around it.

6.2 Wayfinding

Darken (who has worked in wayfinding and related areas for many years [Darken 93, Darken 96]) and Peterson define *wayfinding* as the **cognitive process of navigation** [Darken and Peterson 15]. It is important to note the difference between the actual motion (as described earlier) and wayfinding. Motion is an engine of navigation, which is usually called travel. However, wayfinding does not "involve movement of any kind only the thoughtful parts that guide movements" [Darken and Peterson 15]. Wayfinding and motion are intertwined in a "complex negotiation that is navigation" [Darken and Peterson 15]. It is also important to understand

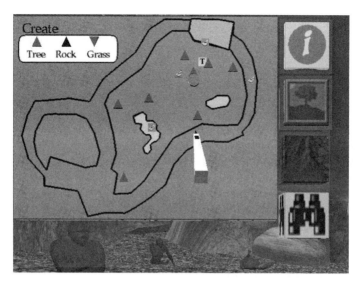

Figure 6.4: Map for stylus pen [Bowman et al. 98].

the mental map (also called cognitive map). This is the representation of the spatial understanding of the subject [Darken and Peterson 15].

6.2.1   Training versus Transfer

Wayfinding can be very useful to transfer spatial understanding to real-life cases. In particular, when dealing with 3D VE to aid real-world scenarios. The type of information provided for wayfinding applications can be divided in two categories [Bowman et al. 04, Darken and Peterson 15]: (1) Navigate through complex environments. It is important to allow the users to view the environment in its entirety. (2) Transfer of spatial knowledge to a real-world scenario: In other words, the ability to use a VE to transfer the spatial layout learned to be used later in the physical world.

In the first category, the notion of large environments will have problems because of its size. The primary reason is that any environment that cannot be viewed from a single vantage point will lack *spatial comprehension*; that is, the ability to "perceive, understand, and recall for future use" [Darken and Peterson 15]. When this problem occurs, it is important to aid the user with cues that yield better spatial understanding. It is important to understand that this problem will occur regardless if the environment was designed for real-world transfer of spatial knowledge or not. The second category of application deals with training that helps real-world scenarios. The fact that VE can be used to help train users for physical environments can be very useful and it has been applied in different domains. However, it is important to understand that there are differences between both types of wayfinding application and the trade-off of training versus performance must be taken into account when designing the VE.

6.2.2 Spatial Knowledge

There are different ways to obtain spatial knowledge about an environment. In a VE, it is possible to introduce many types of cues that are harder to add in the real-world (unless aided by an augmented reality application). How we acquire spatial knowledge is critical for wayfinding. There are three categories: landmark knowledge (or direct environmental knowledge), survey knowledge (e.g., maps), and procedural knowledge [Bowman et al. 04, Darken and Peterson 15].

The first type of spatial knowledge is landmark knowledge. Lynch's book, *The Image of a City* provided ways to decompose a city[2] [Lynch 60]. The different elements that provide direct environmental exposure are [Lynch 60, Bowman et al. 04, Darken and Peterson 15]:

- Landmarks are important objects that provide information about the environment. They are also directional, as the object itself may represent a cue "from one side but not another" [Darken and Peterson 15]. Examples of landmarks are the US White House, the Eiffel Tower, Big Ben, and the Washington monument. For example, "La Moneda" (presidential house of the government of Chile) provides a cue that a person is in the middle of Santiago, also known as "el centro" (downtown or city center). In a VE, artificial landmarks can provide clues to the user.

- Routes (or paths) connect landmarks either directly or indirectly via other routes.

- Nodes are the joints between routes.

- Districts are independent regions within a city, separated from other parts of the city.

- Edges are the the city boundaries. Examples of edges are rivers or a fence line [Darken and Peterson 15].

The second type of spatial knowledge is survey knowledge [Bowman et al. 04]. There are different sources that can be used for this type of spatial understanding, such as video, maps, images, sound (e.g., speech), and VEs. For example, maps can be used either for planning or concurrent with the navigation. One of the first questions a user may have is "where am I?, where am I facing?" [Darken and Peterson 15]. Planning a trip, beforehand, requires geocentric perspective. For

---

[2]Lynch published a follow-up article [Lynch 84].

this type of case, there is no need to go from egocentric to geocentric perspective because this happens outside of the environment. However, when the map is needed to be used within the environment, there are a few considerations that are needed and the problem is not trivial. For example, tasks that require only an egocentric reference frame, such as targeted search tasks, are best when using a forward-up[3] map [Aretz and Wickens 92, Darken and Cevik 99, Darken and Peterson 15]. In contrast, when performing tasks that require "information from the world reference frame" [Igarashi et al. 99], it is best to use a north-up[4] alignment [Aretz and Wickens 92, Darken and Cevik 99, Darken and Peterson 15]. People with high spatial abilities can perform well with any type of map [Darken and Cevik 99]. The study by Darken and Cevik provided additional recommendations, which are complemented by previous studies [Levinew et al. 84, Peruch et al. 86, Rossano and Warren 89]. The transformation from egocentric to geocentric perspective is not the only problem when dealing with maps but it is "the biggest part of it" [Darken and Peterson 15]. Additional research about maps and navigation has been done, including topics about teleoperated robots [Chen et al. 07], 3D mobile maps [Nurminen 08], and 3D virtual environments [Burigat and Chittaro 07], among others [Bowman et al. 99b, Chittaro et al. 05, McGahan 14]. Additional survey knowledge is available, such as Google StreetView™ and the possibilities that devices such as augmented glasses (Google Glass™) provide additional methods of spatial understanding [Darken and Peterson 15].

The third category is called procedural knowledge. This plays a role in spatial knowledge, which describes the "sequence of actions required to follow a certain path or traverse paths between different locations" [Bowman et al. 04]. For example, a user learning the steps needed to go from his/her house to the supermarket. Munro and colleagues provide additional information about spatial knowledge, including locomotion spatial understanding and other relevant information [Munro et al. 14].

Reference frames are also important to understand in relation to spatial knowledge for egocentric and exocentric (where the cognitive map is located [Thorndyke and Hayes-Roth 82]) information transfer, and how theses points of view affect the judgments and decisions of users, as described below [Bowman et al. 04]:

- **Egocentric:** This is a first-person point of view. This point of view provides useful information, which includes distance and orientation. The decisions made during this type of reference frame are [Bowman et al. 04]:

  - Station Point (from the perspective of the eye).

  - Retinocentric (retina).

---

[3]Forward-up map: "The top of the map shows the environment in front of the viewer" [Darken and Peterson 15]. In other words, this map is always rotated to align with the forward position of the user [Darken and Cevik 99].

[4]The north-up alignment approach has the north always on top [Darken and Cevik 99].

- Headcentric (head).
- Bodycentric (torso).
- Proprioceptive, visual and non-visual cues from body parts.

- **Exocentric:** This is a third-person point of view. In this reference frame, the coordinates are defined external to the body. The coordinates are [Bowman et al. 04]:

  - Shape of object.
  - Orientation of object.
  - Motion of object.

Finally, once spatial knowledge is understood, there is still a question of how this information is organized in the mental model of the user [Darken and Peterson 15], which is called the cognitive map [Tolman 48]. The most common spatial knowledge model is Landmark, Route, Survey (LRS) [Siegel and White 75, Thorndyke and Goldin 83]. The LRS model has been extended to have a hierarchical model [Stevens and Coupe 78, Colle and Reid 98]. For additional information about cognitive maps, including additional citations see [Darken and Peterson 15].

There are articles about spatial understanding, which includes topics such as large-scale virtual environments [Darken et al. 98], route knowledge [Gale et al. 90], spatial knowledge in virtual mazes [Gillner and Mallot 98], spatial understanding from maps and navigation [Richardson et al. 99], and misaligned maps [Rossano and Warren 89], among others [Pick and Acredolo 83].

6.2.3 Navigation Model

Decomposing tasks may lead to better assistance or training. However, as Darken and Peterson pointed out, the attempt to find a general model for any task is difficult [Darken and Peterson 15]. Jul and Furnas do have a "relative complete" [Darken and Peterson 15] model, in particular, the inclusion of motion components into the process [Jul and Furnas 97]. This model, shown in Figure 6.5, provides a way to plan for navigation and demonstrates that this is not a serial process. At any point, a user may change the goal and proceed to another place. Finally, additional work has been attempted to model navigation (in some cases specific to an environment) [Darken 96, Spence 99, Chen and Stanney 99, Calton and Taube 09].

6.2.4 Wayfinding Strategies

There are different strategies to support wayfinding from the user-centered and environment-centered perspectives. Some strategies can be used in a regular desktop or mobile 3DUI while others are more useful in immersive systems [Bowman

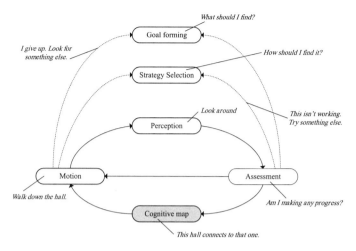

Figure 6.5: A model navigation adapted from [Jul and Furnas 97, Darken and Peterson 15].

et al. 04]. One of the support strategies is **environment-centered** wayfinding. The environment design includes legibility techniques and real-world principles. The legibility technique, drawn from *The Image of the City* [Lynch 60], provides a way to decompose an environment (see Section 6.2.2), among other design considerations. Another important design feature is to include real-world ideas, such as natural environments, architecture design patterns, and color and texture, as it is described in [Bowman et al. 04]. The environment-center has artificial cues that can aid wayfinding, such as maps, compasses, signs, reference objects, artificial landmarks, audio, and olfactory cues, described further in [Bowman et al. 04]. The other support strategy is **user-centered** wayfinding, which aids human-sensory systems. The cues for user-centered strategies are:

- Field of view: A larger FOV in complex environments becomes more useful. While it is not conclusive if a smaller FOV will inhibit wayfinding [Bowman et al. 04], the amount of head turns to search for a target may increase when less information is available to the user. Roy and colleagues noted that increased familiarity of the VE may help to adapt when "reduced amount of navigational information is provided and lead to an increase in the rate at which spatial knowledge is developed" [Ruddle et al. 98]. Péruch and colleagues showed that there was little difference between different degrees of FOVs (40°, 60°, and 80°) [Péruch et al. 97].

- Motion cues: These types of cues provide the ability for users to judge depth and direction of movement [Bowman et al. 04]. Motion cues are visual, such as real-motion objects observed with the user's peripheral vision, as well as non-visual motion cues. Vestibular[5] cues, which provide real-motion information, are important for users in the egocentric point of view. Lack of these cues may negatively impact the cognitive map [Bowman et al. 04]. Harris and colleagues, based on their finding, suggested to add vestibular cues (at least 25% of visual cues) [Harris et al. 99]. Lécuyer and colleagues concluded, based on their user studies, that combining visual and haptic cues required longer processing time; however, they also found that it did improve the perception of self-motion and reduced underestimation "of the angles that the turns made in the visual navigation" [Lécuyer et al. 04]. Finally, it is important to note that some of the motion cues may be harder to implement in a 3D desktop system in comparison to an immersive system.

- Presence: This is the notion of being there, immersed in the VE. Usoh and colleagues showed that the awareness of presence increases when the user associates himself with the virtual body avatar [Usoh et al. 99]. In their study, they also found that real walking provides a better immersion feeling. A case for neuro-scientist to take this problem of immersion has been proposed [Sanchez-Vives and Slater 05]. For additional information, see [Schilbach et al. 06, Riva et al. 07, Blanke and Metzinger 09].

- Multisensory: Providing cues using different types of output can be useful [Bowman et al. 04]. Audio can provide additional spatial understanding about the environment [Davis et al. 99]. For a user study comparing unimodal visual condition versus audio-visual conditions, see [Frassinetti et al. 02].

- Search strategies: Bowman and colleagues provide excellent points as different techniques to aid the user when searching content [Bowman et al. 04]. One example is to use search patterns like search-and-rescue pilots perform. For additional information, see [Bowman et al. 99a, Bowman et al. 04].

Additional information for related topics are suggested to the reader, such as exploration with HMD in limited space [Williams et al. 07], body-based information during navigation [Ruddle 13], and moving in cluttered space [Ruddle and Jones 01], among others [Witmer and Singer 98, Williams et al. 06, Ruddle and Lessels 06, Ruddle and Lessels 09].

6.3   3D Navigation: User Studies

Since the days of the animated film, "A Computer Animated Hand," the development of the Sensomora Simulator by [Heilig 62, Burdea and Coiffet 03], and

---

[5]The vestibular system provides the sensory system, which provides balance and spatial orientation to most mammals [Lowenstein 74, Wikipedia 15m].

Side Note 6.1: Navigation Terminology

As stated in the early part of this chapter, navigation is made of two components. The engine of navigation, called travel, which allows the user to move around the virtual environment. The wayfinding is a cognitive process (aided by different cues) which allows the user to create a mental map. Terminology is important to keep a standard definition across publications and applications. In the case of navigation, there are times that the terminology is misused, as happens to all of us at times, creating confusion for the reader or user of the application. While route finding is related to wayfinding because users will look for cues and understanding to determine a route, they are not interchangeable. The same is true for travel. While navigation includes travel and wayfinding, travel is just the engine that allows the movement. Having said this, it is true that navigation, in most cases applies to both components (travel and wayfinding), making it difficult to break them down. Therefore, if one refers to navigation, even if both components are clearly active, it is suggested to determine the primary goal: travel or wayfinding. Darken and Peterson provid additional information in their recent chapter [Darken and Peterson 15].

the contributions by Ivan Sutherland [Sutherland 63, Sutherland 65], the field of CG^6 led practitioners and researchers to look for ways to push the envelope further. One of these challenges has been to push the state-of-the-art for 3D navigation.

3D navigation (some work overlaps with 3D interactions) has been used in a variety of domains. Note that not all the 3D navigation studies include 6-DOF. In some domains, having 4-DOF may be enough, as already described in Section 6.1.1. For example, [Sultanum et al. 13] studied 3D navigation for geological outcrops with only 4-DOF.

This section covers different examples of 3D navigation, in particular 3D travel. Some of the interaction techniques discussed in Chapter 5 can serve as a foundation for 3D navigation. We described a partial list of relevant literature on the topic of navigation. The following partial list covers some that have been used for 3D navigation:

- Medicine.

- Large-scale virtual environments.

- Geographical environments.

- Geological environments.

---

[6] See http://design.osu.edu/carlson/history/lessons.html.

- Astronomy.

- Other types of scientific visualization.

- Dynamic 3D worlds.

- City models.

- Energy management systems.

- Video games.

6.3.1   Search during Navigation

One of the common tasks in 3D navigation is to search for objects. As it is described in Section 6.1.1, there are two types of search: naïve and primed. This was first studied for large virtual worlds by [Darken and Sibert 96]. The study looked at wayfinding (see Section 6.2) for search and exploration. They found that if no visual cues or directional guides are given, users will tend to become disoriented [Darken and Sibert 96]. Another important finding was that users tend to follow natural paths (e.g., coast line). This work was followed up by [Bowman et al. 99b].

[Bowman et al. 99b] described a testbed evaluation for virtual environments. This included selection, manipulation, and travel experiments. In the travel experiment, which is of interest to this chapter, they performed naïve search and primed search, as described in [Darken and Sibert 96, Bowman et al. 04]. In this study [Bowman et al. 99b], users were provided with flags, with numbers 1-4. In addition, the target was marked with a painted circle consisting of a 10-meter radius (large) or a 5-meter radius (small). For the naïve search, the targets were in numerical order, with a low accuracy (large circle) required. The targets were not all visible during the naïve search. In the primed search, all the objects were visible and they were not sorted in numerical order. The required accuracy was changed to a 5-meter radius (small circle). Seven different travel techniques were used in this between-subjects experiment. For the naïve search, the gaze-directed technique [Bowman et al. 97] was the fastest out of the seven techniques tested. Right after the gaze-directed technique, pointing [Bowman et al. 97] and go-go [Poupyrev et al. 96] techniques came second. For the primed search, gaze-directed and pointing techniques were significantly faster than the HOMER [Bowman et al. 04] approach. In both cases, the map technique was found to be the slowest one [Bowman et al. 99b]. At the end of the experiment, the authors concluded that pointing gave the best results for navigation [Bowman et al. 99b].

6.3.2 Additional User Studies for Navigation

3D navigation has benefited from previous work in related areas. The most closely related areas are 3D interaction and virtual devices. The Sketchpad provided a way forward for UIs [Sutherland 63]. Also, early studies by Nielson and Olsen [Nielson and Olsen Jr 87], which provided direct "Manipulation Techniques for 3D Objects," and Chen and colleagues, who studied 3D rotations, provided the groundwork for more recent developments [Chen et al. 88]. Multi-touch interactions and techniques are described in Chapter 8 and virtual devices in Chapter 27. This section describes user studies in reference to 3D navigation.

When working in large-scale environments, with multiple displays, [Ruddle et al. 99] looked at the effect between head-mounted and desktop displays. Each participant, a total of 12 subjects, traveled long distances (1.5 km) [Ruddle et al. 99]. Two interesting findings were found in this study. First, participants "developed a significantly more accurate sense of relative straight-line distance" when using the HMD [Ruddle et al. 99]. Second, when subjects used the desktop display, they tended to develop "tunnel vision," which led to missing targets [Ruddle et al. 99]. Santos et al. studied the difference between 3D navigation with a non-stereo, desktop display versus a HMD[7] [Sousa Santos et al. 08]. In this comparison study (42 subjects), the subjects were divided into non-experienced and experienced gamers, as well as three levels for their stereoscopic usage (none, moderate, experienced). The experienced gamers group performed differently, with respect to how many objects were caught in the game when using the desktop display [Sousa Santos et al. 08]. This indicated that their previous skills helped this group of subjects to perform the task. This is due to their familiarity with similar environments. No statistical difference for the groups were found when they used the HMD. Santos et al. found that users preferred the desktop display [Sousa Santos et al. 08].

A usability study conducted by [Fu et al. 10] looked at large-scale 3D astrophysical simulations. Their navigation approach used different gestures and touch widgets to allow different actions in a multi-dimensional world, to study astrophysics. Users found tasks using multi-touch very intuitive and useful for the specific-domain tested. This study did not include a quantitative analysis, but did show that users (16 participants) found the use of multi-touch intuitive. The rotations were performed with one finger, with a movement that was horizontal for the rotation about the Y axis, vertical for the rotation about the X axis, and diagonal pan to rotate about an arbitrary axis on the XY-plane. Rotations were also performed with different gestures, with five (or four) fingers in the same direction. Translations and scale gestures were also provided.

The WiiMote has been a popular device for 3D navigation. A study using Google Earth compared two different configurations for the WiiMote [Sousa Santos et al. 10]. To move front/back, left/right, the first configuration used the

---

[7]HMD are stereo.

accelerometer and the second configuration used the IR sensor. The rest of the movements in Google Earth were shared by both configurations. The study found that the accelerometer configuration showed a statistically significant improvement, with respect to the other configuration [Sousa Santos et al. 10]. A similar study used the WiiMote to compare three different techniques for video game navigation [Williamson et al. 10]. The objective was to navigate while avoiding some objects. The first technique used the accelerometer sensor, the second technique used the WiiMote for head-tracking using the IR sensor, and the third technique combined the prior techniques, adding a Kalman filter [Zarchman and Musoff 09]. Techniques two and three were also modified to provide alternate versions, which used the Nintendo WiiMote MotionPlus (gyroscope sensor). The third method (hybrid) was preferred when performing the maneuver and aversion tasks. When comparing the techniques with or without the MotionPlus, users preferred the MotionPlus for the evasion task but not for the maneuver tasks [Williamson et al. 10].

In a comparative study, Lapointe et al. [Lapointe et al. 11] looked at the interactions of 3D navigation with 4-DOF. The devices compared for this study were a keyboard, a mouse, a joystick, and a GamePad. Their quantitative study showed that the mouse significantly outperformed the other devices [Lapointe et al. 11]. In another comparison study, [Beheshti et al. 12] studied the difference between a mouse using a desktop display and a multi-touch tabletop.[8] In their study, the tabletop (multi-touch) outperformed the desktop (mouse); however, this difference was not statistically significant [Beheshti et al. 12]. Furthermore, there was no spatial difference between genders [Beheshti et al. 12]. This result is in contrast to other studies that have showed a significant difference between genders in similar environments [Czerwinski et al. 02, Chai and Jacobs 10, Lawton 94, Astur et al. 98].

In a game study by Kulshereshth and LaViola Jr., they evaluated performance benefits when using a head-tracking device [Kulshreshth et al. 13]. From a total of 40 subjects, half of them used the head-tracking device to assist them in playing four games given by the experimenters. The other half did not use the head-tracking device. The games tested were Arma II, Dirt2, Microsoft Flight, and Wings of Prey [Kulshreshth et al. 13] using a PC and an Xbox 360 controller. The subjects were divided into two groups: Casual and experienced gamers. The casual gamers reported a significant preference for the head-tracking device when playing Dirt2, providing a more engaging user experience. The experienced gamers reported a significant preference for the head-tracking device when playing Microsoft Flight, providing a more engaging user experience. The study also showed that experienced gamers showed a significant improvement when using the head-tracking device for Arma II and Wings of Prey compared to a traditional game controller. Their analysis found that experienced gamers may benefit by

---

[8]Microsoft Surface, first generation.

using a head-tracking device in certain scenarios, such as FPS and air combat games [Kulshreshth et al. 13].

Yu and colleagues conducted an experiment, titled "FI3D: Direct-Touch Interaction for the Exploration of 3D scientific Visualization Spaces," where they studied 3D navigation using touch [Yu et al. 10]. The technique used in [Yu et al. 10] allowed users to navigate in 3D. The virtual world was a representation of scientific data. Users navigated using single-touch gestures or the mouse. The objective was to test a 7-DOF that included X, Y, Z translations; yaw, pitch, and roll rotations; and scaling (the 7th degree) to zoom in or out of the screen. Their approach [Yu et al. 10] limited the touch to one finger interaction in most instances and provided the use for an additional touch to create specific constraints to aid the movement. Their study showed that the mouse had a faster time for translation and rotation, but only the improvement in rotations was statistically significant for the mouse. The case of the scale (zoom in/out), showed a significant difference between both input devices, with the mouse having a faster action time [Yu et al. 10]. Their method concentrated on visualization of data, consisting of visualization spaces where (most) data had pre-determined spatial meaning [Yu et al. 10]. This required the user to support the mental model of a dataset [Kosara et al. 03].

Some contributions provided interesting techniques for 3D navigation, which are worth mentioning in this section. For example, in 1997, Hanson and Wernert developed methods for constrained 3D navigation using 2D controllers [Hanson and Wernert 97]. Another technique was to use Tangible User Interfaces (TUI), as shown by [Wu et al. 11].[9] The NaviRadar, a pedestrian feedback system for navigation, provided tactile feedback to the users [Rümelin et al. 11]. A very interesting approach for WIM[10] is the work by [Coffey et al. 12a]. Their approach used WIM slices to interact with sections of the world [Coffey et al. 12a]. Real-world metaphors have also been used. For example, the Segway PT, two-wheel ride,[11] was used as inspiration in [Valkov et al. 10] for 3D traveling. There have also been techniques to explore cities [Ropinski et al. 05]. A different approach was to use sketching for 3D navigation. Hagerdorn and Döllner studied a sketch-based approach to accomplish navigation tasks [Hagedorn and Döllner 08]. McCrae and colleagues studied a multi-scale 3D navigation approach [McCrae et al. 09]. Different camera techniques have been used for 3D navigation, such as the two-handed Through-The-Lens technique [Stoev et al. 01], HoverCam [Khan et al. 05], controlled camera animation [Santos et al. 11], and Navidget [Hachet et al. 09]. Navigation for time-scientific data was studied by Wolter et al. [Wolter et al. 09]. Visual memory for 3D navigation was also explored [Remazeilles et al. 06]. Many other studies have proposed techniques for 3D navigation tasks [Russo dos Santos et al. 00, Sommer et al. 99, Bowman et al. 97, Edelmann

---

[9]See also [Guéniat et al. 13].
[10]See [Bowman et al. 04, Chapter 5]. For additional references about related work about this topic, see [Coffey et al. 12a].
[11]See http://www.segway.com.

et al. 09, Hachet et al. 06, Tan et al. 01, Vallance and Calder 01, Yu et al. 12, Jackson et al. 12, Boyali and Kavakli 11, Fitzmaurice et al. 08, Chen et al. 88, Nielson and Olsen Jr 87, Saona-Vazquez et al. 99].

Medicine visualization requires navigation in some cases. There have been different types of work in this area. In "3D Navigation in Medicine" [Haigron et al. 96] provided some very interesting pointers for domain-specific navigation. For example, the FOV needed in endoscopy is different from a generic VE. The reason is that an endoscopy visualization requires a wide-angle camera to study a region in detail. Another interesting approach was to use a 2D colon to guide the navigation inside of a 3D colon by [Meng and Halle 04]. Some of the 3D interaction in medicine can provide a foundation to develop further travel interaction, such as the examples described in [Gallo et al. 08, Lundstrom et al. 11].

We have covered different examples of 3D navigation and how some of those have been used to validate the navigation with subject experiments. We have also covered in this section that even 3D interaction techniques can serve as a foundation of 3D navigation systems. We covered different domains, which included: medicine [Haigron et al. 96, Kosara et al. 03, Meng and Halle 04, Gallo et al. 08, Lundstrom et al. 11], large-scale virtual environments [Ruddle et al. 99], geographical and geological environments [Camiciottoli et al. 98, Chen et al. 08, Sousa Santos et al. 10, Beheshti et al. 12, Sultanum et al. 13, Doulamis and Yiakoumettis 13], other scientific visualizations [Wolter et al. 09, Fuchs and Hauser 09, Yu et al. 10, Yu et al. 12, Coffey et al. 12a, Kosara et al. 03], astronomy [Fu et al. 10], dynamic 3D worlds [Russo dos Santos et al. 00], city models [Ropinski et al. 05], energy management systems [Naef and Ferranti 11, Apostolellis et al. 12], video games[12] [Williamson et al. 10], TUIs [Wu et al. 11] , and others [Abásolo and Della 07, Trindade and Raposo 11, Robertson et al. 97, Darken and Banker 98].

Further Reading

There are several publications about wayfinding, some of them already cited in this chapter [Darken 96, Darken and Sibert 96, Lawton 94, Chen and Stanney 99, Chen and Stanney 99, Darken and Peterson 15]. For travel, some additional information is found in [Bowman et al. 04]. Also, in the first edition of the *Handbook of Virtual Environments*, there is a chapter that talks about locomotion interfaces [Hollerbach 02].

---

[12]See games such as Doom, Quake, and Microsoft Flight Simulator.

Exercises

1. Implement a 3D scene in your favorite game engine (or graphics rendering library) that allows users to find multiple targets (see Chapter 21 to create the scene with Unity).

2. Following the previous exercise, implement at least two devices that provide the engine of navigation (travel). Also, record different 3D characteristics that are quantifiable (e.g., time to find an object.)

3. Once both previous exercises have been completed, add visual cues to aid wayfinding for the subjects (see Chapter 3). Perform a pilot-study. Field provides excellent examples for different types of statistical analyses [Field 09].

7

Descriptive and Predictive Models

On the other side I landed in a wilderness. I came
to the open gate of mathematics. Sometimes I think
I have covered the whole area, and then I suddenly
discover a new path and experience fresh delights.
—M.C. Escher

7.1 Introduction

Modeling is important in the development of any human-computer interaction.
For the particular topic of the book, it is also quite useful to use existing models
or create new models for input interaction. For example, say you want to model
multi-touch interaction. How can this be achieved? What method to use? Before
creating a new model, it is important to understand the most-used models in HCI.

A model allows a real problem (physical or non-physical) to be a representation of a real entity. In simpler words, as described by MacKenzie, a model
is a simplification of reality [MacKenzie 12]. A descriptive model is a "loose
verbal analogy and methaphor" [Pew and Baron 83], which describes a phenomenon [MacKenzie 12]. A predictive model (e.g., bimanual control) is expressed by "closed-form mathematical equations" [Pew and Baron 83], which
predict a phenomenon [MacKenzie 12] (e.g., Fitts' law).

Given the topic of the book, the models described in this chapter deal with
input devices interaction and the models that are used for input devices. A few
predictive and descriptive models are described and further reading is provided.

7.2   Predictive Models

Some important predictive models for input interaction are Fitts' law, Hick-Hyman law, linear regression model, keystroke-level model (KLM). The most important predictive model in HCI is Fitts' law and it is very active in the current research work.

Information theory in the 1940s gave rise to information models of psychological processes in the 1950s, giving rise to terms like probability, redundancy, bits noise and channels for experimental psychologists that needed to measure and model human behavior [MacKenzie 92, MacKenzie and Buxton 92].

7.2.1   Fitts' law

Fitts' law is one of the most used works in HCI. Fitts' law is given by Equation 7.1. Gary Olson summarized the law by saying: "The law states that the time it takes to move to a target is a function of the length of the movement and the size of the target" [Olson 08]. In other words, the bigger the target and the closer the target, the faster it is acquired [MacKenzie 92, MacKenzie and Buxton 92]. This has given rise to many findings like the importance of items along the edges [Walker and Smelcer 90]. Equation 7.1 describes that the movement time (MT) is equal to logarithmic result of twice the distance ($2A$) divided by the width of target (W), multiplied by the sum of empirical constants ($a + b$). Olson provides some very interesting facts about findings that were guided by Fitts' law [Olson 08]:

- The edge of the display is infinite size, therefore accessing items on the edges is always faster. The Mac Operating System (OS) has used their top menu on the edge for a long time but it wasn't the case for Microsoft Windows. However, we can see the evolution of Windows. Walker and Smelcer said that the "system that maximizes the percentage of menu items with borders will have a decided advantage over other menu systems" [Walker and Smelcer 90].

- Pop-up menus make the movement cost to get to the menu zero. To minimize the movement inside of the pop-up menu, a pie menu or linear menu is ideal. The most common one is the linear menu that we see by right clicking the mouse either on Windows or Mac OS X. Walker and Smelcer concluded that "it may be more efficient to place menus at the top of the window, backed by an impenetrable border, in multi-tasking" [Walker and Smelcer 90]. For an optimization of walking-menus and pop-up menus, see [Walker et al. 91].

- Selection becomes faster and easier as expanding items are closer, which is the example of the Mac OS X dock bar, as shown in Figure 7.1. McGuffin and Balakrishnan found that "when users expect the target to expand, they can select a single, isolated expanding target faster than a non-expanding static target" [McGuffin and Balakrishnan 05].

Figure 7.1: Dock bar (Mac OS X) with magnification.

$$MT = a + b \, \log_2 \left(\frac{2A}{W} \right) \tag{7.1}$$

Other than Fitts himself, the expert on Fitts' work is Scott MacKenzie,[1] as he has shown in his body of work, including his Ph.D. dissertation [MacKenzie 91], his book, *Human-Computer Interaction: An Empirical Research Perspective* [MacKenzie 12], and "Fitts' law as a Research and Design Tool in Human-Computer Interaction" [MacKenzie 92], among others [MacKenzie 89, Soukoreff and MacKenzie 04]. In the past decade, Soukoreff and MacKenzie looked at the impact of 27 years of research and how to use this law in HCI [Soukoreff and MacKenzie 04].

Fitts proposed that the human motor system is analogous to a communication channel. Fitts used the communication channel capacity using Shannon's theorem 17 [Shannon 63, pp. 100–103], where the information capacity (C in bits/s) "of a communication channel of bandwidth" (B in $1/s$ or Hz) multiplied by the logarithmic result of the signal power (S) divided by the noise power (N) plus one [MacKenzie 89, MacKenzie 92, MacKenzie 12], as shown in Equation 7.2.

$$C = B \, \log_2 \left(\frac{S}{N} + 1 \right) \tag{7.2}$$

Fitts' law was presented in two studies. In the first study, in 1954, users alternated tap on target of a given width (W) separated by a given amplitude (A) showing target acquisition [Fitts 54], as shown in Figure 7.2. The idea was for users to tap each plate as fast as possible, hitting the center part of the plate (black) [Fitts 54, MacKenzie 92]. The subjects were tested for 2 days using a 1-oz stylus and 1-lb stylus. Each subject performed the test 16 times, with four different width measurements (0.25, 0.50, 1.00, 2.00 inches). Using the width and amplitude, Fitts calculated the binary index of difficulty[2] (*ID*), as shown in Equation 7.3. For example, for $W = 0.25$ and $A = 2$, the result is 4. A modified version of the previous equation was introduced by [MacKenzie 92] to improve the information-theoretic analogy, as shown in Equation 7.4, which is the recommended index of difficulty to use [Soukoreff and MacKenzie 04]. To obtain the binary index of performance[2] (*IP*), using the base two logarithmic result of the width (W) divided by twice the amplitude (A), multiply by $\frac{1}{t}$, which is the average movement time [Fitts 54], as

---

[1] http://www.yorku.ca/mack/
[2] Notice that Fitts refers to *ID* as I_d and *IP* as I_p in his 1954 publication.

shown in Equation 7.5. We can also see that the index of difficulty (*ID*) divided by the movement time (*MT*) equals the binary index performance (*IP*), as shown in Equation 7.6. Using the data provided in [Fitts 54], MacKenzie used regression analysis to find the correlation between *MT* on *ID*, yielding $r = .9831$ ($p < 0.001$). In general, the model consistently correlated above 0.9000 [MacKenzie 92]. It is also important to note that the mean value of the index of performance (*IP*) was 10.10 bits/s in Fitts' experiment [Fitts 54], which is claimed to be "the information-processing rate of the human motor system" [MacKenzie 92]. Note that it is more commonly called throughput (*TP* in bits/s). Using regression (*MT* on *ID*), a prediction equation was derived by [MacKenzie 92], as shown in Equation 7.7.

$$ID = -\log_2\left(\frac{W}{2A}\right) = \log_2\left(\frac{2A}{W}\right) \tag{7.3}$$

$$ID = \log_2\left(\frac{2A}{W} + 1\right) \tag{7.4}$$

$$IP = -\frac{1}{t}\log_2\left(\frac{W}{2A}\right) = \frac{1}{t}\log_2\left(\frac{2A}{W}\right) \tag{7.5}$$

$$IP = \frac{ID}{MT} \tag{7.6}$$

$$MT = 12.8 + 94.7ID \tag{7.7}$$

In the experiment conducted by Fitts in 1964, he asked the participants to hit the center of the left or right plate according to the stimulus light, as shown in Figure 7.3. Fitts concluded that "processing feedback in serial tasks introduced a small delay" [Fitts 64]. Using an adjustment of accuracy for the width (W_e) after adjusting the percentage of error, it is possible to calculate the throughput using the index difficulty with its adjustment (ID_e), as shown in Equation 7.8. The width after adjusting the error rate is calculated by Equation 7.9, which is a 4% error rate multiplied by the standard deviation (SD_x) of the selection coordinates of a subject [MacKenzie 12, pp. 251–252]. This "captures what a participant actually did, rather than what he or she was asked to do" [Mukundan 12, p. 252]. The effective target width (W_e) "derives from the distribution of hits" [MacKenzie 92], as it is expressed by Welford in *Fundamentals of Skill* [Welford 68, pp. 147–148]. The basic concept for having this correction is because of the noise that is produced, as explained by [Fitts 64, Shannon 63, Welford 68, MacKenzie 92]. Finally, The effective index of difficulty adjustment is given by Equation 7.10. The effective index is recommended but there are arguments against using it, as expressed by [Zhai et al. 04].

$$TP = \frac{ID_e}{MT} \tag{7.8}$$

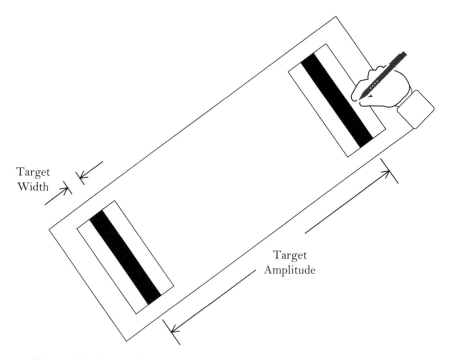

Figure 7.2: Fitts serial task. Adapted from [Fitts 54] and [MacKenzie 92].

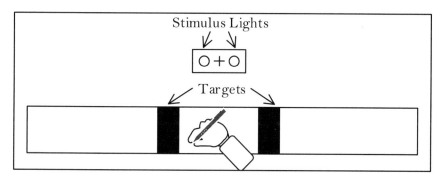

Figure 7.3: Fitts discrete task. Adapted from [Fitts 64] and [MacKenzie 92].

$$W_e = 4.133 \times SD_x \qquad (7.9)$$

$$ID_e = log_2 \left(\frac{A}{W_e} + 1 \right) \qquad (7.10)$$

Soukoreff and MacKenzie published "Towards a standard for pointing device evaluation, perspective on 27 years of Fitts' law research in HCI," which describes recommendations for using Fitts' law [Soukoreff and MacKenzie 04]. They provide seven recommendations [Soukoreff and MacKenzie 04]:

1. Researches should use the Shannon formulation of the index of difficulty, as shown in Equation 7.4.

2. A variety of distances (D) and target widths (W) are needed to have a representative and wide range of ID values (2 to 8). It is recommended that each subject is presented between 15 to 25 times. Finally, it is important to collect movement time (MT).

3. It is important to collect movement end-point and error rates. This suggests that no filtering of data should be performed, except for outliers. Typical outliers includes a subject double-clicking the target by accident.

4. It is suggested to use the end-point data collected (see previous item) for adjustment. Using the end-point position standard deviation (σ), the effective width (W_e) is calculated as $W_e = 4.133\sigma$. Another option is to use the error rate collected (see previous item) to approximate accuracy as shown in the Equation 7.11, shown below:

$$W_e = \begin{cases} W \times \frac{2.066}{z(1-Err/2)} & \text{if } Err > 0.0049\% \\ W \times 0.5089 & \text{otherwise} \end{cases} \tag{7.11}$$

The index of difficulty can be used with the adjusted width and distance. The distance (D) can be computed as the effective distance (DE) if movement end-point data was collected. The index of difficulty is shown below, in Equations 7.12 and 7.13, depending on if the effective distance is available:

$$ID_e = log_2\left(\frac{D}{W_e} + 1\right) \tag{7.12}$$

$$ID_e = log_2\left(\frac{D_e}{W_e} + 1\right) \tag{7.13}$$

5. Use least-square linear regression to find the intercept (a) and the slope (b) in the Fitts' formula $MT = a + b \times ID_e$. This helps to find if there is a relationship between MT and ID_e, which is called the goodness of fit. It is recommended that a positive intercept should be 400 ms or less. A negative intercept should not exceed -200 ms. Most statistical packages can perform the test to see if the intercept is statistically different from zero [Field 09, pp. 198-207].

6. For movement time prediction, the movement time should use *ID* and not *IDₑ*, which was used to find the *a* and *b* values (see previous item), as shown in the formula below:

$$MT_{predicted} = a + b \times ID \qquad (7.14)$$

7. It is recommended to use *throughput* (*TP*), if the analysis required is to compare "two more experiment conditions" [Soukoreff and MacKenzie 04]. Use the mean of means to calculate the dependent measurement of *TP*, as shown in Equation 7.15, where "*y* is the number of subjects, and *x* represents the numbers of movement conditions" [Soukoreff and MacKenzie 04], as shown below:

$$TP = \frac{1}{y} \sum_{i=1}^{y} \left(\frac{1}{x} \sum_{j=1}^{x} \frac{ID_{e_{ij}}}{MT_{ij}} \right) \qquad (7.15)$$

These recommendations just covered the surface of the suggestions made by [Soukoreff and MacKenzie 04], where they provide further explanation, which includes the reason behind each of the seven suggestions. Their recommendation to go forward with the standard (ISO9241-9) [International Organization for Standardization 00, International Organization for Standardization 07, International Organization for Standardization 12] is understood by their statement: "One way or another, meaningful progress in this field with regards to Fitts' law will be hampered until, one way or another, we all conform to a standard kind" [Soukoreff and MacKenzie 04].

There have been some different takes on Fitts' law and its use ([Zhai et al. 04, Drewes 10]). In 2013, Hoffman said that MacKenzie's formulation was invalid [MacKenzie 89, MacKenzie 92], in a published article in the *Journal of Motor Behavior* [Hoffmann 13]. This researcher claimed that MacKenzie's formulation [MacKenzie 89, MacKenzie 92] was invalid providing a series of arguments, such as "the use of effective target width may have (but not always) the effect of improving regression correlation, and dominates the effects of the additive +1 term" [Hoffmann 13], which is in Shannon's formulation proposed by MacKenzie [MacKenzie 89, MacKenzie 92]. In 2013, MacKenzie published a response to Hoffman, where he debunked the arguments provided by Hoffmann, showing the problems with the arguments [MacKenzie 13]. Some of the deficiencies of Hoffman's arguments [Hoffmann 13] mentioned by MacKenzie [MacKenzie 13] include: (a) "Human movements are not electronic signals" [MacKenzie 13] as stated by Hoffman. (b) The argument that +1 term [Shannon 63] is invalid versus the +0.5 term [Welford 68] as valid, has no merit. MacKenzie provides concrete evidence about the invalid assumptions in [Hoffmann 13], concluding that "the Shannon formulation is reaffirmed to provide better predictions than the Fitts or

Welford formulation" [MacKenzie 13] and the standard in HCI. While there may be some different takes, MacKenzie's formulation has prevailed in HCI and it has demonstrated its use in many user studies.

An interesting discussion is Fitts' law (that uses distance and width) versus Woodworth (that uses form and scale) [Woodworth 99]. Woodworth's work is beyond the scope of this book (see [Meyer et al. 88]) but a comparison is discussed by [Guiard 09], where he puts into perspective the differences of both, with certain favoritism (based on his evidence) that the $F \times S$ approach seems more appropriate than the $D \times W$ approach. Both of them have certain deficiencies as perceived by [Guiard 09]. Following the work by [Guiard 09] and previous Fitts' law literature (already described in this section), Wobbrock and colleagues looked at effects for $F \times S$ versus $D \times W$ (or $A \times W$, where A is distance and W is size) [Wobbrock et al. 11] and concluded that Fitts' dimensionality (1D vs. 2D) is largely invariant. It also concluded that bivariate end-point deviation ($SD_{x,y}$) models 2D data better, while univariate (SD_x) can be used in both but "ignores deviation in the orthogonal task dimension" [Wobbrock et al. 11]. Wobbrock and colleagues provide a few formulas, which are then also recommended in their guidelines

i The univariate standard deviation is shown in Equation 7.16, as described by [MacKenzie 92, MacKenzie and Isokoski 08, Soukoreff and MacKenzie 04], which states that "SD_x is the standard deviation of end-point coordinates along the axis of motion" [Wobbrock et al. 11].

$$SD_x = \sqrt{\frac{\sum\limits_{i=1}^{N} (x_i - \bar{x})^2}{N-1}} \qquad (7.16)$$

ii The bivariate standard deviation for two dimensions, shown in Equation 7.17.

$$SD_{x,y} = \sqrt{\frac{\sum\limits_{i=1}^{N} \left(\sqrt{(x_i - \bar{x})^2 + (y_i - \bar{y})^2} \right)^2}{N-1}} \qquad (7.17)$$

iii An example from the bivariate standard deviation shown in Equation 7.17, increased to 3D, as shown in Equation 7.18.

$$SD_{x,y,z} = \sqrt{\frac{\sum\limits_{i=1}^{N} \left(\sqrt{(x_i - \bar{x})^2 + (y_i - \bar{y})^2 + (z_i - \bar{z})^2} \right)^2}{N-1}} \qquad (7.18)$$

iv Throughput (bits per seconds) designated as TP_{avg} [Wobbrock et al. 11, Soukoreff and MacKenzie 04], as described in Equation 7.19. This formula provides the entire throughput over all the subjects [Wobbrock et al. 11].

$$TP_{avg} = \frac{1}{N} \sum_{i=1}^{N} \left(\frac{ID_{e_i}}{MT_i} \right), \text{ where } N = |A| \times |W| \qquad (7.19)$$

Based on their finding, Wobbrock and colleagues provide the following recommendations [Wobbrock et al. 11]:

1. Either use $F \times S$ design by "choosing one level of [size] A" [Wobbrock et al. 11] while modifying width W or $A \times W$ design isolating "a middle [size] A while retaining all [width] W values" [Wobbrock et al. 11].

2. In the case of 2D pointing, calculate the bivariate deviation $SD_{x,y}$. However, if there is a significant difference in the univariate deviation SD_x, it must be reported as well.

3. When comparing a one-dimensional (1D) task with a 2D task, use TP_{avg} using univariate end-point deviation SD_x to make sure "throughputs across dimensionalities agree best" [Wobbrock et al. 11].

4. "Comparisons should generally not be drawn across throughput calculations approaches" [Wobbrock et al. 11].

5. It is recommended to use ring-of-circles found in the ISO 9241-9 for 2D pointing, as shown in Figure 7.4.

Fitts' law, as already stated, is the most widely used model in HCI. Some of these include: Mackenzie and Buxton that extended Fitts' law to 2D [MacKenzie and Buxton 92], Zhai and colleagues looked at 3D target acquisition [Zhai et al. 94], Klochek and MacKenzie looked at the difference performance of a mouse and a GamePad in 3D VE [Klochek and MacKenzie 06], and haptics and 3D stereoscopic [Chun et al. 04], among others [Kabbash et al. 93, Campbell et al. 08]. Recent work includes FittsTilt by MacKenzie and Teather that looked at the application of Fitts' law with tilt-based devices [MacKenzie and Teather 12], the modeling of finger touch using Fitts' law [Bi et al. 13], 3D selection by pointing [Teather and Stuerzlinger 14], and Paul Lubos who showed "that the main factor causing errors in 3D selection is the visual perception and not, as presumed, the motor movement direction during selections" [Lubos 14], among others [Fares et al. 13, Teather and MacKenzie 14, Zeagler et al. 14].

MacKenzie noted in his book [MacKenzie 12] that the success of Fitts' law is in great part because of the early endorsement in the seminal book *The Psychology of Human-Computer Interaction* [Card et al. 83].

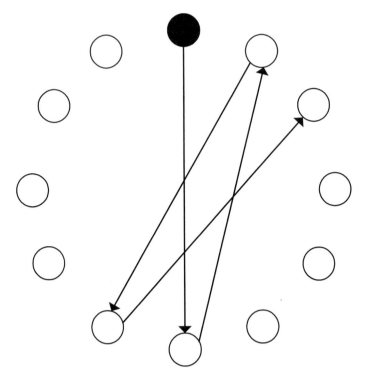

Figure 7.4: Ring-of-circles. Adapted from ISO 9241-9.

7.2.2 Choice Reaction Time: Hick–Hyman Law

The Hick-Hyman law, developed by Hick in 1952 [Hick 52] and Hyman in 1953 [Hyman 53], is another important model in HCI but not as widely used as Fitts' law. Hick-Hyman law can be described as the average reaction time given a set of choices with equal probability. In other words, it can be said that this law shows the time it takes a user to make a decision based on the set of choices. The Hick-Hyman law is a prediction model, where each stimuli n_i has a one-to-one relationship with a response N_i, as described[3] by Equation 7.20, where a and b are empirically determined constants [MacKenzie 12]. Card and colleagues found that reasonably constant values where $a \approx 200$ ms and $b \approx 150$ [Card et al. 83, p. 76]. Note that RT has units of bits, similar to Fitts' law [MacKenzie 12]. Figure 7.5 illustrates an example where this law is applicable, where each key is connected to a light bulb and the user can turn on/off each of those light bulbs.

---

[3]The model is sometimes described as $RT = a + b \log_2(n)$, or without an intercept [MacKenzie 12, Card et al. 83, Welford 68].

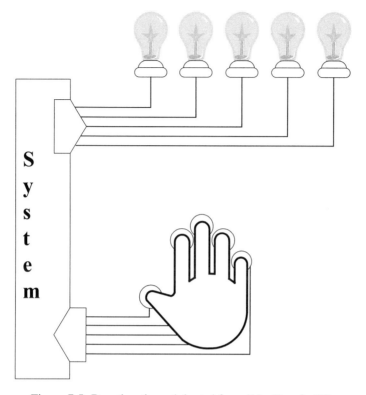

Figure 7.5: Reaction time. Adapted from [MacKenzie 12].

$$RT = a + b \log_2(n+1) \qquad (7.20)$$

Choice reaction time provides a way to calculate the information H when there are some choices more likely to happen than others. The information (H) is calculated as shown by Equation 7.21. An example provided by [MacKenzie 12] is an English keyboard system with 26 letters. The probability of typing a ($p = 0.0810$) is more likely to happen than the letter q ($q = 0.0010$) in the English language [MacKenzie 12]. Silfverberg and colleagues study text prediction on mobile phones using the British national Corpus[4,5] [Silfverberg et al. 00]. Recently, Liu and Räihä studied text prediction speed for Chinese characters [Liu and Räihä 10]. The Hick-Hyman law has not gained momentum as Fitts' law has because the model has limited use [MacKenzie 12].

---

[4]Ftp site: ftp://ftp.itri.bton.ac.uk/
[5]Web site:http://www.nltg.brighton.ac.uk/nltg/

$$H = \sum_i p_i \log_2 \left(\frac{1}{p_i} + 1 \right) \tag{7.21}$$

7.2.3   Keystroke-Level Model (KLM)

Card and colleagues designed Keystroke-Level Model (KLM), a predictive model that analyzes human performance [Card et al. 80]. This was later described in their seminal book *The Psychology of Human-Computer Interaction* [Card et al. 83, ch. 8]. This model predicts error-free expert behavior completion times using task or series of sub-tasks, method used, command language of the system, motor skill of the user, and responsive time of the system [MacKenzie 12]. KLM only predicts the time to execute a given task, not the time that it takes to acquire it [Card et al. 83, p. 260]. While the KLM cannot predict the method (it just predicts the time), another model by Card et al. is able to predict the method, which is called Goals, Operators, Methods, and Selection (GOMS) [Card et al. 83]. This book will not cover GOMS but for further information about this model, see [Card et al. 83, Chapter 5] or [Dix et al. 04, Chapter 12].

KLM provides an analysis tool for "the time it takes a user to perform a task with a given method on an interactive computer system" [Card et al. 80]. However, there are many types of performance metrics that are important when looking at performance, which includes time, errors, learning, functionality, recall, concentration, and acceptability [Card et al. 80] (see [Nielsen 94]). Therefore, KLM provides one of the dimensions of human–computer performance. There is also no single type of task, as it depends on the interactive system. Finally, it is also important to know that there are different types of users, with different skills and expertise [Card et al. 80]:

- Knowledge about different types of tasks.

- Knowledge about other systems.

- Motor skills for different input devices.

- Technical abilities.

- Experience with the system.

A task in its most basic form is composed of a time to acquire plus the time to execute, as shown in Equation 7.22. However, KLM only predicts the execution time unit. The acquisition time "depends on the characteristics of the larger task situation in which it occurs" [Card et al. 83, p. 261]. The execution time depends on the system command language but it "rarely takes over 20 sec" [Card et al. 83, p. 261]. Two assumptions are made in this model [Card et al. 83]: (1) The

Table 7.1: KLM Operators and Values [Card et al. 80].

Operator	Description	Time (sec)
K	PRESS A KEY OR BUTTON Pressing a modifier key (e.g.,) counts as a separate operation. Times varies with typing skills:	
	Best typist (135 wpm)	0.08
	Good typist (90 wpm)	0.12
	Average skilled typist (55 wpm)	0.20
	Average non-secretary typist (40 wpm)	0.28
	Typing random letters	0.50
	Typing complex letters	0.75
	Worst typist (unfamiliar with keyboard)	1.20
P	POINT WITH A MOUSE Empirical value based on Fitts' law. Range from 0.8 to 1.5 seconds. Operators do not include the button click at the end of pointing operation.	1.10
H	HOME HAND(S) ON KEYBOARD OR OTHER DEVICE	0.40
$D(n_D, l_D)$	DRAW n_D STRAIGHT-LINE SEGMENTS OF TOTAL LENGTH l_D. Drawing with the mouse constrained to a grid.	$0.9n_D + 0.16l_D$
M	MENTALLY PREPARE	1.35
R(t)	RESPONSE BY SYSTEM Different commands require different response times. Counted only if the user must wait.	t

execution time is the same regardless of how the task is acquired. (2) Acquisition time and execution time are independent.

$$T_{unit\text{-}task} = T_{acquire} + T_{execute} \qquad (7.22)$$

KLM: Operators and Encoding Methods

The operators are part of KLM. The operators provided by Card and colleagues were designed primarily for text-editing and document management [Card et al. 80]. Later, we will look at some modern ways to use KLM proposed by [MacKenzie 12], in Section 7.2.3. The operators are shown in Table 7.1. This includes motor control operators: keystroking (K), pointing (P), homing (H), and drawing (D), one mental (M) operator, and a system response operator (R). The operators added together yield the total task execution time ($T_{execute}$), as shown in Equation 7.23, for example, $T_K = n_K \times t_K$, which is the number of n_K keystrokes multiplied by the time t_H. The pointing (P) operator can be calculated using Fitts' law. The homing[6] (H) operator is the time that it takes to go from one device to another device. With the data from their own experiments, using GOMS in [Card et al. 83, Ch. 5] and [Card et al. 83, Ch. 7], they determined the constant for t_H was 0.4 seconds for the movement that it takes to go from the keyboard to the mouse. The drawing (D) operator represents the user drawing a set of straight-line segments with a mouse device. For this, the drawing (D) operator takes two arguments: "the number of segments (n_D and the total length of all segments (l_D" [Card et al. 83, p. 263]. The mental operator (M) describes the time it takes the user to prepare to perform a task. This is a simplification of the mental process and the suggested time of 1.35 seconds is based on the experiments found in other experimental data they had [Card et al. 80, Card et al. 83]. Finally, the response time $R(t)$ operator is the time that the user waits for the system to perform the operator.

$$T_{execute} = T_k + T_p + T_h + T_d + T_m + T_r \qquad (7.23)$$

Methods represent a sequence of operators. To illustrate how to encode a method with its operators, take for example a command *LIST* in a computer system. To access the *LIST* command, the user needs to type it and hit the RETURN key. This method is encoded as **MK**[*L*] **K**[*I*] **K**[*S*] **K**[*T*] **K**[*RETURN*], which can be abbreviated as **M 5K**[*LISTRETURN*] [Card et al. 83]. Another example that demonstrates how to encode a method is shown in Table 7.2 [Card et al. 83]. In this example, to accomplish Task T_1, the user has to reach for the mouse, select a word, switch both hands to keyboard (homing), press the F1 key to replace the text, modify "WORLD" into "World" and save the changes with the F2 key. If we look at the execution time of this task, then we can aggregate the keystrokes to produce: $T_{execute} = 2t_M + 8t_K + 2t_H + t_P$. In other words, the user had to switch devices twice ($2t_H$), think twice (mental operator) about the replace and saving action ($2t_M$), point once (t_P), and a total of 8 keystrokes $8t_K$, which included the selection of the word. Note that in this model, the keyboard is used for the word selection, a task nowadays delegated to the mouse in most cases. One may decide to encode the method only with the physical actions or include the mental operators. Card and colleagues provide a heuristic in [Card et al. 83, p. 265], with five rules:

- Use **Rule** 0 to encode the candidate mental operator (M).

    Rule 0: Insert each mental operator (M) in front of each keyboard operator (K), if they are not part of a proper string, such as text or numbers. Place M before P for select commands only.

---

[6]Referred to in [Card et al. 83] as "home."

Table 7.2: Task T_1 [Card et al. 83].

Grab mouse:	H[*mouse*]
Point word:	P[*word*]
Select word:	K[*WORLD*]
Home on keyboard (switch):	H[*keyboard*]
Replace word:	K[*F*1]
Type new word:	5K[*World*]
Save:	K[*F*2]

Rule 1: Delete the mental operator (M) if the operation is anticipated. In other words, if M is between two physical operators where the operation is anticipated.

Rule 2: Delete all mental operators (M) except for the first one, if a string is part of a cognitive unit, such as the name of a command.

Rule 3: If the keyboard operator (K) is the command terminator (e.g., ENTER key), delete the mental operator (M) in front of K.

Rule 4: If the keyboard operator terminates a constant string, such as a command name, delete the M in front of K. Otherwise, if the keyboard operator terminates a variable string, keep the mental operator.

KLM: Modern Use

The seminal paper by Card and colleagues was published more than 35 years ago [Card et al. 80]. It is quite understandable that the operators needed at that time were limited compared the type of operators needed today because of user interfaces available now. Therefore, newer research has adapted operators to fit newer devices. This makes KLM still a valid model today as it was 35 years ago. For example, in 2006, Hinckley and colleagues demonstrated the use of a "springboard" interface for the use of tablet computers using the KLM model [Hinckley et al. 06]. MacKenzie provided some updated equations for the pointing operator using Fitts' law [MacKenzie 12], as shown in Equation 7.24 (where $a = 0.159$ and $b = 0.204$). MacKenzie provided very insightful information about a modern approach to KLM and used it with predictive text in his book [MacKenzie and Teather 12] (among articles co-authored by MacKenzie).

$$t_P = a + b \times \log_2 \left(\frac{A}{W} + 1 \right) \tag{7.24}$$

7.2.4 Other Models

There are additional models in HCI. Some of the models are described below [Hinckley and Widgor 12, MacKenzie 12]:

- Linear regression: This model describes the relationship between an independent predictor variable (x), a dependent human-response variable (y), where the slope of the relationship is m, and the y intercept is b [MacKenzie 12], as shown in Equation 7.25. The objective is to "find the coefficients m and b" [MacKenzie and Teather 12], which minimizes "the squared distances (least squares) of the points from the line " [MacKenzie 12]. This process is called linear regression. For additional information, see [MacKenzie 12, Field 09, Wilcox 11].

$$y = mx + b \qquad (7.25)$$

- Steering law: Accot and Zhai proposed this law that describes the movement time for a cursor to move in a narrow tunnel [Accot and Zhai 97, Hinckley and Widgor 12]. One example where this law can be applied is a pull-down menu for navigation. The general steering law is given by Equation 7.26, where $v(s)$ is the tangential velocity, ρ is the radius of curvature, and $W(s)$ is the width of the path. Given that this law is used for GUIs, the authors [Accot and Zhai 97] provided a concrete example. Figure 7.6 shows the menu with a width (w) and a height (h), where the user starts navigating at top (MENU) and moves to an menu option (option n) at which point the user scrolls to the right to the next menu. Using their experiment results, they derived that the time it takes (T_n) to select the nth sub-menu is given by the vertical part of the equation: $a + b\frac{nh}{w}$, plus the horizontal part of the equation: $a + b\frac{w}{h}$, which yields Equation 7.27. Finally, if the user navigation is a straight line in a pull-down menu, it can be expressed as a "linear function of A and W" [Hinckley 08], as shown in Equation 7.28. Additional reading about minimum-jerk law, which describes "dynamics of motions that lack a continuous accuracy constraint" [Hinckley and Widgor 12] is found in [Viviani and Flash 95], among other related publications [Viviani and Terzuolo 82, Viviani and Flash 95, Lank and Saund 05].

$$v(s) = k\rho(s)W(s) \qquad (7.26)$$

$$
\begin{aligned}
T_n &= a + b\frac{nh}{w} + a + b\frac{w}{h} \\
&= 2a + b\left(\frac{n}{x} + x\right) \text{ where } x = \frac{w}{h} \qquad (7.27)
\end{aligned}
$$

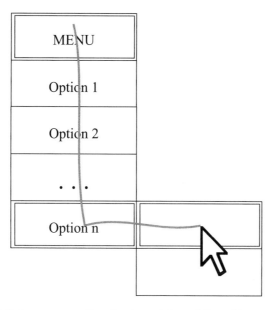

Figure 7.6: Pull down menu. Steering law. Adapted from [Accot and Zhai 97].

$$MT = a + b \times \frac{A}{W} \qquad (7.28)$$

- Skill acquisition (power law): [Newell and Rosenbloom 80]. This law dates back to the 1920s, as far as Newell was able to find [Newell 94]. The automation of skills procedural memory is usually given in the form of $T = aP^b$ [Hinckley and Widgor 12], where T is the time to perform a task and P is the amount of practice, with observed data of factor a and exponent b. The law describes the non-linear relationship between skill and practice. MacKenzie provides the equation using $y = b \times x^a$, where x is the practice-independent variable (regressor) and y is the performance-dependent variable [MacKenzie 12]. MacKenzie has used the power law for mobile input text [MacKenzie et al. 01].

  - If we are looking for the time T_n that it takes to complete the task ("time per task" [MacKenzie 12]) then the equation can be expressed as shown in Equation 7.29, where T_1 is the time for the first trial, n is the trial number, and a is a negative constant (given that acquisition time decreases with practice) [MacKenzie 12].

$$T_n = T_1 \times n^a \qquad (7.29)$$

- If we are looking for the speed, which describes "the task per unit time" [MacKenzie 12], then the equation can be reformulated to S_n as the speed of the nth trial, S_1 as the speed of the first trial, n as the trial number, and a is a constant between 0 and 1 (which reflects that with longer practice, the learning return decreases) [MacKenzie 12], as shown in Equation 7.30.

$$S_n = S_1 \times n^a \qquad (7.30)$$

- A final note about the two previous equations is that the constant a is a "constant setting the shape of the curve" [MacKenzie 12].

7.3   Descriptive Models

This section covers descriptive models. In many publications words like "design space, framework, taxonomy, and classification" [MacKenzie 12] are used. As noted in the beginning of this chapter, we are concerned with models that can be used for input devices. A small subset of the models in HCI are covered. The reader is referred to [MacKenzie 12, Dix et al. 04, Jacko 12] among others.

7.3.1   Bi-Manual Interaction

Humans have used both hands when needed to perform some specific task [MacKenzie 12]. While typing is possible with one hand, both hands seems to be the most effective way to type for most users, when using a PC keyboard. For example, when using a hammer a user may need to hold the nail with the non-dominant hand, while hitting the nail with a hammer, in the dominant hand. While both hands are very useful, it is also important to mention that users prefer to do some tasks only with one hand, as it is with multi-touch gestures (see Chapter 8) as opposed to performing a two-hand gesture. This topic is expanded in Chapter 8 (see Section 8.3.6).

Psychology researchers studied bi-manual behavior years before HCI researchers. For example, in 1979, Kelso et al. studied the coordination of two-handed movements [Kelso et al. 79]. In their work, they found that while the kinematic movements of the hands are different, the movements of both hands are synchronized for certain tasks. In their own words: "The brain produces simultaneity of action as the optimal solution for the two-handed task by organizing functional groupings of muscles," which act as a single-unit [Kelso et al. 79]. Another example of psychology that deals with two hands is the work by Wing [Wing 82]. He studied the timing and coordination of repetitive tasks using both hands. While he used only four subjects, the study led to the conclusion that there may be a difference between synchronous movements versus asynchronous movements [Wing 82]. The users did report that synchronous movements in bi-manual tasks were easier [Wing 82]. In general, studies have shown that most tasks are asymmetric [MacKenzie 12]. Studies have also shown that while hands work together, they have different roles to "perform different type of tasks" [MacKenzie 12].

Later, in 1987, Guiard proposed a model for bi-manual action [Guiard 87]. His model makes two assumptions: First, the hand represents a motor (people having two motors), which serve to create a motion. Second, the motors cooperate with each other, forming a kinematic chain; one hand articulates the movement of the other hand. Guiard's model describes the "inter-manual division of labor" [Guiard 87]. Guiard's model is the basis for much of the HCI research work about bi-manual interaction.

In 1986, Buxton and Myers published a study for bi-manual input [Buxton and Myers 86]. They found that users benefited by using both-hands, because of the efficiency of hand motion in bi-manual actions [Buxton and Myers 86]. Later, in 1993, Kabbash, MacKenzie, and Buxton [Kabbash et al. 93] studied the use of preferred and non-preferred hands. They found that the non-preferred hand performs better in tasks that do not require action (e.g., scrolling). The preferred hand was found to be better for fine movements. This meant that each hand has "its own strength and weakness" [Kabbash et al. 93]. Figure 7.7 shows an example of a bi-manual task and the difference between both hands. The following describes the roles and actions for each hand [MacKenzie 12, Kabbash et al. 93, Guiard 87] (adapted from table in [MacKenzie 12, Chapter 7]):

- Non-preferred hand:

    - Leads the preferred hand.

    - Provides a spatial frame of reference for the preferred hand.

    - Achieves non-fine movements.

- Preferred hand:

    - Follows the other hand.

    - Utilizes a frame of reference set by the non-preferred hand.

    - Achieves fine movements.

Later, in 1994, Kabbash, Buxton, and Selen published "Two-Handed Input in a Compound Task" [Kabbash et al. 94]. This is a significant contribution, as it is the first publication to adapt the bi-manual model by Guiard [Guiard 87]. The experiment had four modes when using the computer: one uni-manual, one bi-manual, with each hand having independent tasks, and two bi-manual, requiring asymmetric dependency. The study found that one of two bi-manual asymmetric modes performed better (as expected by them) than the other methods. This

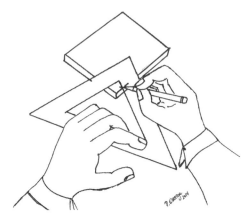

Figure 7.7: Bi-manual interaction [MacKenzie 12]. Drawing courtesy of Patty Melo.

method is called the **toolglass** technique, previously published by Bier et al. [Bier et al. 93], which provided the use of additional widgets for the user's interactions. The reader should look at [Leganchuk et al. 98] to read more about the benefits of two-handed input.

The bi-manual model has been used for multi-touch devices, such as [Benko et al. 06, Yee 04, Moscovich and Hughes 08b]. Benko et al. showed that the **dual finger stretch** technique was found to provide a simple and powerful interaction [Benko et al. 06]. Moscovich and Hughes found that indirect mapping of multi-touch input was compatible (one hand versus two hands) in most cases [Moscovich and Hughes 08b]. They also found that "two hands perform better than one at tasks that require separate control of two points" [Moscovich and Hughes 08b]. Mackenzie provided some very interesting notes about the fact that scrolling is well suited for the right hand [MacKenzie 12]. However, the early introduction of Microsoft's IntelliMouse provide too hard for people to abandon. The reader is invited to see a very interesting personal note in MacKenzie's book, which describes his trip to Microsoft in 1998 with an idea for left-handed buttons to perform difference actions [MacKenzie 12]. In Chapter 8, we cover bi-manual input for pen and multi-touch.

7.3.2   Three-State Model for Graphical Input

Bill Buxton developed the three-state model [Buxton 90]. The elegance of this model is at par with the great models and law that we have in HCI. His motivation at the time is best expressed with a small fragment of his paper that said: "All input devices are not created equal in their capabilities, nor input techniques" [Buxton 90, p. 1]. With this said, he showed that it was possible to express certain types of

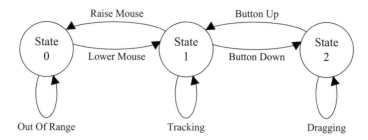

Figure 7.8: Three state model. Adapted from [Buxton 90].

input devices with three states, where some states may have multiples of them. The three states mentioned in [Buxton 90] as shown in Figure 7.8 are the following:

State 0: Out of range. For example, picking the mouse up and placing it back down in the middle of the mouse pad.

State 1: Tracking. For example, the tracking of the mouse cursor as it moves on a display.

State 2: Dragging. For example, moving an object or set of objects on the display with the mouse, possibly by having one of the mouse buttons pressed.

It is possible to have multiple states of the same type. For example, if it is desired to move a set of files from one folder to another, the user may press the left button while dragging the mouse, representing one of the multiple **State** 2. The other option maybe to duplicate the items with the right button while dragging the objects into another folder, making this another **State** 2, as shown in 7.9. Bill Buxton provided additional information about the type of states that a device may use [Buxton 90]. In addition, Buxton described the type of operations (like drag) with their allowable states. For example, the mouse drag operation uses **State** 1 and **State** 2; in contrast, writing with a digital pen uses the three states [Buxton 90]. Bill Buxton also has additional information in his manuscript[7] to describe this model and many additional topics that he has worked on over the years [Buxton 11]. As expressed in Chapter 27, the three-state model has proved to be very useful with some instances where it has fallen short [Hinckley et al. 10a].

---

[7]Online only: http://www.billbuxton.com/inputManuscript.html

Side Note 7.1: About Paul M. Fitts

Little is known about Paul M. Fitts. He was born in 1912 and died at an early age (1965). We were able to dig some information by asking around different organizations where he studied or worked as well as some sites [Staal 14, Wikipedia 15g], including an image provided by the US Air Force (see Figure 7.10). He obtained his doctoral degree from the University of Rochester (1938). He was a psychologist (lieutenant colonel) in the US Air Force from 1941 until 1946. During his time in the US Air Force, Fitts was given the post of psychology branch director of "Wright Field's Aeromedical Laboratory and was charged with coordinating the study of engineering psychology" [Staal 14] in 1954. Paul M. Fitts may have been one of the most important contributors to HCI. Other interests included pilot attention (early work on eye-tracking) [Staal 14]. He was the president of division 21 of the American Psychological Association (1957-1958) and the president of the Human Factors and Ergonomics Society (1962-1963).

  With the help of the United States Air Force History division, we were able to find additional information about Paul M. Fitts. He was a high school science teacher during 1934-1935 and an assistant professor at the University of Tennessee 1938-1941. Before entering the US Air Force, he worked one year as a test construction analyst. After his military service, he worked at the AeroMedical Laboratory between 1946-1949. Right after that, between 1949-1958, he went back to academia as a professor of psychology and Director of the Aviation Psychology Laboratory, Ohio State University. He was the major advisor for 21 Ph.D students. In 1958, he moved to the University of Michigan, as a professor of psychology. This was his last full-time position before his death. During the early 1960s, he received two awards: Exceptional Service Award (US Air Force) in 1960 and the Franklin V. Taylor award (Society of Engineering Psychologist) in 1962. He also consulted for many external companies between 1946 and 1963, including Boeing Aircraft Company, IBM, Lockheed, Office of Naval Research, General Electric, and General Motors, among others. He co-authored at least 45 journal articles and books and 36 government and other reports.

Continues on next page

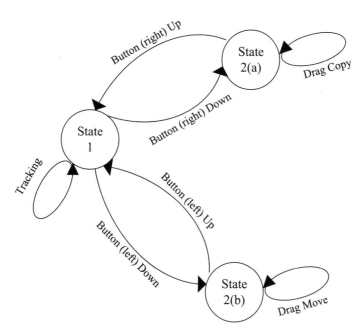

Figure 7.9: Three-state model with multiple states. Adapted from [Buxton 90].

Figure 7.10: Paul M. Fitts (Courtesy of US Air Force).

Further Reading

A recently published article by MacKenzie talks more about the Shannon index of difficulty [MacKenzie 13]. Additional information about models are found in [Dix et al. 04, MacKenzie 12]. Additional information about Paul M. Fitts, including newly found documents are available on our site.

Exercises

1. Implement the ring of circles using Figure 7.4 as an example. Use two different devices to conduct a small pilot study. Field provides excellent examples for different types of statistical analyses [Field 09].

2. Implement a similar Dock Bar, as shown in Figure 7.1. A an interesting pilot study would be to compare the magnified icon bar versus a non-magnified one.

8

Multi-Touch

Everything, including touch, is best for something and
worst for something else.

—Bill Buxton

8.1 Introduction

With the release of the Apple iPhone in 2007, a new mark in multi-touch was set.
This phone alone may have marked the beginning of multi-touch "everywhere"
– pervasive multi-touch in our daily lives. However, multi-touch has a long and
rich history of development that is important to mention. It is also important to
mention current trends in multi-touch as well as the technology behind some of
the multi-touch hardware.

Multi-touch displays come in many flavors. The most representative type of
multi-touch has been the smartphone, with the introduction of the Apple iPhone.
Other types seen in daily use are tablets, such as the Apple iPad. The introduction
of Microsoft Windows 7 and Windows 8 opened a possibility to use multi-touch
displays with a desktop PC. For public spaces, vertical displays can be a solution
for multi-user interaction. Finally, another modality is to have tabletop displays
(horizontal) that will act just as a desk (e.g., Microsoft Surface). Multi-touch has
even been extended to work with stereo vision [Hachet et al. 11].

To take into perspective the history of multi-touch, Table 8.1 provides a look at
the milestones in multi-touch technologies[1] [Microsoft 14e]. Additional entries
can be found in Bill Buxton's "Multi-Touch Systems that I Have Known and
Loved" [Microsoft 14e] and Geoff Walker "Touch Sensing" [Walker 14].

---

[1]The table is built in its majority using the history notes from Bill Buxton (http://www.billbuxton.
com/multitouchOverview.html) and some entries from [Walker 14].

Table 8.1: History of Multi-Touch. Adapted from [Microsoft 14e].

Year	Name	Description
1960	Single Touch	Single Touch (not pressure-sensitive), developed at IBM, the University of Illinois, and Ottawa, Canada. The development occurred in the second part of the 1960s.
1965	Royal Radar	The Royal Radar Establishment in United Kingdom (E.A Johnson) published applications for a transparent touch screen using multi-capacitance (projected capacitive) on a CRT monitor for air-traffic control.
1972	PLATO IV Touch Screen Terminal	The invention of flat-panel plasma display, which included a 16x16 single touch (not pressure-sensitive) touch screen. This machine included real-time random-access audio playback and many other features. The touch panel worked by using beams of infrared light in horizontal and vertical directions. When the infrared light was interrupted at a point, it triggered the touch [Ebeling et al. 73].
1978	Vector Touch	One-Point Touch Input of Vector Information for Computer Displays [Herot and Weinzapfel 78]. It included the ability to detect 2D position of touch, 3D force, and torque.
1979	Camera-based	Sperry Rand developed a touch display using a camera-based optical system.
1981	Tactile Array Sensor for Robots	Multi-touch sensor for the use of robotics to enable different attributes, such as shape and orientation. This consisted of an array of 8x8 sensors in a 4-inch-square pad [Wolfeld 81].
1982	Flexible Machine Interface	The first multi-touch system developed by Nimish Mehta at the University of Toronto. The system consisted of a frosted-glass panel, producing black spots in the back of the panel. This allowed simple image processing, marking white spots as non-touch and black spots as touch.
1983	Soft Machines	Soft Machines: A Philosophy of User-Computer Interface Design by Nakatani et al. provides a full discussion about the properties of touch screen. The attributes discussed outline certain contexts and applications where they can be used [Nakatani and Rohrlich 83].
1983	Video Place - Video Desk	A multi-touch vision-based system [Krueger et al. 85], allowing the tracking of hands and multiple fingers. The use of many hand gestures currently ubiquitous today, was introduced by Video Place. These included pinch, scale, and translation.
1983	Infrared Touch	Hewlett-Packard used the infrared touch in one of its products, as shown in Figure 8.1
1984	Multi-Touch Screen	Multi-touch screen using capacitive array of touch sensors overlaid on a CRT. It had excellent response. This machine was developed by Bob Boie and presented at SIGCHI in 1985.

Continued on next page

Table 8.1 – *Continued from previous page*

Year	Name	Description
1984	Window KeyPad	Advertisement of Projected Capacitive by Ronald Binstead. He provides a history and a series of patents, which were later acquired by 3M [Binstead 07]. See Figure 8.2.
Mid-1980s	MicroTouch Systems	MicroTouch (later acquired by 3M) introduced their first commercial surface-capacitive touch system.
1985	Zenith	Robert Adler, who invented the TV remote control "clicker" in 1956, also invented a surface acoustic wave.
1985	Multi-Touch Tablet	Lee, Buxton, and Smith developed a multi-touch tablet with the capability of sensing not only location but degree of touch for each finger. The technology used was capacitive [Lee et al. 85]. It is important to note that the development of this tablet started in 1984, when the Apple Macintosh was released.
1985	Sensor Frame	Paul McAvinney at Carnegie-Mellon University. This multi-touch tablet, which read three fingers with good accuracy (errors could occur if there were shadows), had optical sensors in the corners of the frame. The sensors allowed the system to detect the fingers when pressed. In a later version, the system could detect the angle of the finger when coming in contact with the display.
1986	Bi-Manual Input	Buxton and Meyers studied the effect of bi-manual multi-touch. One task allowed positioning and scaling, while the hand performed the selection and navigation task. The results reflected that continuous bi-manual control provided a significant improvement in performance and learning [Buxton and Myers 86]. The control was very easy to use.
1991	Bidirectional Displays	Buxton and colleagues, Xerox PARC used a high-resolution 2D a-SI scanner technology with an added layer to make them displays.
1991	Digital Desk Calculator	Wellner developed a front projection tablet top system that sensed hands and fingers, as well as a set of objects. He demonstrated the use of two-finger scaling and translation [Wellner 91].
1992	Simon	IBM and Bell South introduced the first smartphone that operated with single-touch.
1992	Wacom Tablet	Wacom released digitizing tablets, which included multi-device and multi-point sensing. The stylus provided position and tip pressure, as well as the position of the mouse-like device, enabling commercial bi-manual support [Leganchuk et al. 98].
1995	Graspable Computing	The foundation of what has become graspable or tangible user interfaces to use with multi-touch devices. [Fitzmaurice et al. 95]. The work by Fitzmaurice included Active Desk as well.
mid-1990s	Dynapro Thin Films	Dynapro started commercializing mutual-capacitance (projected capacitive). The technology was later renamed by 3M as near-field imaging.

Continued on next page

Table 8.1 – *Continued from previous page*

Year	Name	Description
1997	The metaDESK	metaDesk was developed by Ullmer et al. [Ullmer and Ishii 97], which demonstrated the use of tangible user interfaces(TUI). This addressed the problem that "dynamic assignment of interaction bricks to virtual objects did not allow sufficient interaction capabilities" [Müller-Tomfelde 10].
1998	Zyntronic	Commercialization of large-format self-capacitive (projected capacitive). Invented by Ronald Beinstead.
1999	Infrared Touch	Invention of waveguide infrared touch between 1997 and 1999 by [Sana 99].
early 2000s	SoundTouch	Sampled bending-wave touch invention, later to be known as Acoustic Pulse Recognition™ by Tony Bick-Hardie.
early 2000s	Sensitive Object	Sampled bending-wave touch invention, later to be known as ReverSys™. It is not clear if SoundTouch or Sensitive Object came first or if they were simultaneous.
2001	Diamond Touch	Diamond Touch addressed the multi-user problem with its multi-touch system [Dietz and Leigh 01].
2003	Planar	Technical paper about in-cell light sensing [Boer et al. 03].
2004	Wacom TouchKO	Multi-touch technology that uses proprietary approach called Reversing Ramped-Field Capacitive (RRFC™) [Microsoft 07].
2005	FTIR	Han introduced FTIR [Han 05].
2006	NXT PLC	Commercialization of real-time bending wave touch called Dispersive Signal Technology™(DST).
2007	Apple iPhone	Apple introduced the iPhone, a smartphone with multi-touch capabilities.
2007	Microsoft Surface Computing	Microsoft released an interactive tabletop surface for multiple fingers, hands, and tangible objects. This led to the later introduction in 2011 of Surface 2.0.
2009	PQLabs	Commercialization of multi-touch infrared
2011	Surface Computing 2.0	Second generation of the Microsoft Surface.
2012	iPhone 5	iPhone 5 with in-cell mutual capacitance (projected capacitive).
2013	Tangible for Capacitive	Voelker et al. developed PUCs. A tangible device for capacitive multi-touch displays [Voelker et al. 13b, Voelker et al. 13a].
2014	Houdini	Hüllsmann and Maicher demonstrated the use of LLP [Hüllsmann and Maicher 14].

8.2   Hardware

This section covers different types of hardware devices for multi-touch technology. In particular, capacitive touch is covered with more detail because of the availability

Figure 8.1: HP 150 Magazine advertisement.

and pervasive use today. The largest emphasis is given to projected capacitive technology as it is the most used today with a lesser emphasis on optical and vision technologies for touch. Some touch technologies are not covered but additional information can be found in [Walker 14].

8.2.1 Projective Capacitive Technology

Projected capacitive (p-cap) technology has become pervasive in the day-to-day use of consumer electronics with the introduction of the Apple iPhone and all the smartphones and tablets thereafter. Geoff Walker (currently at Intel), an expert on multi-touch technologies, has predicted[2] p-cap significant growth in the coming years for commercial applications [Walker 14, p. 99]. This is in addition to the adoption that it has enjoyed since the introduction of the iPhone in 2007.

We cannot be certain if touch input was measured using capacitive technology before the 1960s but it is the earliest record we were able to find. The first p-cap display was used for air-traffic control in the United Kingdom (see Table 8.1) in

---

[2]We don't like to make predictions with technology but rather see the amount of work that has come before it. This tells us that the technology may be on good ground. However, new technologies are coming online every day so it is hard to be sure what will be the most adapted technology in years to come. With this said, we do take Walker's prediction very seriously because of his experience.

Figure 8.2: Window keypad 1984. (With permission from Ronald Binstead and BinsteadDesigns.com).

1965. For an additional time line of different touch technologies and major events, see Table 8.1. Projected capacitive technology (in particular, mutual-capacitance) has created certain expectations by users since the introduction of the iPhone, such as multi-touch capabilities, extremely light-touch, extremely smooth and fast scrolling,[3] and effortless, among others [Walker 14]. One of the trends with capacitive displays is to improve the use of multi-touch p-cap and digital pen. For example, Microsoft has used p-cap for multi-touch with the electromagnetic (EM) pen-digitizer[4] [Walker 14]. Touch and pen are not the only multi-modal input found with p-cap. For example, a point of sale (POS) uses IR technology for the touch while combining it with pressure-sensing piezoelectronics. This helps the system to know that the user is touching the display and it removes false-positive touches. Additional mid-air approaches (e.g., Leap Motion) is another option of making touch a multi-modal input device.

P-cap detects the touch "by measuring the capacitance at each addressable electrode" [3M 13], as shown in Figure 8.4. In other words, if a finger or a

---

[3]This is not always the case due to problems with hardware or software.
[4]Wacom is the dominant vendor of EM pen-digitizers.

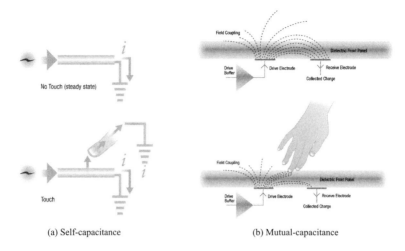

(a) Self-capacitance   (b) Mutual-capacitance

Figure 8.3: Multi-touch capacitance technology.

†: ©2014 3M.All rights reserved.
3M, the 3M logo, and
other 3M marks are owned by 3M.

Side Note 8.1: Piezo Electronics

A piezoelectric sensor is used to measure changes in pressure, acceleration, force, or strain using the piezoelectronic effect [Wikipedia 15h]. This measurement is done by converting those changes into electrical charges, which is called piezoelectricity, which is the electric charge that accumulates in certain solid materials after applying mechanical force to them [Wikipedia 15j].

---

conductive stylus gets closer to the electrode, it disturbs the electromagnetic field. When this occurs, the change in capacitance allows the touch to be detected with a specific location, with coordinates X and Y. P-cap has two main forms of sensing the touch: Self-capacitance and mutual-capacitance, shown in Figures 8.3a and 8.3b, respectively.

Self-Capacitance

In the case of self-capacitance, the measurement of the electrode is with the ground. One option is to use a multi-pad with addressable electrodes (single layer), with a connection for each of them, as shown in Figure 8.5b. While this allows a multi-touch approach, screens greater than 3.5 inches become challenging because

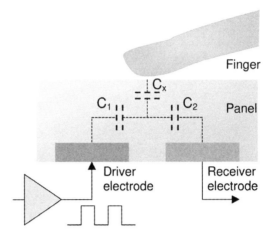

Figure 8.4: Projected capacitive working principle [Hainich and Bimber 11].

of the individual connection between the electrode and the controller. A second option is to use the row and column approach (dual layer), as shown in Figure 8.8a. However, this approach has "ghost" points, as shown in Figure 8.8b, because the electronics are not able to measure each individual intersection (the electronics can only measure each electrode). This limits the approach to a single or dual touch screen because it can provide false positive points, known as "ghost" points. When using the row and column approach, the system can determine which is the closest location. Then, using interpolation, the system can determine the location of a touch. The fact that self-capacitance is not ideal for multi-touch does not mean it cannot be used. Given its lower cost, if the device requires two finger interactions for basic gestures, it is possible to remove the "ghost" points at the software level. For example, a zoom gesture can be recognized because the points will be moving toward or away from each other (zoom in or out).

The p-cap sensor provides the information to the controller (explained in Section 8.2.1) to determine the contact point. In self-capacitance touch displays, a single or dual layer of transparent conductors is configured with electrodes. It is important to remember that each electrode is measured individually. Figure 8.6 provides a view of a dual-layer approach.

Mutual Capacitance

Mutual capacitance exists when two objects hold charges. Projected capacitance displays create mutual capacitance between columns and rows, where each intersects the other object, as shown in Figure 8.5b. In other words, an intersection between the electrodes measures the contact point. This is "accomplished by driving a single X electrode, measuring the capacitance of each Y (intersecting)

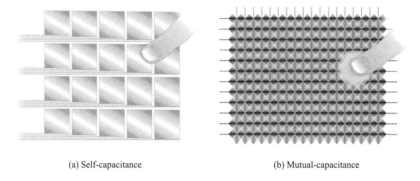

(a) Self-capacitance   (b) Mutual-capacitance

Figure 8.5: Multi-touch capacitance technology.

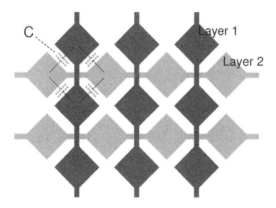

Figure 8.6: Projected capacitive touch panel [Hainich and Bimber 11].

electrode" [Walker 14, p. 40], repeating it for each X electrode until is complete. The system is able to measure multiple touches simultaneously during each screen scan. When the finger touches down near an intersection, the mutual capacitance is reduced, causing the threshold to indicate that a touch has occurred. The correct measurement of mutual-capacitance makes it very reliable and the preferred technology for multi-touch interaction. This avoids the "ghost" points from self-capacitance and provides accurate point detection as shown in Figure 8.7.

Each p-cap surface works with a controller. This controller excites the X electrode and measures the capacitance of the Y electrode. The analog values are converted using an analog-to-digital converter (ADC) running on a DSP chip. This DSP chip runs algorithms to remove undesired touches near the edges of the display ("grip suppression") and removal of unintended[5] touches ("palm rejection") [Wang and Blankenship 11, Walker 14]. Some of the examples driven by innovations on p-cap controllers are the significant increase in signal-to-noise ratio (SNR), which allows to use a passive stylus of 2mm tip [Walker 14]. The largest vendors of these types of controllers are Atmel, Cypress, and Synaptics.

The p-cap sensor in a self-capacitance touch display uses a single or dual layer of transparent conductors configured with electrodes. The most common approaches for placing the electrodes are [Walker 14]:

- **Rows and columns**: This approach utilizes an insulating layer, film, or glass substrate to spatially separate rows and columns of the electrode.

- **Diamond pattern**: This approach utilizes a diamond pattern of squares rotated at a 45°angle. These are connected "at two corners via a small bridge" [Walker 14]. It is important to note that the diamond pattern approach may use two spatially separated layers making the process straightforward. However, to make the displays thinner, a solution is to use a single co-planar layer but this requires additional processing [Walker 14].

There are different approaches on how to stackup mutual-capacitance. The most common case is to start (on top) with the cover glass ("lens"), decoration layer, optically clear adhesive (OCA) layer, diamond shape spatially separated Y electrodes (for sensing), touch-panel glass, diamond shape spatially separated X electrodes (for driving), LCD top polarizer, color filter glass, color filter, liquid crystal, thin-film transistor (TFT), and TFT array glass (at the bottom of this stack) [Walker 14]. Additional layers below that last layer mentioned (TFT array glass) are also present, such as bottom polarizer and backlight, among others [Walker 14]. Glass substrate is used for the touch screen but in some larger mobile devices, two layers of polyethylene terephthalate film (PET) film are used for each set of electrodes (X and Y) [Walker 14].

One of the problems for mobile devices, with the stack just described is the number of layers of glass, in particular, the fourth sheet of glass. The first two sheets are used for the LCD and the next layer is the protective and decorative sheet covering the LCD. The fourth layer of glass can be avoided by either using the "one-glass-solution" or the "on-cell" (also known as embedded touch) solution. As Walker describes, both of these are in direct competition [Walker 14]. The "one-glass-solution" adds the touch module to the decorative sheet. The "on-cell" solution removes the fourth sheet by placing the electrodes on the color-filter sheet, which is below the LCD's top polarizer [Walker 14]. Both solutions provide a lighter and thinner device using different techniques. In the commercial side, the "one-glass-solution" provides a continue streamline of revenue for touch

---

[5]However, having the ability to have access to those points may be a feature that a developer may want. See Section 2.2.2.

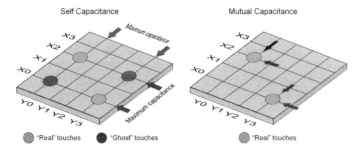

Figure 8.7: Self-capacitance and mutual-capacitance. (With permission from Geoff Walker).

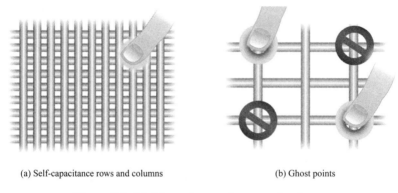

(a) Self-capacitance rows and columns   (b) Ghost points

Figure 8.8: Multi-touch capacitance technology.

†: ©2014 3M.All rights reserved.
3M, the 3M logo, and
other 3M marks are owned by 3M.

manufactures while the "on-cell" solution provides a continued streamline of revenue for the LCD manufacturers [Walker 14].

Finally, it is important to mention that while p-cap technology uses transparent conductors with indium tin oxide (ITO), there is another alternative. This is the use of 10-micron copper wire. The copper wire is not transparent but for larger displays, the current diameter becomes harder to be seen by the user. This is the primary reason that is used, since building large displays (40 inches or larger) with ITO increases the cost, reduces the quality of touch, and it really becomes unfeasible to do it at this time. For additional information and informative figures, the reader is referred to [Walker 14].

Surface Capacitive

Surface capacitive was introduced by MicroTouch Systems, which later was acquired by 3M and integrated into the 3M Touch Systems division. This technology is currently phasing out but there are places where it is still in use. For example, the gambling industry uses surface capacitive displays for their games.[6] This technology has advantages as its drag performance with their smooth surface is ideal and it is highly sensitive [Walker 14]. However, it does not support multi-touch, it is not as durable compared to other glass-based touch devices, and cannot be used with mobile devices [Walker 14].

The technology uses a conductive coating driven by an alternating current (AC) signal (1-2 volts in the range of 30-100 KHz) to each of the corners of the layer [Walker 14]. When the user touches the display, a small amount of current flows to the four corners. The contact point is determined by the current supplied to each of the corners, providing the magnitude proportional to the location of the contact point [Walker 14]. An improved version, invented by Touch Konnection Oasis (see Table 8.1) and commercialized by Wacom, is called reversing ramped capacitive (RRFC™). This technology solves the problems of surface-capacitive touch but it is still a single-touch device. To read more about surface capacitive, see [Walker 14, pp. 47-50].

8.2.2 Optical Touch Surfaces

Optical touch surfaces provide an alternate way to detect contact points. Optical approaches use image processing to determine the location and type of interaction with the surfaces. The basic concept of optical touch surfaces is to emit IR light and determine the X and Y position that is being covered by the finger. The case for the multi-touch, while similar, uses additional information to obtain the simultaneous multi-touch, which will be described later in this section.

The first type of optical touch was the PLATO IV (see Table 8.1), which provided a small grid for touch interaction. In 1983, HP introduced a 9-inch model CRT with touch capabilities, using optical touch technology. This technology has evolved, but there are some common advantages that it has offered. Most importantly, it scales well for larger displays, it can withstand direct sunlight (great for outdoors), and it does not require any substrate [Walker 14]. The evolution of the optical touch started with single-touch, moved to a 1.5-touch[7] from ELO TouchSystems [TouchSystems 09], and finally evolved into a multi-touch system. The latter is described in more detail next.

The optical (IR) multi-touch supports over 32 simultaneous contact points. While the concept is similar to the one for single-touch, the controller will use all the information available from all the receivers to capture the shadows of the objects [Walker 14]. PQ Labs[8] is one of the vendors of this technology and the one that holds a patent describing the functioning of their system [Lu 13]. The

---

[6]This may change over time as multi-touch games are desired in this industry; however, the gambling regulations makes the adoption of new technology slow.

[7]It provides some limited 2D interactions.

[8]http://pqlabs.com

system works by emitting light from an IR LED while detecting it with two IR receivers (or photo-detectors). This produces a one pixel image (usually converted to gray-scale), which shows the shadows of the objects between the IR emitted and the IR receivers [Walker 14]. By repeating this in extremely short intervals, simultaneous objects can be tracked with mathematical functions, such as the one described in PQ Labs patent [Lu 13]. The experience of the multi-touch will be determined by the implementation of the recognition algorithms provided by the controller. This technology offers object recognition, simultaneous contact points, and the system can scale to a larger display with less effort than other technologies. Nevertheless, there are some problems with optical multi-touch systems [Walker 14]: (1) performance issues (jitter and slower response, among others). (2) pre-touch problems. (3) minimum size for touch object. (4) inadequate use for some applications, such as a white-board, because of the low-resolution; (5) issues 1-3 also prevent optimal use for white-boards (or similar applications). PQ Labs does claim to have overcome some of these issues. However, neither [Walker 14] nor us have been able to verify those claims. Like in any decision when purchasing technology, it is important to understand, in our opinion, that marketing claims may not always go hand-in-hand with the actual specifications of the product. With this said, optical multi-touch technology does offer value and it should be explored further as one option, if the use requires the use of large displays. Additional approaches to optical tracking includes PIN-Diode Optical by Baanto[9] (ShadowSense™) and Planar Scatter Detection (in-glass solution) by FlatFrog.[10]

8.2.3 Vision-Based Optical

Another alternative to touch, popular in universities and large displays, is vision-based multi-touch technology, which utilizes cameras to obtain the contact-points (and other) objects positions. Vision-based optical technology provides additional features not available in regular multi-touch systems. One example is the ability to use tangible objects of any type. It is important to note that there have been advances in tangible technology for capacitive displays [Voelker et al. 13a]. In addition, depending on the configuration of the camera and the implementation of the computer-vision algorithms, it is also possible to detect objects and people beyond the normal use of a surface touch (e.g., mid-air interactions).

Frustrated Total Internal Reflection

The frustrated total internal reflection (FTIR) approach [Han 05] is based on the optical total internal reflection within an interactive surface. The electromagnetic waves are transmitted into the transparent surface given the following two conditions:

---

[9]http://flatfrog.com
[10]http://flatfrog.com

1. If the refractive index of the inner material is higher than the outer material.

2. If "the angle of incidence at the boundary of the surface is sufficiently small" [Müller-Tomfelde 10].

A common FTIR configuration uses a transparent acrylic pane. This pane injects infrared light using strips of LEDs around its edges. When the user touches down, the light escapes, and therefore, it reflects the surface display to be captured by a camera set perpendicular to the panel. In other words, the infrared light is "brought into the surface from the side where it is trapped" [Hülsmann and Maicher 14] until a user presses down onto the surface. Also, since the acrylic is transparent, the projector can be in the back of the panel. A computer vision algorithm is applied to obtain location and other features of the touch [Müller-Tomfelde 10].

Diffused Illumination

The diffuse illumination (DI) approach produces infrared light below its surface. DI uses a projector and an infrared-sensitive camera on the back of the surface. The infrared lighting is also placed behind the projection surface (opposite in this case to FTIR) "to be brightly lit in the infrared" [Müller-Tomfelde 10]. Given this configuration, DI technology allows for robust tracking of fingers and physical objects (tangibles). The advantage of physical objects, which use fiducial markers or size of their shape, gives a clear edge to DI technology. This approach also has the potential for hovering interaction.

A similar approach is called diffuse surface illumination (DI) that distributes the IR light across a surface with the acrylic containing "small reflective particles" [Walker 14]. DSI provides a similar approach to DI but with an uniform effect.

Laser Light Plane

The laser light plane (LLP) is another approach of an optical multi-touch system (see a variation to this approach, called LLP+ [Park and Han 10]). The LLP dates back to 1972 by Johnson [Fryberger and Johnson 72]. One of the major advantages that it has over DI and FTIR is that it is the most inexpensive system to build, as seen in [Hülsmann and Maicher 14], while remaining very effective.

The LLP system directs the infrared light above the surface. This gets "scattered at every touch point" [Hülsmann and Maicher 14]. The major advantage to infrared light is that it gets scattered above the display during the user's interaction. This enables fast and reliable tracking of fingers and tangibles, regardless of how fast the movements are from the user. This is because the image is rich in contrast.

The LLP can use acrylic surfaces as well, such as stable glass panes, which are less expensive than acrylic panes. Also, by using lasers, the "illumination becomes independent from the tabletop size" [Hülsmann and Maicher 14].

Side Note 8.2: The Buxton Chess Player's Syndrome

Some multi-touch devices, in particular optical- and vision-based devices, can recognize a touch before the user makes contact with the surface. While this may be a desired outcome for a hover gesture, it is not a feature desired for a touch event. This is what Bill Buxton calls the *chess player's syndrome*. This refers to the lack of agreement between the human and the computer on whether you have touched the screen or not (provided by Ken Hinckley).

The approach described in this section makes reference to the system used in Houdini [Hülsmann and Maicher 14]. There are alternative approaches to LLP, which can be found in *Exploring Multi-Touch Interaction* [Kaindl 10].

Integrated Cameras

MultiTouch[11] Ltd. developed an integrated camera system for multi-touch called MultiTaction™. This high-performance display is bulky and expensive but it has its niche applications given the strengths of this system [Walker 14]: immunity to external light, unlimited number of touch points and users, object-recognition (either with markers or shape-recognition), IR-emitting stylus ready, and it is great for multi-user interactive walls.

8.3   Multi-Touch and Its Applications

This section covers different techniques for multi-touch or techniques that can be extended for multi-touch. It also explains basic concepts of multi-touch implementation that are commonly found in different platforms.

8.3.1   Basics of Multi-Touch

It is important to understand traces before thinking about gestures. There are libraries that supply a limited number of gestures built-in.[12] Nevertheless, it is important to understand how to work with points and traces to create new APIs and move the state-of-the-art forward when it comes to multi-touch gesture recognition.

   The fundamental concept of multi-touch, at the programming level is that it works with the basic notion that a finger or multiple fingers move across the display. This is usually denoted by three states (events): down, moving, and up.

---

[11] http://www.multitaction.com

[12] Some third party libraries may claim to have multiple gestures but failed to recognize the gestures (which we experienced in one of our projects).

The complete movement is considered a trace, which starts at the moment the user touches the surface (down), moves the finger (moving), and lifts the finger (up). This mode is usually called raw touch to make a distinction of gesture recognition. Depending on the driver of the multi-touch system, or the software layer for the raw multi-touch API, there may be some small differences, including additional states (events) and data. For example, The WINAPI (Microsoft Windows 7 and higher[13]) provides the x and y coordinate of the display, the contact size (c_x and c_y), timestamps, and most importantly, an identification number (id) that identifies the trace, among other data fields [Kiriaty et al. 09]. The most important data fields required for a multi-touch system to be effective are the identification (id) and the screen coordinates (x and y). Each driver (or API if working at a higher level) will handle multi-touch data, therefore it is important to know your device. For example, a driver may report every point even if the user is not moving their fingers. This is great because it will allow the higher-level API or the application to know that the user is not moving and decide upon that information.

8.3.2 Multi-Touch Gestures and Design

After working with raw data, it is possible that the system may required gestures. Building your own gesture is a very interesting process because it allows different techniques and algorithms to be used, created, or modified.

It is important to know what a multi-touch gesture is before building it. If we look at the dictionary, a gesture is "a movement of part of the body, especially a hand or the head, to express an idea or meaning" [Stevenson and Lindberg 10]. Lü and Li defined a gesture in Gesture Coder (see Chapter 10) as "A multi-touch gesture consists of a sequence of finger configuration changes, and each finger configuration might produce a series of repetitive motions. A motion is repetitive when any of its segments triggers the same type of action as its whole" [Lü and Li 12]. Additional definitions can be found, for example the one provided by Apple in one of their patents [Apple Inc., Elias, John, Greer, Haggerty, Myra, Mary, Westerman, Wayne, Carl 07].

It is important to know that the definition should be decided on by the developer or designer but in time, it is likely that an accepted definition will emerge as the primary one. While it is possible for this book to give a definition for a multi-touch gesture, it is more interesting for the designer or developer to define what the gesture is. Some possible definitions are:

1. A multi-touch gesture starts when a user touches the surface and continues until the last finger has been lifted, as long as it has been recognized.

2. A multi-touch gesture starts when it is recognized and lasts until the gesture hits a value of decay $\{if(g < decay(g))\ g = nullptr;\}$.

---

[13]Microsoft Windows 8 has new functionality not available in Windows 7.

3. A multi-touch gesture starts when it is recognized and lasts until a new gesture is detected by a value of strength $\{if(g < strength(g_{new}))\ g = g_{new};\}$. This allows for continued strength.

4. A gesture is only recognized when the user has completed the gesture.

The most common gesture definition for strokes (e.g., letters and symbols) is 4. For multi-touch gestures where the fingers are involved (no pen or tangible objects), definitions 2 and 3 provide a clear path for good design. However, definition 3 proves to be more difficult to program. The first definition, while valid, is the most trivial definition, and in practice makes the interaction less fluid because if the user wants to do pinch and later swipe without lifting their fingers, the second interaction will not be recognized. At the end of the day, it all depends on the design of the application or the options provided by the API being used. Of course, the definition may change as soon as you introduce multi-modal interaction, for example, the use of multi-touch with either a pen, tangibles, or INS sensors. One of the recommendations by [Bowman et al. 04, p. 179] is to "match the interaction technique to your device," which is also explained further in [Zhai 95]. Several other questions when designing multi-touch gesture interactions are important, such as: (1) Do we impose a set of fixed gestures for the user or let the user create their own gestures? (2) Do we treat taps as gestures or a different entity all together? (3) Are multi-touch gestures natural or learned? The answers depend on the application and the needs of the developer. Question 3 is described in Section 8.3.5.

8.3.3   Touch Properties

Previously, we explored basic aspects of a multi-touch device and multi-touch gesture design. It is important to expand on some properties, as explained by Hinckley and Wigdor [Hinckley and Widgor 12]:

- **Touch versus multi-touch**: A touch device will only allow one touch as opposed to a multi-touch device that will allow two or more touches. The type of a touch device also varies as described in Section 8.2.

- **Touch data**: In Section 8.3.1, we described the typical raw data for multi-touch devices. However, this is not always the case. Some devices only provide a limited amount of information, such as the DiamondTouch surface [Dietz and Leigh 01]. Devices like the DiamondTouch only provide 1.5 DOF, such as bounding box. While some devices may not offer 2 DOF, they still can implement multi-touch gestures [Forlines and Shen 05].

- **Pressure and contact area**: The sensing of pressure and contact area are related. While contact area may be a surrogate of pressure, it is not equivalent. Pressure is the physical force applied onto the surface by the user.

The contact area, as the name implies, is the measurement of the user's surface area when the finger touches the surface. If the user presses hard onto the surface, it is likely to produce a larger area size; however, a user may produce a large area size by pressing softly. Take for example, placing the entire hand, very softly, onto the display. This will produce a large area size but will not determine if the user did it softly or hard. Another example offered by Hinckley and Wigdor is someone with long nails. His or her touch will produce a large area size but the actual force applied may have been light [Hinckley and Widgor 12]. While they are not equivalent, the fact that area size can be a delegate for pressure is a useful feature. For example, Benko and colleagues used the contact area to simulate pressure [Benko et al. 06], called SimPress (Simulated Pressure). This technique required users to "apply a small rocking motion with their finger in order" [Benko et al. 06] to click. Other examples include [Forlines and Shen 05, Davidson and Han 08]. There are touch devices that can sense pressure. Ramos and colleagues found that six pressure levels are optimal with appropriate visual feedback for users to discern [Ramos et al. 04]. An application created by Ramos and Balakrishnan includes Zliding (fluid zooming and sliding) [Ramos and Balakrishnan 05], among others [Ramos and Balakrishnan 07]. The new Apple Mac Book is built-in with "force touch" for the trackpad, which will provide a new dimension to developers.

- **Hand postures and shape-based input**: The ability to recognize shapes beyond the normal contact points of multi-touch is important. Early work by Krueger explored the interaction of the user's hands by using their silhouettes [Krueger 91]. However, this is not a trivial problem, in particular when dealing with capacitive multi-touch surfaces. For example, when using tangible objects, capacitive devices have problems maintaining contact size points, let alone the inability to recognize the gesture. An excellent effort and possibly a way forward with tangibles in capacitive multi-touch displays is the work by [Voelker et al. 13b, Voelker et al. 13a]. It is true that with vision-based systems, shape recognition presents less of a challenge but capacitive multi-touch is pervasive today (e.g., iPad). For example, Cao and colleagues created ShapeTouch, a prototype that allows the system to respond to an event of each individual[14] shape, as opposed to a centralized event system as a typical multi-touch system would operate [Cao et al. 08]. An approach to handle different types of inputs, such as shape-recognition, is found in "A Framework for Robust and Flexible Handling of Inputs with Uncertainty" [Schwarz et al. 10].

- **Beyond the display**: With devices like Microsoft Kinect, and Leap Motion among others, the extension of multi-touch is a critical design feature,

---

[14]This is an excellent approach to event recognition.

when available. In particular, with work being done with mid-air interaction [Walter et al. 13, Ni et al. 11], it is also important, as different types of displays and projections start working in tandem [dos S Chernicharo et al. 13]. Wilson and Benko expanded the interaction using depth cameras in [Wilson and Benko 10a]. Another example is multi-point feedback with mid-air gestures [Carter et al. 13a]. The most critical aspect is "to provide new capabilities that are differentiated well from direct touch and other inputs" [Hinckley and Widgor 12].

• **Additional information about the finger**: In an effort to enrich the user interaction, obtaining additional information about the type of finger being used [Lepinski et al. 10], the orientation of the finger [Wang et al. 09], and which user it belongs to [Holz and Baudisch 10, Holz and Baudisch 13], is additional information that can enhance the user's experience. The effort to recognize properties has primarily used vision-based touch devices or complementary cameras. For example, Murugappan and colleagues used depth cameras to differentiate users and recover touch posture [Murugappan et al. 12]. While vision-based has been used, efforts to find information using capacitive displays have also tried to obtain additional information. One example of the use of finger identification and capacitive touch displays is the effort by Harrison and colleagues, which employed the Touché [Sato et al. 12], which is a swept frequency capacitive sensing (SFCS) [Harrison et al. 12]. Additional information can be found in "Understanding Touch" [Holz and Baudisch 11].

• **Parallax**: Parallax error is a mismatch between the position sensed by the input device and the position perceived by the user. *Display parallax* "is the displacement between the sensing and display surfaces" [Hinckley and Widgor 12]. In general, 2 mm or less parallax error is acceptable. *Transducer parallax* is "any additional parallax error that may result from the offset between the tip of a mechanical intermediary and the actual component that is sensed" [Hinckley and Widgor 12].

• **Latency**: Input delays on an interactive system will produce a frustrating user experience. This is even more apparent on direct interaction, such as multi-touch display. Latency is the measurement of time that occurred since the initial physical action by the user is executed and the time that the system executes the action. It is important to keep the latency as small as possible to prevent the degradation of the user's experience. In general, between 75 ms to 100 ms is recommended for the user's experience not to degrade [Card et al. 91, MacKenzie and Ware 93, Hinckley and Widgor 12]. Additional information can be found about the user's perception about time and latency in the book titled *Designing and Engineering Time: The Psychology of Time Perception in Software* [Seow 08].

Table 8.2: Taxonomy of Surface Gestures [Wobbrock et al. 09]. With permission from ACM.

Dimension	#	Type	Description
Form	F_1	Static pose	Hand pose is held in one location
	F_2	Dynamic pose	Hand pose changes in one location
	F_3	Static pose and path	Hand pose is held as hand moves
	F_4	Dynamic pose and path	Hand pose changes as hand moves
	F_5	One-point touch	Static pose with one finger
	F_6	One-point path	Static pose and path with one finger
Nature	N_1	Symbolic	Gesture visually depicts a symbol
	N_2	Physical	Gesture acts physically on objects
	N_3	Metaphorical	Gesture indicates a metaphor
	N_4	Abstract	Gesture-referent mapping is arbitrary
Binding	B_1	Object-centric	Location defined w.r.t object features
	B_2	World-dependent	Location defined w.r.t world features
	B_3	World-independent	Location can ignore world features
	B_4	Mixed-dependencies	World-independent plus another
Flow	W_1	Discrete	Response occurs after the user acts
	W_2	Continuous	Response occurs while the user acts

Note: **w.r.t** means "with respect to"

8.3.4   Multi-Touch Taxonomy

In Section 2.7, we described how useful taxonomies are. In that particular section, we described input device taxonomies. In this section, we will describe taxonomies as it refers to multi-touch gestures. Some of the taxonomies were created during user-defined studies (e.g., [Wobbrock et al. 09]), which are described in Section 8.3.5.

Wobbrock and colleagues established a taxonomy for surface gestures, as shown in Table 8.2. The classification was done manually by the authors of "User-Defined Gestures for Surface Computing" [Wobbrock et al. 09]. This taxonomy provides four dimensions: forms (F), nature (N), binding (B), and flow (W), with each type. For simplicity, the taxonomy table provides a code for each type, starting with the letter identifying the dimension (F, N, B, W) with an index number (e.g., static pose is F_1).

This taxonomy (Table 8.2) provides an adequate breakdown of the gestures, as shown in their study [Wobbrock et al. 09]. In their study (see Section 8.3.5), they found that simpler gestures were physical gestures as opposed to the more complex gestures that were metaphorical and symbolic gestures [Wobbrock et al. 09]. This taxonomy is best placed in the context of their study, described in Section 8.3.5. The dimension and its type are discussed next [Wobbrock et al. 09]:

- **Form**: The form dimensions apply only to one hand. If the gesture requires two-hands, each hand is treated separately. The one-point contact is considered a gesture (F_5 and F_6), which are special cases of static pose (F_1) and static pose and path (F_3).

- **Nature**: The emphasis of this dimension are objects that are more "natural" to the users, which may represent the physical world or a metaphor. There are four types listed in Table 8.2, which are symbolic, physical, metaphorical, and abstract gestures. *Symbolic gestures* (N_1) are visual representations of an image, for example, tracing a caret (^) or the right-hand pointing (☞) to indicate an object to the right. *Physical gestures* (N_2) are meant to interact the same way you would interact with physical objects ("same effect on a table with physical objects" [Wobbrock et al. 09]). *Metaphorical gestures* (N_3) describe actions using something else to represent them. An example is bringing the index finger, middle finger, and ring fingers toward the thumb, which may represent grasping an object. Another example is a user simulating walking using two fingers on the surface. This all depends on the user, as "the answer lies in the user's mental model" [Wobbrock et al. 09]. The final type of gesture in this dimension is the *abstract gesture*. These gestures represent an abstract idea, such as triple-tapping an object to delete it.

- **Binding**: These types of gestures affect an object or the world (e.g., camera). *Object-centric gestures* affect the object. For example, rotating an object (two-finger rotation), which affects the object but not the world. *World-dependent gestures* affect the entire VE (world). For example, tapping on an object on a corner and dragging the object off-screen. *World-independent gestures* "require no information about the world" [Wobbrock et al. 09] and can happen anywhere. The only exception is temporary objects that are not part of the world environment. *Mixed dependencies gestures* are gestures that while they may affect an object with one hand, the other hand may be anywhere on the display. An example is using a two-hand gesture, with one hand in one object and the other one outside of the object.

- **Flow**: This dimension of gestures describes the flow of gestures as either discrete or continuous, previously noted by [Wu et al. 06, Baudel and Beaudouin-Lafon 93] and described in this taxonomy defined by [Wobbrock et al. 07]. A *discrete gesture* is "delimited, recognized, and responded to as an event" [Wobbrock et al. 09]. For example, a question mark to request help from the system. A *continuous gesture* is considered to be ongoing, such as a resize gesture.

The taxonomy provided by Wobbrock and colleagues provided a great classification for multi-touch gestures. Some other researchers have used this taxonomy.

One of the examples is the work by Buchanan and colleagues (see 8.3.5), which looked at how to define multi-touch gestures for 3D objects [Buchanan et al. 13]. It is possible to find ways to extend or improve this taxonomy. For example, Ruiz and colleagues added a classification of action (e.g., answer call) or navigation (next) for mobile interaction [Ruiz et al. 11]. Grijincu and colleagues provided an alternate classification based on [Wobbrock et al. 07], which looked to provide less ambiguity [Grijincu et al. 14]. Finally Cohé and Hachet provided additional dimensions for 3D manipulations [Cohen et al. 00].

8.3.5   Are Multi-Touch Gestures Natural?

What is learned and what is not for us humans is beyond the scope of this book. However, it is important to understand if we can consider multi-touch gestures natural or not. A great example given by MacKenzie is that if we consider a light switch on/off functionality, is there a natural spatial relationship that the light and the switch share [MacKenzie 12]? In the United States, the light is off when the switch is down but in the United Kingdom it is on if it is down. Therefore, this is just a learned, cultural behavior that one assumes. In general, it is hard to determine what user interfaces provide natural behavior with the users. It may depend on the previous learned skills that the user has and the cultural behavior. This is important because there has been a growth in the term natural user interface (NUI) to describe the interaction of new devices (e.g., multi-touch) compared to older devices like the mouse. However, I think more important if a gesture is natural[15] or not, the right question is if the it is intuitive to the user. This word is defined in the dictionary as "using or based on what feels to be true even without conscious reasoning". Therefore (as stated already), we can ask if the device is intuitive to most users. Or a better question could be if the device is usable (see Section 1.2.1). One anecdotal example is one of the co-author's father[16] who had trouble using the computer but when devices like the Apple iPhone and the iPad were introduced, he found it much easier working with the new type of devices. We like to think that it has to do with the idea of Mark Weiser, that as technology becomes less visible, the more useful it becomes [Weiser 91]. One particular study by Wobbrock, Morris, and Wilson showed among other important findings that multi-touch interaction is not uniform but there are some gestures more common than others among people that never used a multi-touch device [Wobbrock et al. 09]. As stated by Hinckley and Wigdor, the study by Wobbrock and colleagues shows that "there is no inherently natural set of gestures" [Hinckley and Widgor 12] beyond the common ones that we have used. We explore this study next, which provides the user study about

---

[15]When I started the idea of this book, I was thinking of having in the title "natural user interfaces"; however, over time, based on my experience and the research that I have read in the past few years, I have become convinced that is not important if it is natural or not, as opposed to intuitive to the user or not – Francisco R. Ortega.

[16]Francisco's dad, who is 70 years old, keeps asking for a new iPhone and a new iPad. As of October 30th, 2015, Francisco's dad has the new iPhone 6

finding a set of gestures and a taxonomy of gestures. This study was an extension of their own previous work [Wobbrock et al. 05].

Wobbrock, Morris, and Wilson recruited non-technical people without experience with multi-touch devices, such as the iPhone or the iPad [Wobbrock et al. 09]. This removed the bias of users already accustomed to certain gestures with their phone or tablets. This study was done with a tabletop surface (Microsoft Surface.[17] Microsoft PixelSense also has large displays).

The approach taken by them ([Wobbrock et al. 09]) was to accept any gesture for a given action, regardless if it was considered to be valid or not. This does allow the experimenter to observe the unrevised behavior of the user [Wobbrock et al. 09]. In order to avoid further bias, they removed any object that may be similar to widgets found in known operating systems, such as Microsoft Windows or Apple Mac OS X. In addition, a generic application was chosen for this experiment (as opposed to a domain-specific application). The participants were given 2D blocks (e.g., squares) for their manipulation. The subjects were asked to perform manipulations with 27 referents. For each of them, they needed to use one-hand and two-hand gestures. It is important to note, as stated already, that this study allowed any gesture because it wasn't recognizing the gestures but only logging the contact points, video recording the users from four different perspectives, and the observations of two experimenters. The 27 commands given rated from 1–5 by the authors included: *move a little* (1.0), *move a lot* (1.0), *select single* (1.0), *rotate* (1.33), *delete* (1.33), *pan* (1.67), *zoom in* (2.00), *zoom out* (2.00), *previous* (3.00), *next* (3.00), *insert* (3.33), *paste* (3.33), *cut* (3.67), *accept* (4.00), *help* (4.33), *task switch* (4.67), and *undo* (5.00) [Wobbrock et al. 09]. The tasks were presented randomly to the users. The task would play a recorded voice. For example, the *pan* task would play: "Pan. Pretend you are moving the view of the screen to reveal hidden off-screen content. Here is an example" [Wobbrock et al. 09]. Once the recorded voice finished playing, the system would perform an animation showing what is expected from the user. The user watches a video with initial and final state of the interaction, showing the objective of the complete interaction needed. Given the 20 participants they had, the 27 gestures, and the two options for one-hand or two-hands, the total gestures were $20 \times 27 \times 2 = 1080$ [Wobbrock et al. 09].

To find the winning gesture from the participants, an agreement value is calculated for each of the referents, providing a percentage consensus. Therefore, for one type of referent, the group size (P_i) of identical gestures is divided by the total proposed set of gestures (P_r), as shown in Equation 8.1. An example of this equation for *select single* interaction is shown in Equation 8.2, where the group had size 11, 3, 3, and 3. In this particular case, two gestures were preferred for the same referent with the gesture having the largest group being selected as the winning one [Wobbrock et al. 09]. A simplified form for Equation 8.1 is shown in Equation 8.3 [Ruiz et al. 11], where t is a task member of the set T, P_i is the "set

---

[17]Not to be confused with their tablet line called Microsoft Surface and Microsoft Surface Pro.

of proposed gestures for t, and P_i is a subset of identical gestures from P_t" [Ruiz et al. 11]. The range for A (in either equation since they are equivalent) is between 0 an 1.

$$A = \frac{\sum_{r \in R} \sum_{P_i \subseteq P_r} \left(\left| \frac{P_i}{P_r} \right| \right)^2}{R}$$ (8.1)

$$A_{select\ single} = \frac{\left(\frac{11}{20} \right)^2 + \left(\frac{3}{20} \right)^2 + \left(\frac{3}{20} \right)^2 + \left(\frac{3}{20} \right)^2}{1} = 0.37$$ (8.2)

$$A_t = \sum_{P_t} \left(\left| \frac{P_i}{P_r} \right| \right)^2$$ (8.3)

Once the analysis was completed, twenty-two gestures were assigned a gesture, the *move a little* and *move a lot* were combined into one. Four tasks were not assigned a gesture. The gesture used for *insert* and *maximize* were primitive gestures of dragging and enlarge, respectively. For the other two tasks, *switch* and *close*, users performed gestures with imaginary widgets which were not available. In summary, a total of twenty-three gestures were mapped. These gestures are shown in Figures 8.9 and 8.10 [Wobbrock et al. 09]. The gestures shown in these figures correspond to the use of one hand and two hands. Some gestures were performed toward the edges of the display or outside of the displays. Gestures that are reversible, such as *zoom in* or *zoom out* are depicted for only one of the directions.[18]

Participants in the study [Wobbrock et al. 09] preferred one-hand gestures in most tasks (25 out of 27). This led Wobbrock, Morris, and David to create the gestures set shown in Figures 8.9 and 8.10 to include 31 one-hand gestures and 17 one-hand gestures. The reason to include two-hand gestures, is that while the users did prefer one-hand for most cases, some of the two-hand gestures had agreement scores that merit their inclusion in the set. Another interesting finding is that users in most cases performed reversible gestures (e.g., zoom in/out) for divided referents. In addition, the subjects did not always agree with the complexity of the referent, which was apparent by comments made by the subjects. Another question that was important to address was of how many fingers are needed for a given interaction. Most users, except for two of them, said that fingers did not matter. Most interesting, was a couple of users that expected the finger to be identified (index vs middle-finger), as in his/her mind, the tap of one finger is different from the tap from another finger. This is a very interesting. While anecdotal at best, it shows the importance of having additional features in multi-touch, other than just x and y position. This study found that 1–3 fingers were considered a single point gesture, while having 5-finger touch or the palm, as something else. It is true

---

[18]This also includes enlarge/shrink and next/previous.

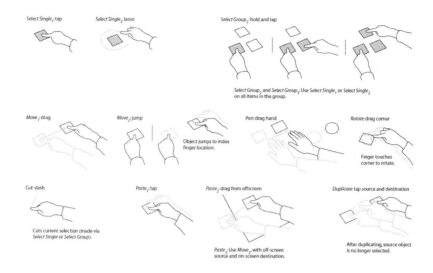

Figure 8.9: User-defined set gesture — Partial set A [Wobbrock et al. 09, Figure 4]. With permission from ACM.

that other systems have used different finger counts to make differentiation of the fingers, however, it is still not clear to us if this was due to the lack of training for the subjects of this experiment or if this could be replicated in other experiments with a different type of subject (e.g., experienced multi-touch users). This is why it is important in HCI to repeat experiments and expand on those experiments as expressed by [Greenberg and Buxton 08]. This has been experimented by others, as will be explained later in this section. Finally, three additional observations were made: (1) Some users had mental models of windows widgets and they acted upon imaginary widgets for some of their referents. (2) Some users performed gestures toward the edge or away from the screen to perform a task (3) A few users performed mid-air gesture interaction when working with the multi-touch. One example was the crossing of their hands denoting an "X" above the surface of the multi-touch display.

Following up their previous study [Wobbrock et al. 09], Morris, Wobbrock, and Wilson expanded their work with "Understanding Users' Preferences for Surface Gesture" [Morris et al. 10]. In this study, they added three sets of gestures by each of the researchers, a unified set of gestures (from the three authors), and user-defined gestures. They recruited twenty-two subjects without experience in multi-touch devices (gender was equally divided). The most interesting finding was that subjects preferred gestures authored by large numbers of people. Subjects also preferred the gestures that were chosen among the three researchers versus the gestures that belonged only to one researcher. Other interesting findings included:

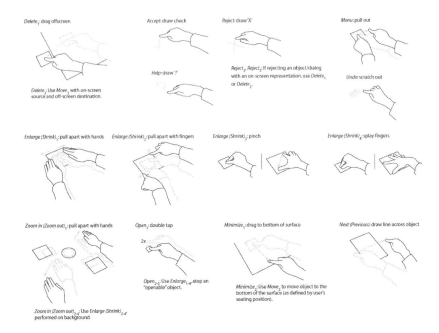

Figure 8.10: User-defined set gesture — Partial set B [Wobbrock et al. 09, Figure 4]. With permission from ACM.

(1) the desire to use one hand; (2) familiar gestures to the WIMP paradigm; (3) efficiency of the gesture (e.g., using one-hand versus two-hands or the number of fingers), among other findings. It was also found that gestures with analogies to the real world or common symbols were more accepted by the users than those that contained metaphors or abstract mapping. To see the new gestures added to their previous gesture set, see [Morris et al. 10].

Another subject study by Cohé and Martin looked at how to understand user gestures using a cube [Cohé and Hachet 12]. In this study, they gave subjects a cube to perform 3D transformations including rotations, translations, and scaling. Rotations are executed in a 90°angle (counterclockwise). Translations are performed twice the size of the cube along the X, Y, and Z axes. Scaling allows a 1.5 factor of the cube. The study was conducted in a scientific museum. Sixteen volunteers participated in the experiment with eleven of them being removed from the dataset due to problems with the equipment's sensitivity. One of their important findings is that physical gestures were preferred in the majority of their transformations. Their study [Cohé and Hachet 12] was expanded by [Buchanan et al. 13].

Another example is the one by Buchanan and colleagues on finding gestures for 3D objects. It expands on [Cohé and Hachet 12] and [Wobbrock et al. 09]. They include different types of 3D objects. Their 3D objects included valves (ball valve, gate valve, butterfly valve, and needle valve), a pull switch, a rotary switch, key switches, a locking clasp and door, a locking knife valve, a wrench, a pickle jar, and a key drawer [Buchanan et al. 13, Figure 2]. This study had 20 participants as in [Wobbrock et al. 09] but their subjects had experience with multi-touch displays. To remove the bias of previous learned experience by the users, they performed two trials: (1) asked them to perform a gesture that they felt appropriate for the task at hand and (2) perform a task as if this was a real object. They defined three types of gestures: (a) metaphorical gestures, which are those that use one-finger or they are representative of the physical motion that is required; (b) proxy gestures, which are those that act like physical motion but do not touch the object; (c) physical gestures, which are those that represent a physical motion on the object. Some of their interesting findings are that while the number of fingers used was "arbitrary in the interpreted gesture" [Buchanan et al. 13], the number fingers is important to indicate the amount of force or control applied to the object. They also found that the number of fingers increased during the first trial and second trial. They found (as expected) that the physical and proxy gestures were higher for trial two. For the second trial, metaphorical gestures were equal to 10.2%, proxy gestures were equal to 24.8%, and physical gestures were equal to 65.0%. However, for the second trial, proxy and physical gestures were higher than expected. For this trial, metaphorical gestures were equal to 41.5%, proxy gestures were equal to 12.2%, and physical gestures were equal to 36.3%. This indicates that for some physical gestures for real-world 3D objects, the use of a physical gesture lends itself better for that type of motion.

The experiment for user-defined gestures has also been studied in devices that use more than touch. For example, Ruiz, Li, and Lank studied motion-gestures with an Android phone (Google Nexus One) [Ruiz et al. 11]. They asked users to find gestures for 19 tasks, which were grouped in two main categories: action and navigation. The action tasks were divided between system/phone and application task. The system/phone task included answering a call, hanging up a call, and voice search, among others. The application task included act on selection. For the navigation tasks, the system/phone tasks included home screen, application switch (next), application switch (previous). For the application, tasks included pan left, pan right, pan up, pan down, zoom in, and zoom out, among others. This experiment allowed them to use similar criteria in other experiments [Wobbrock et al. 05, Wobbrock et al. 09, Buchanan et al. 13, Cohé and Hachet 12]. For example, one very common gesture for answering the phone was picking up the phone toward the user's ear. To hang up the phone, the users took the phone away from the ear and placed it face down. Their users were "very receptive to using motion gestures" [Ruiz et al. 11].

The most important lesson from the experiments described in this section is that users prefer their own gestures. In cases where this is not a feasible option, the best option is to create a gesture-set from as many users as possible, leaving as a last resort the design of gestures by a designer. Of course, if that is the option, a few designers working on a set is better than one, as was shown by [Morris et al. 10]. Other studies have asked users to create their own gestures. For example, Frisch and colleagues [Frisch et al. 09] asked users to define gestures for diagram editing and diagram sketching as an alternative to sketching with pen on a white-board. Seventeen participants of this study were asked to perform gestures for 14 operands using either one-hand, two-hands, and two-hands with pen and touch, for a total possible of ($17x14x3$) 714 gestures (however the actual recorded number was 658 gestures). In their study, they mapped a gesture to a referent, creating a set of gestures with fourteen elements [Frisch et al. 09]. Valdes and colleagues also studied user-gestures [Valdes et al. 14]. A more general discussion, questioning naturalism in 3D user interfaces, published in the *Communication of the ACM*, provides some interesting arguments [Bowman et al. 12]. The memorability study by Nacenta and colleagues is analyzed next [Nacenta et al. 13].

Gesture Memorability

Nacenta and colleagues conducted a study of memorability of pre-designed gestures versus user-defined gestures [Nacenta et al. 13]. While other similar efforts [Wobbrock et al. 09] concentrated in finding out if user-defined gestures are preferred or not, the study by Nacenta and colleagues concentrated on the question of memorability of gestures: "Can users remember gestures they define themselves better than pre-designed or arbitrarily assigned set?" [Nacenta et al. 13]. Their study included three experiments [Nacenta et al. 13]. A follow-up study was conducted later [Grijincu et al. 14].

The study was conducted with 6, 8, and 18 subjects for each experiment, which included four-day sessions with three applications: image editing, web browsing, and word processing [Nacenta et al. 13]. This included three phases: learning, reinforcement, and testing gestures for user-defined set, pre-defined set, and random set. The learning/creation phase was used to teach the users about the subjects or to allow them to create their own gestures. The reinforcement allowed them to practice what was just learned. The next day, the users were asked to recall the gestures and use them (testing phase). This last set represented pre-defined gestures to allow for a baseline and provided a different set of gestures for the third application. A four-day trial always includes the testing phase the day after the learning and reinforcement phase, as shown below:

- Day 1 (40 minutes)

    - Learning: user-designed gestures

    - Reinforcement: user-designed gestures

- Day 2 (60 minutes)

    - Testing: user-designed gestures

- Learning: pre-designed gestures
- Reinforcement: pre-designed gestures

• Day 3 (60 minutes)

- Testing: pre-designed gestures
- Learning: random gestures
- Reinforcement: random gestures

• Day 4 (40 minutes)

- Testing: random design gestures

Each of the experiments they tried in [Nacenta et al. 13] allowed them to conclude very interesting findings, which agree with similar findings in [Wobbrock et al. 09], as well as other studies. The most important finding in our opinion is the recall rate difference of 24% between user-defined and pre-designed gestures. User-defined gestures were easier for the subjects to recall. This difference was consistent among different time lapses for the users. In addition, users perceive an advantage when utilizing user-defined gestures. The possible explanation given by Nacenta and colleagues is that subjects recall user-designed gestures more than other sets of gestures because of their own pre-established memory association [Nacenta et al. 09]. As already stated in this section, user-designed sets are not always a possibility. If that is the case, it is best to either collect the right gesture set from a user study (or rely on the previous studies (e.g., [Wobbrock et al. 09]) or newer ones that emerged). The other alternative if those options are not feasible is to design the gestures with a few experts. This should yield a better gesture set.

8.3.6 Touch: Multi-Modality

Multi-modality interaction refers to the use of more than one device or type of interaction. A very common approach is the use of two devices, as it is with the pen and touch interaction. One of the reasons that two-device interaction is popular is because humans do many type of tasks with both hands. One of the major inspirations for the work of two-handed input is due to the publication by Guiard in 1987 titled "Asymmetric Division of Labor in Human Skilled Bimanual Action: The Kinematic Chain as a Model" [Guiard 87]. This is covered in more detailed in Chapter 7. However, the amount of work for pen and touch deserves to be mentioned here with the emphasis on one of those devices being a multi-touch input system. Multi-touch technology has not displaced the pen. On the contrary, the study of pen and touch working together has increased in the past few years. [Hinckley et al. 10a, Hinckley et al. 10b, Hinckley et al. 10c]. This section covers the multi-modality of multi-touch, in particular, touch and pen.

Side Note 8.3: Native Dual Mode

Lenny Engelhard, from http://www.n-trig.com, created a native dual-mode digitizer for pen and multi-touch [Engelhardt 08]. The device, named N-trig DuoSense™, provides a multi-touch capability using an ITO capacitive sensor with N-trig proprietary electronics and DSP algorithms that enable pen input (passive). The device aims to achieve dual modality of pen and touch, with palm rejection and other features at the firmware level. They also provide some multi-touch gestures available at the firmware. As we have seen in this chapter, the combination of pen and touch is important and companies will continue to push the envelope to make the input devices more reliable.

While this part of the book covers in detail "Pen + Touch = New Tools" by Hinckley and colleagues [Hinckley et al. 10c], the study of two-hand input has been studied for many years. In 1986, Buxton and Myers studied two-handed input [Buxton and Myers 86]. They used a PERQ I workstation by PERQ System Corp. The devices used were a graphics tablet (with four buttons) and a slider device. The keyboard was removed for the purpose of this study. The graphics tablet (Bit Pad-1) was used in absolute mode to control the tracker (cursor) having a direct mapping with the display. The slider box used a proportional (relative) motion, having the effect of a one-dimensional mouse. Buxton and Myers conducted two experiments. The first experiment needed to determine if users would use two hands or one. None of the users were told that both devices could be used at the same time. The most important observation was that almost all the users (all but one of them) used both hands simultaneously. The second experiment, having established that users will use both hands, needed to determined if they were common tasks where users would prefer the two-handed approach. The specific task chosen was to have the screen partition in two, with the top part of the display showing a partial document (80 x 24 lines) and the bottom part showing one line with the task for the user to perform. The selection was done with the puck on the graphic tablet. The user was required to navigate the document to find the line since the actual word was never shown in the display to force the user to perform the action. One group of subjects used one hand and the other group used two hands. An interesting result of this experiment was that the two-handed approach outperformed the one-handed approach both for experts and novices: (1) experts outperformed their peers by 15%. (2) novices outperformed their peers by 25%. Another interesting result is that the gap between experts and novices was reduced when using two hands. The gap between experts and novices when using two hands was 32% ($p = 0.02$) as opposed to an 85% ($p = 0.05$) gap for the use of one hand. Also, experts using one-hand outperformed novices using two-hands by only

12%. This means that partitioning navigation and selection tasks "between the two hands results in improved performance for experts and novices" [Buxton and Myers 86]. A final observation in their experiment was that the use of two hands was more simultaneous in the first experiment compared to the second one. They attributed this to the task of the second experiment being more difficult [Buxton and Myers 86]. Later in 1993, Bier and colleagues provided specific UI that can exploit the use of two-handed interaction with their multi-handed interfaces in "Toolglass and Magic Lenses: The See-Though Interface" [Bier et al. 93]. Around the same time, Chatty also provided user interfaces for two hands [Chatty 94a, Chatty 94b].

In the 1990s, additional efforts were made to study two-handed interactions. For example, Kabbash and MacKenzie looked at the human performances using input devices with the preferred and non-preferred hands [Kabbash et al. 93]. Using a Fitts' law (see 7.2.1) study with all right-handed subjects, they asked the subjects to perform *point-select* and *drag-select* tasks using either: (1) a standard mouse; (2) Wacom tablet with stylus (model SD42x) used in absolute mode and a pressure sensitive stylus; (3) a Kensington trackball on a Apple Macintosh II. The first group had the input devices mentioned to the right of the keyboard while the second group had the input devices to the left of the keyboard. Their study led them to find that when tasks have equivalent difficulty, the preferred-hand (the right-hand for this experiment) had an advantage for target width but the non-preferred hand had an advantage for amplitude [Kabbash et al. 93]. This extended the findings by [Todor and Doane 78]. Another interesting effort was to provide a mouse for the non-preferred hand, called *PadMouse* [Balakrishnan and Patel 98]. Hinckley and colleagues published "Cooperative Bimanual Action" [Hinckley et al. 97]. This study further supported Guiard's Kinematic Chain [Guiard 87]. One of the hypotheses provided by Hinckley and colleagues was: "The hard task is asymmetric and the hands are not interchangeable" [Hinckley et al. 97]. In particular, their study led them to believe that lateral asymmetry has several qualities: (1) In mass asymmetry, where subjects were holding the tool, tremors were visible in the left hand; however, the greater mass helped to reduce the instability. (2) Having the right view of the objects was important because when the object visibility was not the best, the performance of the task would suffer. (3) Referential task: The task becomes easier to perform when the user is able to manipulate one object while holding a stationary object with the other hand. Additional findings were also aligned with [Guiard 87]. Later, Hinckley and colleagues extended the three-state model designed by Bill Buxton [Buxton 90] to include bi-manual input [Hinckley et al. 98]. Leganchuck, Zhai, and Buxton studied the manual and cognitive benefits of bi-manual input [Leganchuk et al. 98]. Their study supported that both two-handed techniques outperformed the one-handed technique. In addition, they found that as tasks become more cognitive demanding, the two-handed approach will yield better results. Two-handed multi-touch was also studied by [Cutler et al. 97]. Their observation also showed that users found two-handed interaction useful. Additional work in the 1990s included [Casalta et al. 99, Balakrishnan and Hinckley 99], among others.

Later in the 2000s and recent 2010s there has been additional work. Balakrishnan and Hinckley looked at the symmetry of bi-manual interaction [Balakrishnan and Hinckley 00]. While their conclusion about symmetry needed further research because of different results in a different study [Peters 81], they are still important to consider. One of their recommendations based on their study is that when both hands are not operating "nearby in the focal visual field should be avoided" [Balakrishnan and Hinckley 00]. Given this observation, the use of both hands for navigation tasks offered the necessary feedback since the flow occurs for the entire display. Another example of using both hands in a symmetrical manner is the use of map navigation. In other words, as stated by the authors: "we see that decreased parallelism does not (except when visual integration is lacking)" [Balakrishnan and Hinckley 00] affect the level of symmetry. Other works include a bi-manual interaction on a tablet top display [Yee 04], the bi-manual curve manipulation [Owen et al. 05], symmetric bi-manual spline manipulation [Latulipe et al. 06], among others [Myers et al. 00, Matsushita et al. 00, MacKenzie and Guiard 01, Butler and Amant 04, Ortega et al. 13b]. Brandl and colleagues provide a very interesting effort about bi-manual pen and touch, published in 2008 [Brandl et al. 08]. We will expand on recent work by Hinckley and colleagues about pen and touch, which provides an insight into multi-modality of both devices [Hinckley et al. 10c].

It is important to see how touch and pen compare to each other. A complete comparison table is found in [Hinckley and Widgor 12, p. 103]. While it depends on the design of either input device, there are some properties that can be compared in the context of a single user: Pen has one well-defined contact point while touch has one or more contact points. In addition, touch may have additional capabilities (depending on the system): (1) shape information [Cao et al. 08], (2) finger orientation [Wang et al. 09]. Occlusion is also a problem for both devices; however, the small tip of the pen produces a much smaller occlusion. For the pen, it is expected that the person will use their dominant hand.[19] In the case of touch, users can use one or two hands. While touch does not have buttons (other than widgets on the displays), pens may have buttons. However, augmenting touch with other devices is possible. In general, touch does not require force (except for resistive touch) but the pen requires a minimal amount of pressure. Elementary actions for touch and pen are different: (a) Touch includes tapping, holding, dragging a finger, and pinching; (b) pen includes tapping, dragging, and drawing a path. False inputs[20] for pen and touch also differ, as shown below [Hinckley and Widgor 12]:

- Touch:

---

[19]In some places, people were forced to use the right hand even if their dominant hand was the left hand. It is possible for a person to write with their non-dominant hand

[20]While those inputs may be considered false positives, to other designers they may be a necessary feature. Hinckley and colleagues stated: "accidental palm contact can be seen as a problem, or it can be viewed as an opportunity" [Hinckley et al. 10c].

- The *Midas touch problem* that happens when "fingers brush screen, finger accidentally rests on screen while holding the device" [Hinckley et al. 10c], among others.
- The *chess player's syndrome*. See Side Note 8.2.
- False contact points when using tangibles in capacitive surfaces (see [Voelker et al. 13a]).

• Pen:

  - Palm creates false inputs. Solutions have been proposed, as in the published worked by [Schwarz et al. 14]. See Side Note 8.4.

    * The actual palm creates one or multiple contact points if it is a multi-touch display, or a false point if it is a touch- or pen-enabled display.
    * Palm makes finger create false contact points because it drags as the user writes.
    * Anecdotally, the Microsoft Surface Pro 3 prevents the palm from producing a false positive input. See the chapter about Windows 8 and the Microsoft Surface palm available on our book website for additional information.

Hinckley and colleagues gave participants a paper notebook to observe their behavior [Hinckley et al. 10c]. Some of the behaviors observed by [Hinckley et al. 10c], shown in Table 8.3, allowed them to pursue some new interactions. The observations clearly show that pen and multi-touch have different roles. The authors point out that their results are not aligned with the results by Frisch and colleagues [Frisch et al. 09], which is discussed later. Hinckley et al. stated that "it would be a mistake" [Hinckley et al. 10c] to treat touch and pen interchangeably since users will already have learned behavior from the normal use of pen and paper. However, there are times that the use of pen and touch can be replaced with each other, for example, when using a radial menu. This led them to try new types of interaction where pen and touch could be combined [Hinckley et al. 10c].

• **Stapler**: This interaction allowed users to group items into a stack. The interaction metaphor uses the "staple" as a hold-and-tap gesture. Using the finger to select items, the user can group them together by using the pen to staple the items. This was rated as one of the favorite tools. (See observation *B7*, in Table 8.3.)

• **X-acto Knife**: This interaction metaphor allowed users to hold an object and cut objects using the pen as the X-acto knife. By allowing the pen to draw any path desired, the user could create very interesting cuts. (See observation *B5*, in Table 8.3.)

Side Note 8.4: Palm Rejection

Palm rejection is needed when using a touch device, in particular a multi-touch surface. It is important to have the option available to the UI designer in case it is a desirable feature. In a recent publication, Schwarz and colleagues provided a palm rejection technique [Schwarz et al. 14]. They identified five properties that allow them to distinguish the palm from a stylus tip: (1) The palm creates a large touch area. (2) The palm generates a segmented set of points in most multi-touch devices. (3) The segmented points tend to be clustered together. (4) The pen has a small and consistent area. (5) The palm moves very little. (6) The palm exists for a longer period of time than the touch of the pen and it happens several seconds before the pen initiates the contact with the surface.

Using their observation, they created a classifier, which led them to build a 97.9% true positive detection, with a very low number of false positives. Their paper provides some additional references for previous work but we believe that their work will create newer solutions, which will help the palm detection problem, as stated by Hinckley and colleagues [Hinckley et al. 10c].

- **Carbon Copy**: This allows the user to copy an object. The user will select the object by holding it with a finger and then proceed to "peel off" a copy with the pen. Note that this is different from copying the object by a menu option, which was provided to the users in this experiment as well. The copy option from a menu divides the process of copying into multiple steps, which include selecting, copying, and positioning. See observation *B2*, in Table 8.3.

- **Ruler**: The user holds the object with index and thumb while using the pen with the preferred-hand to stroke along the object. See observation *B4*, in Table 8.3.

- **Brushing**: The user holds an image and strokes the pen on the canvas to create a brush effect. The user may continue to brush the image to erase selected parts, which is similar (without the complexity) to the tool in Adobe called *Art History*.

- **Tape Curve**: The user draws with the pen while using the non-preferred hand to hold the "tape curve." Once the finger is lifted, the drawing reverts to freehand ink state. This is a common technique used by artists to produce straight lines. Hinckley et al. goes more in detail about this technique

Table 8.3: Paper Notebook User Behaviors [Hinckley et al. 10c]

B#	Type	Description
B0	Specific Roles	Subjects used the pen to write while working with images with their fingers.
B1	Tuck the Pen	Subjects tucked the pen between their fingers. This allowed them to move clippings with the same hand.
B2	Hold Clippings	Using their non-preferred hand, subjects held objects for short period of times.
B3	Hold while Writing	Hold a clip with non-preferred hand while writing with their preferred hand.
B4	Framing	Using their thumb and index finger to "focus attention on a source object" [Hinckley et al. 10c].
B5	Scrops	Subjects cut clippings with preferred hand. They used their non-preferred hand to hold the object.
B6	Extended Workspace	The user's workspace was extended beyond the notebook, which included additional clippings, and unused pages, among others.
B7	Piling	Subjects created piles of clippings.
B8	Drawing along Edges	Two subjects draw along the edge of a clipping.
B9	Hold Page while Flipping	Subjects hold part of the notebook with their non-preferred hand, while flipping a group of pages with their preferred hand, while tucking the pen

and they also pointed to "digital tape drawing" [Balakrishnan et al. 99] for additional information.

In addition to the techniques described above, Hinckley and colleagues added some additional enhancements to the pen + touch interaction, based on some of their observations (Table 8.3). One of them was to create a new object via the **bezel menu**, extending bezel-crossing gesture [Roth and Turner 09] while adapting the concept of marking menus and its considerations about novice-to-expert transitions in [Kurtenbach and Buxton 91]. This bezel menu is accessed by sliding a finger across this semi-transparent strip on the top of the display. Once the finger moves across this semi-transparent bar, the complete menu appears in the top of the display. Once the menu is open, the user may select any option available on this menu by tapping the option, which is the "novice" mode. For example, they could create a *post-it note* by tapping into the post it icon. This menu contains an "expert" mode as well, that allows the user to continuously move across the bezel menu to select the appropriate action. Additional interactions that combined pen and touch included flipping pages and extended workspace [Hinckley et al. 10c]. **Flipping between distal locations** supported the observation (B9) of users that held a page while flipping. This technique was implemented in a dual-display view requiring the user to rest a finger (non-preferred hand) near the margin of the page while flipping with the other hand. The **cross-screen pinch** allowed the user to zoom the current view to extend the workspace. While the user zooms with two fingers in this dual-view mode, he/she could also make notes with the pen.

Hinckley and colleagues showed that multi-modality improves user interaction and that multi-touch is not the whole story [Hinckley et al. 10c]. We agree with this premise. In general, Hinckley et al. found that one or more pen strokes "act in reference to an item" [Hinckley et al. 10c]. In general, users found that their approach "to combined pen and touch interaction" [Hinckley et al. 10c] was appealing. Hinckley and colleagues remind us of the gesture trap: "each additional gesture that one adds to a system proportionally reduces the value of all of the other gestures" [Hinckley et al. 10c]. Having stated the gesture trap, it is still important to keep working on multi-modality gestures to find the ones that work either for all systems or are specific to some domain. Hinckley et al. continues to expand on the work of pen and touch with his latest effort "Sensing Techniques for Tablet+Stylus Interaction" [Hinckley et al. 14].

Frisch and colleagues found [Frisch et al. 09] some interesting findings for multi-modal (pen + touch) interaction for diagram-editing and diagram sketching as an alternative to sketching with pen on white-board. In general, they found that one-hand interaction dominates most of the tasks, except for some tasks, such as scaling and zooming. This is aligned with [Wobbrock et al. 09]. Frisch and colleagues found that two-hand gestures rated high for users when "*moving a group of nodes*" [Frisch et al. 09]. However, some differences with [Hinckley et al. 10c] were that users did not perform many combination gestures with pen and touch. However, this could be explained because [Hinckley et al. 10a], based on their observations (see Table 8.3), were able to create gestures that utilized pen and touch. Frisch and colleagues were performing a different type of work, which is the user-design set of gestures similar to [Wobbrock et al. 09].

The bi-modal interaction of pen and touch is one of many bi-modal options. Many other types of interactions are important. Additional reading on other types of interactions includes free-air and multi-touch [Moeller and Kerne 12], gaze and touch [Pfeuffer et al. 14], pen and touch for games [Hamilton et al. 12], pen and touch for problem solving [Zeleznik et al. 10], gyroscope and touch [Ortega et al. 15], among others [Hasan et al. 12, Ruffieux et al. 13].

8.3.7   More about Touch

To achieve better user interaction between the screen and the user, studies like [Wang et al. 09, Wang and Ren 09, Wilson et al. 08, Cao et al. 08, Benko et al. 06] provided a different take on how touch information can be used. For example, Wang and colleagues studied finger orientation for oblique touches [Wang et al. 09]. Their study looks at property of touch to determine if the finger is oblique when touching the surface. In another study, Benko and Wilson studied dual-finger interactions (e.g, dual-finger selection, dual-finger slider, etc.) [Benko et al. 06]. Additional work dealing with contact shape and physics can be found in [Wilson et al. 08, Cao et al. 08]. In a very comprehensive review of finger input properties for multi-touch displays, [Wang and Ren 09] provided additional suggestions about touch, which another study made use of [Wang et al. 09]. Their suggestions were [Wang and Ren 09]:

• Five fingers provide different abilities and can be utilized for target selection.

• The index finger, middle finger, and the ring finger provide a more precise selection.

• Other features of touch are useful to extract finger properties. This includes:

  – Shape of finger contact area.

  – Size of contact area.

  – Orientation of contact finger.

Other studies looked to see when rotations, translations, and scaling actions are best if kept separate or combined [Nacenta et al. 09, Hancock et al. 07]. If combined actions are chosen, the user's ability to perform the operations separately may be limited [Nacenta et al. 09]. Additional studies have looked at when to use the uni-manual or bi-manual type of interaction [Kin et al. 09, Moscovich and Hughes 08a] for multi-touch. Some studies have concluded that one-hand techniques are better suited for integral tasks (e.g., rotations), while two-hand techniques are better suited for separable tasks [Kin et al. 09, Moscovich and Hughes 08a].

8.3.8   Multi-Touch Techniques

Hancock et al. provided algorithms for one, two, and three-touches [Hancock et al. 07]. This allowed the user to have direct simultaneous rotation and translation. The values that are obtained from initial touches T_1, T_2, and T_3 and final touches T_1', T_2', and T_3' are Δyaw, Δroll, and Δpitch, which are enough to perform the rotation on all three axes, and Δx, Δy, Δz to perform the translation. A key part of their study showed that users preferred gestures that involve more simultaneous touches (except for translations). Using gestures involving three touches was always better for planar and spatial rotations [Hancock et al. 07].

A different approach is presented in RNT (Rotate 'N Translate) [Kruger et al. 05], which allows planar objects to be rotated and translated, using the concept of friction. This meant that the touch was performed opposing the objects' movement or direction, causing a pseudo-physics friction. This concept was also referred to as "current." This particular algorithm is useful for planar objects and it has been used in other studies (e.g., [Reisman et al. 09]).

The spatial separability problem when dealing with 3D interactions (for multi-touch displays) was studied in [Nacenta et al. 09]. The authors proposed different techniques that helped the user perform the correct combination of transformations [Nacenta et al. 09]. The combination of transformation included scaling, translation + rotation, and scaling + rotation + translation, among others. From the proposed techniques in [Nacenta et al. 09], two methods yielded the best results. They were magnitude filtering and first touch gesture matching [Nacenta et al. 09]. Magnitude filtering works similarly to snap-and-go [Nacenta et al. 09], but it does not snap to pre-selected values or objects. It also introduced the concept of catch-up. This concept allowed "continuous transition between the snap zone and the unconstrained zone." [Nacenta et al. 09]. The other technique, first touch gesture matching, worked by minimizing "the mean root square difference between the actual motion and a motion generated with a manipulation subset of each model" [Nacenta et al. 09]. Their algorithm selects the correct technique using best-fit error and the magnitude of the transformation [Nacenta et al. 09].

8.4 Figures of Large Tabletop Displays

The following images represent some large tabletop displays (see Figures 8.11–8.14)

Figure 8.11: Smart box (CITE) – Courtesy of Marc Erich Latoschik.

Figure 8.12: Smart box (CITE) – Courtesy of Marc Erich Latoschik.

Figure 8.13: XRoads (CITE) – Courtesy of Marc Erich Latoschik.

Figure 8.14: XRoads (CITE) – Courtesy of Marc Erich Latoschik.

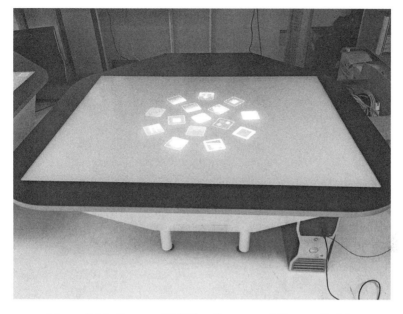

Figure 8.15: Synergy (CITE) – Courtesy of Shamus Smith.

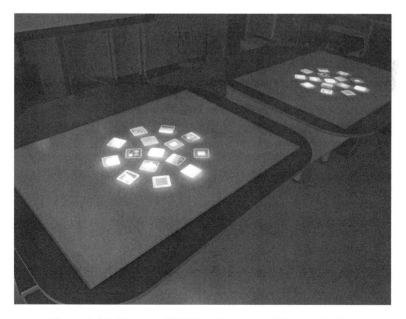

Figure 8.16: Synergy (CITE) – Courtesy of Shamus Smith.

Figure 8.17: 3D Stereo (CITE) – Courtesy of Will Rourk.

Figure 8.18: PQ Labs panel + display – Courtesy of Will Rourk.

Further Reading

If you need to read more about multi-touch hardware, see *Displays* by [Hainich and Bimber 11]. Chapter 2 on *Interactive Displays* provides a detailed understanding about different types of touch technology and the sustainability of certain touch technologies [Walker 14]. A great source for multi-touch is the *Information Displays* magazine, which is freely available at http://informationdisplay.org. This magazine is full of information about displays, which in some cases, includes multi-touch. For example, in the July/August 2014 issue (Vol. 30, No. 4), an article titled "New Trends in Touch" describes the current direction of touch. One of these is the use of the active-pen (used for the Microsoft Surface Pro). The pen provides very important characteristics, as already described in this chapter.

There are plenty of websites and books that described touch. One book that has been very useful is *Introducing Windows 7 for Developers* [Kiriaty et al. 09], which contains two chapters about multi-touch for the WINAPI. Qt framework also has its own wrapper for multi-touch (which in Windows uses the WINAPI) and plenty of documentation on their site (http://www.qt.io/developers/). Petzold provides some information for touch for people using the Windows Runtime (WinRT) [Petzold 13]. For recognition of multi-touch gestures using raw-touches, see Chapter 10 in this book. There are many additional readings. For example, age-related differences between touch surfaces and mouse [Findlater et al. 13], touch keyboard for non-alphanumeric input [Findlater et al. 12], and kids and touch [Anthony et al. 12, Anthony et al. 13b, Anthony et al. 13a]. In Chapter 10, Side Note 10.1, the topic of touch and kids is briefly covered.

Exercises

1. Using the knowledge gained in Section 8.2, create a survey report with the current multi-touch surfaces that are commercially available today. Create a table to compare the different attributes.

2. Create a small pilot where you ask subjects to perform different actions with multi-touch and pen. You can perform a paper-based prototype. The information provided in this chapter should be enough to conduct this pilot study but you can read further [Wobbrock et al. 09, Hinckley et al. 10c, Hamilton et al. 12]. This will help you to find a gesture set.

3. Repeating the previous exercise, try to create a pilot study that is domain-specific. This will help you to find a gesture set for a domain-specific environment.

4. Implement a multi-touch application that will allow you to record all the traces from the user. Following either one of the two previous exercises, now

perform a pilot study with the actual application. Note that you don't have to implement gestures. You have to provide the ability for the user to perform a user-based gesture to perform an action. For example, you may ask a user to duplicate a copy of a sphere with a gesture. However, the gesture does not need to be recognized. Ideally, you want to provide the illusion of the gesture being recognized. The idea of the exercise is to reproduce Wobbrock's experiment [Wobbrock et al. 09] in a different context.

9

Multi-Touch for Stereoscopic Displays

Dimitar Valkov

Always think of what is useful and not what is beautiful. Beauty will come on its own accord.
—Nikolai Gogol

9.1   Understanding 3D Touch

Notwithstanding the initial excitement around multi-touch interfaces it has quickly become apparent that using touch as the primary input modality poses (even in 2D contexts) some fundamental limitations for traditional interface design [Benko and Wigdor 10, Müller-Tomfelde et al. 10]. Some of the most important problems are the missing hover, occlusion and precision problems and – depending on the implementation – missing or non-adequate visual feedback. In particular, the size of the human fingers and the lack of sensing precision make precise touch screen interactions difficult [Benko et al. 06, Holz and Baudisch 10]. The approaches to handle this can be roughly separated into two groups. Approaches from the first group try to shift the problem into the interface design space. Therefore, *precise selection* is distinguished as a new interface requirement, which demands additional functionality and thus an extended set of interaction metaphors or techniques.

Characteristic for the second group of solutions is that they try to overcome or reduce the problem by modeling the user perception and action during the touch. Thus, these approaches try to identify a set of traceable features, which may help to better recognize the intended touch position. Examples of such features are the orientation of the user's finger [Holz and Baudisch 10] or visual features on the upper finger surface [Holz and Baudisch 11]. The primary benefit of these approaches over the pure "brute-force" interface solutions is that they help to understand the mechanics of a touch gesture, when used for input, and provide indications which help to identify the sources of the inaccuracy in traditional touch devices. Recent work has also identified the hand pre-shaping as a valuable source of information in this regard [Daiber et al. 12b]. Indeed, as the investigations of many neuro-psychological and robotic research groups have shown, there is a strong correlation between the course of hand shaping and the object, which is subject to interaction [Daiber et al. 12b, Santello et al. 02].

Extending the interaction environment to the third dimension usually intensifies the impact of these issues on the user experience and satisfaction [Schöning et al. 09] and introduces new problems which are negligible in monoscopic contexts. In this chapter we examine these problems in more detail and consider several high-level approaches to address them. Furthermore, we investigate the effect of stereoscopic parallax on the touch precision and discuss some of the design implications for designing stereoscopic 3D touch interfaces.

9.1.1 Problems with Stereoscopic Touch Interfaces

Recently many approaches for extending multi-touch interaction techniques to 3D applications with *monoscopic* rendering have been proposed [Hancock et al. 07, Martinet et al. 10, Reisman et al. 09, Wilson et al. 08]. For instance, Hilliges et al. [Hilliges et al. 09] have tested two depth sensing approaches to enrich the multi-touch interaction space beyond the touch surface in a tabletop setup with monoscopic projection. Hancock et al. [Hancock et al. 07] have introduced the concept of *shallow-depth 3D*, i.e., 3D with limited depth, in order to extend the interaction with digital 2D surfaces and have developed one, two, and three fingers interaction techniques for object selection and manipulation in this context. Martinet et al. [Martinet et al. 10] have designed a multi-view direct and a single-view indirect technique for 3D object positioning, and Reisman et al. [Reisman et al. 09] propose an energy-minimization technique for adapting 2D interaction to 3D transformation. The benefits of using physics engines for multi-touch input specification are discussed by Wilson et al. [Wilson et al. 08], and the interaction with objects with negative parallax on a multi-touch tabletop setup is further addressed by Benko et al. [Benko and Feiner 07], who have proposed the *balloon selection* metaphor to support precise object selection and manipulation in augmented reality setups.

In 2007 Grossman and Wigdor [Grossman and Wigdor 07] provided an extensive review of the existing work on interactive surfaces and developed a taxonomy to classify the current work and to point out new directions. This framework takes into account the perceived and the actual display space, the input space and the physical properties of an interactive surface. As shown in their work, 3D volumetric visualizations are rarely being considered in combination with 2D direct surface input. More recent surveys, e.g., Argelaguet and Andujar [Argelaguet and Andujar 13], still identify 3D direct touch interaction as a promising research direction, which is still not sufficiently investigated.

Direct touch interaction with *stereoscopically* rendered scenes introduces new challenges, as described by Schöning et al. [Schöning et al. 09]. In their work an anaglyph- or passive polarization-based stereo visualization was combined with FTIR-based touch detection on a multi-touch enabled wall, and approaches based on mobile devices for addressing the formulated parallax problems were discussed. A similar option for direct touch interaction with stereoscopically rendered 3D objects is to separate the interactive surface from the projection screen, as proposed by Schmalstieg et al. [Schmalstieg et al. 99]. In their approach, the user is provided with a physical *transparent prop*, which can be moved on top of the object of interest. This object can then be manipulated via single- or multi-touch gestures, since it has almost zero parallax with respect to the prop. Nevertheless, this requires instrumentation again, which may defeat some of the benefits of touch interaction.

9.1.2 Parallax Problem

Stereoscopic perception requires each eye to see a slightly different perspective of the same scene, which results in two distinct projections on the display. Depending on the disparity between the two projections, virtual objects can be presented with *positive*, *negative*, or *zero* parallax, resulting in different visual impressions.

- If objects are rendered with *zero* parallax they appear aligned with the plane of the display surface and are therefore perfectly suited for touch-based interaction [Schöning et al. 09]. Unlike the positive and negative parallax half-spaces, the zero parallax plane poses considerable constraints on the placement, dimensions, and form of the objects, and therefore contradicts the benefits of using stereoscopy, or 3D in general. In this context the question arises how sensitive humans are with respect to misalignment between visually perceived and tactually felt contact with virtual objects. For example, if an object is rendered at some small distance in front of the display surface, is the user going to move her finger through the object until she receives tactile feedback due to the contact with the display, and how small may this distance be? In particular, this may allow touch (and possibly multi-touch) interaction within stereoscopic environments without losing the advantages of common 2D techniques. While it is reasonable to assume that users tolerate a certain amount of misalignment between the perceived visual depth and the exact point at which haptic feedback is received [Valkov et al. 12], similar effects may lead to misalignment between perceived and actual object depth depending on object size, form, texture, etc. This may then infer the perceived alignment between two objects or between an object and the plane of the display surface. Nevertheless, if 2D interaction is intended or the displayed virtual objects have no associated depth information (e.g. UI widgets), the zero parallax plane may provide superior user experience compared with alternative depth distributions.

- Objects displayed with *positive parallax* are perceived to be behind the screen surface. These objects cannot be accessed directly, since the user's reach is limited by the display. Since the display surface usually has no visual representation in a stereoscopically rendered scene, trying to reach an object with strong positive parallax may become unnatural and in some cases even harmful. Nevertheless, if the object is close to the surface – rendered with shallow depth – the only effect is that the user receives haptic feedback shortly before its visual representation is reached, i.e., the points of receiving haptic and visual feedbacks are spatially misaligned. In Section 9.5 we discuss the problem in more detail and make the first steps toward determining within what range this misalignment is still unnoticeable for the user. For objects rendered with *strong positive* parallax, indirect techniques might be more adequate. For instance, one could cast a virtual ray from the camera's origin through the on-surface touch point and determine the first object hit by that ray or use some abstract interface widget [Daiber et al. 12a] to virtually move the user's touches in the 3D space below the surface. Even though such techniques are indirect, it is often claimed that users experience them to be "natural" and "obvious" [Bowman et al. 04, Daiber et al. 12a].

- Objects that appear in front of the projection screen, i.e., objects with *negative parallax*, introduce the major challenge in this context. When the user wants to interact with such an object by touching, she is limited to touching the area behind the object, since most touch-sensitive screens capture only direct contacts, or hover gestures close to the screen. Therefore the user has to penetrate the visual objects to reach the touch surface with her finger. In addition to the fact that users commonly consider this as unnatural (or not intuitive), the stereoscopic perception may be disturbed, since the user's visual system is fed with contradicting information. If the user penetrates an object while focusing on her finger, the stereoscopic effect for the object would be disturbed, since the user's eyes are not accommodated and converged on the projection screen's surface. Thus the left and right stereoscopic images of the object's projection would appear blurred and could not be merged anymore (Figure 9.1 (a)). However, focusing on the virtual object would lead to a disturbance of the stereoscopic perception of the user's finger, since her eyes are converged to the object's 3D position (Figure 9.1 (b)). In both cases the stereoscopic impression may be lost due to these artifacts.

Another significant problem with stereoscopic touch interfaces is the discrepancy between the disparity and occlusion cues. Indeed, as illustrated in Figure 9.2 (b) if the user's finger penetrates the object in the last phase of the touch gesture, binocular disparity cues are suggesting that her finger is already behind

Side Note 9.1: Accommodation-Convergence

Accommodation-Convergence or simply accommodation reflex is the reflex of the eye to focus on an object. It consists of 2 simultaneous actions: (a) *vergence* is the simultaneous movement of both eyes, such that their optical axes cross on the object and thus allow stereoscopic vision, (b) *accommodation* of each eye's lens shape and pupil size, such that the object is in focus. With real objects both actions are coherent, i.e., the vergence distance and lenses' focal length are highly correlated. Nevertheless, stereoscopic displays only simulate the effect of the vergence reflex by providing each eye with different (slightly shifted) projection. In contrast, the eyes' lenses are always accommodated to the display surface.

This is a common problem with virtually any stereoscopic display technology. Nevertheless, with touch interfaces the problem is sharply intensified, since at some point the user's finger and the aimed object are at the same depth (i.e. same vergence distance), but the eye lenses have to be focused either on the finger or on the display.

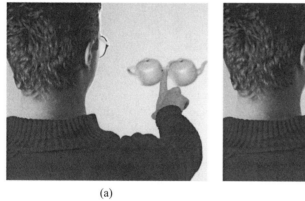 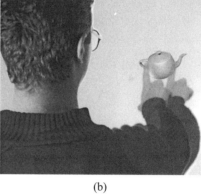

(a) (b)

Figure 9.1: Illustration of the accommodation-convergence problem; The user is either focused on the finger (a), which makes the selection ambiguous, or on the object (b), which disturbs the visual perception of the finger.

the object. Nevertheless, the stereoscopic projection on the display surface cannot occlude the finger (or any object for that matter) in front of it. Thus, the finger is occluding parts of the object, and occlusion cues are confirming that the object is in front of the screen (Figure 9.2 (a)). Since occlusion cues usually dominate over disparity, disparity cues may be ignored and the images for the left and the

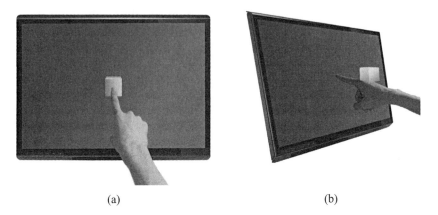

(a)   (b)

Figure 9.2: Illustration of the occlusion problem; while the occlusion cues (a) indicate that the user's finger is in front of an object, binocular disparity cues (b) are suggesting that the user's finger is behind the object.

right eye may not be merged any more, which results in loss of the stereoscopic impression. In both cases touching an object may become ambiguous. However, as discussed in detail in Section 9.5, users have difficulties precisely estimating the depth of an object, which is displayed close enough to the surface, when they try to touch it.

9.1.3   Design Paradigms for Stereoscopic Touch Interaction

While one could simply use a 3D tracking technique to capture the user's finger or hand motions in front of a display surface, it has been shown that touching an intangible surface (i.e., *touching the void*) leads to confusion and a significant number of overshooting errors [Chan et al. 10], and passive haptic has the potential to considerably enhance the user experience with touch- or grasp-based interfaces. Furthermore, touch interaction is nowadays becoming a standard for most mobile devices or tabletop setups, thus a change to other technology is usually not desirable, and sometimes not possible.

Existing approaches to deal with the problems of touch interaction in stereoscopic contexts could be roughly separated into three distinct paradigms (cf. Figure 9.3): "Move the *surface*," "Move the *touches*," and "Perceptual illusions," which are briefly discussed in the following.

Move the Surface Paradigm

The main point in the *move the surface* concept is that one can decouple the interactive surface from the display and move it freely in the 3D volume above the display. One possibility to achieve this is to use a multi-touch enabled transparent prop [Schmalstieg et al. 99, Valkov et al. 10], which can be aligned with a floating

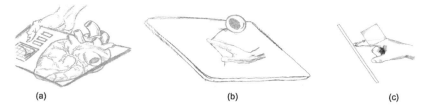

(a)   (b)   (c)

Figure 9.3: Illustration of the three design paradigms for touch interaction with stereoscopic content: (a) "move the surface" paradigm; (b) "move the touch" paradigm, and (c) "perceptual illusions" paradigm

---

Side Note 9.2: Transparent Props

One of the main problems with a transparent prop is that the user is usually holding it at arm's length and the display surface is far behind the prop. While the stereoscopic projection could be tuned such that an object appears on the transparent prop's surface the discrepancy between vergence and accommodation depths is usually so strong that the objects cannot be merged any more.

Another significant problem with both transparent props and tangible views is that one has to precisely track both the prop and user's fingers on top of the prop, which is a challenging task and current solutions are usually very limited and prone to errors.

---

object and used as input to interact with this object in place. Thus, the user interacts "directly" with the object through the prop and receives haptic feedback. Nevertheless, since the objects aligned with the prop are projected with very large disparity, the users often have considerable problems maintaining the fusion of the images for the left and the right eyes. This is further impaired by even very small scratches on the surface of the prop, which may distract the eye accommodation on the top of the prop instead of on the display surface. Another recently published alternative is to use opaque props and a top projection exactly on the surface of these props, i.e., to use tangible views [Spindler et al. 10]. Nevertheless, to our best knowledge the "tangible views" have not been considered with stereoscopic projections.

Move the Touches Paradigm

With the second paradigm the touches are "moved" into the 3D space above or below the display surface by using the on-surface 2D positions of multiple touch points to calculate a 3D position of a distant cursor [Benko and Feiner 07, Strothoff et al. 11]. As with the touch precision, the approach shifts the problem into the interface design space by defining the *stereo touch* as distinct input modality. Examples of interface techniques based on this approach are the *balloon selection* metaphor [Benko and Feiner 07], the *triangle cursor* [Strothoff et al. 11], the *fishnet* metaphor [Daiber et al. 12a], and many more [Hachet et al. 11, Cohé et al. 11, Song et al. 12]. The main drawback of these techniques is that 2D interaction on the surface of the display is either not supported or realized with a different set of techniques, which leads to frequent switching between different interaction modes. Nevertheless, interaction techniques based on this paradigm could be both faster and more precise than in-air free hand gestures. Two examples of such techniques are presented in Sections 9.3 and 9.4.

Perceptual Illusions

Use of perceptual illusions to manipulate the properties of the rendered scene or parts of it in such a way that the user's finger is redirected onto the display surface while reaching to touch a floating object, is the core idea of the last paradigm. The essential part of this approach is that such manipulations have to be imperceptible for the user, i.e., the visual effects of their application must remain below her perceptual detection threshold. Indeed, as shown by Dvorkin et al. [Dvorkin et al. 07], there is only a (small) finite number of parametric functions for ballistic arm motions which are selected and parameterized according to the arm and object positions prior to the execution. Thus, if the user detects a change in the scene she would abort the entire gesture and "reprogram" a new gesture rather than adjust the current one. This usually takes more than 200*ms* [Dvorkin et al. 07] and may thus significantly impair performance. Perceptual illusions for 3D touch interaction are discussed in detail in Sections 9.5 and 9.5.9. While the next chapters describe particular incarnations of the presented design paradigms we first concentrate on the effect of parallax shifts on the touch precision.

9.2 Touching Parallaxes

In the monoscopic case the mapping between an *on-surface touch point* and the *intended* object point in the virtual scene is straightforward, but with stereoscopic scenes this mapping introduces problems. In particular, since there are different projections for each eye, the question arises where users touch the surface when they try to "touch" a stereoscopic object. In principle, the user may touch anywhere on the surface to select a stereoscopically displayed object. However, according to observations we have made, it appears most reasonable that users try to select a stereoscopically rendered object by touching:

- **the midpoint between the projections for both eyes** – the so called *middle* eye projection

---

Side Note 9.3: Eye Dominance

As with handedness, eye dominance is formed in early childhood and manifests itself in the fact that humans preferably use one of the eyes when the task is reduced to 2D. Common examples are pointing, aiming before rolling a bowling ball, looking through a telescope, etc.

Eye dominance can easily be determined with the so-called hole-in-the-card test (also known as the Dolman method). For this test the subject is given a card with a small hole in the middle, and is instructed to hold it with both hands and to view a distant object through the hole with both eyes open. The observer then slowly draws the card back to the head while keeping the object in view. While doing this he unintentionally converges to the dominant eye.

- **the projection for the *dominant* eye**

- **the projection for the *non-dominant* eye**

- **the orthogonal projection of the object onto the touch surface** – i.e., the object's *shadow*

A precise mapping between a touch and an object is important to ensure correct selections, in particular in a densely populated virtual scene, where a great number of objects are distributed over a relatively small space. In order to allow the user to select arbitrary objects, a certain area of the touch surface, which we refer to as *on-surface target*, must be assigned to each object. Therefore, it is important to know where the user will touch the surface for a given object. Recent research has indicated that neither of the targets listed above is fully correct, and users tend to touch between the projections for the two eyes with an offset toward the projection for the dominant eye. Indeed, as can be seen in Figure 9.4 users with left eye dominance and with right eye dominance tend to choose the same strategy to select a stereoscopic object on a two-dimensional touch surface.

Interestingly the touch precision is also affected by the parallax. As illustrated in Figure 9.4 the touch points for negative and positive parallax are more scattered than the touch points on the zero parallax plane, although the size of the projected images for objects behind the screen are smaller than the size of the projections for objects on the surface. Furthermore, the touch points on the planes in front of and behind the display surface are comparably scattered, although the projected images for objects in front of the screen are greater than those of the object behind. This indicates that touching objects displayed with positive or negative stereoscopic parallax on a 2D surface induces more imprecision than touching objects with zero parallax. Furthermore, as one can see in the figure, imprecision increases with stereoscopic parallax, in particular for objects displayed with negative parallax.

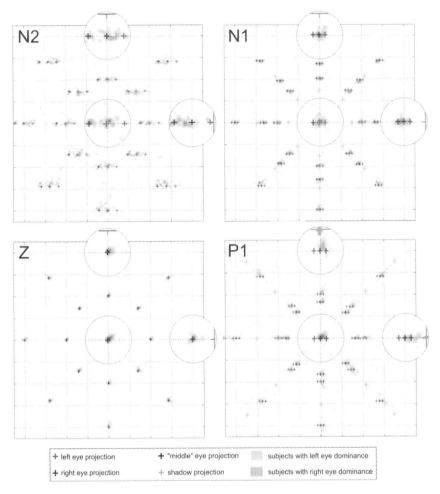

Figure 9.4: Typical touch results from a 3D touch precision experiment: (top left) shows the touch locations for strong negative parallax, (top right) for negative parallax, (bottom left) for condition zero, and (bottom right) for condition positive parallax.

In addition, users tend to perform more slowly for objects with strong negative parallax. This is in particular due to the fact that for objects in front of the screen most users perform a "usual" point gesture until they reach the visual representation of the object and then move the finger slowly through it until it reaches the interactive surface. Thus the balance between ballistic and correction phases is different, leading to degradation in performance. In contrast, some users are "surprised by the surface" while performing some of the touch gestures in order to select objects behind the surface. This may lead to decreased performance times, but also degrades the precision of the touch gesture, since in these cases, the gesture ended prematurely, without users fully executing the slower and more precise *correction phase*. Furthermore, since the motion of a user's arm during a touch gesture may differ very much among users and for different object positions, the prematurely ended gestures may lead to "random touches."

In order to quantify the discussed issues, we have conducted some experiments (e.g. [Valkov et al. 11]). Not surprisingly the results have confirmed that the middle eye and the dominant eye targets are best guesses for the location of the on-surface touch targets for stereoscopic objects, but the calculated mean distances to the actual touch points are still rather large. For instance, the mean distance between the dominant eye targets and the corresponding touch points was in all cases more than 2 cm. Furthermore, as discussed above, observations of the subjects during the experiment reveal that during most of the trials they neither touched the dominant nor the middle eye target, but rather a point "in-between" both touch targets, which raises the question of whether we can do better than this in predicting the actual on-surface touch point.

Therefore, one can express the position P_{IMD} of the actual touch point, which we call *intermediate* target point (IMD), as a linear blend between the positions of the dominant eye target P_{DE} and the middle eye target P_{ME}:

$$P_{\text{IMD}} = P_{\text{ME}} + \alpha \cdot (P_{\text{DE}} - P_{\text{ME}})$$

The parameter $\alpha \in [0, 1]$ determines the position of the point P_{IMD} according to the segment $(P_{DE} - P_{ME})$. For instance, for $\alpha = 1$ the IMD coincides with dominant eye target, whereas for $\alpha = 0$ it coincides with the middle eye target.

With this parameterization we can finally express the optimal position of the on-surface target point. Let P_{CAM} be the camera position, v its normalized right vector and d the user's inter-pupillar distance (usually hard-coded to 6.5 cm). The on-surface touch point P_{TOUCH} for an object at position P is then:

$$P_{\text{TOUCH}} = (1-k)(P_{\text{CAM}} \pm v \cdot \alpha \cdot \frac{d}{2}) + k \cdot P$$

with

$$k = \frac{h_{\text{CAM}}}{(h_{\text{CAM}} - h)}$$

where h and h_{CAM} are the depths of the object and the camera, i.e., their distance to the display surface. The $\pm$ sign in the equation above captures the user's eye dominance. In a right-handed coordinate system (e.g., OpenGL) the on-surface touch point has to be calculated with a positive camera offset for users with right-eye dominance and with negative camera offset for users with left-eye dominance.

Apparently, the optimal α may be influenced by several parameters such as the parallax, the user's handedness, performance speeds and preferences, eye

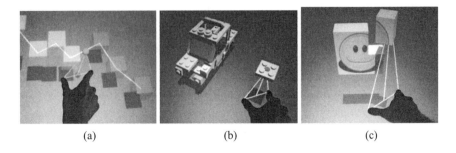

(a)   (b)   (c)

Figure 9.5: Three typical tasks with the triangle cursor metaphor: (a) following a predefined path; (b, c) completing a small 3D model.

dominance, etc. Nevertheless, values between 0.45 and 0.55 are a reasonable initial guess and could decrease the overall error rates significantly, especially if the user's eye dominance is known.

9.3   Multi-Touch above the Tabletop

In the previous sections we have discussed the main problems when interacting with stereoscopically rendered 3D objects and how the on-surface touch point depends on the object's position when the user directly touches through the object to the display surface. Nevertheless, directly touching a floating object usually only works in a small vicinity (about ± 5 cm) in front of and behind the display surface.[1] For objects further away above or below the interactive surface, indirect techniques are usually more appropriate. In this and in the following sections we present two techniques, specially designed for these scenarios.

9.3.1   Triangle Cursor

Triangle cursor (Figure 9.5) is an indirect selection and manipulation metaphor for objects rendered stereoscopically above an interactive tabletop's surface [Strothoff et al. 11]. The metaphor is designed to overcome the occlusion artifacts and fat finger problem [Holz and Baudisch 10] usually accompanying similar interaction techniques [Benko and Feiner 07, Coffey et al. 12c]. In its basic implementation 4-DOF are supported, i.e., 3D position and yaw rotation. Since the technique is usually controlled only with the dominant hand it could easily be extended to support further actions. For instance, pitch and roll rotations could be mapped to a trackball metaphor controlled with the non-dominant hand. We came up with the idea for our triangle cursor technique when we examined how well existing

---

[1]How to extend this range is discussed in more detail in Section 9.5.

selection techniques for multi-touch surfaces would work combined with a display using a stereoscopic projection.

Triangle cursor is a particular incarnation of the "move the touches" paradigm and thus uses an indirect approach to specify a 3D position above the tabletop display. Instead of specifying the 3D position directly (with, e.g., a free-hand technique) the user only interacts with the zero parallax plane, i.e., the table surface. This essentially splits the 3-DOF positioning task into a 2-DOF positioning task on the table surface and a 1-DOF task to select the desired height above the table. Even though triangle cursor uses this indirect approach, it allows the user to combine the position specification with the height specification into a single 3-DOF task .

A spherical cursor is used to represent the currently selected 3D position. An isosceles triangle is displayed between two touch points and perpendicular to the table surface with the 3D cursor attached to the apex (Figure 9.5).

When the user touches the surface at two points an isosceles triangle is displayed with the two base vertices at the touch positions. The triangle's altitude is displayed to provide additional visual feedback to the user. The altitude's base point represents the 2D position on the surface and is located at the midpoint between the user's fingers. The altitude's length is equal to the height above the surface. When the user touches the surface at two points an isosceles triangle is displayed with the two base vertices at the touch positions. The triangle's altitude is displayed to provide additional visual feedback to the user. The altitude's base point represents the 2D position on the surface and is located at the midpoint between the user's fingers. The altitude's length is equal to the height above the surface. The use of the midpoint between the two fingers has two benefits for accurately specifying the position on the surface – first, the point of interest is not occluded by the user's fingers and second, the movement speed of the midpoint can be reduced by a factor of up to 2 by moving a single finger [Benko et al. 06].

The triangle's position can be controlled by moving the fingers on the surface (2-DOF). The height above the surface (1-DOF) is controlled by the distance between the two fingers and independent of their absolute positions. When the fingers are moved the triangle is scaled according to the distance between the fingers.This behavior resembles the usual scaling gesture that is used in many multi-touch applications, and the user can effectively scale the triangle and accordingly the height above the surface. It is possible to use triangle cursor with two hands or with two fingers of the same hand, in most cases the index finger and the thumb of the dominant hand. When using a single hand the height of the interaction space is limited by the amount the user's fingers can be spread apart. As shown by Hancock et. al. [Hancock et al. 07], similar to real tables rich interactions with digital tables can be implemented by limiting the interaction to a shallow area above the table. The use of a stereoscopic projection already limits the maximum height at which objects above the table can be visualized, depending on the user's point of view. Initial tests have shown that mapping the distance between the fingers to the altitude of the triangle using a quadratic function allows users to cover the interaction space required by most applications. Close to the table surface the users have fine control over the height changes, while they are still able to access the upper boundary of the interaction space.

To accommodate differences in hand size or applications that require a fine level of control in a deeper interaction space the metaphor could be extended to allow a change of the base-to-altitude mapping or adding a height offset while using it.

Moscovich et al. [Moscovich and Hughes 08a] have shown that positioning and rotating the hand and adjusting the span of the fingers are compatible and can be combined into a uni-manual manipulation task. A yaw rotation around an axis perpendicular to the table surface can be applied using the relative position of the touch points and midpoint. A rotation of the fingers around the midpoint is mapped to a rotation around the axis defined by the triangle's altitude. Thus the technique is particularly well suited for tasks which require fluent 3/4 DOF control, such as 3D path following or construction (cf. Figure 9.5).

To select an object the spherical cursor has to intersect the object as illustrated in Figures 9.5a and 9.5b. When the user triggers the selection the object is attached to the spherical cursor and is moved and rotated with it until it is deselected. To trigger the selection a technique like *SimPress* clicking [Benko et al. 06] or a simple tap with a finger of either the dominant or non-dominant hand can be used.

Extension to 6 DOF

With the possibility to control 3-DOF position and yaw orientation with only two fingers of a single hand, we explored an extension of the technique to simultaneously control the other 2-DOF of the orientation.

To control the pitch and roll rotation a trackball metaphor could be used. When the user touches the surface with the free hand a trackball is displayed at the touch point. The movement of the touch point is mapped to the rotation of the trackball and accordingly to the orientation of the selected object. The combination of triangle cursor with orientation and a trackball results in a bi-manual 6-DOF interaction technique (cf. Figure 9.6b).

9.3.2   Balloon Selection

Balloon selection [Benko and Feiner 07], illustrated in Figure 9.6a, offers a similar selection mechanism that decomposes the 3-DOF positioning task into a 2-DOF positioning and a 1-DOF height adjustment task.

A spherical cursor (*balloon*) is displayed to show the currently selected 3D position. The user can specify the position on the surface with the first touch. Using a second touch point the user can change the cursor's height by varying the distance between the two touch points. As the original version of balloon selection does not offer support for an additional specification of the orientation, one can expand the technique. If the user rotates the second touch point around the primary touch point

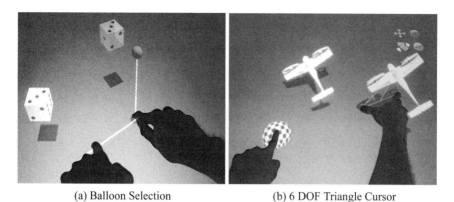

(a) Balloon Selection   (b) 6 DOF Triangle Cursor

Figure 9.6: The two "move the touches" techniques: (a) balloon selection and (b) the extended version of the triangle cursor.

the rotation is applied to the currently selected object. Nevertheless, this extension, although straightforward, may be suboptimal for the technique, since it may change the underlying mental model of the user. Furthermore, it also introduces some interference between setting the height of the balloon and changing its orientation. Indeed, since users are usually not able to move their finger in a perfect circle around a fixed point, changing the orientation will inevitably lead to altering the height of the balloon.

9.3.3 Triangle Cursor vs. Balloon Selection

Our studies have indicated that most of the users have the subjective feeling of being faster with triangle cursor than with balloon selection, when performing a path-following or construction tasks, and have rated the positioning precision as equal. All users have appreciated the fact that triangle cursor provides a smooth single motion to control all degrees of freedom with a single hand, and they have rated it as more appropriate for the path-following task. Nevertheless, some users have described the balloon selection as having a simpler mental model, clearly separating surface positioning from changing the height. Indeed the subjective user comments have indicated that the extension of balloon selection to support yaw rotation leads to difficulties separating the yaw rotation from height changes. Nevertheless, none of our test users rated this as a problem, and most of them intuitively overcame this by first adjusting the object's orientation and then its height. Quantitative evaluations (cf. Figure 9.7) have largely confirmed these subjective estimations for a synthetic docking task and a more real world-like construction task. As one can see in this figure users are able to perform the

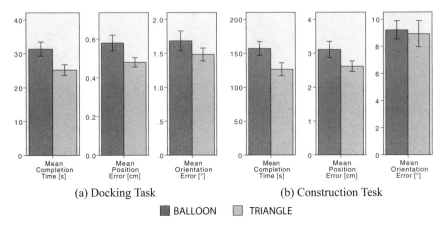

(a) Docking Task   (b) Construction Tesk

■ BALLOON   □ TRIANGLE

Figure 9.7: Comparison of balloon selection and triangle cursor for: (a) docking task (moving a die) and (b) construction task (build a 9-piece puzzle). Error bars = ± SE.

synthetic die moving task about 20% faster with our triangle cursor than with the similar balloon selection technique. The increase in speed did not come at the expense of precision, as the positioning and orientation errors were either nearly identical for both techniques or slightly in favor of triangle cursor. In the more complex puzzle task, which more closely resembles what a real-world task could be like, we were able to achieve nearly identical results. Triangle cursor is again about 20% faster while maintaining a similar precision.

As triangle cursor is more complex and multiple degrees of freedom are controlled at the same time using a single hand one could expect it to be less precise than balloon selection. The results show that this is not the case. On average, triangle cursor even outperformed balloon selection by a small margin. We believe that this is the result of using the midpoint of two touches that allow a more stable control of the cursor position on the surface—one of triangle cursor's initial design ideas.

One of the advantages of triangle cursor is the ability to directly approximate the desired height by spreading the two fingers the right amount apart before touching the surface. Most users were able to approximately *guess* the right height to perform a selection after they had completed several trials. This is one of the main reasons why triangle cursor outperformed balloon selection. After the initial guess only a small correction phase is required for triangle cursor, whereas a larger height change for the cursor of balloon selection was required. Furthermore, the users utilized the time while they were moving the selected object from the starting position to the target, i.e., the users adjusted the spread of their fingers so that the cursor approximately matched the target's height at the end of the gesture. Thus, only a small additional adjustment of the cursorÃŢs position and orientation was necessary once the target position was reached. In contrast, with balloon selection most users had more difficulty in adjusting the height and orientation while moving, so that either a larger correction at the target position was necessary or the users performed the task with discrete phases for moving and adjusting the height and orientation, leading to higher times to complete the tasks.

Although triangle cursor is an indirect interaction technique, it is usually not perceive as such. The combination of orientation, position on and height above the surface in a single-handed technique results in fluid motions. This is particularly observable during the more complex tasks. Nevertheless it should be noted that it is sometimes awkward to use triangle cursor for rotations with large angles. Indeed, the user has to stop during the rotation, reposition his hand, and select the object again to resume the rotation. We observed that users who seemed more comfortable with touch interaction quickly learned to plan ahead and oriented their hand to *grab* the object so that no or only one re-selection was necessary. Other users always grabbed the objects in the same way and were forced to re-select the object more often. While some users reported the re-selection step as slightly disturbing, their results show that they still performed faster than with balloon selection, which usually does not need the additional re-selection step.

9.3.4   Design Considerations

In this section we discuss several design considerations for using triangle cursor within more complex interfaces and briefly consider possible variations suitable for different application requirements.

Widget vs. Tool

In an application where the user manipulates a single or just a few objects over a longer period of time or a continuing sequence of manipulations is necessary it might be beneficial to modify triangle cursor and use it as a manipulation widget. When the user removes his fingers from the surface while an object is selected, the widget remains visible. Thus it acts as a handle, and the user can instantly *grab* it to continue manipulating the object, without needing to re-select the object first. A separate gesture, like tapping on the widget, could be used to deselect the object and dismiss the widget, when it is no longer used. However, in a dense visualization environment, where a large number of selectable objects or two objects that are very close to each other are manipulated, the widgets might occlude other widgets or could be hit accidentally by the user while trying to perform a new selection.

Supporting Multiple Users

The techniques could easily be extended to support multiple users. Using an existing technique that is able to identify to which user each touch point belongs, multiple tools can be active at the same time – one for each pair of touches of the same user that are in close proximity.

The fact that triangle cursor is typically operated using a single hand can aid in the assignment of touches to the users. For example, the touch detection for a tabletop based on the rear diffuse illumination principle can be extended to also detect the users' hands above the surface. While this information does not provide a complete user identification, it is sufficient to decide which touches belong together, so that multiple users can use multiple triangle cursors at the same time.

The widget variants described above could be especially useful for tasks that require multiple users to collaborate. For instance, a selected object could be moved and then passed on to another user.

While the techniques could be extended to multiple users, special considerations to extend stereoscopic displays to multiple users have to be made. A possible solution using a combination of shuttering and polarization has been proposed by Fröhlich et. al. [Fröhlich et al. 05].

Conflicts with Other Touch Gestures

While not a considerable problem for balloon selection, triangle cursor might conflict with other touch gestures, for instance the most common camera navigation gestures pan, pinch, and rotate. This is especially apparent for the pinch gesture that is commonly used to adjust the camera zoom or scale objects, as triangle cursor was designed to resemble the scale gesture for height changes.

In applications where there is a clear separation between objects that can be manipulated and a static environment this could provide a context to decide whether the user wants to select an object or perform a camera navigation action. For instance, if the shadows of selectable objects are displayed below them they provide a visual cue for the user where to initiate a triangle cursor gesture. When two touches are registered by the system and the midpoint between the touches lies inside an object's shadow, triangle cursor is initiated. When the user touches an *empty* spot, a camera navigation action can be performed. A good example of this is a geographic information system (GIS) application with a predefined landscape and movable building models. When the user touches next to a building triangle cursor is used, and when the user touches on the landscape a pinch gesture can be used to scale the landscape, respectively zoom in or out.

Different Height Mappings

In the setup used in our experiments we used a quadratic function to map the distance of the user's fingers on the surface to the height of the cursor above the surface. While the use of a quadratic function to map the 1D finger distance to height is adequate for the most common application tasks, as it had the highest level of precision close to the surface and it was still possible to precisely reach the *highest* points necessary, there are, applications where there is another *reference height*. Imagine an application in which the user controls a group of aerial vehicles that are displayed above a map. It would make sense to place the map in the zero parallax plane and show the aerial vehicles actually *above* the surface. If all vehicles operate at a common flying altitude the range with the most precise height control should be around that altitude and the height mapping function should be adapted accordingly.

In some applications there might be more than one reference height. In this case a switching mechanism to select different height mappings could be added to the application. Another possibility is to extend the interface by another gesture to change the height of an object while it is selected. A sliding gesture might be used to move the selected object up or down without changing the distance between the two fingers which define the height. Changing the distance of the fingers would then result in a manipulation relative to the new height.

Nevertheless, one has to consider that a changing height mapping might cancel out the benefit of the triangle cursor technique, being able to *guess* the right finger placement to get close to the desired selection height.

9.4 Interaction with Virtual Shadows

While the two techniques presented in the previous section map the touches directly to a 3D position and orientation above the tabletop, here we present a conceptually different approach suitable for interaction with objects stereoscopically rendered below the interactive surface, e.g., in the so-called *fish tank* virtual reality setup. Both techniques make use of virtual shadows to access the otherwise unreach-

(a) The Void Shadows Technique

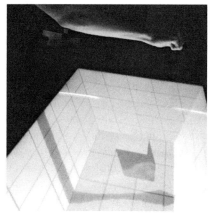
(b) The Shadow Hand Technique

Figure 9.8: Illustration of the two shadows interaction techniques: (a) the void shadows technique and (b) the shadow hand technique.

able objects, but make use of an orthogonal mental concept. The *void shadows* technique, illustrated in Figure 9.8a, uses the object's shadow as proxy for interaction on the display surface, while the *shadow hand* (Figure 9.8b) technique casts a shadow from the user's hand into the scene that acts as a distant cursor for interaction.

Void Shadows

In the *void shadows* (cf. Figure 9.8a) interaction, each interactive object casts a shadow on the touch-enabled display [Giesler et al. 14]. An object's geometry, orientation, and spatial location in the scene controls its shadow's shape and size and helps the user to identify which object is represented. In order to interact with an object, the user manipulates the associated shadow. Therefore, *void shadows* uses the objects' fake shadows as mental model, similar to the shadow metaphor of Herndon et al. [Herndon et al. 92]. Furthermore, the display surface is typically invisible in 3D stereo applications. However, *void shadows* visualizes the interactive shadows on the zero parallax plane, which is aligned to the display surface. Thus, the metaphor implicitly associates some semantical meaning with the interactive surface and facilitates planning and execution of the touch gesture [Valkov et al. 14].

With this technique touch and multi-touch gestures performed on a virtual shadow are transferred to the object casting this shadow. For instance, if the user moves a void shadow on the surface with one finger, the object will be translated in the X/Y-plane, while the shadow always remains under the user's finger. If she scales the shadow up or down with two fingers by a stretch or pinch gesture, the associated object will be lifted or lowered, respectively, in the Z-coordinate. Furthermore, rotating the shadow on the display surface with two fingers will rotate the object around the Z-axis. As with the triangle cursor and balloon selection techniques, void shadows separates the degrees-of-freedom between different modes in order to reduce unwanted operations [Martinet et al. 10, Nacenta et al. 09]. Obviously, users can move both fingers simultaneously, combining position, rotation, and height manipulation at the same time.

The *void shadows* metaphor uses a non-realistic shadow rendering technique, i.e., the shadows are always projected orthogonally onto the touch surface. As Figure 9.9a shows, this projection is controlled by an imaginary plane above the touch surface, called the *shadow plane*, in which each object is represented by a single point. By construction, the shadow volume is generated by this point and the object's silhouette. The void shadow is then the intersection of this shadow volume and the zero parallax plane on the touch surface. To simplify the understanding of the shadow–object link even further, the part of the shadow volume under the display surface is rendered with a semi-transparent light gray color. With decreasing distance to the display surface, objects generate a more obtuse angled shadow volume, which results in a larger shadow. In contrast, objects that are more

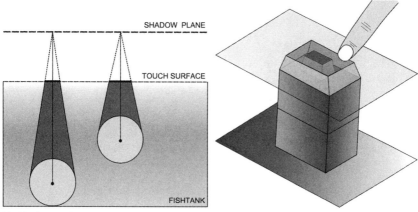

(a) Shadow and Shadow Volume Construction   (b) Nested Shadows for Stacked Objects

Figure 9.9: Illustration of the *Void Shadows* concept. Each interactive object casts a shadow onto the touch sensitive display surface. *(a)* From a projection of the object's center onto an imaginary shadow plane the void shadows are cast onto the interactive surface; the shadow volume under the surface is rendered to highlight the link between the object and its shadow. *(b)* Stacked objects have different shadows, which may be manipulated independently.

distant from the surface will generate a more acute angled volume and therefore a smaller shadow (cf. Figure 9.9a).

Furthermore, if objects are stacked on top of each other, the resulting void shadows will be nested (cf. Figure 9.9b). Nevertheless, it is still possible to select and manipulate individual objects by touching the associated shadow. For instance, touching the innermost shadow will select the bottom-most object, while touching the outermost shadow will select the topmost object. Of course, since the shadows are by their nature 2D projections of 3D geometry, there will always be constellations of objects where the shadows are not clearly separable, e.g., stacked objects having different size or geometry. Nevertheless, in many real-world applications such object arrangements are rather rare. Furthermore, the technique may be extended to compensate for this, e.g., by allowing to modify the height of the shadow plane.

Void shadows is primarily designed for objects at positive parallax, i.e., below the screen surface, but may also work for objects at negative parallax, i.e., above the surface. In this case, the shadow plane is conceptually below the display surface (at the same distance), and the shadow volume is rendered above the surface. However, objects that are located above the display may occlude the interactive shadow. To address this, objects above the display may be rendered semi-transparently. Thus,

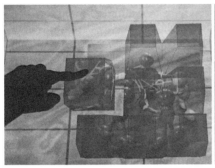 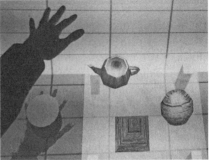

(a) Occlusion in Void Shadows   (b) Object Penetrating the Shadow

Figure 9.10: Illustration of some typical design problems with the void shadows and shadow hand techniques: (a) occlusion due to too many void shadows and (b) an object higher than the cursor penetrates the shadow hand.

the void shadows appear "inside the objects" (but are still correctly ordered due to the stereoscopic cues) and are still accessible in full size for interaction.

However, since each object casts a shadow onto the display surface, the metaphor might involve a limitation on the number of objects in the scene, i.e., the shadows may block the user's view of the objects, an extreme case is shown in Figure 9.10a. As an extension it might be possible to track the user's hands in order to detect a non-interactive user state or to hide shadows of unselected objects during interaction.

9.4.1 Shadow Hand

The *void shadows* technique uses the objects' shadows as metaphor for interaction and allows users to directly select an object by touching its associated shadow. The *shadow hand* is a shadow-based in-air interaction technique, based on the work of Hilliges et al. [Wilson et al. 08], that uses an orthogonal approach. With the technique the user's hand casts a virtual shadow into the scene and activates an invisible distant cursor with an offset below the tabletop surface, which can be positioned in the vicinity of an object for selection. An object is then selected with a grasp gesture,[2] which couples the distant hand representation, i.e., the "cursor" to the object and allows to move the object freely in the scene by mapping the hand movements to equivalent object translations, after which the object can be released by opening the hand. A visual feedback for selectable objects in the vicinity of the distant cursor is usually helpful, such that users can adjust their hand position in

---

[2]Hilliges et al. have initially proposed a pinch gesture, which can be detected with a simple and robust computer vision algorithm, but also causes some usability issues [Wilson et al. 08]

order to select the intended object. Intuitively the shadow of the user's hand has to be projected on the topmost object. Nevertheless, this makes it very difficult to distinguish which object is selected, if the objects are stacked on top of each other. Alternatively one could allow objects which are higher than the distant cursor to penetrate the projected hand shadow as illustrated in Figure 9.10b. This could improve the user's estimation of the current cursor position.

Typical implementations of the technique are based on the Kinect sensor mounted above the tabletop display, and tracks the user's hand and projects the masked depth image as texture from the sensor position into the scene to simulate the shadow. After detection of the user's hand in the depth image, the implementation analyzes the convex hull and convexity defects to classify a hand as opened or closed. The detected hand center is used as the cursor position. Since in this case the depth image is affected by noise, a dynamic filter as jitter compensation for precise positioning tasks and fast object movement should be used. This kind of filter applies a stronger filtering factor during slow hand motions and a weaker filtering factor during quick hand motions. However, as the user's hand alters its shape during the transition from a closed to an opened state, the hand's center and therefore the distant cursor are suddenly moved, which results in a displaced object upon releasing. In order to compensate for this, one can take the most recent position from a history stack, i.e., the position just before the hand changes its state, which in our evaluations resulted in surprisingly correct object placement and grabbing. Users who have tested the technique described this as magical snapping effect and they had the feeling that the shadow hand technique automatically snaps the object into the intended position.

9.4.2   Shadow Hand vs. Void Shadows

In our formal evaluations (cf. Figure 9.11) we have shown that users were able to perform positioning tasks much more precisely with the *void shadows* technique than with the shadow hand technique, while they needed comparable or even shorter time for task completion. Surprisingly, the precision of the in-air technique was relatively high, with a mean position error below 1 cm in the docking task, indicating that the described shadow hand implementation provides sufficient compensation for the noise of the Kinect sensor. In the synthetic docking task users were at mean 28% more precise with *void shadows* and the users tended to perform about 10% faster. This was confirmed in more complex tasks, that more closely resemble what a real-world task could be like. During this experiment, *void shadows* performed more than twice as fast. Therefore, the question arises why the task completion times are different for both scenarios.

Observation of participants show that *void shadows* was primarily fast for object selection, since users could directly select the intended object on the surface. We also observed that most users separated the positioning task into a 2-DOF task in the first phase to move the object close to the target position and then switched to a 1-DOF task to adjust to the correct height, although all participants were aware of the fact that *void shadows* supports 3DOF positioning by moving two fingers simultaneously. In contrast, observation of participants during the experiments revealed that the in-air interaction technique performed slower during the object selection and target correction phase, since the participants had to adjust to the indirect hand shadow proxy. Furthermore, we observed that the in-air technique was maintaining a fast speed between start and end for object movement, since the participants usually moved the object to the approximate height of the target during positioning and therefore made frequent use of the 3-DOF of the in-air technique in the ballistic phase of the motion. Nevertheless, the participants then reduced the motion again to a sequence of 1 or 2-DOF tasks during the correction phase. Thus the choice of an appropriate task should be made in relation to the average object translation needed for the application. At the current state, *void shadows* seems to be particularly appropriate for applications where many relatively short and precise object translations are required.

Nevertheless, it should be noted that the different sensor technologies (30 Hz hand detection with Kinect vs. up to 200 Hz touch detection) might have influenced the results for task completion time. On the other hand, these are currently the state-of-the-art technologies at the consumer market in their respective domains.

Subjectively most users find it appealing to interact with the shadow casting in-air technique, although they sometimes have problems in mentally connecting the shadow to a specific light source. Furthermore, many users prefer *void shadows* over in-air interaction in terms of speed and precision, but the in-air technique in terms of pleasure.

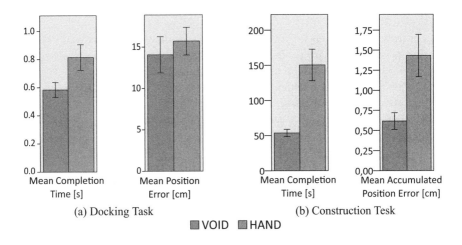

Figure 9.11: Comparison of void shadows and shadow hand techniques for: (a) docking task (moving a box) and (b) construction task (build a 9-piece puzzle). Error bars = ± SE.

9.5 Perceptual Illusions for 3D Touch Interaction

As mentioned earlier, the main benefit of multi-touching stereoscopic objects is that it allows us to get closer to the basic goal of "natural" interaction by building upon skills which humans have developed in their everyday lives interacting with real-world objects. In particular, the user perceives virtual objects stereoscopically, i.e., with their associated depth properties, while she is able to interact with those objects with her own hands and fingers and thus receives direct or indirect haptic feedback.

The lack of haptic feedback is a common issue for interaction with virtual content which may reduce the "naturalness" of the interaction and often increases the amount of overshooting errors and reduced precision [Bowman et al. 04]. Specialized hardware devices exist which use mechanical or ultrasound actuators, e.g., [Carter et al. 13b, Kim et al. 13, Rekimoto 13], to provide active haptic stimuli. Although these technologies can provide compelling stimulation, they are usually cumbersome to use and have a limited application scope [Carter et al. 13b].

In fully immersive or HMD environments *passive haptic* feedback, which is provided by physical props registered to virtual objects, has been shown to be beneficial [Insko et al. 01]. For instance, a user might touch a physical table while viewing its (potentially different) representation in the virtual environment. Nevertheless, until now only little effort has been undertaken to extend this approach into non-HMD, projection-based setups. Theoretically, the display itself might serve as physical prop and provide passive feedback for the objects visually aligned with its surface (as is the case in 2D visualizations). At the same time the point of finger or palm contact with the display can be tracked and used as input for interaction, which adds a powerful extension to this approach. Going a step further, one may separate the touch and the visualization surfaces, e.g., using a *transparent prop* as proposed by Schmalstieg [Schmalstieg et al. 99], which considerably increases the interaction volume in which touch-based interaction is available. An alternative approach would be to move the virtual objects to the display surface, but with the important requirement that all object or scene manipulations are applied imperceptibly for the user. While this requirement would lead to relatively shallow object distribution within the stereoscopic volume in front of and behind the display, it allows us to combine stereoscopic visualization with direct object manipulation and haptic feedback in a single interaction interface. Thus the sacrifice of available depth range allows us to greatly improve the user's interaction experience, providing her with haptic *and* stereoscopic cues, but without losing the directness of the interaction. In a more general sense, our concept is following the *perceptual illusions* paradigm for interface design. Interfaces based on this paradigm benefit from illusions which arise from misinterpretation of (deliberately manipulated) sensory information by the brain. In the domain of virtual reality the "redirected walking" technique is a remarkable example which is based on this paradigm [Razzaque 05]. By ingenious manipulations of the virtual camera this technique reroutes the user to walk in circles while she believes devoutly she is walking in a straight line. Although walking and pointing (or touching) are quite different activities, there are some similarities in the nature of the perceptual inconsistencies, which makes such perceptual illusions feasible in the context of 3D stereoscopic touch interaction. In particular, the approach is strongly motivated by the findings of many perception research groups, revealing that there is a certain amount of induced object or scene manipulations which (although perceivable) cannot be reliably detected by the human visual system. Thus either the entire scene or a single object could be manipulated with some technique such that this manipulation remains below the threshold of our attentional awareness. From these considerations the desire for *usable* manipulation techniques arises which may be applied to the virtual scene and benefit the user in the context of 3D stereoscopic touch interaction.

Since we are mainly targeting on augmenting pure virtual objects floating in front of or behind the display surface with passive tactile feedback, we can manipulate the properties of either an object or the entire virtual scene in such a way that:

1. At the moment when the user reaches the display surface the intended object is aligned with this surface, such that tactile feedback is received (exactly) at this moment.

2. The application of the manipulation technique remains imperceivable for the user, i.e., it remains below her perceptual detection threshold.

Obviously, manipulation may be applied during different phases of the overall interaction process, and different phases may require different types of manipulation techniques or different settings for the same manipulation technique in order to achieve the desired result.

In this section we discuss the applicability of the *perceptual illusions* paradigm to allow users to interact with stereoscopically displayed objects when the input is constrained to a 2D touch surface. Therefore we discuss a number of possible manipulation techniques as well as their benefits and constraints. In particular, we discuss the human sensitivity to the detection thresholds for the misalignment between visual and tactile contact as well as the user sensitivity to small induced depth shifts applied while the user reaches for an object on the display surface. In general, there is a usable range stretching in front of and behind the display surface, in which both *scene* and *object shifts* cannot be detected reliably, i.e., an object could be imperceptibly moved closer to the display surface while the user is reaching out to touch it, and thus at the moment of touch passive haptic feedback is provided.

Figure 9.12: Illustration of the user interaction states with a stereoscopic multi-touch enabled display.

9.5.1   User Interaction States

During observations of many users participating in numerous demonstrations and evaluations with the 3D touch setups in our laboratory, we were able to identify some typical user behavior patterns. Similar to interaction with large public displays, users change between different states of involvement [Vogel and Balakrishnan 04]. Nevertheless, in contrast to public displays where the focus is on different levels of user involvement and attracting the user's attention is one major goal, in most non-public interfaces the user already intends to interact with the proposed setup or environment in order to fulfill her tasks. To generalize these empiric observations we adapt Norman's interaction cycle [Norman 98] resulting in the definition of three typical interaction states as shown in Figure 9.12.

In the *observation* state the user is at such a distance from the display that the whole scene is in her field of view. In this state often the goal of the intended interaction is formed and different strategies to achieve this goal are formulated. Thereafter, and after the most promising strategy is selected, the global task is subdivided into subtasks. The significance of this phase may vary widely with the setup, e.g., size, form, position, and orientation of the display, as well as with the particularities of the specific task and interaction interface. For instance, with our approximately 3 *m*-wide stereoscopic interactive wall the user usually remains beyond arm-reach distance in order to keep track of the scene as a whole, i.e., to get the big picture, and to identify new areas or objects for further local interaction. In contrast, with an usual 65" tabletop setup, where a large portion of the scene is within the field of view of the user, this phase is entered only once at the beginning of the interaction.

The user is in the *specification* state while she is within arm-reach distance from the surface but still not interacting. Thus, the objects or tasks to be performed have already been selected, but the corresponding actions have not yet been performed. We have observed that the user spends only a short period of time in this state, plans the local input action, and speculates about the system's reaction. For small vertical displays and tabletops the user usually never returns to the observation phase, once she has entered the specification. In contrast, in large vertical display environments, where the display size makes it impossible for the user to see the entire scene at once when she is close enough to interact, the user may be forced to go back to the observation phase in order to recapitulate the current results and plan the next local interaction. In the observation state the user is usually approximately $1.5-2m$ away from the interactive surface, whereas during the specification state she is within $50-60cm$ distance from the screen. Thus, a key feature of the transition between the observation state and the specification state is that *real* walking (as opposed to virtual traveling metaphors) is involved.

Finally, in the *execution* state the user performs the actions planned in the specification state. Here it must be mentioned, that the execution itself is, in this sense, a process rather than a static state. With touch-based interfaces the user is applying an input action while simultaneously observing and evaluating the result of this action and correcting the input in a series of mutually connected interactive *micro-cycles* or *tonic* action. Nevertheless, further subdivision of the interaction beyond this merely generalized *execution* state might quickly become a complex and controversial task, which is far beyond the scope of this chapter. Once the execution of the current action is finished, the user may return to the specification and thereafter to the observation state to evaluate the results at a higher level with respect to the global task.

While the described user interaction states and the transitions between them are similar for different kinds of tasks and visualizations, the time spent in each state and the number of transitions between them heavily depends on the application scenario and setup. Nevertheless, there are some high level tendencies. For instance, users frequently switch between specification state and execution state, while changes between observation state and specification state are rather rare or completely missing (indicated by the size of the arrows in Figure 9.12), depending on the display size, orientation, and interaction goal. In tasks in which only local interaction is required or the entire display size is in the user's field of view, users usually do not need to switch back to the observation state at any time. In contrast, in front of a large vertical display and especially in scenarios where some interrelations between the scene objects exist, the users frequently step back to get the big picture after a partial task is considered finished. Furthermore, it is likely that the observed phases and user behavior are affected by the parameters of the particular visualization, i.e., brightness or contrast of the projection, the type of the presented virtual scene, etc. In particular, with vertical wall-size displays the user is more likely to step back at some point, if the scene contains objects rendered with negative parallax, as when there are only objects with zero or positive parallax.

The goal of this heuristic is not to provide a universal description of users' behavior while interacting with stereoscopic visualizations, but it illustrates many aspects involved in this process.

9.5.2   Manipulation Techniques

In this section we are looking at some instances of the perceptual illusions paradigm , which might be useful for the problem at hand. Therefore we are considering techniques which manipulate the parameters of a particular object, of the virtual scene, or of the visualization itself, such that the object, which is intended to be touched, appears closer to the display surface after application of the technique. The application of a technique should be imperceptible for the user in a wide depth range. Thus we are looking for techniques which will allow us to manipulate the perceived depth of the object of interest, while maximizing at the same time the available depth vicinity in front of and behind the display in which scene objects may be placed. In the following, possible manipulation techniques which likely satisfy these requirements are considered, and the constraints for their applicability are discussed.

Manipulation of the Visualization Parameters

The first group of manipulation techniques deals with manipulation of the parameters which are characteristic of the stereoscopic visualization, i.e., virtual inter-ocular distance (IOD) and focal length. One can align the object of interest to the plane of the display surface by adjusting the focal length of the virtual camera in such a way that the object in question moves to zero parallax (Figure 9.13b). In this case, all objects in front of the intended one will have negative parallax, all objects behind it will have positive parallax and all objects at the same depth will lie on the zero parallax plane. One advantage of this technique is that objects keep

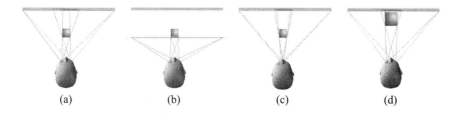

(a)   (b)   (c)   (d)

Figure 9.13: Illustration of different manipulation techniques: (a) neither the scene nor the visualization parameters are manipulated; (b) 3D scene rendered stereoscopically with manipulated focal distance; note how the projections for the left and for the right eye are aligned; (c) manipulated IOD, since the scene is rendered with smaller IOD, the projections for the left and for the right eye are closer to each other; (d) object shift – the object is shifted closer to the display surface and scaled accordingly, so that the size of the projection remains the same, while the stereoscopic disparity has changed.

their relative distances to each other, since they are not moved within the scene. In addition, perspective distortion, lights, or shadows remain unchanged. However, with objects vastly scattered in depth, this technique could move the perceived depths of some objects too close or too far away from the observer, i.e., on strong parallax, causing uncomfortable viewing conditions. Furthermore, our preliminary tests have shown that misalignment of the depth of the zero parallax plane with the user's head-plane distance leads to substantially impaired viewing adaptation and thus to strong eye strains and exhaustion.

Another approach is to modify the inter-ocular distance (IOD) between the camera for the left and the camera for the right eye, i.e., to modify the stereoscopic disparity of the scene objects as shown in Figure 9.13c. Again, perspective distortion, lights, or shadow cues remain unchanged. Nevertheless, gradual reduction of the IOD to 0 will effectively lead to monoscopic visualization, which contradicts the benefits of the interface itself. On the other hand, increasing the IOD beyond some value usually leads to merging problems and diplopia. Again, frequent variation of the IOD usually results in strongly disturbed viewing conditions, which quickly result in eye strain.

Manipulation of the Spatial Parameters

Instead of altering the stereoscopic parameters of the visualization, one could simply shift either the object of interest or the entire scene to the desired position, as illustrated in Figure 9.13d. Shifting the entire scene has the advantage that the spatial relations between the objects remain unchanged. In particular, since the light sources are usually considered as part of the scene, lighting and shadows do not change either. Nevertheless, motion of an object close to the edge of the screen may easily be detected, since the bezel of the display provides a non-manipulative reference for the object's position. Moving a single object can reduce this problem, especially if the object is far away from the display's edge. While changes in the object's shading and its shadow's position or form may reveal its motion, there is a wide range of applications, e.g., GUI elements or chemical visualizations, where the objects and lighting are primarily synthetic and the inter-object relation is not important. In applications where this is not the case, the visualization framework could still compensate for these changes by altering the shading algorithm or fitting the shadow volume calculations for this particular object. In addition, there is a wider range of manipulations applicable to a single object (Figure 9.13d). For instance, it could be moved along some curved path or along the line between its center and the position of the virtual camera, its size could be changed during the shift, etc.

The crucial point here is the moment in which the manipulation is applied. Since touching is only a small part of the interaction process, we can assume that the user already has built a *cognitive map* of the environment. In this case changing the position of an object would be perceived as object motion within a

Side Note 9.4: Imperceptible Shift

At first glance, the idea to imperceptibly shift a stereoscopic object or the scene in depth looks like contradicting its own benefits. On one hand, we claim that binocular disparity cues are precise enough to significantly increase the user's understanding for a 3D scene, i.e., understanding "where the objects are" in the world and relative to each other. On the other hand, we suggest to either shift the virtual scene or to change the depth of one particular object and assume that the user's depth perception is imprecise enough to not recognize this.

The coherence of both assumptions lies in the understanding that human perception of self motion and position (whether we consider displacement of the person itself, e.g., locomotion, or motion of some body part) is mainly dominated by *exteroceptive* environmental stimuli; thus it is predominantly ruled by cues and landmarks extracted from the environment [Berthoz 00]. Our *proprioception* gives us some sense of the relative position and motion of the parts of our body and lets us approximate the result of a particular effort. The results of such approximations are then fed in complex feed-back and feed-forward control paths and mixed together with signals resulting from the evaluation of the related exteroceptive stimuli, which results in generation of corrective muscle signals. Thus we do not have some "global positioning" sensation, but predominantly judge our own position, speed and direction based on the perceived environmental cues, which we have already classified (due to experience or learning) as static [Berthoz 00]. While large discrepancies between proprioceptive and exteroceptive cues might be communicated to cognitive networks at higher hierarchical levels and thus become available to our awareness, many investigations have shown that there is a certain amount of mismatch, which is below the threshold of our conscious perception [Bruder et al. 12, Chan et al. 10].

static scene rather than scene motion while the object is remaining static. Thus the spatial understanding of the scene would not be disturbed even if the object motion is detected. Furthermore, the total arm movement during reaching for an object consists of two distinct phases. During the *ballistic* phase the hand is moved close to the target, and during the subsequent *correction* phase the error between the hand or finger and the target is minimized under control of visual, haptic, and proprioceptive feedback. Thus the mechanical control in the correction phase, i.e., which muscle-control signal must be applied and what the result would be is only approximative. Therefore, we expect that if we slightly move the target within the correction phase, the arm control would change to accommodate the new target position. Since reaching is a very low-level task, controlled through the dorsal visual pathway, we expect that the user will not consciously detect the motion, provided it remains within certain thresholds.

Considering the user interaction states and transitions between them, one can see that there are mainly two instances where a manipulation might be applied – (1) while the user remains in one particular state, (2) during transitions from one state to another. Though it is possible to manipulate an object's spatial parameters by applying temporal drifts, while the user's attention is focused on an object, it has been shown that the magnitude of such drifts has to be very small in order for the manipulation to remain imperceptible [Razzaque 05]. This makes temporal drifts mostly impractical. Thus, we could basically apply manipulations during transitions between states, which we consider in detail in the following sections.

9.5.3   Scene Shifts while Moving toward the Surface

First we will consider the transition between the observation state and the specification state, which is characteristic for interaction with large vertical display environments such as power-walls, CAVEs, etc. As mentioned previously, a characteristic for the transition between these two states is that walking is involved, i.e., while in the observation state the user is about $1.5 \text{ m} - 2$ m away from the surface, such that the entire display is in her field of view, and she is at arm-reach distance (about $0.5 \text{ m} - 0.6$ m) when in the specification state. Thus the user has to make a couple of steps toward the display in order to switch from observation to specification state, and vice versa.

As mentioned previously, exteroceptive environmental stimuli usually dominate the proprioception. Moreover, it has been shown that visual information

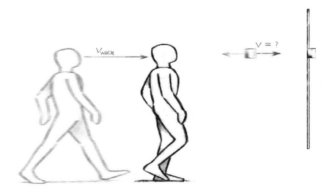

Figure 9.14: Illustration of object/scene shifts while walking. While the user is walking toward the display surface either an object or the entire virtual scene is shifted in or against the walking direction with a fraction of the walking speed.

mostly dominates *extraretinal* cues, such as proprioception, vestibular signals, etc., in a way that humans usually experience difficulties in detecting induced discrepancies between visually perceived motion and physical movement of their body (e.g., [Kohli et al. 05]). In this context, the question arises, if and how much a virtual scene can be imperceptibly shifted in depth during a user's transition from the observation state to the specification state. As illustrated in Figure 9.14, one can slightly translate the virtual scene in, for instance, the same direction as the user's motion and with speed proportional to the user's motion speed, while she is approaching the screen. Thus, an object of interest, which has negative parallax, may be shifted toward the interactive surface, where the user would receive passive haptic feedback if she touches it.

In most stereoscopic display setups the user's head motions in the real world are captured by a tracking system and mapped to translations (and rotations) of the virtual camera so that the virtual scene appears static from the user's point of view. Since humans usually tolerate a certain amount of instability of the virtual scene, we can describe our deliberately induced scene motion as instability with a translation shift $T_{shift} \in \mathbb{R}^3$, i.e., if $P \in \mathbb{R}^3$ is the *perceptually stable* position of an arbitrary object and $P_{shift} \in \mathbb{R}^3$ is the shifted position of the same object, then:

$$P_{shift} = P + T_{shift}$$

In most cases no scene shifts are intended, thus $T_{shift} = 0$. Nevertheless, due to latency, jitter, drift, and the finite resolution of the real-world position, measured by any tracking system, $T_{shift} = 0$ is merely a theoretical concept, thus one usually has:

$$\begin{aligned}
T_{shift} &= \pm \varepsilon_{tracker} \\
&= \pm (\varepsilon_{lat} + \varepsilon_{drift} + \dots) \\
&\approx 0
\end{aligned}$$

In our setup we want to induce depth shifts in the same or in the opposite direction as the motion of the virtual camera, which are considerably larger than the tracker's imprecision $\varepsilon_{tracker}$. Therefore, we define the *scene shift factor* $\rho \in \mathbb{R}$ as the amount of virtual camera motion used to translate the scene in the same or in the opposite direction, i.e.,

$$T_{shift} = \rho \cdot T_{camera}$$

with $|\rho \cdot T_{camera}| \gg |\varepsilon_{tracker}|$.

In the most simple case the user moves orthogonally to the projection screen, and her motions are mapped one-to-one to virtual camera translations. In this case a shift factor of $\rho = 0.3$ means that, if the user walks 1 m toward the projection screen, the scene will be translated 30 cm in the *same direction*, while with $\rho = -0.3$ the scene will be translated 30 cm *opposite* to the user's walking direction.

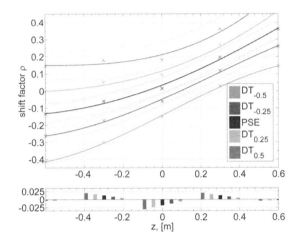

Figure 9.15: Fitted polynomial functions for $DT_{\pm 0.50}(z)$, $DT_{\pm 0.25}(z)$, and $PSE(z)$ (top) and the fitting residuals (bottom). The x-axis shows the objects' start position z, the y-axis shows shift factors ρ. The light curves show the 75% confidence intervals.

Figure 9.15 shows a third-order polynomial interpolation of the relation between the detection thresholds, the points of subjective equality and parallax. Differences within the range defined by these thresholds cannot be detected reliably. For instance, for the 0 cm start parallax subjects had problems in discriminating scene translations with shift factor ρ between -0.15 and 0.18. Thus subjects could not reliably detect if a virtual object initially aligned with the plane of the display surface moved 18 cm in the same direction during 1 m forward movement. Similarly, we could move the same virtual object up to 15 cm against the user while she was walking 1 m toward the display surface, and this motion was still indistinguishable in 75% of the cases. The possible object shifts for 1 m subject motion are illustrated in Figure 9.16.

The results show that subjects generally had problems to detect even large shifts of the stereoscopic depth of rendered objects during active movements, i.e., when approaching the projection wall by walking. Figure 9.15 (a) shows that for objects on the projection surface subjects are generally accurate at detecting scene motions corresponding to shift factors outside the interval between $\rho = -0.150$ and $\rho = 0.181$. Interestingly for objects starting with negative parallax the users tend to underestimate the distance to the object, while for objects starting with positive parallax distances are generally overestimated. Thus objects presented in front of the projection wall are perceived spatially more stable, if they are moved with the walking direction and vice versa.

Side Note 9.5: Perceptual Detection Threshold

A common way to test the perceptual thresholds of particular visual stimulus is to conduct a 2-Alternatives-Forced-Choice (2AFC) experiment. In this kind of experiment the participant is exposed to particular magnitude of the tested stimulus and has to decide if the magnitude is larger or smaller then the magnitude of a reference. The perceptual detection threshold $DT_{\pm 0.5}$ is then defined as the lowest intensity at which a stimulus can be detected at least 50% of the time; thus at least 75% of the answers were correct. Alternatively one can define a tighter detection threshold, in which the stimulus is detected at least 25% of the time, i.e., at least 62.5% of the subject estimations were correct. Obviously these are the detection thresholds $DT_{\pm 0.25}$.

In the case of object shifts, we let the participants walk toward the projection wall, where an object was displayed stereoscopically with some starting parallax. While she was walking toward the wall we applied a shift factor on the object. The participant had then to decide if the object moved in the walking direction or in the opposite direction. A psychological sigmoid function of the type $\frac{1}{1+e^{b \cdot p+c}}$ with parameters $a, b \in \mathbb{R}$ was fitted in the mean results for each shift factor.

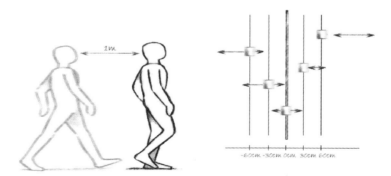

Figure 9.16: Illustration of the imperceptible scene shift ranges. The arrows indicate the maximal scene shift for 1 m walking distance, which the user will not be able to reliably detect. The objects are distributed in depth according to their starting parallax.

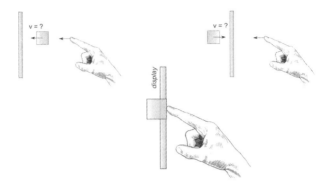

Figure 9.17: Illustration of object/scene shifts during touch. While the user is using a touch gesture either an object or the entire virtual scene is shifted with or against her finger with a fraction of the finger's speed.

9.5.4   Object Shifts during Touch

In the previous section we have discussed how objects could be imperceptibly shifted, while the user is walking toward the display surface. Nevertheless, this has very limited application. As mentioned in Section 9.5.1 users spend most of their time in the *specification* and *interaction* states, which are in some setups the only reasonable user states, and frequently change from one state to the other. The specification might be considered as a form of *passive* interaction state, in which the actions necessary to fulfill the task are specified and the objects subject to these actions are identified. In the subsequent interaction state the user *actively* performs these actions, modifying this way the properties of the virtual scene or of a particular object, and compares the results with the results previously anticipated. Since touch-based interaction is the focus of this chapter, the set of actions considered is dominated by point, touch, and grasp gestures. In the specification phase the user identifies the next object to be touched or grasped and the specific type of touch or grasp gesture to be performed. In this context then the change from specification state to interaction state usually manifests itself by the user simply reaching out to touch or grasp the intended object. As in the previous section it seems worthwhile to investigate the possibility to imperceptibly manipulate the depth of a stereoscopic object while the user is reaching out to touch it, as illustrated in Figure 9.17, since this could allow us to shift that object to the surface and thus provide haptic feedback at the moment of touch. While it is likely that the possible magnitudes of such subtle manipulations are very small, there is a range of applications – discussed briefly in the following section – in which *shallow-depth 3D*, i.e., 3D interaction with limited depth, would be sufficient [Hancock et al. 07]. In contrast to the scene manipulations while the user approaches the surface, as considered in Section 9.5.3, manipulations applied while the user is reaching out to touch an object are not limited to large vertical display setups. Thus, techniques relying on this kind of manipulation have potential to bring stereoscopic touch interaction to a larger set of hardware setups, including tabletops and tilt displays.

9.5.5 Application Space

As indicated by Hancock et al. [Hancock et al. 07] there are multiple application domains in which *shallow-depth 3D* would be sufficient. Assuming there is a usable range of imperceptible misalignments between visual and tactile touch (cf. Section 9.5.8), one could extend those applications with stereoscopic visualization without a need for complex 3D tracking of the user's finger. Through small induced object motions these ranges could be considerably increased. Although this comes at the cost of adding 3D finger tracking, in contrast to alternative techniques both direct object manipulation *and* haptic feedback are provided without additional instrumentation of the user (e.g., haptic gloves, phantoms, etc.).

For instance, a map viewer could render markers or widgets stereoscopically above the display in order to improve visibility and (especially if head tracking is supported) reduce occlusion artifacts. Those widgets, if rendered within some range, would still be accessible for touch interaction. Going a step further, one could overlay the map itself on a (possibly flattened) height model in order to improve spatial understanding of the representation. Many applications, such as the 3D desktops with stacked items on a tabletop setup, or graph visualizations in which highlighted nodes are rendered with different depths, may benefit from the same approach. The combination of stereoscopic touch interaction with the tangible views paradigm [Spindler et al. 10] might also lead to a range of valuable interfaces. For instance, in a medical visualization a stereoscopic representation on the top of the tangible prop would support the tracking of long structures (e.g., veins, nerves) while touch interaction could be used to change the visualization properties at the same time (e.g., zooming, transparency).

In general, there is a wide range of applications, especially in urban planning or data visualization domains, in which shallow-depth 3D is sufficient, but may still benefit from additional stereoscopic cues and more natural interaction interfaces.

9.5.6 Manipulation of Stereoscopic Objects

In order to move an object to the display surface one could shift either only the object of interest or the entire scene to the desired position. As already discussed, shifting the entire scene has the advantage that the spatial relations between the objects remain unchanged. In particular, since the light sources are usually considered as part of the scene, lighting and shadows do not change either. However, our initial evaluations revealed a significant reduction of the perceptual detection thresholds. For instance, if we start the manipulation 10 cm before the user's finger reaches the object, we could only move the object 0.5 cm against or

0.7 cm with the finger, which is far below the requirements of most applications and – as discussed in Section 9.5.8 – might be achieved without any manipulation. Thus, although this technique proved suitable on a large display, which covers more than 60° of the user's horizontal field of view while the user walks toward the display, it seems to be inappropriate for manipulation of the stereoscopic depth while performing a touch gesture, especially in setups with limited display size, e.g., tabletops or desktop displays.

Moving a single object can reduce this problem, in particular if the object is far away from the display edge. Nevertheless, since changes in the object's shading and its shadow's position and form may reveal the motion, the application should compensate for this.

9.5.7   Generalized Scaled Shift Technique

In order to be able to imperceptibly shift an object to the display surface it can be moved along the line between its origin and the position of the virtual camera. Here, we consider the intermediate point between the cameras for the left and for the right eye as camera position. While this ensures constant orientation of the object during translation, it still changes the size of its projection onto the image plane. Thus one has to simultaneously adjust the object's scale factor during translation relative to its motion. This reduces the number of motion cues on which the user may rely while still allowing us to use a number of visually different objects (e.g., different forms, textures, etc.). This is particularly important because imperceptible scene or object manipulations should only be applied in the correction phase due to the fact that the user focuses the object intensively during reaching in the ballistic phase , but pays less attention to the object during error correction and refinement in the correction phase. Indeed, once initiated the

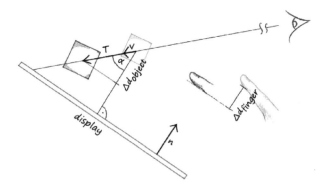

Figure 9.18: Illustration of the generalized scaled shift technique. The object to be manipulated is moved along the ray from the camera to its own position, such that its distance to the screen surface is proportional to the finger's depth.

ballistic phase is carried out without further assistance from the visual system, which is usually scanning for changes in the scene. In the correction phase the vision is switched back and forth between the object and the user's finger, which allows manipulations. Since the correction phase is entered shortly before reaching the object, stronger manipulations are desired to move objects with strong parallax to the display surface. To provide smooth, undetectable manipulation we move the object depending on the motion of the user's fingertip.

In our technique (illustrated in Figure 9.18), which we call *generalized scaled shift* technique, we ignore the exact position and motion vector of the finger and take into account only its orthogonal distance d_{finger} to the display surface. The object in question is then moved along the vector defined by its position and the position of the virtual camera, $v \in \mathbb{R}^3, \|v\|_2 = 1$, such that its depth change is a fraction of the finger's depth change, thus:

$$\Delta d_{\text{object}} = \sigma \cdot \Delta d_{\text{finger}}$$

with *shift factor* $\sigma \in \mathbb{R}$. Similar to the ρ-shifts described in the previous section positive values ($\sigma > 0$) move the object of interest in the same direction as the finger, while for negative values ($\sigma < 0$) the object is moved in the opposite direction. For example, with shift factor $\sigma = 0.5$ the object is moved with half of the speed of the pointing finger in the *same direction* as the finger, while with $\sigma = -0.5$ the object is moved in the *opposite direction*.

Thus, if $\Delta d_{finger} = d_{finger}^{old} - d_{finger}^{new}$ is the relative depth motion of the user's finger, the total object translation $T \in \mathbb{R}^3$ could be expressed as:

$$T = \frac{\sigma \cdot \Delta d_{finger}}{\cos(\alpha)} \cdot v$$

where $\cos(\alpha)$ (cf. Figure 9.18) could be expressed as dot product of the motion vector v and the display normal vector n, i.e., $\cos(\alpha) = -v \cdot n$. Since we are using a right-handed coordinate system, centered in the middle of the display, one has $n = (0 \ 0 \ 1)^T$, thus with $v = \frac{P_{object} - P_{camera}}{\|P_{object} - P_{camera}\|_2} = (v_x \ v_y \ v_z)^T$, the above equation could be expressed as:

$$T = \frac{\sigma \cdot \Delta d_{finger}}{-v_z} \cdot v$$

After unwinding the normalization we obtain

$$T = \frac{\sigma \cdot \Delta d_{finger}}{d_{camera} - d_{object}} \cdot \left(P_{object} - P_{camera}\right)$$

with P_{object} and P_{camera} representing the 3D positions of the object and the virtual camera, respectively. The right side of the equation consists of two main components. The left term defines the amount of object motion as part of the camera to object vector and is only dependent on the depth relations between the finger, the object, and the virtual view point. Since the objects and view point positions are known a priori, one only needs to determine the proximity of the finger to the display surface in order to apply the technique. This greatly reduces the requirements of the finger tracking hardware, since only the finger depth, i.e., its distance to the display, has to be tracked precisely, which could be achieved with different techniques, e.g., [Daiber et al. 12b, Nickel and Stiefelhagen 03].

The right term defines the scale and the direction of the object motion and captures the dependency on the head-tracking technique, if used. Indeed, in a head-tracked setup the position of the virtual view point is constantly adjusted to the user's head position, thus P_{camera} and d_{camera} in the above equation might change between frames. This may lead to small sidewards offsets, which may reveal the manipulation on a static background.

The new scale factor s_{new} of the object could be calculated as

$$s_{new} = s_{old} \cdot \frac{d_{new}}{d_{old}}$$

with $d_{old} = \|P_{old} - P_{camera}\|_2$ denoting the old distance between the object and the camera and $d_{new} = \|P_{new} - P_{camera}\|_2$ the new distance between the translated object and the camera.

In a *2AFC* task the subjects had to decide whether an object appeared to be moving toward or against their fingertip while performing a touch gesture. One interesting result of our evaluation is that the detection of induced object shifts does not depend on the display tilt angle. The relation between the detection thresholds $DT_{\pm 25}$ and the points of subjective equality and parallax are shown in Figure 9.19.

Similar to the results in the previous section, subjects judged static objects with positive parallax as moving with their finger and thus underestimated the distances to those objects. In contrast, static objects starting with negative parallax were judged as moving against the user's finger, which indicates that the subjects overestimated the distances in these cases. The point of subjective equality for shift factors of objects starting on the zero plane is not significantly different from zero, which indicates that subjects are more sensitive to the motion direction in these cases. Considering Figure 9.19 one can see that a vertical line segment between $DT_{\pm 0.25}$ defines the interval of possible shift factors, which may be applied to an object with given parallax. While for the proposed technique we only consider shifts, which move the objects closer to the surface (positive for objects with negative parallax and vice versa), one may consider moving the objects in either direction. A free-hand interaction technique may, for example, manipulate objects with negative parallax to move closer to the hand, while the user is grasping for them, thus reducing the overall magnitude of the hand motion. Alternatively a "smart" technique could selectively move an object closer or further away from the user's finger or from the interactive surface, depending on its accessibility

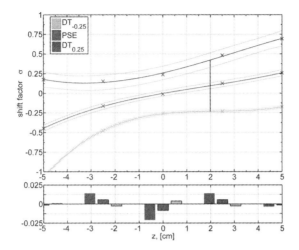

Figure 9.19: Fitted polynomial functions for $\sigma_{max}(z)$, $DT_{\pm 0.25}(z)$, and $PSE(z)$ (top) and the fitting residuals (bottom) for the generalized scaled shift technique. The x-axis shows the object's depth position z, the y-axis shows shift factors σ. The solid curves show fitted polynomial functions and the dotted curves show the 75% confidence intervals.

or appropriateness for the current task. Overall, there is a range of possible applications for these and similar kinds of imperceptible object motions, which might be usable for interactive applications.

On the practical side, the subjects' inability to discriminate small induced object manipulations is quite interesting since it allows users to interact with objects within shallow depth directly, and without noticeable impact on their performance, provided the accuracy is adjusted according to [Valkov et al. 11].

As shown in the next section, users are quite inaccurate in determining an object's depth at the end of the correction phase if tangible feedback is missing. Thus, the technique provides options to extend the so defined depth vicinity in which the user cannot determine if she first touched the display or the object. In particular, objects with negative or zero parallax, i.e., in front of or on the display surface, could be moved with the user's finger by about 33% of the total finger motion without the user noticing it. For instance, starting the manipulation when the pointing finger is at about 10 cm in front of the screen for an object at depth 3.3 cm will allow us to move the object exactly onto the display surface at the moment of touch contact, while this motion will remain imperceptible for most users. Although this comes at the cost of additional hardware equipment, it opens a range of new opportunities. For instance, combined with the approach proposed by Wilson and Benko [Wilson and Benko 10b], one could use stereoscopic rendering, thus augmenting non-planar content on the available surfaces or add objects

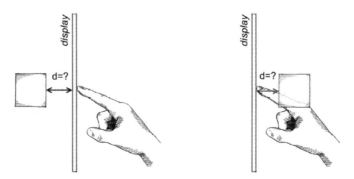

Figure 9.20: Illustration of misalignment between visually perceived and tactually felt contact with a virtual object.

floating in front of or beyond those surfaces. By shifting the virtual objects or application of some morphing technique on more complex surfaces, one could enable touch interaction while still providing passive haptic feedback in such a setup. Furthermore, the behavior of the PSE might indicate that one *needs to add some object manipulations* in order to enhance the interaction. In particular, since users apparently judge static objects as moving, one may need to move those objects to make them appear more static. As our initial user evaluation revealed, this was in fact the case with our setup (this is described in detail in Section 9.5.9).

Some users were initially confused when they were instructed to touch an object which is floating in front of the screen. Nevertheless, after a few touches most of them adapted to the task and usually didn't consider it unnatural or inconvenient. Moreover disparity cues are used for planning a pointing gesture on a very basic cognitive level. Therefore it might be possible to detect such thresholds that are independent from the cultural or educational background of the user.

9.5.8   Discrimination of Stereoscopic Depth

In the last few sections we have considered the human ability to discriminate induced depth shifts of either a single virtual object or the entire scene and have discussed a range of potential applications which may benefit from such techniques. Here we want to discuss the human ability to discriminate depth misalignment between visually perceived and tactually felt contact with a virtual object, without manipulating its properties in any way (illustrated in Figure 9.20). While this would supposedly reduce the depth of the available interaction volume, it also allows touch-based stereoscopic interaction without any further hardware devices. Moreover, existing 2D interaction techniques might be reused in stereoscopically rendered shallow depth 3D environments without modification, while the user may still benefit from the additional visual cues. One of the interesting observations in

Section 9.1 was that users have quickly adapted to the task of touching stereoscopic objects which were floating in front of or behind the display. One obvious reason for this is that the display surface has neither visual representation nor associated meaning in a stereoscopic context. On the other hand, it also means that there is some spatial displacement between the point at which the user sees that she is touching the object and the point at which she feels the touch. Interestingly, most of the users find nothing wrong with the interaction itself and consider a touch gesture finished when haptic feedback is received, although in some cases they have to pass their pointing finger through the visual representation of the object (for objects displayed with negative parallax) or never reach this visual representation (for positive parallax, cf. Figure 9.20). While this might be a remarkable exception to the general rule that vision usually dominates extraretinal cues, one must take into account the fact that the visual cues are in this case contradictory, too. Indeed, when reaching out to touch an object rendered with negative parallax, at some moment the binocular disparity cues are suggesting that the user's finger is behind the object. At the same time the finger is occluding parts of the object, since the display surface is behind it. This ambiguity is further enhanced by the missing haptic feedback which is expected when touching an object. Thus, while the user's finger has already reached the object and even gone beyond the point of initially expected contact, the user is misinterpreting the visual cues and usually continues the touch until either the discrepancies become too large or until some additional, clearly distinguishable cue (such as the sense of touching something) prevails, solving the ambiguity in either direction. While of particular interest, the question at which depth the discrepancy becomes too large and thus available for our attention is not easily answered. Depending on the object's size, visual appearance, or on-screen position, as well as on the interaction context and the touch-environment settings, e.g., display size, tilt angle, or user position, the importance of a single cue might differ significantly. Nevertheless engaging this effect would allow us to enlarge the interaction volume defined by the detection thresholds for the scaled shift techniques, since the objects do not need to be perfectly aligned with the display surface at the moment of touch.

Our experiments have shown that the object's size had a strong correlation with the users ability to discriminate depth misalignments. In particular, user's have problems in detecting positive parallaxes for large objects and negative parallaxes for small objects. One can explain the difference with occlusion of the objects by the finger. Objects with size of, for instance, $2\,cm$ are in large part occluded by the finger such that depth impression is disturbed on negative parallaxes. This led to more uncertainty in discrimination for these objects. With increased object size stereoscopic perception had more surface to rely on, providing a more accurate detection even if a subject's finger occluded a part of the surface.

On the practical side, the subjects' inability to discriminate depth misaligments motivates the possibility to design 3D interfaces without modifications of existing interaction techniques or the hardware. For instance, an interface designer could place some small widgets or anchors in front of the screen in order to improve their visibility and accessibility. Users could then directly interact with those widgets without noticeable impact on their performance, provided the accuracy is adjusted according to [Valkov et al. 11]. The detection thresholds define the narrow depth vicinity in which such objects could be scattered, i.e., if object size is under $3.5\,cm$, they may be placed at most at $4.35\,cm$ in front of the screen surface, but only at $1.3\,cm$ behind it. As discussed previously, this depth vicinity could be further extended by application of imperceptible object shifts.

9.5.9   Object Attracting Shift

While the results presented in the previous section motivate the applicability of the generalized scaled shift technique, there are a number of additional problems which arise when designing a practical interaction metaphor based on this technique. For instance, if objects are close to each other or overlapping, moving only one of them will be instantly noticed by the user. Especially in cases of textured objects in dense visualizations, moving one of them will gradually cover a larger or smaller part of the texture pattern on the other object, which may easily be detected. In addition, with multiple layered objects application of the scaled shift technique may lead to objects overlapping in depth or even switching their z-order. These and similar problems are inherent to all interfaces, in which a 3D interaction space is compressed to a 2D surface. Nevertheless, many investigations (most prominently [Oh and Stuerzlinger 05, Teather and Stuerzlinger 07]) have shown that 2D interaction with the topmost or with the closest visual surface in a 3D scene usually outperforms pure 3D interaction, which is the basis of the "magic" 3D interaction paradigm [Oh and Stuerzlinger 05]. Furthermore, in a head-tracked setup the user will most probably adjust her point of view and reduce the touch gesture to a 2D pointing task instead of touching a fully occluded object. The "magic" 3D interaction paradigm becomes even more important in the context of shallow depth visualizations.

A more significant problem with the interaction technique used in our experiment is the fact that the intended object should be known exactly prior to the application of the technique. Depending on the application this is often a non-trivial precondition. Relaxing the condition that the object be known exactly to an approximation of some volume in which it may reside simplifies the problem significantly. In this case, one could use a heuristic based on the last few positions of the finger and the current head orientation in order to determine safely and sufficiently early a volume in which the intended object resides [Nickel and Stiefelhagen 03, Stellmach and Dachselt 12].

In this section we present the *object attracting shift technique*, which is designed to alleviate these and similar problems. The core idea of the attracting shift technique, illustrated in Figure 9.21, is that a *generalized scaled shift* with maximal shift factor σ_{max} is applied to the object, which the user is intending

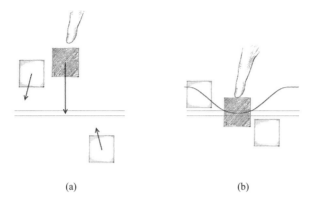

(a)   (b)

Figure 9.21: Illustration of the attracting shift technique: (a) objects close to the intended one are also moved, but with reduced shift factors; (b) at the end of the touch gesture the intended object is aligned with the zero parallax plane. The curve illustrates the distribution of relative shifts to nearby objects.

to touch, and to all objects around this one manipulations with decreasing shift factors are applied. Thus figuratively the intended object (the *attractor*) to which the strongest shift factor is applied "attracts" all objects around itself.

With $P_0 \in \mathbb{R}^3, P_0 = (x_0\ y_0\ z_0)^T$ denoting the position of the attractor and $P \in \mathbb{R}^3, P = (x\ y\ z)^T$ denoting the position of an arbitrary object around P_0 we can then express the shift factor σ as

$$\sigma = \sigma_{max}(z) \cdot \alpha(r_{xy})$$

with $r_{xy} = \sqrt{(x-x_0)^2 + (y-y_0)^2}$ denoting the projected distance between P_0 and P. In the above equation $\sigma_{max}(d)$ denotes the maximal shift factor, which could be imperceptibly applied to an object starting at distance d from the display surface. The function $\alpha(r_{xy})$ determines the amount of maximal shift to be applied to an object depending on its distance from the attractor, i.e., the intended object. Reflecting on the form of $\alpha(r_{xy})$ one can see that it has to be (strictly) decreasing, with maximum of 1 at $r_{xy} = 0$. For our purpose, a Gaussian curve is a reasonable choice. Thus we have

$$\sigma = \sigma_{max} \cdot e^{-1.39\frac{r_{xy}^2}{R^2}}$$

with cut radius $R \in \mathbb{R}$ denoting the radius at which the strength of the applied shift factor falls below 25%.

As discussed in Section 9.5, the maximal shift factor, which can be imperceptibly applied to an object starting at distance z from the display surface is defined by the detection thresholds $DT_{\pm 0.25}(z)$ (cf. Figure 9.19). For instance,

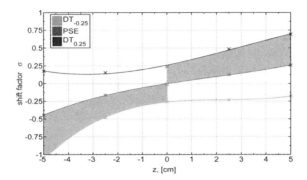

Figure 9.22: Illustration of the available shift factor space $\sigma_{max}(z)$. The solid lines show the fitted polynomial functions for $DT_{\pm 0.25}(z)$ and $PSE(z)$ for the generalized scaled shift technique. The shaded area represents the available shift factors, which could be applied to imperceptibly manipulate an object.

for objects starting 2 cm in front of the surface, i.e., with negative parallax, one could apply shift factors between -0.23 and 0.42 without the user noticing the motion. Since we are currently only interested in moving the objects closer to the display surface, we only consider positive shift factors for objects with negative parallax and negative shift factors for objects with positive parallax. This new shift factor space is illustrated by the shaded area in Figure 9.22. Objects aligned with the display surface should not be manipulated. Thus the maximal applicable shift factor σ_{max} could be defined as:

$$\sigma_{max}(z) = \begin{cases} DT_{0.25}(z) & z > 0 \\ 0 & z = 0 \\ DT_{-0.25}(z) & z < 0 \end{cases}$$

Considering this definition of $\sigma_{max}(z)$ and the detection thresholds $DT_{\pm 0.25}$ reported in the previous chapter one can see that unscaled application of σ_{max} allows shifting an object to the opposite side of the display and that even the partial application of σ_{max}-shifts may align an object to the display surface. Thus the precise knowledge of the intended object is not needed. The system only has to determine and manipulate *some* object near the intended one. The nearby objects will then be attracted by this one, albeit with smaller shift factors, and will probably end up aligned with the display or very close to it, too. As shown in Figure 9.22, the detection thresholds are decreasing when objects get closer to the display surface. Thus manipulating an object farther alway from the display surface will push all near objects closer to the surface. Recalling from Section 9.5.7 that $\Delta d_{object} = \sigma \cdot \Delta d_{finger}$, we could then express the new depth of an arbitrary object as function of its depth, distance to the attractor, and finger motion. An illustration of the object displacement for fixed $\Delta d_{finger} = 3cm$ and varying d_{object}

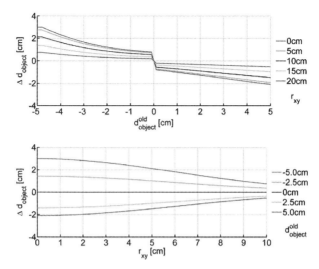

Figure 9.23: Illustration of the absolute object motion for finger motion $\Delta d_{finger} = 3\,cm$ as a function of object's start parallax (top) or distance to the attractor (bottom).

or r_{xy} is shown in Figure 9.23. As one can see in these figures, objects never switch their z-order, and the absolute object motions are sufficient to bring them to the zero parallax plane (and beyond, if desired). Interestingly, it seems to be a "best" cut radius for the techniques at about $2°$ (about $5cm$ at $1m$ distance) visual angle, which coincides with the foveal vision. Radii above or below this increase the chance that the user detects the object's motion. Nevertheless, it is currently not clear how this value depends on the scene or the setup's parameters.

None of the participants in our evaluations reported having problems with the stereoscopic impression, and most of them described the presented content as realistic. Upon request the participants were able to determine the exact depth of an object and some were surprised how the manipulation redirected their finger to the surface. Though we explained that we slightly move the objects during the touch gesture, some of the participants were confused, since they never "saw" objects changing their depth position.

As we already discussed, application of certain undetectable object manipulations aid the user's perception while reaching for virtual objects and may redirect her finger to the display surface, where tactile feedback is provided. With the attracting-shift technique we have relaxed the inherent pre-condition that the intended object should be known in advance, which makes the technique far more practical. In contrast to alternative techniques that may be used for interaction with stereoscopic content, which either lack haptic feedback (e.g., free-hand, in-air interaction) or require additional instrumentation (e.g., tangible views), the proposed approach brings together direct-touch interaction with haptic feedback at the sacrifice of depth.

Talking about interaction with stereoscopic content one is tempted to fit the approach in the 3D user interface domain; however, an interface designer should not forget that the presented technique per se is inherently two-dimensional. Thus there is no way for the system to determine at the end of the touch which object was intended, if multiple objects were displayed on top of each other. Nevertheless, as discussed earlier, "magic 3D" and "shallow depth" are two powerful notions, suitable in many application scenarios.

Considering Figure 9.22 again, one can see that a vertical line segment between $DT_{+0.25}$ and $DT_{-0.25}$ defines the interval of possible shift factors, which may be applied to an object with given parallax. While for the attracting shift technique we only consider shifts which move the objects closer to the surface (positive for objects with negative parallax and vice versa), one may consider moving the objects in either direction. A free-hand interaction technique may – for example – manipulate objects with negative parallax to move closer to the hand while the user is grasping for them and thus reduce the overall magnitude of the hand motion. Alternatively a "smart" technique could selectively move an object closer or farther away from the user's finger or from the interactive surface, depending on its accessibility or appropriateness for the current task. Overall, there is a range of possible applications for this and similar kinds of imperceptible object motions, which might be usable for interaction design.

On the practical side, the formulation of the scaled shift technique as a function of only the depth of the subject's finger and the extent of the $DT_{\pm 0.25}$ ranges for different parallaxes make it possible to reduce the required precision of the finger tracker. Indeed, since the $DT_{\pm 0.25}$ ranges allow shifting an object to the opposite side of the display, one can use slightly smaller values as σ_{max} for manipulation, such that incorrectly large values of Δd_{finger} are still imperceptible. The manipulation of the object should then be stopped, when its depth reaches zero. In contrast to the precision, the tracker's speed should be as high as possible. In particular, since the typical duration of a touch gesture is between 0.5 and 1.5 seconds, and the technique is applied at the very end of this gesture, one has to provide at least 60 fps for reasonably smooth object motions. Otherwise, the motion of the object will be either jerky, which could then be easily detected, or no shift could be applied at all.

Further Reading

The content of this section is mostly based on the work we have done with Klaus Hinrichs, Alexander Giesler, and Sven Strothoff [Valkov et al. 14, Valkov et al. 11, Valkov et al. 12, Strothoff et al. 11, Giesler et al. 14], where the results from the user evaluations are discussed in great detail, and some additional design implication are presented.

In 2013 Argelaguet and Andujar [Argelaguet and Andujar 13] published an in-depth survey of 3D object selection techniques for virtual environments, which takes into account different aspects of the visio-motor coordination, display types, and input devices. An essential concept in this context is the *continuous interaction space* defined by Marquardt et. al. [Marquardt et al. 11]. The concept is extended in the context of stereoscopic projections by Jackson et al. [Jackson et al. 12]. Coffey et al. [Coffey et al. 12a] proposed a multi-surface, multi-touch VR interface, where the content is presented stereoscopically on a vertical display and the user interacts with its monoscopic "shadow" on a multi-touch enabled tabletop. Some recent work [Simeone and Gellersen 15] indicates that such interfaces might be beneficial, especially in dense visualizations, where occlusion poses a significant challenge for direct interaction techniques.

Exercises

1. Implement a triangle cursor for interaction with objects with *positive* parallax in a fishtank tabletop setup. What is different compared to the original triangle cursor?

2. Why is the void shadow technique using a "fake" light source for each object? What happens if one uses a simple omni-directional point light?

3. Implement the attracting shift technique. Why is it important that the user doesn't perceive the objects shifts? How could one extend the technique to support multiple touch points?

10

Pen and Multi-Touch Modeling and Recognition

Writing means sharing. It's part of the human condition to want to share things — thoughts, ideas, opinions.

—Paulo Coelho

10.1   Introduction

This chapter describes some examples for pen and multi-touch modeling and recognition. An in-depth look at Petri Nets modeling for input devices is found in Chapter 11. Input device modeling is not a recent phenomenon. After the introduction of the Sketchpad in 1962 by Ivan Sutherland, it was a matter of time until someone would imagine a model for pen interaction. In 1968, William E. Newman published *A System for Interactive Graphical Programming*, which describes a state-diagram with the flow of a model. Later, in 1990, the seminal work by Bill Buxton showed us what a descriptive model can be for the input devices of that era (e.g., mouse, pen, single-touch) with his publication titled "A Three-State Model of Graphical Input" [Buxton 90]. Another model for input interaction was published by Myers [Myers 90].

There have been various methods proposed to achieve touch gesture recognition, including the use of finite state machines [Hong and Huang 00, Hong et al. 00], hidden markov models (HMM) [Sezgin and Davis 05], neural networks [Pittman 91], dynamic programming [MacLean and Labahn 10], featured-based classifiers [Rubine 91], and template matching [Kara and Stahovich 05, Wobbrock et al. 07, Anthony and Wobbrock 10, Li 10]. Thorough reviews can be found in [Johnson et al. 09, Tappert et al. 90, Plamondon and Srihari 00].

Some of the methods used in handwriting recognition [Tappert et al. 90] serve as a foundation for gesture recognition techniques [Blumenstein et al. 03].

Side Note 10.1: Touch for Young Children

Lisa Anthony and her colleagues have been working to understand the interaction between touch devices and younger children. This is very important work because it provides a road map for gesture recognizers to adapt to unintentional touches. This is not only helpful for applications targeted for kids but it also helps recognizers to adapt to different users, including users with disabilities. Some of the interesting findings are that kids touch outside of the screen (intentional and unintentional) and produce larger *holdovers* ("an unintentional touch in the location of the previous target" [Anthony et al. 13b]) making it harder to recognize the desired target, among others [Anthony et al. 12]. Some of the challenge is even more evident for the youngest age group (ages 7 to 10) [Anthony et al. 13b]. Based on various studies by Lisa and colleagues, a set of guidelines has been suggested [Anthony et al. 12, Anthony et al. 13b, Anthony et al. 13a]. The guidelines are [Anthony et al. 13a]: (1) Provide visual feedback for surface gestures interaction on mobile device. (2) Do not include unfamiliar gestures. (3) Test new gesture sets with the target recognizer in advanced. In her site (http://lisa-anthony.com), you can find additional information about her projects, which includes Mobile Touch and Gesture Interaction for Children (MTAGIC) [Anthony et al. 12, Anthony et al. 13b, Anthony et al. 13a, Brown and Anthony 12].

While handwriting recognition efforts date as far back as the 1950s [Tappert et al. 90], it has been the work of Rubine [Rubine 91] that has been used as a foundation by some in the gesture recognition area [Signer et al. 07, Wobbrock et al. 07]. The Rubine algorithm used a simple training technique with specific features [Rubine 91].

10.2 The Dollar Family

The dollar ($) family of algorithms started with $1 algorithm [Wobbrock et al. 07]. The "$ algorithms"[1] is a partial list of techniques derived or inspired by work from the $1 algorithm [Wobbrock et al. 07], such as [Kratz and Rohs 11, Kratz and Rohs 10, Anthony and Wobbrock 10, Li 10, Vatavu et al. 12]. The $1 algorithm [Wobbrock et al. 07] provided a simple way to develop a basic gesture-detection method. In contrast, algorithms based on hidden Markov models or neural networks [Pittman 91] involved a high level of complexity for the developer and the system

---

[1] Referred to as the dollar family by their authors.

as well. The $1 algorithm provided a very fast solution to interactive gesture recognition with less than 100 lines of code [Wobbrock et al. 07] and required a simple training set. However, it is not meant for the recognition of multi-touch gestures. This does not diminish in any way the importance of the $1 algorithm, because there are several features that make it important. Some examples are the obvious resampling of the gesture, the indicative angle ("the angle formed between the centroid of the gesture and [the] gesture's first point" [Wobbrock et al. 07]), and the re-scaling and translation to a reference point to keep the centroid at (0,0). The $1 algorithm was in part inspired by the publications titled *SHARK2: A Large Vocabulary Shorthand Writing System for Pen-Based Computers* [Kristensson and Zhai 04] and *Cursive Script Recognition by Elastic Matching* [Schomaker and Segers 99]. The goals of the $ family of algorithms are described below:

- Present an easy-to-implement stroke recognizer algorithm.

- Compare $1 with other sophisticated algorithms to show that it can compare certain types of symbols.

- Understand gesture recognition performance for users, recognizer performance, and human subjective preferences.

- Input device agnostics.

The $N algorithm [Anthony and Wobbrock 10], with double the amount of code (240 lines), improved the $1 algorithm [Wobbrock et al. 07] to allow single strokes and rotation invariance discrimination. For example, to make a distinction between A and $\forall$, rotation must be bounded by less than $\pm90°$ [Anthony and Wobbrock 10]. The $N algorithm [Anthony and Wobbrock 10] was extended primarily to allow single strokes to be recognized. This algorithm provided support for automatic recognition between 1D and 2D gestures by using "the ratio of the sides of a gesture's oriented bounding box (MIN-SIDE vs MAX-SIDE)" [Anthony and Wobbrock 10]. In addition, the algorithm provided recognition for a subset of templates to optimize the code. This reduction of templates was done by determining if the start directions are similar and by computing the angle formed from the start point through the eighth point. A common feature of the $1 and $N algorithms [Wobbrock et al. 07, Anthony and Wobbrock 10] is the utilization of the golden section search [Press et al. 07].

Other methods similar to the $1 [Wobbrock et al. 07] and $N [Anthony and Wobbrock 10] algorithms have been implemented. For example, the *protractor gesture recognizer* algorithm [Li 10] works by applying a nearest neighbor approach. This algorithm is very close to the $1 algorithm [Wobbrock et al. 07] but attempts to remove different drawing speeds, different gesture locations on the screen, and noise in gesture orientation. The study by Vatavu et al. (referred to as $P), used the concept of a cloud of points to recognize strokes [Vatavu et al. 12]. Additional algorithms provide great resources for future work. Dean Rubine provided an excellent set of features to be tested with multi-touch data. In addition to the Rubine algorithm [Rubine 91], the work of Wang et al. [Wang et al. 09] can be used to find whether or not the gesture was created with fingers in an oblique position. Finally, $P [Vatavu et al. 12] provided a great direction for multi-touch recognition.

10.2.1 $1 Recognizer

The $1 algorithm also known as **$1 UniStroke Recognizer** was published by Wobbrock and colleagues in 2007. The $1 UniStroke Recognizer can be found at http://depts.washington.edu/aimgroup/proj/dollar/. This is a very interesting algorithm and the important elegance of this work can be recognized by the different modifications based on this original work, and the number of citations that it receives.

Limitations

Before we describe the $1 algorithm, it is important to understand its limitations. The most obvious limitation is that $1 does not recognize multiple strokes. A single stroke does not allow the user to lift the pen from the device. For example, an exclamation point requires a multi-stroke. Also, the fact that $1 is rotation invariant, it cannot recognize the letter A versus the symbol ∀ ("for all"). However, this can be fixed by creating two separate templates. Also, the recognizer does not use time as a criterion. Finally, $1 algorithm requires templates to find the closest match in 2D Euclidean!space. Wobbrock and colleagues find this to be a limitation because as the template set grows, so does the complexity of the algorithm (running time) [Wobbrock et al. 07].

Algorithm

Algorithm 10.1 (recognizer), which is similar to the one in the original publication [Wobbrock et al. 07] but reflects our implementation. This algorithm is divided into four parts:

1. Resampling.

2. Rotate based on "indicative angle."

3. Scale and translate.

4. Find the optimal angle for the best score.

Resampling, as shown in Algorithm 10.2, is the first block required for this algorithm. $1 needed to resample because each hardware has different sampling rates and the movement of users may differ from shape to shape (e.g., speed).

Algorithm 10.1 $1 Algorithm: Recognizer

Require: PointList (pts) ; boolean (useProtractor).
Require: ARange = Deg2Rad(45.0); APrecision = Deg2Rad(2.0).
Require: w = h = 250
Require: Diagonal = $sqrt(w^2, h^2)$; HalfDiagonal = $0.5 * Diagonal$
 1: $pts \leftarrow Resample(pts, NumPoints)$
 2: $rad\_decimal \leftarrow IndicativeAngle(pts)$
 3: $pts \leftarrow RotateBy(pts, -rad\_decimal)$
 4: $pts \leftarrow ScaleTo(pts, BoudingRectangleSize)$
 5: $pts \leftarrow TranslateTo(pts, Point0, 0)$
 6: $b \leftarrow +\infty$
 7: $u \leftarrow -1y$
 8: **for** $i \leftarrow 0$ to $pts.size() - 1$ **do**
 9:     **if** $useProtractor$ **then**
10:         $d \leftarrow OptimalCosineDistance(pts)$
11:     **else**
12:         $d \leftarrow DistanceAtBestAngle(pts, ARange, -ARange, APrecision)$
13:     **if** $d < b$ **then**
14:         $b \leftarrow d$ // Best Distance
15:         $u \leftarrow i$
16: **if** $U = -1$ **then**
17:     **return** $Pair < "NoMatch", 0.0 >$
18: **else**
19:     **if** $useProtractor$ **then**
20:         $1.0/b$
21:     **else**
22:         $1.0 - b/HalfDiagonal$
23:     **return** Pair<$pts[u].shapeName()$, b>

Given **M** original points ($PathLength(points)$) divided by $\mathbf{N}^2$ (where $N = 64$ was found to be adequate), gives each increment **I** between each **N** new points. If the distance covered exceeds **I**, a new point is added through linear interpolation. This allows us to have exactly N points to measure the distance from the candidate $C[k]$ to a template $T_i[k]$ for $k = 1$ to N.

The second step for this algorithm is to rotate the candidate based on an indicative angle. An indicative angle is defined by $1 algorithm as the "angle formed between the centroid of the gesture $(\bar{x}, \bar{y})$ and the gesture's first point" [Wobbrock et al. 07]. Once the indicative angle is calculated, the shape is rotated to 0°. First, the **IndicativeAngle** (Algorithm 10.4) function yields the angle in radians to be passed to the function **RotateBy** (Algorithm 10.5. In other words,

---

[2]Given that zero is the starting index in the code, the division is $\frac{M}{(N-1)}$.

Algorithm 10.2 $1 Algorithm: Resampling

Require: PointList (pts) ; int (n).
1: $I \leftarrow PathLength(pts)/(n-1)$ // interval length
2: $D \leftarrow 0.0$
3: $newpts[0] \leftarrow pts[0]$
4: **for** $i \leftarrow 1$ to $pts.size() - 1$ **do**
5:    $d \leftarrow Distance(pts[i-1], pts[i])$
6:    **if** $(D+d) \geq I$ **then**
7:       $q.x \leftarrow pts[i-1].x + ((I-D)/d) * (pts[i].x - pts[i-1].x)$
8:       $q.y \leftarrow pts[i-1].y + ((I-D)/d) * (pts[i].y - pts[i-1].y)$ // q is a Point(x,y)
9:       $newpts.push\_back(q)$
10:      $pts.insert(i,q)$ // Insert q at position i. In other words, q will be the next i in pts
11:      $D \leftarrow 0.0$
12:   **else**
13:      $D \leftarrow D+d$
14: **if** $newpts.size() == n-1$ **then**
15:    $newpts.push\_back(pts[pts.size()-1])$ // We fall behind because of rounding error
16: **return** $newpts$

Algorithm 10.3 $1 Algorithm: Centroid

Require: PointList (pts)
1: $x \leftarrow y \leftarrow 0.0$
2: **for** $i \leftarrow 0$ to $pts.size() - 1$ **do**
3:    $x \leftarrow x + pts[i].x$
4:    $y \leftarrow y + pts[i].y$
5: $x \leftarrow x/pts.size()$
6: $y \leftarrow y/pts.size()$
7: **return** $Point(x,y)$

Algorithm 10.4 $1 Algorithm: IndicativeAngle

Require: PointList (pts)
1: $c \leftarrow Centroid(pts)$
2: **return** $atan2(c.y - pts[0].y, c.x - pts[0].x)$

(RotateBy) requires the value returned by the **IndicativeAngle** with a negative sign in front ($points = RotateBy(Points, -radians)$).

Algorithm 10.5 $1 Algorithm: RotateBy

Require: PointList (pts), double (θ) // θ is the indicative angle.
1: $c \leftarrow Centroid(pts)$
2: **for** $i \leftarrow 0$ to $pts.size() - 1$ **do**
3:     $q.x \leftarrow (pts[i].x - c.x) * \cos(\theta) - (pts[i].y - c.y) * \sin(\theta) + c.x$
4:     $q.y \leftarrow (pts[i].x - c.x) * \sin(\theta) - (pts[i].y - c.y) * \cos(\theta) + c.Y$
5:     $newpts.push\_back(q)$
6: **return** $newpts$

Once the shape has been rotated by the indicative angle, scaling and translation follows, as step 3. First, the candidate shape is non-uniformly scaled to a reference square using the **ScaleTo** function. This does create some limitations due to the rotation invariance. Once the candidate gesture is rotated, there is no guarantee that the given candidate **C** will align with a template **T**. A simple approach is a brute-force approach. However, this approach proves to be expensive for gesture recognition. $1 recognizer selected the golden section search (GSS) algorithm [Press et al. 07], using the golden ratio $\phi = 0.5(-1 + \sqrt{5})$. The reason is that it is expected that the candidate will compare more dissimilar templates than similar ones. The GSS performs better in this case. If it was the other way around, the hill-climbing approach would be a better choice because it performs better similar gestures.

In their experiment, for a 480 similar gesture sample, "no match was found beyond $\pm 45°$ from the indicative angle" [Wobbrock et al. 07]. This allowed them to bound GSS to $\pm 45°$ and a $2°$ threshold. This gives a guarantee of GSS of having no more than 10 iterations.

Once scaled, the candidate gesture is translated to a reference point so its centroid $(\bar{x}, \bar{y})$ is at $(0,0)$ using the **TranslateTo** function.

The last step allows us to recognize the correct template given a candidate gesture. Given that all templates T_i and the current candidate **C** have been re-sampled, rotated, scaled, and translated, this step can match the candidate to a template. The function **Recognize** allows the candidate to find the best matching template using two additional functions: **DistanceAtBestAngle** and **DistanceAtAngle**. Each of these functions can be described with Equations 10.1 and 10.2, respectively. Note that Equation 10.1 starts with index 1 but the code starts with index 0. The complete source code can be found in the $ family (https://depts.washington.edu/aimgroup/proj/dollar/), which includes source code and complete pseudo-code.

$$d_i = \frac{1}{n} \sum_{k=1}^{N} \sqrt{(C[k]_x - T_i[k]_x)^2 + (C[k]_y - T_i[k]_y)^2} \tag{10.1}$$

$$score = 1 - \frac{d_i^*}{\frac{1}{2}\sqrt{size^2 + size^2}} \qquad (10.2)$$

10.2.2 $1 Recognizer with Protractor

Looking at some of the limitationed mentions for $1, Yang Li realized that candidate **C** needed to be sped up when comparing the set of templates **T** in "Protractor: A Fast and Accurate Gesture Recognizer" [Li 10]. The $1 recognizer grows linearly as the number of templates needed to compare to a given candidate. Protractor remains constant regardless of the number of templates.

Protractor removes factors such as speed, gesture location on the display, and noise in gesture orientation. The difference with $1 recognizer is that the preprocessing converts the 2D data points to a uniform vector. Then protractor resamples a gesture into a fixed equidistant number of points **N** ($N = 16$), similar to the $1 algorithm and translates them to make the centroid coordinates (0,0). This last step reduces the speed and screen location limitations of $1.

Protractor has two options. Either orientation-invariant or orientation-sensitive. The former rotates the gesture by its indicative angle. This makes all the templates have zero indicative orientation. If protractor is set to orientation-sensitive, then protractor aligns the indicative angle of a given gesture with one of eight base cardinal orientation: North, South, East, West, NorthWest, North East, South West, South East. This allows protractor to discerned up to eight different gesture orientations. However, if the developer specifies the same shape for each of those eight categories, then protractor behaves orientation-invariant. Note that while $1 rescale points to fit a reference square, protractor does not. This allows us to preserve the aspect ratio for a gesture. This also helps with one-dimensional gestures, such as vertical or horizontal lines.

10.2.3 $N Recognizer

The $N algorithm by Anthony and Wobbrock [Anthony and Wobbrock 10] is an extension of the original $1. This recognizer addressed some of the limitations of the original work by Wobbrock et al. [Wobbrock et al. 07]. One of the major limitations of $1 is the lack of multi-stroke recognition. Two examples for a multi-stroke symbol are the exclamation point "!" and the letter "X." $N also improves the recognition of one-dimensional symbols, for example, a vertical or horizontal lines. In addition, the fact that the $N is able to recognize shapes with different rotations, such as "A" and "∀", it makes the $N more powerful. The contributions of $N algorithm can be summarized as follows:

1. Multi-stroke representation as a set of unistrokes. This includes the representation of all possible stroke orientation.

2. The recognition of one-dimensional figures.

3. The use of constraint rotation invariance to allow the recognition of additional symbols.

4. Evaluation of $N using algebra symbols by middle-school and high-school students.

Limitations

While $N algorithms solve some of the problems of $1, this comes at a cost of new limitations. One of the major limitations is that $N cannot deduce complicated gestures, for example, a scratch-out gesture for erasing. Also, given the nature of $N uni-stroke permutations which it allows to recognize a candidate symbol drawn with fewer strokes (e.g., 1-stroke "D" vs 2-strokes "D"), while a candidate symbol with more strokes will not match unless the strokes are drawn in the same direction. Another limitation is that it lacks scale or position awareness. Finally, while $N has made improvements in speed, if templates are larger than thirty and some of those templates with more than five strokes, the recognition process will probably experience a slow response.

While the limitations make it less powerful than some of the state-of-the-art hand-writing or sketch systems, the goal still remains the same: to provide a simple algorithm while still a fast and accurate recognizer. It is also known that gestures need to be simple, distinct, and quick to execute [Anthony and Wobbrock 10].

Algorithm

The first step in $N is to store each multi-stroke as a set of uni-stroke permutations: in other words, each possible combination of a gesture order and direction. An example is a multi-stroke "X," which requires two initial input contacts from the user (for one backward slash and one forward slash). The "X" creates 8 different permutations. In order to create the permutations, the authors used *Heap Permute* [Heap 63, Wikipedia 15b] (see about permutations in [Levitin 12, pp. 144–149]). While this causes a combinatorial explosion, this is mitigated because most symbols require few strokes. In addition, this is done before recognition (only runs once). Each component stroke is treated as a dichotomous variable ([0,1]) [Anthony and Wobbrock 10], in which each bit can represent either forward (0) or reverse (1). At recognition time, the $N algorithm connected the uni-strokes drawn to form a multi-stroke, which is then preprocessed (using similar steps to $1) and compared to "uni-stroke permutations using Euclidean distances as in $1" [Anthony and Wobbrock 10]. For additional information see the pseudo-code in [Anthony and Wobbrock 10] and the website (with source code) at http://depts.washington.edu/aimgroup/proj/dollar/ndollar.html. A modified version of the $ N algorithm, which uses the protractor concept was published later [Anthony and Wobbrock 12].

10.2.4 $ Family: $P and Beyond

One of the problems with $N is the memory and running time complexity explosion, which makes it NP-complete [Cormen et al. 09, Ch. 34]. However, in practice, $N provides a feasible solution because the permutations are pre-computed and the number of templates is kept low. However, a solution to this data explosion was offered in the algorithm called $P [Vatavu et al. 12].

$P algorithm represents gestures as a "cloud of points," making it insensitive to the direction of stroke or the order of stroke [Vatavu et al. 12]. The algorithm tries to find a match between a candidate gesture C and a template, where the function M associates each point $C_i \in C$ with exactly one point $T_j \in T$, $T_j = M(C_i)$ [Vatavu et al. 12].

Ideally, the amount of points between T and C will have the same amount of points. However, this is not always true in a real-time environment. Nevertheless, for this discussion, you can assume that the amount of a pair of points are equal for T and C. Using an inspiration from the original $ algorithm ($1) and the proportional shape distance of Shark^2 [Kristensson and Zhai 04], Vatavu and colleagues used the sum of Euclidean distances for all pairs of points of M, as shown in Equation 10.3 [Vatavu et al. 12] (where $i = j$).

$$\sum_{i=1}^{n} ||C_i - T_j|| = \sum_{i=1}^{n} \sqrt{(C_i.x - T_j.x)^2 + (C_i.y - T_j.y)^2} \qquad (10.3)$$

Vatavu and colleagues provided a set of greedy algorithms to test which one was the best candidate for $P. They chose to use a modified version of greedy-2, as they called it, with weights (named greedy-5). The algorithm is best expressed by them in the following quote (from greedy-2) [Vatavu et al. 12]:

> For each point in the first cloud (C_i), find the closest point from the second cloud that hasn't been matched yet. Once point C_i is matched, continue with $C_i + 1$ until all points from C are matched ($i = 1 \ldots n1$). The complexity is $O(n^2)$ as for every point from C a linear search needs to be performed in T.

Greedy-5 is similar to the algorithm just stated, but it uses weight (defined in Equation 10.5) in the formula, as shown in Equation 10.6. This algorithm running time is $O(n^{2+\varepsilon})$. This algorithm is dependent "on the direction of matching" [Vatavu et al. 12]. This means that the implementation must return (Equation 10.4):

$$\min(\text{Greedy-X}(C,T), \text{Greedy-X}(T,C)) \qquad (10.4)$$

$$w_i = 1 - \frac{i-1}{n} \qquad (10.5)$$

Side Note 10.2: A Brave New World

Multi-touch, pen, and other modern input devices have created a set of challenges to designers, developers, and researchers. This chapters deals with multi-touch and pen. In particular, the recognition of touch points. In this new world of modern input devices, Wigdor and Wixon published a book title *Brave NUI World: Designing Natural User Interfaces for Touch and Gesture* [Wigdor and Wixon 11]. Several issues are covered, including chapters such as "Fat Fingers", "No Touch Left Behind: Feedback is Essential", and "Touch versus In-Air Gestures", among others [Wigdor and Wixon 11].

$$\sum_{i=1}^{n} \left(w_i \cdot ||C_i - T_j|| \right) \tag{10.6}$$

This new algorithm in the $ family, $P, provides multiple benefits over its predecessors. First, given that the new algorithm does not require permutations, the memory is linear for training set T ($O(T)$). It also allows the algorithm to be run for sets of uni-strokes or multi-strokes. As already mentioned, another benefit is the direction invariance that it has. It's running time is faster than $O(n^{2.5})$. Finally, maybe the largest benefit of $P and possibly of the entire $ family is the possibility to keep extending this recognizer into other devices, domains, and dimensions. The $ family is probably one of the simplest yet most elegant solutions to recognition. Table 10.1 provides a basic cheat sheet for the $ [Vatavu et al. 12].

10.3   Proton++ and More

There are several types of pen or touch recognizers. In this section we briefly described Proton and Proton++. Additional multi-touch recognizers exist such as Gesture Coder (which creates FSM by demonstration) [Lü and Li 12] and GestIt (which uses low-level Petri Net (PN) using tokens as points in a trace) [Spano et al. 13].

Proton and Proton++ provide a way to recognize multi-touch interaction using RegEx. This approach allows people to define gestures using regular expression gestures. For example, the scale gesture is noted using RegEx as [Kin et al. 12b, Kin et al. 12a]: $D_1^s M_1^s * D_2^a (M_1^s | M_2^a) * (U_1^s M_2^a * U_2^a | U_2^a M_1^s * U_1^s)^3$. In Proton++ [Kin et al. 12a], they also provide a way to include time into gestures, which was a

---

[3]D=Down, M=Move, U=Up; s=shape, b=background, a=any (a|b).

Table 10.1: Cheat Sheet for the $-family: $1, Protractor, $N, and $P.

Criteria	$1	Protractor	$N	$P
❶ Gesture types				
recognizes single strokes	✓	✓	✓	✓
recognizes multi-strokes	✗	✗	✓	✓
is scale-invariant	✓	✓	✓	✓
is rotation-invariant	✗	✓	✓	✓
is direction-invariant	✓	✗	✗	✓
❷ Performance				
user-dependent accuracy (st†)	99.5% ✶	99.4% ✶	98.0%	99.3% ✶
user-independent accuracy (st†)	97.1% ✶	95.9%	95.2%	96.6%
user-dependent accuracy (mt‡)	✗	✗	97.0%	98.4% ✶
user-independent accuracy (mt‡)	✗	✗	96.1%	98.0% ✶
algorithmic complexity	$O(n \cdot T \cdot R)$	$O(n \cdot T)$	$O(n \cdot T \cdot S! \cdot 2^S)$	$O(n^{2.5} \cdot T)$
memory to store the training set	$O(n \cdot T)$	$O(n \cdot T)$	$O(n \cdot T \cdot S! \cdot 2^S)$	$O(n \cdot T)$
❸ Code writing				
needs rotation search (GSS)	yes ✐	no	yes ✐	no
needs sped-up preprocessing	no	no	yes ✐	no
approx. # of lines of code	100 ✐	50	200 ✐ ✐	70

NOTES:

[1] n is the number of sampled points; T = the number of training samples per gesture type; R = the number of iterations required by the golden section search (GSS) algorithm used by $1 (experimentally set to 10 [Wobbrock et al. 07]); S = the number of strokes in a multistroke; $S! \cdot 2^S$ = the number of different permutations of stroke ordering and direction needed by $N [Anthony and Wobbrock 10];

[2] A ✐ symbol means more coding is required. A ✶ indicates best recognition performance.

† single strokes (st).

‡ multi-strokes (mt).

feature missing from the first effort (Proton). We have to say that, besides the $ family, Proton++ seems to show lots of promise. We recommend the reader to look in detail at both publications [Kin et al. 12b, Kin et al. 12a].

Side Note 10.3: The Fat Finger Problem

The "fat finger" problem, covered in *A Brave NUI World* [Wigdor and Wixon 11], is created by two issues: (1) A large area produced by the user's finger that is in contact with the surface device. (2) The occlusion of the pixel(s) produced by the finger on the surface device creates a visual problem for the user because he/she cannot see the object. The trivial solution to this problem is to make all the objects larger. However, this limits the ability for the UI as only fewer objects can be placed on the screen, among other limitations.

The book *A Brave NUI World* provides a set of guidelines to avoid this problem [Wigdor and Wixon 11, Ch .13]: (a) Make objects larger, with a minimum of 1.6 cm for large touch surfaces and 0.9 cm for small surfaces. (b) Consider user perception to adjust the touch point. Ideally, a pilot-study may provide sufficient data to see how the users are selecting a target for a given application. (c) use iceberg targets, which provide a larger selection area for smaller targets. (d) Reduce the role of the land-on event (in a touch system). In other words, changing the UI to accommodate confirmation of the target. For example, if a user touches an object but moves his/her finger away to the right of the display while still touching the surface, then the system can recognize the user changed his/her mind about the original target. If the user touches the target and lifts the finger, then it can be assumed that the target was the intended selection. For additional information see [Holz and Baudisch 10, Yatani et al. 08].

A note of caution when moving from different multi-touch surfaces (or different systems): What worked for a mobile phone is not always transferable to a large multi-touch display. An example given in [Wigdor and Wixon 11] is the producers of the game Halo. Moving from a PC to a game console, the user interaction had to be changed.

10.4 FETOUCH

This section covers Feature Extraction Multi-Touch System (FETOUCH) from its first iteration[4] to the final one that runs on a multi-threaded application. This section is meant to show you how to work with simple feature extractions while demonstrating the iteration that goes into finding a solution.

When using raw touch data, most systems where multi-touch is available (e.g., iOS, Windows) provide a **trace**, which contains a set of points with coordinates

---

[4]FETouch initial fefinitions were partially inspired by a problem description created by Greg Hamerly.

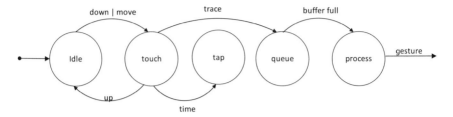

Figure 10.1: State machine.

x and y. In addition, the system will generate a **timestamp** for each point and a unique **ID**, which indicates the trace that it belongs to. The system generates events when the trace is activated (finger down), moved (finger moving), and deactivated (finger up). Each touch includes the ID that is given at the moment of TOUCH-DOWN, to be used during the TOUCHMOVE, and to end when TOUCHUP has been deactivated. The ID gives us a way to group points from each finger. For specific information on how Windows 7 handles multi-touch technology, please see[5] [Kiriaty et al. 09].

FETOUCH combines feature extraction with a FSM [Sipser 06], as shown in Figure 10.1. The idea is to allow a state machine to keep control of the process while the detection takes place. The input device's state starts as idle. Here we have a state transition to the touch state with either down or move events. Once the finger has been lifted, we have a state transition back to idle with the UP event. Once the touch state has been reached, the decision must be made to identify it as either a tap (e.g., double tap, two-finger tap) or a trace. After testing the system, it was noticed that differentiating taps from gestures was unnecessary because the tap can be part of the set of gestures to recognize. Nevertheless, maintaining control of the states with a FSM is still useful.

When a point is detected, then the data is added to a thread-safe queue[6] [Williams 12]. The queue is used to continue storing the traces while a specific window (buffer) of data is processed. Once the queue is full, a transition will take place to the "process" state, where Algorithm 10.6 takes over.

Figure 10.2 gives more details about the queue and how we are using it. On the left side of the figure, a three-finger gesture is performed by a user. The data points are stored in the buffer as those points are coming in. The window must be of a large enough size to detect a gesture (e.g., N = 64). By having this buffer, the user can perform multiple gestures while keeping his or her hands on the display (if desired). Figure 10.2 shows this thread-safe queue with a window size, for a given gesture.

Algorithm 10.6 detects swipe (translation), rotate, and pinch in/out (zoom in/out). If a system does not provide traces, one of the many clustering techniques

---

[5]Windows 8 has additional features. Refer to msdn.microsoft.com.
[6]The reader can find ready-to-use thread-safe data structures.

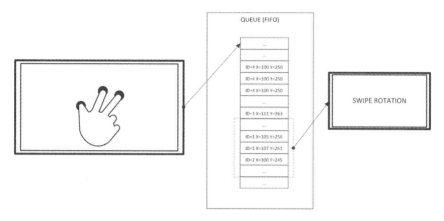

Figure 10.2: Queue.

available can be used to create them [Gan et al. 07]. Given the critical nature of a real-time application, any necessary pre-computations must be performed while the traces are added to the queue. This is why, when running the algorithm, it is expected that the grip will have been pre-computed.

The primary motivation is to lower the running time of the gesture detection in order to use it with demanding 3D applications. Therefore, the running time of the algorithm is as important as the complete utilization of all the resources available in the system. In this context, it is important to note that the gesture detection runs in its own thread. For more details about this multi-threaded approach, a C++ implementation can be found in [Williams 12] or a more detailed explanation with Java code can be found in *The Art of Multiprocessor Programming* [Herlihy and Shavit 08]. The final iteration of **FETOUCH** runs in parallel.

Algorithm 10.6 starts by popping the buffer window in line 1. Since the data is collected offline, the buffer is divided into a top half and bottom half buffer (initial and final states). Before explaining the algorithm in more detail, the following variables are defined next: traces, grip, trace vector, spread, and angle rotation.

Traces is a set that contains information for the path taken by each finger. In other words, for each finger, a set of properties is pre-computed, which is called **trace** in the algorithm. For example, the x and y coordinates are the average of a given trace, as shown in Equations 10.8 and 10.9 (for the y coordinate, replace the "x" for the "y"). Note that the variable n in the formulas refers to the total x and y points for a given trace. Because the buffer is divided into two snapshots, each snapshot has its own average. A **grip** is defined by the average of all points in each snapshot, as shown in Equation 10.10. A **trace vector** is defined as trace minus the grip, as shown in Algorithm 10.6, lines 12 through 15. The **spread** is given by lines 18–19 in Algorithm 10.6, which calculate the spread as the average difference between the grip point and the touch vector. Finally, the **angle rotation** is the average of the angle obtained by the formula $atan2$ (see Equation 10.7) [Dunn and

Parberry 11]. This is the angle between the final touch vector and the initial touch vector.

$$atan2(y,x) = \begin{cases} 0, & x=0, y=0, \\ +90°, & x=0, y>0, \\ -90°, & x=0, y<0, \\ arctan(y/x), & x>0, \\ arctan(y/x)+180°, & x<0, y\geq0 \\ arctan(y/x)-180°, & x<0, y<0. \end{cases} \tag{10.7}$$

Finally, the chosen gesture is given by any of the three distance variables (swipeDistance, rotDistance, or zoomDistance) with the highest value found, as shown in Algorithm 10.6. The swipe distance is given by the spread of the first trace and the grip. The rotate distance is given by the arc length. This is calculated using average angle obtained in line 20 and the radius of the swipe distance. Remember that *atan2* [Dunn and Parberry 11] values range between $\pm\pi$. In order to obtain the distance, the proper factor 2 must be multiplied, as shown in Equation 10.11. The zoom distance is given by the average final spread distance and the average initial spread distance.

Once everything is computed in the for loop, all we have left to do is to determine the correct gesture. The gesture detected is assigned according to the highest distance value of the swipe distance, rotation distance, or zoom distance. Additional information can be obtained for specific detected gestures. For example, if the gesture detected is a zoom gesture, the direction of the zoom can be obtained. While the primary goal of the algorithm is to find the correct gesture, additional information is important to be precise about the gesture. Algorithm 10.6 concentrates on finding the gesture type.

$$iTrace[id].x = \frac{1}{n/2} \sum_{i=0}^{\frac{n}{2}-1} trace[id][i].x \tag{10.8}$$

$$fTrace[id].x = \frac{1}{n/2} \sum_{i=\frac{n}{2}}^{n-1} trace[id][i].x \tag{10.9}$$

$$iGrip.x = \frac{1}{n/2} \sum_{t\in\textbf{iTrace}} iTrace[t].x \tag{10.10}$$

$$rotDistance = \frac{\Theta}{360} 2\pi r \tag{10.11}$$

10.4.1 FETOUCH+

FETOUCH allowed the understanding of working with specific features when using touch. However, the need for a real-time algorithm that would allow gesture

---

Algorithm 10.6 Gesture Detection

Require: TouchCount > 0

1: $traces \leftarrow traceQueue.getWindow()$
2: $iTrace \leftarrow traces.getHalf()$
3: $fTrace \leftarrow traces.getHalf()$
4: $iGrip.x \leftarrow iTrace.getGrip.x$
5: $iGrip.y \leftarrow iTrace.getGrip.y$
6: $fGrip.x \leftarrow fTrace.getGrip.x$
7: $fGrip.y \leftarrow fTrace.getGrip.y$
8: $ivFirst.x \leftarrow iTrace[1].x - iGrip.x$
9: $ivFirst.y \leftarrow iTrace[1].y - iGrip.y$
10: $swipeDistance \leftarrow sqrt(ivFirst.x^2 + ivFirst.y^2)$
11: **for** $t \leftarrow 1$ to $traces.Count$ **do**
12: $\quad iv.x \leftarrow iTrace[t].x - iGrip.x$
13: $\quad iv.y \leftarrow iTrace[t].y - iGrip.y$
14: $\quad fv.x \leftarrow fTrace[t].x - fGrip.x$
15: $\quad fv.y \leftarrow fTrace[t].y - fGrip.y$
16: $\quad di \leftarrow sqrt(iv.x^2 + iv.y^2)$
17: $\quad df \leftarrow sqrt(fv.x^2 + fv.y^2)$
18: $\quad iSpread \leftarrow iSpread + di$
19: $\quad fSpread \leftarrow fSpread + df$
20: $\quad angle \leftarrow atan2(fv.y - iv.y, fv.x - iv.x)$
21: $\quad rotAngle \leftarrow rotAngle + angle$
22: $iSpread \leftarrow iSpread/traces.Count$
23: $fSpread \leftarrow fSpread/traces.Count$
24: $rotAngle \leftarrow rotAngle/traces.Count$
25: $zoomDistance \leftarrow fSpread - iSpread$
26: $rotDistance \leftarrow rotAngle/360.0 * 2 * \pi * swipeDistance$
27: **return** Gesture With Highest Distance

---

detection was imperative. This is why FETOUCH+ was developed. This new approach took the ideas from the off-line algorithm and tested them in real-time. FETOUCH+ was developed with Windows 7 using the multi-touch available in the WINAPI [Kiriaty et al. 09], Microsoft Visual Studio (using C# 4.0 language), and a 3M M2256PW multi-touch monitor. This time, the use of C# **Tasks** [7] gave the process a multi-thread approach while keeping the implementation simpler. The testing and implementation was performed in C#, and the description of the algorithm is specific and provides details about how to implement it in other languages.

---

[7]Task is a higher level of implementation for using threads.

Figure 10.3: Rotation gesture.

There are some definitions similar to FETOUCH. Nevertheless, it is important
to state them again, as they encapsulate the new algorithm with small differences.
First, raw touch data [Kiriaty et al. 09] (e.g., Windows, iOS) was used to capture
data points stored in a set called **trace**. A **trace** starts when a user presses with one
finger and continues until the user removes the finger from the device. Figure 10.3
shows a rotation gesture with two fingers. This constitutes two traces. Each **trace**
has a unique identifier (**id**) and contains a set of points with 2D coordinates (**x,y**)
and a timestamp **t**, for each point. The general events provided are the initial touch
of a trace (TOUCHDOWN), the movement of the trace (TOUCHMOVE), and the
end of the touch (TOUCHUP). A **trace point** structure contains coordinates **x** and
y, timestamp t_0, count **c** (indicating how many continuous points are found in the
same location), Boolean **p** (indicating if the touchpoint was already processed) and
the last timestamp t_1. The **trace point** is also referred to as TOUCHPOINT. An
additional data structure with the name of TRACE is also stored. This contains
id for the unique identifier, the initial timestamp t_i, the final timestamp t_f, and the
Boolean **d** to see if the trace is ready for deletion. For additional information on
how Windows 7 handles the touch API, see [Kiriaty et al. 09].

It is important to keep the touch events and gesture detection in different thread
processes [Williams 12]. Therefore, all the active traces are stored in a concurrent
hash map and a concurrent arraylist (vector) to keep the set of touch points of a
given trace. Once data points are processed, they can be safely removed. The
advantage to having them in different threads (other than speed) is to have a real-
time approach to gesture detection. A buffer with a maximum size of **windowSize**
is defined. This means that when the buffer is full, it needs to perform the gesture
detection while still allowing touch events to execute. During test trials, it was
found that the windowSize works best for $N = 32$ or $N = 64$.

TOUCHDOWN is the initial event that fires when a trace begins. This means
that a user has pressed a finger on the multi-touch device. The event fires for

each new trace. There is room to further improve the performance of the gesture detection system by creating additional threads for each trace. The first trace is stored in the vector **vtrace**, during this event. The vector is kept in a hash map **mtrace**, which contains a collection of all traces. For the first trace, The timestamp t_0 is equal to the timestamp t_1.

As the user moves across the screen (without lifting his or her fingers), the event that fires is TOUCHMOVE (Listing 10.7). In line 3 of Listing 10.7, a method called *removeNoise* is invoked by passing the previous and current traces. It is important to note that the algorithm may benefit from removing the noise or undesired points from the data while it is running. For example, one may consider that noise occurs if a new touch point is within $\pm \mathbf{d}$ of a previous point, where $\mathbf{d}$ is a pre-calculated value depending on the size of the screen (e.g., 2). If the noise variable is true, the counter **c** and the timestamp $\mathbf{t_1}$ need to be updated for this trace, as shown in lines 5–6. Otherwise, the touch point is added to the vector. At the end of the procedure, in line 13, the map is updated (depending on the implementation and language, this may be skipped). The noise removal depends on the actual requirement of the system.

Algorithm 10.7 TOUCHMOVE

1: $trace \leftarrow TRACE(id)$
2: $vtraces \leftarrow mtraces.find(id)$
3: $noise \leftarrow removeNoise(trace, vtrace)$
4: **if** *noise* **then**
5:     $trace.c+ = 1$
6:     $trace.t_1 = trace.requestTimeStamp()$
7: **else**
8:     $trace.t_1 \leftarrow trace.requestTimeStamp()$
9:     $trace.t_0 \leftarrow vtraces[length-1].t_0$
10:     $vtrace \leftarrow mtraces.getValue()$
11:     $vtrace.push\_back(traces)$
12: $mtraces.insert(id, vtrace)$

The final event is when the user removes his or her finger. Since the gesture detection algorithm may still be running, the data is marked for deletion only. Once Algorithm 10.8 finishes, the process can safely delete all the data touch points that have been used.

Algorithm 10.8 detects translation (swipe), rotation, and zooming (pinch). Once the buffer is full, the window of touch data is split into two lists named **top** and **bottom**. This creates an initial and a final snapshot to work with.

Algorithm 10.8 requires pre-computed values, grip points, and average touch points (described below) before it can execute. The choices to pre-compute the values can be done in the TOUCHMOVE event or by firing a separate process before Algorithm 10.8 starts. The values for Algorithm 10.8 are stored in the **top** and **bottom** structures, respectively.

The features identified in each gesture are **grip**, **trace vector**, **spread**, and **angle rotation**. A **grip** is the average of all points in each top and bottom list. A **trace vector** is a **trace** minus the **grip**, as shown in Algorithm 10.8, lines 11 through 14. The **spread** is calculated in lines 15–18 of Algorithm 10.8 as the average distance between the **grip point** and **the touch vector**. The **angle rotation** is given by the average of the angles obtained by *atan2* [Dunn and Parberry 11], which is the angle between the final touch vector and the initial touch vector. This is exactly the same as in FETOUCH.

To select the correct gesture, the algorithm finds the highest value from the three distance variables: swipeDistance, rotDistance, or zoomDistance. The definition of the swipe distance is the spread of the first trace and the grip. The rotate distance is calculated to be the arc length, which is given by the radius of the swipe distance and the average angle, shown in lines 19–20 of Algorithm 10.8. It is important to note that *atan2* [Dunn and Parberry 11] values range between $\pm\pi$. This is why there is a factor of 2 in line 26 (just like in FETOUCH). Finally, the zoom distance is defined as the difference between the average final spread distance and the average initial spread distance. FETOUCH+ demonstrates the ability to find features that can be used to detect a gesture. This is an alternative to using template matching. For an expanded discussion, see [Ortega et al. 13a].

10.4.2   Implementation: FETOUCH++

After testing FETOUCH and FETOUCH+, a few modifications were required to have a more optimized system. This is an enhanced version of FETOUCH+, meant to find additional features. This implementation is referred to as FETOUCH++. All the concepts of FETOUCH+ apply in FETOUCH++.

The first objective was to find the lowest number of points required to be able to output a gesture while the gesture was active. The number found was 32, as shown in Listings 10.2 and 10.3. It is important to note that if the number of gestures to be recognized increases from the set tested on, this parameter may need to be increased to 64.

A small difference from FETOUCH+, during the onDown event, is the finger count (fingers++), as shown in Listing 10.1. The idea is that while the traces can determine how many fingers are currently being used, there is a need to keep a separate value of the number of fingers touching the screen, to run the clean-up process, in the onUp (Listing 10.2) event. Of course, this depends on the definition of a multi-touch gesture. In the case of FETOUCH++, the gesture recognition is defined as active, while fingers are on the surface display. The partial recognition will be fired every N samples (e.g., 32) to see if a gesture can be detected, as shown in Listing 10.3. The onUp event also fires the recognition method.

The recognition of FETOUCH++ is very similar to FETOUCH+. First, the split function (Listing 10.4) divides the points for each trace into two halves (top and bottom). This is performed in parallel using the **Task** class from C#. An example

Algorithm 10.8 GestureDetection

1: $top \leftarrow traces.getTop(windowSize)$
2: $bottom \leftarrow traces.getBottom(windowSize)$
3: $tGrip.x \leftarrow top.getGrip.x$
4: $tGrip.y \leftarrow top.getGrip.y$
5: $bGrip.x \leftarrow bottom.getGrip.x$
6: $bGrip.y \leftarrow bottom.getGrip.y$
7: $spread.x \leftarrow iTrace[1].x - iGrip.x$
8: $spread.y \leftarrow iTrace[1].y - iGrip.y$
9: $swipeDistance \leftarrow sqrt(spread.x^2 + spread.y^2)$
10: **for** $t \leftarrow 1$ to $traces.Count$ **do**
11:     $i.x \leftarrow tTrace[t].x - tGrip.x$
12:     $i.y \leftarrow tTrace[t].y - tGrip.y$
13:     $f.x \leftarrow bTrace[t].x - bGrip.x$
14:     $f.y \leftarrow bTrace[t].y - bGrip.y$
15:     $di \leftarrow sqrt(i.x^2 + i.y^2)$
16:     $df \leftarrow sqrt(f.x^2 + f.y^2)$
17:     $iSpread \leftarrow iSpread + di$
18:     $fSpread \leftarrow fSpread + df$
19:     $angle \leftarrow atan2(f.y - i.y, f.x - i.x)$
20:     $rotAngle \leftarrow rotAngle + angle$
21: $iSpread \leftarrow iSpread/traces.Count$
22: $fSpread \leftarrow fSpread/traces.Count$
23: $rotAngle \leftarrow rotAngle/traces.Count$
24: $zoomDistance \leftarrow fSpread - iSpread$
25: $rotDistance \leftarrow rotAngle/360.0 * 2 * \pi * swipeDistance$
26: **return** Gesture With Highest Distance

of extracting the top half is shown in Listing 10.5. Once this is completed, the split function calculates the features to be used with the recognition process by calling the method *getFeatures*, as shown in Listing 10.6. In conclusion, FETOUCH++ has allowed the possibility to investigate further features that can be helpful for multi-touch devices.

Listing 10.1: FtFeatureMatch (onDown)

```
1  private void OnDown(WMTouchEventArgs e)
2  {
3      fingers++;
4      incPoints();
5      M.Point p = new M.Point(e.LocationX, e.LocationY, e.Id);
6      map.Add(e.Id, p);
7  }
```

Listing 10.2: FtFeatureMatch (onUp)

```
1  private void onUp(WMTouchEventArgs e)
2  {
3      incPoints();
4      M.Point p = new M.Point(e.LocationX, e.LocationY, e.Id);
5      map.Add(e.Id,p);
6      fingers--;
7      if (localPoints >= 32 || fingers == 0)
8          recognize();
9      if (fingers == 0)
10         cleanUp();
11 }
```

Listing 10.3: FtFeatureMatch (onMove)

```
1  private void onMove(WMTouchEventArgs e)
2  {
3      incPoints();
4      M.Point p = new M.Point(e.LocationX, e.LocationY, e.Id);
5      map.Add(e.Id,p);
6      if ( localPoints >= 32)
7          recognize();
8  }
```

Listing 10.4: FtFeatureMatch (Slit)

```
1  private void split(int half,int tCount)
2  {
3      int avgHalf = half;
4      Task<Point>[] taskSplitArray = new Task<Point>[tCount * 2];
5      int[] keys = mapTraces.getKeys();
6      int i = 0;
7      foreach (int k in keys)
8      {
9          taskSplitArray[i] = Task<Point>.Run(
10             () => { return BreakTop(k, avgHalf); } );
11         taskSplitArray[i+1] = Task<Point>.Run(
12             () => { return BreakBottom(k, avgHalf); });
13         i += 2;
14     }
15     Task<Point>[] t = {
16         Task<Point>.Run( () => { return getFeatures(taskSplitArray)↩
                ;} ) };
17     Task<Point>.WaitAll(t);
18 }
```

Listing 10.5: FtFeatureMatch (BreakTop)

```
1  private Point BreakTop(int trace,int avgHalf)
```

```
2   {
3       int half = getHalf(trace, avgHalf);
4       Points pts = new Points(avgHalf);
5       float avgX = 0;
6       float avgY = 0;
7       for (int i = 0; i < half -1; i++)
8       {
9           Point p = mapTraces[trace][i];
10          pts.addPoint(p);
11          avgX += p.X;
12          avgY += p.Y;
13      }
14      mapTop = new MapPoints();
15      mapTop.AddPoints(trace, pts);
16      Point avgPoint = new Point(avgX / half, avgY / half); ;
17      avgPoint.CountFromAverage = half;
18      return avgPoint;
19  }
```

Listing 10.6: FtFeatureMatch (Features)

```
1   private GestureDetected getFeatures(Task<Point>[] taskSplitArray)
2   {
3       traceFeatureList = new TraceFeatureList();
4       for (int i = 0; i < taskSplitArray.Length; i += 2)
5       {
6           Point p = taskSplitArray[i].Result;
7           Point p2 = taskSplitArray[i + 1].Result;
8           Point p3 = new Point((p.X + p2.X) / 2, (p.Y + p2.Y) / 2);
9           TraceFeatures tf = new TraceFeatures();
10          tf.addFeature(TraceFeatures.FeatureType.topAvg, p);
11          tf.addFeature(TraceFeatures.FeatureType.bottomAvg, p2);
12          tf.addFeature(TraceFeatures.FeatureType.Avg, p3);
13          traceFeatureList.traceFeatures.Add(tf);
14      }
15      return traceFeatureList.getGestureDetected();
16  }
```

Further Reading

It is very important to understand touch. Holz and colleagues provide a set of publications expanding the knowledge of touch [Holz and Baudisch 13, Holz and Baudisch 11, Holz and Baudisch 10]. Understanding the difference between oblique and non-oblique touch is also important [Wang and Ren 09]. Also, the *Brave NUI World* contains a series of guidelines and tips about multi-touch (and other modern input devices) [Wigdor and Wixon 11].

For pen and touch recognition, some classic and seminal works include the Rubine classifier [Rubine 91], Shark[2] [Kristensson and Zhai 04], and *Cursive Script*

Recognition by Elastic Matching [Tappert 82], among others. For the $P algorithm, it is important to read about matching algorithms and related topics [Cormen et al. 09, Papadimitriou and Steiglitz 98].

Exercises

1. The $ family currently provides different implementations for their algorithms. Try comparing the different ones and understand how they work.

2. Using the idea of FETouch++, develop a series of other features to extract that can help you determine additional gestures. It is important to implement this with parallelism in mind. However, it is first to test the features without the additional complexity. Therefore, try to extract features using a sequential algorithm.

3. Following the previous exercise, now implement your algorithm in parallel.

11

Using Multi-Touch with Petri Nets

In 1941, I was so excited about my father's report on
Konrad Zuse's programmable computer that I could
not stop thinking about it.
—Carl Adam Petri

Input systems formalism is not recent. The pioneer work by Newman (1968) used a state diagram to represent a graphical system [Newman 68]. The seminal work by Bill Buxton in "A Three-State Model of Graphical Input" [Buxton 90] demonstrated that input devices, such as mouse, pen, single-touch, and similar ones, needed only three states to be described. Around the same time as Buxton's work, a well-rounded model for input interactions was published by Myers [Myers 90].

Multi-touch gesture detection, or detection of touch events, has been explored. In 2013, Proton and Proton++ showed the use of Regular Expressions (RegEx) to accomplish gesture detection [Kin et al. 12a]. Lao et al. [Lao et al. 09] used state-diagrams for the detection of multi-touch events. Context-free grammar was used by Kammer et al. to describe multi-touch gestures without taking implementation into consideration [Kammer et al. 10]. Gesture Coder [Lü and Li 12] created FSMs by demonstration[1] to later use them to detect gestures. Gesture Works and Open Exhibits by Ideum used a high-level language description, using XML, called Gesture Markup Language (GML). A rule-based language (e.g., CLIPS) was used to define the Midas framework [Scholliers et al. 11].

Petri Nets have also been used to detect gestures. Nam et al. showed how to use colored petri nets (CPN) to achieve hand (data glove) gesture modeling and recognition [Nam et al. 99], using HMM to recognize gesture features that are then fed to a PN. PNs have been shown to be applicable in event-driven systems [Hamon et al. 13], which is another reason they are interesting to use for modeling modern input devices. Spano et al. [Spano et al. 12, Spano et al. 13] showed how to

---

[1] Training methods.

use non-autonomous PNs [David and Alla 10] (low-level PNs), for multi-touch interaction. Also, Hamon et al. [Hamon et al. 13] expanded on Spano's work, providing more detail to the implementation of PNs for multi-touch interactions. This chapter deals with modeling multi-touch (with the option to extend it to other input devices) using PN.

11.1   Background

In the early years of the 1960s, Dr. Carl Adam Petri defined a general-purpose mathematical model.[2] PN is a model-oriented language. The model describes the relationship between conditions and events [David and Alla 10]. This provides a solution to a central challenge of computer science (as well as other fields, such as engineering), which is the construction of systems that can be specified, verified, and executed, while providing a solid mathematical framework.

PN is defined as a five tuple $N = (P, T, F, W, M_0)$, which is the net structure. Places **P** and transitions **T** are finite sets of places and transitions. The set of arcs is defined as $F \subseteq (P \times T) \cup (T \times P)$. The weight function **W** is defined as $F \to \{1, 2, 3, \ldots\}$. The dynamics definition (the dynamic state of the net) has the following rules [Chang 11]:

- A transition t is enabled if for each input place p, it has a minimum of tokens $w(p, t)$, the weight of the arc from p to t.

- If the transition t is enabled, then the transition may be fired.

- When an enabled transition t fires, then t removes $w(p, t)$, from each input place p of the given t. Once removed, the token $w(p, t)$ is added to each output place p for the given p.

The definition presented represents the spirit of the PN created by Dr. Petri,[3] and it is what the literature may refer to as low-level PNs. HLPNs[4] were created out of the necessity to have a more expressive model, while keeping the formal mathematical idea of Dr. Petri. The difference between the low-level PN and HLPN could be seen as the difference between assembly language and high-level languages, such as Java or Python.[5] As stated, HLPNs have many variations [David and Alla 10]. We have adopted a HLPN called predicate transition net (PrT Net), which was formulated by Genrich [Genrich 87]. For a basic introduction to PNs, please see [Reisig 12]. For a detailed view of other HLPNs, see [David and Alla 10]. For a general quick overview, the reader is referred to [He and Murata 05, Murata 89].

---

[2]Dr. Petri created the net to visualize the chemical process in 1939 [Reisig 12].
[3]Other definitions can be found. See Reisig [Reisig 12].
[4]There are many HLPN types.
[5]This analogy is not meant to be an exact comparison.

11.1.1   Graphical Representation

PNs have the advantage of having a graphical representation of their mathematical model. In the case of a HLPN, the net consists of places represented by circles or ellipses, transitions represented by rectangles or squares, and arcs represented by arrows. Places are discrete states, which can store, accumulate, or provide information about their state. A transition can produce, consume, transport, or change data. The arcs provide the connections between places and transitions, or transitions and places. It is important to note that an arc cannot connect a transition to a transition or a place to a place. Note that the letter labels found in the images in this chapter are not part of the graphical representation but are used to described the example. These letter labels are placed there to identify the *places* with a label (e.g., A, B, ...), for clarity.

11.1.2   Formal Definition

The HLPN used for the entire chapter is Predicate Transition Net (PrT Net) [Genrich 87]. The Prt Net is defined as a tuple (N, Σ, λ). This contains the Net **N**, the specifications Σ, and the inscription λ. The Net **N** is formed with places **P**, transitions **T**, and connecting arc expressions (as functions **F**). The following is a detailed definition:

- N represents the PN, which is defined by a three-tuple $N = (P, T, F)$.
  - $F \subset (P \times T) \cup (T \times P)$.
  - $P \cap T = \emptyset$.

- The specification Σ represents the underlying representation of type of tokens.[6]
  - $\Sigma = (S, \Omega, \Psi)$.
  - Ω contains the set of token operands.
  - Set Ψ defines the meaning and operations in Ω. In other words, the set Ψ defines how a given operation (e.g., plus) is implemented.

- λ defines the arc operation.
  - $\lambda = (\phi, L, \rho, M_0)$.
  - ϕ is the association of each place $p \in P$ with tokens.
  - L is the labeling inscription for the arc expressions, such as $L(x, y) \iff (x, y) \in F$.
  - The operation of a given arc (function) is given by $\rho = (Pre, Post)$.

---

[6]Tokens may be referred to as "sorts."

- There are well-defined constraint mappings associated with each arc expression, such as $f \in F$.
- The **Pre** condition allows the HLPN to enable the function, if the Boolean constraint evaluates to true.
- Then, the **Post** condition will execute the code if the function is enabled (ready to fire).
- Finally, the initial marking is given by M_0, which states the initial state of the HLPN.

The dynamic semantics of a Prt Net is defined [Chang 11] as follows:

- Markings of Prt Net is the mapping $M : P \rightarrow Tokens$. In other words, places map to tokens, which is defined in the specification Σ.

- The variable e denotes the instantiation of expression e with α, where e can be either a label expression or a constraint. Therefore, the occurrence mode of N is a substitution $\alpha = \{x_1 \leftarrow c_1, \ldots, x_n \leftarrow c_n\}$.

- For a given marking M, a transition t in T, and an occurrence mode $\alpha\_enabled$, t is enabled if and only if:

  - $\forall p \in P(\bar{L}(p,t):\alpha \subseteq M(p)) \wedge R(t) : \alpha$ where: $\bar{L}(x,y)$
  $$= \begin{cases} L(x,y), & \text{if } (x,y) \in F \\ \varnothing, & \text{otherwise} \end{cases}$$

- If t is $\alpha\_enabled$ at M, t may fire in occurrence mode α.

- An execution sequence $M_0[t_0 > M_1[t_1 > \ldots$ is either finite when the last marking is terminal (no more transitions are enabled), or infinite.

- The behavior of the net model is the set of all execution sequences, starting from M_0.

11.2   PeNTa: Petri Nets

The explosion of new input devices has added many challenges to the implementation of input componenets for user interfaces. **Petri Net Touch (PeNTa)** addressed this problem by offering a mathematical approach to modeling input, using HLPN (Prt Net).

Side Note 11.1: Developers and Petri Nets

In the obscurity of a small room of a computer science department, there is a small group of people working with Petri Nets. Computer science has considered Petri Nets a very specialized field, useful software verification, and specification. Of course, this is a very important matter when we deal with software.

There is one underlying benefit of learning Petri Nets (and High-Level Petri Nets) to developers. When I became interested in Petri Nets and after reading some books on the topic, I took a class under Dr. Xudong He. Besides the simplicity of using set theory to define the use of PN and HLPN, it was something else that caught my attention. The distributed fact of PN makes the developer think about keeping everything local to the function, which provides better parallelism. Because of this "atomicity" within the function it is true that Petri Nets are distributed in nature. In this highly parallelized world of today's computing, Petri Nets offer not only a formal way to define software specification (and provide validation) but also, change the mind-set of developers.

–Francisco R. Ortega

11.2.1 Motivation and Differences

It is important to note that this approach is not targeted toward the end-user. The target audiences for **PeNTa** are four: (1) Software developers who would like to graphically model multi-touch interactions. (2) Framework developers[7] who wish to incorporate modern input devices to their libraries. (3) Domain-specific language (DSL) developers who create solutions for domain-experts. (4) Researchers in the HCI field.

There are several reasons why using this approach may be the preferred one for some developers or researchers. The first difference to consider is between low-level PN vs. HLPN. The major difference is that HLPN have "complex data structures as data tokens, and [use] algebraic expressions to annotate net elements" [Nets-Concepts 00]. This is similar to the difference between assembly language versus a high-level language (e.g., Python). For the complete standard defining HLPN, see [Nets-Concepts 00]. HLPN is still mathematically defined as the low-level Petri Net but it can provide "unambiguous specifications and descriptions of applications" [Nets-Concepts 00].

There are further reasons that were considered when picking the use of HLPN to model multi-touch interactions. These reasons might be better understood when **PeNTa** is placed in the context of other existing approaches for input mod-

---

[7]Library and/or language developers also fit in this category.

eling: Proton and Proton++ [Kin et al. 12a], Gesture Coder [Lü and Li 12], and GestIT [Spano 12, Spano et al. 13, Hamon et al. 13]. While **PeNTa** offers more expressiveness and distributed capabilities, simultaneously providing a solid mathematical framework, the work offered by Proton++, Gesture Coder, and GestIT offers great insight into modeling multi-touch interaction, with different benefits that must be evaluated by the developer. Finally, it is important to note that the work of **PeNTa** is inspired in part by Proton and Proton++.

The question still may remain for some readers: Why use HLPN to define multi-touch interactions? PNs provide graphical and mathematical representations that allow verification and analysis; furthermore, they provide a formal specification that can be executed. This is important. They can be used to specify, to verify, and to execute. Petri Nets also allow distributed systems to be represented. Finally, a finite state machine can be represented as a PN, but a PN may not be represented as a FSM. In other words, PNs have more expressive representational power.

Proton and Proton++ offer a novel approach to multi-touch interaction using RegEx. Such an approach offers an advantage to those who are proficient with regular expressions. However, there may be some disadvantages in using RegEx for our goals. Expressions of some gestures can be lengthy, such as the scale gesture [Kin et al. 12a]: $D_1^s M_1^s * D_2^a (M_1^s | M_2^a) * (U_1^s M_2^a * U_2^a | U_2^a M_1^s * U_1^s)^8$. Spano et al. [Spano et al. 13] presented additional differences between PNs and the use of RegExs in Proton++. Another potential disadvantage of using RegExs is that some custom gestures may become harder to represent.

The Gesture Coder method offers a great approach to creating gestures by demonstration. PeNTa could also create a HLPN using machine learning. The representation of the training for the Gesture Coder results in a FSM. FSMs can become large and do not provide the expressive power and distributed representation of HLPNs.

GestIT is the closest approach to PeNTa. GestIT uses low-level PNs. The approach of GestIT is similar to Proton++, but it uses a PN. The trace is broken down into points and the gesture becomes a pattern of those points. The expressiveness of HLPNs allow the Proton++ technique to be used. However, this author chose to define the tokens as individual traces. GestIT represents a valuable contribution, but it lacks the expressiveness of HLPN using data structures in tokens, which are essential in PeNTa. Nonetheless, GestIT can provide some great ideas to further improve PeNTa.

PeNTa includes a novel approach by using HLPN (in specific, Prt Net) for multi-touch recognition, including the definition required for HLPN to work with multi-touch. PN allows formal specifications to be applied to multi-touch, and perhaps other modern input devices (e.g., Leap Motion), and enables a distributed framework while keeping the approach simpler (in comparison to low-level PNs). This means that by encapsulating complex data structures in tokens and allowing

---

[8]D=Down, M=Move, U=Up; s=shape, b=background, a=any (a|b).

algebraic notation and function calling in the transitions of a PN, the modeling is not restricted to one individual approach. Furthermore, the data structure kept in each token maintains history information that may be useful for additional features. However, note that the historical reason must be self-contained, otherwise the HLPN formal model is violated.

11.2.2   HLPN: High-Level Petri Nets and IRML

PeNTa is defined using HLPN [Genrich and Lautenbach 81, Liu et al. 11, Genrich 87], consisting of the Prt Net definition [Genrich 87]. The model is defined as $HLPN = (N, \Sigma, \lambda)$. This contains the Net **N**, the specifications Σ, and the inscription λ.

The Net **N** is formed with places **P**, transitions **T**, and connecting arc expressions (as functions **F**). In other words, a PN is defined as a three-tuple $N = (P, T, F)$, where $F \subset (P \times T) \cup (T \times P)$. Petri Nets' arcs can only go from **P** to **T**, or **T** to **P**. This can be formally expressed, stating that the sets of places and transitions are disjointed, $P \cap T = \emptyset$. Another important characteristics of Petri Nets is that they use multi-sets[9] (elements that can be repeated) for the input functions, $(I : T \to P^\infty)$ and output functions, $(O : P \to T^\infty)$ [Peterson 81].

The specification Σ defines the underlying representation of tokens. This is defined as $\Sigma = (S, \Omega, \Psi)$. The set S contains all the possible token[10] data types allowed in the system. For the particular case of multi-touch in **PeNTa**, the data type is always the same,[11] which is a multi-touch token **K**, as shown in Table 11.1. The set Ω contains the token operands (e.g., plus, minus). The set Ψ defines the meaning and operations in Ω. In other words, the set Ψ defines how a given operation (e.g., plus) is implemented. In the case of **PeNTa**, which uses Prt Net, the operations use regular math and Boolean algebra rules. This is the default for **PeNTa** tokens, which is of signature (S, Ω).

The inscription λ defines the arc operation. This is defined as $\lambda = (\phi, L, \rho, M_0)$. The data definition represented by ϕ is the association of each place $p \in P$ with tokens. This means that **places** should accept only variables of a matching data type. **PeNTa** has token **K**, which represents the multi-touch structure. The inscription also has labeling **L** for the arc expressions, such as $L(x, y) \iff (x, y) \in F$. For example, a transition that goes from place B to transition 4 will be represented as $L(B, 4)$. The operation of a given arc (function) is defined as $\rho = (Pre, Post)$. These are well-defined constraint mappings associated with each arc expression, such as $f \in F$. The **Pre** condition allows the HLPN model to enable the function, if the Boolean constraint evaluates to true. The **Post** condition will execute the code if the function is enabled (ready to fire). Finally, the initial marking is given by M_0, which states the initial state of **PeNTa**.

---

[9] Also known as bag theory.

[10] Some Petri Nets' publications may refer to tokens as "sorts."

[11] This is up to the designer. If the designer wants to create additional tokens, it is also possible.

Table 11.1: Multi-Touch Data Structure.

Name	Description
id	Unique Multi-Touch Identification
tid	Touch Entry Number
x	X display coordinate
y	Y display coordinate
state	Touch states (DOWN, MOVE, UP)
prev	Previous sample
get(Time t)	Get previous sample at time **t**
tSize	Size of sample buffer
holdTime	How many milliseconds have passed since last rest
msg	String variable for messages

Dynamic Semantics

In order to finalize the formal definition of the HLPN used in **PeNTa**, there are some basic details about the dynamic aspects of these Prt Nets. First, markings of HLPN are mappings $M : P \rightarrow Tokens$. In other words, places map to tokens. Second, given a marking M, a transition $t \in T$ is enabled at marking M iff $Pre(t) \leq M$. Third, given a marking M, α_t is an assignment for variables of t that satisfy its transition condition, and A_t denotes the set of all assignments. The model defines the set of all transition modes to be $TM = \{(t, \alpha_t) | t \in T, \alpha_t \in A_t\} \iff Pre(TM) \leq M$. An example of this definition is a transition spanning multiple places, as shown in Figures 11.1 and 11.2 (concurrent enabling). Fourth, given a marking M, if $t \in T$ is enabled in mode α_t, firing t by a step may occur in a new marking $M' = M - Pre(t_{\alpha_t}) + Post(t_{\alpha_t})$; a step is denoted by $M[t > M'$. In other words, this is the transition rule. Finally, an execution sequence $M_0[t_0 > M_1[t_1 > \ldots$ is either finite when the last marking is terminal (no more transitions are enabled) or infinite. The behavior of a HLPN model is the set of all execution sequences, starting from M_0.

11.2.3   PeNTa and Multi-Touch

A multi-touch display (capacitive or vision-based) can detect multiple finger strokes at the same time. This can be seen as a finger trace. A **trace** is generated when a finger touches down onto the surface, moves (or stays static), and is eventually lifted from it. Therefore, a trace is a set of touches of a continuous stroke. While it is possible to create an anomalous trace with the palm, **PeNTa** takes into consideration only normal multi-finger interaction. However, the data structure (explained in detail later) could be modified to fit different needs, including multiple users and other sensors that may enhance the touch interaction. Given a set of traces, one can define a **gesture**. For example, a simple gesture may be two fingers

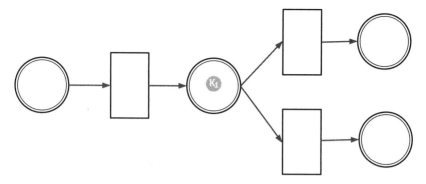

Figure 11.1: Parallel PN: State 1.

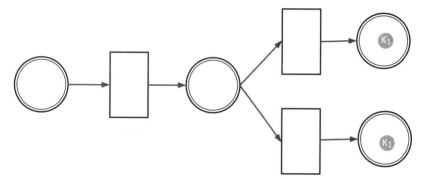

Figure 11.2: Parallel PN: State 2.

moving on the same path, creating a **swipe**. If they are moving in opposite ways (at least one of the fingers), this can be called a **zoom out** gesture. If the fingers are moving toward each other, then this is a **zoom in** gesture. A final assumption that **PeNTa** makes for multi-touch systems is the following: if a touch interaction is not moving, it will not create additional samples but increment the holding time of the finger. Note that this is not inherently true in all multi-touch systems. For example, in native WINAPI (Windows 7) development, samples are generated, even if the finger is not moving, but holding. To adjust this characteristic of the WINAPI to PeNTa assumption, the samples are just filtered by creating a small threshold that defines the following: If the finger is not moving or if it is moving slightly, a counter is incremented.

11.2.4   Arc Expressions

Each arc is defined as a function **F**, which is divided into two subsets of inputs **I** and outputs **O**, such that $F = I \cup O$. In the inscription ρ of this HLPN, the arc expression is defined as **Pre** and **Post** conditions. Simply put, the **Pre** condition either enables or disables the function, and the **Post** condition updates and executes call-back events, in the HLPN model.

Each function **F** is defined as $F = Pre \cup Post$, forming a four-tuple $F = (B, U, C, R)$, where **B** and **U** are part of the **Pre** conditions, and **C** and **R** are part of the **Post** conditions. **B** is the Boolean condition that evaluates to true or false, **R** is the *priority function*, **C** is the call-back event, and **U** is the update function.

The Boolean condition **B** allows the function to be evaluated using standard Boolean operators with the tokens, in C++ style (e.g., $T_1.state == STATE.UP$). If no condition is assigned, the default is *true*. The priority function **R** instantiates a code block, with the purpose of assigning a priority value to the arc expression. The call-back event **C** allows the Petri Net to have a function callback with conditional *if* statements, local variable assignments, and external function calling. This can help to determine which function should be called. If no callback event is provided, then a default *genericCallBack(Place p, Token t)* is called. The update function **U** is designed to obtain the next touch sample using $update(T_1)$, or setting a value to the current sample of a given token using $set(T_1, TYPE.STATE, STATE.UP)$.

Places and transitions in **PeNTa** have special properties. This is true for **P**, which has three types: *initial*, *regular*, and *final*. This allows the system to know where tokens will be placed when they are created (*initial*) and where the tokens will be located when they removed (*final*).

Picking the next transition or place for the case when there is one input and one output is trivial (the next **T** or **P** is the only available one). However, when there are multiple inputs or outputs, picking the next one to check becomes important in a PN implementation [Mortensen 01]. The "picking" algorithm used in **PeNTa** is a modified version of the one by Mortensen [Mortensen 01]. The algorithm combines the random nature found in other CPN [Jensen and Kristensen 96] selection and the use of *priority functions*. The algorithm sorts the neighboring **P** or **T** by ascending value, given by the priority function **R**, and groups them by equivalent values, (e.g., $G_1 = 10, 10, 10, G_2 = 1, 1$). The last **P** or **T** fired may be given a higher value if found within the highest group. Within each group, the next **P** or **T** is selected randomly. Also note that the algorithm presented here is just one of many possible ones. Given the flexibility of Petri Nets and the amount of work available in this field, the developer may wish to modify or change the algorithm in its entirety. The important part of the algorithm is how to pick the next transition, doing so in a way that does not violate PNs or Prt Nets.

Tokens and the Structure

A powerful feature of HLPNs is their discrete markings, called **tokens**. This feature allows the marking of different states and the execution of the PN. When tokens go through an input function **I** or output function **O**, they are consumed. For **PeNTa**'s particular modeling requirements, the token is a representation of a data structure that defines a **trace**, as shown in Table 11.1. This data structure contains the current sample and a buffer of previous samples (**touches**).

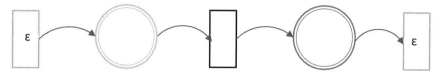

Figure 11.3: Cold transitions (Entry and Exit).

When tokens are consumed into a transition, the **Post** condition creates a new token. If the desired effect is of a parallel system, as shown in Figure 11.1, then a transition can create N number of tokens based on the original one. In Figure 11.2, token K_1 is cloned into two identical tokens. To represent the new tokens, different colors were chosen in Figures 11.1 and 11.2.

The only token data type for **PeNTa** is a multi-touch structure, type **K**, as shown in Table 11.1. The identification given by the system is denoted as **id**. Depending on the system, this may be a unique number while the process is running (long integer type), or as a consecutive integer, starting from $1 \ldots m$, lasting through the duration of the gesture performed by the user. The latter definition is also contained in the variable **tid**. Display coordinates are given by **x** and **y**. The **state** variable represents the current mode given by DOWN, MOVE, and UP. The **holdTime** helps to determine how many milliseconds have lapsed, if the user has not moved from his or her current position on the display. This data structure assumes that a new sample only happens when the user has moved beyond a threshold. Finally, this data structure acts as a pointer to previous history touches in a buffer of size η. Therefore, the buffer (if it exists) can be accessed with the function $get\,(Time\,\imath)$ or the previous sample with the variable **prev**.

In HLPNs, at least one initial Marking M_0 needs to be known, which is the initial state of **PeNTa**. In the case of simulations (which is discussed later), this is not a problem. For the case of real-time execution, the initial marking must have empty tokens. This is solved by the concept of hot and cold transitions [Reisig 12], represented by ε. A hot transition does not require user input. A cold transition requires user (or external system) input. Therefore, in **PeNTa**, the model defines entry and exit cold transitions, as shown in Figure 11.3.

11.2.5 A Tour of PeNTa

A tour of **PeNTa** is needed to better explain how it works. Take for example, an interaction that has two possible gestures using two fingers: swipe and zoom. A swipe implies that the user moves two fingers in any direction. Therefore, the callback required is always the same, which is a function that reports the direction of the swipe. In the case of the zoom, zoom-in and zoom-out could be modeled separately or together. In the case of the example shown in Figure 11.4, zoom is configured as one entity.

The example shown in Figure 11.4 is created for two-finger gestures. The figure has places, arcs, transitions, and two tokens (K_1, K_2), representing two active traces in place **C**. For this particular example, Figure 11.4 has additional graphical representations, which are letter labels in places, numbers in arcs, and transitions with names. This is done to make the example easier to follow. However, those additional items in the graph are not part of the actual Prt Net. In addition, Table 11.2 shows each arc expression with its Boolean condition and the tokens that are required to fire (e.g., two tokens). The system starts with an empty initial marking (no tokens), while it waits for the user input. Once the user touches down onto the surface, tokens are created (using cold transitions) and placed in **START**. Given that the tokens will start with a DOWN state, they will move from place **A** into place **C**, using transitions 1 and 2. The first arc just consumes the token, and arc 2 updates the token with the next touch data sample into place **B**. Once in place **B**, since the token was updated with the touch sample, **PeNTa** infers the next transition using the constraint provided. It has two options, either arc 3 or arc 4. Assuming that the state is MOVE, now each token is moved into place **C** with an updated touch data sample. Now, we are at the point shown in Figure 11.4. PeNTa infers the next step. This is where the picking algorithm explained earlier comes into play. For this example, **MOVE'**, **ZOOM**, **SWIPE**, and **UP** have priority function values 1, 10, 10, and 2, respectively. This means the groups with **ZOOM** and **SWIPE** are the first to be checked for constraints, since they have the highest values. **PeNTa** will randomly pick either one and check if it can be enabled (fired) based on the Boolean condition. Assume, for example, that it picks **SWIPE** and the Boolean condition is *true*. It is *true* if two tokens are in place **C**, both tokens are in state **MOVE**, and the function *isSwipe* is true, which is an external C++ method. If the value is true, then it will call back a swipe function, passing a copy of the token data, and then update it to the next sample via arc 12. This finally brings back both tokens into place **C**. At some point, the tokens will have the **UP** state, and they will move to place **E** and place **F**.

While the example presented in Figure 11.4 shows the interaction model in a single PN for various gestures, it is possible to create individual PNs, as shown in Figure 11.5, and combine them in a set of PNs. For example, individual PNs (PN_i) can form a model $P = (PN_1, PN_2, PN_3, ...PN_n)$, which, once constructed, can be executed. Each PN_i can run in parallel and disable itself when the corresponding condition is not met.

11.2.6   Simulation and Execution

PNs could be used for analysis (e.g., linear temporal logic), simulations, and execution. However, the initial motivation for **PeNTa** was simulation and execution. Nevertheless, analysis could be performed if needed, but it is beyond the scope of this book.

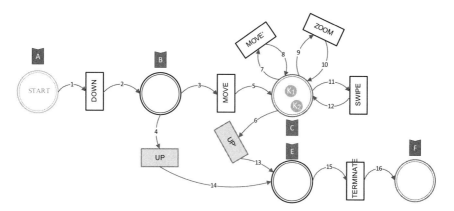

Figure 11.4: Multiple gestures in PeNTa.

Table 11.2: Transitions.

Arc	From	To	Condition	Token Count
1	A	Down	K.state == DOWN	1
2	Down	B	update(T)	1
3	B	Move	K.state == MOVE	1
4	B	UP	K.state == UP	1
5	Move	C	update(T)	1
6	C	UP	K.state == UP	1
7	C	Move	K.state == MOVE	1
8	C	Move	update(T)	1
9	C	Zoom	K.state == MOVE && IsZoom(K_1, K_2)	2
10	Zoom	C	Update(K_1, K_2)	2
14	Swipe	C	K.state == MOVE && IsSwipe(K_1, K_2)	2
15	Swipe	D	Update(K_1, K_2)	2
17	UP	E	K.state == UP	1
18	UP	E	K.state == UP	1
19	E	Terminate	true	1

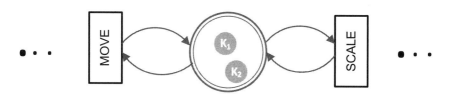

Figure 11.5: Partial Petri Net for scale.

There are different ways to simulate **PeNTa**. Non-user-generated data could be used for the simulation, providing an initial marking with a history of the possible samples. Another option is to record the user interaction, creating tokens and a buffer to feed those tokens. There are multiple ways to go about this, but two ways are very common: store the data in a transactional database or in plain text files. The former can be very useful if the set is large and different conditions may need to be applied.

Execution is the primary purpose of **PeNTa**. Given a well-defined model, this can run in real-time, using **PeNTa**, which has already been defined. As stated before, **PeNTa** needs additional entry and exit **cold** transitions, if there are additional inputs involved.

Further Reading

An introduction to formal methods called "A specifier's introduction to formal methods" provides a basic understanding about the development of systems via formality [Wing 90].

The best introduction to Petri Nets is called *Understanding Petri Nets* [Reisig 12]. Additional books include *Discrete, Continuous, and Hybrid Petri Nets* [David and Alla 10] and an edited book called *High-Level Petri Nets* [Jensen and Rozenberg 91]. Additional tutorials are available, such as "Petri Nets and Industrial Applications: A Tutorial" [Zurawski and Zhou 94].

12

Eye Gaze Tracking as Input in Human–Computer Interaction

Imago animi vultus est, indices oculi. (The countenance is the portrait of the soul, and the eyes mark its intentions.)

—Marcus Tullius Cicero

12.1   Principle of Operation

In the context of HCI applications, Eye Gaze Tracking (EGT) systems are primarily used to determine, in real time, the point-of-gaze (POG) of the subject's eye on the computer screen. The Point-Of-Gaze (POG) is commonly derived through geometric considerations driven by knowledge of the direction of the optical axis of the eye (OAE), i.e., the 3-dimensional vector indicating the direction in which the user is aiming his/her gaze. The determination of the OAE is estimated from real-time analysis of the image of the eye captured by an infrared video camera. The analysis is based on the location of two critical landmarks in the image: the center of the pupil and the center of the reflection of infrared light on the cornea of the eye (also known as the "glint"). The relative position of these two landmarks, with respect to each other, within the image of the eye captured by the infrared camera is a function of the OAE and, combined with geometrical knowledge obtained in a calibration session, prior to EGT use, can reveal the POG of the subject. Figure 12.1 illustrates the process for POG determination as a block diagram.

The corneal reflection (CR) appears as a compact cluster of particularly high intensity (closer to white) pixels in the gray scale images captured by the infrared

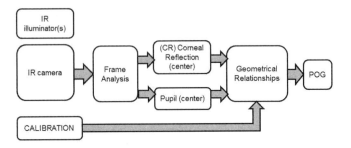

Figure 12.1: Process followed for determination of the point-of-gaze (POG).

video camera. Therefore, it should be possible to isolate this cluster by setting an appropriately high threshold. Once the cluster is isolated, the approximate centroid can be estimated and used as the CR landmark.

The determination of the pupil and its centroid may require a more involved approach. Ordinarily, the pupil will appear as a dark circle (or ellipse due to the angle in which its image is captured) because it is, in fact, an opening into the eye, which does not have internal illumination. Under these circumstances, the pupil will appear as a circle or ellipse of particularly low intensity (closer to black) in the image captured by the camera. This so-called "dark pupil" could then be isolated by setting a low threshold. There are instances, however, in which the retina, in the back section of the inside of the eyeball, reflects light (particularly infrared) and will actually appear as a circle of high intensity, although typically not as high as the glint. This is the so-called "bright pupil," which would require a high threshold for its isolation. This is, in fact the reason for the "red eye" phenomenon that may appear in standard flash photography, when the powerful light of the flash reaches the fundus of the eye of the subject and its red components are reflected by the retina in such a way that the reflection travels outwardly through the pupil and reaches the camera. It should be noted, however, that this effect requires the source of light and the camera to be nearly collinear, which is achieved by placing the light source (e.g., the flash) very close to the image capturing device (i.e., camera), and both of them as close as possible to an axis that is perpendicular to the pupil and crosses it through its center, i.e., the optical axis of the eye (which defines the direction of gaze). Therefore, the bright pupil appears when infrared illumination is applied in that same axis ("on-axis illumination"). Figure 12.2 [Joshi and Barreto 07] shows an image where the bright pupil and the corneal reflection are apparent.

Ebisawa and Satoh devised an efficient approach to facilitate the isolation of the pupil in the images of the eye recorded by an infrared camera [Ebisawa and Satoh 93, Ebisawa 98]. The method consists of acquiring pairs of eye images comprising a "bright pupil" image and a "dark pupil" image, and calculating the

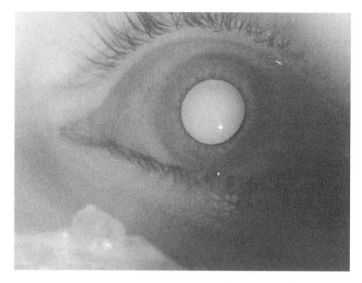

Figure 12.2: Example of eye image showing the bright pupil and the corneal reflection or "glint" [Joshi and Barreto 07].

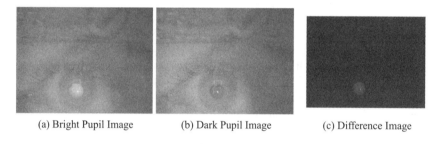

(a) Bright Pupil Image   (b) Dark Pupil Image   (c) Difference Image

Figure 12.3: Bright pupil and dark pupil images. Also shown is the corresponding difference image [Joshi and Barreto 07].

"difference image" (bright minus dark), in which the pupil area will stand out from the rest of the frame more than in either one of the individual (bright or dark) images. Figure 12.3 shows examples of a "bright pupil" image and a "dark pupil" image [Joshi and Barreto 08]. It also shows the resulting "difference image," where the pupil stands out clearly from the very dark background determined by all the pixels in the frame whose appearance is unchanged by the slight displacement of the infrared source used to capture the bright pupil (collinear with the camera axis) and the dark pupil (IR source displaced from the camera axis).

The requirement of providing infrared illumination along the camera axis ("collinear") in order to capture the bright pupil image properly is sometimes ful-

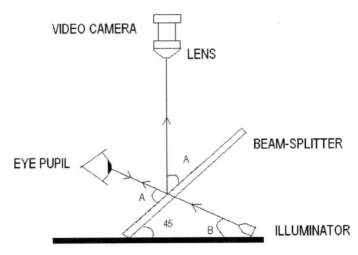

Figure 12.4: Diagram showing the use of a beam-splitter to achieve collinear IR illumination and recording [Joshi and Barreto 08].

filled by setting up a distribution of IR LEDs around the camera, for remote (desk) EGT systems. For head-worn systems, however, the dimensions are smaller and it may be necessary to use an infrared beam-splitter that will allow the passage of the IR illumination to the eye and reflect the image of the eye to a camera mounted perpendicularly, in a collinear manner. This arrangement is diagrammed in Figure 12.4 and an example of its practical implementation [Joshi and Barreto 08] is shown in Figure 12.5. In this case, the "ON-AXIS" IR source (for bright pupil) is placed right in front of the user's eye, while the "OFF-AXIS" IR source (for dark pupil) is displaced about 1.5 cm. toward the subject's nose.

Once the centers of the pupil and the corneal reflection have been located in the IR camera image, the direction of gaze and, therefore, the point of gaze in a plane such as the computer screen in front of the user, can be determined as the intersection of the optical axis of the eye (in the direction of gaze) and the plane in question [Ware and Mikaelian 87, Hutchinson et al. 89, Jacob 91, Jacob 93, Lankford 00, Sibert and Jacob 00, Sibert et al. 01]. Evidently, calculation of this intersection requires knowledge of the location of the plane with respect to the eye, which is normally obtained through a calibration process executed prior to the use of the EGT system. The calibration process relies on instructing the user to direct his/her gaze to pre-established points on the screen, on locations that are known to the calibration program. Therefore, the computer will have those (usually 5 or 9) pairs of calibration target screen coordinates and the associated directions of gaze recorded while the subject was known to be looking at each target. Guestrin and Eizenman have written a comprehensive paper in which they describe the general theory involved in the remote gaze estimation from knowledge of the pupil center and corneal reflection(s) [Guestrin and Eizenman 06]. In their paper they address

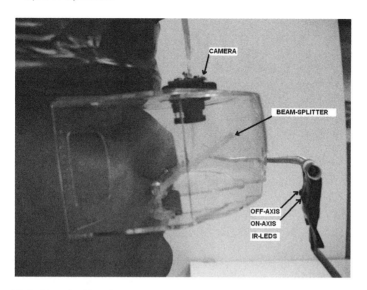

Figure 12.5: Practical implementation of the arrangement diagrammed in Figure 12.4 [Joshi and Barreto 08].

the determination of the POG for several cases, starting with the simplest scenario involving one camera and a single illuminator (light source), but also covering the cases with multiple light sources and/or multiple cameras. They indicate that "Using one camera and one light source, the POG can be estimated only if the head is completely stationary. Using one camera and multiple light sources, the POG can be estimated with free head movements, following the completion of a multiple-point calibration procedure. When multiple cameras and multiple light sources are used, the POG can be estimated following a simple one-point calibration procedure" [Guestrin and Eizenman 06]. This observation highlights the interplay of calibration points and simultaneous images available during the EGT system operation, which determines the degrees of freedom involved in the determination of the POG. This is one of the reasons why contemporary EGT systems have escalated in complexity, commonly involving multiple cameras. In some instances the multiplicity of cameras serves the purpose of providing simultaneous data from both eyes of the subject (binocular EGTs), and in other cases they contribute additional information for purposes such as head tracking, which expands the robustness of the EGT operation with respect to translations and rotations of the head of the subject.

Side Note 12.1: Early EEG-Based "Eye Tracking" Approach

While most contemporary EGT systems used in human–computer interaction applications rely on the non-invasive and unobtrusive use of infrared video cameras and illuminators, early attempts to use the direction of gaze of a user to interact with a computer explored other interesting avenues. In particular, Erich E. Sutter proposed [Sutter 84, p. 92] an ingenious system that flickered different regions of the screen at different frequencies. Therefore, depending on the specific region of the screen on which the user is fixating his / her gaze, the EEG recorded from the occipital area of the user's scalp would have a predominant visual evoked potential (VEP) component at a frequency matching that of the flicker in the observed region. This revealing frequency can be determined, in real time, by means of discrete frequency analysis of the EEG signal, yielding an identification of the region where the user is placing his/her gaze, i.e., performing a low-resolution form of "eye gaze tracking" within the computer screen.

12.2 Post-Processing of POG Data: Fixation Identification

During the normal examination of a visual scene, the eye exhibits two types of movements: saccades and fixations. A saccade is a rapid, ballistic motion that moves the eye from one area of focus of the visual scene to another. Each saccade can take 30 to 120 ms, traversing a range of $1°$ to $40°$ visual angle [Sibert and Jacob 00, Sibert et al. 01]. During a saccade vision is suppressed. Upon completion of a saccade the direction of gaze of the eye experiences a period of relative stability known as a fixation. A fixation allows the eye to focus light on the fovea, which is a portion at the center of the retina that contains a higher density of photoreceptors and is, therefore, capable of higher-resolution image sensing. The typical duration of a fixation is between 200 to 600 ms [Jacob 91, Sibert and Jacob 00, Sibert et al. 01]. However, even during a fixation, the eyes still perform small, jittery motions, usually less that $1°$ in size. These movements are necessary so as to prevent the loss of vision that could result from constant stimulation of the retinal receptors [Martinez-Conde et al. 04]. The short movements that take place during a fixation, called "fixational eye movements," may be of different types [Martinez-Conde et al. 13]. Carpenter [Carpenter 88] identified 3 types: "tremors" (low amplitude, e.g., $0.004°$ and last a few milliseconds [Yarbus 67]), "slow drifts" (amplitude from $0.03°$ to $0.08°$ and last up to a few seconds [Ratliff and Riggs 50]) and "microsaccades" (spike-like features with amplitudes of up to $0.2°$ and a duration from 10 to 30 ms [Engbert 06]).

One of the immediate uses of eye gaze tracking technology as an input methodology for human-computer interaction is, of course, the control of the screen cursor with the eye gaze. For this particular purpose, it is necessary to separate the gaze fixations from the transient saccades. Since, as pointed out above, the gaze exhibits several sharp and short movements, even within a fixation, such fixation identification process requires detailed consideration. Salvucci and Goldberg studied a number of popular approaches to the fixation identification task and proposed a taxonomy for these methods, in terms of how they utilize spatial and temporal information [Salvucci and Goldberg 00]. Their taxonomy differentiated algorithms that used EGT spatial information as: velocity-based, dispersion-based, and area-based. Similarly, they distinguished between two types of algorithms, according to their use of temporal characteristics of the EGT traces: duration-sensitive and locally adaptive. In their article, the authors review and evaluate 5 representative algorithms: the velocity-threshold identification (I-VT), the hidden Markov model identification (I-HMM), the dispersion-threshold identification (I-DT), the minimum spanning tree identification (I-MST), and the area of interest identification (I-AOI). These 5 representative algorithms were analyzed and compared in terms of their interpretation speed, accuracy, robustness, ease of implementation, and parameter setting. Overall, these authors found that both I-HMM and I-DT provide accurate and robust fixation identification. I-MST also provided robust results, but was found to be the slowest method from all those tested. I-VT was the simplest method to implement but its performance may produce multiple indications for a single fixation ("blips"), particularly when the gaze velocity hovers near the threshold used in this method. Finally, I-AOI was found to exhibit the poorest performance among the methods evaluated and the authors discouraged its use. Chin developed a practical, real-time, fixation identification algorithm, (for the purpose of screen cursor control), that analyzed POG data reported by a desktop, monocular, EGT system, 60 times per second [Chin 06]. This fixation identification algorithm utilized temporal and spatial criteria to determine whether or not a fixation had occurred. More specifically, the algorithm extracted a 100 ms moving window (temporal threshold) of consecutive POG data points (POGx, POGy), and calculated the standard deviation of the x- and y-coordinates of these points. If both standard deviations were less than the coordinate thresholds associated with $0.5°$ of visual angle (spatial threshold), then it was determined that the onset of a fixation had occurred, and the points used to represent the fixation were the coordinates of the centroid of the POG samples received during the 100 ms window analyzed, (Fx, Fy). If it was determined that a fixation had not occurred, then the window was advanced by one data point and fixation identification was performed again. This algorithm is further illustrated by the flowchart shown in Figure 12.6.

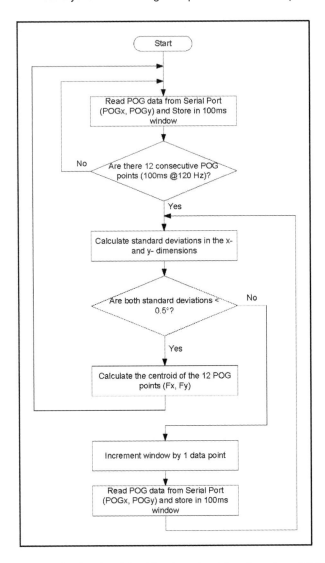

Figure 12.6: EGT fixation identification algorithm flowchart [Chin 06].

12.3   Emerging Uses of EGT in HCI: Affective Sensing

Clearly, one of the key benefits derived from the operation of an EGT system is the knowledge, in real time, of the point-of-gaze of the eye(s) of the subject. In the context of human–computer interaction this POG movement knowledge has primarily been exploited to provide an alternative mechanism of control of the screen cursor in a graphical interface. GUIs have become almost universally prevalent as the WIMP paradigm has replaced text-based interfaces in almost all computer systems. This has, without a doubt, simplified the access to computer applications, to the point at which young children can use many of the applications available in tablets and smartphones. Unfortunately, this has simultaneously presented new obstacles for the computer interaction of individuals with different abilities. In particular, individuals with motor disabilities may not have the capability to move and activate ("click") the screen cursor in a GUI. Therefore, the pointing capabilities obtained with EGT systems have been used as a helpful substitute for the motor abilities normally exercised in moving the screen cursor. In using an EGT system for cursor control the user provides voluntary and overt information to the computer system, just as it is provided with the use of a mouse.

However, embedded in the process of estimating the POG of the user's eye is an additional set of sources of information that the computer could utilize. Studies have verified that information provided by most EGT systems can, in fact, be used advantageously by a computer system seeking to improve the user's experience by taking into account his/her affective state. The sub-field of affective computing has been pursuing such enhancement in the interaction between computer systems and their users since the mid 1990s. In 1997, in her pioneering book *Affective Computing*, Rosalind Picard envisioned a new era of computing in which computers would be much more than mere data processors [Picard 97]. On the wake of the "artificial intelligence" revolution, which focused on enabling computers to "learn" (i.e., "machine learning"), the computers that Picard envisioned could not only learn and interact with humans intelligently, but they would also be able to interact with them at an affective level, defining "affective computing" as "computing which relates to, arises from, or deliberately influences emotions." In analyzing the specific capabilities that a computer would require to fulfill Picard's description, Hudlicka proposed that the following are the key processes involved [Hudlicka 03]:

1. Affect sensing and recognition (affective information from user to machine).

2. User affect modeling / machine affect modeling.

3. Machine affect expression (affective information from machine to user).

EGT systems provide the computer with data which can be used to tackle the first of these processes: Affective sensing, which was identified by Picard as one the key challenges that must be conquered to bring the full promise of affective computing concepts to fruition [Picard 03].

Most of us can attest to some clear, involuntary, and inconcealable changes in our bodies as reactions to strong emotional stimuli: Our hearts may change their pace during climactic moments in a sports event we witness; our hands may turn cold and sweaty when we are scared; we may feel "a rush of blood to the head," when we get into a strong argument. These are perceptions of the actual reconfiguration of our organism that takes place as a reaction to the psychological stimuli listed. Further, we are also capable of identifying an affective shift in another human being by sensing his/her physiological reconfiguration (e.g., seeing the redness in the face of an angry colleague). Physiological affective sensing proposes that computers could, potentially, measure these physical quantities from their users and utilize those measurements to assess their affective states. The reconfiguration experienced by a human subject as a reaction to psychological stimuli is controlled by the autonomic nervous system (ANS), which innervates many organs all over the body. The ANS can promote a state of restoration in the organism, or, if necessary, cause it to leave such a state, invoking physiologic modifications that are useful in responding to external demands. These changes in physiological variables as a response to manipulations of the psychological or behavioral conditions of the individual are the object of study of psychophysiology [Hugdahl 95].

The autonomic nervous system coordinates the cardiovascular, respiratory, digestive, urinary, and reproductive functions according to the interaction between a human being and his/her environment, without instructions or interference from the conscious mind [Martini et al. 01]. According to its structure and functionality, the Autonomic Nervous System (ANS) is studied as composed of two divisions: the sympathetic division and the parasympathetic division. The parasympathetic division stimulates visceral activity and promotes a state of "rest and repose" in the organism, conserving energy and fostering sedentary "housekeeping" activities, such as digestion [Martini et al. 01]. In contrast, the sympathetic division prepares the body for heightened levels of somatic activity that may be necessary to implement a reaction to stimuli that disrupt the "rest and repose" of the organism. When fully activated, this division produces a "flight or fight" response, which readies the body for a crisis that may require sudden, intense physical activity. An increase in sympathetic activity generally stimulates tissue metabolism, increases alertness, and, overall, transforms the body into a new status, which will be better able to cope with a state of crisis. Parts of that re-design or transformation may become apparent to the subject and may be associated with measurable changes in physiological variables.

The alternated increases in sympathetic and parasympathetic activation provide, in principle, a way to assess the affective shifts and states experienced by the subject. So, for example, sympathetic activation (in general terms) promotes the secretion of adrenaline and noradrenaline, inhibits bladder contraction, promotes the conversion of glycogen to glucose, inhibits peristalsis and secretion, dilates the bronchi in the lungs, accelerates the heartbeat, inhibits the flow of saliva, reduces the peripheral resistance of the circulatory system, and, importantly for this discussion, dilates the pupils of the eyes. In contrast, parasympathetic activation (in general terms) stimulates the release of bile, contracts the bladder, stimulates peristalsis and secretion, constricts the bronchi in the lungs, slows the heartbeat, and stimulates the flow of saliva.

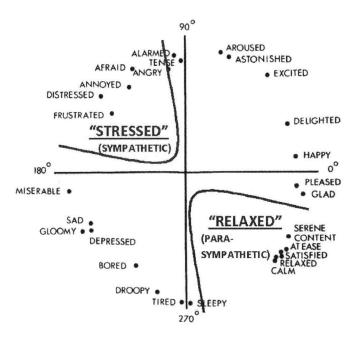

Figure 12.7: Sympathetic ("STRESSED") and parasympathetic ("RELAXED") activations in the Circumplex Model of Affect. Adapted from [Russell 80].

Therefore, an approach to affective sensing based on physiological measures targets specifically the changes in observable variables introduced by sympathetic activation. Figure 12.7 shows the Circumplex Model of Affect [Russell 80] with the regions associated with sympathetic ("stressed") and parasympathetic ("relaxed") predominance overlaid. This combined diagram provides a rationale for the proposal of detecting sympathetic activation to alert the computer that the user is evolving from the comfortable, "relaxed" states in the lower-right quadrant, toward the "stressed" states in the upper-left quadrant.

It has been proposed that sympathetic activation detection can help the implementation of affective computing concepts in some key applications. For example, that will be the case of intelligent tutoring systems, where it is important to distinguish if the student is relaxed/calmed or if he/she is becoming stressed/frustrated, etc.

The sympathetic and parasympathetic divisions of the ANS innervate organs all over the body. Therefore, there are, in principle, many physiological measurements that could be monitored for detection of sympathetic activation. However, in the context of practical human–computer interactions, and keeping in mind the goal of making the affective sensing implementation as unobtrusive as possible, the list of physiological variables that are viable is reduced. This has promoted interest in taking advantage of the impressive advances in current eye gaze tracking technology. Modern EGT systems provide robust and unobtrusive tracking for sustained eye monitoring and even re-acquisition of the subject's eye without requiring the subject's awareness or cooperation. This suggests that the monitoring of multiple eye parameters (all of them measurable through a high-speed EGT system) may be a viable way to detect sympathetic activation due to stress in the computer user. For a computer user, the sympathetic activation could arise because of (negative) stress or distress, frustration, etc. Therefore, in an affective computing system the detection of sympathetic activation could trigger the implementation of corrective measures to mitigate such distress.

Specifically, there are at least two physiological variables that are observable in the eyes of the computer user by means of a high-speed eye gaze tracking unit:

A **Pupil Diameter Variations**: It is well documented that the pair of agonist/antagonist muscles that control the pupil diameter are under complementary control of the sympathetic and parasympathetic divisions of the ANS [Steinhauer et al. 04]. Similarly, variations of pupil diameter under changes of mental workload and in response to auditory affective stimulation have been analyzed. More specifically, the pupil diameter variations in response to affective stimulation of a computer user have been studied [Barreto et al. 07a, Barreto et al. 07b, Gao et al. 09, Gao et al. 10, Ren et al. 13, Ren et al. 14].

B **Characteristics of Eye Saccades and Fixational Eye Movements (transient deflections of the eye gaze)**: The muscles that control the eye movements (and therefore the direction of gaze) are also innervated by the third cranial nerve, which provides the parasympathetic control to the contractor pupillae muscle, responsible for the constriction of the pupil [Martini et al. 01]. Several characteristics of the eye saccades have been found to correlate well with varying levels of difficulty in mental tasks performed by experimental subjects. Typically the difficulty levels of the tasks were manipulated in terms of the associated mental workload. However, the intended increase of mental workload is likely to have been associated with increased stress, concurrently.

The monitoring of pupil diameter for stress detection has a clear anatomical and physiological rationale. The diameter of this circular aperture is under the control of the ANS through two sets of muscles. The sympathetic ANS division, mediated by posterior hypothalamic nuclei, produces enlargement of the pupil by direct stimulation of the radial dilator muscles, which causes them to contract [Steinhauer et al. 04]. On the other hand, pupil size decrease is caused by excitation of the circular pupillary constriction muscles innervated by the parasympathetic fibers. The motor nucleus for these muscles is the Edinger–Westphal nucleus located in the midbrain. Sympathetic activation brings about pupillary dilation via two mechanisms: (i) an active component arising from activation of radial pupillary dilator muscles along sympathetic fibers and (ii) a passive component involving inhibition of the Edinger–Westphal nucleus [Bressloff and Wood 98].

The pupil has been observed to enlarge with increased difficulty in mental tasks where the workload is manipulated as independent variable (frequently "N-back" tasks), but one should keep in mind that such tasks are also likely to produce an affective reaction (e.g., stress) in the subjects. Furthermore, there have been other experiments in which pupil diameter has been found to increase in response to stressor stimuli that do not cause a differential mental workload. Partala and Surakka used sounds from the International Affective Digitized Sounds (IADS) collection [Bradley and Lang 99] to provide auditory affective stimulation to 30 subjects, and found that the pupil size variation responded to affectively charged sounds [Partala and Surakka 03].

Those observations were confirmed in the experiments by Gao and colleagues, which also used affective stimulation that did not explicitly increase the mental workload [Gao et al. 09, Gao et al. 10]. They used a computer-based version of the "Stroop Color-Word Interference Test," originally devised by J.R. Stroop [Stroop 35]. The efficacy of this stress elicitation method has been previously established by Renaud and Blondin [Renaud and Blondin 97] and its psychological, physiological, and biochemical effects in subjects have been validated by Tulen's group [Tulen et al. 89]. They found that the Stroop test induced increases in plasma and urinary adrenaline, heart rate, respiration rate, electrodermal activity, electromyography, feelings of anxiety, and decreased finger pulse amplitude. All these are consistent with sympathetic activation associated with mental stress. Further, Insulander and Johlin-Dannfelt verified the electrophysiological effects of mental stress induced by a Stroop test implementation very similar to Gao's and found that "Mental stress-with an emotional component, as elicited by the Stroop conflict word test, had pronounced effects on the electrophysiological properties of the heart, most markedly in the sinus and AV nodes and to a lesser degree in the ventricle" [Insulander and Johlin-Dannfelt 03].

The Stroop Color-Word Interference Test [Stroop 35], in its classical version, requires that the font color of a written word designating a color name be stated verbally. Gao and colleagues created an interactive computer version that requires the subject to click on a screen button with the correct answer [Gao et al. 09, Gao et al. 10]. If the subject cannot make a decision within 3 seconds, the screen automatically changes to the next trial, which intensifies the stress elicitation [Renaud and Blondin 97]. In each Stroop trial, a word presented to the subject designates a color that may ("Congruent") or may not ("Incongruent") match the font color. Congruent trials are not expected to elicit an affective response. In contrast, the internal contradiction induced in the subject during incongruent trials produces an affective response (sympathetic activation) associated with a stressor stimulus. Figure 12.8 shows the timeline followed during each complete experimental session, for each participating subject in Gao's experiments. There

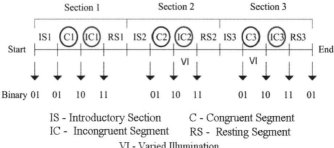

Figure 12.8: Timeline of the stress elicitation experimental protocol [Gao et al. 10].

are 3 consecutive sections. In each section, there are four segments including: 1) 'IS' — An introductory segment to establish an appropriate initial level for his/her psychological state, according to the law of initial values (LIV) [Stern et al. 01]; 2) 'C' — a congruent segment, comprising 45 Stroop congruent word presentations (font color matches the meaning of the word), which are not expected to elicit significant stress in the subject; 3) 'IC' — an incongruent segment of the Stroop test (font color and the meaning of the 30 words presented differ), to induce stress in the subject; 4) 'RS' — a resting segment to act as a buffer between the sections of the protocol.

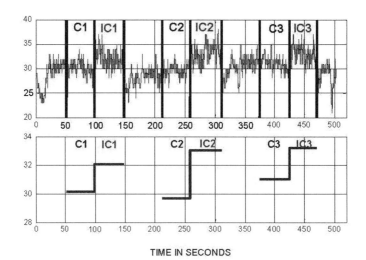

TIME IN SECONDS

Figure 12.9: Pupil diameter variations (above) and mean values (below) originally observed during the protocol [Barreto et al. 07b].

Previous work on pupil monitoring for affective sensing has sought to distinguish between the congruent (relaxation) and incongruent (stress) experimental segments. The initial approach focused on the mean pupil diameter differences between congruent and incongruent experimental segments. An example of these mean values is shown in Figure 12.9. Originally, a single feature from each segment of pupil diameter (PD) data, which was the normalized mean PD value in each segment, was extracted and used in conjunction with 10 other normalized features obtained from GSR, blood volume pulse (BVP), and skin temperature (ST) signals recorded concurrently. The classification of experimental segments on the basis of those multiple features revealed:

A Segment (congruent vs. incongruent) classification by a Support Vector Machine achieved 90.10% average accuracy using all 11 features, but decreased to 61.45% if the information from the pupil diameter (PD mean feature) was removed (not provided to the classifier) [Zhai and Barreto 06].

B The receiver operating characteristic (ROC) curve for the Pupil Diameter (PD) mean feature had an area $AUROC\_PDmean = 0.9647$, which was much higher than even the second-best feature ROC, from the GSR signal ($AUROC\_GSRmean = 0.6519$) [Barreto et al. 07a].

More recent studies by Ren et al. have confirmed these observations [Ren et al. 13, Ren et al. 14]. However, it has also been realized that the Stroop elicitation paradigm may present some limitations, as the low intensity of the stimulation may not actually trigger a stress response in some subjects. Further, the artificial (uncommon) environment in which the subject is asked to take the Stroop Test seems to raise the baseline of sympathetic activation in some of the subjects. This may result in the collection of physiologic data where the differential affective response of some subjects is actually very small.

Early studies in pupil diameter monitoring for stress detection took place in controlled conditions where the amount of illumination impinging on the retina of the experimental subject was kept approximately constant. In uncontrolled (real) scenarios, the pupil diameter may also decrease due to increased illumination, according to the pupillary light reflex (PLR). To address this Gao et al. [Gao et al., 2009] used an adaptive signal processing approach to account for the effect of illumination changes on pupil size variations, so that the processed pupil diameter signal would reflect primarily the changes in pupil diameter due to affective responses, (designated as the "pupillary affective response" or PAR). Figure 12.10 shows a block diagram indicating how an adaptive transversal filter (ATF), adapted using the H-infinity algorithm, was set up for this task [Gao et al. 09]. This architecture, which follows the general structure of an adaptive interference canceller (AIC) [Widrow and Stearns 85], requires a "reference noise" signal, obtained from the same source (but not necessarily identical) as the noise that pollutes the signal of interest, in order to remove that noise. In this case the signal of interest is the component in the measured pupil diameter variations that is due to the pupillary affective response, while the noise is the component in the measured pupil diameter variations that is due to the pupillary light reflex. Therefore, Gao and colleagues placed a photo sensor in the forehead of the subject and used the corresponding signal as "noise reference."

The left panel of Figure 12.11 shows one example set of the signals processed by the adaptive interference canceller. The second plot is the illumination intensity recorded by the photo sensor. The two increases in illumination observed in segments IC2 and C3 were introduced deliberately (turning on a desk lamp) to test the robustness of the process to illumination changes. The output from the adaptive interference canceller, labeled MPD (bottom-left plot), is further processed by half-wave rectification and a sliding median filter, to yield the bottom trace of the right panel, the processed modified pupil diameter (PMPD), which was used as an indication of sympathetic activation, i.e. stress.

It should be noted that the PMPD signal rises over the zero level almost only exclusively during the Stroop Incongruent (stress) segments (after the initial adaptation of the AIC), as expected. Feeding the mean level of PMPD during each segment, along with the other 9 features obtained from GSR and BVP into a support vector machine, achieved an average accuracy of 76.67% in the classification of segments ("stress" vs. "relax"). In this case, also, the classification accuracy dropped to 54.44% if the PMPDmean feature was not used, while a classifier using this single normalized feature, "PMPDmean," resulted in an average accuracy of 77.78% [Gao et al. 10]. Furthermore, the ROC curve obtained for the normalized PMPDmean had, again, a much larger area, $AUROC\_PMPDmean = 0.9331$, than the second-best ROC curve, obtained from the mean GSR average value in each segment, $AUROC\_GSRmean = 0.6780$ [Gao et al. 09]. These observations confirm the strong potential that the pupil diameter signal captured by an EGT instrument seems to have for affective sensing of a computer user.

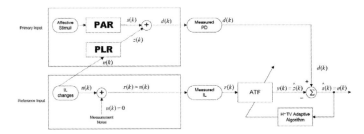

Figure 12.10: Adaptive interference canceller (AIC) architecture used to minimize the negative impact of the pupillary light reflex (PLR) on affective assessment by pupil diameter monitoring [Gao et al. 10].

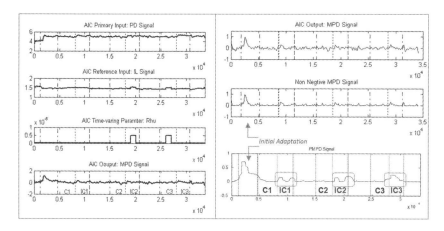

Figure 12.11: Process of the original pupil diameter signal (top-left) by the adaptive interference canceller and subsequent sliding window median analysis to result in the PMPD signal (bottom-right) that indicates the emergence of sympathetic activation ("stress") in the incongruent Stroop segments (IC1, IC2 and IC3). [Gao et al. 09].

It was previously pointed out that, even while humans attempt to pay attention to a stationary target (i.e., during a "fixation"), our eyes must continue to perform small movements, shifting the gaze around the target, so that the image projected onto the retina is never constant. These compensatory movements that occur during a "fixation" are called "fixational eye movements" (FEMs). FEMs had been traditionally classified as "tremors" [Yarbus 67], "slow drifts" [Ratliff and Riggs 50], and "microsaccades" [Engbert 06]. Recently, however, Abadi and Gowen differentiated a fourth type of fixational eye movement, which they called "saccadic intrusions" (SIs), with these characteristics: "conjugate, horizontal saccadic movements which tend to be 3-4 times larger than the physiological microsaccades and take the form of an initial fast eye movement away from the desired position, followed, after a variable duration, by either a return saccade or a drift" [Abadi and Gowen 04].

Eye movements are affected by the psycho-physiological state of the subject. For example, Ishii and colleagues have attempted to evaluate mental workload by analyzing pursuit eye movements [Ishii et al. 13]. Most importantly, tremors, slow drifts and microsaccades are involuntary [Carpenter 88, Martinez-Conde et al. 04] and saccadic intrusions are also involuntary [Abadi and Gowen 04]. That is, we do not perform them or regulate their characteristics (timing, speed, amplitude, etc.) under conscious control. Their properties at any given time, therefore, are dependent on the autonomic nervous system of the subject, as the pupil diameter is.

The properties of (regular) saccades are also defined, in part, by involuntary processes. "The decision to initiate a saccade is under voluntary control, however, once the saccade is initiated the speed that the eye moves is completely involuntary, with no central CNS influence" [Connel and Baxeddale 11]. These authors found that alteration of the ANS by an increasing dose of buprenorphine in 16 volunteers, induced a (dose dependent) decrease in saccadic velocity, peaking around two hours post dose.

Therefore, both (regular) saccades and saccadic intrusions (SIs) have variations in their characteristics that depend on the psycho-physiological state of the subject, as pupil diameter variations do. Tokuda proposed the analysis of SIs as an advantageous alternative to the measurement of pupil diameter variations to evaluate mental workload. In their studies they used an (auditory) N-back task to manipulate mental workload and found that both pupil diameter and occurrence of SIs correlated well with the degree of difficulty of the N-back task. It should be noted that, while the more difficult (larger N) N-back task was meant to manipulate the mental workload, large N tasks are also likely to induce a stressful response in the subject, which could also be the cause for the increase in pupil diameter and in the occurrence of SIs.

Similarly, a study used eye tracking (among other measures) to evaluate the psycho-physiological response of anesthesiologists during the simulation of a critical incident endangering the patient (progressive anaphylaxis, reaching severe anaphylaxis) [Schulz et al. 11]. While this study meant to evaluate workload, it used an independent variable (inclusion or exclusion of the simulation of a critical incident) that clearly altered the stress level in the anesthesiologists participating as subjects, concurrently. These researchers confirmed an increase in pupil diameter in the sessions that included the simulated critical incident, and saw the pupil size vary in correlation to the progressive severity of the critical incident, so that "the simulator conditions explained 92.6% of the variance in pupil diameter." It was also found that "assessment of duration of fixation (time between regular saccades) as a function of simulator state by mixed models revealed a highly significant association ($p < 0.001$). The independent variable 'simulator state' explained 65% of the variance during incident scenarios" [Schulz et al. 11].

These findings lend additional credibility to the emerging utilization of EGT systems to obtain implicit information about the affective state of a computer user, defining a new avenue for research into the additional potential of EGT technology as input mechanism in human–computer interaction.

Further Reading

To help appreciating the evolution of EGT systems for HCI, it is interesting to read one of Robert Jacob's earliest reports on EGT [Jacob 90].

In 2007 Andrew Duchowski published a comprehensive book on EGT methodology [Duchowski 07] that can be consulted to obtain more detailed information on multiple aspects related to these instruments.

Finally, an interesting comparison of the origins (1990) of these technologies in HCI with a current state of the art can be obtained by reading Heiko Drewes' contribution [Drewes 15] to the book on *Interactive Displays* edited by Bhomik.

Exercises

1. Create a survey report with the current EGT commercially available EGT systems. Create a table to compare the different attributes found on those commercial EGT systems, including prices.

2. According to the study by Guestrin and Eizenman (2006), what is the minimum set of requirements for estimating the point of gaze, if the head of the subject cannot be expected to be perfectly stationary:

    a Using only one camera and one light source.

    b Using one camera and multiple light sources, after a multi-point calibration.

    c Using multiple cameras and multiple light sources, after a single-point calibration.

    d Using multiple cameras and multiple light sources, after a multi-point calibration.

3. To obtain a "bright pupil" image it is necessary that:

    a The IR illuminator and the IR camera are placed on the same axis (collinear).

    b The IR illuminator and the IR camera are placed on perpendicular axes.

    c The IR illuminator is displaced about 1.5 cm from the camera axis.

    d The "on-axis" illuminator and the "off-axis" illuminator are turned on alternatively.

4. The rationale for monitoring the pupil diameter readings provided by an EGT system to detect the emergence of stress in a computer user is that:

    a Stress is associated with activation of the parasympathetic division of the ANS, which activates the muscles that make the pupil dilate.

    b Stress is associated with activation of the parasympathetic division of the ANS, which activates the muscles that make the pupil reduce its size.

    c Stress is associated with activation of the sympathetic division of the ANS, which activates the muscles that make the pupil reduce its size.

    d Stress is associated with activation of the sympathetic division of the ANS, which activates the muscles that make the pupil dilate.

13

Brain–Computer Interfaces: Considerations for the Next Frontier in Interactive Graphics and Games

Frances Lucretia Van Scoy

> The interpretation of human thought from brain activity, without recourse to speech or action, is one of the most provoking and challenging frontiers of modern neuroscience.
>
> —Lorina Naci

13.1   Introduction

Gesture and speech are the main ways humans interact with each other. Yet humans often have rich inner lives as they communicate with themselves within their own heads by thoughts.

Speculative fiction has long described mind-to-mind communication between sentient beings. On being transported to a future time, the protagonist of Isaac Asimov's *Pebble in the Sky* first feared that mind-reading existed in that time and was relieved to learn that chess was still popular, showing that thoughts were still private. Others of Asimov's books address the disruptive nature of telepathy.

Can humans use technology to communicate with software using their minds?

13.2   Neuroscience Research

Recent developments in neuroscience research suggest that electrical activity within the brain may provide a way other than gesture and speech for humans to communicate with computer software.

All of the studies described in this section are invasive or use large expensive equipment and therefore aren't feasible for application in constructing brain–computer interface (BCI). However, they provide an indication of what might eventually be feasible using low-cost devices of the near future.

13.2.1   Invasive Research

An example of a very invasive study of the use of the brain to control movement of a cursor is that conducted by an interdisciplinary team of researchers led by Jeremiah Wandera at the University of Washington [Wander et al. 13].

Controlling Movement of a Cursor on a Video Display

The seven test subjects all had epilepsy and received surgically implanted electrodes to collect data to identify the focus of their seizures. The experimental recordings were done without interfering with the clinical recordings over several days for each subject. The specific task performed by the test subjects was controlling the vertical movement of a cursor as it moved from the left screen edge to the right screen edge at constant horizontal velocity. The goal was to guide the cursor to a specific one of two targets near the right edge of the screen. The researchers observed different brain activity in the learning phase, when subjects were learning how to control the cursor, and the automatic phase, when subjects were able to control the cursor without much effort. They reached two conclusions.

1. Although the task did not involve physical movement by the subject, in the learning phase of the experiment the parts of the brain that control physical activity were involved.

2. During the automatic phase, once the test subject had learned how to cause the cursor to hit the target reliably, activity in those parts of the brain decreased significantly.

Controlling a Prosthetic Hand and a Robotic Arm

Early research in neuroprostheses, electronic brain implants, was described in an unsigned *Nature* editorial [unsigned editorial 06]. One of these projects was led by John P. Donoghue of Brown University [Hochberg et al. 06]. His group implanted sensors in the motor cortex of a subject with tetraparesis, partial loss of voluntary motor control in both arms and both legs, due to damage to the spinal cord three years earlier. They translated the electrical signals in the motor cortex into commands to operate a prosthetic hand and a multi-jointed robotic arm. The subject was able to complete simple tasks of control of the hand and the arm merely by thinking about the desired actions. This research underlies the work of the company BrainGate.

Selecting Keys

The other project, conducted at Stanford [Santhanam et al. 06], implanted electrode arrays in the dorsal premotor cortex of monkeys. Their results showed the feasibility of this approach for attaining keyboard input of about 15 words per minute, an improvement on similar previous work.

13.2.2   EEG Research

One noninvasive approach to capturing brain signals used in clinical or research settings is electroencephalogram (EEG). Teplan described "the essentials of EEG measurement" in his 2002 paper [Teplan 02].

Two examples of experiments studying EEG data to detect specific brain activity of test subjects are described below.

Controlling a QuadCopter

Five test subjects at the University of Minnesota were able to fly an AR Drone quadcopter through suspended hoops in a gymnasium [LaFleur et al. 13]. This extended their previous work of moving a virtual helicopter in 2D space.

Transferring Bits between Test Subjects

In a proof of the concept of transmitting specific brain activity between subjects [Grau et al. 14], one subject, the emitter, was connected to an EEG system and was shown zeroes and ones one at a time on a screen. The bits were chosen to encode the words "hola" or "ciao." He was instructed to think about moving his feet when shown a zero and to think about moving his hands when shown a one. The resulting data were sent via email to the location of three other subjects, the receivers. The data from the emitter were translated into biphasic transcranial magnetic stimulation pulses that stimulated an occipital cortex site (specific to each receiver). The intent was that a receiver subject (with eyes closed) would experience the sensation of light when a one was sent from the emitter and no sensation of light when a zero was sent. The receivers were able to decode the cortical signals to identify which word had been sent by the emitter.

13.2.3   fMRI Research

A second noninvasive way of collecting brain signaling data is magnetic resonance imaging (MRI). The European Magnetic Resonance Forum has produced a peer-reviewed overview of magnetic resonance imaging (MRI) [Rinck 14] that is available online.

Examination of vendor price lists shows that the cost of an MRI machine is generally between $500,000 and $3,000,000 US dollars.

Generating Text from fMRI Data

Carnegie-Mellon researchers Tom Mitchell and Marcel Just presented test subjects with 60 drawings and noun labels [Mitchell et al. 08]. The subject looked at a drawing-label pair for 3 seconds and was asked to think about properties of the object. One example was that a person viewing a drawing of a castle might think of cold, knights, and stone. They predicted and verified magnetic resonance imaging (MRI) activation for thousands of concrete nouns for which fMRI data was not yet available. Pereira, Detre, and Botvinick, researchers at Princeton, used the fMRI data from Mitchell and Just as the basis for their work in mapping functional brain scan data to text [Pereira et al. 11]. They used a generative approach in which they generated a verbal description from an fMRI image. They analyzed 3500 Wikipedia articles and, using unsupervised machine learning techniques, created a topic model of each article. They divided Mitchell's fMRI data into a training set and a testing set. Working with the topic models and the training set they developed a mapping from the topic models to the brain scans. Then they inverted the mapping from topic models to brain scans in order to map the testing fMRI images to topics. The result was that they were able to generate appropriate text based on the earlier brain scans. By using a topic model their work suggests applicability to recognition of abstract concepts with no natural visual representation. In a Princeton University news release [Kelly], senior researcher Matthew Botvinick, said:

> "If we give way to unbridled speculation, one can imagine years from now being able to *translate* brain activity into written output for people who are unable to communicate otherwise, which is an exciting thing to consider."

Connecting Images from fMRI Data

A paper by Berkeley researchers [Kay et al. 08] begins "Imagine a general brain-reading device that could reconstruct a picture of a person's visual experience at any moment in time" and ends "We are therefore optimistic that the model-based approach will make possible the reconstruction of natural images from human brain activity." In the paper they describe their work with quantitative receptive-field models.

Miyawaki et al. [Miyawaki et al. 08] explained the weaknesses of the quantitative receptive-field models used by Kay and retinotopy, the mapping of visual stimuli from the retina to neurons, and then described their work. fMRI data was collected as a subject was presented with 440 different random 10x10 images. Then the subject was shown 10x10 images of five letters of the alphabet and five geometric shapes, each shown between six and eight times. Using the fMRI data from the random images and the letters and shapes they were able to construct which scan data came from seeing each letter or shape.

Recognizing Yes-No Answers to Questions

Naci, Cusack, Jia, and Owen at the University of Western Ontario explored techniques that might enable a patient in a coma to communicate without using gestures or speech [Naci et al. 13]. Healthy test subjects answered yes-no questions while undergoing an fMRI scan. They compared their results with earlier results by [M. et al. 07] in which they had subjects imagine playing tennis or walking through their house in order to cause different regions of the brain to be active in each yes or no response.

They wrote:

> "Although MRI is more costly than EEG, fMRI BCIs may offer novel and unique opportunities . . . , especially for patients in a complete locked-in state (CLIS), who do not respond with EEG-based systems. CLIS patients, who have entirely lost all motor abilities . . . , have not been able to communicate via EEG BCIs . . . . The lack of a priori knowledge about their level of cognitive capacities and communicative intent, as well as their varying levels of arousal, constitute major hurdles in building appropriate BCI systems for communicating with this patient group. Hence, the strengths of the technique reported here, especially its ease of use, robustness, and rapid detection, may maximize the chances that any nonresponsive patient will be able to achieve brain-based communication."

Locating Personality Models in the Brain

A multi-university, multi-disciplinary team [Hassabis et al. 13] based their work on the premise that individual behavior is based on individual personality which is based on cognitive and behavioral tendencies. They used fMRI scanning to determine the regions of the brain which store personality information about other individuals and which are active when a subject is predicting the behavior in a specific situation of someone whose personality traits are known to the user.

Subjects were shown photographs and statements about the personalities of four people, fictitious characters whom the subjects were led to believe were real. The individuals were described in such a way that the subjects could easily identify each as being low or high in agreeableness and in extraversion. Then the subjects were asked to think about twelve specific locations such as a bar or a bank. Next each subject was given an event such as "Dave" is in a bar when someone spills a drink and was asked to think for ten seconds about what Dave would think and feel about the event and how he would respond. Twelve of these events were presented to each subject.

In the fMRI data, "[d]ifferent patterns of activation in the anterior mPFC [medial prefrontal cortex] could reliably distinguish between the different people whose behavior was being imagined. We then examined how the brain represents 2 major traits: agreeableness and extraversion. Agreeableness was associated with unique patterns of BOLD [blood oxygen level-dependent] response in the dorsal mPFC and LTC [lateral temporal cortex], whereas extraversion was associated with the pCC [posterior cingulate cortex]." They suggested that "a possible inability to build accurate personality models of others" may be a cause of some social cognition disorders and that future related research might result in treatment.

13.3 Implications of EEG- and fMRI-Based Research for the Brain–Computer Interface

13.3.1 Implications of Constructing Text or Images from Brain Scan Data

These projects of constructing text or images from brain scan data have several implications for use of brain data in user interfaces.

First they demonstrate the importance of interdisciplinary teams of researchers. The Princeton researchers [Pereira et al. 11] were in psychology and neuroscience and used previous work of Carnegie-Mellon researchers. The CMU group [Mitchell et al. 08] included researchers from computer science and from cognitive science. One of the Berkeley researchers [Kay et al. 08] is a physicist.

Second the initial work of one group used fMRI data collected elsewhere (at CMU) for a different purpose and made publicly available. This suggests that for researchers who don't yet have collaborators with access to fMRI systems it might be both possible and prudent to design studies that can reuse others' published fMRI data to confirm or refute their hypotheses.

Third if this line of research is successful it changes everything in user interfaces. If affordable accurate wireless technology becomes available, truly hands-free user interfaces can become routine. Dictation systems that use thought rather than finger and hand movements or speech can become commonplace, resulting in privacy and possibly faster speed, and can eliminate the need for training in "touch typing." When combined with algorithms to generate images from specific brain activities, the process used by creative writers changes dramatically.

In a 1992 interview [King] television writer and novelist Sidney Sheldon described his writing process:

> "I start with a character and I dictate to a secretary. I don't start with any plot at all. In a sense, I am the reader as well as the writer, because I don't know what is going to happen next. At the end of the day when I read the pages my secretary has typed, there are situations and characters there I didn't know existed when I began dictating that morning. So it is an exciting way to work."

Elsewhere he said that in his imagination he observed what his characters said and did and then described this to his secretary.

A hardware/software system that could capture what Sheldon saw and heard and generate a rough draft either in written words or in images and spoken words would be a dramatically different and powerful system.

Sue Grafton said in a 2010 interview for *Writer's Digest* magazine [Jordan] concerning the protagonist of her projected 26 volume series of mystery novels:

> "In my mind, I am only privileged to know what she chooses to share, and she assures me that some things are just not my business, thank you. I don't tell her. She tells me. I discover things about her in the process of writing. I don't have a great scheme afoot. I try to keep honest, I try not to repeat myself. I try to let her evolve as she will, not according to my dictates. It's a very odd process."

Development of a brain–computer interface that captures what a writer sees or hears via imagination while drafting a story is a challenging project but may be feasible within ten years.

But what would a brain-signal-based system constructed for a writer be like?

13.3.2   Implications of Personality Models for Digital Games

Neuroscience research in personality models [Hassabis et al. 13] may be applicable to new developments in games that rely on social simulation. Although the Hassabis paper doesn't suggest an application of their research to digital social simulation games, it may provide a neuroscience basis for future development of such games. The goal is to develop tools and approaches for developing games in which the player can make meaningful choices that change the direction of the narrative of the game.

ABL and Façade

Mateas and Stern, creators of the social simulation game Façade, described their goals for the impact of player choices on the plot of playing of a game [Mateas and Stern 00]:

The player's actions should have a significant influence on what events occur in the plot, which are left out, and how the story ends. The plot should be generative enough that . . . full appreciation of the experience requires the story be played multiple times. Change in the plot should not be traceable to distinct branch points; the player will not be offered an occasional small number of obvious choices that force the plot in a different direction. Rather, the plot should be smoothly mutable, varying in response to some global state which is itself a function of the many small actions performed by the player throughout the experience.

That writing such a game is a huge job is an understatement. Using conventional techniques many scenes must be written which a player who plays the game only once will never see. For example, Mateas and Stern wrote five hours of dialog for *Façade* but only 20 minutes are presented to the player in a typical playing (Mateas, 2000). The branching storylines of Bioware's *Star Wars: The Old Republic* were written by 20 writers taking 60 staff-years of work [Orland]. Game logic must be very complex in keeping track of states. Perhaps most importantly, emergent game play is nearly impossible. That is, a player can only have the experiences constructed by the game designers rather than new experiences not predicted by the designers but logical outcomes of game play.

ABL (A Behavior Language) is the implementation language of Façade (see https://abl.soe.ucsc.edu/index.php/Main_Page).

Comme il Faut and Prom Week

Two new social simulation game platforms which allow for emergent game play are Comme il Faut, by researchers at the University of California, Santa Cruz, and Versu.

Comme il Faut [McCoy et al. 14] is an artificial intelligence narrative platform that supports the construction of games whose characters have emotions, values, and personalities. They form relationships with other characters and retain memories of past interactions. Attitudes of characters toward each other shift as game play progresses and cause characters to change how they respond to each other. *Prom Night* [McCoy et al. 13] is a game developed in parallel with Comme il Faut as both a proof of concept of CiF and as a driver of changes to CiF. *Prom Night* takes place the week of the prom. Eighteen high school students try to attain their social goals for finding a date for the prom.

Versu and Blood & Laurels

Versu is an interactive narrative system by Richard Evans and Emily Short [Evans and Short]. They describe Versu as "an improvisational play, rather than an interactive story" and "an agent-driven simulation in which each of the NPCs make decisions independently." In "Versu, the game designer is a writer putting together both a broad narrative and also a richly interactive experience, in which fictional people have motives and emotions and beliefs" (Nelson, 2014). Versu uses Praxis, a logic programming language which was developed by Richard Evans and has similarities to Prolog. The concepts behind Praxis are described by Evans in his paper "Computer Models of Constitutive Social Practice" [Evans]. Graham Nelson developed the programming language Prompter, which is translated into Praxis, with two goals: "to enable faster development, and to make Versu content more human-readable." [Nelson]

Emily Short has described some of the complexity of game play in games implemented in Versu [Short]:

> Evaluations, and the reasons which justify the evaluations, can be communicated from one character to another. For example: in an early play-test, I was wondering why the doctor was being so rude to me when I had never spoken to him before. I found out, after much debugging, that the reason for his rudeness was that I had been mean to the butler, and the butler had been gossiping about me in the kitchen.

The first Versu game or story released was *Blood & Laurels* by Emily Short [Suellentrop]. Chris Suellentrop has described this as a "novel, even radical, form of digital storytelling with text" and written "*Blood & Laurels* is interesting in its own right but even more so for the promise of what might come after it."

Implications of Comme il Faut and Versu

The existence of the software platforms Comme il Faut and Versu suggest these questions:

Can future neuroscience research shape which attributes are modeled in social simulation games? Can future social games be developed that use neuroheadsets as input devices? And, in particular, can the emotional state of the player be used to control complex game play?

13.4   Neuroheadsets

A pragmatic question is: Is there, or will there be, brain signal capturing technology that is affordable both for game developers and for game players?

Fortunately for researchers outside of medical centers, low-cost devices for capturing EEG data are available.

13.4.1   Some Available Devices

Several companies promote low-cost neuroheadsets that provide access to raw EEG data. This information is current as of January 2015. Some examples are:

Side Note 13.1: Looking back

While, due to space restrictions, this chapter has not included detailed descriptions of the pioneering efforts by several research groups around the world during the 1980s, 1990s, and early 2000s, choosing instead to address recent developments and prospects for the future, the interested reader is directed to the 2006 Special Issue on Brain-Computer Interfaces of the *IEEE Transactions on Neural Systems and Rehabilitation Engineering* (Vol. 14, Number 2, June 2006). This special issue presents a panoramic view of the state-of-the-art in BCI technologies, summarizing the key outcomes of the Third International Meeting on Brain–Computer Interface Technology held at the Rensselaerville Institute, Rensselaerville, NY, in June 2005. As such, the 30 peer-reviewed research communications and 4 workshop summary papers in the special issue provide a detailed report of the developments in prestigious BCI research centers at Berlin, Seattle, Aalborg, Graz, Geneva, Florida, and Wadsworth, among others.

– Armando Barreto

- EE = Emotiv Epoc.

- EI = Emotiv Insight.

- IM = InteraXon Muse.

- NM = NeuroSky MindWave.

Each of these neuroheadsets reports data from different channels as shown in Table 13.1. A diagram showing the locations of these channels is found in [Oostenveld and Praamstra 01].

The Emotiv headsets report data from these channels: *AF3, F7, F3, FC5, T7, P7, O1, O2, P8, T8, FC6, F4, F8*, and *AF4*. The price of an Emotiv EPOC is $399, and that of EPOC+ is $499 (US dollars). The EPOC+ has a sampling rate twice that of the EPOC. The EPOC+ is Bluetooth-enabled. For either headset there is

Table 13.1: Channels Reported by Each Neuroheadset System.

	AF3	F7	F3	FC5	T7	P7	O1	O2	P8	T8	FC6	F4	F8	AF4	Pz	TP9	FP1	FP2	TP10
EE	✓	✓	✓	✓	✓	✓	✓	✓	✓	✓	✓	✓	✓	✓					
EI	✓				✓					✓				✓	✓				
IM																✓	✓	✓	✓
NM																			

a cost of an additional $300 US dollars for firmware allowing the user to capture raw EEG data.

The Emotiv Insight reports data from these channels: AF3, AF4, T7, T8, Pz. It is scheduled for release in April, 2015. No price has been announced.

The InteraXon Muse reports data from these channels: TP9, FP1, FP2, TP10. The price of an InteraXon is $299 US dollars. A developer API and access to raw EEG data are available.The NeuroSky MindWave Muse is priced at $79.99 US dollars. Rather than reporting data from the channels, it returns data about waveform frequencies and shape (alpha, beta, delta, and theta). Software developer kits for major platforms are available without charge.

13.4.2   An Example: Controlling Google Glass with MindRDR

A recent technology article [Boxall] described work using Google Glass and a "telekinetic headband" from NeuroSky by This Place, a London digital design agency. They have written software called MindRDR that uses EEG signals from the NeuroSky headband to control the Glass. When the user imagines being fearful or anxious Glass takes a picture.

13.5   A Simple Approach to Recognizing Specific Brain Activities Using Low-End Neuroheadsets and Simple Clustering Techniques

A presentation at the 2008 meeting of the Society for Science, Literature, and the Arts led to the thought by the author of this chapter of the possibility of a future non-invasive brain-scan-based system that could take thoughts of a writer and form them into a rough draft of a short story or a novel chapter. She wondered, could the moving images I see and the voices of the characters I hear in my head as I write a story be turned into digital files that I could transcribe or edit?

In fall 2012 West Virginia University senior undergraduates Timothy Hitrik, Aaron Westbrook, Jacob Satterfield, and Anders Kane approached her about advising their two-semester senior capstone project of developing some simple games using brain signals captured by an Emotiv Epoc neuroheadset. They succeeded in constructing some simple thought-controlled games.

In summer 2013 she acquired an Emotiv Epoc headset for her lab. West Virginia Wesleyan College sophomore Eric Harshbarger worked with her to try to differentiate individual words when thought. They wrote a simple cluster analysis program to find centroids for the samples, points in 14-dimensional space. Thoughts of "tree" when he thought about the tree on which his mother hangs her bird feeder and "dog" when he thought about his black Labrador retriever were

Figure 13.1: EEG.

easy to distinguish as were "bark" when he thought about the bark on the tree in his yard and "bark" when he thought about the "bark" of his black Lab. They then tried to move a cartoon figure around the screen by thought and quickly realized that they could not reliably distinguish among the compass directions north, east, south, and west, likely because as compass directions the concepts were too closely related.

In academic year 2014 another group of WVU senior computer science majors, Kathleen Baker, Tyler Durham, Corey Kouns, and Jian Zhang, extended the project to recognize ideas that a nursing home resident with aphasia might want to communicate, such as being thirsty or needing to use the bathroom.

Also in summer 2014 Harshbarger returned to the lab and worked with graduate student Taylor Cutlip and the author to do a proof of concept on ordering pizza by thoughts, using a newer model of the neuroheadset, the Emotiv EEG. They built a list of forty pizza toppings based on menus from two chains and one independent pizzeria. They modified their software to construct a centroid for each of the forty toppings in the observed EEG data. They were able to distinguish among thoughts of most toppings in their test data with some exceptions. For example, the pizzeria's spicy Italian sausage and the pepperoni of the two chains were indistinguishable. That is not surprising, since the two concepts are very similar.

13.6 Using EEG Data to Recognize Active Brain Regions

Adrian Owen's laboratory at the University of Western Ontario whose work using fMRI to detect brain activity in locked-in patients was described earlier [M. et al. 07], is now using EEG for similar research [Wilson 15]. This *New Scientist* article says, "it's early days and Owen's work is unpublished as yet. *We have had some successes*, is all he will say for now."

This group is using a new EEG device called g.Nautilus from g.tech.The company builds models with 8, 16, or 32 channels, priced between 8,000 and 20,000 euros.

13.7 Conclusion

The technology for brain-computer interfaces for personal computers is almost ready for use. However, the trend toward fewer EEG channels rather than more in low-end headsets should be reversed to improve the quality of the data. The price of the neuroheadset with software or firmware to capture raw EEG is somewhat high but doable for individual faculty labs. The price of the Emotiv system is high for personal use, but the NeuroSky headset is affordable at under $100. The recent unpublished work by Adrian Owen's laboratory suggests that results as good as those obtained by fMRI may also be attainable by portable EEG systems with sophisticated software. The price of the headset they use is high but it could be a useful platform for capturing data for testing new algorithms. There are exciting possibilities for future brain–computer interfaces, and work by researchers using current neuroheadsets will prepare the community to develop truly useful and affordable brain-computer based systems. And, it is important for user interface researchers to remain current with research in neuroscience. For example, will magnetoencephalography have an impact on the work described in this chapter [M. et al. 14]?

Further Reading

[Brunner et al. 13] have written a survey of "seven major BCI platforms," including BCI2000, OpenViBE, and pyff.

Two open-source EEG hardware projects are openEEG and OpenBCI. The Wikipedia article "Comparison of consumer brain–computer interfaces" may be useful in comparing available and affordable EEG systems.

A good introduction to the mathematics of neuroscience is: Peter Dayan and Laurence F. Abbott *Theoretical Neuroscience: Computational and Mathematical Modeling of Neural Systems*

Exercises

1. fMRI data files collected by Marcel Just et al. at Carnegie Mellon University are available at http://www.cs.cmu.edu/afs/cs.cmu.edu/project/theo-81/www/

   Download some of this data and experiment with ways to access and use it.

2. Play several games that involve text input or insight into the behavior of non-player characters. As you play, think about the nature of the use of a brain–computer interface in playing a future version of the game. Some suggested games to play are *Zork*, *Galatea*, *Façade*, and *Blood & Laurels*.

Part II

Advanced Topics

14

Introduction to 3D Math for Input Devices

Steven P. Landers & David Rieksts

> You have to learn the rules of the game. And then you
> have to play better than anyone else.
>
> —Albert Einstein

14.1 Introduction

The purpose of this chapter is to cover the basics of the math that goes into working with 3D input devices. These sections are intended to give a brief overview. If you would like a more formal treatment of these subjects, please see the suggested readings. Some topics, such as 3D rotations and quaternions are not covered, since they are already covered in Part II.

14.2 Axis Conventions

Coordinates in 3D are represented by three numbers. Each one of these numbers corresponds to one of the three axes that form the basis for the 3D coordinate system. These axes are called X, Y, and Z. These three axes are orthogonal, which intuitively means that a value on one axis does not share any information with a value on another axis; they are completely separate.

While these basics of 3D coordinates are set in stone, there are many different conventions that determine which of the three directions each axis measures. These directions are right, up, and forward. If an axis measures the reverse of one of these, we would say it measures left, down, or backward, respectively. One example of an axis convention would be deciding that X represents right, Y represents up,

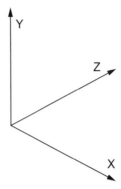

Figure 14.1: Example of a 3D coordinate system.

and Z represents backward. There is one other piece of information that is usually included with an axis convention; if you were to group all sets of axes by whether or not they can be rotated to one another, you would find that there are only two groups of axis conventions. One set is called right-handed; it is called this because if you hold your right hand out in the direction of an axis and then sweep your palm toward the next axis (e.g., from X in the direction of Y, from Y in the direction of Z, from Z in the direction of X), your thumb would be pointing in the direction of the third axis. The example given before is a right-handed coordinate system. The second group is called left-handed, because you are able to perform the same process described above with the axes in this group, but with your left hand instead. Handedness is an important aspect of a coordinate system because it defines which direction rotations will go in that system. It should also be noted that any single swap or negation of a set of axes will change the handedness.

Here are examples of a few coordinate systems used by popular programs and fields:

- OpenGL: X is right, Y is up, Z is backward (right-handed)

- DirectX and Unity: X is right, Y is up, Z is forward (left-handed)

- Unreal Engine: X is forward, Y is right, Z is up (left-handed)

- Land vehicles: X is forward, Y is left, Z is up (right-handed)

- Air and sea vehicles: X is forward, Y is right, Z is down (right-handed)

14.3   Vectors

Intuitively, a vector represents the direction and distance needed to get from one point to another. The vector is only concerned with the direction and distance of

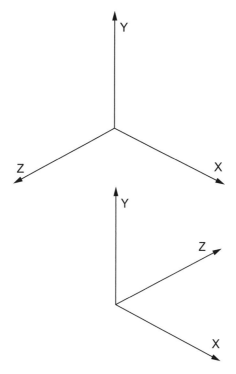

Figure 14.2: Left-handed system (on left) vs. right handed system.

the destination relative to the start. It is not concerned with the path taken. For example, if we want to get from the origin (0, 0) to the point (2, 3), we can go along the straight line which goes through those two points, or we can go in the x-direction for two units and then go in the y-direction for three units, or we can first go in the y-direction for 2 units, then the x-direction for two units, and then in the y-direction for another unit. All these paths are represented by the same vector since the destination is the same direction and distance from the start.

Also, note that the start and destination are not important in and of themselves, only the direction and distance from the start to the finish. For example, to get from $(0,0)$ to $(1,0)$, from $(2,2)$ to $(3,2)$, from $(-1,1)$ to $(0,1)$ or from $(949,-125)$ to $(950,-125)$ all have the start and destination the same distance and direction from each other. So, they would all be represented by the same vector.

This allows us to view all vectors as equivalent to some vector starting at the origin. All of the examples in the paragraph above are equivalent to the vector from $(0,0)$ to $(1,0)$. Thus, a vector can be written as an ordered n-tuple without fear of ambiguity, though normally the symbols () are replaced by <> to make it clear that it is referring to a vector. For instance, the vector from $(0,0)$ to $(1,0)$

can be represented by <1,0>.

In $\mathbb{R}^2$, a vector can be thought of as an ordered pair $<a_1, a_2>$ with special operations associated with it. Similarly, in $\mathbb{R}^3$, a vector can be thought of as an ordered triple $<a_1, a_2, a_3>$.

14.3.1 Equality

Two vectors $v = <a_1, a_2, \ldots, a_n>$ and $u = <b_1, b_2, \ldots, b_n>$ are said to be equal if their components are equal, that is, if $a_1 = b_1, a_2 = b_2, \ldots, a_n = b_n$.

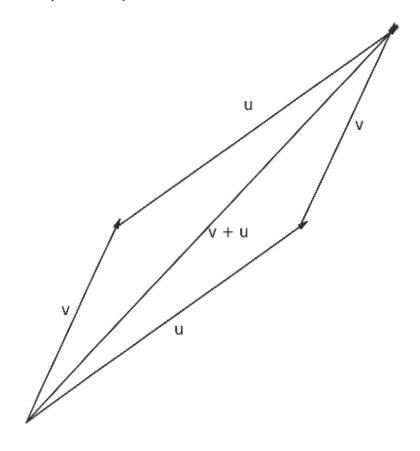

14.3.2 Addition

The addition of two vectors $v = <a_1, a_2, a_3>$ and $u = <b_1, b_2, b_3>$ is defined to be the vector $v + u = <a_1 + b_1, a_2 + b_2, a_3 + b_3>$. Notice that since addition of real numbers is commutative, vector addition is also commutative. So, $v + u = u + v$.

14.3.3   Scalar Multiplication

Given a real number r and a vector $v = \langle a_1, a_2, \ldots, a_n \rangle$, the scalar product of r and v is defined as $r \cdot v = \langle r \cdot a_1, r \cdot a_2, \ldots, r \cdot a_n \rangle$. Scaling a vector changes the distance, but not the direction of the vector.

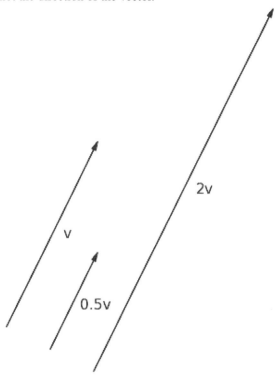

14.3.4   Negation and Subtraction

Given a vector $v = \langle a_1, a_2, \ldots, a_n \rangle$, the negation of v is $-v = (-1) \cdot v = \langle -a_1, -a_2, \ldots, -a_n \rangle$. This represents a movement of the same distance in the opposite direction. So, if v represents the movement from point A to point B, -v represents the movement from point B to point A.

Given two vectors $v = \langle a_1, a_2, \ldots, a_n \rangle$ and $u = \langle b_1, b_2, \ldots, b_n \rangle$, the subtraction of u from v is defined as the subtraction of the individual components (or alternatively as addition of v and the negation of u), $v - u = \langle a_1 - b_1, a_2 - b_2, \ldots, a_n - b_n \rangle = v + (-u)$.

14.3.5   Basis Vectors

The formal definition for a basis of a vector space is that a set of vectors $S = \{v_1, v_2, \ldots, v_n\}$ form a basis for the vector space V over $\mathbb{R}$ if

1. If for any scalars $a_1, a_2, \ldots, a_n$, $a_1 \cdot v_1 + a_2 \cdot v_2 + \ldots + a_n \cdot v_n = 0$ implies $a_1 = a_2, = \ldots = a_n = 0$. (S is **linearly independent**)

2. For any vector v in V, there exist scalars $a_1, a_2, \ldots, a_n$ such that $v = a_1 \cdot v_1 + a_2 \cdot v_2 + \ldots + a_n \cdot v_n$. (S **spans** V)

Intuitively, a set of vectors is a basis if you can get from any point to any other point by scaling and adding the vectors in the set and there are no unnecessary vectors in the set.

The most commonly used basis vectors of $\mathbb{R}^2$ are $\{<1,0>,<0,1>\}$. The most commonly used basis vectors of $\mathbb{R}^3$ are $\{<1,0,0>,<0,1,0>,<0,0,1>\}$. Notice that these vectors represent movements along the axes of their space and thus represent the basic directions that can be taken in their spaces.

14.3.6 Magnitude

The **magnitude** or **length** or **norm** of a vector v in $\mathbb{R}^3$ is defined as the Euclidean norm: $\|v\| = \sqrt{(a_1^2 + a_2^2 + \ldots + a_n^2)}$.

14.3.7 Unit Vector and Normalization

A unit vector is a vector which has a length of 1. Given a vector u, there is a unit vector, denoted Ãż, in the same direction as u. It is found by the process of normalization. To normalize u, multiply u by the reciprocal of the magnitude of u. That is, $\hat{u} = \frac{1}{\|u\|} \cdot u$.

14.3.8 Dot Product

The dot product of two vectors $v = <a_1, a_2, \ldots, a_n>$ and $u = <b_1, b_2, \ldots, b_n>$ is defined by $v \cdot u = \|v\| \cdot \|u\| \cdot \cos(\theta)$ or alternatively $v \cdot u = a_1 \cdot b_1 + a_2 \cdot b_2 + \ldots + a_n \cdot b_n$, where θ is the angle between v and u. Because of these two definitions, it is easy and fast to use the dot product to calculate the angle between two vectors.

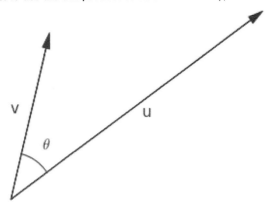

14.3.9 Cross Product in $\mathbb{R}^3$

The cross product is commonly used to find a vector which is perpendicular to two given vectors.

The formal definition of the cross product of a vector v with a vector u is, $v \times u = \|v\| \cdot \|u\| \cdot \sin(\theta) \cdot n$ where θ is the angle between v and u and n is the unit vector perpendicular to a and b which completes a right-handed system. An alternative formulation is $v \times u = <a_2 \cdot b_3 - a_3 \cdot b_2, a_3 \cdot b_1 - a_1 \cdot b_3, a_1 \cdot b_2 - a_2 \cdot b_1>$. The latter formulation is more computationally efficient. As with the dot product, the two separate definitions make it easy to compute the unit vector which is perpendicular to v and u.

14.4 Matrices

A matrix is a mathematical object which consists of numbers or other mathematical objects arranged in rows and columns. The size of a matrix is a pair of numbers representing the number of rows and the number of columns. For example, an $n \times m$ matrix has n rows and m columns. A matrix is known as a square matrix if the number of rows is the same as the number of columns, that is if $n = m$. Two matrices A and B are said to be the same size if they have the same number of rows and the same number of columns.

The numbers in the matrix are known as elements of the matrix. Given a matrix A, the element of A that is in row number i (commonly called the ith row) and column number j (commonly called the jth column), subscripts are used to denote the elements row and column, a_{ij}. A typical $n \times m$ matrix then looks like the following,

$$A = \begin{pmatrix} a_{11} & a_{12} & \dots & a_1 m \\ a_{21} & a_{22} & \dots & a_2 m \\ \vdots & \vdots & \vdots & \vdots \\ a_{n1} & a_{n2} & \dots & a_{nm} \end{pmatrix}$$

14.4.1 Transposition

The transpose of an $n \times m$ matrix,

$$A = \begin{pmatrix} a_{11} & a_{12} & \dots & a_1 m \\ a_{21} & a_{22} & \dots & a_2 m \\ \vdots & \vdots & \vdots & \vdots \\ a_{n1} & a_{n2} & \dots & a_{nm} \end{pmatrix}$$

is an $m \times n$ matrix whose rows are the columns of A and whose columns are the rows of A. That is,

$$A^T = \begin{pmatrix} a_{11} & a_{21} & \cdots & a_{n1} \\ a_{12} & a_{22} & \cdots & a_{n2} \\ \vdots & \vdots & \vdots & \vdots \\ a_{1m} & a_{2m} & \cdots & a_{nm} \end{pmatrix}$$

14.4.2 Trace

The trace of an $n \times n$ square matrix is defined as the sum of the elements of the matrix such that the number of the row to which it belongs and the number of the column to which it belongs are the same. That is, $\mathrm{tr}(A) = \sum_{i=1}^{n} a_{ii}$.

14.4.3 Addition

If two matrices A and B are the same size, addition is defined as the addition of their elements individually. That is, if

$$A = \begin{pmatrix} a_{11} & a_{12} & \cdots & a_{1m} \\ a_{21} & a_{22} & \cdots & a_{2m} \\ \vdots & \vdots & \vdots & \vdots \\ a_{n1} & a_{n2} & \cdots & a_{nm} \end{pmatrix}$$

$$B = \begin{pmatrix} b_{11} & b_{12} & \cdots & b_{1m} \\ b_{21} & b_{22} & \cdots & b_{2m} \\ \vdots & \vdots & \vdots & \vdots \\ b_{n1} & b_{n2} & \cdots & b_{nm} \end{pmatrix}$$

then the sum of A and B is defined as

$$A + B = \begin{pmatrix} a_{11}+b_{11} & a_{12}+b_{12} & \cdots & a_{1m}+b_{1m} \\ a_{21}+b_{21} & a_{22}+b_{22} & \cdots & a_{2m}+b_{2m} \\ \vdots & \vdots & \vdots & \vdots \\ a_{n1}+b_{n1} & a_{n2}+b_{n2} & \cdots & a_{nm}+b_{nm} \end{pmatrix}$$

This is commonly called entrywise addition.

14.4.4 Scalar Multiplication

Given a real number c and an $n \times m$ matrix A,

$$A = \begin{pmatrix} a_{11} & a_{12} & \cdots & a_{1m} \\ a_{21} & a_{22} & \cdots & a_{2m} \\ \vdots & \vdots & \vdots & \vdots \\ a_{n1} & a_{n2} & \cdots & a_{nm} \end{pmatrix}$$

scalar multiplication is defined as

$$A = \begin{pmatrix} c \cdot a_{11} & c \cdot a_{12} & \cdots & c \cdot a_{1m} \\ c \cdot a_{21} & c \cdot a_{22} & \cdots & c \cdot a_{2m} \\ \vdots & \vdots & \vdots & \vdots \\ c \cdot a_{n1} & c \cdot a_{n2} & \cdots & c \cdot a_{nm} \end{pmatrix}$$

14.4.5 Matrix Multiplication

While it may be tempting to define multiplication as element-wise multiplication (this type of multiplication is called the Hadamard product, the Schur product, or the entrywise product), the more common definition is different. Two matrices A and B can be multiplied if the number of columns of the left matrix is equal to the number of rows of the right matrix. For instance, if we want to multiply A and B as $A \cdot B$, the number of columns of A must be equal to the number of rows of B. If A is an $m \times n$ matrix and B is an $n \times p$ matrix then the resulting matrix C will be an $m \times p$ matrix. The product $A \cdot B$ is defined as $c_{ij} = \sum_{r=1}^{n} a_{ir} \cdot b_{rj} = a_{i1} \cdot b_{1j} + a_{i2} \cdot b_{2j} + \ldots + a_{n1} \cdot b_{nj}$. In other words, the element c_{ij} is the dot product of the ith row of A and the jth column of B. It is important to note that matrix multiplication is not commutative. In other words, $A \cdot B$ need not be equal to $B \cdot A$. The following equation can help visualize this.

$$\begin{pmatrix} \cdot & \cdot & \cdot & \cdot & \cdot & \cdot \\ \cdot & \cdot & \cdot & \cdot & \cdot & \cdot \\ a_{i1} & a_{i2} & \cdot & \cdot & \cdot & a_3 \\ \cdot & \cdot & \cdot & \cdot & \cdot & \cdot \end{pmatrix} \begin{pmatrix} \cdot & b_1 j & \cdot & \cdot \\ \cdot & b_2 j & \cdot & \cdot \\ \cdot & \cdot & \cdot & \cdot \\ \cdot & \cdot & \cdot & \cdot \\ \cdot & b_{nj} & \cdot & \cdot \end{pmatrix} = \begin{pmatrix} \cdot & \cdot & \cdot & \cdot \\ \cdot & \cdot & \cdot & \cdot \\ \cdot & c_{ij} & \cdot & \cdot \\ \cdot & \cdot & \cdot & \cdot \end{pmatrix}$$

For example, if

$$A = \begin{pmatrix} -11 & -3 & 2 \\ 7 & 0 & 1 \end{pmatrix}$$

$$B = \begin{pmatrix} -15 & 6 & -10 & 7 \\ 10 & 13 & 4 & 5 \\ -12 & 2 & -11 & 14 \end{pmatrix}$$

and we let $C = A \cdot B$, the elements in bold are used for the calculation of c_{11}.

$$A = \begin{pmatrix} \mathbf{-11} & \mathbf{-3} & \mathbf{2} \\ 7 & 0 & 1 \end{pmatrix} B = \begin{pmatrix} \mathbf{-15} & 6 & -10 & 7 \\ \mathbf{10} & 13 & 4 & 5 \\ \mathbf{-12} & 2 & -11 & 14 \end{pmatrix}$$

So, $c_{11} = (-11) \cdot (-15) + (-3) \cdot 10 + 2 \cdot (-12) = 111$.

Doing the rest of the calculations, we have:

$$c_{12} = (-11) \cdot 6 + (-3) \cdot 13 + 2 \cdot 2 = -101$$
$$c_{13} = (-11) \cdot (-10) + (-3) \cdot 4 + 2 \cdot (-11) = 76$$
$$c_{14} = (-11) \cdot 7 + (-3) \cdot 5 + 2 \cdot 14 = -64$$
$$c_{21} = 7 \cdot (-15) + 0 \cdot 10 + 1 \cdot (-12) = -117$$
$$c_{22} = 7 \cdot 6 + 0 \cdot 13 + 1 \cdot 2 = 44$$
$$c_{23} = 7 \cdot (-10) + 0 \cdot 4 + 1 \cdot (-11) = -81$$
$$c_{24} = 7 \cdot 7 + 0 \cdot 5 + 1 \cdot 14 = 63$$

Thus,

$$C = \begin{pmatrix} 111 & -101 & 76 & -64 \\ -117 & 44 & -81 & 63 \end{pmatrix}$$

14.4.6 Identity Matrix

An $n \times n$ matrix I_n with all 1's on the diagonal and 0's everywhere else is known as an **identity matrix**. More precisely, the elements of an identity matrix are defined as $a_{ij} = 1$ if i = j and $a_{ij} = 0$ if i $\neq$ j. To understand why it is called an identity matrix, recall that 1 is known as the multiplicative identity because it has the property that for any real number a, $a \cdot 1 = a$ and $1 \cdot a = a$. Identity matrices have a similar property. If A is an $n \times m$ matrix and B is an $m \times n$ matrix, then $I_n \cdot A = A$ and $B \cdot I_n = B$.

Additionally, if we are only concerned with $n \times n$ square matrices, I_n acts as a true identity as $I_n \cdot A = A = A \cdot I_n$ when A is an $n \times n$ matrix.

Frequently, the subscript is omitted and I is assumed to be the identity matrix with the size which is required to complete the multiplication. For example, if A is a 3×5 matrix and we are interested in $A \cdot I$, I must be the 5×5 identity matrix or I_5.

14.4.7 Determinant

An $n \times n$ matrix A is said to be **invertible** if there exists a matrix A^{-1} such that $A \cdot A^{-1} = A^{-1} \cdot A = I$. The matrix A^{-1} is called the **inverse** of A. This property is useful because given matrices A and C and the equation $A \cdot B = C$, we can find B by multiplying both sides of the equation on the left by A^{-1}.

The **determinant** of a square matrix A (written det(A)) is a number which is used to determine whether or not a matrix is invertible. For a 1×1 matrix, this is easy because for 1×1 matrices, matrix multiplication is just the standard multiplication of real numbers. Thus, a 1×1 matrix is invertible if and only if its one entry is non-zero. For larger matrices, this same idea holds: a square matrix is invertible if and only if $det(A) \neq 0$.

For a 2×2 matrix

$$A = \begin{pmatrix} a & b \\ c & d \end{pmatrix}$$

the determinant is $a \cdot d - b \cdot c$.

Given a square matrix A, the **minor** of the element a_{ij} (written M_{ij}) is defined as the determinant of the matrix that results from deleting the ith row and jth column. For example, if

$$A = \begin{pmatrix} 2 & 5 & 3 \\ 1 & 6 & 2 \\ 2 & 1 & 3 \end{pmatrix}$$

then the minor of element a_{11} is the determinant of the matrix

$$\begin{pmatrix} 6 & 2 \\ 1 & 3 \end{pmatrix}$$

which is $6 \cdot 3 - 2 \cdot 1 = 16$.

The **cofactor** of a_{ij} is $C_{ij} = (-1)^{(i+j)} \cdot M_{ij}$. Notice that finding the cofactor given the minor is simply a matter of multiplying by either 1 or -1. The following matrix offers an alternative way to remember which number to multiply the minor by in order to get the cofactor.

$$\begin{pmatrix} 1 & -1 & 1 & -1 & 1 & -1 & \cdots \\ -1 & 1 & -1 & 1 & -1 & 1 & \cdots \\ 1 & -1 & 1 & -1 & 1 & -1 & \cdots \\ -1 & 1 & -1 & 1 & -1 & 1 & \cdots \\ \vdots & \vdots & \vdots & \vdots & \vdots & \vdots & \ddots \end{pmatrix}.$$

Notice, that thus far we can only calculate the cofactors of a 3×3 matrix because to calculate the cofactors of a 4×4 we would need the determinant of a 3×3 matrix. The following definition will allow us to calculate the cofactors and determinant for any $n \times n$ matrix.

The determinant of an $n \times n$ matrix is given by $det(A) = a_1 j \cdot C_1 j + a_2 j \cdot C_2 j + \ldots + a_{nj} \cdot C_{nj}$ or alternatively $det(A) = a_{i1} \cdot C_{i1} + a_i \cdot C_{i2} + \ldots + a_{in} \cdot C_{in}$. In this way, it is possible to calculate the determinant of a matrix through recursive calculation of its cofactors.

14.4.8 Transformation Matrices

Note that a vector of dimension n can be thought of as a $n \times 1$ matrix (called a **column vector**) or a $1 \times n$ matrix (called a **row vector**). Now, if this column vector is multiplied by an $m \times n$ matrix on the left, the result will be a $m \times 1$ vector. In this way, the matrix can transform one vector into another vector. Also, note that if the matrix is an $n \times n$ matrix, the vector will transform into a vector of the same dimension.

Two special types of matrix transformations are rotations and reflections. For a 2-dimensional column vector $\begin{pmatrix} x \\ y \end{pmatrix}$, a **clockwise rotation** is given by the 2×2 matrix

$$\begin{pmatrix} \cos(\theta) & \sin(\theta) \\ -\sin(\theta) & \cos(\theta) \end{pmatrix}$$

and a **counter-clockwise rotation** is given by the 2×2 matrix

$$\begin{pmatrix} \cos(\theta) & -\sin(\theta) \\ \sin(\theta) & \cos(\theta) \end{pmatrix}$$

where θ is the angle of rotation.

In 3-dimensional space, not only the angle of rotation, but also the axis of rotation must be defined. Thus, if you wish to rotate a vector about a unit vector $<a_1, a_2, a_3>$ by the angle θ, the matrix used will be

$$\begin{pmatrix} a_1^2 \cdot (1 - \cos(\theta)) + \cos(\theta) & a_2 \cdot a_1 \cdot (1 - \cos(\theta)) - a_3 \cdot \sin(\theta) \\ a_1 \cdot a_2 \cdot (1 - \cos(\theta)) + a_3 \cdot \cos(\theta) & a_2^2 \cdot (1 - \cos(\theta)) + \cos(\theta) \\ a_1 \cdot a_3 \cdot (1 - \cos(\theta)) - a_2 \cdot \sin(\theta) & a_2 \cdot a_3 \cdot (1 - \cos(\theta)) + a_1 \cdot \sin(\theta) \end{pmatrix}$$

$$\begin{matrix} a_3 \cdot a_1 \cdot (1 - \cos(\theta)) + a_2 \cdot \sin(\theta) \\ a_2 \cdot a_3 \cdot (1 - \cos(\theta)) - a_1 \cdot \sin(\theta) \\ a_3 \cdot a_3 \cdot (1 - \cos(\theta)) + \cos(\theta) \end{matrix}$$

14.4.9   Reflection Matrices

In 2-dimensional space, a **reflection** about a line going through the origin is given by the matrix

$$\left(\frac{1}{(\|l\|)} \right) \cdot \begin{pmatrix} l_x^2 - l_y^2 & 2 \cdot l_x \cdot l_y \\ 2 \cdot l_x \cdot l_y & l_y^2 - l_x^2 \end{pmatrix}$$

where $l = <l_x, l_y>$ is a vector that is on the line.

14.4.10   Eigenvalues, Eigenvectors

For square matrix A and a vector v, if there is a real number λ such that $A \cdot v = \lambda \cdot v$.

The vector v is known as an **eigenvector** (or characteristic vector) of A. The number λ is known as an **eigenvalue**. Eigenvectors and eigenvalues are important because they represent vectors whose direction is not changed by a particular matrix transformation. (The prefix eigen- comes from the German eigen which means "own").

The equation for eigenvectors can be reworked as follows: $A \cdot v = \lambda \cdot I \cdot v$ and thus $(\lambda \cdot I - A) \cdot v = \mathbf{0}$, where $\mathbf{0}$ is the vector of all zeroes and the same dimension as v. There is a theorem which states that the equation $B \cdot v = 0$ has only the trivial solution (that is, the only solution is the zero vector) if and only if $det(B) \neq 0$. This means that to find non-zero eigenvalues we can find the roots of $det(\lambda \cdot I - A) = 0$. This equation is known as the characteristic equation and expanding the equation results in a polynomial known as the characteristic polynomial.

Once this polynomial is solved and the eigenvalues are known, the eigenvectors can be found by solving the system of equations that results from the equation $A \cdot v = \lambda \cdot v$ for each eigenvalue λ. For example, if

$$A = \begin{pmatrix} a_{11} & a_{12} & a_{13} \\ a_{21} & a_{22} & a_{23} \\ a_{31} & a_{32} & a_{33} \end{pmatrix}$$

is known and λ is known, then we can take a generic vector $v = \begin{pmatrix} v_1 \\ v_2 \\ v_3 \end{pmatrix}$ and we will get the following system of equations:

$$a_{11} \cdot v_1 + a_{12} \cdot v_2 + a_{13} \cdot v_3 = \lambda \cdot v_1$$
$$a_{21} \cdot v_1 + a_{22} \cdot v_2 + a_{23} \cdot v_3 = \lambda \cdot v_2$$
$$a_{31} \cdot v_1 + a_{32} \cdot v_2 + a_{33} \cdot v_3 = \lambda \cdot v_3.$$

In theory this will allow the eigenvalues and eigenvectors of any matrix to be approximated with a numerical root finding algorithm and solving a system of equations. In practice, using the determinant is only efficient for small matrices. Numerical methods are usually used to approximate the eigenvalues and eigenvectors of large matrices.

14.5 Axis Angle Rotations

Any 3D rotation can be represented by an axis of rotation, and an angle about that axis, as shown here:

$$aa_{axis} = (x, y, z)$$
$$aa_{angle} = angle$$

There is also a more compact form that is less convenient to use in computations, if an application calls for speed to be traded for storage space:

$$aa = (x, y, z) \times angle$$

One way to conceptualize this form of rotation is to imagine a toothpick being stuck into the object you are rotating, with the toothpick being placed exactly along the vector specified by the axis, and then the toothpick being twisted by the specified angle. The object should at that point be rotated the appropriate amount.

This form is inconvenient for combining rotations together and for rotating vectors, though conversion to and from quaternions is a very simple process, as this representation is similar to the quaternion representation of rotations in many ways. However, data in this form can be much easier to understand, as it as not as abstract as a quaternion.

14.6   Two-Vector Orientation

While not a convenient way to store a rotation (angular difference), a set of two vectors can be used to represent an orientation (angular position). Two orthogonal vectors given in a known coordinate system is enough to define how a reference frame is oriented with respect to the coordinate system. A coordinate system is typically defined by three axes/vectors, but for storage reasons, you can omit one of the three axes and recalculate it as needed by taking the cross product of the remaining two vectors. Which two vectors are kept is a matter of convention and does not affect what this representation is capable of.

Example: Orientation Vectors Given in a 3D Coordinate System

This form is convenient if vector math is needed to extract components of the orientation. For example, if we had a reading of the orientation of a spinning top and we wanted to figure out how much the top was tilting so we would know if it was close to falling over, we would take the dot product between the "up" vector from our two-vector orientation and the vertical axis of our coordinate system, and from this we could derive our tilt angle.

This form of orientation can be calculated from any other form by rotating each axis of the coordinate system by the other form of orientation.

14.7   Calibration of Three-Axis Sensors

A common tool used in 3D input applications is a three-axis sensor: a device which measures some physical quantity on three separate directional axes. Examples of some three-axis sensors which are useful in 3D input are accelerometers (devices which measure acceleration), magnetometers (devices which measure magnetic field), and gyroscopes (devices which measure rotation about an axis). Data obtained from these sensors will typically need to be calibrated before it can be used as desired. Though these sensors measure very different physical quantities, the values that are needed to calibrate them are the same.

14.7.1 Bias

Bias can be a significant source of error in sensor readings. Bias is the value a sensor reads when it should be reading zero on all axes. It is a constant offset of a sensor's data. To model this, assume we have a raw vector sensor reading s_{raw} and we want to find the final vector sensor reading s_{final}. We further assume that no other sources of error are present. We can then model bias as:

$$s_{final} = s_{raw} - s_{bias}$$

where s_{bias} is our bias vector.

Calculating the bias happens differently depending on the sensor. For example, if a sensor is expected to read around zero on each axis at rest, like a gyroscope, you can simply average a collection of gyroscope readings at rest and use this as your bias. In actuality, a gyroscope does not read zero at "rest" when on Earth because it is also sensing the rotation of Earth itself, but for many applications this is small enough to be ignored. On the other hand, a magnetometer or accelerometer does not read zero at rest, so for these sensors it is necessary to rotate them around and collect a cloud of readings. So long as these are roughly evenly distributed around the bias, the average of these should yield the bias.

14.7.2 Scale

Scale errors can also contribute significantly to sensor error. Scale is how stretched or squished the data on a sensor's axis is. To correct for errors like this, we introduce a scale matrix which has a corrective value for each axis. If an axis has no scale error, it will have a scale value of 1; if it is stretched, it will have a value below 1 to bring it back in line, and if squished it will have a value above 1. The scale matrix would look like this:

$$s_{scale} = \begin{bmatrix} s_{scalex} & 0 & 0 \\ 0 & s_{scaley} & 0 \\ 0 & 0 & s_{scalez} \end{bmatrix}$$

To apply this to our calibration model, we assume that bias and scale are the only error sources. Our model would then look like this:

$$s_{final} = s_{scale} \times (s_{raw} - s_{bias})$$

Calculating scale can be a little more involved than calculating bias. For the case of sensors whose output is directly related to their current orientation (accelerometers and magnetometers), it is possible to gather a cloud of data from the sensor and to use the size (width, length, height) of the cloud on each axis to determine the scale values. However, this is not possible with a gyroscope, as the readings of a gyroscope correspond directly to its motion. For a gyroscope, an external truth measurement would be needed to determine the scale. For example, you could use a turntable that spins at a known rate, $rate_{known}$, and compare it to the reading of rate from a gyroscope axis, $rate_{gyro}$. The scale for that gyroscope axis would then be $rate_{known}/rate_{gyro}$.

14.7.3　Cross-Axis Effect and Rotation

Though these typically have a smaller impact on error than bias and scale, cross-axis effect and rotation can be important to consider if you want to get the highest level of accuracy from your sensor. Cross-axis effect is a type of error experienced by sensors when their axes are not perfectly orthogonal, or when an axis on a sensor measures some part of the data on another axis in addition to measuring its own data. A matrix which corrects for cross-axis effect only would look like this:

$$s_{cross} = \begin{bmatrix} 1 & -s_{12} & -s_{13} \\ -s_{21} & 1 & -s_{23} \\ -s_{31} & -s_{32} & 1 \end{bmatrix}$$

where each off-diagonal value in the matrix represents the portion of one axis' data that needs to be removed from another.

　　Rotation is an error experienced by a sensor when all of its data is rotated by some constant amount away from what it should be reading. To learn about rotation matrices, refer to the matrix section of this chapter. We can take scale, cross-axis effect, and rotation into account with a single matrix by doing the following:

$$s_{correction} = s_{rotate} \times s_{cross} \times s_{scale}$$

Our final calibration model based on this matrix looks like this:

$$s_{final} = s_{correction} \times (s_{raw} - s_{bias})$$

One way to calculate cross-axis effect is to put the sensor in a situation where one axis should be reading zero, and another axis will be reading a large value. Call the "zero" axis reading s_{zero}, and the other axis reading s_{large}. The cross-axis value that would be calculated for the "zero" axis based on the other axis would be $-s_{zero}/s_{large}$.

　　Calculating rotation is trickier, as there would be no indication from the data itself as to whether a rotation would be necessary or not. Calculating rotation of a sensor's data would require sampling from the sensor at several points where the correct reading is known, and detecting whether the data is experiencing a constant rotation overall.

14.8　Smoothing

A common problem when working with measured data is that it can be noisy or jittery. There are many filters you can apply to data to smooth it, though often they will have some trade-off with some other area of performance in exchange for reducing noise, such as a reduction in responsiveness or fluidity of motion. Low-pass filter and oversampling are examples of ways to smooth the data. Those examples are described below. Additional methods include average filter and median filter, which are available in the online resources.

14.8.1 Low-Pass Filter

One of the simplest forms of smoothing is a low-pass filter, also sometimes referred to as a running average. A low-pass filter creates a smoothed reading by summing some portion of the previous smoothed reading and some portion of new measured data. The two portions must add up to one complete new reading. In other words, if you take $\frac{3}{4}$ of the previous smoothed reading, you must take $\frac{1}{4}$ of the new measured data. Given that you have a which represents the amount of the previous smoothed reading to be used, our low pass filter would look like this:

$$smoothed_{new} = smoothed_{last} \times a + measured_{new} \times (1 - a)$$

What this does can be thought about in two ways. It can be thought of as a continual averaging of measured values, with older measurements gradually being filtered out as new ones join the smoothed value. It can also be thought of in terms of frequency, as this type of filter is designed to block high frequencies while allowing low ones through, hence the name "low-pass filter."

Low-pass filters can introduce a time delay into a stream of data, so there is a trade-off between smoothness and responsiveness.

14.8.2 Oversampling

Another simple way to smooth measured data is to oversample the data. Oversampling simply means that more than one sample of measured data is taken, and the set of samples are averaged and presented as a single sample. This has the effect of causing a data stream to give fewer but cleaner samples. Oversampled readings can be more responsive than low-pass filtered readings because they are based entirely on fresh data, but oversampled data does not provide as smooth of a response as a low-pass filter. Instead, if higher oversampling rates are used, data can become quantized, and a smooth transition between samples will be lost. Whether this is a good trade-off depends on your application, and some accuracy sensitive applications like gyro-compassing and inertial positioning rely on heavy oversampling.

Further Reading

A great book that covers 3D mathematics needed for computer graphics is *3D Math Primer for Graphics and Game Development* [Dunn and Parberry 11]. **Please note** that this chapter contained additional information that was cut due to space. You can find additional topics that relates to this topic on the book's website.

Exercises

1. Determine whether a coordinate system where X is up, Y is left, and Z is backward is right-handed or left-handed.

2. Find the determinant of $A = \begin{pmatrix} 8 & 9 & 3 \\ -5 & 5 & 7 \\ -5 & 7 & 4 \end{pmatrix}$.

3. Find the eigenvalues of $A = \begin{pmatrix} 1 & 4 \\ -4 & -7 \end{pmatrix}$.

   (Hint: It may be useful to use the quadratic formula: $x = \frac{-b + \sqrt{b^2 - 4 \cdot a \cdot c}}{2 \cdot a}$
   when $a \cdot x^2 + b \cdot x + c = 0.)$

4. Estimate the scale and bias for a three axis sensor which gave the following data points: $(-1, 4, 5)$, $(7, 4, 5)$, $(3, 6, 5)$, $(3, 2, 5)$, $(3, 4, 10)$, $(3, 4, 0)$.

5. What angle of rotation does the following quaternion (in w,x,y,z form) represent, and about what axis: $(0, 1, 0, 0)$?

6. Imagine an object facing forward, with its top up. Your goal is to rotate the object so it is facing up, with its top facing right. You may make $90°$ rotations about two different axes to achieve this. What axes would you use, and which direction about them do you rotate?

7. Given Euler angles that use rotations about Y, then Z, then X, what axis would using a $90°$ rotation cause on gimbal lock?

8. Given the vector $(1, 0, 0)$, what axis angle rotation would you use to rotate the vector to $(0, 1, 0)$?

15

Introduction to Digital Signal Processing

A signal is comprehended if it serves to make us notice the object or situation it bespeaks. A symbol is understood when we conceive the idea it presents.
—Susanne Langer

15.1 Introduction

In this chapter, the basic knowledge about digital signal processing will be described. If you want to use inertial sensors for your work, or need to deal with any type of digital signals, you need to understand how to process, filter, and interpret your data. If you are familiar with digital signal processing, you can skip this chapter. In this chapter, general operations in signal processing, like sampling, aliasing, and transforming, will be introduced. An effort has been made to avoid bringing up the concepts in a complicated mathematic form. Instead this chapter attempts to simply provide general explanations about basic digital signal processing concepts.

15.2 What Is a Signal?

In signal processing, a signal is a function that carries information about the operation of a system [Priemer 91]. There are many forms of signals in nature, such as acoustic signals and electromagnetic signals. The signals contain the data that show the patterns of variations of physical quantities. Although not all the signals are in electrical quantities, we can convert them to electrical quantities by using sensors. In this way, the information can be stored, analyzed, manipulated,

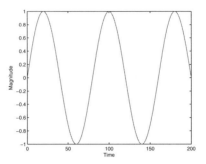

Figure 15.1: Continuous signal.

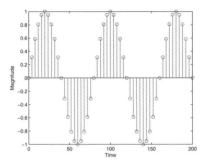

Figure 15.2: Discrete signal.

and transmitted. For example, the pattern for the rotation of a moving object can be considered as a signal and it can be converted to an electrical form by a gyroscope sensor. The details about the gyroscope sensor will be discussed later. Signal processing is a science that deals with analyzing signals. It involves different operations such as noise reduction, filter design, data acquisition, feature detection, etc. Signal processing deals with different types of signals. Signal processing is classified into two major categories: "digital signal processing" and "analog signal processing." Analog signals are continuous in time and also can have any value of amplitude. Analog signal processing deals with analog signals. A signal can be discrete in time and/or amplitude. Sampling operation produces discrete time signals and the quantization process produces discrete amplitude signals. Do not be worried if you are not familiar with sampling and quantization processes. We will explain these terms in Sections 15.8 and 15.11. The digital signal term is used for signals that are discrete in both time and amplitude. Figures 15.1 and 15.2 represent the continuous and discrete sinusoidal signal.

For presenting the continuous time signals, notation $x(t)$ is used, where the t is time. The notations $x(kT)$ or $x[kT]$ are used for the discrete time signals, where T presents the time increment and k is an integer number which can have the following values:

$$k = (..., -3, -2, -1, 0, 1, 2, 3, ...)$$

The available time points in the discrete time signal are calculated in Equation 15.1. For example, if $T = 3$, values of the signal are available every 3 seconds.

$$t = kT \qquad (15.1)$$

15.3 Classification of Signals

The signals are categorized based on their specifications. In this section, some of the fundamental classes of signals are introduced.

- Discrete time and continuous time signals : The discrete signals can take values only at some specific time points, while the continuous signals are defined throughout continuous time intervals.

- Discrete value and continuous value signals: If a signal can takes all values, it is a continuous value signal. In contrast, if a signal can take just a specific set of values it is called a discrete value signal. Later in this chapter, we will discuss the process of converting continuous value signals to discrete value signals.

- Deterministic and random signals: The deterministic signals can be expressed by a definite mathematical description. Signals of this class take values that can be forecast by their definition, for any time. Contrary to deterministic signals, there are signals that cannot be expressed by a certain mathematical model. These signals are usually expressed based on their probability of occurrence. Their values at specific times cannot be fully predicted.

- Periodic and non-periodic signals: A signal is called periodic if there is a repetitive pattern in fixed time frames of the signal. In other words, signal $x(t)$ is periodic when there is constant T so that:

$$x(t) = x(t + T) \qquad (15.2)$$

If we cannot find any value of T to satisfy the above equation, the signal is called non-periodic.

- Odd and even signals: A signal is called even (or symmetric) if it satisfies the following condition for all t), as shown in Equation 15.3. The odd signal is a signal that satisfies for all t, as shown in Equation 15.4.

$$x(t) = x(-t) \qquad\qquad (15.3)$$

$$x(t) = -x(t) \qquad\qquad (15.4)$$

15.4 Applications of Digital Signal Processing

Digital signal processing (DSP) has many applications in several fields of technology. Audio (for example music or speech) can be stored and transmitted with digital techniques. Different types of signal processing operations are performed for the recoding and transmission of music. These operations are used for different reasons including noise reduction, adding special effects to the sound, improving the quality of transmission, and modifying the quality of spectral characteristics of the sound. When the audio signal is transmitted digitally, it is less sensitive to distortion and a weakened signal can be amplified without distortion [Chen 00]. The speech recognition technology uses signal processing operations. DSP is very useful for processing of biomedical signals. The different biomedical data such as magnetic resonance imaging (MRI), functional magnetic resonance imaging (fMRI), electroencephalograph (EEG), and electrocardiograph (ECG) are frequently corrupted with noises and artifacts. To interpret such biomedical signals, we need to perform several DSP operations such as filtering, noise cancellation, and extracting some specifications [Chang and Moura 10].

Navigation is another area of use for DSP. The Global Navigation Satellite System (GNSS) data can be processed in real time by utilizing DSP [MacGougan et al. 05]. The GPS systems use the DSP techniques to improve reliability. Radar and sonar systems also use DSP operations [Stranneby 01].

DSP is used extensively in the telecommunications field. Data compression, error correction, and dual tone multi-frequency (DTMF) are examples of tasks that can be implemented with digital techniques.

Storing pictures in digital format enables us to perform several types of manipulations, such as image enhancement, compression, and restoration. Different features of a picture, such as edges, colors, and shades, can be manipulated easily by using digital techniques.

Analysis of seismic data is carried out by using digital signal processing techniques. Natural phenomena like earthquakes or volcanic eruptions and man-made explosions produce waves that are called seismic waves. The seismic data is studied to find out information about the structure of the Earth's interior and types of material in the Earth. The automotive industry, robotics, vibration study of bridges and tall buildings, and defense applications are other areas of utilization of digital signal processing.

Side Note 15.1: Signal Processing Toolbox

MATLAB®provides a "Signal Processing Toolbox" that can help you to practice DSP. The toolbox provides functions to generate, measure, filter, and visualize different types of signals. This toolbox can be used to generate, compare, and analyze signals in both time and frequency domains. It also includes further features such as Fourier transform, filter design, and feature extraction.

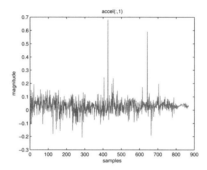

Figure 15.3: Noisy signal.

15.5 Noise

In signal processing, the term noise refers to the undesirable information that appears added to the signal of interest. Noises interfere in almost all of the physical quantities measurements and communications. Noise can corrupt or obscure the signal of interest. One of the fundamental operations in signal processing is to distinguish between diverse signal components to separate the noise from the signal data. In some experiments the signal and noise can be distinguished based on frequency analysis. To illustrate how noise can corrupt the signal of interest, we proceed with an example. Figure 15.3 shows a signal that is contaminated with noise. A noise reduction process was applied to this data and the result is shown in Figure 15.4. Comparing these two figures, it clearly can be seen that the presence of noise obscures the data and it is critical to denoise the signal to be able to interpret the data.

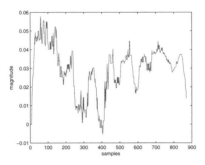

Figure 15.4: Denoised signal.

Depending on the system, noise has different types of sources. It might arise from sources such as the following:

- Random motions of electrons (thermal noise)

- Motion or vibration of the sources (acoustic noise)

- Electronic devices such as diodes (shot noise)

- Electrical power fluctuations (electromagnetic noise)

- Magnitude and phase distortion in communication processes (channel distortion)

- Digitalization process noise (quantization noise)

Noise can be categorized based on its frequency into different categories including narrow-band noise, white noise, impulsive noise, transient noise pulses, and colored noise.

White noise is a random signal with constant power density in the whole frequency spectrum. In contrast to white noise, the spectrum of colored noise is not flat. The impulse noise is short time on-off signal and transient noise pulse is a long duration noise consisting of a short sharp pulse that is followed by decaying low frequency fluctuations [Vaseghi 08].

15.6   Signal Energy and Power

Energy and power are two important terms in signal processing. In signal processing, for a discrete time signal, the energy is defined in Equation 15.5:

$$E = \sum_{n=-\infty}^{\infty} |x[n]|^2 = \lim_{N \to \infty} \sum_{n=-N}^{N} |x[n]|^2 \qquad (15.5)$$

A signal can be categorized based on its energy into two categories of energy signal and power signal [Proakis 96]. When energy of a signal is in the $0 < E < \infty$ interval, the signal belongs to the energy signal category. These signals have finite energy and are limited in time. In contrast, in the power signal category, signals have infinite energy and are not limited in time. But these signals can have either infinite or finite average power. The average power of a discrete time signal is defined as Equation 15.6:

$$P = \lim_{N \to \infty} \frac{1}{2N+1} \sum_{n=-N}^{N} |x(n)|^2 \tag{15.6}$$

When the energy of a signal is finite, the average power would be zero, so the average power for the energy signals is zero.

15.7 Mathematical Representation of Elementary Signals

It would be difficult to understand the digital signal processing concepts without having mathematical knowledge about signals. In this section, some of the common elementary signals and their mathematical representations will be introduced. These basic signals are: impulse function, unit step function, ramp function, cosine function, exponential function, and Gaussian function. These functions play a critical role in signal processing and often are used to model more complex signals.

As was stated earlier, the notation $x[t]$ is used for mathematical representation of a signal. The variable t is an independent variable. For the continuous time signals, this variable can take any value in the $(-\infty, \infty)$ interval. For the discrete signal the variable t gets values so that $t = nT$.

15.7.1 The Impulse Function

The impulse function (δ) is one of the basic sequences. The mathematical representation of this function is shown in Equation 15.7:

$$\delta[k] = \begin{cases} 0 & k \neq 0 \\ 1 & k = 0 \end{cases} \tag{15.7}$$

This function gets the value equal to 1 for $k = 0$ and zero for the other points. This function is depicted in the Figure 15.5.

15.7.2 The Unit Step Function

The unit step function gets zero value for the negative time points and one for the positive time points. The mathematical description of this function is introduced in Equation 15.8 and Figure 15.6 shows its graphical representation.

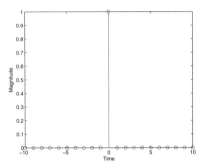

Figure 15.5: Delta signal.

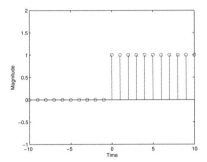

Figure 15.6: Uni tstep signal.

$$u[k] = \begin{cases} 0 & k < 0 \\ 1 & k \geq 0 \end{cases} \tag{15.8}$$

15.7.3   The Cosine Function

The cosine signal, or sine signal, is one of the most popular signals. The general mathematical description for the cosine signal is shown in Equation 15.9.

$$x[t] = A\cos[wt + \phi] \tag{15.9}$$

where A is the amplitude of the signal. This constant controls the magnitude of the signal so that the signal will oscillate in the $[-A, A]$ interval. w is the radian frequency or angular frequency of the signal. The w is calculated with Equation 15.10, where the T is the period of the signal.

$$w = \frac{2\pi}{T} = 2\pi f \tag{15.10}$$

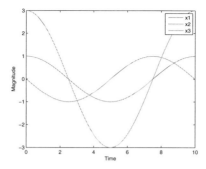

Figure 15.7: Cosine signal.

The term ϕ is the phase-shift of the cosine signal in radians. To depict the effect of amplitude and phase shift, the following three cosine equations are shown in Figure 15.7.

$$x_1[t] = cos[0.2\pi t]$$
$$x_2[t] = 3cos[0.2\pi t]$$
$$x_3[t] = cos[0.2\pi t + \pi/2]$$

As can clearly be seen, the function $x_2[t]$ oscillates between $[-3, 3]$ while the two other functions oscillate in the $[-1, 1]$ interval. The signal $x_2[t]$ also does not have any phase shift with respect to the $x_1[t]$. Contrary to $x_2[t]$, signal x_3 has $\pi/2$ phase shift with respect to x_1.

15.7.4 Exponential Function

The general form for the exponential function is written in Equation 15.11:

$$x[t] = Ca^t \tag{15.11}$$

The a is a real number and based on the value of this parameter the function gets different shapes. Figures 15.8, 15.9, 15.10, and 15.11 illustrate the exponential function for four different values of parameter a.

15.7.5 Ramp Function

The ramp function is the integral of the unit step function. This sequence is defined in Equation 15.12:

$$x[t] = \begin{cases} t & k \geq 0 \\ 0 & t < 0 \end{cases} \tag{15.12}$$

This sequence is shown in Figure15.12.

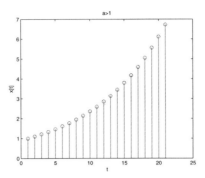

Figure 15.8: Exponential function for (a) equal to 1.1.

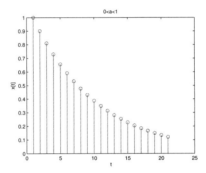

Figure 15.9: Exponential function for (a) equal to 0.9.

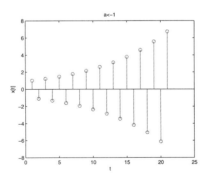

Figure 15.10: Exponential function for (a) equal to -1.1.

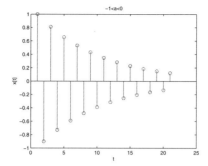

Figure 15.11: Exponential function for (a) equal to −0.9.

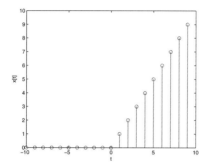

Figure 15.12: Ramp function.

15.7.6 Gaussian Function

The Gaussian function (or normal probability density function) is a symmetric bell-shaped function. The mathematical representation of this function is shown in Equation 15.13:

$$X[t] = ae^{-\frac{(x-b)^2}{2\sigma^2}} \tag{15.13}$$

Figure 15.13 shows the Gaussian function, where $a = 1, \sigma = 1$ and $b = 5$.

15.8 Sampling Theorem

In the real world, signals are continuous or analog. Analog signals are continuous in both magnitude and time. In order to process the signals with computers, since the computers cannot deal with the time continuous form of signals, it is necessary to convert them to the discrete time form. As was mentioned before, the discrete time signal can be represented mathematically as a sequence of numbers. These

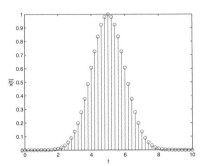

Figure 15.13: Guassian function.

sequences are called digital signals. You might ask how a time continuous signal can be converted to a sequence of numbers. This process is quite simple. To perform this conversion, you just need to record the amplitude of the continuous signal at equal time intervals.

The process which converts a continuous-time signal to a discrete-time signal is called sampling. In the sampling process, a continuous signal's amplitude is periodically recorded at equal time intervals. Each of these recorded values is called a sample. The time interval between the capture of any two sequential samples is called "sampling interval" and usually shown by "T." The number of recorded samples per second is called the "sampling frequency" and it is represented by f_s, as shown in Equation 15.14:

$$f_s = \frac{1}{T} \tag{15.14}$$

To clarify the sampling concept, lets continue with an example. Assume the $x(t)$ is a continuous sinusoidal signal with the following mathematical representation:

$$x(t) = \sin(2\pi 0.075t)$$

The $x(t)$ is plotted in Figure 15.14. The sampling process with $f_s = 3.35$ Hz was applied on this signal. The result is shown in Figure 15.15. As can be seen, in this figure the points are not connected and the information about the time point between consecutive samples is not available. We just record the amplitude of the $x(t)$ every 0.29850 second. To illustrate how the recorded discrete time signal changes by different sampling frequencies, we repeat the sampling process with sampling rate equal to 1.025 samples per second. It means the samples were recorded every 0.9756 seconds. The result is depicted in Figure 15.16.

Comparing Figures 15.15 and 15.16, it is evident that there are more samples in Figure 15.15. The reason is the difference in sampling rates. Figure 15.15 shows samples obtained with a sampling rate more than three times higher than the sampling rate for Figure 15.16. So we conclude that with a bigger sampling

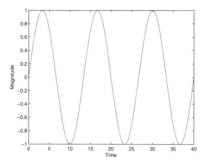

Figure 15.14: Continuous signal $x(t) = \sin(2\pi 0.075t)$.

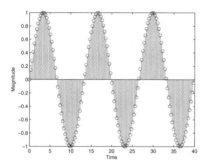

Figure 15.15: Discrete signal $x_1[n] = \sin(2\pi 0.075nT), T = 0.0975$.

rate, the recorded discrete signal will have more points. As was mentioned earlier, the discrete time signals are stored as mathematical sequences in the computer. Having more points in the sequence means the computer needs more storage to store them. If you look at Figure 15.16, you can visually reconstruct the continuous

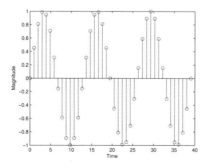

Figure 15.16: Discrete signal $x_2[n] = \sin(2\pi 0.075nT), T = 0.29850$.

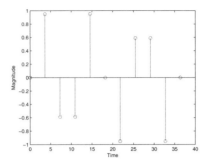

Figure 15.17: Discrete signal $x_3[n] = \sin(2\pi 0.075nT), T = 3.63$.

$x(t)$. Although it has fewer points, compared to Figure 15.15, it still has enough points to carry the necessary information from the continuous signal and at the same time it needs less storage to be stored or transmitted.

Now, this raises the question: how low can the sampling frequency be? To answer this question let's repeat our sampling process with a new sampling rate $f_s = 0.275$ Hz. The result is named $x_3[n]$ and shown in Figure 15.17. If we want to reconstruct the $x(t)$ by using signal $x_3[n]$, the result would not be similar to the original $x(t)$ signal. It means this low sampling rate caused loss of necessary information. So, which sampling rate should be chosen to have the minimum number of samples, and at the same time be able to reconstruct the correct signal? To answer this question, we will introduce the Nyquist–Shannon theorem in the following section.

15.9 Nyquist–Shannon Theorem

To ensure that the digital signal contains enough information to reconstruct the original continuous signal, it is necessary to preserve the samples with the proper sampling rate. As you learned in the previous section, we follow two goals in choosing the proper sampling rate, which are:

- Retaining adequate information in the discrete signal to reconstruct the original signal.

- Recording the minimum number of required samples.

The Nyquist–Shannon sampling theorem simply finds the minimum sampling frequency, in a way that both goals are achievable. Based on the Nyquist–Shannon sampling theorem, if f_{max} is the highest frequency component in the original signal, the sampling process should be performed with a sampling rate greater than or equal to $2f_{max}$ [Orfanidis 98], as is shown in Equation 15.15.

$$f_s \geq 2f_{max} \qquad (15.15)$$

Therefore the sampling interval should be chosen as Equation 15.16:

$$T \leq \frac{1}{2f_{max}} \qquad (15.16)$$

The minimum allowed sampling rate, based on the Nyquist–Shannon theorem, is equal to $2f_s$ and is known as the Nyquist rate. The value of $\frac{f_s}{2}$ is called "Nyquist frequency" or "folding frequency" and it determines the endpoints of the "Nyquist frequency interval" as it is shown in Equation 15.17:

$$\text{Nyquist Interval} = [\frac{-f_s}{2}, \frac{f_s}{2}] \qquad (15.17)$$

For example for a sinusoidal waveform with the highest frequency component equal to 4 Hz, we need to record it at least with the sampling rate of 8 samples per second to be able to reconstruct it. However, if we sample it with a frequency higher than 8 Hz, there will be more information about the signal available and we can reconstruct it more precisely. Note that if the signal is sampled at any frequency lower than 8 Hz, for example 6 Hz, then there are not enough samples to show the variations in the signal correctly.

15.10 Aliasing

The aliasing phenomenon occurs when the sampling is performed with an insufficiently high frequency. In such a condition, the reconstructed signal is different from the original continuous signal. In aliasing, some components which were not present in the original signal might be seen in the reconstructed signal. Furthermore, some of the frequencies of the original signal might be lost in the reconstructed signal. Assuming $x(t)$ is given by:

$$x(t) = sin(2\pi 60t)$$

The $x(t)$ was sampled with a low sampling frequency and after that the signal was reconstructed from the recorded samples. In Figure 15.18 the sold line (blue in color plate) is the $x(t)$, the dots are stored samples and the dash line (red in color plate) shows the reconstructed signal from the recorded points. It can be clearly seen that the reconstructed signal is different from the original $x(t)$.

15.11 Quantization

After the sampling process is performed, we have a signal which is discrete in time but continuous in amplitude. The amplitudes of the samples, at this point,

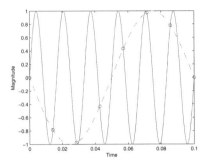

Figure 15.18: Aliasing phenomenon.

could take on any value. To present these values to a computer as a binary word, there is only a finite number of bits available. So, we do not have any choice but to use this finite number of bits to preserve the sequence of signal value, which are not restricted. In fact, we need to discretize the recorded amplitudes. The process of discretization of recorded amplitude values is called "quantization." Thus, in quantization a large set of values is expressed by a limited set of available binary words.

The device that performs this process is called a quantizer. In the quantization process, the numbers get rounded to the nearest quantization level or truncated. Consequently, there is a discrepancy in the signal before and after the quantization process, which is called quantization error.

Assuming there are N bits to represent the data, we have 2^N binary words to represent the sequence values. The signal level represented by each binary word is called a quantization level. These levels can range from zero to $2^N - 1$, or -2^{N-1} and $+2^{N-1}$. The difference between two consecutive levels is called resolution or quantization step. The quantization step is calculated as Equation 15.18:

$$\Delta = \frac{x_{max} - x_{min}}{2^N - 1} \tag{15.18}$$

where x_{max} and x_{min} are maximum and minimum values of signal respectively.

15.12   Fourier Analysis

The Fourier analysis is a mathematical tool to decompose a signal to its component frequencies. It was named after a French mathematician and physicist, Jean Baptiste Joseph Fourier. In 1807, he published a paper claiming that any continuous periodic signal can be expressed as the sum of sinusoidal waves. In fact, the Fourier process decomposes the signal to its sinusoidal components. In this way, the signal can be represented in the frequency domain. Based on the type of input signal, the general Fourier analysis can be broken down into four categories, including:

- Fourier Series (FS)

- Fourier Transform (FT)

- Discrete Fourier Transform (DFT)

- Discrete-Time Fourier Transform (DTFT)

Fourier series (FS) and the Fourier transform (FT) operations are applied to the continuous time signals in a way that in the FS the input signal is a finite length (periodic) signal while in the Fourier transform the input signal is an infinite length (aperiodic) signal. As an example of periodic continuous signal we can name the cosine waves. These waves have a repetitive pattern from negative infinity to the positive infinity. The Gaussian function is an example of an aperiodic continuous signal that extends from negative infinity to positive infinity without repetition in the pattern [Smith 97].

For both discrete Fourier transform and discrete-time Fourier transform, the input signal must be a discrete time signal. The difference between the discrete Fourier transform and discrete-time Fourier transform is in the length of the input signal. For the discrete Fourier transform the input must be a finite length sequence, while infinite length is assumed for the discrete-time Fourier transform.

One of the most popular operations in digital signal processing is the frequency analysis of finite discrete time signals. Therefore, we continue with a description of the discrete Fourier transform (DFT) and skip the other three categories of Fourier analysis. If you are interested in the mathematical descriptions of the skipped categories, there are plenty of references in Fourier analysis to study.

15.12.1 Discrete Fourier Transform

The discrete Fourier transform (DFT) converts a discrete time finite-duration signal from the time domain to the frequency domain. In this section the DFT procedure will be discussed. Because we just intend to introduce the common digital signal processing operations without entering into mathematical details, we do not explain the origin of the DFT formula. You just need to know that the DFT operation provides the frequency spectrum of the discrete signal preceded by it. Then you can analyze or manipulate the signal based on its frequency.

Assuming $x[n]$, is the finite-duration sequence with length N, for $n = 0, 1, 2, ...,$ $N - 1$, the definition of the discrete Fourier transform of $x[n]$ is given by Equation 15.19:

$$X[k] = \sum_{n=0}^{N-1} x[n]e^{-jwkn} \tag{15.19}$$

where $X[k]$ represents the DFT of sequence $x[n]$. Similar to $x[n]$, the $X[k]$ is a finite sequence of $X[0], X[1], X[2], ..., X[N-1]$. The variable w is defined as:

$$w = \frac{2\pi}{N} \tag{15.20}$$

The variable j in the DFT formula is defined by Equation 15.21:

$$j = \sqrt{-1} \tag{15.21}$$

As you know, the Euler formula converts the complex exponential function to the trigonometric functions as Equation 15.22:

$$e^{-j\theta} = \cos(\theta) - j\sin(\theta) \tag{15.22}$$

Using the Euler formula, the DFT equation can be expressed by Equation 15.23:

$$X[k] = \sum_{n=0}^{N-1} x[n](\cos(wkn) - j\sin(wkn)) \tag{15.23}$$

which can be written as:

$$X[k] = \sum_{n=0}^{N-1} x[n](\cos(\frac{2\pi kn}{N}) - j\sin(\frac{2\pi kn}{N})) \tag{15.24}$$

The $X[k]$ appears in the complex form with real and imaginary parts. These parts show the magnitude and phase as Equation 15.25:

$$X[k] = X_{real}[k] + jX_{imag}[k] \tag{15.25}$$

The phase is defined as:

$$X_{phase}(k) = \tan^{-1}(\frac{X_{imag}[k]}{X_{real}[k]}) \tag{15.26}$$

and the magnitude is:

$$X_{mag}(k) = |X[k]| = \sqrt{(X_{real}[k])^2 + (X_{imag}[k])^2} \tag{15.27}$$

Both n and k indices are from 0 to $N-1$ and it means that the input consists of N samples and the DFT process delivers the frequency spectral components at N equally spaced points. If the sampling frequency for the signal x is equal to f_s, the frequency spacing between adjacent results of the DFT is calculated by Equation 15.28:

$$df = \frac{f_s}{N} \tag{15.28}$$

The df is the frequency spacing between the consecutive outputs of DFT. The frequency spectrum provided by the DFT consists of N points at the following frequencies:

$$f(k) = \frac{kf_s}{N} \quad k = 0, 1, 2, ..., N-1. \tag{15.29}$$

15.12.2   Inverse Discrete Fourier Transform

Converting the signal with DFT to the frequency domain does not cause loss of signal information. It just changes the presentation form of the signal. As was stated, a signal can be expressed by a sum of the various exponential sequences, each representing a different frequency. The DFT process output is the N complex numbers that contain the magnitude and phase for the exponential sequences that form the sum. The frequency domain representation of the signal can be converted to the time domain by inverse DFT transformation. The mathematical expression of the inverse DFT is shown in Equations 15.30 and 15.31:

$$x[n] = \frac{1}{N} \sum_{k=0}^{N-1} X[k] e^{j2\pi kn/N} \quad n = 0, 1, 2, ..., N-1 \tag{15.30}$$

or

$$x[n] = \frac{1}{N} \sum_{k=0}^{N-1} X[k] (\cos(\frac{2\pi kn}{N}) + j\sin(\frac{2\pi kn}{N})) \tag{15.31}$$

15.13   Fast Fourier Transform

Although the DFT is a fundamental method to compute the frequency components of the signal, the computational complexity of this method is fairly high. Computing the frequencies directly from the DFT formula may be slow, to the extent that it would not be considered a practical method. For a N-point DFT, the complexity is $O(n^2)$. The Fast Fourier Transform (FFT) is an algorithm for computing the DFT results which is more efficient. The FFT method reduces the computational complexity to the $O(n \lg n)$.

15.14   z-Transform

The z-transform is a general representation of the discrete time Fourier transform in terms of complex exponential signals. The z-transform can be calculated for many sequences for which the Fourier transform does not exist [Mitra and Kuo 06]. Furthermore, by utilizing the z-transform, we are able to convert linear difference equations to linear algebraic equations. Then the linear algebraic equations can be easily solved with algebraic manipulations. The z-transform is also reversible and it is possible to recover the time domain signal from its z-transform by applying the inverse z-transform operation. In this section, the z-transform is introduced and some properties of z-transform are reviewed. Next, the convergence condition for the z-transform and the inverse z-transform are discussed.

15.14.1   Definitions

The z-transform of the discrete-time signal, $x[n]$, is defined as Equation 15.32:

$$X(z) = \sum_{n=-\infty}^{\infty} x[n] z^{-n} \tag{15.32}$$

where n is an integer and z represents a complex variable. In general, the complex variable z can be written as Equation 15.33:

$$z = Ae^{j\phi} = A(\cos\phi + j\sin\phi) \tag{15.33}$$

where A is the magnitude and ϕ is the phase of z. As can be seen from the z-transform definition, this transform is a power series representation of a discrete-time signal. The exponent of z represents the location of each sample in the sequence and the coefficient of z shows the weight of each sample [Strum and Kirk 88]. If $x[n]$ is defined only for $n \geq 0$, the z-transform is called single-sided z-transform and defined as Equation 15.34:

$$X(z) = \sum_{n=0}^{\infty} x[n] z^{-n} \tag{15.34}$$

To clarify the z-transform concept, we proceed in this section with a few examples.

- Example 1

The sequence $x[n]$ consists of following values in the interval of [0,5].

$$x[n] = [3, 2, 1, 4, 5, 0]$$

The z-transform of the above sequence is calculated as:

$$X(z) = \sum_{n=0}^{5} x[n] z^{-n} =$$
$$3z^0 + 2z^{-1} + 1z^{-2} + 4z^{-3} + 5z^{-4} + 0z^{-5} =$$
$$3 + 2z^{-1} + 1z^{-2} + 4z^{-3} + 5z^{-4} \tag{15.35}$$

- Example 2

For $x[n] = A\delta[n]$ the z-transform is calculated as following

$$X(z) = \sum_{n=-\infty}^{\infty} A\delta[n] z^{-n} = Az^0 = A \tag{15.36}$$

- Example 3

For the step sequence, $x[n] = Au[n]$, the z-transform is obtained as:

$$X(z) = \sum_{n=-\infty}^{\infty} Au[n]z^{-n} = A\sum_{n=0}^{\infty} (z^{-1})^n = \frac{A}{1-z^{-1}} \tag{15.37}$$

- Example 4

To calculate the z-transform of the sequence $x[n] = Aa^n u[n]$, we have:

$$X(z) = \sum_{n=-\infty}^{\infty} Aa^n u[n]z^{-n} = A\sum_{n=0}^{\infty} (az^{-1})^n = \frac{A}{1-az^{-1}} \tag{15.38}$$

- Example 5

For the complex exponential sequence,

$$x[n] = \begin{cases} e^{-anT} & ,n \geq 0 \\ 0 & ,n < 0 \end{cases}$$

the z-transform is obtained as:

$$X(z) = \sum_{n=0}^{\infty} e^{-anT} z^{-n} = \sum_{n=0}^{\infty} (e^{-aT}z^{-1})^n = \frac{1}{1-(e^{-aT}z^{-1})} = \frac{z}{z-e^{-aT}} \tag{15.39}$$

- Example 6

For the cosine sequence

$$x[n] = \begin{cases} \cos(n\Theta) & ,n \geq 0 \\ 0 & ,n < 0 \end{cases}$$

the z-transform is calculated as follows:

$$X(z) = \sum_{n=0}^{\infty} \cos(n\Theta)z^{-n}$$

Based on the Euler relation, the cosine sequence can be written as

$$\cos(n\Theta) = \frac{e^{jn\Theta} + e^{-jn\Theta}}{2} \tag{15.40}$$

So we have

$$X(z) = \frac{1}{2}\left(\frac{z}{z-e^{j\Theta}} + \frac{z}{z-e^{-j\Theta}}\right) \tag{15.41}$$

15.14.2   z-Plane

The complex number z can be represented in a complex plane so that the horizontal axis is assigned to the real part and the vertical axis shows the imaginary part.

The unit circle in the z-plane is centered in the origin of the plane with unit radius. Its mathematical description is shown in Equation 15.42:

$$z = e^{j\phi} \tag{15.42}$$

15.14.3   Region of Convergence

The region of convergence (ROC) of a z-transform is the region of the complex z-plane where that z-transform exists. For a z-transform to converge, it must have this condition:

$$\left| \sum_{n=-\infty}^{\infty} x[n]z^{-n} \right| < \infty \tag{15.43}$$

The region of convergence is the range of z values that satisfies Equation 15.43. To illustrate the ROC concept, we proceed in this section with a simple example.

- Example

Assuming $x[n]$ is the following sequence,

$$x[n] = (-0.2)^n u[n]$$

The z-transform for this sequence is:

$$X(z) = \sum_{n=-\infty}^{\infty} (-0.2)^n u[n]z^{-n} = \sum_{n=0}^{\infty} (\frac{-0.2}{z})^n = \frac{1}{1+0.2z^{-1}} = \frac{z}{z+0.2}$$

Now we calculate the region of convergence for $X(z)$:

$$\frac{z}{z+0.2} < \infty \Rightarrow |z| > 0.2$$

It means that the z-transform converges just outside the circle in the z-plane with radius equal to 0.2.

15.15   Convolution

Convolution can be considered as one of the basic operations in the signal processing field. From the mathematical point of view, the convolution of two functions is defined as shifting one of the functions over other functions and computing their overlaps. To perform such operations the integral of the product of these functions is calculated while one of them is reversed and shifted.

Assuming x and h are two functions, their convolution is described as Equation 15.44:

$$x * h = \int_0^t x(\tau)h(t - \tau)d\tau \tag{15.44}$$

The convolution operation is shown with the $*$ symbol. The convolution operation can also be defined over an infinite range as:

$$x * h = \int_{-\infty}^{\infty} x(\tau)h(t - \tau)d\tau \tag{15.45}$$

The convolution operation also can be expressed in the discrete time domain as shown in Equation 15.46:

$$y[n] = x * h = \sum_{k=-\infty}^{\infty} x[k]h[n - k] \tag{15.46}$$

To understand the concept of convolution, let's continue with one example of discrete convolution.

- Example 1: Assuming the x and h functions are defined as:

$$x[n] = \begin{cases} 1 & n = 0 \\ 2 & n = 1 \\ 3 & n = 2 \\ 0 & otherwise \end{cases}$$

$$h[n] = \begin{cases} 1 & n = 0 \\ 2 & n = 1 \\ 0 & otherwise \end{cases}$$

These functions are depicted in Figures 15.19 and 15.20.

Then the convolution of x and h functions, (y), is calculated as:

$$y[0] = \sum_{k=-\infty}^{\infty} x[k]h[0 - k] = x[0]h[0] = 1 \times 1 = 1$$

$$y[1] = \sum_{k=-\infty}^{\infty} x[k]h[1 - k] = x[0]h[1 - 0] + x[1]h[1 - 1] = 1 \times 2 + 2 \times 1 = 4$$

$$y[2] = \sum_{k=-\infty}^{\infty} x[k]h[2 - k] = x[0]h[2 - 0] + x[1]h[2 - 1] + x[2]h[2 - 2]$$
$$= 1 \times 0 + 2 \times 2 + 3 \times 1 = 7$$

$$y[3] = \sum_{k=-\infty}^{\infty} x[k]h[3 - k] = x[0]h[3 - 0] + x[1]h[3 - 1] + x[2]h[3 - 2] + x[3]h[3 - 3]$$
$$= 1 \times 0 + 2 \times 0 + 3 \times 2 = 6$$

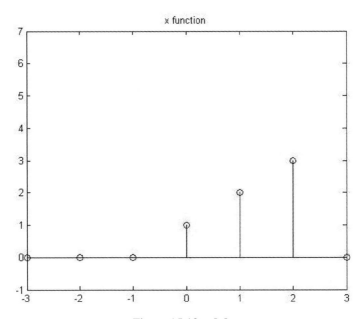
Figure 15.19: x[n].

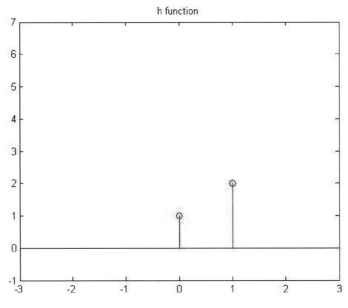
Figure 15.20: h[n].

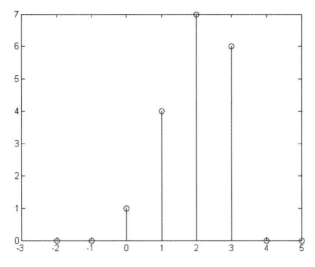

Figure 15.21: y[n]=x[n]*h[n].

Function y is shown in Figure 15.21 and can be expressed as:

$$y[n] = \begin{cases} 1 & n = 0 \\ 4 & n = 1 \\ 7 & n = 2 \\ 6 & n = 3 \\ 0 & otherwise \end{cases}$$

In digital signal processing the convolution concept is used to describe the relationship between the system input signal $x(t)$ and output of the system, $y(t)$, for the linear systems [Haykin and Van Veen 07]. The impulse response of a system $h(t)$, is defined as output of the system if the input is the impulse function. The output of linear systems can be expressed as the convolution result of the input signal with the impulse response of the system.

Further Reading

This chapter briefly describes digital signal processing. However, this topic requires further reading. A great book that cover this topic is *Digital Signal Processing: DSP and Applications* [Stranneby 01] and *DSP First: A Multimedia Approach* [McClellan et al. 98]. They are both great books. DSP is a topic that is much easier to grasp since it is discrete. Therefore, we don't have to worry much about integrals and derivatives, as one has to in analog signals.

16

Three-Dimensional Rotations

I've learned over the years that it doesn't matter where
you pitch in the rotation. For me, preparation is everything.

—Cory Lidle

16.1 Introduction

This chapter provides the background information about the concepts of three-
dimensional rotation, Euler rotation, and quaternions.

16.2 Three-Dimensional Rotation

The three dimensional space (R^3) can be expressed using a Cartesian system
defined by three mutually perpendicular axes passing through the origin point.
These axes are called the X-, Y-, and Z-axes. Each point in such space is presented
by three elements as:

$$A = (x_1, y_1, z_1) \qquad (16.1)$$

Each point can be presented as a vector from the origin to that point. Figure 16.1
depicts a point in the three-dimensional space.

An object can rotate around each of these orthogonal axes. One of the most
common convention (used in airplanes states is the rotation about the X-axis, called
roll; rotation about the Y-axis is called pitch; and yaw refers to rotation about
Z-axis. See Chapter 20 for alternative conventions. These rotations are shown in
Figures 16.2, 16.3, and 16.4.

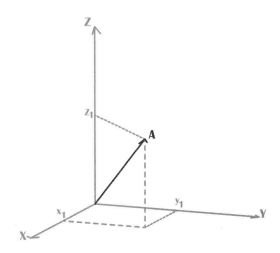

Figure 16.1: Three-dimensional reference frame.

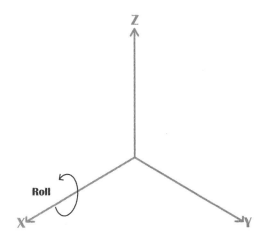

Figure 16.2: Roll.

16.3   Coordinate Systems

The three-dimensional rotation can be described using two reference frames. These reference frames are the inertial and the body-fixed frames. Each of these frames is an orthogonal, right-handed Cartesian frame. In the following these frames are described.

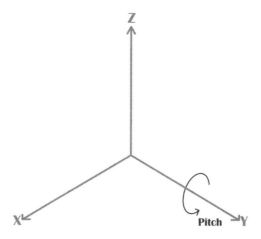

Figure 16.3: Pitch.

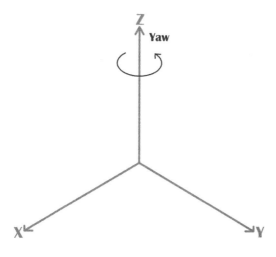

Figure 16.4: Yaw.

16.3.1   Inertial Frame

The origin of this frame is located at the center of the Earth.The X-axis passes
through the equator and the Z-axis passes through the Earth's axis. The Y-axis is
orthogonal to the other two axes.

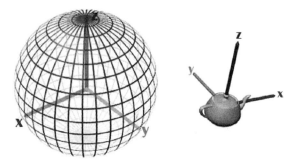

Figure 16.5: Inertial and body-fixed reference frames.

16.3.2 Body-Fixed Frame

The origin of the body-fixed frame is located at the center of gravity of the rotating object and the Z-axis is perpendicular to the object. The X- and Y-axes are orthogonal in a horizontal plane. When the object rotates, this frame rotates with respect to the inertial frame. If the inertial sensors are attached to the rotation object, using this reference frame is required. Figure 16.5 depicts the inertial and body-fixed frames for a rotation object.

16.4 Euler Angles

Euler angles are used to represent the rotation in three-dimensional Euclidean space. The Euler theorem states that [Kuipers 99] "Any two independent orthogonal coordinate frames can be related by a sequence of rotations (not more than three) about the coordinate axes, where no successive rotations may be about the same axes." Based on the Euler rotational theorem, any rotation can be expressed with three rotational angles. These rotational angles are called Euler angles and defined as:

ϕ represents rotation about x-axis
θ represents rotation about y-axis
ψ represents rotation about z-axis

16.4.1 Rotation Matrices

Euler angles present the orientation of an object, with respect to a known coordinate system, using combination of rotations about different axes. The rotation around each axis can be expressed mathematically with rotation matrices. The rotation matrices are defied as:

Rotation matrix about x-axis:

$$R_x(\phi) = \begin{bmatrix} 1 & 0 & 0 \\ 0 & \cos(\phi) & \sin(\phi) \\ 0 & -\sin(\phi) & \cos(\phi) \end{bmatrix} \tag{16.2}$$

Rotation matrix about y-axis:

$$R_y(\theta) = \begin{bmatrix} \cos(\theta) & 0 & -\sin(\theta) \\ 0 & 1 & 0 \\ \sin(\theta) & 0 & \cos(\theta) \end{bmatrix} \tag{16.3}$$

Rotation matrix about z-axis:

$$R_z(\psi) = \begin{bmatrix} \cos(\psi) & \sin(\psi) & 0 \\ -\sin(\psi) & \cos(\psi) & 0 \\ 0 & 0 & 1 \end{bmatrix} \tag{16.4}$$

Multiplication of a rotation matrix with a vector rotates the vector. Assuming V is a vector in $\mathbf{R}^3$, if V rotates about a single axis a new vector would be created. This new vector can be calculated as:

$$V' = R_n(\theta)V \tag{16.5}$$

where θ is the angle of rotation and n is the axis of rotation. Any rotation can be performed using a sequence of three rotations about the coordinate axes [Perumal 11]. There are twelve different rotation sequences with three Euclidean axes. These twelve sequences are:

XYZ YZX ZXY
XZY YXZ ZYX
XZX YXY ZYZ
XYX YZY ZXZ

Any rotation with three degrees of freedom can be expressed using one of the above sequences. To understand how each sequence rotates the objects, we explain one of the sequences here. The sequence XYZ means that initially rotation happens around the X-axis, then there is a rotation about the new Y-axis followed by a rotation about the new Z-axis. Notice that with three axes fifteen more sequences are possible with consecutive rotation around the same axis. Since consecutive rotation around the same axis reduces the degrees of freedom, these possible sequences are ignored. To apply a sequence of rotation like XYZ, the related rotation matrices should be multiplied as

$$R_{XYZ} = R_X(\phi)R_Y(\theta)R_Z(\psi) =$$

$$\begin{bmatrix} 1 & 0 & 0 \\ 0 & \cos(\phi) & \sin(\phi) \\ 0 & -\sin(\phi) & \cos(\phi) \end{bmatrix} \begin{bmatrix} \cos(\theta) & 0 & -\sin(\theta) \\ 0 & 1 & 0 \\ \sin(\theta) & 0 & \cos(\theta) \end{bmatrix} \begin{bmatrix} \cos(\psi) & \sin(\psi) & 0 \\ -\sin(\psi) & \cos(\psi) & 0 \\ 0 & 0 & 1 \end{bmatrix} =$$

$$\begin{bmatrix} \cos(\theta)\cos(\psi) & \cos(\theta)\sin(\psi) & -\sin(\theta) \\ \sin(\phi)\sin(\theta)\cos(\psi) - \cos(\phi)\sin(\psi) & \sin(\phi)\sin(\theta)\sin(\psi) + \cos(\phi)\cos(\psi) & \sin(\phi)\cos(\theta) \\ \cos(\phi)\sin(\theta)\cos(\psi) + \sin(\phi)\sin(\psi) & \cos(\phi)\sin(\theta)\sin(\psi) - \sin(\phi)\cos(\psi) & \cos(\phi)\cos(\theta) \end{bmatrix}$$

In a general form, the rotation matrix for a sequence of rotations is expressed as

$$R_{abc} = R_a(\theta)R_b(\theta)R_c(\theta) \qquad (16.6)$$

Where each of a, b, and c can be X, Y, or Z. Matrix R_{abc} is also called the direct cosine matrix (DCM) which is expressed in terms of Euler angles.

16.4.2 Gimbal Lock

A ring that can rotate freely around an axis is called a gimbal. To represent the three-dimensional rotation, three gimbals are used in a way that each of the gimbals can rotate about one of the X-, Y-, or Z-axis. Each gimbal can rotate freely about its respective axis. These gimbals are placed together in a way that when the outer gimbal rotates all the other gimbals rotate with it. Rotating the intermediate gimbals does not affect the outer gimbal but the innermost gimbal follows its rotation. Finally the innermost gimbal rotates without affecting the other gimbals. The combination of these three gimbals is shown in Figure 16.6. The gimbal lock phenomenon happens as a result of a series of rotations that align the two axes of the three gimbals into the same direction. In other words, it is possible that because of a sequence of rotation, two of the axes are driven into a parallel direction, then these two axes rotate in the same plane, which causes loss of one degree of freedom. This phenomenon is shown in Figure 16.7. To avoid the gimbal lock problem the three-dimensional rotation can be expressed using quaternions (see Side Note 16.1). The next section, describes how to use quaternions to represent three-dimensional rotation.

16.5 Quaternions

Quaternions can be used to express the rotation . The advantage of using quaternions over Euler angles for rotation is that the singularity problem can be avoided. Additionally, operation with quaternions do not need trigonometric functions, which simplifies the process of filter implementation for real-time applications.

In this section the concept of quaternions and quaternion mathematics is described and eventually it is explained how a quaternion is used to represent the three-dimensional rotation.

16.5.1 What Are Quaternions?

In 1843, quaternions were invented by Hamilton. Quaternions are hyper complex numbers of rank four. In quaternions, three imaginary parts are defined, presented by i, j, and k elements. We have the following relations for these basic elements:

$$i * i = i^2 = -1 \tag{16.7}$$

$$j * j = j^2 = -1 \tag{16.8}$$

$$k * k = k^2 = -1 \tag{16.9}$$

$$i * j * k = -1 \tag{16.10}$$

Quaternions can be expressed in different notations. A quaternion can be expressed as linear combination of four elements as:

$$q = (q_0, q_1, q_2, q_3) = q_0 + iq_1 + jq_2 + kq_3 \tag{16.11}$$

Figure 16.6: Three gimbals.

Figure 16.7: Gimbal lock effect.

Side Note 16.1: Quaternions and Gimbal Lock

The statement: "Quaternions avoid gimbal lock" can be misrepresented. Gimbal lock in the mathematical sense is about non-unique factorization of rotation matrix into a product of coordinate-axis rotations. That is, Euler angles provide a many-to-one mapping onto the rotations. Unit-length quaternions are a double-covering of the rotations, so if you stick to a hemisphere (in 4D), you have a one-to-one mapping. However, if you try to factor a quaternion into a product of 3 coordinate-axis quaternions, you have the same problem with non-unique factoring. See additional information in [Eberly 14].

---

where q_0 is the real part which is called scalar, and the rest are the imaginary parts of the quaternion, which Hamilton called vectors. q_0, q_1, q_2, and q_3 are real numbers. A quaternion may also be represented as a scalar and a vector as:

$$q = (q_0, \vec{\mathbf{q}}) \tag{16.12}$$

The vector part, $\mathbf{q}$, is a vector in $\mathbf{R}_3$:

$$\vec{\mathbf{q}} = iq_1 + jq_2 + kq_3 \tag{16.13}$$

The i, j, and k elements are used to represent the standard orthogonal three-dimensional basis as the following vectors:

$$i = (1,0,0) \tag{16.14}$$

$$j = (0,1,0) \tag{16.15}$$

$$k = (0,0,1) \tag{16.16}$$

Quaternion Equality

Two quaternions are equal if and only if their corresponding components are equal. Considering two p and q quaternions as:

$$q = q_0 + iq_1 + jq_2 + kq_3$$
$$p = p_0 + ip_1 + jp_2 + kp_3$$

Then q is equal to p if and only if:

$$q_0 = p_0$$
$$q_1 = p_1$$
$$q_2 = p_2$$
$$q_3 = p_3$$

Quaternion Addition

The sum of two quaternions follows the same rule for addition of complex numbers. This rule says that the corresponding components should be added as:

$$q + p = (q_0 + p_0) + i(q_1 + p_1) + j(q_2 + p_2) + k(q_3 + p_3) \tag{16.17}$$

Quaternion Multiplication

The multiplication rule to obtain the product of a scalar by a quaternion is simple. Each component of a quaternion should be multiplied by the scalar. If p is a quaternion and a is a scalar, then the product of p and a is given by:

$$ap = ap_0 + iap_1 + jap_2 + kap_3 \tag{16.18}$$

However, the multiplication of two quaternions is not that straightforward. Its rule is similar to polynomial multiplication, considering the multiplicative properties of i, j, and k as the following:

$$i^2 = j^2 = k^2 = ijk = -1 \tag{16.19}$$

$$ij = k = -ji \tag{16.20}$$

$$jk = i = -kj \tag{16.21}$$

$$ki = j = -ik \tag{16.22}$$

The above products are not commutative, therefore the quaternion multiplication cannot be commutative either. Now, using the above fundamental rules, the product of two quaternions is defined. The symbol $\otimes$ is used for quaternion multiplication.

$$
\begin{aligned}
p \otimes q = {}&(p_0 + ip_1 + jp_2 + kp_3) \otimes (q_0 + iq_1 + jq_2 + kq_3) \\
= {}& p_0 q_0 + ip_0 q_1 + jp_0 q_2 + kp_0 q_3 \\
&+ ip_1 q_0 + i^2 p_1 q_1 + ijp_1 q_2 + ikp_1 q_3 \\
&+ jp_2 q_0 + jip_2 q_1 + j^2 p_2 q_2 + jkp_2 q_3 \\
&+ kp_3 q_0 + kip_3 q_1 + kjp_3 q_2 + k^2 p_3 q_3
\end{aligned}
$$

Considering the fundamental rules, the product of two quaternions would be expressed as:

$$
\begin{aligned}
p \otimes q = {}&(p_0 + ip_1 + jp_2 + kp_3) \otimes (q_0 + iq_1 + jq_2 + kq_3) = \\
& p_0 q_0 + ip_0 q_1 + jp_0 q_2 + kp_0 q_3 + ip_1 q_0 - p_1 q_1 + kp_1 q_2 - jp_1 q_3
\end{aligned}
$$

$$+ jp_2 q_0 - kp_2 q_1 - 1 p_2 q_2 + ip_2 q_3 + kp_3 q_0 + jp_3 q_1 - ip_3 q_2 - p_3 q_3 \tag{16.23}$$

The above expression can be rewritten as:

$$
\begin{aligned}
p \otimes q = {}& p_0 q_0 - (p_1 q_1 + p_2 q_2 + p_3 q_3) + p_0 (iq_1 + jq_2 + kq_3) + q_0 (ip_1 + jp_2 + kp_3) \\
& + i(p_2 q_3 - p_3 q_2) + j(p_3 q_1 - p_1 q_3) + k(p_1 q_2 - p_2 q_1)
\end{aligned}
\tag{16.24}
$$

Quaternion Conjugate

The conjugate operation for the given quaternion, q, is defined as:

$$p = p_0 + ip_1 + jp_2 + kp_3$$

$$p^* = p_0 - ip_1 - jp_2 - kp_3 \tag{16.25}$$

p^* denotes the conjugate of p.

Quaternion Norm

The norm of a quaternion p, denoted as $|p|$ or $\mathbf{N}(p)$, is a scalar and is defined as

$$|p| = \sqrt{p^*p} = p_0^2 + p_1^2 + p_2^2 + p_3^2 \tag{16.26}$$

When the norm of a quaternion is equal to 1, the quaternion is called a unit or normalized quaternion. The product of unit quaternions and inverse of unit quaternion are also unit quaternions. A unit quaternion can be written as

$$q = [q_0, \vec{\mathbf{q}}] \tag{16.27}$$

where:
$q_0 = \cos(\frac{\theta}{2})$ and $\vec{\mathbf{q}} = \hat{u}\cos(\frac{\theta}{2})$ u is a three-dimensional vector with length 1 and θ is the rotational angle. Therefore the unit quaternion can be expressed as:

$$q = \cos(\frac{\theta}{2}) + i\sin(\frac{\theta}{2}) + j\sin(\frac{\theta}{2}) + k\sin(\frac{\theta}{2}) \tag{16.28}$$

And the conjugate of quaternion can be written as:

$$q = \cos(\frac{\theta}{2}) - i\sin(\frac{\theta}{2}) - j\sin(\frac{\theta}{2}) - k\sin(\frac{\theta}{2}) \tag{16.29}$$

Quaternion Inverse

The inverse of a quaternion p is denoted as p^{-1} and, based on the definition of inverse, we should have

$$p^{-1}p = pp^{-1} = 1$$

Using the norm and conjugate tools, the above statement can be expressed as

$$p^{-1}pp^* = p^*pp^{-1} = p^*$$

In the previous section we noticed $pp^* = \|N(p)\|^2$, so inverse formula can be written as:

$$p^{-1} = \frac{p^*}{\|N(p)\|^2} = \frac{p^*}{|p|^2} \tag{16.30}$$

If the quaternion is a unit quaternion, then the norm is equal to 1; therefore the inverse quaternion would be equal to quaternion conjugate.

$$p^{-1} = p^*$$

16.5.2   Quaternion Rotation

We previously explained how a three-dimensional rotation can be expressed using rotation matrices. It was shown there that a vector can be rotated by multiplying it by a rotation matrix. Rotations also can be accomplished using quaternions. A three-dimensional vector v can be rotated around axis $\hat{u}$ by an angle of θ, using unit quaternion $q = \cos(\frac{\theta}{2}) + \hat{u}\sin(\frac{\theta}{2})$. The rotated vector v' is described as

$$v' = q \otimes v \otimes q^* \qquad (16.31)$$

where, q^* is the conjugate of quaternion q and v' is the rotated version of vector v about axis of q. Axis q can be each of X-, Y-, or Z-axes. The quaternion for rotation about each of these axis is expressed as

$$q_x = \cos(\frac{\phi}{2}) + i\sin(\frac{\phi}{2}) + j\sin(\frac{0}{2}) + k\sin(\frac{0}{2}) = \cos(\frac{\phi}{2}) + i\sin(\frac{\phi}{2}) \qquad (16.32)$$

$$q_y = \cos(\frac{\theta}{2}) + i\sin(\frac{0}{2}) + j\sin(\frac{\theta}{2}) + k\sin(\frac{0}{2}) = \cos(\frac{\theta}{2}) + j\sin(\frac{\theta}{2}) \qquad (16.33)$$

$$q_z = \cos(\frac{\psi}{2}) + i\sin(\frac{0}{2}) + j\sin(\frac{0}{2}) + k\sin(\frac{\psi}{2}) = \cos(\frac{\psi}{2}) + k\sin(\frac{\psi}{2}) \qquad (16.34)$$

Equation 16.31 can be defined in a general form as:

$$v' = R_Q v \qquad (16.35)$$

where R_Q is the rotation matrix corresponding to the quaternion. The general form of this rotation matrix is expressed as [Wheeler and Ikeuchi 95]

$$R_Q = \begin{bmatrix} q_0^2 + q_1^2 - q_2^2 - q_3^2 & 2q_1q_2 - 2q_0q_3 & 2q_1q_3 + 2q_0q_2 \\ 2q_0q_3 + 2q_1q_2 & q_0^2 - q_1^2 + q_2^2 - q_3^2 & -2q_0q_1 + 2q_2q_3 \\ -2q_0q_2 + 2q_1q_3 & 2q_0q_1 + 2q_2q_3 & q_0^2 - q_1^2 - q_2^2 + q_3^2 \end{bmatrix} \qquad (16.36)$$

As was explained earlier, there are twelve forms of rotation sequences with three degrees of freedom. To express the quaternion rotation of each sequence, we should multiply the corresponding quaternion representations of each of the axes involved.

Further Reading

To see an expanded topic about quaternions, see *Quaternions and Rotation Sequences* [Kuipers 99]. It includes some advanced special topics in spherical trigonometry, along with an introduction to quaternion calculus and perturbation theory. For a simple description of quaternions and general 3D mathematics needed for computer graphics, see [Dunn and Parberry 11]. An excellent book about quaternions is called *Visualizing Quaternions* [Hanson 06]. Finally, Eberly has written many books covering different aspects of computer graphics, which includes quaterions. Eberly's latest book, *GPGPU: Programming for Games and Science* provides an excellent section on rotations [Eberly 14, pp. 288–317].

17

MEMS Inertial Sensors and Magnetic Sensors

> Everything was sensory and I never saw the structure in anything.
>
> —Gill Kane

17.1   Introduction

Inertial sensors consist of accelerometer and gyroscope sensors. A unit with gyroscopes and accelerometers is also called an inertial measurement unit (IMU). These sensors can be utilized for motion detection applications. Inertial sensors are also used in combination with magnetometer sensors to achieve better measurements.

Advances in MEMS technology have revolutionized the inertial sensors industry. MEMS sensors have significant advantages over non-MEMS sensors in terms of size, energy consumption, reliability, and cost. The emergence of miniaturized MEMS inertial sensors has provided the possibility of adopting such sensors in the expanded range of consumer electronic products.

In this chapter the basic principles of accelerometer, magnetometer, and gyroscope sensors are described and their error sources are introduced.

17.2   Inertial Sensors

Inertial sensors function based on inertial forces. These sensors capture the external motion forces acting on them. These forces consist of acceleration and angular rotation. The measured forces are used to calculate the acceleration and angular rotation of the body. Knowing the acceleration forces acting upon the body, it should be possible (in theory) to determine the translational motion of the body.

Accelerometers sensors respond to the forces associated with acceleration and gyroscopes sensors are sensitive to the angular rotations.

Inertial sensors have various applications in different areas. These sensors are applied for navigations video gaming interface, automotive, motion detection for health monitoring, monitoring of machinery vibration, mobile phones, vibration detection of buildings, sports training, etc. [Maenaka 08] [Bhattacharyya et al. 13].

The combination of accelerometers and gyroscopes is called IMU. Sometimes the IMU has magnetometers in addition to accelerometers and gyroscopes. The IMU is commonly used to measure the inertial forces in three dimensions. In the following, accelerometer and gyroscope sensors are described.

17.2.1   Accelerometers

Accelerometers detect the acceleration due to external forces acting on objects. The output of an accelerometer is a combination of the acceleration due to Earth's gravity and the linear acceleration due to motion. Each sensor responds to the acceleration along a specific axis. In the past, accelerometers could sense the acceleration in just one axis, but recently tri-axis accelerometers have become available in the market. To measure the acceleration in three dimensions with one-axis accelerometer, three accelerometers were used. These sensors were positioned so that their sensitive axes were oriented east-west, north-south, and vertically. The tri-axis accelerometer has three orthogonal axes that can sense the acceleration forces in three dimensions.

The acceleration associated with external forces acting on an object can be explained by Newton's second law of motion: "A force F acting on a body of mass m causes the body to accelerate with respect to the inertial space" [Titterton and Weston 04].

The mathematical representation of Newton's second law of motion is shown in Equation 17.1, where a is the acceleration and m represents the mass. The force (F) is what causes acceleration to the body. The force origin can be either the result of body motion or Earth's gravity (g).

$$F = ma \qquad (17.1)$$

A basic form of accelerometer consists of a small mass that is connected to a case through a spring. The mass is also called proof or seismic mass. Figure 17.1 shows the basic form of the accelerometer.

When an external force is applied to the case, because of the mass inertia, it shows resistance against the movement. Consequently, it creates tension or extension in the springs, and the mass position with respect to the case will change. The mass displacement makes the output of the sensor vary. This variation is used to measure the acceleration [Titterton and Weston 04].

Figure 17.2 depicts the accelerometer when a force is applied to it along its sensitive axis.

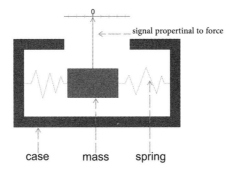

Figure 17.1: Basic accelerometer.

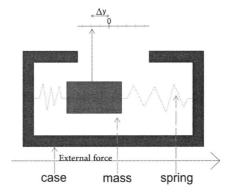

Figure 17.2: Accelerometer response to the external forces.

There are also MEMS accelerometers that are built based on other techniques such as capacitive-based displacement accelerometers, piezoelectric and piezoresistive-based accelerometers, and resonant element accelerometers. [Nikolic and Renaut 0].

17.2.2 Gyroscopes

Gyroscope sensors are devices to measure the angular motion of an object. The sensor output is proportional to its rotation. Some gyroscopes measure the angular velocity (rate gyroscopes) while other gyroscopes measure the orientation (angle gyroscopes).

Gyroscopes have been made based on different technologies. These sensors can be categorized into three major groups including mechanical gyroscopes,

---

Side Note 17.1: Calibration Process

Before performing any process on the inertial sensors, it is important to calibrate them. The calibration equation for the inertial sensor output can be expressed as:

$$G_c = [M].(S.[G_r + b]) \tag{17.3}$$

Where G_c is the calibrated data, G_r is raw data, S is the scale factor, b represents the bias, and M is misalignment matrix. Each of these variables can usually be found in the sensor data sheet.

---

optical gyroscopes, and MEMS gyroscopes.

Mechanical gyroscopes typically consist of a spinning wheel mounted in two gimbals. The wheel can rotate in three axis. It works based on the effect of conservation of angular momentum.

There are two types of optical gyroscopes including fiber optic gyroscopes (FOG) and ring laser gyroscopes (RLG) [Woodman 07]. FOGs use a coil of optical fiber and two light beams to measure rotation. Two light beams, in opposite directions, are entered into the coil and travel at constant speed. When the sensor is rotating, the light traveling in the direction of rotation traverses a longer path compared to the light traveling in the opposite direction. This is called the "Sagnac effect." By measuring the path length, the angular rate of rotation can be computed. Ring laser gyroscopes consist of a closed loop tube with three arms. At each corner of the tube a mirror is placed and the tube is filled with helium-neon gas. These sensors also work based on the "Sagnac effect."

MEMS gyroscopes work based on the Coriolis effect. If a mass m is moving with velocity v in a reference frame rotating at angular velocity w, then a force F will work upon the mass as shown in Equation 17.2. These sensors measure the Coriolis acceleration acting on a vibrating element which is used as proof mass [Shaeffer 13]. The vibrating elements are available in the form of a tuning fork or a vibrating wheel. All MEMS gyroscopes are rate gyroscopes.

$$F = -2m(w \times v) \tag{17.2}$$

MEMS gyroscopes have many advantages compared to mechanical and optical gyroscopes. MEMS gyroscopes have low power consumption, small size, low weight, and low maintenance cost, among other features.

17.3 MEMS Inertial Sensor Errors

Inertial sensors suffer from several sources of errors. The error origin can be an environmental disturbance (such as temperature, magnetic field, or air pressure), measurement equipment, or random noises [Dorobantu and Gerlach 04].

The inertial sensor errors can be classified into two major categories, including systematic (deterministic) errors and random (stochastic) errors. Both types of errors affect the accuracy of inertial sensor measurements. Therefore, to enhance the performance of the inertial sensors it is necessary to detect and compensate for such errors [Zander 07].

Systematic errors can be estimated by reference measurement. The calibration process is used to estimate and compensate systematic errors. Scale factor, constant bias, misalignment, nonlinearity, and sign asymmetry are categorized as systematic errors. Unfortunately, even after the calibration process the data extracted from the sensors are contaminated with other types of errors.

Random noises consist of high-frequency and low-frequency components. To remove the high-frequency noises different noise removal techniques have been used, such as Wavelet, low pass filters, and neural networks. The low-frequency noises are modeled using random processes. Different random processes are utilized to model the inertial sensor's low-frequency noises such as random walk, constant random, and Gauss–Markov random processes [El 08a].

To extract accurate and meaningful data from the sensor output, it is necessary to compensate all types of errors; otherwise the results would not be reliable. Some types of common inertial sensor errors are described next.

17.3.1 Angle Random Walk

Angle random walk (ARW) is the white noise added on the sensor output. This noise usually results from the power supplies or semiconductor devices. The power spectral density of angle random walk is shown in Equation 17.4, where Q is the angle random walk coefficient.

$$s(f) = Q^2 \tag{17.4}$$

17.3.2 Rate Random Walk

Rate random walk (RRW) is a random noise with unknown origin [El 08b]. The power spectral density of this noise is:

$$s(f) = \frac{k^2}{2\pi} \frac{1}{f^2} \tag{17.5}$$

where k is the rate random walk coefficient.

17.3.3   Flicker Noise

Flicker noise is a non-stationary noise whose power spectra is proportional to f^{-1}. The power spectrum shows that most of the power of this noise appears in low frequencies.

17.3.4   Quantization Noise

Quantization noise is the result of the digitalization process. A finite number of bits is used for storing the signal values, so information is lost and the digital signal is slightly different compared to the original analog signal.

17.3.5   Sinusoidal Noise

The sensor's output exhibits an additive sinusoidal noise component. The reason is because these sensors work around a resonant frequency. Therefore, a pseudo-deterministic sinusoidal noise is seen in the output signal.

17.3.6   Bias Error

Bias error is a nonzero output signal which appears in the sensor output when input is zero. The bias offset causes the sensor output to offset from the true data by a constant value. This error is not dependent on external forces applied to the sensor. Bias error can be divided into three categories, including a static part (or bias offset), a random part (or drift), and a temperature dependent part [Naranjo and Hgskolan 08]. The static bias and temperature bias can be compensated in the calibration process. Static bias can be measured by averaging the sensor output for a zero input signal. To compensate for this bias, it should be subtracted from the output data. The drift bias has a random nature and cannot be fixed in the calibration process. It should be treated as a stochastic error. Bias error is presented in Figure 17.3.

17.3.7   Scale Factor Error

The scale factor error is linear deviation of the input-output gradient from unity. Similar to the bias error, the scale factor error can be divided into a static part, a drift part, and a temperature-dependent part. This effect is depicted in Figure 17.4. This error may arise from aging or manufacturing tolerance. [Grewal et al. 07] To compensate for the scale factor error the data should be multiplied with a constant factor [Zander 07].

17.3.8   Scale Factor Sign Asymmetry Error

The scale factor sign asymmetry effect is the spontaneous change of at least one point in the measurement curve. This error is shown in Figure 17.5.

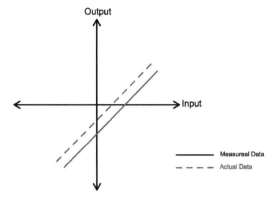

Figure 17.3: Bias error.

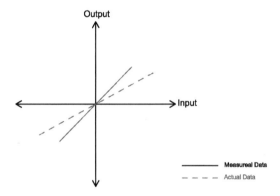

Figure 17.4: Scale factor error.

17.3.9 Misalignment (Cross-Coupling) Error

This error is a systematic error and comes from the misalignment of the sensitive axes of the sensor with respect to the axes of the body frame [Groves 13]. This error appears because of manufacturing imperfection and can be compensated through the calibration process. Figure 17.6 shows the sensor's X, Y, and Z axis misalignment with respect to the body frame.

17.3.10 Non-Linearity Error

The scale factor phenomenon does not always happen in a linear form; sometimes it appears in the form of second or higher order function [Lawrence 98]. This effect happens because of the material properties and geometric shape of the sensor [Zander 07]. This effect is shown in Figure 17.7.

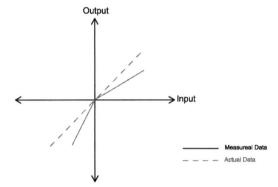

Figure 17.5: Scale factor sign asymmetry error.

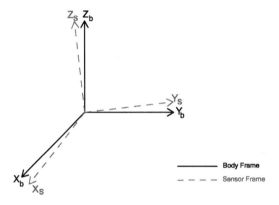

Figure 17.6: Axis misalignment.

17.3.11   Dead Zone Error

The dead zone effect is an apparent discontinuity in the output data. The sensor does not sense the applied forces in the interval in which the discontinuity happens. This interval is called a "dead zone." Figure 17.8 depicts the dead zone effect.

17.3.12   Temperature Effect

Changes in the environment temperature affect the output of MEMS sensors. A temperature sensor is usually added to the inertial measurement units to be used for compensating the temperature effect.

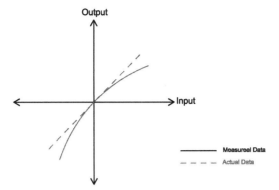

Figure 17.7: Non-linearity error.

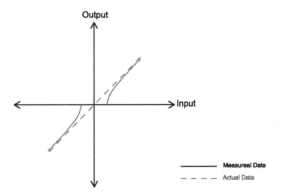

Figure 17.8: Dead zone error.

17.4 Magnetometers

For centuries, navigators have been acquainted with the Earth's magnetic field effect. The earliest evidence about compass navigation is ascribed to the Chinese and dated 250 years B.C. [Campbell 03]. Traditional magnetometers (compass) were simple instruments that pointed approximately to magnetic north. A small magnetized arrow aligns itself to be parallel with the horizontal component of the Earth's magnetic field.

The Earth's magnetic field is produced by the Earth and also interacting fields from the Sun, called the solar wind. The solar wind is the stream of high-energy charged particles, which are released outward from the Sun continuously. To explain the source of Earth's magnetism, many hypotheses have been asserted. But only the "Dynamo Effect" mechanism is now considered plausible [Campbell 03]. The Earth is composed of four layers, including outer crust, mantle, outer core, and inner core. The temperature at the mantle layer, at the boundary with the

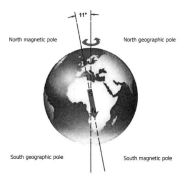

Figure 17.9: Geographic and magnetic poles.

outer core, is over 4000° Celsius, which is hot enough to liquefy the outer core. The outer core consists of molten iron. In this theory, the Earth's magnetism is attributed to the convection currents of molten iron in this layer.

The north pole of the Earth's magnet is on the side of geographical south and vice versa. The geographical north and south axis, which is defined by the Earth's rotational axis, does not coincide with the axis of the Earth's magnet [Butler 92]. The best approximation of discrepancy between magnetic pole and geographical pole is 11.5°. This is so-called magnetic declination. Figure 17.9 presents the location of geographic and magnetic poles.

Three-axis MEMS magnetometers provide more information than traditional magnetometers. They measure the magnitude and direction of two horizontal and one vertical component of the magnetic field. The tri-axis magnetometer projects Earth's field vector in three orthogonal vectors. This data can be described in two ways:

- Magnetic field can be described by three orthogonal components. In this arrangement, the positive values point northward in X-axis, eastward in Y-axis, and downward in Z-axis. It uses the right-hand system to present the magnetic field. Figure 17.10. illustrates this presentation of magnetic field. The total field strength is calculated as:

$$F = \sqrt{X^2 + Y^2 + Z^2} = \sqrt{H^2 + Z^2} \qquad (17.6)$$

- In the second representation, the components include the horizontal magnitude (H), the declination angle (D), and the inclination angle (I). The inclination angle is the angle between horizontal plane and the field vector, which measures positive downward. The declination and the inclination angles can be computed by following equations.

$$X = H\cos(D) \qquad (17.7)$$

$$Y = H \sin(D) \tag{17.8}$$

$$D = \arctan(\frac{Y}{X}) \tag{17.9}$$

$$I = \arctan(\frac{Z}{H}) \tag{17.10}$$

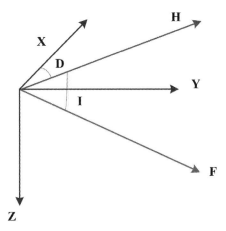

Figure 17.10: Earth's magnetic vector.

17.5 MEMS Magnetometer Errors

MEMS magnetometers are subject to bias error, scale factor error, misalignment errors, and stochastic noise [Ji et al. 11] [Renaudin et al. 10]. Furthermore, the local magnetic fields can disturb the sensor output. Such disturbance is categorized into groups as [Garton et al. 09]:

- Soft iron disturbance: Soft iron disturbance is caused by the ferromagnetic objects in the vicinity of the magnetometer. These objects can distort the direction of the magnetic field.

- Hard iron disturbance: Hard iron effect is the result of the presence of any permanent magnetic field surrounding the sensor. The permanent magnetic field causes a constant bias on the sensor output.

Magnetometer Soft and Hard Iron Compensation

If a magnetometer, which has already compensated for the soft and hard iron effects, is turned around on the vertical axis about 360 degrees in a horizontal surface then plotting of the X axis with respect to the Y axis would be a circle

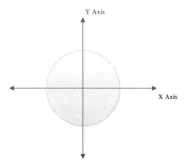

Figure 17.11: Magnetometer without presence of hard and soft iron disturbances.

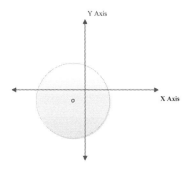

Figure 17.12: Hard iron effect on magnetometer.

centered in zero [Säll and Merkel 11]. Figure 17.11 depicts the ideal plot of the X axis with respect to the Y axis when hard and soft iron disturbances are removed. Presence of hard iron error would shift the center of the circle, as is shown in Figure 17.12. In fact the hard iron effect adds offset to the data. This offset can be compensated in the calibration process by measuring the maximum and minimum values for each axis after turning the sensor about 360 degrees. If the maximum and minimum values for each specific axis are the same with different signs, then there is not hard iron error. Otherwise offset is calculated and removed with the following steps for each axis:

- $sum = data_{maximumvalue} + data_{minimumvalue}$

- $bias = sum/2$

- $data = data - bias$

Soft iron disturbance would change the circle to the elliptic shape as depicted in Figure 17.13.

To perform the soft iron correction it is recommended to carry out the hard iron and tilt correction prior to the soft iron to adjust the origin of the ellipse at the

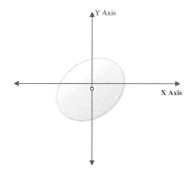

Figure 17.13: Soft iron effect on magnetometer.

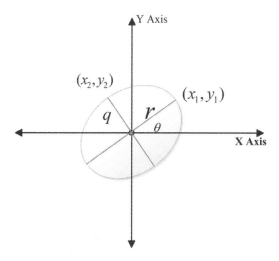

Figure 17.14: Soft iron effect on magnetometer.

center (Figure 17.14). A simple approach to make up for soft iron is presented here [Konvalin 09].

First the rotation angle from X axis is calculated as:

$$r = \sqrt{(x_1^2 + y_1^2)} \qquad (17.11)$$

$$\theta = \arcsin(\frac{y_1}{r}) \qquad (17.12)$$

Now, the rotation matrix is defined as:

$$R = \begin{bmatrix} \cos\theta & \sin\theta \\ -\sin\theta & \cos\theta \end{bmatrix} \qquad (17.13)$$

Original Data

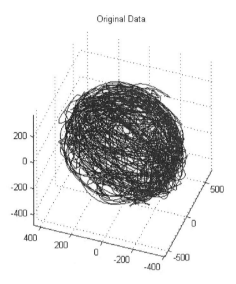

Figure 17.15: Soft and hard Iron effect on magnetometer data.

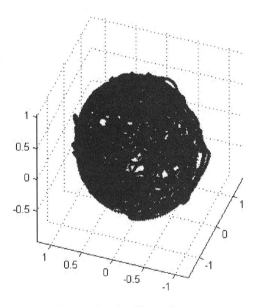

Figure 17.16: Sphere fitted calibrated magnetometer data.

Now the ellipse should turn using rotational matrix. Once the rotation is done the major and minor axes of the ellipse are aligned with the X and Y axes.

$$\hat{v} = Rv \tag{17.14}$$

The next step is to scale the major axis of the ellipse to reshape it to a circle. The scale factor is calculated as:

$$S = \frac{q}{r} \tag{17.15}$$

Figure 17.15 shows the recorded output of a magnetometer which is not compensated for the soft and hard iron effect after moving the sensor randomly in different orientations. It can be seen that the data lie on an ellipsoid instead of a sphere. To correct, the data ellipsoid form should be transformed to a sphere. In [Yury 09] a MATLAB®program is provided to fit an ellipsoid to a sphere. The compensated data are shown in Figure 17.16.

Further Reading

Describing the techniques for implementing and evaluating inertial MEMS sensors was skipped in this chapter. If you are interested in MEMS inertial sensors design and instrumentation, you can find related information in the book *Strapdown Inertial Navigation Technology* [Titterton and Weston 04].

18

Kalman Filters

> It's not about how much movement you do, how much interaction there is, it just reeks of credibility if it's real. If it's contrived, it seems to work for a while for the people who can't filter out the real and unreal.
>
> —Fred Durst

18.1   Introduction

Kalman filtering is an advanced approach for controlling complex and dynamic systems. One Kalman filtering applications is fusing inertial and magnetic sensors data to produce reliable measurements. Many people believe this is a very complicated approach and give up learning and using this filter. In this chapter the background theory of Kalman filtering is described in a simple way, avoiding deep and complicated mathematical explanation. Once you understand how it works, you can implement it for your system. Notice that even if you cannot conceive how it works, you can implement it for your system by following the filter's steps.

18.2   Least Squares Estimator

The Kalman filter is a least squares error estimator. An estimator is a statistic that uses the observed data to calculate an estimate of a given quantity. In this section, the concept of least squares estimator is described.

The least squares (LSQ) is a recursive algorithm to design linear adaptive filters. One of its variations is known as recursive least squares (RLS). The LSQ approach is a method for estimating optimal data from noisy data [Grewal and Andrews 11]. The algorithm computes the filter coefficients that minimize the cost function which is the sum of weighted error squares. The RLS algorithm defines error as the discrepancy between the desired signal and the actual signal. This method was first

403

published by Andien-Marie Legendre, but it is mostly attributed to Carl Friedrich Gauss. Gauss describe this method in the following way: "the most probable value of the unknown quantities will be that in which the sum of the squares of the differences between the actually observed and the computed values multiplied by numbers that measure the degree of precision is a minimum" [Simon 06].

A system can be described in matrix form [Sorenson 85], as shown in Equation 18.1. This equation can be written as shown in Equation 18.2, where Z is the observed dependent signal, x represents the original signal which carries the information and v is the measurement error.

$$
\begin{bmatrix} z_1 \\ z_2 \\ z_3 \\ \vdots \\ z_l \end{bmatrix} = \begin{bmatrix} h_{11} & h_{12} & h_{13} & \cdots & h_{1n} \\ h_{21} & h_{22} & h_{23} & \cdots & h_{2n} \\ h_{31} & h_{32} & h_{33} & \cdots & h_{3n} \\ \vdots & \vdots & \vdots & \ddots & \vdots \\ h_{l1} & h_{l2} & h_{l3} & \cdots & h_{ln} \end{bmatrix} \begin{bmatrix} x_1 \\ x_2 \\ x_3 \\ \vdots \\ x_l \end{bmatrix} + \begin{bmatrix} v_1 \\ v_2 \\ v_3 \\ \vdots \\ v_l \end{bmatrix} \tag{18.1}
$$

$$
Z_k = H x_k + v_k \tag{18.2}
$$

The overall objective is to estimate values of vector x, which is represented with $\hat{x}$ notation, in a way that minimizes the estimated measurement error $(H\hat{x} - Z)$. To solve the problem of finding $\hat{x}$ Gauss assume the signal x and the observed data to be linearly related.

The difference between measured data and calculated data is called the residual. In the least-squares method, the best estimation minimizes the sum of the squares of the residuals, as shown in Equation 18.3.

$$
\varepsilon^2(\hat{x}) = (H\hat{x} - Z)^2 = \sum_{i=1}^{m} [\sum_{j=1}^{n} h_{ij}\hat{x}_j - z_i]^2 \tag{18.3}
$$

To minimize the error it is required to find the value of $\hat{x}$ [Grewal and Andrews 11] such that:

$$
\frac{\partial \varepsilon^2}{\partial \hat{x}_k} = 0 \tag{18.4}
$$

or

$$
2\sum_{i=1}^{m} h_{ik}[\sum_{j=1}^{n} h_{ij}\hat{x}_j - z_i] = 2\sum_{i=0}^{m} h_{ij}H\hat{x} - z_i = 0 \tag{18.5}
$$

Equation 18.5 can be written as Equations 18.6, 18.7 and 18.8. Equation 18.7 is called the normal form for linear least squares problems [Grewal and Andrews 11].

$$
2H^T[H\hat{x} - z] = 0 \tag{18.6}
$$

$$
H^T H\hat{x} = H^T z \tag{18.7}
$$

$$\hat{x} = (H^T H)^{-1} H^T z \qquad (18.8)$$

18.3 Kalman Filters

The Kalman filter was named after Rudolf Emil Kalman. He was born in 1930 in Hungary and emigrated to the United States during World War II [Grewal and Andrews 11].

He completed his bachelor's and master's degrees in electrical engineering at Massachusetts Institute of Technology and received his PhD at Columbia University in 1957. His famous paper describing a recursive estimator was published in 1960 [Kalman 60]. The estimator is called the Kalman filter and also is known as linear quadratic estimation.

The Kalman filter has been applied in a wide range of applications and research areas, including economic modeling, process control, navigation, tracking objects, and earthquake prediction [Gibbs 11]. It has been used notably in the area of navigation, estimation, and tracking.

The Kalman filter is a recursive algorithm which measures consecutive noisy data samples over time and estimates the variables in a way that minimizes the mean square error. The Kalman filter algorithm consists of the following two steps:

- Prediction (or Time Update) step.

- Correction (or Measurement Update) step.

In the prediction step, the Kalman filter predicts the state of the system and calculates the error covariance for the next step. In the correction step, the filter incorporates received measurements to correct its prediction. In general, the prediction step is responsible for forecasting the state of the system ahead in time and the correction step adjusts the prediction by applying the real measurement at the time.

The Kalman filter estimates the state of a system at a time (t+1) by using the state of the system at time (t). The prediction-correction cycle is depicted in Figure 18.1.

18.4 Discrete Kalman Filters

The discrete Kalman filter, which is applicable for linear systems, is described in this section. The discrete Kalman filter is much more frequently used than the continuous Kalman filter. Even in applications in which the system's model is continuous, because the measurement is mostly performed in a discrete manner, the discrete Kalman filter is often used.

In order to apply the Kalman filter, it is necessary to find the mathematical description of your system. This mathematical description is called the "system model." This model relates inputs of the systems to the outputs with some differential equations. Sometimes it is difficult to find the mathematical model for the system. To understand the "system model," you need to have knowledge about the state-space representation. The system model for the discrete time linear systems can be described by the state transition Equation 18.9:

$$x_{k+1} = Ax_k + w_k, \qquad k \geq 0 \tag{18.9}$$

where x_k is the state vector at time k, which is an $(n \times 1)$ column vector. A is the state transition matrix, which is an $(n \times n)$ matrix, and w_k represents the zero-mean state noise vector, which is $(n \times 1)$ column vector.

The Kalman filter minimizes the effect of the noise w on the signal x. The state variable, x_k, describes a physical quantity of the system such as velocity, position, force, etc. The matrix A has constant elements. The Kalman filter formulation assumes that the measurement is linearly related to the states as indicated in Equation 18.10:

$$Z_k = Hx_k + v_k \tag{18.10}$$

where z_k is measurement of x at time k, which is an $(m \times 1)$ column vector. H represents the observation matrix, which is an $(m \times n)$ matrix, and v_k is the zero-mean measurement noise, which is an $(m \times 1)$ column vector. The matrix H includes constant elements and represents how each state variable is related to the measurements.

The Kalman filter was developed under the following assumptions:

- The initial state, x_0 is uncorrelated to both the system and measurement noises with known mean and covariance as described in Equations 18.11 and 18.12:

$$\mu_0 = E[x_0] \tag{18.11}$$

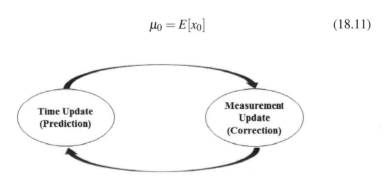

Figure 18.1: Kalman filter cycle.

Side Note 18.1: Finding Q and R matrices

Performance of Kalman filtering depends on determining correct values for R and Q matrices. Errors in R and Q matrices would result in producing unacceptable output. Some may find it challenging to find the correct values for R and Q. To simplify the process of finding appropriate values for these matrices, one can initially guess some reasonable values for R and Q matrices. These values should be tuned experimentally until the correct output from the filter is determined.

$$P_0 = E[(x_0 - \mu_0)(x_0 - \mu_0)^T] \qquad (18.12)$$

You might have forgotten about some statistical theories. Therefore in order to help you recall some of the necessary background theory, a brief review is brought here.

The notation $E(X)$ is the expected value of variable X. The expected value for the discrete random variable X which can take values of $x_1, x_2, ..., x_n$ is defined by Equation 18.13.

$$E[X] = \sum_{i=1}^{n} x_i p_i \qquad (18.13)$$

where p_i is the probability of the x_i.

The covariance of two variables x and y shows how these two variables change together and is calculated as Equation 18.14.

$$\sigma(x, y) = E[(x - E(x))(y - E(y))] \qquad (18.14)$$

For a vector X a covariance matrix is defined as:

$$\sigma(X, X) = E[(X - E(X))(X - E(X))^T] \qquad (18.15)$$

- The process noise, w_k, and measurement noise, v_k, are zero-mean, uncorrelated with known covariance matrices which are described from Equation 18.16 to Equation 18.20.

$$E[w_k] = 0 \qquad (18.16)$$

$$E[w_k w_j^T] = \begin{cases} Q_k & \text{if } k = j, \\ 0 & \text{if } k \neq j \end{cases} \qquad (18.17)$$

$$E[v_k] = 0 \tag{18.18}$$

$$E[v_k v_j^T] = \begin{cases} R_k & \text{if } k = j, \\ 0 & \text{if } k \neq j \end{cases} \tag{18.19}$$

$$E[w_k v_j^T] = 0 \qquad \text{for all k and j} \tag{18.20}$$

In a Kalman filter, it is assumed that the noise is Gaussian and has the normal distribution with zero mean. So the covariance is the only thing that needs to be calculated. R and Q are the covariance matrices of v_k and w_k, respectively. These matrices are diagonal matrices which means all the non-diagonal elements have zero value. The covariance matrix is a matrix whose elements are the variances of variables. For example, if the measurement noise vector, v_k , has m elements $v_1, v_2, ..., v_m$ and $\sigma_1^2, \sigma_2^2, ..., \sigma_m^2$ are the variances of each noise components, respectively, then covariance matrix R is calculated as Equation 18.21:

$$R = \begin{bmatrix} \sigma_1^2 & 0 & \cdots & 0 \\ 0 & \sigma_2^2 \cdots & 0 \\ \vdots & \vdots & \ddots & \vdots \\ 0 & 0 & \cdots & \sigma_m^2 \end{bmatrix} \tag{18.21}$$

As it was mentioned earlier, the prediction or time update is the first step of filter. The time update is responsible for predicting the state of the system and error covariance ahead in time. The state of the system is a vector that contains as elements the variables of interest. The results of this step are called "priori estimates." 18.22 and 18.23 are the two prediction equations:

$$\hat{x}_{k+1}^- = A.\hat{x}_k + B.u_k \tag{18.22}$$

$\hat{x}_{k+1}^-$ is the prediction of the system for the time $(k+1)$, while the system is at time k.

$$P_{k+1}^- = A.P_k.A^T + Q \tag{18.23}$$

At this step, the filter projects the error covariance estimates, P_{k+1}^-, from the time step k to the time step $(k+1)$.

At the correction step, the filter utilizes the result from the prediction step in combination with measurements received at time k to update its first prediction. The results of the measurement update step are called a "posteriori" estimates. At the beginning of the measurement update step the filter gain, which is called Kalman gain, K_k, is calculated as shown in Equation 18.24

$$K_k = P_k^- .H^T .(H.P_k^- .H^T + R)^{-1} \tag{18.24}$$

The Kalman gain is the variable weighting factor that is updated in each time step. It is used to update the state of the system, combining the new measurement, z_k, with the state prediction, $\hat{x}_k^-$, as shown in Equation 18.25:

$$\hat{x}_k = \hat{x}_k^- + K_k(z_k - H\hat{x}_k^-) \tag{18.25}$$

It can be seen, from Equation 18.25, that the corrected state of the system is the predicted state modified by a correction component. The correction component is correlated to the disparity between the predicted state and the measured state. The term $(z_k - H\hat{x}_k^-)$ is known as the measurement residual and indicates the discrepancy between the measurement of the system at time k and the prediction of the system for time k. The H is the matrix that relates the state of the system to the measurement.

The final step of the measurement update is the error covariance update. The error covariance reflects the degree of precision of the estimator. Larger error covariance indicates a larger estimator error and a small error covariance implies a small error in the estimation process. The error covariance is updated as shown in Equation 18.26:

$$P_k = (I - K_k H)P_k^- \tag{18.26}$$

As stated earlier, in the prediction step, the error covariance was predicted. Then in the correction step, the predicted error covariance was utilized to compute the Kalman gain. The recursive flow chart of the discrete Kalman filter is shown in Figure 18.2.

To summarize this discussion, to implement a Kalman filter for your system, you need to perform the following steps:

1. Extract the system equations.

2. Find A (state transition), H (observation), Q (process noise covariance), and R (measurement noise covariance) matrices.

3. Set initial values for the state vector and error covariance matrix.

4. Compute the Kalman gain.

5. Update the expected value of the state vector using measurements and Kalman gain.

6. Update the error covariance matrix.

7. Predict the state vector for the next time step.

8. Estimate the error covariance matrix for the next time step.

9. Loop to step 4.

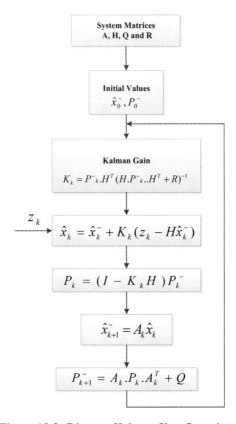

Figure 18.2: Discrete Kalman filter flow chart.

18.5   Extended Kalman Filters

As discussed earlier, the Kalman filter is a solution for linear systems that estimates the state of the system. The general Kalman filter cannot be considered as an appropriate approach when the dynamic or observation models are non-linear. Being restricted to the linear systems, the filter would not be applicable for the wide range of applications in which the system or observation models are non-linear. To be able to address the non-linear restriction of the Kalman filter algorithm, the extended Kalman filter was developed. The extended Kalman filter was developed by Stanley F. Schmidt. He applied this filter for processing the non-linear navigation equations for the Apollo project [Kleinbauer 04].

In the extended Kalman filter, the state and the observation models are describe by Equations 18.27 and 18.28:

$$x_{k+1} = f(x_k) + w_k \tag{18.27}$$

$$z_k = h(x_k) + v_k \tag{18.28}$$

where w_k and v_k represent the process and observation noises, respectively. Both noises have zero mean. In these equations, f is the non-linear function that projects the state at the previous time step to the current time step and h is the non-linear function that relates the state of the system to the measurement. Comparing Equations 18.27 and 18.28 with the Kalman filter state and observation equations, it can be observed that the linear matrix equations Ax_k and Hx_k have been substituted by the non-linear functions $f(x_k)$ and $h(x_k)$.

Similar to the general Kalman filter, the extended Kalman filter is a recursive predictor, which consists of two steps, including prediction (or time update) and correction (or measurement update). The algorithm for extended Kalman filter is similar to the Kalman filter algorithm with minor variations.

The time update equations for extended Kalman filter consist of prediction for state and error covariance as shown in Equations 18.29 and 18.30. Despite its similarity to the Kalman filter model, the matrix A in not seen directly in the Extended Kalman filter model. We should derive this matrix by linearizing the non-linear model.

$$\hat{x}_{k+1}^- = f(\hat{x}_k) \tag{18.29}$$

$$P_{k+1}^- = A.P_k.A^T + Q_k \tag{18.30}$$

Finally, the measurement update equations for the extended Kalman filter are shown in Equations 18.31, 18.32, and 18.33.

$$K_k = P_k^-.H_k^T.(H_k.P_k^-.H_k^T + R_k)^{-1} \tag{18.31}$$

$$\hat{x}_k = \hat{x}_k^- + K_k(z_k - H\hat{x}_k^-) \tag{18.32}$$

$$P_k = (I - K_k H_k)P_k^- \tag{18.33}$$

The matrix A and H are computed by linearizing the functions f and h, as shown in Equations 18.34 and 18.35, respectively.

$$A = \frac{\partial f}{\partial x} \big|_{x=\hat{x}_k} \tag{18.34}$$

$$H = \frac{\partial h}{\partial x} \big|_{x=\hat{x}_k} \tag{18.35}$$

Further Reading

Kalman filters can be difficult to model. It is our hope to expand this topic further in a different book (with a different take from what is currently available). Currently, the book *Kalman Filtering: Theory and Application* [Sorenson 85] discusses the model development in detail as well as exploratory data analysis to define the model structure. For additional information about Kalman filtering, see *Advanced Kalman Filtering, Least-Squares and Modeling: A Practical Handbook* [Gibbs 11]. A very complete book is *Fundamentals of Kalman Filtering: A Practical Approach* [Zarchman and Musoff 09]. Finally, additional books with MATLAB® exercises include *Introduction to Random Signals and Applied Kalman Filtering* [Brown and Hwang 12] and *Kalman Filter for Beginners with MATLAB® Examples* [Kim and Huh 11].

19

Quaternions and Sensor Fusion

The true portrait of a man is a fusion of what he thinks
he is, what others think he is, what he really is and
what he tries to be.

—Dore Schary

19.1   Introduction

In Section 19.1, sensor fusion and Kalman filters will be described using hand-motion tracking as the example. This chapter goes in depth on the use of quaternions and sensor fusion.

This chapter assumes that the MEMS has a gyroscope, accelerometer, and magnetometer sensors. Although the rotational motion can be computed by integrating gyroscope data, the results drift over time. The explanation for this phenomenon is that the integration accumulates the noise over time and turns noise into the drift, which yields unacceptable results. **Roll** and **pitch** rotations can be calculated using accelerometer data, but the results would be noisy. Furthermore, in order to measure rotation around the Z-axis (**yaw**), the other sensors need to be incorporated with the accelerometer. The magnetometer sensor can be used in cooperation with inertial sensors to measure the yaw angle.

Neither the accelerometer nor the gyroscope provides accurate rotation measurements alone. This is the reason, for implementing a sensor fusion algorithm in order to compensate for the weakness of each sensor by utilizing other sensors, as shown in Figure 19.1.

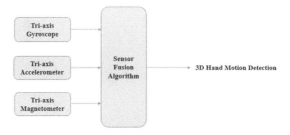

Figure 19.1: Sensor fusion for the Hand Motion Detection Project.

19.2   Quaternion-Based Kalman Filter

As described in Chapter 16, three-dimensional rotation can be represented using quaternions. In the case of the hand-motion tracking example, there are two frames including the Earth frame and the hand-fixed frame. If we called the Earth frame, frame A and the hand frame, frame B, the orientation of hand frame relative to Earth frame can be calculated through a rotation around vector $\vec{a}$ in Earth frame. These two reference frames are depicted in Figure 19.2.

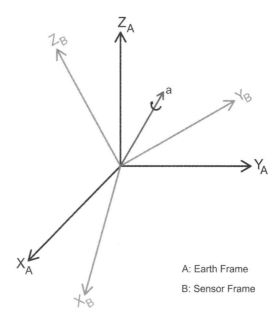

Figure 19.2: Hand and inertial reference frames.

The quaternion describing the orientation of frame B with respect to frame A is shown in Equation 19.1, where θ is the rotation angle around a vector defined in frame A. Then a_x, a_y, and a_z are components of a unit vector $\vec{r}$ in the Earth frame. Interestingly, the orientation of Earth frame (A) relative to the sensor frame (B) is the conjugate of the orientation of the sensor frame relative to the inertial frame. The conjugate is shown in Equation 19.2.

$$
{}^{B}_{A}\hat{q} = [q_0, q_1, q_2, q_3] = [\cos\frac{\theta}{2}, -a_x\sin\frac{\theta}{2}, -a_y\sin\frac{\theta}{2}, -a_z\sin\frac{\theta}{2}] \tag{19.1}
$$

$$
{}^{B}_{A}\hat{q} = {}^{A}_{B}\hat{q} = [q_0, -q_1, -q_2, -q_3] \tag{19.2}
$$

Another property of quaternions, used for indicating rotation, is expressing a compound quaternion as a quaternion product. For instance, for the orientations ${}^{B}_{A}\hat{q}$, the compound orientation is defined in Equation 19.3.

$$
{}^{B}_{A}\hat{q} = {}^{B}_{C}\hat{q} \otimes {}^{C}_{A}\hat{q} \tag{19.3}
$$

If v is a vector in frame A, this vector can be represented in coordinate frame B by rotating the vector about a quaternion q as shown in Equation 19.4. In this equation, vector $\vec{v}$ is written in quaternion form so that it contains zero for the first element as shown in Equation 19.5. The rotation matrix is defined in Equation 19.6.

$$
v_{rotated} = {}^{B}_{A}\hat{q} \otimes v \otimes {}^{A}_{B}\hat{q}^{*} \tag{19.4}
$$

$$
v = [0, v_x, v_y, v_z] \tag{19.5}
$$

$$
R_Q = \begin{bmatrix} 2q_0^2 - 1 + q_1^2 & 2(q_1 q_2 + q_0 q_3) & 2(q_1 q_3 - q_0 q_2) \\ 2(q_1 q_2 - q_0 q_3) & 2q_0^2 - 1 + q_2^2 & 2(q_3 q_2 + q_0 q_1) \\ 2(q_1 q_3 + q_0 q_2) & 2(q_2 q_3 - q_0 q_1) & 2q_0^2 - 1 + q_3^2 \end{bmatrix} \tag{19.6}
$$

19.2.1 Prediction Step

The tri-axis gyroscope data is used as an input for the prediction step. The gyroscope records the angular rate about x-, y-, and z-axis of the sensor frame. These angular rotation rates will be symbolized with w_x, w_y, and w_z notations. To represent the angular rate in quaternion format, the following vector is defined by Equation 19.7 [Suh 10]. The objective is to calculate the angular change in reference to the Earth frame using the angular rate in sensor frame representation. The equation describing the rate of change of orientation in the Earth's frame relative to the change in sensor frame, as shown in Equation 19.8, where, $^S_E\dot{q}$ is the rate of rotational change of the sensor frame relative to the Earth frame, and $^S_E\hat{q}$ is the normalized previous estimate of orientation.

$$\vec{w}_{Sensor} = \begin{bmatrix} 0 & w_x & w_y & w_z \end{bmatrix} \tag{19.7}$$

$$^S_E\dot{q} = (\frac{1}{2})^S_E\hat{q} \otimes w_{Sensor} \tag{19.8}$$

The rate of change of orientation in the sensor frame relative to the Earth frame at time t is calculated using Equation 19.9. By integrating the rotational variations, $^S_E\dot{q}_t$, over time the orientation of the sensor frame relative to Earth frame at time t is calculated using Equation 19.10, where Δt is the sampling period and the state of system is ^S_Eq. Having ^S_Eq as the state of the system, the equation can be rewritten as shown in Equation 19.11. Finally, the state transition matrix (A) is defined by Equation 19.12.

$$^S_E\dot{q}_t = (\frac{1}{2})^S_E\hat{q}_{t-1} \otimes w_{Sensor_t} \tag{19.9}$$

:

$$^S_Eq_t = ^S_E\hat{q}_{t-1} + ^S_E\dot{q}_t\Delta t \tag{19.10}$$

$$x_t = x_{t-1} + ^S_E\dot{q}_t\Delta t = A.x_{t-1} \tag{19.11}$$

$$A = \begin{bmatrix} 1 & -\frac{1}{2}.\Delta t.w_x & -\frac{1}{2}.\Delta t.w_y & -\frac{1}{2}.\Delta t.w_z \\ \frac{1}{2}.\Delta t.w_x & 1 & \frac{1}{2}.\Delta t.w_z & -\frac{1}{2}.\Delta t.w_y \\ \frac{1}{2}.\Delta t.w_y & -\frac{1}{2}.\Delta t.w_z & 1 & \frac{1}{2}.\Delta t.w_x \\ \frac{1}{2}.\Delta t.w_z & \frac{1}{2}.\Delta t.w_y & -\frac{1}{2}.\Delta t.w_x & 1 \end{bmatrix} \tag{19.12}$$

Process Noise Covariance Matrix

To describe the process noise, the covariance matrix of the input vector can be calculated using Equation 19.13. For the vector $\vec{X}$, the covariance matrix which is a 4×4 diagonal matrix is calculated as shown in Equation 19.14.

$$\vec{X} = \begin{bmatrix} 0 \\ w_x \\ w_y \\ w_z \end{bmatrix} = \begin{bmatrix} x_1 \\ x_2 \\ x_3 \\ x_4 \end{bmatrix} \tag{19.13}$$

$$Q = E((X - E(X))(X - E(X))^T) \tag{19.14}$$

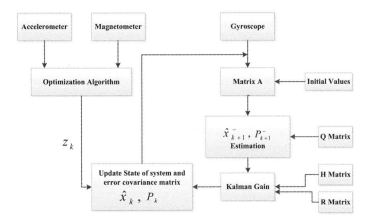

Figure 19.3: Discrete Kalman filter block diagram.

19.2.2 Correction Step

The sensor unit records nine-dimensional data from the gyroscope, the magnetometer, and the accelerometer. If the nine-dimensional data is used as an observation vector, the measurement equation would be non-linear and a heavy computational process would be needed. Therefore, it was suggested [Yun et al. 03] that just data recorded by the accelerometer and the magnetometer be used as observation data to determine the orientation. The quaternion vector which corresponds to the orientation of the sensor frame relative to the Earth frame is calculated using accelerometer and magnetometer data.

The magnetometer records the direction and magnitude of Earth's magnetic field and the accelerometer measures the gravity direction in the sensor reference frame. The orientation of the sensor frame relative to the Earth frame can be extracted using the recorded field's direction in the sensor frame. However for any sensor measurement, an unique sensor's orientation cannot be obtained. It is necessary to compute a unique true quaternion orientation to be used as the observation vector in the Kalman filter. To obtain such a quaternion, use optimization algorithms [Madgwick et al. 11]. In this research two optimization algorithms: gradient descent optimization and Gauss–Newton optimization methods, were chosen to calculate the quaternion vector from accelerometer and magnetometer data. Figure 19.3 depicts the block diagram for the quaternion-based Kalman filter using an optimization algorithm to calculate the observation vector.

19.2.3 Observation Vector Using Gradient Descent Optimization

Gradient descent is an optimization algorithm to find a local minimum of functions. This algorithm starts with an initial value of the solution and iteratively moves to values that minimize the cost function.

In our case, the process seeks an optimized solution for the orientation of the sensor relative to Earth frame, $_E^S\hat{q}$, using a predefined direction of Earth field $^E\hat{d}$, and the field direction measured in the sensor frame $^S\hat{S}$, as defined by Equation 19.15, where the objective function is described by Equation 19.16. The vectors $^E\hat{d}$ and $^S\hat{S}$ and $_E^S\hat{q}$ are defined in Equations 19.17, 19.18, and 19.19. Using these three vectors on the equations just mentioned, the function f is defined by Equation 19.20.

$$min f(_E^S\hat{q}, ^E\hat{d}, ^S\hat{S}) \tag{19.15}$$

$$f(_E^S\hat{q}, ^E\hat{d}, ^S\hat{S}) = _E^S\hat{q}^* \otimes ^E\hat{d} \otimes _E^S\hat{q} - ^S\hat{S} \tag{19.16}$$

$$^E\hat{d} = \begin{bmatrix} 0 & d_x & d_y & d_z \end{bmatrix} \tag{19.17}$$

$$^S\hat{S} = \begin{bmatrix} 0 & s_x & s_y & s_z \end{bmatrix} \tag{19.18}$$

$$_E^S\hat{q} = \begin{bmatrix} q_1 & q_2 & q_3 & q_4 \end{bmatrix} \tag{19.19}$$

$$f(_E^S\hat{q}, ^E\hat{d}, ^S\hat{S}) = \begin{bmatrix} 2d_x(\frac{1}{2} - q_3^2 - q_4^2) + 2d_y(q_1q_4 + q_2q_3) + 2d_z(q_2q_4 - q_1q_3) - s_x \\ 2d_x(q_2q_3 - q_1q_4) + 2d_y(\frac{1}{2} - q_2^2 - q_4^2) + 2d_z(q_1q_2 + q_4q_3) - s_y \\ 2d_x(q_1q_3 + q_2q_4) + 2d_y(q_3q_4 - q_1q_2) + 2d_z(\frac{1}{2} - q_2^2 - q_3^2) - s_z \end{bmatrix} \tag{19.20}$$

The gradient descent algorithm for the n iteration is defined by Equation 19.21, where μ is the adaptation step size and $_E^S\hat{q}_0$ is the initial value for orientation. The gradient of surface representing the objective function is defined by Equations 19.22 and 19.23.

$$_E^S q_{k+1} = _E^S\hat{q}_k - \mu \frac{\nabla f(_E^S\hat{q}, ^E\hat{d}, ^S\hat{S})}{\|f(_E^S\hat{q}, ^E\hat{d}, ^S\hat{S})\|}, k = 0, 1, 2, ..., n \tag{19.21}$$

$$\nabla f(_E^S\hat{q}, ^E\hat{d}, ^S\hat{S}) = J^T(_E^S\hat{q}, ^E\hat{d}) f(_E^S\hat{q}, ^E\hat{d}, ^S\hat{S}) \tag{19.22}$$

$$
J(^S_E\hat{q},{}^E\hat{d}) =
\begin{bmatrix}
2d_yq_4 - 2d_zq_3 & 2d_yq_3 + 2d_zq_4 & -4d_xq_3 + 2d_yq_2 - 2d_zq_1 \\
-2d_xq_4 + 2d_zq_2 & 2d_xq_3 - 4d_yq_2 + 2d_zq_1 & 2d_xq_2 + 2d_zq_4 \\
2d_xq_3 - 2d_yq_2 & 2d_xq_4 - 2d_yq_1 - 4d_zq_2 & 2d_xq_1 + 2d_yq_4 - 4d_zq_3
\end{bmatrix}
$$

$$
\begin{matrix}
-4d_xq_4 + 2d_yq_1 + 2d_zq_2 \\
-2d_xq_1 - 4d_yq_4 + 2d_zq_3 \\
2d_xq_2 + 2d_yq_3
\end{matrix}
$$

$$(19.23)$$

The step-size μ is defined by Equation 19.24, where $^S_E\dot{q}_{w,t}$ is the rotation rate calculated using gyroscope measurements, Δt is the sampling rate.

$$
\mu_t = \alpha \left\| {}^S_E\dot{q}_{w,t} \right\| \Delta t, \alpha > 1 \tag{19.24}
$$

The objective function f, and the Jacobian J can be simplified if it is defined that the direction of field has components only in one or two axes of the Earth frame. In utilized sensor unit, the gravity vector in Earth frame can be defined by Equation 19.25 and the accelerometer vector in the sensor frame is defined by Equation 19.26. Then the objective function f, and the Jacobian J can be rewritten as shown in Equations 19.27 and 19.28, respectively.

$$
{}^E\hat{g} = \begin{bmatrix} 0 & 0 & 1 & 0 \end{bmatrix} \tag{19.25}
$$

$$
{}^S\hat{accel} = \begin{bmatrix} 0 & a_x & a_y & a_z \end{bmatrix} \tag{19.26}
$$

$$
f_g({}^S_E\hat{q},{}^S\hat{accel}) =
\begin{bmatrix}
2(q_1q_4 + q_2q_3) - a_x \\
2(0.5 - (q_2)^2 - (q_4)^2) - a_y \\
2(q_3q_4 - q_1q_2) - a_z
\end{bmatrix}
\tag{19.27}
$$

$$
J_g({}^S_E\hat{q},{}^E\hat{g}) =
\begin{bmatrix}
2q_4 & 2q_3 & 2q_2 & 2q_1 \\
0 & -4q_2 & 0 & -4q_4 \\
-2q_2 & -2q_1 & 2q_4 & 2q_3
\end{bmatrix}
\tag{19.28}
$$

The magnetic vector in the Earth frame can be described by Equation 19.29. The magnetometer measurement vector in the sensor frame is represented by Equation 19.30. Then using these two vectors, the f and J can be written as shown by Equations 19.31 and 19.32, respectively.

$$
{}^E\hat{mag} = \begin{bmatrix} 0 & 0 & b_y & b_z \end{bmatrix} \tag{19.29}
$$

$$
{}^S\hat{mag} = \begin{bmatrix} 0 & m_x & m_y & m_z \end{bmatrix} \tag{19.30}
$$

$$f(_E^S\hat{q},{}^E b,{}^S m\hat{a}g) = \begin{bmatrix} 2b_y(q_1q_4 + q_2q_3) + 2b_z(q_2q_4 - q_1q_3) - m_x \\ 2b_y(0.5 - (q_2^2) - (q_4^2)) + 2b_z(q_1q_2 + q_3q_4) - m_y \\ 2b_y(q_3q_4 - q_1q_2) + 2b_z(0.5 - (q_2^2) - (q_3^2)) - m_z \end{bmatrix} \quad (19.31)$$

$$J(_E^S\hat{q},{}^E b) = \begin{bmatrix} 2b_yq_4 - 2b_zq_3 & 2b_yq_3 + 2b_zq_4 & 2b_yq_2 - 2b_zq_1 \\ 2b_zq_2 & -4b_yq_2 + 2b_zq_1 & 2b_zq_4 \\ -2b_yq_2 & -2b_yq_1 - 4b_zq_2 & 2b_yq_4 - 4b_zq_3 \end{bmatrix}$$
$$\begin{bmatrix} 2b_yq_1 + 2b_zq_2 \\ -4b_yq_4 + 2b_zq_3 \\ 2b_yq_3 \end{bmatrix} \quad (19.32)$$

Neither the accelerometer measurements nor the magnetometer measurements can provide the unique attitude. To achieve a unique orientation, both measurements and references should be combined as shown by Equation 19.33.

$$f_{g,b}(_E^S\hat{q},{}^S a\hat{c}cel,{}^E m\hat{a}g,{}^s m\hat{a}g) = \begin{bmatrix} f_g(_E^S\hat{q},{}^S a\hat{c}cel) \\ f_b(_E^S\hat{q},{}^E m\hat{a}g,{}^S m\hat{a}g) \end{bmatrix} \quad (19.33)$$

$$Jg,b(_E^S\hat{q},{}^E m\hat{a}g) = \begin{bmatrix} J_g^T(_E^S\hat{q}) \\ J_b^T(_E^S\hat{q},{}^E m\hat{a}g) \end{bmatrix} \quad (19.34)$$

19.2.4   Observation Vector Determination Using Gauss–Newton Method

The Gauss–Newton algorithm is a technique for solving non-linear least square problems. In this case, the Gauss–Newton algorithm is used to minimize the cost function which is defined by the differences between the known gravitational and Earth magnetic vectors and the sensors (accelerometer and magnetometer) readings transformed to the Earth frame.

The data from the accelerometer and the magnetometer are used as observation vectors. The accelerometer and magnetometer vectors in the body frame are symbolized as shown by Equation 19.35 and 19.36. The same acceleration and magnetic vectors in the Earth frame are represented by Equations 19.37 and 19.38. Combining the two vectors in each reference frame, the following measurement vectors are constructed, as shown by Equations 19.39 and 19.40. The rotation matrix that rotates the body vector to the Earth vector, in quaternion form, is defined by Equation 19.41, where matrix M is described by Equation 19.42.

$$A_{Body} = (a_{xb}, a_{yb}, a_{zb}) \quad (19.35)$$

$$M_{Body} = (m_{xb}, m_{yb}, m_{zb}) \quad (19.36)$$

$$A_{Earth} = (0, g, 0) \tag{19.37}$$

$$M_{Earth} = (m_{xE}, m_{yE}, m_{zE}) \tag{19.38}$$

$$y_{Earth} = (0, g, 0, m_{xE}, m_{yE}, m_{zE}) \tag{19.39}$$

$$y_{Body} = (a_{xb}, a_{yb}, a_{zb}, m_{xb}, m_{yb}, m_{zb}) \tag{19.40}$$

$$R_t = \begin{bmatrix} M_t & 0 \\ 0 & M_t \end{bmatrix} \tag{19.41}$$

$$M_t = \begin{bmatrix} q_4^2 + q_1^2 - q_2^2 - q_3^2 & 2(q_1 q_2 - q_3 q_4) & 2(q_1 q_3 + q_2 q_4) \\ 2(q_1 q_2 + q_3 q_4) & q_4^2 + q_2^2 - q_1^2 - q_3^2 & 2(q_2 q_3 - q_4 q_1) \\ 2(q_1 q_3 - q_2 q_4) & 2(q_3 q_2 + q_1 q_4) & q_4^2 + q_3^2 - q_1^2 - q_2^2 \end{bmatrix} \tag{19.42}$$

The Gauss–Newton optimization method is used to minimize discrepancies between actual and computed measurement vectors as shown by Equation 19.43. The Gauss–Newton method executes the iteration defined by Equation 19.44. Where J_k is the Jacobian of ε calculated in q_k and is calculated using Equation 19.45. The computed Jacobian matrix computed is shown by Equation 19.46.

$$\varepsilon = y_{Earth} - R_t . y_{Body} \tag{19.43}$$

$$q_t = q_{t-1} - (J_t^T . J_t)^{-1} . J_t^T . \varepsilon \tag{19.44}$$

$$J_t(q_k(t)) = \frac{\partial(\varepsilon)}{\partial(q_k(t))} = -[(\frac{\partial R}{\partial q_1} . y_{Body(t)})(\frac{\partial R}{\partial q_2} . y_{Body(t)})(\frac{\partial R}{\partial q_3} . y_{Body(t)})$$

$$(\frac{\partial R}{\partial q_4}) . y_{Body(t)}] \tag{19.45}$$

$$J_t(q_k(t)) = -2 \begin{bmatrix} (q_1 a_{xb} + q_2 a_{yb} + q_3 a_{zb}) & (-q_2 a_{xb} + q_1 a_{yb} + q_4 a_{zb}) \\ (q_2 a_{xb} - q_1 a_{yb} - q_4 a_{zb}) & (q_1 a_{xb} + q_2 a_{yb} + q_3 a_{zb}) \\ (q_3 a_{xb} + q_4 a_{yb} - q_1 a_{zb}) & (-q_4 a_{xb} + q_3 a_{yb} - q_2 a_{zb}) \\ (q_1 m_{xb} + q + 2 m_{yb} + q_3 m_{zb}) & (-q_2 m_{xb} + q_1 m_{yb} + q_4 m_{zb}) \\ (q_2 m_{xb} - q_1 m_{yb} - q_4 m_{zb}) & (q_1 m_{xb} + q_2 m_{yb} + q_3 m_{zb}) \\ (q_3 m_{xb} + q_4 m_{yb} - q_1 m_{zb}) & (-q_4 m_{xb} + q_3 m_{yb} - q_2 m_{zb}) \end{bmatrix}$$

$$\begin{bmatrix} (-q_3 a_{xb} - q_4 a_{yb} + q_1 a_{zb}) & (q_4 a_{xb} - q_3 a_{yb} + q_2 a_{zb}) \\ (q_4 a_{xb} - q_3 a_{yb} + q_2 a_{zb}) & (q_3 a_{xb} + q_4 a_{yb} - q_1 a_{zb}) \\ (q_1 a_{xb} + q_2 a_{yb} + q_3 a_{zb}) & (-q_2 a_{xb} + q_1 a_{yb} + q_4 a_{zb}) \\ (-q_3 m_{xb} - q_4 m_{yb} + q_1 m_{zb}) & (q_4 m_{xb} - q_3 m_{yb} + q_2 m_{zb}) \\ (q_4 m_{xb} - q_3 m_{yb} + q_2 m_{zb}) & (q_3 m_{xb} + q_4 m_{yb} - q_1 m_{zb}) \\ (q_1 m_{xb} + q_2 m_{yb} + q_3 m_{zb}) & (-q_2 m_{xb} + q_1 m_{yb} + q_4 m_{zb}) \end{bmatrix} \tag{19.46}$$

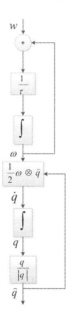

Figure 19.4: Filter process model.

19.3   Quaternion-Based Extended Kalman Filter

The system model for implementing the quaternion-based extended Kalman filter is designed based on the approach proposed in [Yun and Bachmann 06]. The process model is depicted in Figure 19.4.

The state vector consists of three angular rate components and four quaternion components as shown in Equation 19.47. According to the process model, there are seven system equations, of which the first three equations are defined by Equations 19.48, 19.49, and 19.50, where τ is the time constant and λ_x, λ_y, and λ_z are white noises. The other four system equations are defined by Equations 19.52, 19.53, 19.54, and 19.55.

$$\hat{x} = \begin{bmatrix} w_x \\ w_y \\ w_z \\ q_1 \\ q_2 \\ q_3 \\ q_4 \end{bmatrix} = \begin{bmatrix} x_1 \\ x_2 \\ x_3 \\ x_4 \\ x_5 \\ x_6 \\ x_7 \end{bmatrix} \qquad (19.47)$$

$$\dot{w}_x = -\frac{1}{\tau}w_x + \frac{\lambda_x}{\tau} \tag{19.48}$$

$$\dot{w}_y = -\frac{1}{\tau}w_y + \frac{\lambda_y}{\tau} \tag{19.49}$$

$$\dot{w}_z = -\frac{1}{\tau}w_z + \frac{\lambda_z}{\tau} \tag{19.50}$$

$$\begin{bmatrix} \dot{q}_1 \\ \dot{q}_2 \\ \dot{q}_3 \\ \dot{q}_4 \end{bmatrix} = \frac{1}{2}\begin{bmatrix} q_1 \\ q_2 \\ q_3 \\ q_4 \end{bmatrix} \otimes \begin{bmatrix} 0 \\ w_x \\ w_y \\ w_z \end{bmatrix} \tag{19.51}$$

$$\dot{q}_1 = -\frac{1}{2}(w_x q_2 + w_y q_3 + w_z q_4) \tag{19.52}$$

$$\dot{q}_2 = \frac{1}{2}(w_x q_1 - w_y q_4 + w_z q_3) \tag{19.53}$$

$$\dot{q}_3 = \frac{1}{2}(w_x q_4 + w_y q_1 - w_z q_2) \tag{19.54}$$

$$\dot{q}_4 = \frac{1}{2}(-w_x q_3 + w_y q_2 + w_z q_1) \tag{19.55}$$

The non-linear process model should be linearized and then discretized through the following steps:

$$\Delta\dot{x} = \frac{\partial f(x)}{\partial x}\Big|_{x=\hat{x}} + \lambda(t) \tag{19.56}$$

$$\Delta x_{k+1} = A\Delta x_k + \lambda_k \tag{19.57}$$

where λ_k is the 7×1 discrete white noise vector defined as:

$$\lambda_{ik} = \begin{cases} \int_{t_k}^{t_{k+1}} e^{-\frac{t_{k+1}-\gamma}{\tau}}\lambda_i(\gamma)d\gamma & i = 1,2,3 \\ 0 & i = 4,5,6,7. \end{cases} \tag{19.58}$$

and A represents the state transition matrix as:

$$A = \begin{bmatrix} e^{-\frac{\Delta t}{\tau}} & 0 & 0 & 0 & 0 & 0 & 0 \\ 0 & e^{-\frac{\Delta t}{\tau}} & 0 & 0 & 0 & 0 & 0 \\ 0 & 0 & e^{-\frac{\Delta t}{\tau}} & 0 & 0 & 0 & 0 \\ -\frac{\hat{x}_5\Delta t}{2} & -\frac{\hat{x}_6\Delta t}{2} & -\frac{\hat{x}_7\Delta t}{2} & 1 & -\frac{\hat{x}_1\Delta t}{2} & -\frac{\hat{x}_2\Delta t}{2} & -\frac{\hat{x}_3\Delta t}{2} \\ -\frac{\hat{x}_4\Delta t}{2} & -\frac{\hat{x}_7\Delta t}{2} & -\frac{\hat{x}_6\Delta t}{2} & -\frac{\hat{x}_1\Delta t}{2} & 1 & -\frac{\hat{x}_3\Delta t}{2} & -\frac{\hat{x}_2\Delta t}{2} \\ -\frac{\hat{x}_7\Delta t}{2} & -\frac{\hat{x}_4\Delta t}{2} & -\frac{\hat{x}_5\Delta t}{2} & -\frac{\hat{x}_2\Delta t}{2} & -\frac{\hat{x}_3\Delta t}{2} & 1 & -\frac{\hat{x}_1\Delta t}{2} \\ -\frac{\hat{x}_6\Delta t}{2} & -\frac{\hat{x}_5\Delta t}{2} & -\frac{\hat{x}_4\Delta t}{2} & -\frac{\hat{x}_3\Delta t}{2} & -\frac{\hat{x}_2\Delta t}{2} & -\frac{\hat{x}_1\Delta t}{2} & 1 \end{bmatrix} \tag{19.59}$$

19.3.1 Measurement Process

The gyroscope, magnetometer, and accelerometer provide a nine-dimensional vector of measurements. If this vector is given directly to the filter as an observation vector, the measurement equations will be non-linear and consequently the filter computational process will be complicated. To simplify the process just the magnetometer and accelerometer data are used to compute the corresponding quaternion. The QUEST algorithm is used for quaternion vector computation. The computed quaternion vector and the gyroscope data are used as the observation vector, which produces linear measurement equations. The discrete measurement equation is:

$$Z_k = H.x_k + v_k \tag{19.60}$$

The observation matrix is given by:

$$H = \begin{bmatrix} 1 & 0 & 0 & 0 & 0 & 0 & 0 \\ 0 & 1 & 0 & 0 & 0 & 0 & 0 \\ 0 & 0 & 1 & 0 & 0 & 0 & 0 \\ 0 & 0 & 0 & 1 & 0 & 0 & 0 \\ 0 & 0 & 0 & 0 & 1 & 0 & 0 \\ 0 & 0 & 0 & 0 & 0 & 1 & 0 \\ 0 & 0 & 0 & 0 & 0 & 0 & 1 \end{bmatrix} \tag{19.61}$$

Process Noise Covariance Matrix

As was described earlier, the process noise covariance matrix is calculated as:

$$Q_i = E[\lambda(t_i)\lambda(t_i)^T] \tag{19.62}$$

$$Q_i = \begin{cases} \sigma_k \delta(t - \tau) & k = j \\ 0 & k \neq j. \end{cases} \tag{19.63}$$

where λ is white, E is the expectation operator, and δ is discrete white noise variance from the system equations. Matrix Q is given as:

$$Q_i = \begin{bmatrix} N_1 & 0 & 0 & 0 & 0 & 0 & 0 \\ 0 & N_2 & 0 & 0 & 0 & 0 & 0 \\ 0 & 0 & N_3 & 0 & 0 & 0 & 0 \\ 0 & 0 & 0 & 0 & 0 & 0 & 0 \\ 0 & 0 & 0 & 0 & 0 & 0 & 0 \\ 0 & 0 & 0 & 0 & 0 & 0 & 0 \\ 0 & 0 & 0 & 0 & 0 & 0 & 0 \end{bmatrix} \tag{19.64}$$

N_1, N_2, and N_3 are calculated as:

$$N_1 = \frac{\sigma_1}{2\tau}\left(1 - e^{-\frac{2\Delta t}{\tau}}\right) \tag{19.65}$$

$$N_2 = \frac{\sigma_2}{2\tau}(1 - e^{-\frac{2\Delta t}{\tau}})$$ (19.66)

$$N_3 = \frac{\sigma_3}{2\tau}(1 - e^{-\frac{2\Delta t}{\tau}})$$ (19.67)

where; σ is the white noise variance and τ is the time constant of the process model.

Measurement Noise Covariance Matrix

The measurement noise covariance matrix is defined as:

$$R_i = E[v(t_k)v(t_k)^T] = \begin{bmatrix} r_1 & 0 & 0 & 0 & 0 & 0 & 0 \\ 0 & r_2 & 0 & 0 & 0 & 0 & 0 \\ 0 & 0 & r_3 & 0 & 0 & 0 & 0 \\ 0 & 0 & 0 & r_4 & 0 & 0 & 0 \\ 0 & 0 & 0 & 0 & r_5 & 0 & 0 \\ 0 & 0 & 0 & 0 & 0 & r_6 & 0 \\ 0 & 0 & 0 & 0 & 0 & 0 & r_7 \end{bmatrix}$$ (19.68)

The values of r_1 to r_7 can be found experimentally.

19.4   Conversion between Euler and Quaternion

The quaternion result computed by the sensor fusion algorithm can be converted to the Euler form as:

$$\phi = \arctan(\frac{2q_1q_2 - 2q_0q_3}{2q_0^2 + 2q_1^2 - 1})$$ (19.69)

$$\theta = -\arcsin(2q_1q_3 + 2q_0q_2)$$ (19.70)

$$\psi = \arctan(\frac{2q_3q_2 - 2q_0q_1}{2q_0^2 + 2q_1^3 - 1})$$ (19.71)

Further Reading

For further information about computing rotational data from inertial and magnetic sensors see "An efficient orientation filter for inertial and inertial/magnetic sensor arrays" [Madgwick 10]. For quaternions, see [Dunn and Parberry 11, Hanson 06].

Part III

Hands-On

20

Hands-On: Inertial Sensors for 3D Input

Paul W. Yost

Do not go where the path may lead, go instead where there is no path and leave a trail.
—Ralph Waldo Emerson

20.1 Introduction

Input devices provide a means of getting data into a computer system so that it may be subsequently used to control some aspect of either the system itself or an application running on that system. Human interface devices (HID) are the most common type of input device and, as the name implies, are used to enable the actions of a human operator to control some aspect of the system or application. Examples of HID devices include mice, keyboards, and joysticks. It should be noted that each of these devices, in their most general form, simply allow a human action to be sensed, communicated to the system, and used by that system in some way. This form holds true regardless of the specific human action being taken, the specific method of sensing that action, the specific communication methods involved, or the end-use of that action within the system. Thus, any human interface device follows the general form:

**human action → sensing device → communication → system input →
application/end-use action**

This can be simplified and abstracted by removing some of the middle details to:

human action → human interface device → application/end-use action

From this diagram it is clear that human interface devices are simply a way of translating human action into corresponding system actions. As we will see in this chapter the input can be as simple as a single action or as complex as full-body actions and gestures.

This chapter will look at the general concept of sensing human motions and using those motions in a variety of ways with a specific focus on using inertial sensor technology for input. The chapter will also provide a practical hands-on look at YEI Technology's 3-Space Sensor devices and PrioVR full-body motion sensing suits.

20.2   Motion Sensing and Motion Capture

Anyone who has seen the 2002 science fiction movie "Minority Report" is likely to remember the scene where Captain John Anderton (played by Tom Cruise) controls the PreCrime computer systems by using only his hands and body. In the film, Captain Anderton sorts through the voluminous onslaught of complex information that is streaming from the PreCogs, mutated humans with special precognitive abilities, by using a variety of body motions, poses, and gestures in a way that seems both fluid and intuitively efficient. While the movie is a work of futuristic science fiction and PreCogs are most certainly not real, some might find it surprising that technologies that enable the type of whole-body motion sensing interface depicted in the movie are not only real, but readily available and becoming increasingly inexpensive. It is also interesting to note that motion sensing technology is often used as part of the movie making process itself. The use of full-body human motion capture technology combined with computer generated characters and digital animation have become an integral part of the film making process.

Both motion sensing and motion capture systems have, at their core, the same concept: sensing movements and using them for some purpose. Since there are some subtle differences in the terms, it will be helpful to define them a bit more precisely.

20.2.1   Motion Sensing

Motion sensing systems are generally considered to be systems that use movement as a direct input source that causes an immediate action to be taken within the system. This could be as simple as a single sensor that triggers an action such as a "wake-up function" or as complex as tracking a sequence of movements using multiple sensors for pointing applications, the recognition of gestures, or full-body motion and pose tracking. Regardless of the complexity of use, it is important to note that motion sensing systems are generally considered to be used for applications that require real-time motion input.

20.2.2   Motion Capture

Motion capture systems, also called mo-cap or mocap systems, are generally considered to be systems that record movement for use as an indirect input source that may be part of a non-real-time process. Examples here would be recording the movements of an actor for later use in rendering a computer generated actor or the recording of the movements of an athlete for later performance analysis. Motion capture systems are generally used to track and record the movements of human performers. A recorded motion capture performance is called a mocap session. It is important to note that motion capture involves the recording of human movements and may be used for either real-time or non-real-time applications.

20.3   Types of Motion Sensing Technology

Currently available motion sensing and motion capture systems can be based upon one or more base technologies. Although the goal of each of the base technologies is the same, each has specific properties and limitations. This section gives a brief overview of each base technology along with a list of advantages and disadvantages for each.

20.3.1   Marker-Based Optical Systems

Optical motion capture systems collect data from one or more image sensors and use this data to attempt to calculate the position and movement of the objects or entities being tracked. There are several ways that this can be achieved, but each optical system, by nature, involves a defined special capture area that is outfitted with one or more fixed image sensors. To achieve large capture areas, capture multiple actors, or capture more data points, additional image sensors are needed and additional processing power is often required to handle the large volume of image data that results. Form-fitting suits with special markers attached are worn by performers to allow the optical tracking of specific points of interest. The attached markers can be either passive markers that reflect light or active markers that produce coded/synchronized/modulated light.

Passive optical systems generally use suits of dark colored form-fitting fabric along with special markers that are coated with retro-reflective material. The imaging cameras usually have a light-source located around or near each imaging camera which causes the light from the camera to strike the retro-reflective material of the markers and be reflected back to each imaging camera. This configuration makes it easier to discern and track just the markers within each image frame. In order to determine the position and motion of the markers, multiple imaging cameras must be used along with multiple-point triangulation algorithms. The recorded data is often in the form of point-cloud data that requires extensive processing and constraint-based filtering to clean-up the data so that marker ambiguity, marker swapping, and marker occlusion effects are minimized.

Active optical systems use suits outfitted with special powered markers that contain electronics and an LED light source. By illuminating each marker one-at-a-time or by individually modulating each marker in a unique way, it is possible to determine the identity and location of each individual marker by processing the image data from multiple cameras and using triangulation algorithms. Active marker systems require much less computationally intensive algorithms than passive marker systems since each marker can be uniquely identified. As such, active systems don't suffer from marker ambiguity or marker swapping, but marker occlusion can still be problematic.

Advantages	Disadvantages
• Positionally accurate when calibrated • Capable of high performance • Allow for flexible use	• High latency • Not easily usable for real-time applications • Must maintain line-of-sight • Multiple performers can be problematic • Limited capture space • Expensive • Possibility of errors due to sensor swapping

20.3.2   Marker-Less Optical Systems

Marker-less optical systems don't require suits with special markers and may use a variety of technologies to extract the pose of the performer. Generally these systems use either multiple imaging cameras or a combination of an imaging camera and a depth-camera. The data from these sources is then processed using a probabilistic approach to extract a best-guess pose given the data available. The most familiar and widely deployed marker-less motion capture system is the Microsoft Kinect. Marker-less systems require significant processing resources and tend to have lower accuracy than marker-based systems due to increased ambiguity caused by the lack of markers and the probabilistic nature of the pose extraction algorithms themselves.

Advantages	Disadvantages
• Positionally accurate under ideal circumstances • Ease of set-up and use • No suit required	• High latency • Special capture space required • Must maintain line-of-sight • Limited capture space • Multiple performers can be problematic • Limited pose / capture possibilities due to nature of processing • Possibilities of errors due to probabilistic nature of processing

20.3.3 Mechanical Systems

Mechanical motion capture systems generally use a mechanical exoskeleton structure that contains potentiometers or other angular position sensing technology to directly measure the joint angles of a performer. As the performer moves, the exoskeleton moves with them and the joint angle sensors track the movements in real-time. These movements can be recorded or reported in real-time using either wireless communication or tethered wired communication. Mechanical motion capture systems don't suffer from the occlusion, line of sight, limited capture volume, or high latency problems associated with optical systems, but they can, due to the exoskeleton itself, impose restrictions on the types of motion that can be performed and tracked.

Advantages	**Disadvantages**
• Low-latency	• Positional errors possible
• Doesn't require line-of-sight	• Limited pose / capture possibilities due to exoskeleton.
• Unlimited capture space	• Cumbersome to set-up.
• Easily supports multiple performers	• No global reference-frame

20.3.4   Magnetic Systems

Magnetic motion capture systems use a fixed magnetic transmitter that consists of three orthogonal magnetic source coils and trackers consisting of three orthogonal sensor coils. The source coils are excited in a sequential pattern that, in turn, is sensed by the coils within the tracker. This produces a sequence of vectors that allows the tracker to compute both its position and orientation relative to that of the fixed transmitter. Since magnetic tracking relies upon this magnetic coupling effect, the capture volumes are generally much smaller than those associated with optical systems and may suffer from accuracy due to both non-linear sensor response near the edges of the capture volume and the affects of ferrous materials or other magnetic sources in or near the capture space.

Advantages	**Disadvantages**
• Low-latency	• Highly limited capture space
• Doesn't require line-of-sight	• Multiple performers not easily supported
• Positional and rotational accuracy	• Errors possible due to limited capture space
	• Errors possible due to magnetic interference

20.3.5   Inertial Systems

Inertial motion capture systems use miniature inertial sensors along with sensor fusion algorithms and filtering algorithms to compute the orientation of the tracker. Some inertial trackers use a 3-axis accelerometer along with a 3-axis gyroscope to compute the orientation. These are called six degree-of-freedom trackers (6-DOF) due to the use of 6 sensing elements and may suffer from accumulating error in the yaw orientation due to drift of the gyroscope over time. More advanced inertial trackers, such as the YEI 3-Space Sensor family of products, add a 3-axis magnetometer to the tracker to eliminate error caused by gyroscopic drift. These are called 9 degree-of-freedom (9-DOF) trackers and they effectively can produce an orientation that is highly accurate and drift free in global-space by using the accelerometer and magnetic north vector to act as external references that work to eliminate the accumulation of gyroscopic drift. Special sensor fusion algorithms work to allow the gyroscope to maintain accuracy during quick movements while using the other sensors to remove orientation drift. The end result is a sensor capable of sensing orientation accurately without drift, even under highly dynamic conditions. By outfitting a performer with inertial trackers, the pose of the performer may be accurately determined in real-time. The sensed pose and movements of the performer may also be used, along with a skeletal model, to compute the relative positions of each tracker.

Inertial systems are self-contained and require no cameras, or other external references, can have unlimited capture volumes, are low-latency, can have zero orientation drift, and can directly measure both the pose and movements of the performer. Inertial tracking has the disadvantages of the possibility of accumulating positional error in the global reference and, when 9-DOF trackers are used, being susceptible to errors caused by magnetic perturbation.

Advantages	Disadvantages
• Low-latency	• Relative positional errors possible due to avatar / performer proportion mismatch.
• Doesn't require line-of-sight	
• Rotational accuracy	• Global avatar positional errors may be accumulated due to integration
• Unlimited capture space	
• Orientations are accurate within global reference-frame	• Errors possible due to magnetic interference
• Multiple performers easily supported	

20.4   Inertial Sensor Configurations for Input

From the previous section, it is clear that motion sensors offer several important advantages over other motion-sensing and motion capture technologies and also have some limitations that some of the other technologies do not. This section will discuss several possible configurations of inertial motion sensors and where each configuration might be most applicable.

20.4.1   Single Sensor Configurations

Single sensor configurations can be used in any application where the orientation of something or the inertial forces acting upon something need to be sensed. Traditionally, aircraft and maritime navigation systems have used single sensor configurations and have referred to them as an IMU or an attitude and heading reference system (AHRS). The key distinction is that IMU units simply provide inertial measurements with no processing or filtering and AHRS systems provide on-board processing. In recent years, the cost of high-quality inertial sensors has dropped to the point where they are being used in all sorts of mass-market and consumer electronic application spaces.

A single 9-DOF inertial sensor can provide a range of useful data such as:

• Absolute orientation in global space

• Relative orientation relative to some defined reference

• Instantaneous angular rates

• Changes in rotation

• Accelerations

• Down vector

• Azimuth (north) vector

It is important to note that with a single 9-DOF sensor only orientation can be accurately sensed. Position estimates can be computed, but these are subject to growing error terms over time since the position is calculated by integrating the acceleration to get a velocity estimate and then integrating the velocity to get a position estimate. Thus, while the orientation may be accurate and drift-free in a 9-DOF sensor, the required double integration needed to compute the position estimate will unavoidably be subject to growing error terms over time. While some applications, such as short-duration gesture recognition, don't need long-term positional accuracy to be successful, in general where positional accuracy is an absolute necessity, another technology must be used to augment the inertial sensors.

Applications that use single sensor configurations: pointing, navigation, gaming, robotic systems, autonomous vehicles, flight systems, sports and fitness, smart-phone orientation detection, data-logging, alignment, and stabilization.

20.4.2 Multiple Sensor Configurations

Multiple sensor configurations offer the same data that is available within a single sensor configuration, but the use of multiple sensors to track different objects can allow additional useful data items to be computed. Since each of two or more sensors can accurately report their own respective orientation, it becomes possible to compute the difference in two orientations quite simply. This can be useful for applications where a simple angle, compound angle, or rotation vector between two things is desired.

Applications that use multiple sensor configurations: sports performance analysis, gesture-based interfaces, tele-presence, robotic tele-operation, industrial telemetry.

20.4.3 Full-Body Sensor Configurations

Full-body sensing is simply an extended case of the multiple sensor configuration in which a performer has sensors placed upon major skeletal segments of their body. This configuration allows accurate full-body tracking and enables many applications. Applications that use full-body sensor configurations: motion capture, full-body sports performance analysis, virtual reality, immersive simulation and gaming, full-body user interfaces and control systems, and ergonomics testing.

20.5 Hands-On: YEI 3-Space Sensors

20.5.1 Overview

The YEI 3-Space Sensor™ product line is a family of miniature, high-precision, high-reliability 9-DOF inertial sensor systems that make it easy to add motion sensing to a project or application with little knowledge of the complexities associated with sensor fusion and filtering algorithms. Each YEI 3-Space Sensor uses triaxial gyroscope, triaxial accelerometer, and triaxial compass sensors in conjunction with advanced processing and on-board quaternion-based Kalman filtering algorithms to determine orientation in real-time in absolute terms or relative to a designated reference orientation.

The product family offers a breadth of communication, performance, and packaging options ranging from the ultra-miniature modules that are embeddable to fully integrated battery-powered wireless and data-logging versions.

The YEI 3-Space Sensor system features are accessible via a well-documented open communication protocol that allows access to all available sensor data and configuration parameters using a variety of communication interfaces. Versatile

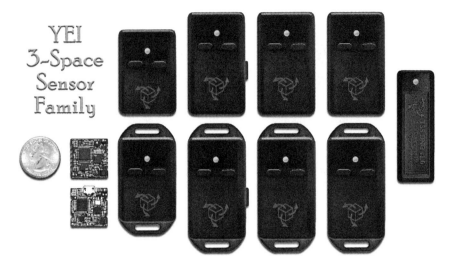

Figure 20.1: YEI 3-Space Sensor family.

commands allow access to raw sensor data, normalized sensor data, and filtered absolute and relative orientation outputs in multiple formats.

The following sections provide a hands-on guide to getting data from the sensors along with a description of some sample applications that serve to illustrate the use of the sensors.

20.5.2   Using a Single YEI 3-Space Sensor

The 3-Space Sensor family can communicate in a variety of ways depending on sensor model, including USB, RS232, 2.4GHz wireless, Bluetooth, SPI, and asynchronous serial UART. Regardless of the model, all 3-Space Sensor family members use the communication interface to send orientation data and component sensor data such as acceleration, and to allow their parameters and settings to be modified.

YEI 3-Space Sensors, as shown in Figure 20.13 are easy to communicate with since they enumerate via USB as a virtual communications port and use an open and well-documented communication protocol. The open protocol features both ASCII and binary communications modes. The ASCII communication mode allows for human-readability and convenience and the binary communication mode is suitable for applications that require lower latency and higher performance. Additionally, YEI 3-Space Sensors can be used in a polled command/response paradigm or configured to automatically stream data asynchronously. To further simplify development, YEI provides an open source 3-Space Sensor API that further simplifies the process of developing with 3-Space Sensors.

For a complete listing of these parameters/data and the commands that are used to access them, see the Protocol Reference in the User's Guide document available on the YEI 3-Space Sensor website.

Data Available

The YEI 3-Space Sensor has many commands that allow access to the inertial data stream coming from the sensor as well as access to configuration parameters and settings of the sensor itself.

YEI 3-Space Sensor family members all can accurately report orientation around 360°for all axes without restriction. The orientation resolution is <0.085°and the accuracy, when calibrated, is ±1°average for all orientations.

All YEI 3-Space Sensor product family members have re-mappable axis assignments and axis directions. This flexibility allows axis assignment and axis direction to match the desired end-use requirements.

The coordinate system axes of the 3-Space Sensor are as follows:

- The positive X-axis points out of the right-hand side of the sensor, which is the side that is facing right when the buttons face upward and the plug faces toward you.

- The positive Y-axis points out of the top of the sensor, the side with the buttons.

- The positive Z-axis points out of the front of the sensor, the side opposite the plug.

The coordinate system axes are illustrated in Figure 20.2:

Bear in mind the difference between coordinate system axes and the axes that are used in protocol data. While they are by default the same, they can be remapped so that, for example, data axis Y could contain data from natural axis X. This allows users to work with data in a reference frame they are familiar with.

To facilitate communication with a YEI 3-Space Sensor, a versatile command set allows access to raw sensor data, normalized sensor data, and filtered absolute and relative orientation outputs in multiple formats including: quaternion, Euler angles (pitch/roll/yaw), rotation matrix, axis angle, two vector (forward/up). Commands are also provided for filter selection, parameter tuning, and other advanced functionality.

For a complete list of the commands, see the Protocol Reference in the User's Guide document available on the YEI 3-Space Sensor website.

20.5.3   Installing a Sensor

Since YEI 3-Space Sensors perform all processing on-board and are designed to enumerate as a standard USB Communication Device Class (CDC) device, they are easy to install and supported on a variety of platforms. Installing a YEI 3-Space Sensor on each of the major platforms is as follows:

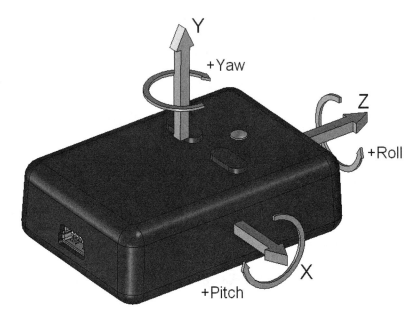

Figure 20.2: YEI 3-Space Sensor — Coordinate system axes of rotation.

Linux

To install a 3-Space Sensor on a Linux system, simply plug the sensor in via an available USB port. The sensor will enumerate and a pseudo-file will be automatically created in the /dev directory that will act as an interface to the device.

If a single device is installed it will likely be accessible via a name such as this:

/dev/ttyACM0

Note that the pseudo-file name will be in the form /dev/ttyACMx where x may change for different installed sensors or devices.

Communication can then be achieved by opening this pseudo-file and writing data to it to send commands and reading data from it to receive command responses.

Mac

To install a 3-Space Sensor on a MAC OS-X system, simply plug the sensor in via an available USB port. The sensor will enumerate and a pseudo-file will be automatically created in the /dev directory that will act as an interface to the device.

If a single device is installed it will likely be accessible via a name such as this:

/dev/cu.usbmodem0

Note that the pseudo-file name will be in the form /dev/cu.usbmodemx where x may change for different installed sensors or devices.

Communication can then be achieved by opening this pseudo-file and writing data to it to send commands and reading data from it to receive command responses.

Windows

To install the sensor on Windows, run the latest 3-Space Sensor installer, which can be found on the YEI Technology 3-Space Sensor website.

This will install the drivers needed to use the 3-Space Sensor, as well as the 3-Space Suite, a program which allows easy experimentation with 3-Space Sensor products and offers an interface to many of the features the sensor offers. It also offers a terminal mode in which you may interface with the sensor using text-based commands.

Once the installation is complete, plug the 3-Space Sensor into one of your computer's USB ports.

If a single device is installed it will likely be accessible as a virtual COM port device via a name such as this:

COM10 – 3 Space Sensor

Note that the com port name will be in the form COMx where x may change to represent different installed sensors or devices.

Communication can then be achieved by opening this virtual com port and sending commands and receiving command responses.

Alternatively, for the quickest way to test the sensor and experiment with it simply run the 3-Space Sensor Suite application that was installed, select the sensor from the COM port pull-down at the bottom of the screen, and click the "Connect" button on the user interface.

20.5.4 Communicating with a Sensor Using Command and Response

The simplest way to communicate directly with a 3-Space Sensor is using a command and response paradigm. With command and response, a command is issued by the host and communicated to the sensor. The sensor then receives that command and replies with a response back to the host. There are two ways to communicate:

- ASCII mode, which is good for use within a terminal program or when troubleshooting, as it takes and returns data in a human readable form.

- Binary mode, which is good for use within a programming language and when speed is important, as it takes and returns smaller, fixed length pieces of data.

The following sections describe the basic process of issuing commands and getting data from a YEI 3-Space Sensors using both ASCII and Binary modes of communication.

Connecting to a Sensor

To connect to a 3-Space Sensor in code, simply open the port.

In Python, the pySerial module can be installed and imported to allow cross-platform access to serial ports. An example of the code for this would look something like this:

Listing 20.1: pySerial Example

```
1  #import the pyserial module
2  import serial
3
4  # Open COM port of 3-Space sensor on your system
5  serial_port = serial.Serial("COM10", timeout=0.1, writeTimeout=0.1)
```

Sending a Command in ASCII Mode

To send a command in ASCII mode, simply send a command string to the sensor as formatted according to the following format:

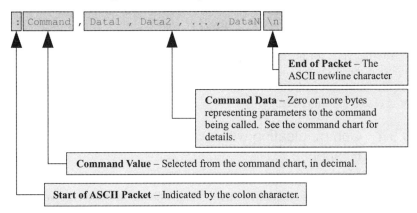

For most commands, this will be a simple string. This string could be typed into a terminal application or it could be sent via code. For example, in Python, sending the command to "Get Tared Orientation as Quaternion" would look like this:

```
1  serial_port.write(":0\n")
```

Receiving Response Data in ASCII Mode

All values are returned in ASCII text format when an ASCII-format command is issued. To read the return data, simply read data from the sensor until a Windows newline (a carriage return and a line feed) is encountered.

For example, in Python, receiving the command data for the command above would look like this:

```
1  command_response = serial_port.readline()
```

This will result in the command_response variable containing a string representation of a quaternion that would be something like this:

```
1  '0.18435,-0.81224,-0.12797,0.53843\r\n'
```

This response string could then be printed or parsed for further use with code something like this:

Listing 20.2: Orientation

```
1  orientation\_quaternion = command\_response.strip().split(',')}
2  print "Orientation Quaternion:",orientation\_quaternion
```

Sending a Command in Binary Mode

To send a command in binary mode, simply send a command string to the sensor as formatted according to the following format:

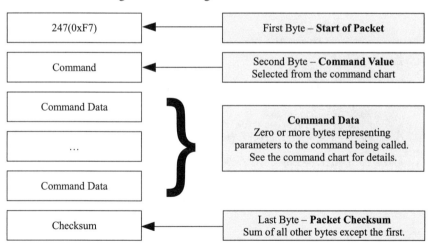

For most commands this will be a short sequence of bytes starting with the start of packet byte and terminated with the checksum.

The checksum is computed as an arithmetic summation of all of the characters in the packet (except the start of packet byte and checksum byte itself) modulus 256. This gives a resulting checksum in the range 0 to 255. The checksum for binary packets is transmitted as a single 8-bit byte value.

For example, in Python, sending the command to "Get Tared Orientation as Quaternion" would look like this:

Listing 20.3: Orientation as Quaternion

```
1  # Parameter-less wired commands the checksum will be the same as the↵
       command
2  write_bytes = chr(0xF7) + chr(0x00) + chr(0x00)
3
4  # Write the bytes to the serial
5  serial_port.write(write_bytes)
```

Receiving Response Data in Binary Mode

When a 3 Space Sensor command is called in binary mode, any data it returns will also be in binary format. For example, if a floating point number is returned, it will be returned as its 4 byte single-precision binary representation.

Keep in mind that integer and floating point values coming from the sensor are sent in big-endian format.

Since the command example above requests a quaternion to be returned, we must read the returned data of 4 individual single-precision floating-point numbers. Fortunately, Python has a module that simplifies reading such binary data and unpacking it into native Python numbers. The code below illustrates the process of reading and unpacking the data from the command issued above:

Listing 20.4: Reading and Unpacking Data

```
1  import struct
2
3  data_struct = struct.Struct('>ffff') # format for 4 floating-point ↵
       values
4
5  # Read the bytes returned from the specified command
6  commandResponse = serial_port.read(data_struct.size)
7
8  # The data must be unpacked from the string using the format above
9  orientationQuaternion = data_struct.unpack(commandResponse)
10
11 print "Orientation Quaternion:",orientationQuaternion
```

Disconnecting from the Sensor

When done communicating with the sensor or before the application exits, it is always good practice to close the virtual communications port of the sensor. This is done the same way as closing other COM ports.

In Python, an example of the code for this would look like this:

```
1  serial_port.close()
```

20.5.5   Communicating with a Sensor Using Streaming Mode

The default mode of communication for the 3-Space Sensor is a call and response paradigm wherein you send a command and then receive a response. The sensor also features a streaming mode where it can be instructed to periodically send back the response from up to 8 commands without any further communication from the host.

Setting Up and Activating Streaming Mode

To activate the streaming mode, use the following steps:

1. **Set up the streaming to call the commands you want data from.**

   First, figure out which commands you want data from. The sensor is capable of streaming inertial data, calculated orientation data, and a wide range of data from other commands. See the 3-Space Sensor User's Manual for a complete list of all valid streaming commands.

   There are 8 streaming slots available for use, and each one can hold one of these commands. These slots can be set using command 80(0x50), with the parameters being the 8 command bytes corresponding to each slot. Unused slots should be filled with 0xff so that they will output nothing. Please note: The total amount of data the 8 slots can return at once is 256 bytes. If the resulting data exceeds this, the set streaming slots command will fail.

2. **Set up the streaming interval, duration, and start delay.** These parameters control the timing of the streaming session. They can be set using command 82(0x52). All times are to be given in microseconds. They control the streaming as follows:

   Interval determines how often the streaming session will output data from the requested commands. For example, an interval of 1000000 will output data once a second. An interval of 0 will output data as quickly as possible. The interval will be clamped to 1000 if the user attempts to set it in the range 1 – 1000.

   Duration determines how long the streaming session will run. For example, a duration of 5000000 indicates the session should stop after 5 seconds. A duration of 4294967295 (0xFFFFFFFF) means that the session will run indefinitely until a stop streaming command is explicitly issued.

   Start Delay determines how long the sensor should wait after a start command is issued to actually begin streaming. For example, a start delay of 200000 means the session will start after 200 milliseconds.

3. **Begin the streaming session.** This can be done using command 85(0x55). Once started, the session will run until the duration has elapsed, or until the

stop command, 86(0x56) has been called. Note that if the sensor is sending large amounts of data the host doesn't have time to collect, this can cause buffer overflows in some communication drivers, leading to slowdowns and loss of data integrity. If the firmware detects that the buffer has overflowed, the asynchronous session will be stopped. If this occurs, this is a sign that the streaming interval is set too low, the program is not collecting data quickly enough, or both.

Streaming Mode Example Code

The sample code below shows how to set up the streaming of two commands: "Get Tared Orientation Quaternion" and "Get Corrected Linear Acceleration in Global Space."

Listing 20.5: Streaming

```
1   #YEI 3-Space Sensor: basic wired streaming mode example
2   import serial
3   import struct
4
5   #function to automatically calculate checksum and send data
6   def send_wired_command(port, data):
7       checksum = 0
8       for d in data:
9           checksum += ord(d)
10      checksum %= 256
11      port.write(chr(0xf7)+data+chr(checksum))
12
13  #open the serial port that matches your sensor
14  serial_port = serial.Serial("COM10", 115200, timeout=1)
15
16  #setup streaming command slots:
17  #   slot0='read tared orientation quaternion', all others empty
18  send_wired_command(serial_port, chr(0x50)+chr(0x00)+chr(0xff)*7)
19
20  #prepare streaming data: data every 20ms, send forever, don't wait ↵
        before starting
21  s_interval_us = struct.pack('>I',20000)
22  s_duration_us = struct.pack('>I',0xFFFFFFFF)
23  s_delay_us = struct.pack('>I',0)
24
25  #set up streaming command
26  send_wired_command(serial_port, chr(0x52)+ s_interval_us + ↵
        s_duration_us + s_delay_us)
27
28  #start streaming command
29  send_wired_command(serial_port, chr(0x55))
30
31  while(True):
32      try:
33          tdata = serial_port.read(16)
34          if len(tdata) == 16:
```

```
35                    data = struct.unpack('>ffff', tdata)
36                    print "Reading:", data
37          except KeyboardInterrupt:
38              break
39
40  #stop streaming
41  send_wired_command(serial_port, chr(0x56))
42  #close port
43  serial_port.close()
44  print "done"
```

20.5.6   Using the 3-Space Sensor API

For convenience and ease of use, YEI also provides a free and open source 3-Space Sensor API to simplify interfacing with sensors. The API provides abstractions for all 3-Space Sensor commands and provides support for both command/response and streamed communication modes. The core 3-Space API is written in C++ and can be used in numerous environments as a DLL, YEI also provides a Python API that is implemented as a wrapper around the DLL. The simple examples below illustrate the use of the 3-Space API and DLL within Python. For full documentation and additional API examples, visit the YEI 3-Space Sensor website.

API Command and Response Mode Example

The example below illustrates using the YEI 3-Space Sensor API to connect to a sensor, send a command and get a response.

Listing 20.6: Connect to Sensor

```
1   # YEI 3-Space Sensor: API command and response example
2   import ThreeSpaceAPI
3   import time
4
5   # Create sensor instance. Opens the port implicitly.
6   sensor = ThreeSpaceAPI.TssSensor("COM10")
7
8   # send command and get response
9   orientationQuaternion = sensor.getTaredOrientationAsQuaternion()
10
11  # print the result
12  print "Orientation Quaternion:",orientationQuaternion
13
14  # sensor object is deleted and the port is closed automatically.
15  print "done"
```

API Streaming Mode Example

The example below illustrates using the YEI 3-Space Sensor API to setup streaming of a command from a sensor and receive the streamed data.

Listing 20.7: Setup Streaming

```python
# YEI 3-Space Sensor: API streaming example
import ThreeSpaceAPI

# Create sensor instance. Opens the port implicitly.
sensor = ThreeSpaceAPI.TssSensor("COM10")

# Setup and start streaming.
s_commands = ThreeSpaceAPI.↵
    TSS_STREAM_TARED_ORIENTATION_AS_QUATERNION
s_interval_us = 20000
s_duration_us = ThreeSpaceAPI.TSS_STREAM_DURATION_INFINITE
sensor.startStreamingWired(s_commands, s_interval_us, s_duration_us)

print "Streaming"
while(True):
    try:
        packet = sensor.getLastStreamingPacket()
        if packet:
            orientationQuaternion = packet[ThreeSpaceAPI.↵
                TSS_STREAM_TARED_ORIENTATION_AS_QUATERNION]
            print "Orientation Quaternion:",orientationQuaternion
    except KeyboardInterrupt:
        break

sensor.stopStreamingWired()

#sensor object is deleted and the port is closed automatically.
print "done"
```

20.5.7 Hands-On: Single 3-Space Sensor Applications

Example: Navigation and Compassing

Since YEI 3-Space Sensors are full 9-DOF solutions, it is possible to extract accurate drift-free orientations in global space. This makes them ideal for navigation applications that require knowledge of both attitude (tilt/roll) and heading. Common navigation applications could include: tilt-compensated compassing, aircraft flight instrumentation, autonomous air/ground/sea vehicle navigation and stabilization, guidance systems, pedestrian navigation and compassing, and other applications that require accurate heading/tilt/roll data.

Since YEI 3-Space Sensors can output orientation as pitch/roll/yaw, and can sense orientation in a global reference frame with down and north as the zero-reference, it becomes almost trivial to implement a typical navigation system. The process is as follows:

1. **Open the 3-Space Sensor for communication**

   This is done using the following commands:

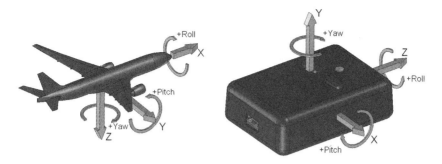

Figure 20.3: Coordinate system axes: Aviation versus YEI 3-Space Sensor.

```
1  #Create sensor instance. Opens the port implicitly.
2  sensor = ThreeSpaceAPI.TssSensor("COM10")
```

Listing 20.8: Untared Orientation

```
1  #Use untared orientation to get global refernce for heading ↩
       and gravity.
2  #Euler orientations are always returned as pitch, yaw, roll.
3  orientation_euler = sensor.getUntaredOrientationAsEulerAngles↩
       ()
```

Note that this example assumes the sensor has enumerated as COM10. This might be different on different systems and installations.

2. **Read the untared orientation as Euler angles**

   The untared orientation gives the orientation of each sensor in global terms, which is what we want since that places azimuth (magnetic north) and down as the zero references. The code to read the untared orientation is as follows:

3. **Put the angles into typical heading and attitude form**

   One thing that must be considered for this example is that the coordinate system axes of the 3-Space Sensor are different from those typically used in aircraft navigation. The figure below illustrates the difference between the two coordinate systems.

   By looking at the differences in the coordinate system axes of the two systems, it is apparent that pitch and roll have inverted positive directions. Because of this, we must invert the data for the pitch and roll axes. The code for this is as follows:

Listing 20.9: Pitch, Roll, and Yaw

```
1  #Pitch and roll must be inverted to match standard aircraft ↩
     system
2  pitch = -math.degrees(orientation_euler[0])
3  roll = -math.degrees(orientation_euler[2])
```

The data range generally used to indicate aircraft heading is also typically reported as a positive number in the range 0 to 360. the code for this is as follows:

```
1  #Convert heading to degrees and 0-360 degree
2  heading = math.degrees(orientation_euler[1])
3      if heading<0:
4          heading += 360
```

4. **Use the results**

In this example, we simply print out the readings for display, but in other applications these could be returned and used for navigation purposes or used as part of a larger system. The code for simple display is as follows:

```
1  print "heading:",heading,"pitch:",pitch,"roll:",roll
```

No matter the application, the 3-Space Sensor makes it easy to get access to the relevant data.

Complete Example

Listing 20.10: Complete Example

```
1  # YEI 3-Space Sensor: Aircraft Navigation Example
2  # Uses command and response to get AHRS output
3
4  import ThreeSpaceAPI
5  import math
6
7  #Create sensor instance. Opens the port implicitly.
8  sensor = ThreeSpaceAPI.TssSensor("COM10")
9
10 while(True):
11     try:
12         #Use untared orientation to get global refernce for heading ↩
             and gravity.
13         #Euler orientations are always returned as pitch, yaw, roll.
14         orientation_euler = sensor.↩
             getUntaredOrientationAsEulerAngles()
15
```

```
16          #convert heading to degrees and 0-360 degree
17          heading = math.degrees(orientation_euler[1])
18
19          if heading<0:
20              heading += 360
21
22          #Pitch and roll must be inverted to match standard aircraft ↩
                system
23          pitch = -math.degrees(orientation_euler[0])
24          roll = -math.degrees(orientation_euler[2])
25
26          print "heading:",heading,"pitch:",pitch,"roll:",roll
27
28      except KeyboardInterrupt:
29          break
30
31  #delete the object when done. Port is closed automatically.
32  del sensor
```

Example: Pointing and User Interface Control

The ability of YEI 3-Space Sensors to accurately determine a drift-free orientation in real-time allows them to be used for an input device. One way that the sensors' orientation output can be used is for pointing applications. For example, a remote control could use 3-Space Sensor technology to control an on-screen pointer in an easy way.

To achieve this, it is necessary to convert the orientation from the sensor into an X/Y location on the screen. This can be done by taring the sensor in the neutral / center-screen orientation and then creating a rotation vector from that neutral orientation. The intersection of this rotation vector and a defined plane representing the screen can then be computed. The X/Y of the computed intersection point can then be used as the pointer location.

1. **Open the 3-Space Sensor for communication**

   This is done using the following commands:

   ```
   1  #Create sensor instance. Opens the port implicitly.
   2  sensor = ThreeSpaceAPI.TssSensor("COM10")
   ```

   Note that this example assumes the sensor has enumerated as COM10. This might be different on different systems and installations.

2. **Tare the sensor with the current orientation**

   Before the main loop starts the sensor is tared to define the zero-reference orientation. Ideally this will be with the sensor pointing toward the center of the screen. This is done using the following commands:

```
1  #Use start orientation as tare.
2  #Assumes sensor is pointed at center of screen during tare.
3  sensor.tareWithCurrentOrientation()
```

Note that in practice, for fixed installations the tared sensor may have its settings committed to non-volatile memory and the sensor tare step could be skipped. For other non-fixed installations, it might be useful to have the user be able to tare the sensor within the main loop through some set-up procedure.

3. **Read the tared orientation from the sensor**

   Since the sensor was tared at the center of the screen, we can now use the getTaredOrientationAsQuaternion method to obtain the rotational offset from the tare orientation. This is done using the following commands:

```
1  #send command and get response
2  orientationQuaternion = sensor.getTaredOrientationAsQuaternion↩
      ()
```

4. **Calculate the rotation vector from the current orientation to the forward vector**

   We convert the current orientation into a rotation vector so that we can later use this rotation vector to compute the intersection with the screen plane. The Python cgkit module is quite useful and is used here to provide a vec3 class that simplifies the code. This rotation vector is computed with the following commands:

Listing 20.11: Compute Forward Vector

```
1  #compute forward vector by finding a rotation to the z-axis
2  forwardVector = cgkit.cgtypes.vec3(0,0,1)
3  rotatedVector = orientationQuaternion.rotateVec(forwardVector)
```

5. **Calculate the intersection point with the screen plane**

   The final step is to calculate the intersection point with the screen (see Figure 20.4). To achieve this, we must scale the vector so that it contacts the plane that is at the distance of the plane of the screen. In practice, the screen plane Z-distance is selected to give the appropriate offsets from the center of the screen.

   In this case a z-distance of 1920.0 is selected so that the computed screen offsets are appropriate for a typical 1920x1080 resolution display. Once the vector is scaled, the Z-plane intersection point is simply the X and Y components of the scaled vector. The code that performs the vector scaling and X/Y component extraction is as follows:

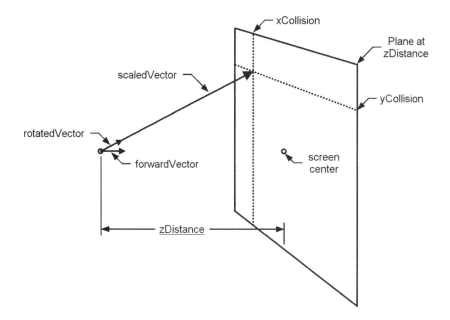

Figure 20.4: Orientation vector used for screen pointer.

Listing 20.12: Compute Scaling Factor

```
1  #compute scaling factor to make vector contact Z plane
2  scaleFactor = zDistance/rotatedVector[2]
3
4  #scale the entire vector by the scale factor
5  scaledVector=rotatedVector*scaleFactor
6  xCollision=scaledVector[0]
7  yCollision=scaledVector[1]
```

6. **Compute the roll angle**

   If desired, the roll angle of the pointer can also be computed and used
   to orient the screen-pointer, or as an additional interface. This is done
   most simply by using the getTaredOrientationAsEulerAngles method and
   extracting the roll angle. The code for this is as follows:

```
1  #read Euler angles to get roll.  Returned as Pitch, Yaw, Roll.
2  orientationEulers = sensor.getTaredOrientationAsEulerAngles()
3  rollAngle = math.degrees(orientationEulers[2])
```

7. **Use the results**

   In this example, we simply print out the readings for display, but in other
   applications these could be returned and used for navigation purposes or

used as part of a larger system. The code for simple display is as follows:

```
1  #display the collision points and roll with the plane at ↩
       zDistance
2  print "x offset:",xCollision,"y offset:",yCollision, "roll:",↩
       rollAngle
```

Complete Example

Listing 20.13: Complete Example 2

```
1  # 3-Space Sensor Example: Single Sensor Used for Screen Pointing
2  import ThreeSpaceAPI
3  import cgkit
4  import math
5
6  #Create sensor instance. Opens the port implicitly.
7  sensor = ThreeSpaceAPI.TssSensor("COM10")
8
9  #Use start orientation as tare.
10 #Assumes sensor is pointed at center of screen during tare.
11 sensor.tareWithCurrentOrientation()
12
13 #Z-distance of plane we want to intersect with.
14 zDistance = 1920.0
15
16 while(True):
17     try:
18         #send command and get response
19         orientationQuaternion = sensor.↩
               getTaredOrientationAsQuaternion()
20
21         #compute forward vector by finding a rotation to the z-axis
22         forwardVector = cgkit.cgtypes.vec3(0,0,1)
23         rotatedVector = orientationQuaternion.rotateVec(↩
               forwardVector)
24
25         #compute scaling factor to make vector contact Z plane
26         scaleFactor = zDistance/rotatedVector[2]
27
28         #scale the entire vector by the scale factor
29         scaledVector=rotatedVector*scaleFactor
30         xCollision=scaledVector[0]
31         yCollision=scaledVector[1]
32
33         #read Euler angles to get roll.  Returned as Pitch, Yaw, ↩
               Roll.
34         orientationEulers = sensor.getTaredOrientationAsEulerAngles↩
               ()
35         rollAngle = math.degrees(orientationEulers[2])
36
37         #display the collision points and roll with the plane at ↩
               zDistance
```

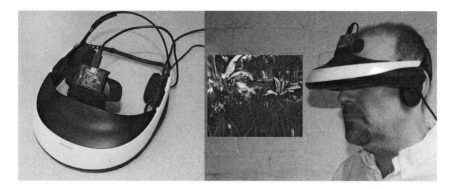

Figure 20.5: YEI 3-Space Sensor for head tracking on a Sony HMZT1 HMD.

```
38          print "x offset:",xCollision,"y offset:",yCollision, "roll:"↩
               ,rollAngle
39
40      except KeyboardInterrupt:
41          break
42
43  #delete the obeject when done. Port is closed automatically.
44  del sensor
```

Example: Virtual Reality Head Tracking

The ability of the 3-Space Sensor to output accurate orientations in real-time makes it ideal for use as an input device for interactive simulation and virtual reality(VR) applications (as shown in Figure 20.5). In VR, for example, it is necessary to accurately track the orientation of the head so that the head-mounted display (HMD) can render a realistic rendered view of the virtual world. To maintain the illusion of immersion it is important for the head orientation sensor to be accurate in all orientations, have fast update rates, be jitter free, and exhibit low-latency. The 3-Space Sensor can be used for HMD head-tracking for VR applications by attaching a 3-Space Sensor to an HMD or by embedding a 3-Space Sensor module within the HMD itself.

Using the 3-Space Sensor for head-tracking is quite simple. Since the 3-Space Sensor can output orientations in real-time as a sequence of quaternions and modern game engines support using quaternions to apply rotations to game objects, implementing head tracking becomes a matter of simply applying the quaternion read from the 3-Space Sensor to the in-game camera for the first-person view that is being rendered.

The process detailed below illustrates the sequence of steps necessary to create a class that reads the tared quaternion orientation from a 3-Space Sensor and subsequently applies that orientation to the view camera within the Unity game engine.

1. **Import the name-spaces required by the Unity Engine**

   For the C# script to access the classes and other data types of the Unity
   Engine they must be imported into the script. The following code allows
   access to the required name spaces, classes, and other data types associated
   with the unity engine.

   Listing 20.14: Unity Engine

   ```
   1  using UnityEngine;
   2  using System.Collections;
   3  using System.Collections.Generic;
   4  using System.Runtime.InteropServices;
   5  using System.Text;
   6  using System;
   ```

2. **Create the class**

   For a class to be used within and access the data and features of the Unity
   Engine, it must inherit from the MonoBehavior class. For us in Unity,
   MonoBehavior is the base class that every script should derive from. Here
   we're calling our class HMD since it will be used for head-tracking of a
   head mounted display.

   The declaration is as follows:

   ```
   1  public class HMD : MonoBehaviour
   2  {
   3    //Place class variables and methods in here.
   4  }
   ```

3. **Declare the DLL functions within the class**

   For the class to access the DLL functions that provide access to the YEI
   3-Space Sensor functionality, we need to import the required DLL functions. In our example, we really only need to access three functions:
   tss_createSensor, tss_removeSensor, and tss_sensor_getUntaredOrientation
   AsQuaternion. These are imported and given the simplified function name
   aliases createSensor, removeSensor, and sensor_getUntaredOrientation
   AsQuaternion, respectively.

   The code for this is as follows:

   ```
   1  [DllImport("ThreeSpaceAPIDLL.dll", CallingConvention = ↩
        CallingConvention.Cdecl,   EntryPoint= "tss_createSensor")↩
        ] private static extern uint createSensor([MarshalAs(↩
        UnmanagedType.LPStr)]String port, ref uint sensor_id);
   2
   ```

```
3  DllImport("ThreeSpaceAPIDLL.dll", CallingConvention = ←
       CallingConvention.Cdecl, EntryPoint= "tss_removeSensor")]←
       private static extern uint removeSensor(uint sensor_id);
4
5  [DllImport("ThreeSpaceAPIDLL.dll", CallingConvention = ←
       CallingConvention.Cdecl, EntryPoint= "←
       tss_sensor_getUntaredOrientationAsQuaternion")] private ←
       static extern uint ←
       sensor_getUntaredOrientationAsQuaternion(uint sensor_id, ←
       float[] orient);
```

4. Declare other variables within the class

The other necessary class variables are declared. These will be used later by the class methods. The code is as follows:

```
1  uint sensor_id;
2  Quaternion tare, offset;
3  GameObject camera;
```

5. Create a method to read the untared orientation from the sensor

Since we need to read the orientation from the sensor in multiple places within the code, it makes sense to define a function that abstracts the process. The basic process is to call the sensor_getUntaredOrientationAsQuaternion DLL function. This function will return after placing the 4 floating point components of the quaternion into the array that was passed by reference. A new Quaternion object is then instantiated with the quaternion components that were read. This Quaternion object is then returned.

```
1  Quaternion getUntaredOrientationAsQuaternion()
2  {
3    float[] orient = new float[4];
4    sensor_getUntaredOrientationAsQuaternion(sensor_id, orient);
5    Quaternion q_orient = new Quaternion(orient[0], orient[1], ←
         orient[2], orient [3]);
6    return q_orient;
7  }
```

6. Create the Start method

In Unity, the Start method is called when a script is first enabled and generally is responsible for initialization and start-up code. In this case we want the Start method to create the sensor object for the specified COM port of the YEI 3-Space sensor and then attach our local camera variable to the game's "Main Camera" object. This code for the Start method is as follows.

Listing 20.15: Create the Start Method

```
1  void Start()
2  {
3    String port = "COM10"; //Change to COM port for sensor
4    Debug.Log ("Opening sensor: " + port);
5    createSensor (port, ref sensor_id);
6
7    //grab the camera object
8    camera = GameObject.Find ("Main Camera");
9  }
```

7. **Create the OnApplicationQuit method**

   Just as the Start method is used to initialize things at start-up, the OnApplicationQuit method is used to clean things up when the application closes. In our case, we simply call the removeSensor function for the opened sensor. This closes the port and performs all the other necessary clean-up tasks. The code is as follows:

```
1  void OnApplicationQuit()
2  {
3    Debug.Log ("Releasing sensor");
4    removeSensor (sensor_id);
5  }
```

8. **Create the Calibrate method**

   The Calibrate method is used to set the zero-reference orientation for the head-tracking sensor. One thing that is important to handle is cases where the sensor may be mounted at an angle on the HMD as shown in Figure 20.6:

   In this case, the tare zero orientation must be rotated by the appropriate offset to account for the mounting angle of the sensor. If the sensor is mounted orthogonally or the offset is not necessary then this step may be omitted or the offset may be set to the identity quaternion.

Listing 20.16: Calibrate

```
1  void Calibrate()
2  {
3    Quaternion q_orient = getUntaredOrientationAsQuaternion ();
4    //this is the place where you indicate the mounting
5    //orientation of the sensor on the HMD
6    //for an orthogonally moutner sensor, this offset would be ↩
         identity
7    //if it were tilted upward at a 30 degree angle on the HMD,
8    //the offset would be Quaternion.AngleAxis (30, Vector3.↩
         right)
9
```

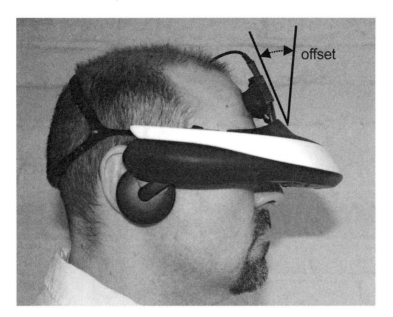

Figure 20.6: Offset angle of head-tracking sensor.

```
10    offset = Quaternion.AngleAxis (30, Vector3.right)
11    //offset = Quaternion.identity; // use this if no offset is ↩
          desired
12
13    //have to take the offset into consideration to find the tare
14    tare = Quaternion.Inverse (q_orient*offset);
15  }
```

9. **Create the Update method**

In Unity, the Update method is called every frame when the script is enabled. In our case, we want to provide a way for a key-press event to invoke the calibration method and a way to read the current orientation from the 3-space sensor, apply the offset orientation if necessary, and apply the resulting orientation to the game's main camera. As described above, the offset orientation may be necessary if the head-tracking sensor is mounted at an angle within the HMD.

The code is as follows:

Listing 20.17: Update

```
1  void Update()
2  {
3      //calibrate once the HMD/sensor is in place
```

```
4    if (Input.GetKeyDown (KeyCode.C))
5      Calibrate ();
6      Quaternion q_orient = getUntaredOrientationAsQuaternion ();
7      q_orient = tare * q_orient * offset;
8      camera.transform.rotation = q_orient;
9    }
```

Complete Example: Head-Tracking in Unity

Listing 20.18: Complete Example (Unity)

```
1    using UnityEngine;
2    using System.Collections;
3    using System.Collections.Generic;
4    using System.Runtime.InteropServices;
5    using System.Text;
6    using System;
7
8    public class HMD : MonoBehaviour
9    {
10     [DllImport("ThreeSpaceAPIDLL.dll", CallingConvention = ←
          CallingConvention.Cdecl, EntryPoint= "tss_createSensor")]
11     private static extern uint createSensor([MarshalAs(UnmanagedType.←
          LPStr)]String port, ref uint sensor_id);
12
13     [DllImport("ThreeSpaceAPIDLL.dll", CallingConvention = ←
          CallingConvention.Cdecl, EntryPoint= "tss_removeSensor")]
14     private static extern uint removeSensor(uint sensor_id);
15
16     [DllImport("ThreeSpaceAPIDLL.dll", CallingConvention = ←
          CallingConvention.Cdecl, EntryPoint= "←
          tss_sensor_getUntaredOrientationAsQuaternion")]
17     private static extern uint ←
          sensor_getUntaredOrientationAsQuaternion(uint sensor_id, float←
          [] orient);
18
19
20     uint sensor_id;
21     Quaternion tare, offset;
22     GameObject camera;
23
24     Quaternion getUntaredOrientationAsQuaternion()
25     {
26       float[] orient = new float[4];
27       sensor_getUntaredOrientationAsQuaternion(sensor_id, orient);
28       Quaternion q_orient = new Quaternion (orient [0], orient [1], ←
            orient [2], orient [3]);
29       return q_orient;
30     }
31
32     void Calibrate()
33     {
34       Quaternion q_orient = getUntaredOrientationAsQuaternion ();
```

```
35
36        //this is the place where you indicate the mounting
37        //orientation of the sensor on the HMD
38        //for a loose sensor, this offset would be identity
39        //if it were tilted downward at a 45 degree angle on an HMD,
40        //the offset would be Quaternion.AngleAxis (-45, Vector3.right)
41        offset = Quaternion.identity;
42        //offset = Quaternion.AngleAxis (-45, Vector3.right);
43
44        //have to take the offset into consideration to find the tare
45        tare = Quaternion.Inverse (q_orient*offset);
46      }
47
48    void Start()
49    {
50      String port = "COM10"; //Change to COM port for sensor
51      Debug.Log ("Opening sensor: " + port);
52      createSensor (port, ref sensor_id);
53
54      //grab the camera object
55      camera = GameObject.Find ("Main Camera");
56    }
57
58    void Update()
59    {
60      //calibrate once the HMD/sensor is in place
61      if (Input.GetKeyDown (KeyCode.C))
62        Calibrate ();
63
64      Quaternion q_orient = getUntaredOrientationAsQuaternion ();
65      q_orient = tare * q_orient * offset;
66      camera.transform.rotation = q_orient;
67    }
68
69    void OnApplicationQuit()
70    {
71      Debug.Log ("Releasing sensor");
72      removeSensor (sensor_id);
73    }
74  }
```

20.5.8   Hands-On: Multiple 3-Space Sensor Applications

Data from Multiple Sensors

Getting data from multiple YEI 3-Space Sensors follows the same process as getting data from a single 3-Space Sensor, but is repeated for each desired sensor. Thus, multiple 3-Space Sensor applications are easily implemented using either direct communication or the 3-Space Sensor API.

Data from multiple 3-Space Sensors can be used independently as two separate sensors for control of distinct elements within the application or they can be used to compute data values that a single sensor alone cannot provide such as difference angles between sensors.

Example: Multiple Sensors for Human Body Input

This example illustrates how to calculate angles between two YEI 3-Space Sensor devices. This is especially useful for organic motion-capture, bio-mechanics studies, sports performance analysis, range-of-motion studies, and ergonomics studies since it is possible to extract human joint-angles from body-worn sensors.

Orientation can also be returned relative to a designated reference orientation. This makes 3-Space Sensor placement and alignment easier since the devices can make use of arbitrarily defined zero-identity orientations which makes perfect physical alignment unnecessary and reduces the difficulty in extracting desired output angles.

The 3-Space Sensor devices can return orientation in a number of formats, including forward and down vectors, thus making it simple to calculate the angle between two of these devices. However, many surfaces, such as those of the human body, may not be flat or smooth, and, thus, we must be able to compensate for the possibility of imperfect sensor placement and alignment. We can use the devices' quaternion orientation output and quaternion operations to account for the human body's irregularities and obtain more accurate forward and down vectors.

The example below illustrates a method for calculating the angles between two 3-Space Sensors (see Figure 20.7) that are attached to the upper-arm and forearm near the wrist, with the LED end of the sensor facing toward the distal (hand end) end of the arm. For convenience, this document assumes the use of two 3-Space Sensors that are being communicated with via wired USB.

The example code below uses the 3-Space Sensor API to read the global orientations from two sensors and then computes the angles between the two orientations. The basic process is as follows:

1. **Open both sensors for communication**

   This is done using the following two commands:

   ```
   1  #create sensor instance. Opens the port implicitly.
   2  sensor1 = ThreeSpaceAPI.TssSensor("COM10")
   3  sensor2 = ThreeSpaceAPI.TssSensor("COM11")
   ```

   Note that this example assumes the two sensors have enumerated as COM10 and COM11, respectively, and might be different on different systems and installations.

2. **Read the untared quaternion orientation for each sensor**

   The untared orientation gives the orientation of each sensor in global terms. Since we're looking for the angle difference between the two physical

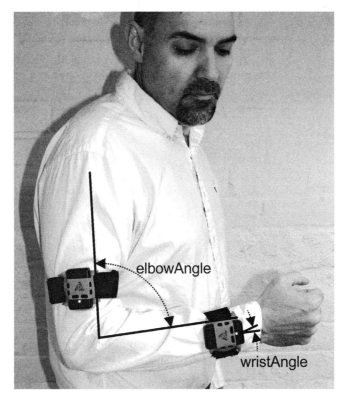

Figure 20.7: Sensor placement for joint angle measurement.

sensors themselves it is appropriate to use the untared sensor orientations. The code to read the two untared orientations is as follows:

```
1  #send command to both sensors and get responses from each
2  orientationQuaternion1 = sensor1.↩
       getUntaredOrientationAsQuaternion()
3  orientationQuaternion2 = sensor2.↩
       getUntaredOrientationAsQuaternion()
```

Note that if the sensors are mounted imperfectly it may be desirable to use a calibration step and the tared orientation of the two sensors.

3. **Calculate the quaternion difference between the two orientations read**

   Since we are interested in the rotational differences between the two sensors, we can calculate the difference between the two orientation quaternions. This is done by computing the difference quaternion between the two quaternions.

A quaternion difference is defined as a quaternion that, when multiplied by a first quaternion (q1), results in the second quaternion (q2)

Thus, to find a quaternion difference qD between q2 and q1, we need to find a quaternion qD such that q2 * qD == q1.

To do this, we can use the multiplicative inverse and solve for qD to get:

qD = inverse(q2) * q1

The code to do this is as follows:

```
1   #compute difference quaternion
2   diffQuaternion = orientationQuaternion2.inverse() * ↩
        orientationQuaternion1
```

Note that quaternion differences are not commutative and different results will be produced depending upon which quaternion is considered the reference quaternion (q1). In this example "sensor1" is the sensor that is placed on the upper arm and "sensor2" is the sensor placed upon the wrist.

4. **Convert the computed quaternion difference into a rotation matrix**

   Converting the quaternion into a rotation matrix is done here as an intermediate step to simplify the decomposition into Euler angles using the toEulerZXY() method built into cgkit's Mat3 object.

   The code to do this is as follows:

```
1   #make difference quaternion into a rotation matrix
2   differenceRotationMatrix = diffQuaternion.toMat3()
```

5. **Decompose the rotation matrix into Euler angles**

   To decompose the rotation matrix into individual Euler angles, we use the toEulerZXY() method of the Mat3 rotation matrix differenceRotationMatrix. This results in the individual X, Y, and Z angles being returned in radians. The code for this is as follows:

```
1   #convert the rotation matrix into Euler angles
2   eulerAngleDifference = differenceRotationMatrix.toEulerZXY()
```

One thing that is important to note is that Euler angle representations inherently are susceptible to gimbal lock due to the mathematics involved with describing an arbitrary rotation as a series of angular offsets around orthogonal axes. Gimbal lock occurs when the compound rotation is decomposed in such a way as to make two of the three axes wind up in a parallel or near parallel orientation. In these orientations, the results of the decomposition become unsuitable for some applications.

One observation that can help is that two of the three axes won't suffer from this behavior as long as the third axis remains sufficiently distant from the ±90° rotation regions. In the decomposition order it is the center axis that must be kept away from the ±90° region for the others to remain stable.

Thus, in the example above where we used the ZXY composition order, we'll get stable Z and Y rotations so long as X stays away from the ±90° region. This is what we want in this particular application because the Z rotational difference is the wrist angle and the Y rotational difference is the elbow angle. Since it is impossible to bend the elbow along the X-axis this solution is general for tracking the elbow rotation and wrist angle.

Note that care must be taken since other joint types and sensor mounting configurations might require different decomposition orders.

6. **The Euler angles that result directly represent the angle differences on each of the axes**

The final step is to extract the desired angles for the joints. This is done by simply pulling the appropriate axis values from the decomposition of the rotational difference and, in this example, converting them to degrees for display and ease of understanding.

The code for this is as follows:

```
1  #elbow angle is the Y axis, convert to degrees
2  elbowAngle = math.degrees(eulerAngleDifference[1])
3
4  #wrist rotation is the Z axis, convert to degrees
5  wristAngle = math.degrees(eulerAngleDifference[2])
6
7  print "Elbow angle:", elbowAngle, "Wrist angle:",wristAngle
```

Complete Example

Listing 20.19: Complete Example

```
1  # 3-Space Sensor Example: Human joint Angles from multiple sensors.
2  # sensor1 is mounted on the upper arm.
3  # sensor2 is mounted on the fore arm on the wrist area.
4
5  import ThreeSpaceAPI
6  import cgkit
7  import math
8
```

```
 9  #Create sensor instance. Opens the port implicitly.
10  sensor1 = ThreeSpaceAPI.TssSensor("COM10") #upper arm sensor
11  sensor2 = ThreeSpaceAPI.TssSensor("COM11") #wrist sensor
12
13  while(True):
14      try:
15          #send command to both sensors and get responses from each
16          orientationQuaternion1 = sensor1.↩
                getUntaredOrientationAsQuaternion()
17          orientationQuaternion2 = sensor2.↩
                getUntaredOrientationAsQuaternion()
18
19          #compute difference quaternion
20          diffQuaternion = orientationQuaternion2.inverse() * ↩
                orientationQuaternion1
21
22          #make difference quaternion into a rotation matrix
23          differenceRotationMatrix = diffQuaternion.toMat3()
24
25          #convert the rotation matrix into Euler angles
26          eulerAngleDifference = differenceRotationMatrix.toEulerZXY()
27
28          #elbow angle is the Y axis, convert to degrees
29          elbowAngle = math.degrees(eulerAngleDifference[1])
30
31          #wrist rotation is the Z axis, convert to degrees
32          wristAngle = math.degrees(eulerAngleDifference[2])
33
34          print "Elbow angle:", elbowAngle, "Wrist angle:",wristAngle
35
36      except KeyboardInterrupt:
37          break
38
39  #delete the object when done. Port is closed automatically.
40  del sensor1
41  del sensor2
```

20.6   Hands-On: YEI Prio for Whole-Body Input

The YEI Prio Suit (see Figure 20.8) is a full-body motion-tracking system based upon high-performance inertial sensors. Since Prio uses inertial sensors, it is able to provide 360 degrees of low-latency, real-time motion tracking without the need for cameras, optics, line-of-sight, or special capture environments.

Prio's motion sensors are placed on key points of your body to capture your movements and translate them on-screen in real-time. Prio is wireless, allows for multiple simultaneous users, and will work anywhere in capture spaces of any size.

Prio is available in three versions, the Core, the Lite, and the Pro, all of which are wireless and compatible with each other. All suits include two hand-controllers with action buttons, triggers, and joysticks. The joysticks let you easily add

Figure 20.8: Prio prototype suit in action.

additional user-interface inputs that can allow users to navigate through large virtual worlds without actually walking, while the buttons and trigger support a familiar user-interface experience.

Development for Prio is simplified by the availability of the multi-layered Prio API stack and drop-in support via pre-built plug-ins for popular game-engines such as Unity Technologies' Unity Engine and Epic Games' Unreal Engine.

Prio is also supported by the freely available YEI Mocap Studio application which will allow users to record and export mocap performances for use in other content pipelines.

20.6.1   Using the Prio API

The YEI Skeletal API is meant to make connecting to and using a Prio suit as easy as possible. In this section, we will show how to use the Prio API to find a suit connected to a PC, prepare it for use, and stream skeleton orientation data from the suit. We will be going over a C++ API use example line by line to show how to accomplish this.

Skeleton Creation

The first step in using a Prio through the YEI Skeletal API is to create a skeleton to work with.

```
1   yei_skeleton_id skel_id = yeiskel_createSkeleton();
```

This code gives the ID of a skeleton object which the API creates. This ID will be passed to any further function that references the skeleton object.

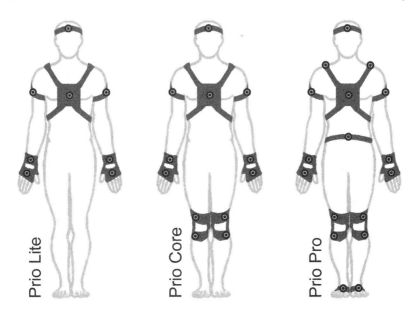

Figure 20.9: Prio suit options.

Skeleton Setup

We have created a skeleton, but currently it is an empty skeleton with no bones. We next need to provide it with a bone heirarchy. While complex bone heirarchies can be set up manually by the user, the API provides methods to easily create standard humanoid bone heirarchies.

```
1   bool is_male = false;
2   int age = 28;
3   yeiskel_createStandardBoneHeirarchyWithAge(skel_id, is_male, age);
```

This code takes simple parameters about the intended user of the Prio, those being the gender and age of the user. In this example, a 28-year-old female is the suit user. It uses these parameters to make an appropriately sized bone hierarchy for the given skeleton.

Prio Connection

We have our skeleton created and bones set up inside it. Now we want our Prio suit to drive the skeleton's bones. To do this, we will add a "PrioProcessor" to our skeleton object.

```
1  yei_processor_id prio_id = yeiskel_addPrioProcessorToSkeleton(↩
       skel_id);
```

This code will find a Prio suit connected to the host PC and hook it up to the skeleton. If none is present, prio_id will be set to an error value. Otherwise, the Prio will be hooked up to drive the skeleton. If the skeleton was set up with a standard bone heirarchy as it was in this example, Prio sensors will be automatically assigned to the appropriate bones.

Prio Calibration

Before we can start getting proper data from the Prio, it needs to be calibrated. This process involves instructing the user to assume a particular pose, after which the sensor data will be adjusted based on the assumption that the user is in the given pose. By default, Prio calibration will be performed by having the user assume the "T" pose, in which the arms are out to the sides with the palms facing down, and the feet are together and facing forward. This process also detects and cancels the user's facing direction, causing bone orientations to be in a reference frame defined by the direction the user was facing during calibration. This is useful if the user needs to face a screen to play a game using the Prio, as the orientation data will be in a reference frame defined by the screen so long as the user faces it as they calibrate. The calling application is responsible for informing the user to assume the given pose, and for allowing the user the appropriate amount of time to enter the pose. Once the user has had time to assume the pose, the following code should be executed.

```
1  yeiskel_calibratePrioProcessor(prio_id);
```

Once this code has been executed, the orientations of each bone should cause the skeleton to be in a perfect "T" pose itself, and all orientation data will have been corrected for the user's facing.

Starting the Prio

Now we need to instruct the PrioProcess to start gathering data from the Prio suit.

```
1  yeiskel_startPrioProcessor(prio_id);
```

Reading the Data

At this point, orientation data will be automatically obtained from the Prio at a regular interval. All that remains is to tell the skeleton to update its bone orientations using the Prio data, and to bring that bone orientation data into our application. In this example, we will only read orientation data from the chest sensor, though in a real application, we would read data from all the bones of our skeleton.

Listing 20.20: Reading Data

```
1  while(true)
2  {
3    yeiskel_update(skel_id);
4    quaternion quat;
5    yeiskel_getBoneOrientation(skel_id, "Chest", &quat);
6  }
```

The "quaternion" structure used here is a container for four floating point values, used here to represent an orientation. A quaternion can be converted to any other major orientation format, including rotation matrix, axis-angle, or Euler angles. The default orientation for a bone is aligned along the z-axis with the front of the bone pointing along the y-axis, and this orientation represents how far the bone has rotated from this point.

Note in the example code above, the orientation quaternion is read for the "Chest" segment of the skeleton. The API allows custom skeletal configurations and naming, but generally, the default skeleton and names can be used. By default, the following bones are available by name in a standard Prio skeleton:

"Chest", "Hips", "Head", "LeftShoulder", "LeftUpperArm", "Left-LowerArm", "LeftHand", "RightShoulder", "RightUpperArm", "Right-LowerArm", "RightHand", "LeftUpperLeg", "LeftLowerLeg", "Left-Foot", "RightUpperLeg", "RightLowerLeg", "RightFoot"

This example showed all that was required to obtain data from a Prio suit in an application using the YEI Skeletal API. There are additional tools the API features which allow for setting name aliases and additional rotation offsets for bones; these tools allow for easy integration with existing skeletal systems in applications such as game engines. Regardless of the application, the API aids in easy integration of Prio.

Complete Example

Listing 20.21: Complete Example

```
1  #include <stdio.h>
2  #include <time.h>
3  #include "yei_skeleton_api.h"
4
5  void main()
6  {
```

```
7     //create a skeleton to work with
8     yei_skeleton_id skel_id = yeiskel_createSkeleton();
9
10    //create a bone heirarchy for the skeleton based on gender and ↩
         age of the user
11    bool is_male = false;
12    int age = 28;
13    yeiskel_createStandardBoneHeirarchyWithAge(skel_id, is_male, age↩
         );
14
15    //find and attach a Prio suit to the skeleton
16    yei_processor_id prio_id = yeiskel_addPrioProcessorToSkeleton(↩
         skel_id);
17
18    //tell the user to get in the T pose
19    printf("When ready, press Enter and return the T pose within 2 ↩
         seconds...\n");
20
21    //wait for enter
22    while(getch()!="\n")
23    {;}
24
25    //sleep for 2 seconds
26    sleep(2);
27
28    //user should be in T pose by now, perform the calibration
29    yeiskel_calibratePrioProcessor(prio_id);
30
31    //start receiving data from the Prio suit
32    yeiskel_startPrioProcessor(prio_id);
33
34    while(true) //for as long as you need suit data for
35    {
36        //apply Prio data to the skeleton
37        yeiskel_update(skel_id);
38
39        //get the chest sensor orientation
40        quaternion quat;
41        yeiskel_getBoneOrientation(skel_id, "Chest", &quat);
42    }
43
44    //delete the skeleton and shut down the API
45    yeiskel_destroySkeleton(skel_id);
46    yeiskel_resetSkeletalApi();
47  }
```

20.6.2 Hands-On: Prio for Full-Body Immersion in Unity

YEI provides easy-to-use drop-in support via a pre-built plug-in for the popular Unity Engine from Unity Technologies. This makes it possible to create games and simulation applications that take advantage of Prio's full-body motion control input with very little programming and just a few simple steps.

The following section describes getting a Prio suit working within the Unity Engine.

1. **Create a new project in Unity**

   To create a new project in Unity, click: **File → New Project**

2. **Import a character model**

   Importing a character model can be done by either dragging the FBX model of a character into the asset directory or by using the Asset→Import New Asset and browsing to the desired character model.

3. **Set the imported model type**

   After the model has been imported it is necessary to set the model up for humanoid animation.

   To do this, go to the import setting and, under "Rig," set the "Animation Type" to be "Humanoid."

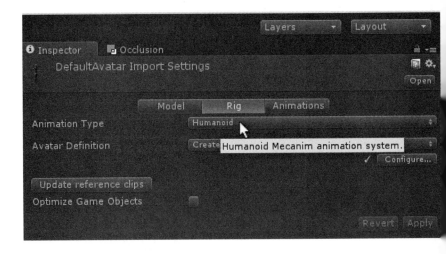

4. **Add the character to the scene**

   To add the character to the scene, simply click and drag the imported character into the scene hierarchy.

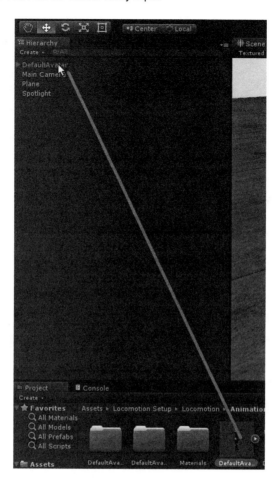

5. **Import the Prio package**

To use the Prio suit within the project, the Prio package needs to be imported. The Prio package allows easy access to the Prio suit functionality with minimal programming.

Import the package by clicking:

Assets → Import Package → Custom Package

and selecting the **PrioRig** component.

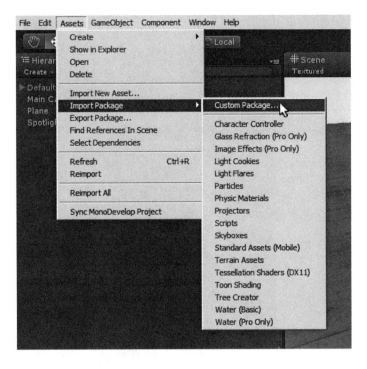

6. **Add the PrioRig component the character**

From the imported package click the PrioRig component script and drag it to the character in the scene view.

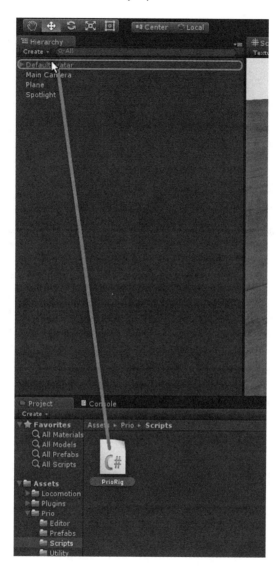

7. **Set up the skeleton properties**

Select the character and set the properties for the suit layout and desired gender and height. This will size the skeleton appropriately and associate the proper suit sensors to the animation rig.

8. **Set up a calibration routine**

To calibrate the suit for use, a calibration routine must be called before the suit is used in the game. In this example, the keyboard character "t" is used to trigger the calling of the Prio default calibration routine.

```
1  using UnityEngine;
2  using System.Collections;
3
4  public class PrioController : MonoBehaviour
5  {
6      //PrioRig Component
7      PrioRig myPrioRig;
8
9      // Use this for initialization
10     void Start ()
11     {
12         //Get the PrioRig component from the character
13         myPrioRig = GetComponent<PrioRig>();
14     }
15
16     // Update is called once per frame
17     void Update ()
18     {
19         //Press "t" to start calibration
20         if(Input.GetKeyDown("t"))
21         {
22             //Starts calibration after a wait time of 2.0 seconds
23             StartCoroutine(myPrioRig.CalibrateSens(2.0f));
24         }
25     }
26  }
27
```

9. **Test the game**

   To test the game, press the play button in the development environment.

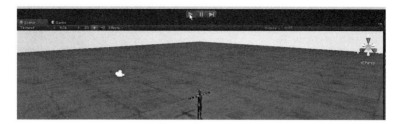

10. **Calibrate the suit**

    Once the game has started, press the "t" key and then stand in the standard T-pose, with feet together and arms straight out to the side, until the calibration completes. This should only take a few seconds.

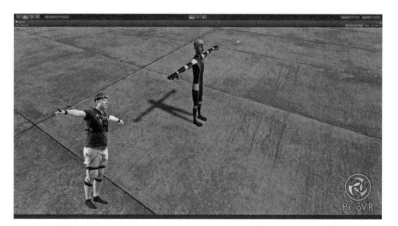

11. **Start moving**

    Now the suit has been associated with the in-game character and the suit's movements will be relayed to the in-game avatar in real-time.

20.6.3   Hands-On: Prio for Full-Body Motion Capture

Both YEI Prio motion sensing suits and YEI 3-Space Sensors can be used to record motion capture performances in a number of ways. YEI provides two options for recording and using motion capture data: YEI 3-Space Mocap Studio and the YEI MotionBuilder Plugin.

YEI 3-Space Mocap Studio

The YEI 3-Space Mocap Studio (see Figure 20.10) is an open-source motion capture application that uses the YEI 3-Space Sensor devices and YEI Prio motion sensing suit devices. The interface is similar to other motion capture applications, but is designed to be more convenient for immediate use with YEI devices since the application was created specifically to support them.

YEI 3-Space Mocap Studio offers point-and-click ease of use and automates much of the discovery and set process on start-up.

YEI 3-Space Mocap Studio can export mocap performance sessions in a variety of standard formats for use in other content pipelines and game engines.

For more information on the YEI 3-Space Mocap Studio, visit the YEI Technology web page.

YEI MotionBuilder Plug-in

YEI also provides a 3-Space TSH Importer Plug-in for the popular MotionBuilder application by Autodesk (see Figure 20.11). The TSH importer allows users to import YEI native TSH motion data files created from the YEI 3-Space Mocap Studio into MotionBuilder.

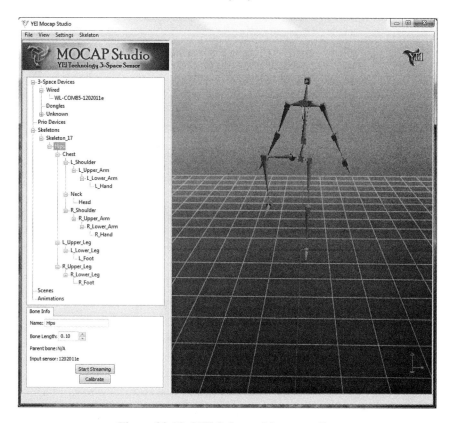

Figure 20.10: YEI 3-Space Mocap studio.

Once installed, the plug-in provides an easy-to-use user interface that allows the user to select files and control import options such as unit conversion, characterization and creation of control-rigs for the imported skeleton(s), and attachments for models.

The MotionBuilder plug-in is provided for free under an open-source license to allow others to expand, enhance, and learn from the script.

For more information on the YEI 3-Space MotionBuilder Plug-in, visit the YEI Technology web page.

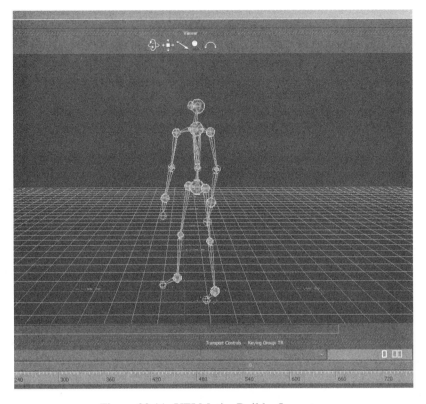

Figure 20.11: YEI MotionBuilder Importer.

Further Reading

A great book that talks about mocop animation, which fits perfectly with this chapter, is *The Mocap Book. A Practical Guide to the Art of Motion Capture* [Tobon 10]. There are additional web references, including from YEI Technology [YEI 15b, YEI 15c, YEI 15d, YEI 15a], Unity [Unity 15b], and general entries from Wikipedia [Wikipedia 15e, Wikipedia 15a].

Exercises

1. Write a program that uses a single YEI 3-Space Sensor to log the opening and closing of a door. Log the time the door was opened and closed and the angle of the door during the event.

2. Write a program that uses the X/Y, and roll angle from a single YEI 3-Space

Sensor to control the user interface of a simple program. Use the X/Y data to control the on-screen cursor position and use the roll angle to allow the modification of data associated with some UI element when the cursor is over that element. For example, make a screen full of shapes and allow the user to select a shape by pointing at it and change the size of the shape by altering the roll of the sensor.

3. Write a program that uses a single YEI 3-Space Sensor to estimate and record the number of steps and the walking heading for each step of a pedestrian wearing the sensor on the leg or foot. Hint: The sensor on the leg will rotate through a repeating orientation pattern and the heading of travel will be along the vector of the leg swing.

4. Write a program that uses a single YEI 3-Space Sensor as a virtual analog joystick by using the tilt of the sensor to control an on-screen cursor. Visualize this with an on-screen cross-hair that moves around the screen in real-time.

5. Write a program that takes the pitch/roll and heading from a single YEI 3-Space Sensor to render an aviation-style attitude indicator display and heading indicator display. The attitude indicator should visualize pitch and roll while the heading indicator should visualize the heading. Both should update in real-time as the 3-Space Sensor is moved.

6. Write a program that uses two YEI 3-Space Sensors, one placed upon the lower-back and one placed upon the upper back, to track the posture of the wearer. Create a visualization of this posture that gives the user a warning if the relative alignment of the two sensors detects a posture misalignment.

7. One powerful use of a full-body motion sensing suit is to be able to detect poses and gestures. Write a program that uses a YEI Prio Suit to detect when the suit-wearer is in a particular pose. Hint: have the Prio suit wearer stand in the desired pose to be matched and store the orientations of each of the relevant bones of the skeleton. To detect subsequent later matches with this pose, find the orientation differences between all of the bone orientations of the real-time pose and those previously stored.

8. Flag-semaphore code is a method of visually conveying messages by placing the arms in particular positions that encode alphabetic characters and other information. Extend the example above by writing a program that detects each of the alphabetic characters of flag-semaphore code and displays the currently detected character on the screen in real-time. See the "flag-semaphore" Wikipedia page at http://en.wikipedia.org/wiki/Flag_semaphore for a description of the poses necessary in flag-semaphore code.

9. Write a Unity program that uses pose detection of just the two arms such that when the arms are in the position required to hold binoculars (hand-binoculars or where both hands are near the eyes and the elbows are out to the sides) the camera on the view-port switches to being a zoomed-in view. Improve this by making the zoom functionality transition smoothly from the normal view to the binocular view. Hint: modify the fieldOfView object variable for the game camera. Look at smoothing the transition from normal to zoomed-in by considering the use of the Mathf.Lerp( ) function.

21

Simple Hands-On Project with Unity3D and Oculus Rift

Nonnarit O-larnnithipong

> To visualize is to see what is not there, what is not real
> – a dream. To visualize is, in fact, to make visual lies.
> Visual lies, however, have a way of coming true.
>
> —Peter McWilliams

Unity, created by Unity Technology, is a popular game development kit designed to be a complete integrated development environment (IDE). Unity provides multi-platform game development (desktops, web browsers, consoles, and mobile devices) for rapid development. Unity is capable of creating the game for either a 2D or 3D VE. This chapter deals with the steps required for a 3D VE. This chapter used Unity Pro version 4. While Unity 5 is the latest development tool, Unity 4 is still pervasive among Unity users. Unity 4 Pro it is still available for users that purchase[1] Unity 5. Also, the concepts of this chapter would apply to newer versions (see Figure 21.1).[2].

21.1   Installation and System Requirements

The latest version of Unity is available at http://unity3d.com/unity/download.[3] Unity is available for both Windows and Mac OS X version. The Unity Pro version

---

[1] Contact Unity to see if both subscription model and perpetual model provide access to Unity 4 pro.

[2] With the difference that some of the options may have changed or been distributed differently in the UI.

[3] You can just visit http://unity3d.com and browse what options they have available.

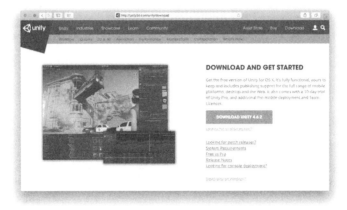

Figure 21.1: Download page on Unity website.

is required for some of the samples provided in this chapter (e.g., Oculus Rift). Unity 5 offers a free version and paid version (exact functionality but different licensing). After finishing download, install the software on your hard drive. The system requirements [UnityTechnologies 15] for Unity[4] 4 installation are:

- **Operating System**: Windows XP SP2+, Windows 7 SP1+, Windows 8, Mac OS X 10.6 or above.[5] (Windows Vista is not supported.)

- **GPU**: Graphics card with DX9 (shader model 2.0) capabilities. Anything made since 2004 should work.

21.2   Getting Started

To start with Unity, open the application from its installed directory. If it is the first time, the Unity License Activation dialog will appear, as shown in Figure 21.2. After the activation is completed, Unity starts with a sample game project. Before creating a game, we should be familiar with the layout of Unity user interface [Blackman 13], as shown in Figure 21.3.

1. **Unity Menu Bar**: It contains all commands and settings used in Unity.

2. **Scene Navigation and Object Transformation Tools**: Scene navigation (left-most) is used to navigate or rotate the scene view. Note that the changes

---

[4]Please check their site for updated requirements.
[5]Version 5 requires Mac OS X 10.8 or above.

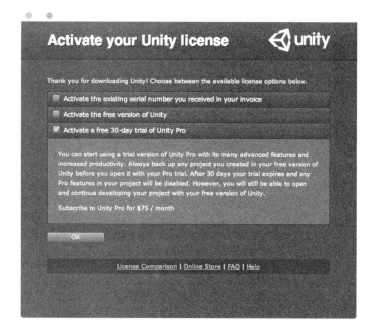

Figure 21.2: Unity Pro license activation options.

do not apply in game view. The object transformation tools, which are translate, rotate, scale, and free-transform, are used to transform the game object. Also note that the tools mentioned here are different in game view.

3. **Play Mode Controls**: It allows the developer to enter or exit the play mode.

4. **Hierarchy**: This shows how objects are oriented in the game. It also indicates (dynamically) the active game objects.

5. **Scene View**: This is the working space to design the game scene.

6. **Game View**: It shows how the game is displayed to the player. The game view depends on the location and direction of the projected camera placed in the game scene.

7. **Inspector**: It allows the developer to customize the features or the properties of the game objects, materials, prefabs, or game components.

8. **Console**: It displays various messages relevant to the game project. This includes warnings and errors. In general, any logging information that is sent to the console during play mode (while the game is running).

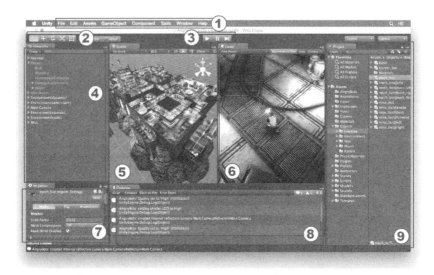

Figure 21.3: Layout of unity user interface.

9. **Project**: It provides the developer a way to manage the files in the game project directory.

21.2.1   Creating a New Project

Create the new project by selecting **File > New Project** on the menu bar. A project wizard will ask for the project name and directory. It also allows the developer to select the essential Unity packages, as shown in Figure 21.4. Set up the defaults for 3D mode and then click the button **Create Project**. The empty project, as shown in Figure 21.5, will be created with one main camera (can be seen in the scene view and also in hierarchy). Move the mouse over the area of **Scene** and try to become familiar with scene navigation by using the mouse.

21.3   Creating Game Scene

The game scene that will be introduced as the sample in this chapter consists of some basic concepts of game creation in Unity. For example, creating terrain, adding 3D objects to the scene, creating a Skybox, and lighting the game scene. For this game scene, an island surrounded by an ocean is used to demonstrate the concepts.

1. First, it is important to create the terrain, which is the base of the entire scene. On the menu bar, select **GameObject > 3D Object > Terrain**. The

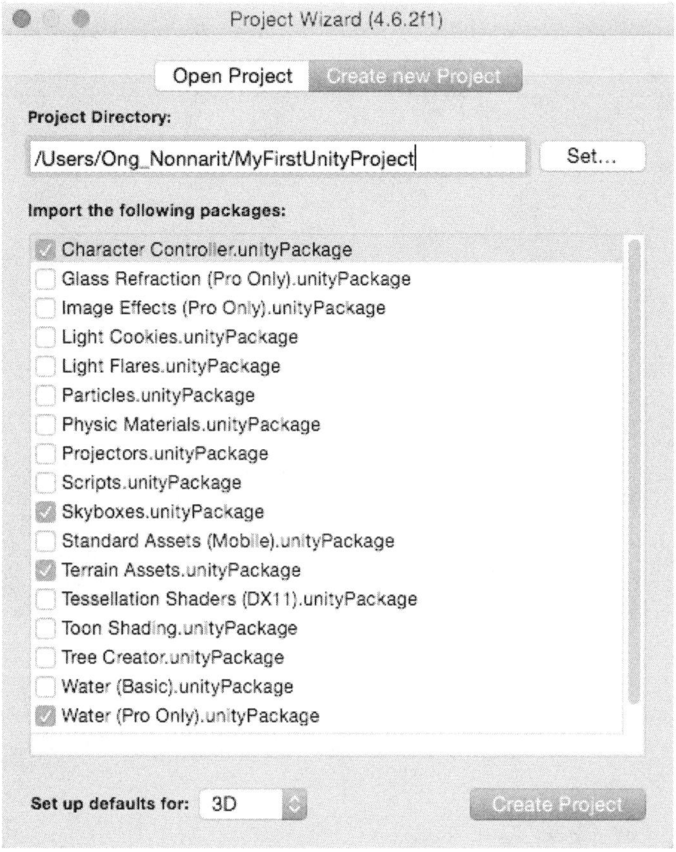

Figure 21.4: Project wizard for creating new project.

Side Note 21.1: Tips: User Interface Layout

The Unity user interface layout can be changed and customized. On the top right corner of the Unity window, there is the drop-down menu labeled *Layout*. It has several layouts for the UI and users can also customize their own UI layout by dragging the panels around.

---

flat gray terrain will appear in the scene view section. Before continuing to the next step, saving the file is needed. Save this game scene by selecting **File > Save Scene** and name it *IslandScene*. Click **Save** to finish. The scene will be saved in the *assets* folder,[6] as shown in Figure 21.6.

---

[6]The folder will contain the Unity icon when viewed in Windows Project Explorer.

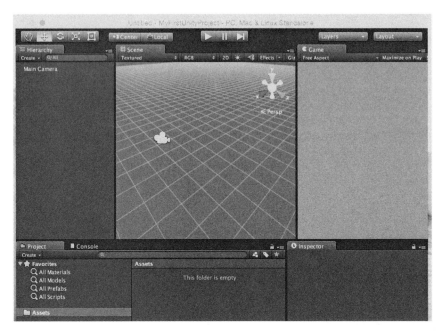

Figure 21.5: The empty project with one main camera.

Side Note 21.2: The Mouse in Unity

- **Left Click**: To select a game object.

- **Left Click and Drag**: To select multiple game objects.

- **Mouse Wheel Scroll**: To zoom in and out.

- **Mouse Wheel Click and Drag**: To pan the scene view.

- **Right Click and Drag**: To rotate the scene view.

---

2. Click at object named Terrain in the hierarchy. Using the Inspector, take a look at several properties and settings of the selected terrain object. Modify the values in the Position in Transform section as $X = -500$, $Y = -10$ and $Z = -500$. In the Terrain (Script) section (below the Transform section), there are seven icons for terrain modification. Click on the gear icon button and modify the terrain width and length to be 1000. The Terrain Inspector

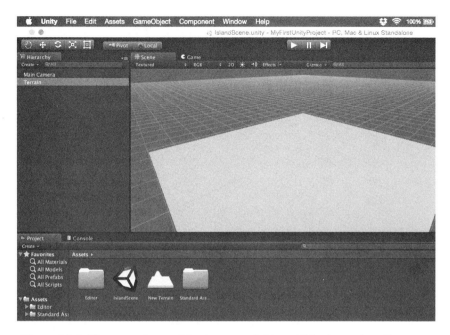

Figure 21.6: The scene is saved in the assets folder within the project directory.

panel is shown in Figure 21.7. This modification results in translating the center of the terrain to the center of the scene and lowering the terrain below sea level (assuming sea level is at Y = 0).

3. Next, we will add a texture[7] to the current terrain. In the Terrain (Script) section, click on the brush icon (the fourth icon). Then, click on the button *Edit Textures*; select *Add Texture* from the drop-down menu. Select the texture *GoodDirt*, as shown in Figure 21.8. This makes the terrain appear as sea sand. Then click *Add*; the first texture you add to the terrain will be considered the base texture for the terrain.

4. To add the ocean to the scene, there is a Prefab[8] already included in Unity. This is included in the original packages selected in the project wizard. On the Project panel, go to folder **Assets > Standard Assets > Water (Pro Only) > Water4**, then drag Prefab *Water4Example (Advanced)* to the scene. Then, at the Transform section on the inspector panel, modify the position **(X,Y,Z) to (0,0,0)** and the scale **(X,Y,Z) to (10,1,10)**, as shown in Figure

---

[7]You may find in some Unity books the term *paint the terrain with texture*. While this is the terminology, we prefer to use "add texture" to the terrain, as it is standard in computer graphics.

[8]A Prefab is an "asset type that allows you to store a GameObject object complete with components and properties" [Unity 15a].

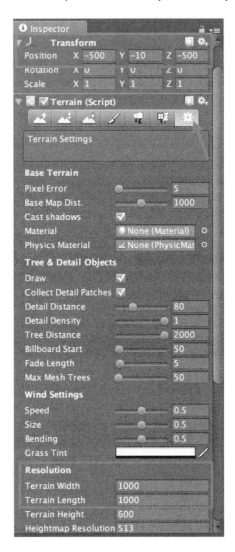

Figure 21.7: Modification of terrain properties on the inspector panel.

21.9.

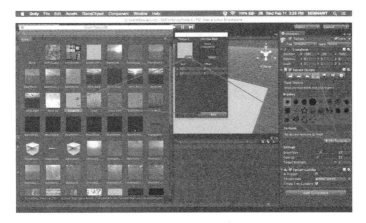

Figure 21.8: Painting textures on terrain.

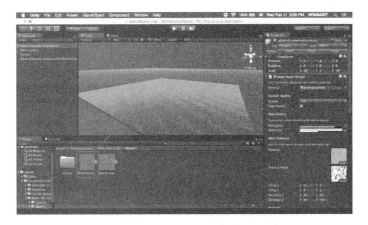

Figure 21.9: Adding the ocean prefab to the scene.

5. The scene now has layers of terrain and an ocean on top. Next, we are going to raise the level of terrain to make it appear as an island surrounded by the ocean. On the Hierarchy panel, select Terrain. Then, in the Terrain (Script) section on the inspector panel, click on the first icon tool; this tool will be used to raise or lower the level of the terrain. Select a brush you prefer, set the proper brush size and opacity, as shown in Figure 21.10. On the scene view, click on any place you would like to raise the terrain level. You can click, hold the mouse button and drag to raise the terrain level higher. The third terrain modification icon tool can be used to smooth the rough surface of the terrain.

6. Next, you can go back to add the terrain with other textures by clicking at

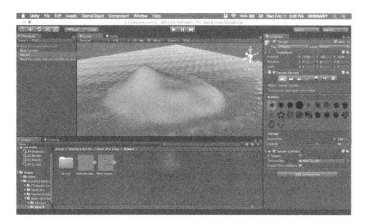

Figure 21.10: Modification of the terrain level.

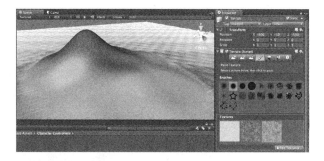

Figure 21.11: Painting the terrain using several textures.

the brush icon and add more textures. For example, the texture named *Grass (Hill)* and *Grass&Rock*, are shown in Figure 21.11. This gives the terrain different textures.

7. Moreover, with the fifth terrain modification icon tool on the Terrain Inspector, we can place trees on the terrain. Click on the button *Edit Trees* and then select *Add Tree*. Choose the *Palm* tree from the list of preloaded GameObjects. You can first adjust the brush size, density of the trees, and its variation, as shown in Figure 21.12, before placing them on the terrain by clicking on the terrain surface.

Figure 21.12: Placing the trees on the terrain.

21.4   Lighting, Camera, and Skybox

There is still more needed to finish our unity game. In this section, we are going to talk about how to create the light and Skybox in the game scene. This will help to make the game more realistic. We will render our scene for the first time. Therefore, we need to put the camera and the character into the scene.

1. Continuing from the previous section, we are going to add the light source that acts like the sunlight for the game scene. On the menu bar, go to **GameObject > Light > Directional Light**. Then, adjust the transform properties of the directional light on the inspector panel as position (X,Y,Z) = (0,100,0) and rotation (X,Y,Z) = (45,-45,0). The rotation of the directional light will affect the direction of light and shadow for the entire game scene acting like the sunlight, as shown in Figure 21.13.

2. Next, we are going to add a camera and a character to the game scene. Before adding the camera, the current *Main Camera* must be removed. Right click on GameObject *Main Camera* on the hierarchy panel and select *Delete*. Then, on the project explorer panel, go to **Assets > Standard Assets > Character Controllers**. Click and drag First Person Controller Prefab to the scene. Then, modify the position in transform section on the inspector panel as $(X, Y, Z) = (0, 15, 0)$ (or any other value you desired). The idea is that the first person controller object appears above the terrain, as shown in Figure 21.14. Otherwise, the character will fall down when entering play mode due to the gravitational effect. This character controller prefab consists of several pre-defined character controller scripts and a built-in camera. Right now, we are ready to render the game scene by clicking on the play button above the scene view. This makes unity enter play mode. What we actually observed is the perspective of the camera attached to the character controller, as shown in Figure 21.15

3. As we can see from Figure 21.15, the sky of the scene is still the plain dark blue background. In this step, we will render the image of the sky at the very far distance of the scene. In Unity, we call this component "Skybox."[9] Exit the play mode by clicking on the Play button again. On the hierarchy panel, expand the GameObject named *First Person Controller* by clicking on the triangular arrow head. Select the GameObject *Main Camera*. On the inspector panel, scroll down to the bottom, click on the button **Add Component > Rendering > Skybox**. On the right of the field *Custom Skybox*, click on the small circle to select the Skybox material named **Sunny1_Skybox**. Enter play mode once again and you will see the sky rendered at the very far distance of the game scene as shown in figure 21.16. You can use mouse and keyboard to navigate the game character through the game scene.

4. Next, we are going to add the shadow and modify its direction. On the hierarchy panel, select the GameObject *Directional Light*. At the Light section on the inspector panel, choose the shadow type as soft shadow. At the transform section above light section, manually modify the X and Y rotation to match the direction of the sun image on the Skybox. The resultant shadow is shown in Figure 21.17.

Now, our game scene is ready and consists of the basic components we need, as shown in Figure 21.18. In the next section, we will discuss how to add the material and the action script to the GameObject.

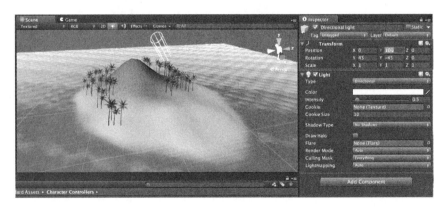

Figure 21.13: Directional light affects the direction of light and shadow for the entire game scene.

---

[9]Which is a common component in most computer graphics engines and game engines.

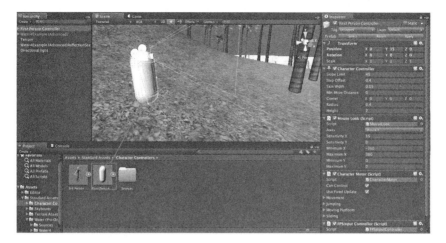

Figure 21.14: Character controller prefab placing on the terrain.

21.5 GameObject and Basic Action Script

In this section, we will cover how to add another GameObject into the game scene and also learn how to create material for the GameObject. The character controller will be able to pick this object. Therefore, the scripts are needed in order to define the action on the GameObject.

1. Add the new GameObject to the game scene. On the menu bar, go to **GameObject > 3D Object > Sphere**. Then, manually adjust the position

Figure 21.15: Game scene rendering in play mode without skybox.

Figure 21.16: Game scene rendering in play mode with Skybox.

Figure 21.17: Angle modification of directional light.

of the sphere at its inspector panel to make it visible on the terrain. We are going to create a beach ball from this sphere. Thus, you may also change its scale to match the proportion of the terrain as we can see in Figure 21.19.

2. Next, we are going to create the material for this sphere. First, at the menu bar, go to **Assets > Create > Material**. This creates the material for the white plain sphere, as shown in Figure 21.20. Give this object the name *BeachBall*.

3. You can see that the *BeachBall* material is now blank. We have to assign the texture to this material before assigning the material to the GameObject. You can import a JPG, PNG, GIF, BMP, or even PSD image file to use as the texture. In this example, you can use whatever file format you like. For completeness, this section contains an example of how to create texture

Figure 21.18: Completed game scene.

Figure 21.19: Adding new GameObject into the game scene.

using Adobe Photoshop.[10] The example uses the Adobe Photoshop default
file format (".psd"). The reason is that this file format retains the highest
resolution. It is also very easy to edit. Having said this, in other engines,
using a ".psd" file is not always a possibility. In those cases, one can choose
a high-resolution format of the desired file type (see Further Reading section
for additional information).

In Photoshop, go to **File > New** in order to create a new image document with
the width and height of 1024×1024 pixels with resolution of 72 pixels/inch.
Then, click OK. You can paint the color stripes similar to Figure 21.21. Save
the image file as *BallTexture.psd* in the *Assets* folder in the Unity Project
directory. It is possible to use other image sizes, such as 512×512 pixels.

---

[10]An alternative to Photoshop is GIMP, an open-source application.

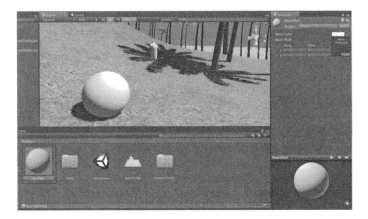

Figure 21.20: Create new material for the GameObject.

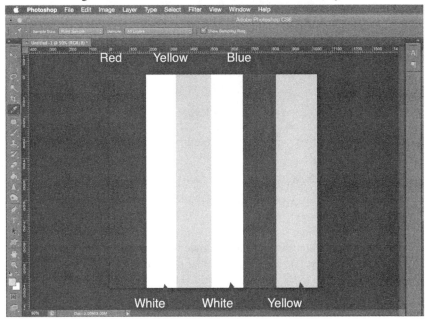

Figure 21.21: Create new texture image using Adobe Photoshop.

4. The texture image file can now be used in the Unity IDE. The texture image
   will be located in the Assets folder (in the Project Explorer panel). Click on
   the material file we created before. Then, click and drag the texture image
   and drop it on the texture of the material (at the inspector panel), as shown
   in Figure 21.22.

Figure 21.22: Assign the texture image to material.

5. The next step is to assign the material to the sphere. Select *GameObject* sphere from hierarchy panel. At the mesh renderer section on the inspector panel, click on the small circle next to the field *Element0* under the materials subsection. Then, select the BeachBall material we have created, as shown in Figure 21.23.

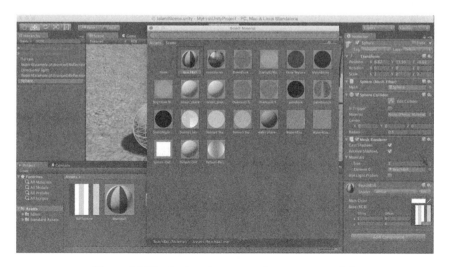

Figure 21.23: Assign the texture image to material.

6. Now, the material is assigned to the sphere. It does appear now as a real beach ball. Next, to work with the beach ball (e.g., rotate the ball), Action Script is required. Select the GameObject sphere at the hierarchy panel. At the inspector panel, scroll down to the bottom and click **Add Component > New Script**. Give the script the name *BallRotate*. select C# (CSharp) language. The script BallRotate.cs will appear in the project explorer panel. Double click the file to open it in MonoDevelop-Unity and replace the existing code with the code in Listing 21.1. Then, click *Save* and go back to Unity. Now, when we enter play mode, the beach ball will rotate. From the code Listing 21.1, in the function *Update()*, the command *transform.Rotate()* is equivalent to when the properties of the GameObject on the inspector are modified. But for this one, the rotation of the GameObject (sphere) is updated regularly. The updates happen in each cycle as defined by Unity. The three inputs of the function *transform.Rotate()* are the angles in degree for the rotation about X, Y, and Z-axis, respectively.

Listing 21.1: BallRotate.cs

```
1
2   using UnityEngine;
3   using System.Collections;
4
5   public class BallRotate : MonoBehaviour {
6
7     void Update () {
8       transform.Rotate (new Vector3 (45, 45, 45) * Time.↩
          deltaTime);
9     }
10  }
```

7. Next, the player controller will need to pick up the beach ball. We will make the beach ball collectible. On the hierarchy panel, select the GameObject *First Person Controller*. On the inspector panel, scroll all the way down and click **Add Component > New Script**. Then, name the script *BallCollect*. Select C# language. Replace the existing code with the code in Listing 21.2. Once completed, save and go back to Unity.

Listing 21.2: BallCollect.cs

```
1
2   using UnityEngine;
3   using System.Collections;
4
5   public class BallCollect : MonoBehaviour
6   {
7     void OnTriggerEnter (Collider other) {
8       if (other.gameObject.tag == "PickUpObject")
9       {
```

Figure 21.24: Creating the tag for the GameObjects.

```
10          other.gameObject.SetActive (false);
11      }
12    }
13  }
```

8. The status of GameObject with the tag "PickUpObject" when the object collider is triggered as shown in Listing 21.2. In other words, the GameObject will disappear when the GameObject collider is triggered (with tag name "PickUpObject"). Now, we have to add the tag to the sphere. Select the GameObject sphere from the hierarchy. At the top of the inspector panel, click on the drop-down menu labeled "Tag." Then, select *Add Tag...* Create the tag with the name "PickUpObject," as shown in Figure 21.24. Go back to the inspector of the sphere again by selecting the sphere (from the hierarchy). Now, click on the drop-down menu labeled "Tag." Then, select *PickUpObject*. At the section called *Sphere Collider* on the inspector, check mark the box label "Is Trigger" to allow the collider to be overlapped by another collider (character collider). Otherwise, the event OnTriggerEnter() will not be possible. After that, we can try running the game in play mode and see whether the beach ball can be collected or not. Copy and paste a number of the beach balls (sphere) on the different positions in the game scene similar to the snapshot in Figure 21.25

21.6   Graphic User Interface (GUI)

In this section, we will continue making the complete game scene example by adding a very simple GUI on the game view. We will create the GUI that indicates the number of the collected beach balls on the upper left of the screen while playing the game.

Figure 21.25: Game scene with multiple collectible objects.

1. Select the GameObject "First Player Controller" from the hierarchy panel.
   On the inspector panel, scroll all the way down to the *BallCollect (Script)*
   section. To edit the script, double click on it. The updated version of the
   code is shown in Listing 21.3. The new variable "count" allows us to track
   the number of beach balls collected. It is incremented by one when the
   object collider with tag named "PickUpObject" is triggered.

Listing 21.3: BallCollect.cs (updated with GUI)

```
1
2   using UnityEngine;
3   using System.Collections;
4
5   public class BallCollect : MonoBehaviour
6   {
7     private int count = 0; // add this line
8
9     void OnTriggerEnter (Collider other) {
10      if (other.gameObject.tag == "PickUpObject")
11      {
12        other.gameObject.SetActive (false);
13        count = count + 1; // add this line
14      }
15    }
16
17    // add this function
18    void OnGUI()
19    {
20      GUI.Box (new Rect (10, 10, 600, 60), "Beach Ball Collected↩
              : " + count.ToString () + "/7");
21      GUI.skin.box.fontSize = 50;
22    }
23
24  }
```

The function *OnGUI()* updates the display of GUI frequently for a small

Figure 21.26: Adjusting the position of the camera.

period of time. The command *GUI.Box()* needs two sets of input. The first one is the position and size of the GUI box to be displayed. To create the GUI box on the screen at coordinate of X = 10 and Y = 10 with the width of 600 and the height of 60, code as that shown in Listing 21.3 is needed. Note that the second input of *GUI.Box()* is the string to be displayed. The listing shows how the static string is concatenated with the variable "count." This allows the GUI to display the current value of the variable "count" along with some fixed words. It is also possible to change the font size of the text in the GUI box.

2. The current setting of the camera provides a first person perspective. However, the camera can be adjusted to provide a different perspective (e.g., third-person). This will allow us to see the character interact with the ball. By expanding GameObject "First Player Controller" on the hierarchy panel, select *Main Camera*. Then, manually adjust the position of the camera by moving it above and behind the character, as shown in Figure 21.26. Unity provides a preview window to see the effect in the rendering based on the new camera position. This is found at the lower right corner of the scene, which provides a preview.

Now, in play mode, the changes are self-evident, with the new GUI and camera position. This is shown in Figure 21.27. The beach ball count is updated as a number of them are collected by the character.

21.7 Oculus Rift Integration for Unity

Oculus Rift is a HMD developed by Oculus VR [Wikipedia 15f]. It is virtual reality display goggles that immerse the users in a true 3D virtual reality environment. With the stereoscopic display, the Oculus Rift mimics the vision of human eyes

Figure 21.27: Complete game scene in unity with GUI.

and makes the users feel like they are standing or being a part of the gaming environment (see Chapter 3). With the INS (e.g., gyroscope sensor) (see Chapters 17 and 20) built into the device, the image displayed on the screen of the Oculus Rift changes according to the movement of the user's head. Thus, the Oculus Rift simultaneously works as an input and output device.

Unity provides support for the Oculus Rift. Unity provides an *Oculus Rift Camera Prefab* to replace the regular *Main Camera*. The Oculus Rift requires Unity Pro version installed (4 or higher). The next example uses Oculus Rift DK2.

21.7.1   Installation and Package Import

1. The first requirement to start with Oculus Rift is to prepare the necessary drivers and software from Oculus. This can be downloaded from **https://developer.oculus.com/downloads**. It is also important to download *Unity 4 Integration* and *Oculus Runtime* for the correct operating system.

2. Install *Oculus Runtime* on the computer where Unity is installed. Then, connect the Oculus Rift to the computer.

3. Open the application called **OculusConfigUtil** from the installed Oculus Runtime directory. Ensure that the Oculus Configuration Utility can detect both "Oculus Rift Sensor" and "Infrared Camera," as shown in Figure 21.29.

4. Open the Unity Game Project, just completed in the previous section. On the menu bar, select **Assets > Import Package > Custom Package**. Choose the file named "OculusUnityIntegration.unitypackage" located in your download directory of Unity 4 Integration. (You may need to extract

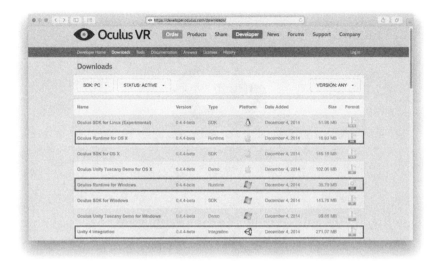

Figure 21.28: Oculus Rift developer website.

the ovr_unity_0.4.4_lib.zip[11] first.) A pop-up window will appear, as shown in Figure 21.30. Click the button *import*. Unity will import the Oculus Rift package into the assets folder (located in the project directory).

21.7.2 Oculus Rift Prefab

After finishing import the Oculus Rift integration package for Unity; a new folder named **OVR** will be located under the folder Assets (on the project explorer panel). That folder contains materials, resources, scripts, and necessary files for Oculus Rift needed for Unity and Oculus Rift to work in tandem. We are going to use OVR Prefab, which is the prefabricated GameObject with complete material and control scripts. The first person controller will be replaced by the stereoscopic camera of the Oculus Rift.

1. On the hierarchy panel, select the GameObject *First Person Controller*. Right click on it and delete it from the game scene. This will be replaced by the Oculus Rift Prefab.

2. On the project explorer panel, Go to **Assets > OVR > Prefabs**. Select *OVRPlayerController.prefab* and drag and drop it on the scene view, as shown in Figure 21.31

---

[11]Remember that versions change over time.

Figure 21.29: Oculus Rift configuration utility.

3. Try to adjust the position of OVRPlayerController to be above the terrain level so that the object will not fall down due to gravity. In play mode, now the game scene is split into two slightly different images, as shown in Figure 21.32.

4. The Skybox and the interaction between the character and the beach ball are lost (deleted in a previous step along with first person controller.). Adding the Skybox is similar to before. Instead of adding it to the main camera of the first person controller, the Skybox is added to both camera views. On the hierarchy, expand *OVRPlayerController* and *OVRCameraRig*. Then select *LeftEyeAnchor*. On the inspector panel, scroll all the way down and

Figure 21.30: Import Oculus Rift package for Unity.

Figure 21.31: Adding OVR player controller to the game scene.

click **Add Component > Rendering > Skybox**. Then, select the Skybox material named **Sunny1_Skybox**. Repeat the same step for *RightEyeAnchor* with the same Skybox material.

5. The next step is make the ball collectible again. On the Hierarchy, select *OVRPlayerController*. Then, at the bottom of the Inspector panel, click **Add Component > Scripts > Ball Collect**. The script, previously created, is now added to the character controller. We can go into play mode and see the result. By navigating through the game scene, the final result shows that both images on the stereoscopic display render the Skybox. The Skybox images are rendered at a very far distance of the scene. The action script is added back to the player controller, and the beach balls are now collectible, as shown in Figure 21.33.

With the example in this chapter, the reader may understand the basic concept of how to get started with Unity by creating a simple interactive Game Scene. For future work, you can replace the game character controller with other preferable 3D models so that the game scene will become more interesting and more realistic. Unity is a powerful game engine that consists of several integrations to support many gaming platforms so it can be considered one of the useful tools to create a human–computer interaction interface.

Figure 21.32: Stereoscopic images using Oculus Rift Integration for Unity.

Figure 21.33: Play mode using Oculus Rift integration with Skybox rendering.

Further Reading

The book called *Beginning 3D Game Development with Unity 4: All-in-One, Multi-Platform Game Development*, second edition by Sue Blackman contains several examples on how to create and develop the game using Unity 4. The author provides useful knowledge, which is necessary for the game creation.

Ogre3D provides a very interesting tutorial about Skyboxes, which can provide a better understanding about them (http://www.ogre3d.org/tikiwiki/Basic+Tutorial+3#SkyBoxes). In addition, *Game Programming Gems 2* provides a chapter titled "Rendering Distance Scenery with Skyboxes," which talks about Skyboxes as well [DeLoura 01, pp. 416–420].

While this chapter provided a hands-on approach to Unity, it is really important to understand how computer graphics works. See Chapter 4 for additional information. Also, *Real-Time Rendering* [Akenine-Möller et al. 08] provides a general overview.

Please note that an updated for Unity 5 will be available on the book's website.

Exercises

1. With the example in this chapter, replace the character mesh with another 3D model that suits the game environment.

2. Add other game objects for collision. The idea is that when the character controller collides with these obstructed game objects, the score of objects collected is decreased.

3. Add an ambient sound to the game scene. For example, a sea's wave noise, wind noise, or a bird noise. This will make the game scene more realistic. Change the mesh and material of the collecting game object. Then, add a sound effect when the character controller hits the game object.

22

Hands-On Approach with Leap Motion

Frank E. Hernandez

> I find languages that support just one programming
> paradigm constraining.
>
> —Bjarne Stroustrup

This chapter deals with the Leap Motion controller. Here we present a hands-on project to get familiarized with the functionality of the Leap Motion controller and learn how to integrate it into your own applications.

22.1   What Is Leap Motion?

Developed by Leap Motion Inc., the Leap Motion controller (see Figure 22.1) is a great addition to the arsenal of any HCI enthusiast and researcher alike. This device allows for tracking of 3D objects in mid-air to a degree of accuracy that allows tracking of individual fingers in the hand [Leap 14b]. The Leap Motion accomplishes this through the use of two infrared cameras arranged so that their field of vision intersects. It has three infrared red IR light-emitting diodes LEDs, two located at each side of each camera and one between the cameras. This creates strong contrast between the object (hand, arm, and finger, among others) of interest and the background [Holz 14]. The images collected are then sent to the software component which keeps an internal model of the object.

Figure 22.1: Leap Motion controller.

22.2 Installation

In this section we will go over the steps needed to get started using the Leap Motion in your project. The steps presented here are for the Leap Motion Software Development Kit (SDK) version 2.2[1] but should be relevant to other versions of Leap Motion. While at first sight it might seem like a long list of steps, do not fret over it as the installation process is quite simple:

1. Go to the Leap Motion setup page: https://www.leapmotion.com/setup

2. Find the "Developer Installer" button and click it. This will take you to the development portal.

3. Once in the developer portal click on the "Sign into download SDK vX.X.X.XXX".

4. Create an account if needed. An account is required to download the SDK.

5. The SDK comes in the form of a compressed archive. Make sure to extract the files.

---

[1] SDK Version: v2.2.2.24469.

Side Note 22.1: Firmware - Windows Only

After going through the steps and performing the setup, there might still be a slight chance that the device will not track any input. If this is the case, the firmware may need to be updated. Follow the following steps to update the firmware:

1. Open "Control Panel" and go to "Devices Manager."

2. Under "Other Devices," search for "WestBridge" with an alert sign on it, as show in Figure 22.2.

3. Follow the steps for firmware in this Leap Motion support document: https://support.leapmotion.com/entries/39199843-Troubleshooting-Guide. Locate the "Firmware Reset Tool."

4. Download the tool and follow the steps to reset your firmware.

5. Your Leap Motion should now detect the hand movements.

---

6. Once uncompressed, make sure to look at the README file for any steps specific to the targeted operating system.

    (a) Windows:

        i. Run Leap_Motion_Installer_version.exe

    (b) Mac OS X:

        i. Open Leap_Motion_Installer_version.dmg

        ii. Run Leap Motion.pkg

    (c) Linux (Ubuntu):

        i. For 32-bit systems, run: sudo dpkg –install Leap-version-x86.deb

        ii. For 64-bit systems, run: sudo dpkg –install Leap-version-x64.deb

7. Follow the steps in the installer.

22.3 Hands-On Mini-Project

The application we will develop in this chapter will track two gestures from the user to minimize and restore all windows on the desktop. We are going to allow the

Figure 22.2: Trouble with Leap Motion firmware.

user to swipe in order to minimize every window on the desktop (to have access to
your desktop). We are also going to write code that will perform a circle gesture to
restore all your windows.

The leap motion site https://developer.leapmotion.com/documentation/cpp/devguide/
Project_Setup.html has a great walk-through on how to set up the developer SDK
with your IDE. Additional help is provided on the book's website about general
help in setting up libraries with different IDEs.

Let us begin by creating a new file and ensure that the application runs until the
user presses enter. Let's do that by typing the code in Listing 22.1

Listing 22.1: LEAP (Basic Setup)

```
1
2   #include <iostream>
3   #include <string.h>
4
5   int main(int argc, char ** argv){
6     std::cout << "Press Enter to quit..." << std::endl;
7     // Keep this process running until Enter is pressed
8     std::cin.get();
9     return 0;
10  }
```

Now we can proceed to connect the Leap Motion controller. In order to accomplish
this, we must create a **Controller** object. As soon it is created, the controller object
will attempt to connect to the Leap Motion. However, this is an asynchronous
process so we'll need to wait until it is connected.

Listing 22.2: LEAP (Controller)

```
1
2   #include <iostream>
3   #include <string.h>
4
5   using namespace Leap;
6
```

```
7   int main(int argc, char ** argv){
8     Controller controller;
9
10    // Keep this process running until Enter is pressed
11    std::cout << "Press Enter to quit..." << std::endl;
12    std::cin.get();
13    return 0;
14  }
```

In order to know when the Leap is connected and can easily handle the interaction with the Leap Motion controller, we will subclass the **Listener**. The listener class provides a set of callbacks to respond to the events dispatched by the controller object. For this project, we will define a simple listener, **LeapListener** (see Listing 22.3), which will only listen to a few events of importance to us. The events we'll care about are:

- **onConnect**: This is dispatched when the controller object detects that the Leap Motion controller is ready. In other words, the connection was established. This is where we'll handle any initialization of our logic.

- **onFrame**: This is dispatched when a new frame of the hand or finger data is available to be consumed. This is where we'll handle all of our logic that deals with interpreting the user's interaction (for each iteration or combination of those) and how to react to each frame (or combination of frames).

- **onDisconnect**: This is dispatched when the Leap Motion controller is unplugged. The clean up logic is performed here.

Listing 22.3: LEAP (LeapListener.h)

```
1   #include <windows.h>
2   #include <shlobj.h>
3   #include <exdisp.h>
4   #include <stdio.h>
5
6   using namespace Leap;
7   using namespace std;
8
9   class LeapListener: public Listener {
10    public:
11      // Will be called when the Leap Motion Controlled is Connected.
12      virtual void onConnect(const Controller&);
13      // Called on every frame, good place to perform our control ↩
            logic.
14      virtual void onFrame(const Controller&);
15      // Will ve called when the Leap Motion Controller is ↩
            Disconnected.
16      virtual void onDisconnect(const Controller &);
17
```

```
18    private:
19        // Needed for our Hands on project.
20        IShellDispatch* _pShell;
21        HRESULT _hr ;
22        bool _bMinimized;
23        void restoreWindows();
24        void minimizeWindows();
25
26    };
```

Once we have defined our header, we can proceed to implement our listener. We
begin by programming the logic for the **onConnect** event. First, we are going to
let the user know that the controller is connected. Then, we can proceed to activate
the gestures that we want to detect. By default, all the gestures are turned off in the
Leap Motion software. Therefore, gestures must be activated one by one. In the
case of this project we will track only the circle and the swipe gestures. Currently,[2]
LeapMotion supports four gestures:

- **Circle**: This gesture is defined as a finger making a circle in mid-air. This is
  recognized as Gesture::TYPE_CIRCLE.

- **Swipe**: This gesture, similar to the multi-touch swipe gesture (see Chapter
  8), is defined as the linear motion of a finger or fingers. This is recognized
  as Gesture::TYPE_SWIPE.

- **Key Tap**: This function is defined as the simulation of a key tap (in mid-air).
  This is recognized as Gesture::TYPE_KEY_TAP.

- **Screen Tap**: This is defined as the horizontal tapping movement of the finger.
  In other words, this is a forward motion as if one was tapping the desktop
  display in front. This is recognized as Gesture::TYPE_SCREEN_TAP.

Listing 22.4: LEAP (LeapListener.cpp - onConnect)

```
1    #include "LeapListener.h"
2
3    void LeapListener::onConnect(const Controller & controller) {
4        std::cout<< "Leap Controller Connected" << std::endl;
5        // In order to use gestures we must first enable the
6        // recognition for each gesture we want in our app.
7        // We are going to be using 2 gestures here:
8        // - Circle and Swipe
9        controller.enableGesture(Gesture::TYPE_CIRCLE);
10       controller.enableGesture(Gesture::TYPE_SWIPE);
11
12       // Initialize the use of COM objects...
13       CoInitialize(NULL);
14
```

---

[2] At the time that this chapter was written.

Side Note 22.2: Listeners — Thread Safety

Note: Keep in mind that listeners run on a separate thread. It is important to ensure that the operations they perform are thread safe. Another option is to poll the frame directly into the controller without the need of the listener. This might be a better option for applications that have a game (or update) loop. However, if recognition is paramount and event listening is important for a design of an application, then thread-safety is paramount [Williams 12].

```
15    // Create a Shell object pointer...
16    _pShell = NULL;
17    _hr = CoCreateInstance(CLSID_Shell, NULL, CLSCTX_SERVER, ↩
          IID_IDispatch, (void**)&_pShell);
18    _bMinimized = false;
19  }
```

Once we have enabled the gestures in Lines 16–17 (Listing 22.4), we can proceed to acquire our shell, which we'll use to minimize and maximize all our windows later on.

Now that the connection logic has been explained, we can program our logic for this project. All of the information is contained inside a **Frame**. Every frame contains information about:

- **Id**: Id of the current frame.

- **Hands**: List of hands currently detected on this frame.

- **Fingers**: List of fingers currently detected on this frame.

- **Tools**: List of tools currently detected on this frame.

- **Gestures**: List of gestures currently detected on this frame.

- **Additional Data Structures**: Additional data structures are available, which include **Arm**, **Bones**, **Image** (single image from camera), among others. However, the Leap Motion does not provide raw data (point of clouds). See Leap Motion support for more information.[3] However, the **Image** provides a raw view of a single frame, where depth and other information can be processed.[4]

---

[3] https://support.leapmotion.com/entries/40337273-Is-it-possible-to-get-raw-point-cloud-data-
[4] See http://ccw1986.blogspot.tw/2014/09/opencvleap-motion-get-depth-image-from.html

For this project, we are only interested in the gestures themselves. Therefore, we won't be needing any additional information from the frame aside from the list of gestures detected. When the Leap Motion fails to recognize a gesture, it will still create a gesture entry for it. This means that we must ensure that we only process valid gestures by calling the **isValid()** function of the gesture (see line 15 in Listing 22.5. Once we are sure that the gesture is valid, if the gesture happens to be a **Swipe** gesture, then we are going to minimize all windows to see our desktop. If it is a **Circle** gesture, we will restore all previously minimized windows back.

Listing 22.5: LEAP (LeapListener.cpp - onFrame)

```
1
2  void LeapListener::onFrame(const Controller & controller) {
3    Frame currFrame = controller.frame();
4    GestureList currGestures = currFrame.gestures();
5
6    bool gestureHandled = false;
7    for(GestureList::const_iterator gl = currGestures.begin(); gl != ↵
       currGestures.end() && !gestureHandled
8      ; gl++){
9      Gesture tempGest = (*gl);
10     if(tempGest.isValid()){
11       switch (tempGest.type()){
12         case Gesture::TYPE_CIRCLE:
13           restoreWindows();
14           gestureHandled = true;
15           break;
16
17         case Gesture::TYPE_SWIPE:
18           minimizeWindows();
19           gestureHandled = true;
20           break;
21
22         default:
23           break;
24       }
25     }
26   }
27 }
```

The code for minimizing and restoring the windows is quite straightforward and is presented in Listing 22.6.

Listing 22.6: LEAP (LeapListener.cpp - Minimize/Restore Windows)

```
1  void LeapListener::minimizeWindows() {
2    if (SUCCEEDED(_hr) && !_bMinimized){
3      // Call minimize all windows.
4      _pShell->MinimizeAll();
5      _bMinimized = true;
```

```
 6      }
 7    }
 8
 9    void LeapListener::restoreWindows() {
10      if (SUCCEEDED(_hr) && _bMinimized){
11        // Restore all minimized windows.
12        _pShell->UndoMinimizeALL();
13        _bMinimized = false;
14      }
15    }
```

Finally, once the Leap Motion controller is disconnected, we need to make sure we deallocate the pointers (that we allocated during onConnect if any). In order to do this, we implement the onDisconnect function of our listener.

Listing 22.7: LEAP (LeapListener.cpp - onDisconnect)

```
1    void LeapListener::onDisconnect(const Controller & controller) {
2      std::cout<< "Leap Controller Disconnected" << std::endl;
3
4      if (SUCCEEDED(_hr)) {
5        // Release the COM object when we're finished...
6        _pShell->Release();
7        CoUninitialize();
8      }
9    }
```

Further Reading

The official Leap Motion developer site [Leap 14a] contains a lot of good examples in C++, JavaScript and C#. It is a good place to continue learning. For those more adventurous readers you can even integrate the Leap Motion controller with the Oculus [Leap 14c] for creating VR applications.

Exercises

1. The hand-tracking data provided by the Leap Motion controller includes vectors for the palm normal and the palm position. Using this information, modify our application to minimize all windows when the user swipes downward, and restores the windows when the user swipes upward.

2. Implement an application that allows you to scroll up or down the content in your web browser.

3. The frame data also contains a list of Pointables which hold information about tools or fingers. Among the information provided by a Pointable is

the tipPosition. Create an application that moves your mouse pointer using your finger.

23

Hands-On Approach with Kinect Sensor v2

Frank E. Hernandez

> When I read commentary about suggestions for where
> C should go, I often think back and give thanks that
> it wasn't developed under the advice of a worldwide
> crowd.
>
> —Dennis Ritchie

This chapter deals with the Kinect sensor v2 from Microsoft. Here we present a hands-on project to get familiarized with some of the functionality of the Kinect sensor v2 and learn how to integrate it into your own applications. Additional information about Kinect sensor v1 is found in various books (e.g., [Catuhe 12]) and brief documentation about Kinect v1 and skeleton data structures is found in Chapter 26.

23.1   What Is the Kinect Sensor?

Released by Microsoft on Novermber 4, 2010, the Kinect sensor (see Figure 23.1) was intended as an addition to the Xbox 360 video game console. The sensor allowed players to control many aspects of their game by using gestures, facial expressions, and voice. This was possible due to the depth sensor, RGB camera, and microphones included in the device (see Chapter 26 for more information). The Kinect placed in the hands of HCI developers is an amazing piece of technology for a relatively low price. This sparked the interest of the open-source community and even a bounty was placed by AdaFruit [Adafruit 10] for the development of open-source drivers, and on November 10, the community delivered. Soon after seeing the popularity of the Kinect, Microsoft launched Kinect for Windows on

Figure 23.1: Kinect v2 (top) and Kinect (bottom)

June 16, 2011, which allowed greater access to the Kinect features, including (near/far modes).

A couple of years later Microsoft released the Kinect sensor v2 to work alongside the Xbox One console. This is a much improved version than the original Kinect, and allows for better tracking and integration with games and application. In this chapter, we will go over the settings, process, and requirements for Kinect sensor v2 (for Windows 8).

The Kinect sensor v2 includes quite a number of improvements over the Kinect v1 [Microsoft 14f]:

- Wider fields of view.

- 3 times depth fidelity.

- 1080 dp HD color camera (1920 x 1080 at 30 or 15 fps based on lighting condition).

- Light independent IR (512 x 424 at 30 fps).

> **Side Note 23.1: Requirements**
>
> Currently the Kinect for Windows SDK is intended for development using the Windows 8, Windows 8.1, or Windows Embedded Standard 8 operating systems. You will also need to install either Visual Studio 2012 or Visual Studio 2013. For more information on the hardware and software requirements, check the website [Microsoft 14c]. Additional information about setting up a Visual Studio environment for different types of projects is found in the book's website.

- Improved microphones. Four microphones inside the microphone bar.

- 25 skeletal joints for six people.

- Thumb tracking and end of hand tracking with hands states (open/closed/lasso).

23.2 Installation

The steps presented here are for the Kinect for Windows SDK but should be relevant to other versions of the Kinect SDK. Note that it is possible to use the Xbox One Kinect for development purposes only. It is recommended to purchase a Windows version of the Kinect v2.

1. Go to the Kinect for Windows page: https://www.kinectforwindows.com

2. Find the tab that says "Develop" on the top and click it. This will show a drop-down menu with more options.

3. Once the tab is open, click on the "Download the SDK" link.

4. Download the SDK installer.

5. Follow the steps in the installer. Once the installer is finished, we are ready to begin developing with your Kinect sensor v2.

23.3 Hands-On Mini-Project

In this section, we will cover how to implement a simple application. This application will allow the user to control the mouse with the Kinect sensor. Also, we will cover how to take advantage of the built-in gesture recognition provided by the SDK. We will use the gestures to signal left and right clicks of a mouse. Let's begin by creating our project:

Side Note 23.2: Drivers Update

Once you have downloaded and installed the SDK, the Kinect might take a few seconds before it starts. When the Kinect v2 runs for the first time in any machine, it will try to get the latest drivers available. This usually takes around 60 seconds.

1. Open Visual Studio and click **File > New > Project** (or simply press Ctrl+Shift+N).

2. Once the "New Project" dialog appears, select Console Application and let's name it "KinectConsolApp."

3. Once done naming it, click "OK."

4. In the "Solution Explorer," right click "KinectConsoleApp" and click "Add Reference." You'll need to add the following references (some may have been added by default):

   • Microsoft.Kinect

   • System.Drawing

   • System.Windows.Forms;

To prevent the application from exiting before a user presses the "Enter" key, we add the following code in "Program.cs" (see Listing 23.1).

Listing 23.1: Kinect (Basic Setup)

```
1   using Microsoft.Kinect;
2   using System;
3   namespace KinectConsoleApp{
4       class Program{
5           static void Main(string[] args){
6               Console.WriteLine("Press Enter To Finish");
7               Console.ReadLine();
8           }
9       }
10  }
```

Currently[1] only one Kinect sensor per system is supported by the API. Therefore, to acquired the Kinect sensor v2, the program must called **Kinect.GetDefault()**. Note that while only one system per computer is supported, a possible work around is to have multiple computer systems connected via fast local area network and

---

[1] At the time of this writing.

then communicate the messages (after processing) to a centralized server. This can be accomplished using sockets [Makofske et al. 04, Stevens et al. 04]. If the **Kinect.GetDefault**() call is successful, it is possible then to get data from the device. Let's now modify the code in 23.1 by updating the code to match the one in Listing 23.2.

Listing 23.2: Kinect (Basic Setup 2)

```
1
2   using Microsoft.Kinect;
3   using System;
4   namespace KinectConsoleApp
5   {
6       class Program{
7           static void Main(string[] args){
8               KinectSensor sensor = KinectSensor.GetDefault();
9               if (sensor != null){
10                  sensor.Open();
11                  Console.WriteLine("Press Enter To Finish");
12                  Console.ReadLine();
13                  sensor.Close();
14              }
15
16          }
17      }
18  }
```

The Kinect sensor provides data through frame sources and the data is contained inside frames. There are two ways to receive data from a frame in Kinect v2, either by polling or via events. In this project we will be receiving our data via events by registering our event handler method with the frame. Currently there are six frame sources [Microsoft 14b]:

- **ColorFrameSource**: Contains information received through the color sensor. It is 1920 x 1080 pixels and runs at a rate of 30 frames-per-second (fps) or 15 fps depending on the lighting conditions of the room. It contains a 1920 x 1080 array of color pixels.

- **InfraredFrameSource**: Contains information received through the infrared sensor. It is 512 x 424 pixels and runs at 30 fps. Contains a 16-bit infrared intensity value and the ambient light is removed which provides a clean IR image.

- **DepthFrameSource**: Contains information received through the IR sensor. It contains 16-bit pixel data in millimeters from the sensor's focal plane. It has a range of 0.5 to 8 meters from the Kinect sensor.

- **BodyIndexFrameSource**: Contains information received through the IR sensor. It contains pixels data with value from 0 to 5. This represents the index of the body a given pixel belongs to. This index matches the index in the body source. Currently only a maximum of 6 bodies can be tracked at a given time. Therefore, a value greater than five means that no body is tracked at that pixel.

- **BodyFrameSource**: Contains information received through the IR sensor. It provides a collection of six **Body** objects with each object containing 25 joints. Each of the joints has a position in 3D space and an orientation. It also has **Hand State** on two bodies (open, close, or lasso). It also includes lean data of the torso with respect to the body.

- **AudioFrameSource**: Contains information received through the microphone bar. It contains audio samples captured over a specific interval of 16 milliseconds. The audio data is associated with an audio beam, which is automatically aimed at the direction of the sound but can also be manually aimed. The audio frame arrives at a rate of 60 fps.

For our application, we will use the **BodyFrameSource** to be able to get the position of the left hand as well as the state it is in. We will take each hand state and map it to a mouse operation.

- **Open**: This is represented by the open hand. If the user has his/her left hand open, we will position our cursor to the location on screen.

- **Closed**: This is represented by the closed hand. If the user has his/her left hand closed, we will perform a left click.

- **Lasso**: This is represented by extending only the index and middle finger in the hand while keeping the rest of the hand closed. If the user has his/her left hand in the lasso, we will perform a right click.

Next, we will implement a new class "MouseController." We are going to implement the event handler method that will be called when a new frame is received from the sensor. In order to accomplish this, the code needs to be modified, as shown in Listing 23.3 (in a file named "MouseController.cs").

Listing 23.3: Kinect (Frame Handling 1)

```
1
2    using Microsoft.Kinect;
3    using System;
4    using System.Collections.Generic;
5    using System.Diagnostics;
6    using System.Drawing;
7    using System.Linq;
8    using System.Text;
9    using System.Windows.Forms;
10
```

```
11   namespace KinectConsoleApp{
12
13       public class MouseController{
14           // Reference to the current sensor used.
15           private KinectSensor m_currSensor;
16
17           // We'll need it for mapping the data received
18           // to other spaces.
19           private CoordinateMapper m_coorMapper;
20
21           public MouseController(KinectSensor sensor)
22           {
23               m_currSensor = sensor;
24               m_coorMapper = m_currSensor.CoordinateMapper;
25
26           }
27
28           public void BodyReader_FrameArrived(object sender, ↩
                 BodyFrameArrivedEventArgs e){
29               // We'll perform our logic here...
30           }
31       }
32   }
```

Every body frame contains information about a maximum of 6 bodies. In order to obtain this information, we must first acquire the frame in our **BR_FrameArrived** method. We are going to acquire this frame by using the *using block*. This will guarantee that the frame is disposed as soon as we are done with it. Kinect will ensure that no frame data is leaked. Therefore, if we don't dispose of the frame, we will not receive any new frames of that specific type from the Kinect sensor. For that same reason we also want to make sure we do not hold the frame for longer than we need to. We must ensure to perform the bare minimum logic needed while we have control of the frame. In our case, all we need is the information about the tracked bodies. The Kinect will always give you a list of 6 **Body** objects regardless of the number of bodies tracked in the frame. This means that we must ensure to pass an array of size 6 to the frame's **GetAndRefreshBodyData** method. In order to accomplish this, we need to modify the code (Listing 23.3). The updated code is shown in Listing 23.4.

Listing 23.4: Kinect (BR_FrameArrived 1)

```
1
2    public void BR_FrameArrived(object sender, BodyFrameArrivedEventArgs↩
         e){
3        bool dataReceived = false;
4
5        Console.WriteLine("Frame Received");
6
7        // Using block automatically disposes the frame.
8        // If the frame is not disposed of you won't be getting any
```

```
9      // more frames of this type.
10     using (BodyFrame frame = e.FrameReference.AcquireFrame()){
11         // Only perform the minimum operations needed and
12         // release the frame.
13         if (frame != null){
14             if (m_bodies == null){
15                 m_bodies = new Body[frame.BodyCount];
16             }
17
18             frame.GetAndRefreshBodyData(m_bodies);
19             dataReceived = true;
20         }
21     }
22     // We'll perform more logic here...
23 }
```

Now that we have our frame data, we need to iterate through our **Body** objects list **m_bodies** and only work with the bodies that are currently tracked. We accomplish this by using its **IsTracked** property. If the body is not tracked, we will just ignore it and move on to the next body. When we find a tracked body, we will get a reference to the left hand. Since each **Body** object provides 25 joints, we will acquire the left hand by using the **JointType.HandLeft**, as shown in line 14 (Listing 23.5). Each joint also contains a **TrackingState**, which lets us know whether the joint is being tracked, inferred, or not tracked. For our project, we'll only care about the left hand if it is being tracked by the system. In this case, we will only perform our mouse operations when we have a high degree of confidence it is the left hand. We'll delegate the interpretation of the hand to our helper method **HandleLeftHand**. The new code is shown in Listing 23.5.

Listing 23.5: Kinect (BR_FrameArrived 2)

```
1   public void BodyReader_FrameArrived(object sender, ↵
        BodyFrameArrivedEventArgs e){
2   ...
3       if (!dataReceived)
4           return;
5
6       foreach (Body mainBody in m_bodies){
7           if (mainBody == null)
8               continue;
9
10          if (!mainBody.IsTracked)
11              continue;
12
13          Joint leftHand = mainBody.Joints[JointType.HandLeft];
14
15          if (leftHand.TrackingState == TrackingState.Tracked){
16              HandleLeftHand(mainBody, leftHand);
17          }
18      }
19  }
```

Before we continue with our implementation of the **HandleLeftHand** helper, we need to add a few more members to our "MouseController" class. In order to map our hand position to screen coordinates, we'll need to know the width and the height of the frame. Even though we know that since it is received through the infrared sensor, its dimensions should be 512 x 424. It is a lot cleaner to get this information from the sensor's **FrameDescription** (lines 18–20 in Listing 23.6). We also want to limit how often we perform a left or right click to one per second. In order to accomplish this we'll take advantage of the **StopWatch** class (lines 22–26 in Listing 23.6).

Listing 23.6: Kinect (MouseController 2)

```
1   ...
2   // Used for cooldown between clicks.
3   private long m_leftClickDelayMillis = 1000;
4   private long m_rightClickDelayMillis = 1000;
5
6   // Used to reduce how ofter we signal for
7   // a left or right click.
8   private Stopwatch m_leftStopWatch;
9   private Stopwatch m_rightStopWatch;
10
11  // We'll need these for scaling our hand
12  // position to our screen coordinates.
13  private int m_frameWidth;
14  private int m_frameHeight;
15
16  public MouseController(KinectSensor sensor){
17      ...
18      FrameDescription frameDes = m_currSensor.DepthFrameSource.↩
            FrameDescription;
19      m_frameWidth = frameDes.Width;
20      m_frameHeight = frameDes.Height;
21
22      m_leftStopWatch = new Stopwatch();
23      m_leftStopWatch.Start();
24
25      m_rightStopWatch = new Stopwatch();
26      m_rightStopWatch.Start();
27  }
```

Listing 23.7: Kinect (HandleLeftHand)

```
1   private void HandleLeftHand(Body mainBody, Joint leftHand){
2       CameraSpacePoint handPosition = leftHand.Position;
3       DepthSpacePoint dsp = m_coorMapper.MapCameraPointToDepthSpace(↩
            leftHand.Position);
4
5       float x = dsp.X / m_frameWidth * Screen.PrimaryScreen.Bounds.↩
            Right;
```

```
6       float y = dsp.Y / m_frameHeight * Screen.PrimaryScreen.Bounds.↩
            Bottom;
7
8       if (mainBody.HandLeftConfidence != TrackingConfidence.High)
9         return;
10
11      if (mainBody.HandLeftState == HandState.Open){
12        Console.WriteLine("Hand Open");
13          Cursor.Position = new Point((int)x, (int)y);
14      }
15      else if (mainBody.HandLeftState == HandState.Closed){
16          Console.WriteLine("Hand Closed");
17          if (m_leftStopWatch.ElapsedMilliseconds >= ↩
                m_leftClickDelayMillis){
18            MouseHandler.PerformLeftClick();
19              m_leftStopWatch.Restart();
20          }
21      }
22      else if (mainBody.HandLeftState == HandState.Lasso){
23          Console.WriteLine("Hand Lasso");
24          if (m_rightStopWatch.ElapsedMilliseconds >= ↩
                m_rightClickDelayMillis){
25            MouseHandler.PerformRightClick();
26            m_rightStopWatch.Restart();
27          }
28      }
29  }
```

The **HandleLeftHand** method takes care of the input logic for our application.
Every **Joint** object has a position in 3D space. In order to translate it to the screen
coordinates, we must first map that position to depth space (lines 2–3 in Listing
23.7). Once we have obtained **DepthSpacePoint**, we can map the 3D values into
the X and Y coordinates of the display (lines 5–6 in Listing 23.7). In order to
maintain a smooth interaction, we will ignore the tracked hand unless it has a high
confidence level (lines 8–9 in Listing 23.7).

Once we have a good confidence level, then we'll look at the hand state to
perform our operations. If the hand state for the left hand is **Open**, then we will
create a new point and set our mouse cursor position to that point on screen (lines
11–14 in Listing 23.7). If the hand state is **Closed**, we signal a left mouse click
(lines 15–21 in Listing 23.7). Since we could potentially receive 30 frames within
a given second, this could lead to 30 mouse clicks sent (each second). In order to
limit this, we will use our **StopWatch** instance. This will limit the user's mouse
clicks to one per second (lines 17–20 in Listing 23.7. We will do the same in the
case that the hand state is a **Lasso**. In order to limit the number of right clicks
sent to one per second, the code also needs to be modified, as shown in lines
22–28 (Listing 23.7). The "MouseHandler" class provides a simple wrapper to the
SendInput function for synthesizing our mouse clicks (see Listing 23.8).

Listing 23.8: Kinect (MouseHandler)

```
1   using System;
2   using System.Collections.Generic;
3   using System.Linq;
4   using System.Runtime.InteropServices;
5   using System.Text;
6   using System.Threading.Tasks;
7
8   namespace KinectConsoleApp{
9       class MouseHandler{
10          [DllImport("user32.dll", SetLastError = true)]
11          static extern uint SendInput(uint nInputs, ref INPUT pInputs↩
                , int cbSize);
12
13          [StructLayout(LayoutKind.Sequential)]
14          struct INPUT{
15              public SendInputEventType type;
16              public MouseKeybdhardwareInputUnion mkhi;
17          }
18          [StructLayout(LayoutKind.Explicit)]
19          struct MouseKeybdhardwareInputUnion{
20              [FieldOffset(0)]
21              public MouseInputData mi;
22
23              [FieldOffset(0)]
24              public KEYBDINPUT ki;
25
26              [FieldOffset(0)]
27              public HARDWAREINPUT hi;
28          }
29          [StructLayout(LayoutKind.Sequential)]
30          struct KEYBDINPUT{
31              public ushort wVk;
32              public ushort wScan;
33              public uint dwFlags;
34              public uint time;
35              public IntPtr dwExtraInfo;
36          }
37          [StructLayout(LayoutKind.Sequential)]
38          struct HARDWAREINPUT{
39              public int uMsg;
40              public short wParamL;
41              public short wParamH;
42          }
43          struct MouseInputData{
44              public int dx;
45              public int dy;
46              public uint mouseData;
47              public MouseEventFlags dwFlags;
48              public uint time;
49              public IntPtr dwExtraInfo;
50          }
51          [Flags]
```

```
52          enum MouseEventFlags : uint{
53              MOUSEEVENTF_MOVE = 0x0001,
54              MOUSEEVENTF_LEFTDOWN = 0x0002,
55              MOUSEEVENTF_LEFTUP = 0x0004,
56              MOUSEEVENTF_RIGHTDOWN = 0x0008,
57              MOUSEEVENTF_RIGHTUP = 0x0010,
58              MOUSEEVENTF_MIDDLEDOWN = 0x0020,
59              MOUSEEVENTF_MIDDLEUP = 0x0040,
60              MOUSEEVENTF_XDOWN = 0x0080,
61              MOUSEEVENTF_XUP = 0x0100,
62              MOUSEEVENTF_WHEEL = 0x0800,
63              MOUSEEVENTF_VIRTUALDESK = 0x4000,
64              MOUSEEVENTF_ABSOLUTE = 0x8000
65          }
66          enum SendInputEventType : int{
67              InputMouse,
68              InputKeyboard,
69              InputHardware
70          }
71
72          public static void PerformRightClick(){
73              INPUT mouseDownInput = new INPUT();
74              mouseDownInput.type = SendInputEventType.InputMouse;
75              mouseDownInput.mkhi.mi.dwFlags = MouseEventFlags.↩
                    MOUSEEVENTF_RIGHTDOWN;
76              SendInput(1, ref mouseDownInput, Marshal.SizeOf(new ↩
                    INPUT()));
77
78              INPUT mouseUpInput = new INPUT();
79              mouseUpInput.type = SendInputEventType.InputMouse;
80              mouseUpInput.mkhi.mi.dwFlags = MouseEventFlags.↩
                    MOUSEEVENTF_RIGHTUP;
81              SendInput(1, ref mouseUpInput, Marshal.SizeOf(new INPUT↩
                    ()));
82          }
83
84          public static void PerformLeftClick(){
85              INPUT mouseDownInput = new INPUT();
86              mouseDownInput.type = SendInputEventType.InputMouse;
87              mouseDownInput.mkhi.mi.dwFlags = MouseEventFlags.↩
                    MOUSEEVENTF_LEFTDOWN;
88              SendInput(1, ref mouseDownInput, Marshal.SizeOf(new ↩
                    INPUT()));
89
90              INPUT mouseUpInput = new INPUT();
91              mouseUpInput.type = SendInputEventType.InputMouse;
92              mouseUpInput.mkhi.mi.dwFlags = MouseEventFlags.↩
                    MOUSEEVENTF_LEFTUP;
93              SendInput(1, ref mouseUpInput, Marshal.SizeOf(new INPUT↩
                    ()));
94          }
95
96      }
97  }
```

Now that we are finished implementing our "MouseContoller," all that remains
is to let our Kinect sensor know that when it receives a **BodyFrame** it must forward
it to our "MouseContoller." In order to accomplish this, we need to create a new
instance of our "MouseController" in your "Program" class (line 10 in Listing
23.8). In order to read the frame from our source, we need to create a frame
reader for the given type. In this case, we created a **BodyFrameReader** instance
and opened the reader from the **BodyFrameSource**. This will give us a reader,
which can be registered with **BR_FrameArrived** method, which is the method
that handles incoming frames (lines 12–13 in Listing 23.9). Once this has been
registered, the application is ready to start with the Microsoft Kinect v2 sensor.

Listing 23.9: Kinect (Basic Setup 3)

```
1
2    using Microsoft.Kinect;
3    using System;
4    namespace KinectConsoleApp
5    {
6        class Program{
7            static void Main(string[] args){
8                KinectSensor sensor = KinectSensor.GetDefault();
9                if (sensor != null){
10                   sensor.Open();
11                   MouseController mouse = new MouseController(sensor);
12                   BodyFrameReader bodyReader = sensor.BodyFrameSource.↩
                         OpenReader();
13                   bodyReader.FrameArrived += mouse.BR_FrameArrived;
14
15                   Console.WriteLine("Press Enter To Finish");
16                   Console.ReadLine();
17                   sensor.Close();
18               }
19
20          }
21      }
22   }
```

Further Reading

The official Kinect site [Microsoft 14d] contains many instructional videos and
samples. The Kinect SDK also installs the Kinect SDK browser, which includes a
good set of sample applications that can be used as starting points for many types
of applications. **C++ samples** will be provided on the book's website. Finally you
can find many interesting projects in [Microsoft 14a].

Exercises

1. In the application we developed in this chapter, we assumed that there would be only one body tracked at any time to control the mouse. However, our current implementation allows a second user to hijack the controls if they come within the range of the Kinect. Modify our code to allow only the first person that was detected to control the mouse.

2. In this chapter, we relied on losing track of the left hand to stop the movement of the mouse. Using the hand states for the right hand, modify the code in order to toggle the control of the mouse on or off depending on the hand state of the right hand. Hence, an open right hand will signal the mouse control to turn on while a closed right hand will signal the mouse controls to turn off.

3. Using what we know about the positions of the joint and the body frame data, create a simple application that recognizes when two players fist bump each other.

4. Using what we know about hand states, develop a simple application that recognizes when two players high five each other.

5. Create a client/server application that relies on messages from the Kinect connected to each computer. The messages need to be relayed to the centralized server.

24

Creating Home-Brew Devices with Arduino Microcontrollers

Sudarat Tangnimitchok

> The two words *information* and *communication* are often used interchangeably, but they signify quite different things. Information is giving out; communication is getting through.
>
> —Sydney J. Harris

There are some instances in which the current input device landscape is not enough to cover the needs of the developer. It is also important to be able to prototype new input devices and combinations of those. There are different ways to address those needs. A common option is to create your own electronics and system drivers to communicate with the host machine [Orwick and Smith 07, Corbet et al. 05]. It is also possible to use Musical Instrument Digital Interface (MIDI) devices to send signals from an input device. MIDI provides a protocol of communication with a set of attributes for a given button (key), such as amount of pressure to the key, if the key has been pressed or not, and the time that a button has been pressed down, among others [Rumsey 94, Messick 98]. Another alternative is to use smaller form-factor computer boards, such as Raspberry Pi or BeagleBone boards. They provide the functionality of a computer (e.g., Linux) with additional inputs. The communication between another computer can vary (e.g., sockets). Finally, working with microcontrollers can also be helpful in creating new input devices. They usually communicate via USB. One of the popular microcontroller board, which is covered in this chapter, is Arduino (typically using Atmel microcontrollers). Note that this chapter uses microcontroller term loosely to refer to the microcontroller chip or the board.

24.1 Microcontroller

Microcontroller is another type of computer on a single integrated circuit, which usually comes in small boards. Microcontroller properties include: small farm factor (size) and low-power consumption. This makes them very popular for control devices, such as home appliances, mobile phone, and modern automobile, among others. While there are many types of microcontrollers in the market, the typical components included on their boards are:

- **Microcontroller chip**: This unit is the main processing core. Its main objective is to perform logical and mathematical tasks. The chip itself contains all of the necessary components, which include: random-access memory (CPU), read-only memory (ROM), and central processing unit (CPU). In addition, most of the microcontroller chip now has electrically erasable programmable read-only memory (EEPROM) integrated inside. The reason that EEPROM is included on the microcontroller chip is due to its flexibility to program and erase as needed.

- **Input and output port (IO port)**: This provides the basic input and output communication channel for the microcontroller. How each input and output channel operates is configured in the microcontroller's firmware. There are different types of ports, including digital IO ports. Some ports are multipurpose pins, which can be used for a variety of devices. Additional functions are also configured in the firmware. These additional functions provide more special features needed to perform advanced operations. For example, one type of port is called pulse width modulation (PWM). This port controls the level of direct current (DC) voltage. Another type of port, called INT, which stands for interrupt, provides real-time access to the controller. Finally, the TX and RX ports, which are the transmitter and receiver ports for serial communication, provide a synchronous form of communication between another device and the controller. Pin No. 2 can be configured as digital IO port(RA0) or analog IO port(A0), as shown in Figure 24.1. This depends on the requirements of the application. Normally, pins have their terminals soldered with connectors. This makes it easier for users to connect external devices (or circuits) with only wires.

- **ADC**: This is a process known to convert analog to digital (using a controller). In other words, ADC converts an analog voltage acquired from an analog input port to a digital number that represents its quantity [Ifeachor and Jervis 02]. The basic principle behind this process is to sample the continuous signal and store it in binary form expressing it as a bit format.

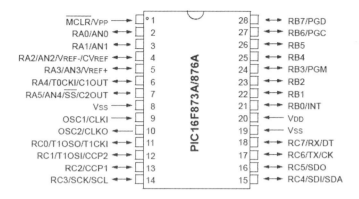

Figure 24.1: Diagram of microcontroller chip of PIC16F876A.

For example, ADC that has 8 bits resolution will have 256 (2^8) possible ways of digital number, 0 to 255, to express the quantity of the input signal. In this case, if the input voltage is ranged from 0–5 volts, then 0-volt is represented by the number 0 and 5-volt is represented by the number 255. The voltage between 0-volt and 5-volt will be between the numbers 0 and 255. Because of this limitation, the input signal that is not an integer will be rounded up; leading to the loss of some data points. That is why, having a higher resolution ADC means increasing the accuracy of converting the analog input signal as well.

• **PWM**: This component has the ability to vary the overall average power of DC voltage output without changing its DC level. In the past, controlling DC voltage was based on the principle of the voltage divider, for instance, using a potentiometer; however, the idea of controlling the DC voltage level using purely electrical signals seems to have much more benefits in terms of speed and reliability. Thus, PWM was introduced. Its basic concept is that instead of feeding a stable DC voltage and changing the voltage level, the same amount of voltage is fed in a pulse signal. By turning on and off between zero and the maximum voltage, the output voltage will vary based on duty cycle, which is the percentage of the high period of the pulse. PWM is usually present on modern microcontrollers, which provides a feature to control a DC device.

• **Serial Interfacing Ports**: This provides a type of communication between the computer (or another microcontroller) and the microcontroller. This is the most common form of communication between the microcontroller and the computer. Additional information about serial communication will be further explained in Section 24.3.

- **Software Environment**: Another component that is not part of the board but plays an important role is the software environment (IDE) provided by the makers of the microcontroller. This helps to build complex projects, which are compiled into executable programs. They also provide the ability to load those executables into the microcontroller. Each family of the microcontroller chip has its own software environment, such as Atmel Studio 6 for Atmel (AVR microcontrollers), MPLAB X IDE for PIC chip family [Microchip 15], or MDK-ARM for Cortex and ARM processor-based chip [KEIL 15].

24.2   Analog Sensor

Analog sensors in general are special kinds of devices capable of sensing some aspect of their environment such as temperature, light, force, or even an angle. They can detect a change in a physical quantity or direction of those features. Analog sensors transform those signals into the corresponding output in the form of electrical signals, which mostly are expressed by the voltage level. The output can be anything whether in discrete form as low and high voltage level, or in an analog form of voltage ranging from zero to its maximum voltage. Even though each type of sensor detects different kinds of features from its environment, they all apply the same basic principle of energy conversion. Therefore, *transducer* whose definition is two-port devices that turn physical energy to electrical energy can be used to describe sensors as well [Wikipedia 15l]. Here are the examples of some interesting analog sensors:

- **IR Sensor**: The word *infrared* means under-red. The translation explains the characteristic of infrared radiation by itself. Its wavelength is found between the visible light and microwave area [Wikipedia 15c]; therefore, its region is under the red spectrum in visible light. Typically, all objects which have a temperature greater than absolute zero will emit infrared radiation as a result of possessing a thermal energy source. Using this basic principle, infrared sensors have two ways to detect the infrared radiation: (1) photo sensitivity or (2) heat. Its typical use can be seen in the remote control devices found for television and other home appliances. Its application includes night vision, aid depth sensing (e.g., Kinect), and detecting astronomical objects that radiate infrared radiation, among others. Infrared (as already mentioned) has become a popular sensor to perceive the distance and depth of objects (including motion). This has been in sensors ranging from Microsoft Kinect (and Kinect 2) and Nintendo WiiMote. This has provided a great new game experience.

- **Ultrasonic Sensor**: This sensor works by emitting a sound wave and then interpreting the echo received back to the sensor, which is the distance that it traveled. This works by collecting the time interval used by the sound wave traveling from the source to the time the echo is received, multiplied by the velocity of the sound (for a particular medium and temperature). This technology is mostly used in a navigation system such as sound navigation and ranging (SONAR) in submarine navigation, or in medical ultrasonography [Wikipedia 15d], which utilizes the ultrasound sensing to create an image from inside the human body. This sensor will be used in this chapter.

- **Piezoelectric Sensor**: This type of sensor transforms the applied force or pressures into an electrical charge. This causes the level of its output signal to change in proportion to its input. In other words, piezoelectric sensors convert mechanical energy into electrical energy. Piezoelectric sensors play an important role in many fields that require pressure detection, for example, touch pad technology used in some touch input devices [Wikipedia 15i]. Some additional information about piezoelectric sensors is found in Side Note 8.1 (Chapter 8).

24.3   Serial Communication

Serial communication provides a form of input and output communication for two devices. Unlike parallel communication, which sends several bits at once, serial communication sends one bit at a time. Therefore, to avoid the confusion between sender and receiver, some ground rules and agreements called "Serial Package" are needed: (1) block of data (data bits); (2) start and stop bit (synchronization bits); (3) error checking (parity bits); (4) transmission speed (Baud rate). The idea is to provide the same protocol properties for both ends. The interface for this type of communication is called universal asynchronous receiver and transmitter (UART), which creates the serial package from the parallel bus and controls the physical hardware lines [JIMB0 15].

24.3.1   Universal Synchronous Receiver/Transmitter

It is the most basic and the most popular interface that is used for serial communication. The primary reason for its popularity is that it is very reliable and low-cost, and requires only two wires without the need of an external clock. The fact that it does not need an external clock means that both devices may even have different types of clock rates. This is what makes the interfaces asynchronous. The port transmitter (TX) and receiver (RX) are typically found in microcontrollers. TX for sending and RX for receiving. Notice that some of the microcontrollers are capable of creating a serial communication through its USB cable as well. The UART is accessed by the microcontroller's API [JIMB0 15].

24.4   Hands-On Project: Ultrasonic Proximity Sensor

We are ready to start with the project. The objective of this project is to provide experience on how to use a microcontroller with additional sensors. The objective is to demonstrate how a proximity sensor can be used with a microcontroller. Using this ultrasonic proximity sensor, it is possible to estimate the distance of an object in front of the sensor while showing the results in the computer. This will provide a way to practice with the concepts already provided in the beginning of this chapter.

24.4.1   Introduction to Arduino

The microcontroller used in this project is the Arduino UNO R3 (see Figure 24.2), which is mainly designed for educational prototyping. Apart from its simplicity of use and its low cost, Arduino UNO R3 is compatible with many add-on devices, such as Infrared Camera, LCD, global positioning system (GPS), and many other analog sensors. This makes it ideal for home-brew input devices [Arduino 15h]. For additional information about its hardware and specification of the board, go to: *http://arduino.cc/en/Main/arduinoBoardUno*. We will discuss the components required for this project.

PINs

All of the pins on Arduino can be configured as digital pins for either input or output. Furthermore, Arduino UNO R3 provides 6 ports of analog input from *A0-A5* ports which users can choose freely. Other useful ports are port *5V* and *GND*, which deliver 5-volt and ground signals, respectively, for an external circuit. The locations of the pins are shown in Figure 24.3 [Arduino 15d]

Arduino Uno

Arduino Uno R3 Front   Arduino Uno R3 Back

Figure 24.2: Front and back view of Arduino UNO R3.

Figure 24.3: Location of pins used in this project.

Software Environment

Arduino UNO R3 board has its own development environment, called Arduino Software IDE. This includes a text editor, compiler for Sketch, among other features. Programs for Arduino are written in C or C++ and they produce a program (named Sketch). Arduino provides a set of libraries to aid developers when using their microcontrollers. The functionalities provided by those libraries include access to the IO digital pins, PWM control, and serial communication [Arduino 15e].

24.4.2   Ultrasonic Sensor

For this project, we used the ultrasonic sensor HC-SR04, which is compatible with Arduino. This is an affordable sensor, integrated with its controlling circuit. This sensor has a range of operation from 2 cm to 400 cm. It has 4 pins which from left to right are "Vcc" for input voltage, "Trig" for Trigger input, "Echo" for output (when echo is received), and "Gnd" for ground. [FREAKS 15], as shown in Figure 24.4.

By supplying a short 10-μs pulse to the *Trig*[1] pin, the sensor will generate an eight-cycle sonic burst of ultrasound at 40 KHz. Then, the sensor will wait for the echo reflected from the distant object to travel back before moving to the next step. After receiving the echo sound wave, the *Echo* pin then provides the output pulse whose length is proportional to the amount of period of time from the moment the pulse is sent off to the moment it is received (in microsecond unit). This is

---

[1]Denoted as *Trig* to denote the triggering of an output from the microcontroller, in this particular case, the triggering of the ultrasound sonic burst.

Figure 24.4: HC-SR04 ultrasonic sensor.

considered the end of the cycle for this process. A timing diagram is shown in Figure 24.5 [FREAKS 15].

The length of the pulse obtained from the *Echo* pin is the parameter required to determine the distance of the target. This is calculated using the basic principle of velocity function [Dunn and Parberry 11, Ch. 11], as shown in Equation 24.1.

$$distance \ = \ velocity \ \times \ \delta time \qquad (24.1)$$

where the length of the pulse is obtained by the velocity times the change in time

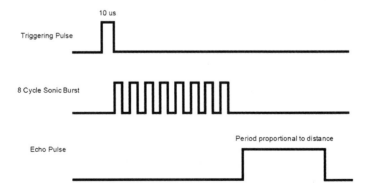

Figure 24.5: Time diagram of HC-SR04 ultrasonic sensor operation.

Side Note 24.1: Ultrasonic Sensors: Combining Input and Output

Some ultrasonic sensors come only with three pins. The two pins used in the demo found in this chapter, *Trig* pin and *Echo* pin are combined into a single pin, usually called *Sig* pin (for signal), and are the same pin (sometimes it's called "Sig" pin). Thus, at first, the pin will act like an input port waiting for the trigger pulse, then turn to be an output pin sending the echo pulse back to the microcontroller.

($\delta time$). The *velocity* variable is the sound velocity in the air at room temperature which is roughly 340 meters per second (or 1130 feet per second in U.S. customary units). The result yields the distance between the object and the sensor. Please note that the sensor uses the metric system. Therefore, conversion is required if U.S. customary units are required.

Therefore, if sound travels 340 meters in 1 second, it takes 29 microseconds to travel 1 centimeter. The same applies in the U.S. system as well, so roughly 74 microseconds are used by sound to travel 1 inch. It is important to remember that the result must be divided by 2. The reason is that the acquired pulse's length contains both departure and returning time of the sound [Arduino 15g]. Thus, the equations used to obtain the results (for this particular example), after passing all of the correct aspect, in our Sketch are:

$$Distance(cm) = \frac{length\ of\ echo\ pulse\ width(\mu s)}{29 \times 2} \qquad (24.2)$$

$$Distance(inches) = \frac{length\ of\ echo\ pulse\ width(\mu s)}{74 \times 2} \qquad (24.3)$$

All of these equations will be processed in Arduino in the form of programming code, which will be discussed further in Section 24.4.4.

24.4.3 Connecting Circuit

Connecting Arduino

The first step is to prepare the working environment for Arduino by installing Arduino IDE and its driver. All the information on where to download its software environment and installation guide can be found at their website at http://arduino. cc/en/Guide/HomePage [Arduino 15c].

Connecting Sensor to Arduino

First, some wires and a breadboard are required for connecting the required circuit for this project, as shown in Figure 24.6. Basically, pin *D2* is selected to send

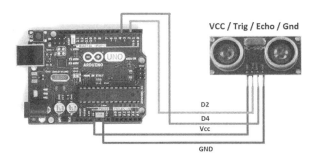

Figure 24.6: Circuit diagram.

Figure 24.7: Completed circuit in top view.

the triggering pulse and pin *D4* for receiving the echo pulse. In addition, two connections are needed to provide power to operate the sensor and ground.[2] Figures 24.7 and 24.8 show the connected circuit using a breadboard in top and side view, respectively.

---

[2]This makes the sensor use the ground as the Arduino board.

Figure 24.8: Completed circuit in side view.

24.4.4 Coding (Sketch)

Typically, microcontrollers work using a routine pattern similar to the game loop pattern. In other words, after some initial setup, a while loop runs *forever*, polling different states of the microcontroller and performing some actions. For example, to blink an LED, the developer may turn the LED after 5 cycles and then turn it back on 5 cycles later. It is important to note that some microcontrollers will allow certain interrupt routines to work in tandem with this loop. This method provides a more robust application, using the interrupts as event handlers. An example is found in the Texas Instruments (TI) TMS320C6713 (or similar TI DSP chips), which uses interrupt to detect a signal from one of their input lines [Chassaing and Reay 11]. Arduino microcontrollers also have interrupt routines (see [Arduino 15a]). Listing 24.1 shows the typical structure used in microcontrollers. The initial setup is used to initialize variables, set Baud rate, and configure ping, among many other operations. The primary reason to run the microcontroller in this continuous loop is to be able to react to changes happening in real time (of course, interrupts may provide a better way to handle certain aspects of the program). When using Arduino IDE, the process is simplified.

Listing 24.1: Typical Structure Used in Microcontroller Software

```
1
2  Setup.......................................
3  ............Initializing Set up............
```

Figure 24.9: How to create the simplest template in Sketch.

```
4     ..........................................
5     ..........................................
6
7     while(1)
8     { ..........................................
9       .........Regular Routine.................
10      ..........................................
11      ..........................................
12      ..........................................
13    }
```

We can start coding now. In Arduino IDE, go to **Main Menu > File > Examples > 01.Basic** and select **BareMinimum**, as shown in Figure 24.9. The BareMinimum example provides the basic structure for a new project. The *setup()* and *loop()* functions are already present in the code, as shown in Figure 24.10. We provide additional details for some of the library functions used in this project [Arduino 15f]:

- **Serial.begin**(): Arduino can operate the serial communication through either TX/RX port or USB cable, which in this case, USB ports are selected here. Moreover, as mentioned in Section 24.3, Baud rate needs to be config-

Figure 24.10: Example of BareMinimum project.

ured in order to successfully perform data transmission in UART interface, which can be set using this function. Not only is it used for starting the communication between the board and the computer but also it is used to set the Baud rate as well. Here it is set at 9600 bps. In other words, the data are transmitted as the speed of 9600 bits per second.

- **Serial.print**(): This function sends text data (American Standard Code for Information Interchange (ASCII) format) to the serial port. This function takes a second argument that allows us to change the base format into binary, hexadecimal, and octal. Binary data can be sent using **serial.write**().

- **pinMode**(): This function provides access to the digital pin settings. In other words, it allows us to configure each pin. For example *pinMode(4,INPUT)* sets the *D4* port as input.

- **digitalWrite()**: This function writes a high or low voltage to a digital pin. If the pin is set as an output, it will provide output voltage (at the level supplied to the board). In Arduino UNO R3, the voltage is 5 volts.

- **delay()**: This function allows the system to delay (pause) execution for a number of milliseconds. This is useful in waiting for an event or data to be transmitted. In essence, this can be used as a timer. For our project, the delay is needed to slow down the flow of data sent to the serial monitor to pause the output on the screen.

- **delayMicroseconds()**: It is similar to the *delay()* function except that the argument of this function receives the time as microseconds.

- **pulseIn()**: This function reads the length of the input pulse on the targeting pin, provided as the first argument. The second argument indicates if the pulseIn function should wait for *HIGH* or *LOW*. A third optional argument provides a timeout in microseconds (default is 1 second). For example *lenPulse = pulseIn(7, HIGH, 500000)*. This indicates that the pulse will be read from pin 7, when the pulse is high, and will time out in .5 seconds. This function returns the length of the pulse in microseconds (or 0 if no pulse).

The code in Listing 24.2 is the source code for this project. All the explanations are described in the comment above or beside the code for better understanding. Type this in your Sketch window and save it to avoid any mistakes.

Listing 24.2: Sketch for Proximity Ultrasonic Sensor

```
1
2   const int Trig = 2;              //Declare D2 as Trigger pin
3   const int Echo = 4;             //Declare D4 as Echo pin
4
5   // Declare necessary variable
6   int interval;
7   long inches;
8   long cm;
9
10  // Initialized setting
11  void setup()
12  {
13    Serial.begin(9600);           //Setting Baud rate
14    pinMode(Trig,OUTPUT);         //Assign D2 to be output
15    pinMode(Echo,INPUT);          //Assign D4 to be input
16  }
17
18  // This part of program will be run repeatedly
19  void loop()
20  {
```

```
21    //Clear signal for the up comming triggering pulse
22    digitalWrite(Trig,LOW);  // Set the voltage output at D2 to be 0 V
23    delayMicroseconds(2);    // delays for 2 microsecond
24
25    //Generating the Triggering Pulse 10 microsecond
26    digitalWrite(Trig,HIGH); //Set the voltage output at D2 to be 5 V
27    delayMicroseconds(10);   //delays for 10 microsecond
28    digitalWrite(Trig,LOW);  //Set the voltage output at D2 to be 0 V
29
30    // Function pulseIn have the ability to read the length of input ↩
          pulse on the targeting pin
31    // then store the pulse length in interval variable
32    interval = pulseIn(Echo,HIGH);
33
34    // Calculating the distance of the targeting object using the ↩
          formula discussed in
35    // ultrasonic sensor section
36    cm = interval/(29*2);
37    inches = interval/(74*2);
38
39    // Send informationtion using serial communication as well as
40    // print out the parameter in Serial Monitor
41    Serial.print(cm);
42    Serial.print(" cm\t");
43    Serial.print(inches);
44    Serial.print(" inch\n");
45
46    delay(100);
47
48  }
```

Uploading Sketch

Additional parts of the Arduino IDE need to be covered to complete this project. By following Figure 24.11, from left to right [Arduino 15b]:

- **Verify**: Checks the syntax and compiles.

- **Upload**: Uploads the executable (sketch) to the Arduino board.

- **New**: It creates a new project (file).

- **Open**: It opens an existing project.

- **Save**: It saves a project.

- **Serial Monitor**: It opens the serial monitor window.

To upload the program to the Arduino board, connect the board to the computer and open Arduino IDE. Then make sure to select the correct device using the menu bar (**Tool > Board**). Then, choose the board in use (from the list). In this project,

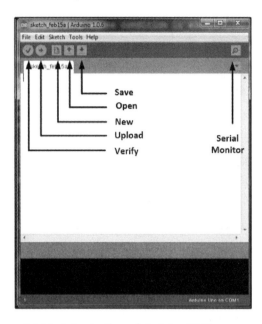

Figure 24.11: Introduction of Arduino IDE components.

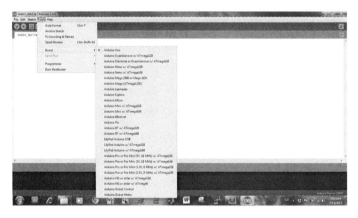

Figure 24.12: Demonstrate where to choose the correct type of board to connect with Arduino IDE.

the board is "Arduino UNO," as shown in Figure 24.12. It is also important to find which port Arduino is connected to In Windows, this can be checked using the device manager. For additional instructions for Windows, Mac OS X, and Linux, see [Arduino 15e]. Once the connection is selected (with the right port number), then the *Upload* will complete the process to load the Sketch into the board.

Figure 24.13: Serial monitor.

Serial Monitor

The serial monitor provides an input and output console. For this project, the serial monitor displays the distance of the object in real time, as shown in Figure 24.13.

24.4.5 Testing the Project

Now, if we move the object away from the sensor and back to the sensor, we can observe the different distances obtained in the serial monitor. In this project we used a tape case as the object. A smartphone is used to display the measurement in order to compare it to the results in the serial monitor. This is shown in Figure 24.14 (to see the values from the serial monitor, see Figure 24.13).

Figure 24.14: Complete proximity ultrasonic sensor.

Further Reading

The official site of Arduino [Arduino 15c] is an excellent source of information, including libraries and many project examples. An excellent book that starts from basic projects to more advanced ones is *Arduino Cookbook Second Edition* [Margolis 11]. For a very basic introduction to sketch programming, see [Monk 11] (with a follow-up book [Monk 13]).

Bowman and colleagues provide additional information about home-brew input devices [Bowman et al. 04]. Finally, Phidgets are a way to use microcontrollers by combining different input devices without the need to program microcontrollers [Greenberg and Fitchett 01, Greenberg and Boyle 02].

Exercises

1. Currently, parameters from a serial port are shown in Serial Monitor Window, which is still the software environment of Arduino. Ideally, to work in a real environment, the Arduino board must communicate with a program (in a host computer). Using serial communication, create a program in your language of choice to talk back and forth with the Arduino board.

2. In this project, we use the digital port to receive the pulse from the echo pin. Instead of using digital pin, try using the analog input port.

Autonomous Bicycle with Gyroscope Sensor

Panuwat Janwattanapong & Mercedes Cabrerizo

The secret of getting ahead is getting started.
—Mark Twain

This chapter illustrates the application of input signals using a control system of an autonomous bicycle. It further illustrates the use of input devices outside of the typical PC or mobile environment. This application focuses on designing an unmanned bicycle and a controller by using a classic control, Proportional derivative controller (PD controller), and applying the method to the AU self-balancing bicycle (AUSB). The main concept applied in this project is the gyroscopic effect. Input data obtained from the gyroscope sensor in the form of an analog signal will be the process variable of the controlling system, which will be captured in a dsPIC microcontroller. This microcontroller will control the output in terms of percentage called PWM with the value accordings to the error obtained from the gyroscope sensor and send this output to control the direction of the flywheel to balance the system.

25.1   Introduction

The AU self-balancing bicycle (AUSB) robot, as shown in Figure 25.1, is one of the challenging problems in the area of control systems. This application is based on the same idea as the inverted pendulum, which is to use the linear control to stabilize the unstable systems. Self-balancing bicycle robot leads us to transform an original bicycle to one that can balance itself without any physical supports or human interaction. Similar to the famous self-balancing bicycle riding robot

Figure 25.1: Image of AU self-balancing bicycle.

called Murata Boy, it can balance itself whether it is stationary, moving, or even when it comes to a stop immediately. The gyroscope sensor will detect the little slanting angle of the bicycle. When the slanting angle is determined, a large disc in the robot's body will rotate and then generate an equal amount of counter force to eliminate the slant. We adapt this control system idea to be used in the AUSB robot.

Gyroscopic effect is the main theory for this application due to its effect and torque production. The gyroscopic effect is focused on and applied to use in stabilization of the unstable bicycle. A mechanical gyroscope [Lam 11] consists of a massive spinning wheel and the free axis that allows the wheel to orient in any direction. The orientation of the wheel will remain fixed unless the external force or torque is applied. Because of the moment of inertia, the high-speed spinning wheel will generate angular momentum and the upward force to compensate the external torque and remain fixed in its same orientation again. The direction of torque vector is also based on the directions of the other vectors. This torque is the key to balancing an object (in this case, the bicycle). There have been different efforts to use the gyroscopic to balance bicycles [Suprapto 06, Thanh and Parnichkun 08]. Than and Parnichkum used the particle swarm optimization-based structure specified method and fuzzy sliding mode control (SMC) on their bicycle, respectively [Thanh and Parnichkun 08]. Their bicycle illustrates an excellent performance.

The AUSB robot also uses the spinning flywheels acting as a mechanical gyroscope to generate the force to maintain the balance of the bicycle. Two same mass and shape flywheels are designed in order to produce more force in both the upper part and lower part of the bicycle. The microcontroller *dsPIC30F4011* is used as the controller module in this system. When the gyro sensor, which is installed in the middle of the bicycle, can detect a little error of slant angle, it results in analog voltage passing the value through the ADC into the microcontroller. The microcontroller calculates the PD controller output to control the speed of the flywheels input motor by adjusting the duty cycle of pulse width modulation (PWM). Since the double flywheels with constant spinning speed are controlled by the PD controller, the slant angle of flywheels is changed. This results in the change of force direction to pull back the bicycle and reduce the error in bicycle slant (making the angle to be zero). This is how the bicycle can maintain balance.

25.2   AU Self-Balancing Bicycle (AUSB)

AUSB can be mainly divided into 3 parts, consisting of a mechanical structure, a controller, and a sensor (or sensors). This section describes those components.

25.2.1   Mechanical Structure

Each flywheel is constructed with 30-mm thickness and the distance between flywheels is fixed at 180 mm apart. Both flywheels are connected to the spinning motors with a specification of 250 watt and 2650 rpm. Note that the two motors' direction of spinning will be in the opposite direction. The rear of each flywheel is connected with a gear train, which is driven forward and back by the *direction control motor* (with a specification of 36 watt and 7000 rpm.

Figure 25.2 reviews the structure and dimensions of the AUSB in CAD drawing. The positions of both flywheels and gyroscope sensor are located above the ground according to Table 25.1.

25.2.2   Controller: dsPIC30F4011

dsPIC30F4011 from Microchip is used as a main controller. Our team [Janwat-tanapong and Ratchatanantakit 12] has designed a multi-purpose printed circuit board (PCB) based on dsPIC30F4011. Overview of the ABAC's PCB layout is shown in Figure 25.3. This 16-bit microprocessor is based on Harvard architecture with 24-bit instruction. Many functions are available such as PWM, UARTS, QEP, I2C, SPI, and ADC/DAC.

25.2.3   Gyroscope Sensor: MicroStrain 3DM-GX1

The main sensor for this project is the gyroscope sensor by Microstrain model 3DM-GX1. Analog output of the Gyro sensor is scaled from 0–5 volts and directly connected to dsPIC30F4011 ADC pin. Figure 25.4 shows the mounting of the gyro sensor on the AUSB.

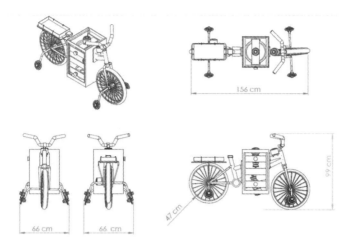

Figure 25.2: AU self-balancing bicycle structure in CAD drawing.

Side Note 25.1: Features Selection

The ABAC's layout PCB is designed based on the features that will be implemented in the system. To optimize the performance and minimize the size of the PCB, some of the features provided from dsPIC30F4011, such as I2C or SPI, are disregarded.

Table 25.1: Flywheel Dimensions.

	Height from Ground	Thickness	Radius
Upper Flywheel	615 *mm*	30 *mm*	150 *mm*
Lower Flywheel	270 *mm*	30 *mm*	150 *mm*

AUSB system uses a gyroscope sensor to mainly detect the leaning angle of the bicycle and return the value of angle to the controller. This value is significantly important to the system and can be considered as the main part of the system.

25.3   Data Processing

This section covers the data processing required for this project.

Figure 25.3: ABAC's PCB: dsPIC30F4011.

Figure 25.4: Gyroscope sensor: MicroStrain 3DM-GX1.

25.3.1   Structure of Data Processing

Figure 25.5 illustrates the flow of the data being processed in the system. The main output signal of this AUSB system is obtained from the gyroscope sensor. The signal generated from the sensor will be in a form of analog signal and then passes through the analog-to-digital converter (ADC), which will be briefly explained (in the context of this project) in the next section. The controller, dsPIC30F4011, computes the input data. First, it attenuates the noise by using

Side Note 25.2: Gyrocope Sensor Selection

The dimension of this gyroscope sensor from Microstrain is considered large, which affects the location of the sensor to be implemented. The AU self-balancing bicycle (AUSB) robot was designed and implemented in 2012 resulting in smaller amount of gyroscope sensor selection. Nowadays the precision and size of gyroscope sensors are greatly optimized, which definitely will improve the overall performance of the system. However, as demonstrated in some of the chapters found in Part II, MEMS with gyroscopes can produce large errors in measurement.

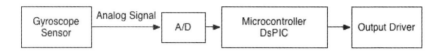

Figure 25.5: Diagram of processing a signal obtained from gyroscope sensor.

the digital filter. Second, it calculates the desired output value. The output signal from the controller in the form of PWM is sent to the driver to stabilize the system.

The gyroscope sensor, Microstrain model 3DM-GX1, is capable of providing both analog and digital output. The main reason that the AUSB system uses analog is due to the noise-to-information ratio. With the analog signal, it is more effective for the digital filter programmed inside the microcontroller to filter out the noise and receive the clear data from the sensor.

25.3.2 Analog to Digital Converter

Analog signal is a continuous time varying signal. In this system, the gyroscope sensor converts the leaning angle of the bicycle into voltage ranging from 0–5V. To be able to compute the data by using the microcontroller, the signal must be converted into a digital signal first by using the analog-to-digital converter implemented in the microcontroller.

The ADC feature introduced in the microcontroller is a 10-bit system. This means the output from the gyroscope sensor consisting of a 0–5V signal will be scaled to a 10-bit value or a value range from 0–1023. For instance, Figure 25.6 briefly demonstrates a conversion of a 4-bit ADC system between analog and digital values.

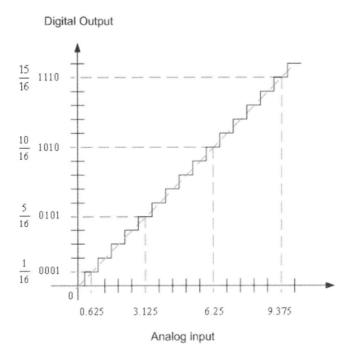

Figure 25.6: Example of ADC scaling.

25.4 System Implementation and Results

This section describes the system implementation and the results, which includes the control system.

25.4.1 Control System of AU Self-Balancing Bicycle (AUSB)

A conventional proportional-derivative controller is used to control the balance position of the AUSB system. Figure 25.7 shows the classical PD controller system. In the control loop, PD controller is used for tracking a set-point, $\theta_{set-point}$, which is the balance position of the bicycle. The controller output, $U(s)$, is calculated in Equation 25.1 and position error is specified in Equation 25.2.

$$U(s) = K_p \theta_{error}(s) + sK_d \theta_{error}(s) \tag{25.1}$$

$$\theta_{error}(s) = \theta_{set-point}(s) - \theta_{lean\,angle}(s) \tag{25.2}$$

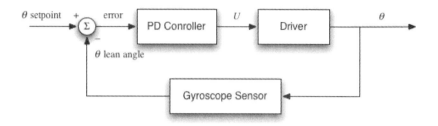

Figure 25.7: Conventional PD controller in AUSB system.

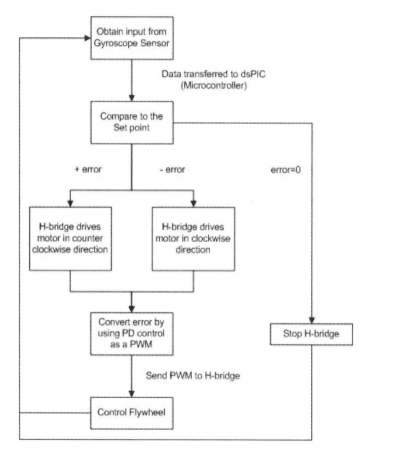

Figure 25.8: Flowchart of AUSB system.

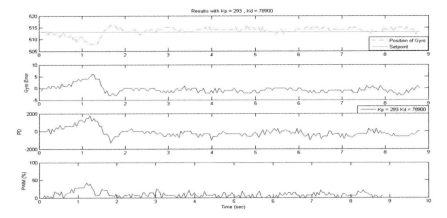

Figure 25.9: Plot of AUSB response.

The variable $\theta_{set-point}$ indicates the balancing position of the bicycle and the variable $\theta_{lean\,angle}$ is the current leaning angle of the bicycle provided by the gyroscope sensor. The difference in both angles is computed as θ_{error}, which needs to be adjusted to balance the AUSB robot. The θ_{error} obtained from Equation 25.2 is then passed through the PD controller to compute for the appropriate value of PWM (U), which will be used to control the driver of the AUSB system. PD controller is mathematically described as shown in Equation 25.1, where K_p represents the proportional gain constant, and K_d represents the derivative gain constant.

25.4.2 Analysis of AUSB System

Section 25.4.1 explains the mechanism of the controller system, which is just a part of the AUSB system. To visualize the overall implementation of AUSB, a flowchart of the system is introduced in Figure 25.8 to illustrate the process of the balancing control.

When the AUSB robot is in the balancing position, $\theta_{error} = 0$, there are 3 possibilities: the bicycle will fall to the left or right of the balancing point, or the bicycle remains in the balancing position. Therefore θ_{error} is classified into 3 cases: *positive, negative,* or *stationary* at balancing point $\theta_{error} = 0$.

Intuitively, when the AUSB robot remains in the balancing position, the system requires no action to preserve the balance. Therefore the microcontroller sends a command to stop the H-Bridge, where H-Bridge is the device that controls the direction of the DC motor attached to the flywheels of this system. When the θ_{error} is *positive*, the microcontroller sends a command to the H-Bridge to drive the DC motor in a counter-clockwise direction. This produces a correct direction of counter torque to place the bicycle back in the balancing position. The same procedure applies when the θ_{error} is *negative* on the H-Bridge. In this case, this will drive the DC motor in the clockwise direction. The amount of PWM is precisely calculated as mentioned in Equation 25.1 and sent to the flywheels.

25.4.3 Result

In order to evaluate the performance of the AUSB with the PD controller, the gains (K_p, K_d) of PD controller need to be varied to analyze and obtain the best result. Only the best optimized gain and result from [Janwattanapong and Ratchatanantakit 12] of the experiments is plotted and shown in Figure 25.9.

With the gain: $K_p = 293$ and $K_d = 78900$, the AUSB is able to balance with the tracking performance as shown in Figure 25.9. The bicycle leaning error is limited to $1.76°$, which is calculated by $\frac{5}{1023} \times 360°$, where 1023 represents the 10-bit system of the gyroscope sensor. These gains settings give an excellent balancing performance.

25.5   Conclusion

The AU Self-Balancing Bicycle is one of the hands-on projects that illustrates the implementation of input devices in a mobile environment. This project focuses on challenging the control theory where the most important parameters are the stability of the system and the computational time of the controller. From Section 25.3, the stability of the AUSB greatly depends on the data obtained from the gyroscope sensor. Theoretically, the data generated will be processed directly by the main controller, but in a practical situation, the data will be altered with artifacts from many sources. The best approach to deal with this situation is to design a high-performance filter while minimizing the computational time.

This indicates that any system dealing with signal and data processing, the foremost procedure that needs to be applied is the preprocessing of signal or data. Signal and data without artifacts will definitely impact the stability and reliability of the implemented algorithm and will improve the output of the system in every aspect.

Further Reading

The principle of AUSB is based on an inverted pendulum control. To understand the mathematical model and the control derivation of the AUSB system is highly challenging. An article,"Simulation Studies of Inverted Pendulum Based on PID Controllers" written by Jia-Jun Wang [Wang 11] will enhance the basic knowledge of conventional PID controllers and the modeling of the system.

To practice simulating the system and controller, http://ctms.engin.umich.edu/ CTMS/index.php?example=InvertedPendulum&section=SystemModeling from [MATWORK 12] provides a great explanation of the inverted pendulum system and provides steps in creating a simulation.

Exercises

1. Explain briefly the control diagram of Figure 25.7. For instance, what are the required parameters of the system and output of the system?

2. Construct a new control diagram using the same PD controller block assuming that the AUSB is changed to an inverted pendulum system. Label all the required parameters on the diagram.

26

Input Implementation Details

Nosotros tenemos la oportunidad de hablar a través del
juego, que es la expresión más natural y genuina. (We
have the opportunity to speak throughout our game,
which is the most beautiful and genuine expression.)
—Marcelo Bielsa

This chapter covers different snippets of code that are useful for certain input
implementation.

26.1 Input Devices

This section covers the implementation of different input devices and techniques.

26.1.1 Device Listeners and Common Interfaces

Input devices comes in different flavors. Some devices may used third-party API,
WINAPI low-level access, or their own proprietary drivers. For this reason, it is
important to have a common design pattern [Gamma et al. 94, Gregoire et al. 11],
known as the observer pattern. Note this is not the only approach that can be
taken (see [Hoste et al. 11, Scholliers et al. 11]. The reason that this pattern is not
always desired is due to the problems inherent in a multi-threaded environment.
Nevertheless, it is a viable option and it is presented here.

The observer pattern allows a central object (subject) to keep a list of depen-
dents (observers). In other words, the device has a listener waiting for an event.
Each device has its own device listener. An example for the 3D mouse is shown in
Listings 26.1, 26.2, and 26.3. The listener (Listing 26.1) provides an interface for
any class that needs to receive the event data input when it triggers. The registry
(Listing 26.2 provides two functionalities: registration to the list of observers

(*registryListener*(...)), and the signaling method for the raw input methods (e.g., WINAPI) to signal an event to all subscribed observers. The concrete implementation is shown in Listing 26.3. Finally, it is important to mention that a common interface was created for all game navigation controllers, which is called **InputPad**. This interface allows users to have common functionalities across devices. The **InputPad** interface is shown in Listing 26.4.

Listing 26.1: Observer Pattern (Listener.h)

```
1   typedef struct DOF6 {
2     int tx;
3     int ty;
4     int tz;
5     int rx;
6     int ry;
7     int rz;
8   } DOFSix;
9
10  typedef struct BDATA {
11    unsigned char p3;
12    unsigned char p2;
13    unsigned char p1;
14  } BData;
15
16  class Win3DXOgreListener
17  {
18  public:
19    virtual bool handleNavigator(int message,DOFSix & D,BData & B) = ↩
          0;
20  };
```

Listing 26.2: Observer Pattern (Registry.h)

```
1   #include "Win3DXOgreListener.h"
2   #include <vector>
3   #include <map>
4
5   class Win3DXOgreEventRegistry
6   {
7       public:
8           static bool registerListener(int inMessage, ↩
                Win3DXOgreListener* inListener);
9
10          static bool signalNavigator(int inMessage, int outMessage,↩
                DOFSix & D,BData & B);
11
12      enum MESSAGES {M_UNKNOWN = 100,M_BUTTON = 101,M_NAVIGATOR = ↩
            102};
13      enum REGISTER {LISTEN_ALL=0};
14
15      protected:
16          static std::map<int, std::vector<Win3DXOgreListener*>> ↩
```

```
                    sListenerMap;
17
18   };
```

Listing 26.3: Observer Pattern (Registry.cpp)

```
1    // Implements the EventRegistry class
2    #include "Win3DXOgreEventRegistry.h"
3    using namespace std;
4    map<int, vector<Win3DXOgreListener*>> Win3DXOgreEventRegistry::↵
         sListenerMap;
5
6    bool Win3DXOgreEventRegistry::registerListener(int inMessage, ↵
         Win3DXOgreListener* inListener)
7    {
8      if (inMessage != REGISTER::LISTEN_ALL) return false;
9      sListenerMap[inMessage].push_back(inListener);
10     return true;
11   }
12
13   bool Win3DXOgreEventRegistry::signalNavigator(int inMessage, int ↵
         outMessage,DOFSix & D,BData & B)
14   {
15     if (inMessage != REGISTER::LISTEN_ALL || sListenerMap.find(↵
           inMessage) == sListenerMap.end())
16       return false;
17     for (auto iter = sListenerMap[inMessage].begin();
18       iter != sListenerMap[inMessage].end(); ++iter)
19     {
20         (*iter)->handleNavigator(outMessage, D,  B);
21
22     }
23     return true;
24   }
```

Listing 26.4: InputPad (Interface)

```
1    #include <string>
2    using namespace std;
3    class InputPad
4    {
5    public:
6      virtual void updateInput(const double,const unsigned long long)=0;
7      virtual string getPlayerName()=0;
8      virtual string getDeviceName()=0;
9      virtual void setPlayerName(const string &  playerName)=0;
10     virtual void setDeviceName(const string & deviceName)=0;
11     virtual void enableInputDevice(bool enabled)=0;
12     virtual void enableWrite(bool enabled)=0;
13   };
```

Figure 26.1: 3D mouse space sensor.[†]

26.1.2   3D Mouse

The 3D mouse by 3DConnexion[1], a division of the popular company Logitech,[2] provides a 6-DOF interaction. The company has reported over one million units sold as of March, 2011.[3]

This 3D mouse, shown in Figure 26.1, provides the three rotations yaw (spin), roll, and pitch (tilt). It also provides three additional movements that can be used for the translations in X, Y, and Z coordinates, which they called pan left/right, pan up/down, and zoom, respectively, as shown in Figure 26.2.

While the device does provide 6-DOF, the user is restricted by the device to small movements in each of the six possible interactions provided by the 3D mouse. Some users have adopted the use of two of these mouses. For example, the movements along the Z axis (zoom) are restricted to approximately 0.5 mm from center to either direction (in/out). The device can be a complement to current navigation techniques. It is used by some 3D CAD and 3D modelers, working in AutoCAD, 3Ds Max, Maya, and other similar tools.

---

[1] See http://www.3dconnexion.com.
[2] See http://www.logitech.com.
[3] See http://bit.ly/1nFpujp.

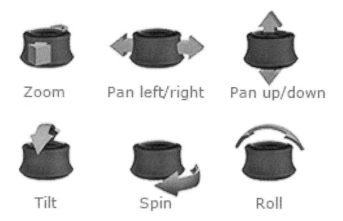

Zoom   Pan left/right   Pan up/down

Tilt   Spin   Roll

Figure 26.2: 3D mouse functions.[†]

Implementation

During the time that the 3D mouse was tested, the SDK provided by 3DConnexion had some problems that remained unresolved (it is possible that an updated SDK may have fixed those problems). However, the other alternative is to use low-level driver (see [Viscarola and Mason 99, Orwick and Smith 07]) support from WINAPI [Petzold 98]. We tested this in Windows 7. The following implementation describes the low-level implementation[4] to access the 3D Mouse.

First, the device must be initialized, as shown in Listing 26.5. In lines 2–5, the process defines a few global variables required for the entire device recognition and device listening at the raw level. Then, the initialize function must be executed, as shown in lines 7–21. If the function is successful, it will return true, as shown in line 20.

After verifying during the initialization process that there is a device, there needs to be a search for the type of device present, which in this case, is the 3D mouse. The actual model is called 3D Mouse Space Navigator. The steps indicated in Listing 26.5 are shown in Listing 26.6. During the for loop included in lines 1–37, the process must determine if the 3D mouse is found, to later register up to 8 devices. First, the process must check if the device type is **RIM_TYPEHID**, which is defined as the constant equal to 2. In line 15, the function *GetRawInput-DeviceInfo*(...), checks to see if the return value is a number greater than zero and the type is equal to **RIM_TYPEHID**. Note that **RIDI_DEVICEINFO** is equal to the hexadecimal number of 2000000B (5366870923 in decimal value). If this is the

---

[4]See http://www.ogre3d.org/forums/viewtopic.php?f=2&t=69156.

case, and the **usUsagePage** = 1 and the **usUsage**, the device is registered into the list **g_RawInpuDevices**. Finally, the devices found are registered using *Register-RawInputDevices*, in line 38, using the list of devices already stored. It is important to note that **g_pRawInputDeviceList** must have its memory released once the process completes using the free method (*free(g_pRaw)*), which is equally important for any other data structure allocated using the C language method *malloc(...)*, when it is no longer needed.

Once the devices are registered, the actual data can be extracted from the device using the Windows event loop available. The actual data can be extracted from the device. The typical error checks are performed in Listing 26.7. The device input data process is shown in Listing 26.8. It is important to note that data packets are not triggered in one cycle, but independent events, which are captured by checking the **bRawData**. This variable is equal to one for the translation movement, equal to two for the rotation movements, and equal to three if the buttons were pressed. This is why lines 8–36 have an if-elseif-else logic, to obtain the data packets. Once the process is completed, there are different options for the developer. For example, the developer may desire to fire each event independently or test some criteria before firing. For example, if **bRotation** and **bTranslation** are true, then the input event is fired. An example of firing the event data listener is shown in line 35. The *signalNavigator(...)* is how the listeners are advised of new device data when fired. This is described in Section 26.1.1, including the listing for the observer pattern, already explained.

Listing 26.5: 3DMouse (Global and Initial Checks)

```
1   ...
2   //Global variables
3   PRAWINPUTDEVICELIST g_pRawInputDeviceList;
4   PRAWINPUTDEVICE     g_pRawInputDevices;
5   int                 g_nUsagePage1Usage8Devices;
6
7   BOOL InitRawDevices()
8   {
9     UINT nDevices;
10    if (GetRawInputDeviceList(NULL, &nDevices, sizeof(↵
          RAWINPUTDEVICELIST)) != 0)
11      return FALSE; // no 3D Mouse Found
12    if ((g_pRawInputDeviceList = (PRAWINPUTDEVICELIST)malloc(sizeof(↵
          RAWINPUTDEVICELIST) * nDevices)) == NULL)
13      return FALSE; // malloc fails
14    if (GetRawInputDeviceList(g_pRawInputDeviceList, &nDevices, sizeof↵
          (RAWINPUTDEVICELIST)) == -1)
15      return FALSE; //fails to get input devices
16
17    g_pRawInputDevices = (PRAWINPUTDEVICE)malloc( nDevices * sizeof(↵
          RAWINPUTDEVICE) );
18    g_nUsagePage1Usage8Devices = 0;
```

```
19    ...
20    RETURN TRUE;
21  }
22  ...
```

Listing 26.6: 3DMouse (Partial Initialize)

```
1   for(UINT i=0; i<nDevices; i++)
2   {
3     if (g_pRawInputDeviceList[i].dwType == RIM_TYPEHID)
4     {
5       UINT nchars = 300;
6       TCHAR deviceName[300];
7       if (GetRawInputDeviceInfo( g_pRawInputDeviceList[i].hDevice,
8         RIDI_DEVICENAME, deviceName, &nchars) >= 0)
9         fprintf(stderr, "Device[%d]: handle=0x%x name = %S\n", i, ↵
              g_pRawInputDeviceList[i].hDevice, deviceName);
10
11      RID_DEVICE_INFO dinfo;
12      UINT sizeofdinfo = sizeof(dinfo);
13      dinfo.cbSize = sizeofdinfo;
14      if (GetRawInputDeviceInfo( g_pRawInputDeviceList[i].hDevice,
15        RIDI_DEVICEINFO, &dinfo, &sizeofdinfo ) >= 0)
16      {
17        if (dinfo.dwType == RIM_TYPEHID)
18        {
19          RID_DEVICE_INFO_HID *phidInfo = &dinfo.hid;
20          fprintf(stderr, "VID = 0x%x\n", phidInfo->dwVendorId);
21          fprintf(stderr, "PID = 0x%x\n", phidInfo->dwProductId);
22          fprintf(stderr, "Version = 0x%x\n", phidInfo->dwVersionNumber↵
                );
23          fprintf(stderr, "UsagePage = 0x%x\n", phidInfo->usUsagePage);
24          fprintf(stderr, "Usage = 0x%x\n", phidInfo->usUsage);
25
26          if (phidInfo->usUsagePage == 1 && phidInfo->usUsage == 8)
27          {
28            g_pRawInputDevices[g_nUsagePage1Usage8Devices].usUsagePage↵
                  = phidInfo->usUsagePage;
29            g_pRawInputDevices[g_nUsagePage1Usage8Devices].usUsage ↵
                  = phidInfo->usUsage;
30            g_pRawInputDevices[g_nUsagePage1Usage8Devices].dwFlags ↵
                  = 0;
31            g_pRawInputDevices[g_nUsagePage1Usage8Devices].hwndTarget ↵
                  = NULL;
32            g_nUsagePage1Usage8Devices++;
33          }
34        }
35      }
36    }
37  }
38  if (RegisterRawInputDevices( g_pRawInputDevices, ↵
        g_nUsagePage1Usage8Devices, sizeof(RAWINPUTDEVICE) ) == FALSE )
39    return FALSE; // fails to register
40  ...
```

Listing 26.7: 3DMouse (Process Input Error Checking)

```
1   RAWINPUTHEADER header;
2   UINT size = sizeof(header);
3   if ( GetRawInputData( (HRAWINPUT)lParam, RID_HEADER, &header,  &size↵
         , sizeof(RAWINPUTHEADER) ) == -1)
4     return; \\error with device
5   }
6   size = header.dwSize;
7   LPRAWINPUT event = (LPRAWINPUT)malloc(size);
8   if (GetRawInputData( (HRAWINPUT)lParam, RID_INPUT, event, &size, ↵
         sizeof(RAWINPUTHEADER) ) == -1)
9     return; \\error with input
10  ...
```

Listing 26.8: 3DMouse (Process Input)

```
1   ...
2   if (event->header.dwType == RIM_TYPEHID)
3   {
4     static BOOL bGotTranslation = FALSE,
5       bGotRotation   = FALSE;
6     static int all6DOFs[6] = {0};
7     LPRAWHID pRawHid = &event->data.hid;
8     if (pRawHid->bRawData[0] == 1) // Translation vector
9     {
10      all6DOFs[0] = (pRawHid->bRawData[1] & 0x000000ff) | ((signed ↵
           short)(pRawHid->bRawData[2]<<8) & 0xffffff00);
11      all6DOFs[1] = (pRawHid->bRawData[3] & 0x000000ff) | ((signed ↵
           short)(pRawHid->bRawData[4]<<8) & 0xffffff00);
12      all6DOFs[2] = (pRawHid->bRawData[5] & 0x000000ff) | ((signed ↵
           short)(pRawHid->bRawData[6]<<8) & 0xffffff00);
13      bGotTranslation = TRUE;
14    }
15    else if (pRawHid->bRawData[0] == 2) // Rotation vector
16    {
17      all6DOFs[3] = (pRawHid->bRawData[1] & 0x000000ff) | ((signed ↵
           short)(pRawHid->bRawData[2]<<8) & 0xffffff00);
18      all6DOFs[4] = (pRawHid->bRawData[3] & 0x000000ff) | ((signed ↵
           short)(pRawHid->bRawData[4]<<8) & 0xffffff00);
19      all6DOFs[5] = (pRawHid->bRawData[5] & 0x000000ff) | ((signed ↵
           short)(pRawHid->bRawData[6]<<8) & 0xffffff00);
20      bGotRotation = TRUE;
21    }
22    else if (pRawHid->bRawData[0] == 3)
23    {
24      DOFSix D;
25      BData B;
26      D.tx = 0;
27      D.ty = 0;
28      D.tz = 0;
29      D.rx = 0;
30      D.ry = 0;
```

```
31      D.rz = 0;
32      B.p3 = (unsigned char)pRawHid->bRawData[3];
33      B.p2 = (unsigned char)pRawHid->bRawData[2];
34      B.p1 = (unsigned char)pRawHid->bRawData[1];
35      Win3DXOgreEventRegistry::signalNavigator(Win3DXOgreEventRegistry↩
            ::LISTEN_ALL,Win3DXOgreEventRegistry::M_BUTTON,D,B);
36    }
37  }
38  ...
```

26.1.3 Inertial Navigation System

INS has become a popular method as an input device (see Part II of this book, in particular Chapters 17 and 20). One of the components is the gyroscope. This type of system also includes accelerometers and compasses. With the advance of MEMS devices, they have become small and pervasive, as seen with the WiiMote, and a standard in many tablets and smartphones, such as the iPhone. This section describes how to implement the MEMS sensor by YEI Technologies,[5] called **3-Space Sensor**. The API provided by YEI Technologies works with C/C++ and Python. The actual API is pure C.

The actual sensor used comes with a wireless dongle that connects up to 15 devices. An example is provided on the book's website, which includes a visualization sample. YEI technologies provide additional software. For example, they provide a suite to do testing, which requires no coding at all. This can be quite useful for understanding the output of the device before creating a prototype. Chapter 20 provides additional information about this sensor.

26.1.4 Microsoft Kinect

A bit of background is required to understand Microsoft Kinect. The original design and intent was the capture of in-air gestures when using the Microsoft XBox 360 video game console. Given the popularity and potential of the Kinect, the working system was reverse-engineered to provide an unofficial API. It is not certain if this led Microsoft to release Microsoft Kinect for Windows, but in any case, the release of Kinect for Windows came with an official SDK provided from Microsoft and a modified firmware that included a feature for the near/far distance detection. This SDK was used for testing. While Microsoft has released the new Kinect 2 for the XBox One video game console, and will be releasing a Kinect 2 for windows soon, note that when the Kinect sensor is mentioned in this chapter, it refers to the Microsoft Kinect (version 1) for Windows.

The Kinect includes a microphone array, an infrared emitter, an infrared receiver, a color camera, and a DSP chip. This all connects using a USB 2 [Catuhe 12]. The use of both cameras allows for 3D vision to be captured. In other

---

[5]See http://www.yeitechnology.com

words, depth can be captured using the Kinect. There are some limitations to the use of the Kinect, which are listed below (adapted from [Catuhe 12]):

- Horizontal viewing angle: 57°.

- Vertical viewing angle: 43°.

- Far mode distance: 1.2 meters to 4.2 meters.

- Near[6] mode distance: 0.4 meters to 3.0 meters.

- Standard depth range: 8000 mm.

- Near mode depth range: 400 mm.

- Temperature: 5° to 35° Celsius.

- Motor controller vertical viewing position: ±28°

One feature provided by the Kinect SDK is the ability to track the human skeleton, called **skeletal tracking**. It allows the tracking of the movements of joints by a user, as shown in Figure 26.3. The tracking can be done for up to six persons simultaneously [Catuhe 12], in its FOV.

The Implementation

The implementation described here is meant to be used by two different applications running in the same system.[7] The primary reason is that developers may prefer to utilized C# code for Microsoft Kinect because of the amount of samples already available; therefore we have provided the code in C#, which sends messages to a WINAPI C++ application. Another reason to keep it in a separate application is that people have used an array of Kinects, using an external process or computer to capture the data, and sent the information to another process (sometimes over a network instead of a process). This provides the flexibility to have different processes in the same computer or across a network.

This implementation was achieved using a WINAPI messaging system to send data between processes, as shown in Listing 26.9. This allows the Kinect process to send messages to an external application running on the same computer. Of course, the implementation of the method **SendMessageTo** could be replaced by another type of system or networking communications (e.g., communication sockets [Makofske et al. 04]).

To perform the 3D navigation using the Kinect, a basic set of gestures was created, as shown in Figure 26.3. In this figure, there are 8 positions where the

---

[6]Only available with firmware update.

[7]The development of the prototype was led by Francisco R. Ortega, with the collaboration of Jose Camino, Karina Harfouche, and Holly Smith.

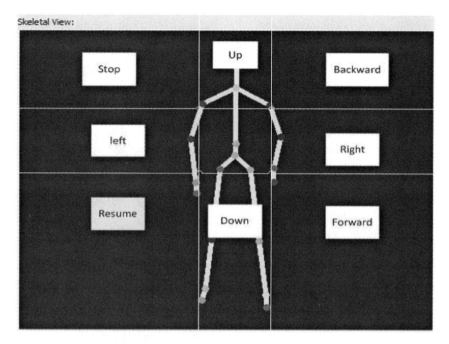

Figure 26.3: C# skeleton viewer (possible gestures).

user can move his or her right or left hand to achieve a desired action. The user was presented with a model of ruins from a ancient civilization, as shown in Figure 26.4, in full screen. The user could also see the different parts of the system if needed,[8] as shown in Figure 26.5. What the user experienced, from his or her point of view, is shown in Figure 26.5.

Listing 26.9: Kinect (WINAPI Messages)

```
 1  private struct COPYDATASTRUCT
 2  {
 3      public IntPtr dwData;
 4      public int cbData;
 5      [MarshalAs(UnmanagedType.LPStr)]
 6      public string lpData;
 7  }
 8  private const int WM_COPYDATA = 0x4A;
 9  [DllImport("user32.dll", SetLastError = true)]
10  static extern IntPtr
11      FindWindow(string lpClassName, string lpWindowName);
12  [DllImport("User32.dll", EntryPoint = "SendMessage")]
13  private static extern int
```

---

[8]Used primarily for development.

```
14      SendMessage(IntPtr hWnd, int Msg, int wParam, ref COPYDATASTRUCT↩
            lParam);
15
16  IntPtr hwnd FindWindow(null, "QTApp:KinectMessageHandler");
17
18  private void sendMessageTo(IntPtr hWnd, String msg)
19  {
20      int wParam = 0;
21      int result = 0;
22
23      if (hWnd != IntPtr.Zero)
24      {
25          byte[] sarr = System.Text.Encoding.Default.GetBytes(msg);
26          int len = sarr.Length;
27          COPYDATASTRUCT cds;
28          cds.dwData = IntPtr.Zero;
29          cds.lpData = msg;
30          cds.cbData = len + 1;
31          result = SendMessage(hWnd, WM_COPYDATA, wParam, ref cds);
32      }
33  }
```

Listing 26.10: Skelton Tracking (Left/Right)

```
1   ...
2   if (yMin != 0.0f && yMax != 0.0f && xMax != 0.0f && xMin != 0.0f)
3   {
4       //sends 'right' command: right hand in right square
5       if (skeleton.Joints[JointType.HandRight].Position.X >= xMax + ↩
            0.3f &&
6           skeleton.Joints[JointType.HandRight].Position.Y < yMax && ↩
                skeleton.Joints[JointType.HandRight].Position.Y > yMin)
7       {
8           sendMessageTo(hwnd,"right");
9       }
10      //sends 'left' command: left hand in left square
11      if (skeleton.Joints[JointType.HandLeft].Position.X <= xMin - 0.3↩
            f &&
12          skeleton.Joints[JointType.HandLeft].Position.Y < yMax && ↩
                skeleton.Joints[JointType.HandLeft].Position.Y > yMin)
13      {
14          sendMessageTo(hwnd, "left");
15      }
16  }
17  ...
```

26.1.5   Keyboard and Mouse

The keyboard and mouse usage and implementation are pervasive. Therefore, very little will be mentioned in this chapter about these input devices. However,

Figure 26.4: Ancient 3D ruins.

additional information is found in Chapter 27. What is more important is how to handle the 3D navigation using a keyboard or a mouse. The following example, in Listing 26.11, demonstrates the interface for keyboard navigation controller.

Listing 26.11: Keyboard (Navigation)

```
1   class KeyPad : public InputPad
2   {
3   public:
4     typedef float real;
5     KeyPad(Navigation * navigation,OIS::Keyboard* keyboard,const ↩
            string & playerName=string("Player"),const string & deviceName↩
            =string("Keyboard"));
6     virtual void updateInput(const double,const unsigned long long);
7     virtual void enableInputDevice(bool enabled){mEnabled = enabled;}
8     virtual void enableWrite(bool enabled){mWriteEnabled = enabled;}
9     virtual void setPlayerName(const string &  playerName) { ↩
            mPlayerName = playerName; }
10    virtual void setDeviceName(const string & deviceName) { ↩
            mDeviceName = deviceName;}
11    virtual string getPlayerName(){ return mPlayerName;}
12    virtual string getDeviceName(){ return mDeviceName;}
13
14  private:
15    //Methods
16    void moveLeft(real f,real t);
17    void moveRight(real f,real t);
```

Figure 26.5: Screen closeup.

```
18    void moveUp(real f,real t);
19    void moveDown(real f,real t);
20    void moveIn(real f,real t);
21    void moveOut(real f,real t);
22    void rotateX(real f,real t);
23    void rotateY(real f,real t);
24    void rotateZ(real f,real t);
25    void rotateInverseX(real f,real t);
26    void rotateInverseY(real f,real t);
27    void rotateInverseZ(real f,real t);
28    Navigation * mNavigation;
29    OIS::Keyboard * mKeyboard;
30    string mPlayerName;
31    string mDeviceName;
32    bool mEnabled;
33    bool mWriteEnabled;
34  };
```

26.1.6   GamePad

The GamePad is a type of video game controller that is the default device for every video console game today. While video games tried different controllers in the late seventies and early eighties, such as the joystick (Figure 26.7a), paddles (Figure 26.7b), and other input devices, the release of the GamePad in the third

Figure 26.6: From the user's point of view.

generation of the NES video game console marked the before and after for game controllers (Figure 26.7c). The GamePad (also called joypad), shown in Figure 26.8a, provides a common form to navigate in virtual worlds. In particular, the XBox 360 controller has become popular among researchers in the past few years (compared to other GamePads), shown in Figure 26.8b. This GamePad comes from the seventh generation of video game consoles [Loguidice and Barton 14]. The evolution of the GamePad has made them an excellent candidate for 3D navigation. The most current GamePad, from the eighth generation, is the XBox One controller, shown in Figure 26.8c.

The Implementation

To use the XBox 360 GamePad in Windows, the use of the Microsoft XInput[9] [Harbour 10, McShaffry 13] library was utilized. XInput is the most current Microsoft library for input devices, in specific, game controllers. Just like in the previous devices already mentioned, the wrapping of the low-level access to

---

[9]See http://msdn.microsoft.com/en-us/library/windows/desktop/ee417014(v=vs.85).aspx

the controller was developed, as shown in Listings 26.12 and 26.13. The actual navigation was configured just like in the keyboard example. Here is a partial sample of the code needed, shown in Listings 26.14 and 26.15. Finally, it is important to normalize the data and smooth the input,[10] to have a more continuous navigation when using the GamePad, as shown in Listing 26.16. The GamePad is covered in depth in Chapter 27.

Listing 26.12: XBox360 Controller (h)

```
1   #define WIN32_LEAN_AND_MEAN
2   // We need the Windows Header and the XInput Header
3   #include <windows.h>
4   #include <XInput.h>
5   // NOTE: COMMENT THE NEXT LINE, IF YOU ARE NOT USING A COMPILER THAT↩
        SUPPORTS #pragma TO LINK LIBRARIES
6   #pragma comment(lib, "XInput.lib")
7
8   class CXBoxController
9   {
10  private:
11    XINPUT_STATE _controllerState;
12    int _controllerNum;
13  public:
14    typedef XINPUT_STATE controllerx_state;
15    CXBoxController(int playerNumber);
16    XINPUT_STATE GetState();
17    bool IsConnected();
18    void Vibrate(WORD leftVal = 0, WORD rightVal = 0);
19  };
```

Listing 26.13: XBox360 Controller (cpp)

```
1   #include "CXBoxController.h"
2   CXBoxController::CXBoxController(int playerNumber)
3   {
4     _controllerNum = playerNumber - 1;
5   }
6   XINPUT_STATE CXBoxController::GetState()
7   {
8     ZeroMemory(&_controllerState, sizeof(XINPUT_STATE));
9     XInputGetState(_controllerNum, &_controllerState);
10    return _controllerState;
11  }
12  bool CXBoxController::IsConnected()
13  {
14    ZeroMemory(&_controllerState, sizeof(XINPUT_STATE));
15    DWORD Result = XInputGetState(_controllerNum, &_controllerState);
16    if(Result == ERROR_SUCCESS)
```

[10]See http://www.altdevblogaday.com/2011/06/16/analog-input-processing/

(a) Atari Joystick   (b) Atari Paddles   (c) Nintendo NES Pad

Figure 26.7: Images.

(a) Sony Dual-Shock (PS1)   (b) Xbox 360   (c) Xbox One

Figure 26.8: Images.

```
17      return true;
18    else
19      return false;
20  }
21  void CXBoxController::Vibrate(WORD leftVal, WORD rightVal)
22  {
23    XINPUT_VIBRATION Vibration;
24    ZeroMemory(&Vibration, sizeof(XINPUT_VIBRATION));
25    Vibration.wLeftMotorSpeed = leftVal;
26    Vibration.wRightMotorSpeed = rightVal;
27    XInputSetState(_controllerNum, &Vibration);
28  }
```

Listing 26.14: Game Navigation Controller(h)

```
1  class XPad : public InputPad
```

```
2   {
3   public:
4     typedef enum {PlayerOne=1,PlayerTwo=2,PlayerThree=3,PlayerFour=4} ↵
          player_number;
5     typedef enum {Analog,Digital} process_type;
6     typedef float real;
7     typedef struct controller_data { ... };
8     typedef struct normalized_data { ... };
9     typedef struct deadzone_data { ... };
10    typedef struct player_data { ... };
11    typedef struct controller_values { ... };
12    ...
13    XPad(...);
14    void setNormalizedDeadZoneL(real v){mDeadzone.left =v;}
15    void setNormalizedDeadZoneR(real v){mDeadzone.right =v;}
16    void setNormalizedDeadZoneTrigger(real v){mDeadzone.trigger =v;}
17    player_data getPlayerData() { return mPlayerData;}
18    void setPolarity(bool p){mPolarity=p;}
19    void setDigital(bool d){mDigital=d;}
20    bool isConnected(){return true;}
21    virtual void updateInput(const double timeSinceLastFrame,const ↵
          unsigned long long cCount);
22    virtual void enableInputDevice(bool enabled){mEnabled = enabled;}
23    virtual void enableWrite(bool enabled){mWriteEnabled = enabled;}
24    virtual void setPlayerName(const string &  playerName) { ↵
          mPlayerName = playerName; }
25    virtual void setDeviceName(const string & deviceName) { ↵
          mDeviceName = deviceName;}
26    virtual string getPlayerName(){ return mPlayerName;}
27    virtual string getDeviceName(){ return mDeviceName;}
28    XINPUT_STATE getState(){ return mPad.GetState();}
29  private:
30    ...
31  };
```

Listing 26.15: Game Navigation Controller(cpp)

```
1   class XPad : public InputPad
2   {
3   public:
4     typedef enum {PlayerOne=1,PlayerTwo=2,PlayerThree=3,PlayerFour=4} ↵
          player_number;
5     typedef enum {Analog,Digital} process_type;
6     typedef float real;
7     typedef struct controller_data { ... };
8     typedef struct normalized_data { ... };
9     typedef struct deadzone_data { ... };
10    typedef struct player_data { ... };
11    typedef struct controller_values { ... };
12    ...
13    XPad(...);
```

```
14    void setNormalizedDeadZoneL(real v){mDeadzone.left =v;}
15    void setNormalizedDeadZoneR(real v){mDeadzone.right =v;}
16    void setNormalizedDeadZoneTrigger(real v){mDeadzone.trigger =v;}
17    player_data getPlayerData() { return mPlayerData;}
18    void setPolarity(bool p){mPolarity=p;}
19    void setDigital(bool d){mDigital=d;}
20    bool isConnected(){return true;}
21    virtual void updateInput(const double timeSinceLastFrame,const ↩
          unsigned long long cCount);
22    virtual void enableInputDevice(bool enabled){mEnabled = enabled;}
23    virtual void enableWrite(bool enabled){mWriteEnabled = enabled;}
24    virtual void setPlayerName(const string &  playerName) { ↩
          mPlayerName = playerName; }
25    virtual void setDeviceName(const string & deviceName) { ↩
          mDeviceName = deviceName;}
26    virtual string getPlayerName(){ return mPlayerName;}
27    virtual string getDeviceName(){ return mDeviceName;}
28    XINPUT_STATE getState(){ return mPad.GetState();}
29  private:
30    ...
31  };
```

Listing 26.16: XBox360 Controller (Smooth Input)

```
1   void XPad::normalizedData(controller_data & data,normalized_data & ↩
        ndata)
2   {
3     //scale data will give you input from -1 to 1
4     //normalized will give you 0 to 1.
5     ndata.LX = NMath<short,real>::scaledData(MINTHUMB,MAXTHUMB,data.LX↩
          );
6     ndata.LY = NMath<short,real>::scaledData(MINTHUMB,MAXTHUMB,data.LY↩
          );
7     ndata.RX = NMath<short,real>::scaledData(MINTHUMB,MAXTHUMB,data.RX↩
          );
8     ndata.RY = NMath<short,real>::scaledData(MINTHUMB,MAXTHUMB,data.RY↩
          );
9     ndata.TL = NMath<short,real>::normalizedData(MINTRIGGER,MAXTRIGGER↩
          ,data.TL);
10    ndata.TR = NMath<short,real>::normalizedData(MINTRIGGER,MAXTRIGGER↩
          ,data.TR);
11  }
12  double XPad::smoothInput(double v,double alpha)
13  {
14    //data is expected to be normalized.
15    if (std::abs(v) < alpha)
16      return make_pair(0,0);
17    double u = NMath<real>::sgn(v) * (std::abs(v) - alpha) / ( 1.0f - ↩
          alpha) ;
18    return std::make_pair(u);
19  }
```

26.2   Multi-Touch Implementation

There are multiple forms used to detect the multi-touch input at the hardware level, as explained in Chapter 8. Once the touches are detected, the data is communicated to the system using different types of drivers or protocols. For example, in vision touch detection, tangible user interface objects (TUIO) are quite popular[11]. The protocol is defined in [Kaltenbrunner et al. 05], and is illustrated with a real user case in the ReactiVision system [Kaltenbrunner 09]. In capacitive systems, it is common to use the drivers provided by the manufacturer or the operating system. For example, the 3M M2256PW multi-touch display comes with its own drivers provided by the manufacturer. In addition, this multi-touch (and others) can work using the WINAPI[12] multi-touch interface. Most languages and API have support for multi-touch. This is true in objective-C for iPad and iPhone, C# for Windows (version 7 or greater) desktop, tablets, phones, and Qt[13] framework. Some of those have support for raw data (points and traces), others for specific types of gestures, and some of them, support both options (raw data and gesture mode).

It is common for raw data to provide trace id, as well as X and Y coordinates. Additional data is obtained depending on the system. For example, in WINAPI, it is possible to obtain a time stamp, as well as the contact size for the X and Y coordinates. It is important to note that the contact size does not provide a lot of information. It fluctuates between low and high levels for the contact size, at least when tested with the 3M display. The gesture mode provides defined gestures to work with. For example, the WINAPI used in Windows 7 provided a very small set of available gestures, which are the most common ones. GestureWorks Core (GWC) provides a richer set of gestures; however, it does create a lot of ambiguity. The raw touch event data provides the opportunity to have custom-made recognition methods, such as the ones described in Chapter 10.

Implementation: Multi-Touch Using Windows 7

When working with multi-touch using the WINAPI, the initialization, the event loop, and the touch event (down, move, and up) are important to explain. To implement a solution with multi-touch using the native calls of Microsoft requires some understanding of the WINAPI. A detailed explanation of this topic is outside the scope of this chapter. The reader is referred to the classic *Windows Programming* book (fifth edition[14]) by Charles Petzold [Petzold 98] and the book by Kiriaty et al. [Kiriaty et al. 09]. Windows 8 has some additional features, which can be accessed using either the WINAPI or the Windows run-time (WinRT) libraries [Petzold 13]. An online supplemental chapter will cover Windows 8 using the Microsoft Surface Pro.

---

[11] See http://tuio.org.
[12] Available in Windows 7 or newer
[13] See Qt-project.org
[14] Note that the next edition does not cover WINAPI.

Listing 26.17 provides the basic initialization of a Windows process and the multi-touch functionality. In this listing, lines 8–17 check all the possible direct input interactions available in Windows 7. For example, these lines check if a pen is available to the system. The one that is of concern to this discussion is the multi-touch functionality. This is checked in line 13. This means that the system must have a multi-touch display attached at the moment of this check. Otherwise, the application will exit. Then, like any typical WINAPI application, the initialization obtains calls in *WinMain*, as shown in Listing 26.18 (line 16).

Once the multi-touch has been initialized, the next step is to receive the messages in the Windows event loop. The *GetMessage(...)* method is seen in Listing 26.18. An alternate way of receiving the messages is using *PeekMessage(...)*. The difference is that by receiving messages, messages are removed. By peeking at a message, the messages are left in the loop. This is very important when working with 3D graphics, as the main event loop may be controlled by another driver. For example, in OGRE, if the developer was to call the *GetMessage(...)* method, it will remove other important messages from Windows. In games, *PeekMessage(...)* is the preferred method [McShaffry 13].

The common way to handle messages in WINAPI is shown in Listing 26.19. With regard to multi-touch events, Listing 26.20 shows the correct form to handle multi-touch data events. If there is multi-touch input data to be processed, then a for loop is executed in lines 15–29. This means that each input is fired independently. Furthermore, each data point in this cycle may have different event modes, which includes down, move, and up. As stated earlier, the down event happens when the finger is pressed for the first time into the display, the move event generates the continuous set of data points while the point has stayed on the touch surface, (regardless of if it is moving or not), and the up event marks the finger's removal from the surface. Each trace is denoted by an id number, in this case, provided by the Windows system. Finally, it is important to deallocate the multi-touch display resource, which had been previously allocated (in the initialization phase), as shown in line 37.

Finally, the events help to handle the multi-touch interaction. The basic interaction generates 2D points. For example, a painting application can be used with this information. The utilization of the 2D point information received depends on the application. FETOUCH (see Chapter 10) stores the points in a hash table (map), where each trace becomes the key, and the value of the map becomes a list of points (in order of arrival). This is later broken in half to compute the gesture. This is really application specific. Listing 26.21 displays an example of using (thread-safe) data structures to store the data points, during the down, move, and up events. Two important aspects about the data touch points must be taken into account. First, the data structures shown are thread-safe, meaning that it is safe to run them in parallel if needed.[15] Second, during the up event, no points are removed from the hash table. This is because it is expected to have another process deal with the points and delete them. Finally, the **Trace** class, in this context, contains information about a data point that belongs to a certain trace.

Listing 26.17: WINAPI (Multi-Touch init)

```
1   BOOL InitInstance(HINSTANCE hInstance, int nCmdShow)
2   {
3     g_hInst = hInstance;
4     g_hWnd = CreateWindow(g_wszWindowClass, g_wszTitle, ←
          WS_OVERLAPPEDWINDOW,
5         CW_USEDEFAULT, 0, CW_USEDEFAULT, 0, NULL, NULL, hInstance, ←
            NULL);
6     if (!hWnd)
7        return FALSE;
8     if (value & NID_READY){ /* stack ready */}
9     if (value & NID_INTEGRATED_TOUCH) {/* integrated touch device in ←
          the PC enclouser */}
10    if (value & NID_EXTERNAL_TOUCH) { /* Touch device is not ←
          integrated in the PC enclouser */ }
11    if (value & NID_INTEGRATED_PEN){/* Integrated pan support is in ←
          the PC enclouser */ }
12    if (value & NID_EXTERNAL_PEN){/* Pan is supported but not as part ←
          of the PC enclouser */ }
13    if (((value  & NID_MULTI_INPUT) == NID_MULTI_INPUT))
14    {
15        if(!RegisterTouchWindow(hWnd, 0))
16           return FALSE;
17    }
18    ...
19    ASSERT(IsTouchWindow(hWnd, NULL));
20    ShowWindow(hWnd, nCmdShow);
21    UpdateWindow(hWnd);
22    ...
23    return TRUE;
24  }
```

---

[15]There is still a synchronization aspect between down, move, and up events.

Listing 26.18: WINAPI (Multi-Touch WinMain)

```
1   int APIENTRY wWinMain(HINSTANCE hInstance,
2                         HINSTANCE hPrevInstance,
3                         LPWSTR    lpCmdLine,
4                         int       nCmdShow)
5   {
6     ...
7     GdiplusStartupInput gdiplusStartupInput;
8       ULONG_PTR            gdiplusToken;
9       MSG msg;
10      HACCEL hAccelTable;
11    //Initialize GDI+
12    GdiplusStartup(&gdiplusToken, &gdiplusStartupInput, NULL);
13
14      ...
15      MyRegisterClass(hInstance);
16      if (!InitInstance (hInstance, nCmdShow))
17          return FALSE;
18    ...
19      // Main message loop:
20      while (GetMessage(&msg, NULL, 0, 0))
21      {
22          if (!TranslateAccelerator(msg.hwnd, hAccelTable, &msg))
23          {
24              TranslateMessage(&msg);
25              DispatchMessage(&msg);
26          }
27      }
28      ...
29    GdiplusShutdown(gdiplusToken);
30    return (int) msg.wParam;
31  }
```

Listing 26.19: WINAPI (Events)

```
1   LRESULT CALLBACK WndProc(HWND hWnd, UINT message, WPARAM wParam, ↵
        LPARAM lParam)
2   {
3       int wmId, wmEvent;
4       PAINTSTRUCT ps;
5       HDC hdc;
6       switch (message)
7       {
8       case WM_COMMAND:
9           ...
10          break;
11      case WM_PAINT:
12          ...
13          break;
14      case WM_TOUCH:
15          ...
16          break;
```

```
17          case WM_DESTROY:
18              ...
19              PostQuitMessage(0);
20              break;
21          default:
22              return DefWindowProc(hWnd, message, wParam, lParam);
23      }
24      return 0;
25  }
```

Listing 26.20: WINAPI (Multi-Touch Touch Events)

```
1   switch (message)
2   {
3   ...
4       case WM_TOUCH:
5           UINT numInputs = (UINT) wParam;
6           TOUCHINPUT* pTIArray = new TOUCHINPUT[numInputs];
7           if(NULL == pTIArray )
8           {
9               CloseTouchInputHandle((HTOUCHINPUT)lParam);
10              break;
11          }
12
13          if(GetTouchInputInfo((HTOUCHINPUT)lParam, numInputs, ↩
                pTIArray, sizeof(TOUCHINPUT)))
14          {
15              for(UINT i=0; i<numInputs; ++i)
16              {
17                  if(TOUCHEVENTF_DOWN == (pTIArray[i].dwFlags & ↩
                        TOUCHEVENTF_DOWN))
18                  {
19                      OnTouchDownHandler(hWnd, pTIArray[i]);
20                  }
21                  else if(TOUCHEVENTF_MOVE == (pTIArray[i].dwFlags & ↩
                        TOUCHEVENTF_MOVE))
22                  {
23                      OnTouchMoveHandler(hWnd, pTIArray[i]);
24                  }
25                  else if(TOUCHEVENTF_UP == (pTIArray[i].dwFlags & ↩
                        TOUCHEVENTF_UP))
26                  {
27                      OnTouchUpHandler(hWnd, pTIArray[i]);
28                  }
29              }
30          }
31
32          CloseTouchInputHandle((HTOUCHINPUT)lParam);
33          delete [] pTIArray;
34          break;
35
36      case WM_DESTROY:
```

```
37        if(!UnregisterTouchWindow(hWnd))
38        ...
39        break;
40     ...
41  }
42  ...
```

Listing 26.21: WINAPI (Multi-Touch down,move,up)

```
1   void OnTouchDownHandler(HWND hWnd, const TOUCHINPUT& ti)
2   {
3       POINT pt = GetTouchPoint(hWnd, ti);
4       unsigned long iCursorId = GetTouchContactID(ti);
5     Trace trace(iCursorId,ti,hWnd);
6     trace.requestTimeStamp();
7     concurrent_vector<Trace> vtrace;
8     vtrace.push_back(trace);
9     mapTraces.insert(pair<unsigned long,concurrent_vector<Trace>>(←↩
          iCursorId,vtrace));
10  }
11
12  void OnTouchMoveHandler(HWND hWnd, const TOUCHINPUT& ti)
13  {
14      unsigned long iCursorId = GetTouchContactID(ti);
15      POINT pt;
16      pt = GetTouchPoint(hWnd, ti);
17    concurrent_unordered_map<unsigned long,concurrent_vector<Trace>>::←↩
          iterator p = mapTraces.find(iCursorId);
18    Trace trace(iCursorId,ti,hWnd);
19    trace.requestTimeStamp();
20    int touchCount = mapTraces.size();
21    int traceSize = p->second.size();
22    Trace lastTrace = p->second[traceSize - 1];
23    ...
24    if (moving)
25      p->second.push_back(trace);
26    else //not moving
27      p->second[traceSize - 1].IncCount();
28  }
29
30  void OnTouchUpHandler(HWND hWnd, const TOUCHINPUT& ti)
31  {
32    //Delete point only if not handled by a external
33    //   resource such as gesture recognition method.
34  }
```

26.3   Working with a 3D Graphics Engine: OGRE

OpenGL is a natural candidate when one thinks about creating graphics because of its close relationship with the GPU. (Big cube of multiple color spheres was tested in OpenGL, as shown in Figure 26.9.) However, to be able to create 3D prototypes, it is better to use an engine. Nowadays, many people are using Unity (which is covered in Chapter 21). However, having the control of complete source code may be of interest to some people. While this book does not provide an introduction to Ogre 3D (visit http://www.ogre3D.org), we decided to provide the interaction needed between Ogre and input devices. This is applicable to other C++ engines that provide ways to handle windows messages.

Ogre 3D is not a game engine but a graphics engine that works on top of OpenGL and DirectX, providing functionality that can help build a game or a 3D prototype. For example, if it is desirable to have a framework that provides a scene graph and collision detection, while still keeping the freedom to code in C++, OGRE is a great option. If a game engine is needed, many engines exist including Unity and Unreal. However, OGRE provides a very capable graphics engine that could run under OpenGL or DirectX and its current development provides a very fast open source engine (see Ogre 3D 2.0 and 2.1). OGRE engine contains a scene controller, as well as other tools. In addition, we can use a third-party exporter, called OgreMax,[16] which allows exporting complete scenes from 3DS Max and Maya to OGRE. This allows a scene to be built with one of those types of software and then exported into a **.scene** (see Listing 26.22) file created by OgreMax. Figure 26.10 shows 3DS Max scene, which can be exported to a **.scene** file using OgreMax.

OGRE: The Implementation

This section outlines the essential issues pertaining to the implementation of a 3D navigation system (in particular concerning input devices and application state management), using OGRE. The OGRE engine is a very well-documented graphics engine. Most of the documentation is found in its online wiki,[17] with some additional information found in [Kerger 10, Grinblat and Peterson 12, Junker 06]. We have used the Advanced Ogre Framework,[18] which provides a simplified starting point for a 3D application. This framework facilitated the use of the OGRE engine for things such as start-up for the engine, and different stages of a 3D application, among other functionalities. The Advanced Ogre Framework provided a state machine to control the different levels of the process. In the case of the code provided below (which was used for an experiment), these were menu state

---

[16] See http://www.ogremax.com.
[17] See http://www.ogre3d.org/tikiwiki/tiki-index.php.
[18] See tutorial in http://www.ogre3d.org/tikiwiki.

Figure 26.9: OpenGL cube of spheres.

(initial state) and game state (experiment mode). A partial listing is provided for the advanced framework definition, as shown in Listing 26.23, and the definition of the menu and game states, shown in Listings 26.24 and 26.25, respectively.

The applications states (menu and game), shown in Listings 26.24 and 26.25, have a few items in common. First, they have access to an advanced framework singleton [Gamma et al. 94] object. In addition, the states share a common interface as shown in Listing 26.26. This provides developers with enter, exit, pause, resume, and update methods. The most important methods here are the enter, which provides the initial configuration needed for the given state (e.g., experiment setup), the exit, to clean up the state, and the update method. The update method is what fires for every frame that is rendered. The input listeners are also shared across states whenever it makes sense. For example, the keyboard is useful in any state (menu and experiment modes).

To have basic input functionalities in OGRE, a third-party library can be used. This library is called object-oriented input system (OIS),[19] which enables the keyboard and mouse. Another alternative for the input is to use the WINAPI, which we have used here for demonstration purposes. It is also needed as OIS does not handle all type of input devices. This is true for many other input device libraries. Finally, it is also possible to use the vendor's own drivers and library to access a device. Below, we provide some sample code.

---

[19]See http://www.ogre3d.org/tikiwiki/tiki-index.php?page=OIS.

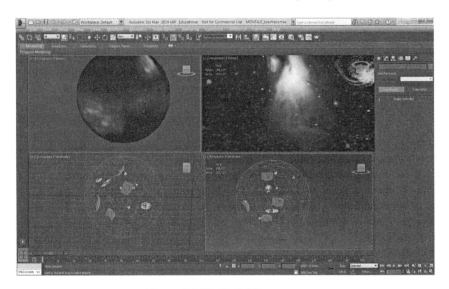

Figure 26.10: 3DS Max scene.

A partial listing showing the wiiMote (lines 7–8), and the 3D mouse (lines 13–22), is shown in Listing 26.27. This is executed in the **OgreFramework** class (from the Ogre Advanced Framework), in a method called *initOgre(...)*. Once OGRE is rendering, for each frame, there needs to be a check if new input event data is available. If it is, then the system fires the appropriate events, as described in previous sections. This happens in the **AppStateManager** class, in a method called *start(...)*. Partial code is shown in Listing 26.28.

Basic collision detection is possible with OGRE without any additional third-party physic engine libraries (e.g., bullet). In OGRE, collision detection is achieved using bounding volumes provided by the SDK. An example is shown in Listing 26.29. For more information about collision detection, see [van den Bergen 04, Ericson 05]. Finally, to achieve GUI buttons and windows in OGRE, the library called MyGui[20] was used.

Listing 26.22: Scene Nodes (Partial XML file)

```
1   <?xml version="1.0" encoding="UTF-8"?>
2   <scene formatVersion="1.0" upAxis="y" unitsPerMeter="1" unitType="↩
        meters" minOgreVersion="1.8" ogreMaxVersion="2.6.1" author="↩
        OgreMax Scene Exporter (www.ogremax.com)" application="3DS Max">
3       <environment>
4           <colourAmbient r="0.333333" g="0.333333" b="0.333333"/>
5           <colourBackground r="0" g="0" b="0"/>
6           <clipping near="0" far="2540"/>
7       </environment>
```

---

[20]See http://mygui.info.

```
8        <nodes>
9          <node name="SPACE">
10              <position x="0" y="0" z="0"/>
11              <scale x="0.5" y="0.5" z="0.5"/>
12              <rotation qx="0" qy="0" qz="0" qw="1"/>
13              <entity name="SPACE" castShadows="true" receiveShadows="↵
                   true" meshFile="SPACE.mesh">
14                  <subentities>
15                      <subentity index="0" materialName="Material#0"/>
16                  </subentities>
17              </entity>
18          </node>
19        <node name="planet_with_craters">
20              <position x="8.23713" y="69.6509" z="-171.328"/>
21              <scale x="0.210295" y="0.210295" z="0.210295"/>
22              <rotation qx="0" qy="0" qz="0" qw="1"/>
23              <entity name="planet_with_craters" castShadows="true" ↵
                   receiveShadows="true" meshFile="planet_with_craters.↵
                   mesh">
24                  <subentities>
25                      <subentity index="0" materialName="↵
                       planet_with_craters"/>
26                  </subentities>
27              </entity>
28          </node>
29        </nodes>
30    </scene>
```

Listing 26.23: OGRE (Advanced Framework (h))

```
1   class OgreFramework : public Ogre::Singleton<OgreFramework>, OIS::↵
        KeyListener, OIS::MouseListener, Ogre::FrameListener, Ogre::↵
        WindowEventListener, Win3DXOgreListener
2   {
3   public:
4     OgreFramework();
5     ~OgreFramework();
6     bool initOgre(Ogre::String wndTitle, OIS::KeyListener *↵
          pKeyListener = 0, OIS::MouseListener *pMouseListener = 0);
7     void updateOgre(double timeSinceLastFrame);
8     bool keyPressed(const OIS::KeyEvent &keyEventRef);
9     bool keyReleased(const OIS::KeyEvent &keyEventRef);
10    bool mouseMoved(const OIS::MouseEvent &evt);
11    bool mousePressed(const OIS::MouseEvent &evt, OIS::MouseButtonID ↵
          id);
12    bool mouseReleased(const OIS::MouseEvent &evt, OIS::MouseButtonID ↵
          id);
13    bool handleNavigator(int message,DOFSix & D, BData & B);
14  private:
15    void windowResized(Ogre::RenderWindow* rw);
16    bool frameStarted(const Ogre::FrameEvent& evt);
17    bool frameEnded(const Ogre::FrameEvent& evt);
18  public:
19    Ogre::Root*              m_pRoot;
```

```
20    Ogre::RenderWindow*          m_pRenderWnd;
21    Ogre::Viewport*             m_pViewport;
22    ...
23  private:
24    ...
25    BOOL InitRawDevices(void);
26    void FreeRawInputDevices(void);
27    OgreFramework(const OgreFramework&);
28    OgreFramework& operator= (const OgreFramework&);
29  };
```

Listing 26.24: OGRE (Menu State (h))

```
1   class MenuState : public AppState
2   {
3   public:
4     MenuState();
5     DECLARE_APPSTATE_CLASS(MenuState)
6     void enter();
7     void createScene();
8     void exit();
9     bool keyPressed(const OIS::KeyEvent &keyEventRef);
10    bool keyReleased(const OIS::KeyEvent &keyEventRef);
11    bool mouseMoved(const OIS::MouseEvent &evt);
12    bool mousePressed(const OIS::MouseEvent &evt, OIS::MouseButtonID ↩
          id);
13    bool mouseReleased(const OIS::MouseEvent &evt, OIS::MouseButtonID ↩
          id);
14    bool handleNavigator(int message,DOFSix & D, BData & B);
15    void notifyMouseButtonClick(MyGUI::Widget* _sender);
16    void notifyComboAccept(MyGUI::ComboBox* _sender, size_t _index);
17    void notifyMessageBoxResult(MyGUI::Message* _sender, MyGUI::↩
          MessageBoxStyle result);
18    void notifyQuestionBoxResult(QuestionPanel* _sender, ↩
          QuestionPanelStyle result);
19    void update(double timeSinceLastFrame);
20  private:
21    bool m_bQuit;
22  };
```

Listing 26.25: OGRE (Game State (h))

```
1   class GameState : public AppState
2   {
3   public:
4     GameState();
5     DECLARE_APPSTATE_CLASS(GameState)
6     void enter();
7     void exit();
8     bool pause();
9     void resume();
10    void moveCamera();
```

```
11    void getInput(const double timeSinceLastFrame,const unsigned long ↩
         long cCount);
12    void getWiiMoteInput();
13    bool getGamePad();
14    bool keyPressed(const OIS::KeyEvent &keyEventRef);
15    bool keyReleased(const OIS::KeyEvent &keyEventRef);
16    bool mouseMoved(const OIS::MouseEvent &arg);
17    bool mousePressed(const OIS::MouseEvent &arg, OIS::MouseButtonID ↩
         id);
18    bool mouseReleased(const OIS::MouseEvent &arg, OIS::MouseButtonID ↩
         id);
19    bool handleNavigator(int message,DOFSix & D, BData & B);
20    void onLeftPressed(const OIS::MouseEvent &evt);
21    void onRightPressed(const OIS::MouseEvent &evt);
22    void update(double timeSinceLastFrame);
23  private:
24    void createScene();
25    void createCamera();
26    void wiiMotionPlus(const wiimote const & remote);
27    double vPrime(double v,double lambda, double vmax);
28    void notifySentenceQuestionPanelResult(SentenceQuestionPanel* ↩
         _sender, QuestionPanelStyle result);
29    ...
30  };
```

Listing 26.26: OGRE (App State Interface)

```
1   class AppState : public OIS::KeyListener, public OIS::MouseListener,↩
         public Win3DXOgreListener
2   {
3   public:
4     static void create(AppStateListener* parent, const Ogre::String ↩
         name) {};
5     void destroy() { delete this;}
6     virtual void enter() = 0;
7     virtual void exit() = 0;
8     virtual bool pause(){return true;}
9     virtual void resume(){};
10    virtual void update(double timeSinceLastFrame) = 0;
11  protected:
12    AppState(){};
13    AppState* findByName(Ogre::String stateName){return m_pParent->↩
         findByName(stateName);}
14    void changeAppState(AppState* state){m_pParent->changeAppState(↩
         state);}
15    bool pushAppState(AppState* state){return m_pParent->pushAppState(↩
         state);}
16    void popAppState(){m_pParent->popAppState();}
17    void shutdown(){m_pParent->shutdown();}
18    void popAllAndPushAppState(AppState* state){m_pParent->↩
         popAllAndPushAppState(state);}
19
```

```
20     ...
21     AppStateListener* m_pParent;
22     Ogre::Camera*   m_pCamera;
23     Ogre::SceneManager* m_pSceneMgr;
24   };
```

Listing 26.27: OGRE (InitOgre)

```
1    Ogre::LogManager* logMgr = new Ogre::LogManager();
2    m_pLog = Ogre::LogManager::getSingleton().createLog("OgreLogfile.log↵
         ",true,true,false);
3    m_pLog->setDebugOutputEnabled(true);
4    m_pRoot = new Ogre::Root(mPluginsCfg);
5    if (!m_pRoot->showConfigDialog())
6      return false;
7    m_wiiMote.ChangedCallback = on_wiimote_state_change;
8    m_wiiMote.CallbackTriggerFlags = (state_change_flags)(CONNECTED | ↵
         EXTENSION_CHANGED | MOTIONPLUS_CHANGED);
9    m_pRenderWnd = m_pRoot->initialise(true, wndTitle);
10   size_t hWnd = 0;
11   OIS::ParamList paramList;
12   m_pRenderWnd->getCustomAttribute("WINDOW",&hWnd);
13   if (!InitRawDevices())
14   {
15     OgreFramework::getSingletonPtr()->m_pLog->logMessage("[3DX] Error ↵
           InitRawDevices()");
16     m_bRawDevicesOn = false;
17   }
18   else
19   {
20     m_bRawDevicesOn = true;
21     Win3DXOgreEventRegistry::registerListener(Win3DXOgreEventRegistry↵
           ::LISTEN_ALL,this);
22   }
23   ...
24   m_pRoot->addFrameListener(this);
25   Ogre::WindowEventUtilities::addWindowEventListener(m_pRenderWnd, ↵
         this);
26   ...
27   return true;
```

Listing 26.28: OGRE (Check Input)

```
1    ...
2    while (!m_bShutdown)
3    {
4      if(OgreFramework::getSingletonPtr()->m_pRenderWnd->isClosed())
5        m_bShutdown = true;
6      if(OgreFramework::getSingletonPtr()->m_pRenderWnd->isActive())
7      {
8        MSG  msg;
9        HWND hwnd;
```

```
10      bool navOn = OgreFramework::getSingletonPtr()->m_bRawDevicesOn;
11      OgreFramework::getSingletonPtr()->m_pRenderWnd->↩
           getCustomAttribute("WINDOW", (void*)&hwnd);
12      if( navOn && PeekMessage( &msg, hwnd, 0, 0, PM_REMOVE ) )
13      {
14        if(msg.message == WM_INPUT)
15        {
16          OgreFramework::getSingletonPtr()->ProcessWM_INPUTEvent(msg.↩
               lParam);
17        }
18        else
19        {
20          TranslateMessage( &msg );
21          DispatchMessage( &msg );
22        }
23      }
24    }
25    Ogre::WindowEventUtilities::messagePump();
26
27    if(OgreFramework::getSingletonPtr()->m_pRenderWnd->isActive())
28    {
29      ... //DO Ogre work.
30    }
31    else
32    {
33      Sleep(1000);
34      sleep(1);
35    }
36  }
37  ...
```

Listing 26.29: OGRE (Collision)

```
1   void CollisionTrigger::onUpdate()
2   {
3     if(!_nodeA || !_nodeB)
4       return;
5     updateActions();
6     if(_nodeA->_getWorldAABB().intersects(_nodeB->_getWorldAABB()))
7       onCollision();
8     else
9       cancelActions();
10  }
11  void CameraCollisionTrigger::onUpdate()
12  {
13    if(!_camera || !_nodeB)
14      return;
15    updateActions();
16    if(_nodeB->_getWorldAABB().intersects( Ogre::Sphere(_camera->↩
          getDerivedPosition(), _cameraRadius) ))
17      onCollision();
18    else
19      cancelActions();
20  }
```

26.4   ECHoSS: Experiment Module

Some of us create 3D environments to perform different types of experiments. This section provides a basic skeleton for experiments using C++. A more generalized version is currently in development. The experiment module, called Experiment Controller Human Subject System (ECHoSS), contained a series of C++ classes and additional configuration files, designed for one of our 3D navigation experiment. The objective is to make the environment suitable for human-subject testing in the area of 3D navigation. The experiment module is composed of a few sub-modules. Those are the experiment controller, experiment device, experiment task, and experiment search object. With this, it is enough to specify a running experiment.

The experiment controller, shown in Listing 26.30, controls a human-subject test. It is composed of devices (e.g., multi-touch) and tasks (e.g., objects to find). The experiment controller can be built by adding devices using *AddExperiment*(...) or by adding training devices by using *AddTraining*(...). Actually, a device can be added by using *AddDevice*(...), since the device can specify if it is a training device or treatment device. Another important method that must be called after starting the experiment (*start*(...)) is the *processNext*() method, which allows the system to go from one device to the other. Depending on the initialization of the experiment controller, the queue holding the devices is determined as follows:

- Training devices will be the first devices to be placed in the queue.

- If controller is not responsible for randomizing the devices,[21] the order of devices will be set by their insertion.

- If controller is responsible for randomizing the devices, then it will perform a random sorting of devices, sorting separately the training devices from the treatment devices.

The experiment device class, as shown in Listing 26.31, allows the control of each treatment (e.g., input device) that will handle a series of tasks. For example, in the case of the experiment, the user must search for five objects. This means that each device contains a series of objectives, defined in the experiment tasks class. This class, as shown in Listing 26.32, provides the definition for a task. In particular, the tasks used in this example add the keyboard task, in addition to the object to be found. However, this is an example for this particular case, since the developer can modify the settings. The actual concrete implementation of the task is defined in the search object class, as shown in Listing 26.33. The specific search object made use of the entities found in OGRE to keep track of the object in question and the marker (e.g., flag) that provides visual feedback to the user. An important part of the task is that it also has knowledge where to place the object to

---

[21]The author chose this option for the experiment.

be searched. This allows the experimenter to move the objects, depending on the treatment and requirements of the experiment. ECHoSS objective is to provide a system for generic human-subject testing, while keeping the requirements separate from the actual 3D implementation.

Listing 26.30: Experiment Controller

```
1   class ExperimentController : public ...
2   {
3   public:
4     typedef boost::system::error_code error_code;
5     typedef enum {Init,Started,Device_Running,Device_Exited,↩
          Device_Exit_By_Time_Expired,Stopped} experiment_state;
6     typedef enum {None,Training,Treatment} experiment_mode;
7     ...
8     ExperimentController(const string & subjectName,const string & ↩
          experimentName, bool shuffleDevices=true, bool, ↩
          shuffleTraining=true);
9     ~ExperimentController();
10    bool AddExperiment(const ExperimentDevice & experimentDevice);
11    bool AddTraining(const ExperimentDevice & experimentDevice);
12    bool AddDevice(ExperimentDevice & experimentDevice);
13    bool start();
14    bool stop();
15    bool pause();
16    bool resume();
17    bool abort();
18    void update(const double timeElapsed,const unsigned long long ↩
          cCount);
19    virtual bool handleExperiment(...);
20    bool isExperimentStarted(){return _guard.mStarted;}
21    bool isDeviceRunning();
22    bool isPaused() { return _guard.mPaused;}
23    bool processNext();
24    bool isNextAvailable();
25    bool getCurrentDevice(ExperimentDevice & dev);
26    string getExperimentName() { return mExperimentName;}
27    inline size_t getTotalObjectCount() { return mTotalObjectCount;}
28    inline bool hasStarted() { return _guard.mStarted;}
29  private:
30    ...
31  };
```

Listing 26.31: Experiment Device

```
1   class ExperimentDevice : public ...
2   public:
3     ...
4     typedef enum {PreInitialized,Initialized,Running,Completed,↩
          CompletedByExpiredTime,Aborted,Paused} device_state;
5     typedef enum {MultiTouch,GamePad,Mouse,Keyboard,Mouse3D,WiiMote,↩
```

```
          LeapMotion,Generic} device_type;
6    ExperimentDevice(ExperimentTimerPtr timer,string & deviceName,↩
          const size_t order,bool isTrainingDevice=false);
7    ExperimentDevice(string & deviceName,const size_t order, bool ↩
          isTrainingDevice=false);
8    typedef vector<ExperimentTask> tasks;
9    ...
10   ExperimentDevice();
11   ~ExperimentDevice();
12   bool start();
13   bool isInitialized();
14   bool addTask(ExperimentTask & task);
15   bool exit();
16   bool pause();
17   bool abort();
18   virtual void update(double timeElapsed,unsigned long cycleCount);
19   bool isTrainingDevice() { return mIsTrainingDevice;}
20   //define copy constructor and equal operator
21   ...
22   virtual bool handleExperiment(...);
23   inline const size_t getOrder()  { return mOrder;}
24   inline const size_t getFoundObjectCount() { return ↩
          mFoundObjectCount;}
25   inline const size_t getFoundObjectWithSentenceCount() { return ↩
          mFoundObjectWithSentenceCount;}
26   inline string getDeviceType() { return mDeviceType;}
27   inline void setDeviceType(const string & deviceType){mDeviceType =↩
          mDeviceType;}
28   ...
29   };
```

Listing 26.32: Experiment Task

```
1    class ExperimentTask : public ...
2    {
3    public:
4      typedef struct view_data
5      {
6        ...
7        Ogre::Vector3 position;
8        Ogre::Quaternion orientation;
9        Ogre::Vector3 direction;
10     }view_data;
11     typedef struct location_data
12     {
13       ...
14       Ogre::Vector3 position;
15       Ogre::Quaternion orientation;
16     }location_data;
17     typedef struct object_data
18     {
19       ...
```

```
20      view_data camera;
21      location_data object;
22      location_data object_flag;
23      bool enabled;
24    }object_data;
25    ExperimentTask(SearchObject * searchObject,const std::string & ←
            taskName, const object_data & objectData=object_data());
26    virtual ~ExperimentTask();
27    typedef enum task_state {Init,Started,Stopped,Aborted,Unkown};
28    void start();
29    void stop();
30    void abort();
31    bool isTaskFinished();
32    bool isHit(){ return mHit;}
33    bool isFound(){ return mFound;}
34    task_state getTaskState() { return mTaskState;}
35    bool isEnabled(){return mIsEnabled;}
36    void setEnabled(bool enabled){enabled = mIsEnabled;}
37    virtual void searchEvent(SearchObject::SearchObjectListener::←
            EventType type, SearchObject* sender, map<string,string> ←
            userData);
38    SearchObject * getSearchObject();
39    void update(double TimeSinceLastFrame,unsigned long cycleCount);
40    string getTaskName(){return mTaskName;}
41    string getKeyboardSentence() { return mKeyboardSentence;}
42    void setKeyboardSentence(const std::string & str) { ←
            mKeyboardSentence=str;}
43    void reset();
44    ...
45  };
```

Listing 26.33: Experiment Search Object

```
1   class SearchObject
2   {
3   public:
4     typedef struct view_data
5     {
6       ...
7       Ogre::Vector3 position;
8       Ogre::Quaternion orientation;
9       Ogre::Vector3 direction;
10    }view_data;
11    typedef struct score_data
12    {
13      ...
14      int score;
15      bool objectFound;
16      bool objectHit;
17      bool flagFound;
18      bool flagHit;
19    }score_data;
```

```
20
21    SearchObject(Ogre::SceneNode* node, Ogre::SceneNode* flagNode);
22
23    virtual ~SearchObject();
24
25      Ogre::SceneNode* getNode();
26      Ogre::SceneNode* getFlagNode();
27
28
29      bool isFound();
30      bool isHit();
31      void update(double timeSinceLastFrame);
32      ...
33    };
34    extern SearchObjects* SearchObjectsCollection;
```

Further Reading

This chapter is a collection of snippets of codes and strategies about input implementation. In our online supplementary, we will discuss further the development of an input framework.

For Windows development, the most important book about WINAPI is *Programming Windows* (fourth edition) [Petzold 98]. Note that the newer edition [Petzold 13], while very useful, covers Windows Runtime (WinRT) with C# (but Petzold provides the C++/CX code in his website http://www.charlespetzold. com). Windows driver development books are also important [Viscarola and Mason 99, Orwick and Smith 07]. For a general overview of Unix/Linux programming, see *The Linux Programming Interface* [Kerrisk 10]. For Linux device drivers, see [Corbet et al. 05]. For MacOSx Internals, see [Singh 06].

For more agnostic platform books, see *3D Game Engine Architecture* [Eberly 05], *3D Game Engine Design* [Eberly 07], *Game Engine Architecture* [Gregory 14], *Design Patterns* [Gamma et al. 94], and *API Design for C++* [Reddy 11], among others [McShaffry 13].

Exercises

1. Implement the observer pattern using multi-threads. Make sure you provide a safe-thread observer pattern.

2. What other design patterns can you use to work with multiple input devices? In particular, which design pattern (or your own approach) may provide a safer environment for multi-threaded application?

3. In the Kinect section of this chapter, we send messages using the WINAPI. Modify the version to send them using sockets.

Part IV

Case Study: Speech as Input

27

Multimodal Human-Like Conversational Interfaces

Ugan Yasavur & Christine Lisetti

> For millions of years mankind lived just like the animals. Then something happened which unleashed the power of our imagination: we learned to talk.
> —Stephen Hawking

Embodied conversational agents (ECAs) are anthropomorphic virtual characters that can exhibit human-like interaction capabilities by using verbal and non-verbal communication via understanding and producing speech, gestures, and facial expressions. Embodied conversational agents are a type of multimodal interface where the modalities are the natural modalities of human conversation: speech, intonation, facial expressions, hand gestures, body movements. This and the next chapter cover conversational interfaces that use ECAs. This chapter provides background information about conversational/dialog systems and ECAs. The next chapter aims to demonstrate how to build conversational systems with ECAs that can handle task-oriented dialogs. We selected real-world health dialog as our example domain.

A substantial amount of research has been conducted on developing conversational interfaces (dialog systems or spoken dialog systems or speech-enabled interfaces) in restricted microdomains (e.g., flight reservations, information provider systems) in the 1990s and early 2000s. Commercial systems have been deployed for reservation/booking, customer center automation, and question answering in the last decade as a result of these early research endeavors [Pieraccini and Huerta 08]. Recently, researchers have mostly concentrated on the development of dialog systems that are able to take initiative, reason and infer in the domain of the system while conducting dialog in microdomains using planning, collaborative problem solving [Allen et al. 06]. In the last decade, there has been a high interest

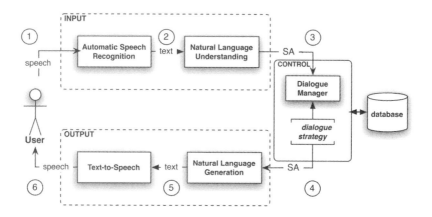

Figure 27.1: Dialog system architecture [Rieser and Lemon 11].

in developing dialog systems in real-world application areas such as personal coaches, companions, and counselors [Catizone et al. 08].

While the current trend in commercial systems involves applying finite state-based system directed dialog strategies, research projects have been moving away from restricted and contrived applications to systems that require flexibility in the management style of the dialog (e.g., personal coaches, virtual companions) [McTear 11].

Although there is no accepted standard for dialog systems design, an end-to-end dialog system architecture (as shown in Figure 27.1) usually includes three modules: input, output, and control [McTear 02, p. 113]. The input module is commonly composed of automatic speech recognition (ASR) and spoken language understanding (SLU). The control module corresponds to the dialog manager, which executes a dialog strategy. The output module consists of a natural language generation (NLG) system and a text-to-speech (TTS) engine. Depending on the domain of interest and application area, there can be specialized components such as domain reasoner, planner, and specialized databases [Ferguson et al. 98]. There are many commercial softwares for automatic speech recognition and text-to-speech engines. The focus of this chapter is the control module, also referred to as the dialog manager.

27.1   Dialog Management Overview

The primary focus of this research is dialog management. The dialog manager maintains an internal state and decides what dialog move (speech act) action to perform next.

There is a wide range of techniques to develop a dialog manager, and the current techniques used in industry are different from the ones used in research. The focus of this research is dialog management.

Research systems aim at conveying natural human behavior such as conversing, reasoning, and inferencing, whereas commercial systems aim at being robust to solve specific tasks (e.g., customer service automation). Commercial systems are widely based on finite state-based [Sutton et al. 98] dialog management to address their objectives in terms of robustness.

In **finite state-based dialog management**, dialog states represent the results of performing a dialog move from some previous state, and each state leads to a set of allowable next dialog moves. The information is thus implicit in the state itself and the relationship it plays to other states. While the finite state-based approach is regarded as a viable option for simple, scripted dialog such as reservation systems, it is not possible to create flexible dialog systems with this approach. Finite state-based approaches have often been compared with plan-based approaches in terms of dialog modeling.

Plan-based dialog management approaches are viewed as more suitable for flexible dialog modeling and research in plan-based models is concerned with reasoning domain actions and the goals to which they contribute [Ferguson et al. 98, Allen et al. 06, Rich et al. 01]. Plan-based approaches are seen as being more opaque than other approaches in terms of development. The plan-based approaches require a considerable amount of procedural processing power. The plan-based operations (e.g., logical inference) are usually designed based on heuristic rules rather than a well-founded theoretical base. Even though the approach provides a solid computational model, it is not entirely clear for these operations how the mental constructs employed in the model correlate to people's actual mental states. However, in plan-based dialog management, the efforts to separate domain-specific task knowledge from domain-independent dialog control logic provide serious potential to create complex dialog systems with a small amount of effort and without expert knowledge [Bohus and Rudnicky 09].

An **information-state (IS) dialog management** approach allows one to combine the two approaches (finite-state and plan-based), using the advantages of each of them. The information-state may include aspects of dialog state as well as mentalistic notions such as beliefs, intentions, plans. *"The term information-state of a dialog represents the information necessary to distinguish it from other dialogs, representing the cumulative additions from previous actions in the dialog, and motivating future action"* [Traum and Larsson 03].

While the information-state approach has been shown to provide a basis for flexible dialog interaction with rich dialog state representation, existing IS-based dialog managers [Traum and Larsson 03, Bos et al. 03] have a number of general limitations that stem from the intuition-based design methodology. From the perspective of system development, the information-state methodology has traditionally been based around a declarative update rule-based design. The functionality of integrating both user dialog and planning system contributions is encoded as the firing of a complex and sequential update rules. While a rule-based approach is useful in working within an overtly declarative programming environment, the operation of resultant rules can become highly opaque. The IS-based dialog management, like plan-based approaches, requires the manual specification of update rules that define an action for all possible dialog situations. It is not practically possible for the designer to anticipate all the possible situations of a dynamic dialog environment. Thus, dialog management requires a strategy that can be generalized to unseen events.

27.1.1   Dialog Management Based on Machine Learning

Recent research in dialog management has turned to automated dialog strategy learning using statistical machine learning techniques (e.g., [Rieser et al. 11a, Young et al. 13, Young et al. 10, Thomson and Young 10]). A major advantage of the **statistical dialog management** approach is that it introduces a principled scientific method for improving dialog strategy design, whereas the previous hand-coded approaches were mainly based on the designer's intuition.

To date, different machine learning methods have been applied [Lemon et al. 07] to automatic dialog management:

- Supervised approaches

- Reinforcement learning-based approaches

[Lemon et al. 07] has listed key potential advantages of the statistical computational learning approaches for dialog system development as following:

- Data-driven development cycle

- Provably optimal action policies

- A precise mathematical model for action selection

- Possibilities for generalization to unseen states

- Reduced development and deployment costs for industry.

Supervised Learning vs. Reinforcement Learning

The nature of a dialog is *temporal* and *dynamic*, and machine learning techniques are well positioned to be able address these aspects of dialog.

Dialog is **temporal** in the sense that how good an action is depends on how the dialog progresses further [Rieser and Lemon 11]. Taking an action affects the state of the dialog and thereby affects the options and opportunities available at later times. Thus, action choice requires foresight and long-term planning with respect to the delayed consequences of actions as specified by the dynamics of the environment. Therefore, it is not possible to present correct input/output move pairs of ideal dialog strategy behavior. Corpus of dialog usually contains annotations of how good the overall performance of a specific dialog was (e.g., task success or user scores), but it does not have any indication about how good a single action was. In other words, it is hard to tell how things should have been exactly done in a particular situation, but it is possible to tell whether the dialog was successful/satisfying overall.

Supervised learning methods do not model dialog as a sequence of actions and they only mimic behavior observed in a fixed dialog corpus. Reinforcement learning (RL), in contrast, models the problem as sequential decision process with long-term planning [Litman et al. 02, Rieser and Lemon 11]. Therefore, reinforcement learning is more suitable than supervised learning to model the temporal aspect of dialog.

Dialog being **dynamic** describes the fact that dialog takes place in interaction with a stochastic environment, where conditions change frequently (e.g., the level of noise) or a dialog partner reacts differently than predicted in a certain situation. This characteristic requires an approach that is robust to unseen states.

In supervised learning, the learner has to be explicitly instructed what to do in a specific situation by presenting as many examples as possible. RL learns by exploration (of uncharted territory) and exploitation (of current knowledge) [Sutton and Barto 98]. The ability to explore allows a system to learn strategies which are more robust to unseen and unpredictable states [Rieser and Lemon 11, Sutton and Barto 98, Young et al. 13]. The ability to exploit current knowledge allows learning by experience.

27.1.2 Dialog Management and Reinforcement Learning

Reinforcement learning (RL) is a sequential decision making, where the RL agent interacts with its environment ([Sutton and Barto 98]). The environment is defined as: "anything that cannot be changed arbitrarily by the agent is considered to be outside of it and thus part of its environment" [Sutton and Barto 98, p. 53]. Reinforcement learning treats dialog strategy learning as a sequential optimization problem, leading to strategies that are globally optimal ([Sutton and Barto 98]). Uncertainty can be explicitly represented in RL.

Within the RL framework for dialog development, dialog strategies are represented as mappings from states to actions within Markov decision processes (MDPs) [Levin et al. 98]. A MDP is formally described by a finite state space S, a finite action set A, a set of transition probabilities T, and a reward function R. The dialog strategy learner can be visualized as an agent traveling through a network of interconnected dialog states (see Figure 27.2) [Rieser and Lemon 11]. Starting in some initial state, the learning algorithm transitions from state to state by taking actions and collecting rewards as it goes along. The transitions are

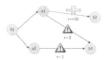

Figure 27.2: Reinforcement learning with MDP [Rieser and Lemon 11].

non-deterministic, since the dialog environment is stochastic and dynamic. RL based on MDPs successfully was used by [Litman et al. 02, Lemon et al. 06, Rieser et al. 11b] for implementation of a statistical dialog manager. They tested their system by comparing standard fixed policies and show that the performance of the learned policy is better than several "standard" fixed policies. In a nutshell, the approach followed by [Litman et al. 02] in the development of the system is:

- Choosing an appropriate reward measure for dialogs, an appropriate representation for dialog states, and designing a dialog policy that maps each state to a set of reasonable actions.

- Building an initial state-based training system that creates an exploratory dataset. Despite being exploratory, this system still provides the desired basic functionality.

- Using these training dialogs to build an empirical MDP model on the state space. The transitions of this MDP is modeling the user population's reactions and rewards for the various system actions.

- Computing the optimal dialog policy according to this MDP.

- Reimplementing the system using the learned dialog strategies.

Recently dialog systems research has become focused on extension of MDP model to handle uncertainty more efficiently, which is partially observable markov decision processes (POMDP) [Young et al. 10, Young et al. 13]. While MDPs assume that the entire state space is fully observable, POMDPs provide a framework for modeling the inherent uncertainty in dialog systems. POMDPs handle uncertainty by representing the current dialog state as a belief state which is a distribution over the possible states. The CLASSIC (Computational Learning in Adaptive Systems for Spoken Conversation) project [Jurcıcek et al. 10] used POMDPs with the information-state approach for dialog management, which aims to develop a data-driven, machine learning-based architecture for robust and more adaptable spoken dialog systems (http://www.classic-project.org). Some of the results they obtained are listed below:

- The hidden information state system (a POMDP system) improves task success by 25% in high-noise conditions, when tested in simulation [Young et al. 10]

- 5% reduction in word error rate when using predictions from a simulated user to re-rank n-best lists of speech recognizer's hypotheses [Lemon and Konstas 09]

- Online reinforcement learning improved the commercial application's completion rate by 10% with real customers [Putois et al. 10]

- A statistical planning approach to natural language generation for information presentation (content planning and attribute selection) outperforms hand-coded policies and a policy learned from human performance. Tested in simulation in the tourist information domain [Rieser et al. 10]

- Adaptive natural language generation using reinforcement learning techniques, evaluation with real users: 12% decrease in time taken, and a 15% increase in task completion rate [Janarthanam and Lemon 10]

Reinforcement learning and MDP can be accepted as state-of-the-art techniques for data-driven spoken dialog system development [Young et al. 13, Frampton and Lemon 09]. Since our example topic is on health dialog systems, the next section covers current methods used in health dialog systems.

27.2 Dialog Management in Health Dialog Systems

Although there is a great interest in developing computer-based conversational systems which can promote healthy behaviors or perform interventions, there is very limited experimentation with the state-of-the-art techniques in health dialog systems area [Coyle et al. 07, Coyle and Doherty 09]. There are many deployed standardized health assessment guidelines that are amenable to computer-based delivery via conversational systems. The guideline that is used in the next chapter is from the National Institute of Health for brief alcohol interventions which is covered in the next section. The next chapter covers the fundamental design approaches for conversational systems that can interview users for any task-based dialog. The approach that is used to design the system is Markov decision processes with reinforcement learning. However, before going straight to the system design, this section covers some of the methods that are used in health dialog systems.

To date there is no system that uses data-driven machine learning-based dialog management approaches in the health domain. The purpose of this section is to review recent health dialog systems in terms of dialog management strategy. Health dialog systems designed usually based on finite state or rule-based approaches.

Therefore, the aforementioned limitations of these approaches also applies to the health dialog systems.

In a recent comprehensive literature review of active assistance technologies in health-related behavior change systems [Kennedy et al. 12], covering articles written between January 2005 and January 2012, 41 health-behavior change systems are identified. Dialog systems and ECAs are identified as emerging technology themes in the behavior change systems field. It is reported that 19 studies out of 41 use dialog systems technology. Among those 19 systems, only 1 system uses speech as an input modality [Levin and Levin 06]. The remaining 19 dialog-based systems use text or menu-based choices as a style of communication. In the same literature review [Kennedy et al. 12], it is reported that 8 of the systems use ECAs [Bickmore 05, Bickmore et al. 11, Turunen et al. 11, de Rosis et al. 06].

There are also dialog systems in other health-related domains such as health and fitness companions [Turunen et al. 11], or virtual support agents for post traumatic stress disorder [Morbini et al. 12]. Although, there has been growing interest to develop multimodal SDS which can converse, guide, assist, or motivate users for different health-related topics [Bickmore et al. 11, Ferguson et al. 10, Morbini et al. 12], to the best of our knowledge, there does not exist any spoken dialog system for the alcohol consumption domain, which is the focus of my research.

Furthermore, dialog management for health-related dialog systems has so far been mostly designed based on *plan-based* dialog management mechanisms such as hierarchical transition networks [Bickmore et al. 11, Bickmore et al. 10], plan-based approaches [Schulman et al. 11], or information-state based approaches [Morbini et al. 12]. These systems usually do not have speech recognition integration. Interaction is usually conducted with menu-based choices, but the system utterances are delivered vocally via text-to-speech or prerecorded voice [Lisetti et al. 13, Bickmore et al. 11].

Other than systems that use menu-based interaction, there are systems that use a different input modality. SimCoach, for example, is a web-based system which uses text as input modality, and an interface with an anthropomorphic ECA which responds to users' questions with answers prerecorded by a human. Whereas human voices are still superior to synthetic ones, using pre-recorded utterances means that the sentences that the system can speak are fixed, as opposed to systems using text-to-speech engines (like ours) which provides the flexibility of adding new sentences for the system to utter automatically, i.e., without the need to prerecord new sentences. SimCoach, designed to provide support and health-care information about post traumatic stress disorder, incorporates the information-state approach [Traum and Larsson 03] with dialog moves with assigned reward values [Morbini et al. 12]. The Companions project includes three different systems in the domain of health and fitness [Turunen et al. 11], and all of them use speech as input modality. The dialog management approach in the Companions project is the information-state approach, and one system (the cooking companion) has an ECA interface.

27.3   Task-Based Spoken Dialog Systems

Dialog or conversational systems can be classified into two main categories based on their dialog management technique, which can be either based on machine learning (e.g., based on reinforcement learning), or hand-crafted (see Section 27.1). Systems based on RL are popular in the SDS community and are reported to work better than hand-crafted ones for *speech*-enabled systems [Young et al. 13, Frampton and Lemon 09] against noisy speech recognition. *Hand-crafted systems*, on the other hand, can be divided into three subcategories, with dialog management approaches using finite states [Sutton et al. 98], plans and inference rules [Ferguson et al. 98, Bohus and Rudnicky 09], or information states. [Traum and Larsson 03] which is covered in Section 27.1.

RL-based dialog systems can learn dialog strategies in a given dialog state from their prior experiences. The idea of having a dialog manager (DM) that can learn interactively from its experience is a cost-effective methodology given the alternative approaches: crafting system responses to all possible user's input using rules and heuristics [Paek and Pieraccini 08]. At best, these rules are based on accumulated knowledge from a trial-and-error experience. At worst, they are based on intuition and limited experience of the designer. Either way, because it is extremely challenging to anticipate every possible user's input, hand-crafting dialog management strategies is an error-prone process that needs to be iteratively refined and tuned [Paek and Pieraccini 08]. That iterative refinement of course requires a substantial amount of time and effort.

The RL-based approach provides the opportunity to automate the design of dialog management strategies by having the system learn these strategies from received reward signals (see Section 27.1.2).

Approaches for dialog systems based on reinforcement learning (RL) use Markov decision processes (MDP) [Singh et al. 02] or partially observable Markov decision processes (POMDP) [Young et al. 10, Williams 08] frameworks to develop robust dialog managers [Frampton and Lemon 09, Young et al. 13]. While both MDP and POMDP require a high amount of data for training, POMDPs usually suffer from scalability issues [Williams and Young 07, Young et al. 10], and optimization algorithms usually become intractable with large numbers of states. However, POMDPs outperform the MDP-based systems [Young et al. 13]. It is possible to find tractable solutions by using some approximation to solve practical problems [Young et al. 10].

RL-based dialog systems are mainly used for slot-filling applications. The domain of the dialog is usually in the tourist information domain, such as finding information about restaurants [Jurčíček et al. 12, Young et al. 10], appointment scheduling [Georgila et al. 10], flight reservations [Henderson et al. 08]. The RL-based dialog management paradigm was also recently used for assistive technologies [Li et al. 13] and health assessments [Yasavur et al. 14].

We will follow the MDP-based approach to avoid the mentioned problems associated with POMDPs. Unlike the very classic dialog strategy learning approaches [Levin et al. 98, Scheffler and Young 02, Levin et al. 97] in which the system literally has no knowledge for dialog action selection in the training stage, the designed system knows taking which actions makes sense in each state despite being non-optimal as in [Singh et al. 02]. For example, taking a farewell action in the beginning of dialog instead of greeting does not make sense. This approach enables us to learn dialog strategies faster from small amounts of dialog corpus than the systems that have absolutely no knowledge of the training. The ideas that are used in [Singh et al. 02] are very good examples of this strategy; as in NjFun [Singh et al. 02] system, the goal is to minimize state space and learn dialog policies from real and small amounts of data.

In the mentioned systems, each piece of information is accepted as a *slot* and all slots need to be filled to complete the task. The total number of slots that current systems can usually handle is less than 5, and the flow of a dialog is determined by the slots that need to be filled [Singh et al. 02, Young et al. 10]. One of the important measures of success of task-based dialogs is their *task completion rate*. When the number of the slots that are needed to be filled increases, the likelihood of successful completion decreases.

27.4   Embodied Conversational Agents

Virtual human-like characters that specifically focus on dialog-based interactions are called **embodied conversational agents (ECAs)**, also known as intelligent Virtual Agents (IVA). ECAs are digital systems created with an anthropomorphic embodiment (be it graphical or robotic), and capable of having a conversation (albeit still limited) with a human counterpart, using some artificial intelligence broadly referred to as an "agent." With their anthropomorphic features and capabilities, they interact using humans' innate communication modalities such as facial expressions, body language, speech, and natural language understanding, and can also contribute to bridging the digital divide for low reading and low health literacy populations, as well as for technophobic individuals [Neuhauser and Kreps 11, Bickmore et al. 09].

One of the most influential works in the study of virtual animated characters established that, when provided with social cues by a computer system, humans react socially similarly to how they would with a human [Reeves and Nass 96]. Because the latest ECAs can use their sophisticated multimodal communication abilities to *establish rapport* [Pelachaud 09, Wang and Gratch 10, Gratch et al. 07a, Prendinger and Ishizuka 05, Huang et al. 11], *communicate empathically* [Prendinger and Ishizuka 05, McQuiggan and Lester 07, Aylett et al. 07, Boukricha and Becker-Asano 07], and *engage in social talk* [Kluwer 11, Bickmore et al. 05, Bickmore 05, Cassell and Bickmore 03], they have become capable of being as engaging as humans — and have even been found more engaging than humans at times [Gratch et al. 07b]. In this discussion, the developed spoken dialog systems have an ECA interface.

Embodied conversational agents (ECA) or virtual humans (VH) and spoken dialog systems (SDS) are two emerging fields of research which, *together*, could bring a revolution to human–computer interaction. Even though the term ECA includes the notion of spoken dialog, SDS and ECA communities still do not have a strong connection. While progress in the spoken dialog system area is complementary for the development of conversational embodied agents, latest findings in SDS research have not been commonly used by ECA researchers (and vice versa).

Indeed, although spoken dialog systems (SDS, henceforth) research has shown in the past few years that using reinforcement learning (RL) with MDPs for dialog management outperforms older hand-crafted rule-based approaches [Frampton and Lemon 09, Young et al. 13], intelligent virtual agent researchers have not yet integrated these results into their dialog systems. ECA-based systems usually involve spoken dialog (versus menu options to choose from), but their dialog management usually still relies on hand-crafted methods [Morbini et al. 12, Bickmore and Gruber 10].

In this project, I bring together the latest progress from the SDS community to the IVA community with the use of RL-based dialog management integrated with a 3D animated character (shown in Figure 27.3). The 3D animated virtual character is an interface for a task-based spoken dialog to deliver brief alcohol interventions to people at-risk of health issues due to excessive alcohol consumption.

From a computer science perspective, my work aims at building a fully implemented system to be used as screening tools to help individuals at risk of health issues, and at evaluating the system in terms of both users' (subjective) acceptance and the dialog system's (objective) performance.

From a health-care perspective, I aim at increasing access to effective evidence-based health interventions with a novel mode of delivery for computer-based health interventions — namely delivering health interventions with a virtual counselor. The screening dialog system brings insight and awareness regarding *alcohol problems* by using the well-established *brief intervention* (BI) counseling approach. BIs are short, well structured, one-on-one counseling sessions, focused on specific aspects of problematic lifestyle behavior. BIs are not only ideally suited for people who drink in ways that are harmful or abusive (which is the current domain of our work), but BIs have also been used successfully for a variety of target problem behaviors (e.g., overeating, lack of exercise). Therefore the results of our research will also have an impact on dialog systems for diverse behavior change interventions for healthy lifestyles. The next section covers brief alcohol interventions which is the topic of the demonstration system.

Figure 27.3: Multimodal embodied conversational agent interface.

27.5   Brief Interventions for Alcohol Problems

Unlike traditional alcoholism treatment, which focuses on helping people who are dependent on alcohol, brief interventions or short, one-on-one counseling sessions are ideally suited for people who drink in ways that are harmful or abusive [Moyer et al. 02]. Brief interventions can be delivered in a few minutes and require minimal follow-up whereas traditional alcoholism treatment takes many weeks or months.

The purpose of brief interventions is different from formal alcoholism treatment. Brief interventions generally aim to moderate a person's alcohol consumption to reasonable levels and to eliminate harmful drinking behaviors (such as binge drinking), rather than to insist on complete avoidance of drinking – although abstinence may be encouraged, if appropriate [Moyer et al. 04]. Reducing levels of drinking or changing patterns of harmful alcohol use helps to reduce the negative outcomes of drinking, such as alcohol-related medical problems, injuries, domestic violence, motor vehicle crashes, arrests, or damage to a developing fetus.

Many of the challenges involved in administering brief interventions — such as finding the time to administer them in busy doctors' offices, obtaining the extra training that helps staff become comfortable providing interventions, and managing the cost of using interventions — may be overcome through the use of technology. Patients are sometimes encouraged to use computer programs in

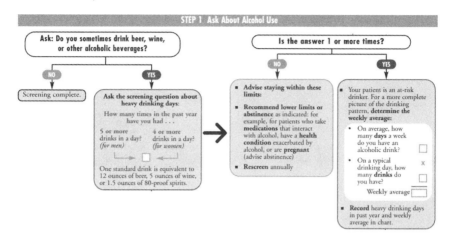

Figure 27.4: First step of alcohol screening and brief intervention [NIAAA 06].

the doctor's waiting room or at home, or to access the intervention through the Internet, which offers privacy and the ability to complete the program at any time of day [Hester et al. 05, Portnoy et al. 08, Mauriello et al. 11].

The current research is focused on delivering interventions by incorporating spoken dialog technology with anthropomorphic user interfaces such as interactive virtual characters [Bickmore et al. 11, Schulman et al. 11, Catizone et al. 08]. Pilot results indicate that although users reported they would be most comfortable consulting with a doctor in person [Gerbert et al. 03], they responded positively to the computerized interventions [Bickmore 05, Schulman et al. 11, Bickmore et al. 09], which were accessible even to those with little computer experience.

According to the clinician's guide for conducting brief interventions [on Alcohol Abuse and (U.S.) 07] from the National Institute on Alcohol Abuse and Alcoholism (NIAAA), a brief intervention can be delivered in three steps;

- Step 1: Asking about Alcohol Use (see Figure 27.4)

- Step 2: Assessing for Alcohol Use Disorders (see Figure 27.5)

  - Assessment of Abuse
  - Assessment of Dependence

- Step 3: Advising and Assisting According to Degree of Alcohol Problem

  - At-Risk Drinkers (see Figure 27.6)
  - Drinkers with Alcohol Use Disorder (see Figure 27.7)

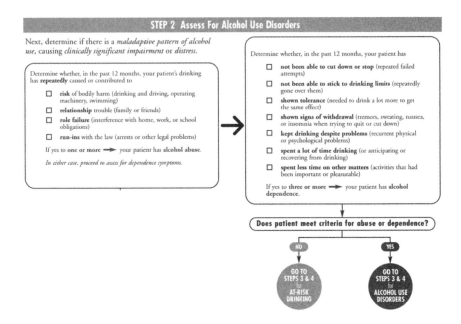

Figure 27.5: Second Step of Alcohol Screening and Brief Intervention [NIAAA 06]

The guide provides two methods for the first step (See Figure 27.4): a single question (about heavy drinking days) or administering a written self-report instrument. The single interview question can be used at any time, either in conjunction with the screening instrument or alone. For this project, the system starts intervention with a single question about alcohol use (e.g., "Do you sometimes drink beer, wine, or other alcoholic beverages?"). If the client's answer is no, there is no need to continue screening. If the client's answer is yes, the system will ask about the amount of alcohol the client consumes to find out if the client is an at-risk drinker (e.g. "How many times in the past year have you had 5 or more drinks in a day?").

If a client is not an at-risk drinker, the system may advise maintaining or lowering drinking limits according to the situation and offer re-screening annually. If a client is an at-risk drinker, to get the complete picture of drinking, the system will ask several questions to query the drinking pattern of a client (e.g., On average, how many days a week do you have an alcoholic beverage?).

In step 2 (see Figure 27.5), the system will try to determine whether or not there is a maladaptive pattern of alcohol use that is causing clinically significant impairment or distress. In this step, the system will try to query if a client has alcohol abuse (e.g., risk of bodily harm, relationship trouble) and alcohol dependence (e.g., kept drinking despite problems, not been able to stick to drinking limits) problem. If a patient does not meet the criteria for alcohol abuse or dependence,

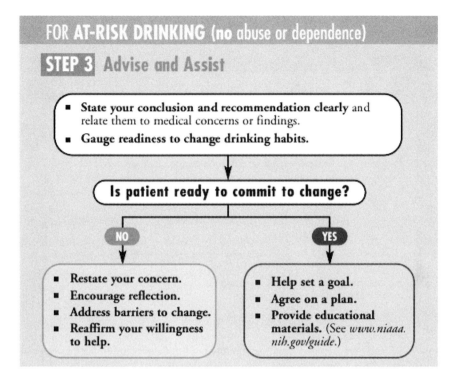

FOR **AT-RISK DRINKING** (**no** abuse or dependence)

STEP 3 Advise and Assist

- **State your conclusion and recommendation clearly** and relate them to medical concerns or findings.
- **Gauge readiness to change drinking habits.**

Is patient ready to commit to change?

NO

YES

- **Restate your concern.**
- **Encourage reflection.**
- **Address barriers to change.**
- **Reaffirm your willingness to help.**

- **Help set a goal.**
- **Agree on a plan.**
- **Provide educational materials.** (See *www.niaaa. nih.gov/guide.*)

Figure 27.6: Third step of alcohol screening and brief intervention for at-risk drinking [NIAAA 06].

the patient is still at-risk for developing alcohol-related problems. If a patient has an alcohol use disorder (dependence or abuse), the next step (step 3) will be different than for at-risk drinkers.

In step 3, if the client is at-risk (see Figure 27.6), the system will state its conclusion according to the guideline and recommend to cut down his/her drinking. Then it will try to assess readiness to change; if the client is not ready to change, the system will restate its concern for the client's health, encourage reflection by asking positive versus negatives of drinking, and reaffirm its willingness to help when the client is ready. If a client is ready to change, the system will set a goal, agree on a change plan, and provide educational materials (e.g., pamphlets). In step 3 for the client who has alcohol abuse or dependence problems (see Figure 27.7), the system will state its conclusion, negotiate a drinking goal, and refer the client to an addiction specialist. A sample brief intervention dialog shown in Table 27.1. The system performs screening in the first step with 3 questions. In the second step, it asks a question for assessing alcohol abuse. Since it elicits indicators of alcohol abuse, it does not ask about alcohol dependence (one indicator is enough

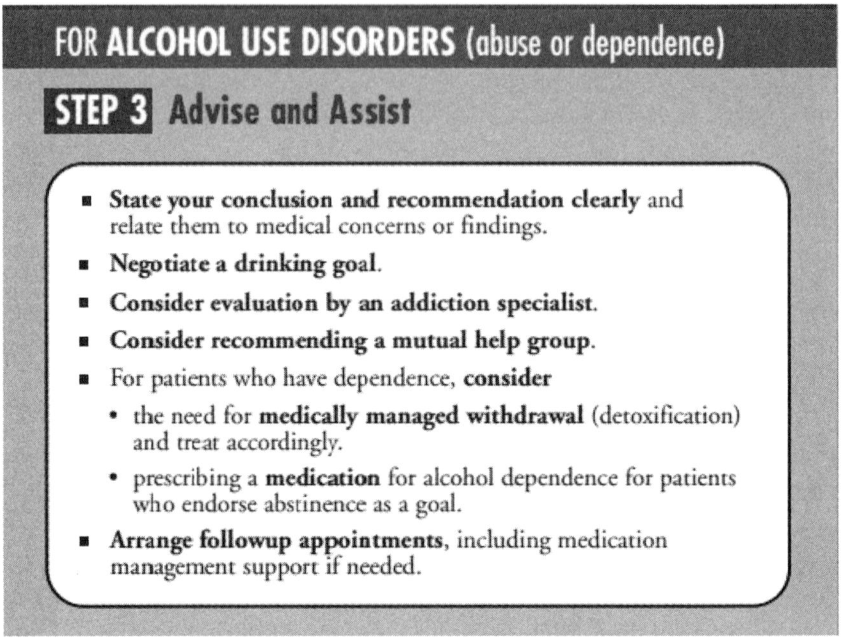

FOR **ALCOHOL USE DISORDERS** (abuse or dependence)

STEP 3 Advise and Assist

- **State your conclusion and recommendation clearly** and relate them to medical concerns or findings.
- **Negotiate a drinking goal.**
- **Consider evaluation by an addiction specialist.**
- **Consider recommending a mutual help group.**
- For patients who have dependence, **consider**
  - the need for **medically managed withdrawal** (detoxification) and treat accordingly.
  - prescribing a **medication** for alcohol dependence for patients who endorse abstinence as a goal.
- **Arrange followup appointments**, including medication management support if needed.

Figure 27.7: Third step of alcohol screening and brief intervention for alcohol use disorders [NIAAA 06].

for abuse) and passes to the next step. Based on the result from step 2, the system delivers step 3 which is for people who have alcohol use disorders. It recommends to getting professional help.

Table 27.1: Sample Dialog: S shows systems utterance and C shows user utterance in Turn Column. Second column shows what user or system utters in each turn. Third column shows in which step the system is operating in terms of Brief Intervention.

Turn	Utterance	Step in BI
S1:	Hi, My name is Lola, I am a virtual character created to have conversations with you and to teach you about healthy lifestyles. Today, I'm here to talk about drinking to figure out if you have any issues. May I ask you a few questions about your drinking?	
C1:	Yes, sure you can.	
S2:	Do you sometimes drink beer, wine, or other alcoholic beverages?	
	Continued on next page	

Table 27.1 – continued from previous page

Turn	Utterance	Step in BI
C2:	Well yes, I drink wine or beer sometimes!	
S3:	How many times in the past year have you had 5 or more drinks in a day?	
C3:	I think around once a week.	
S4:	Actually, consuming more than 4 drinks on any single day is classified as heavy drinking. So it seems like you are sometimes going above heavy drinking limits? Is that right?	
C4:	Yes, that's correct.	
S5:	How frequently do you have an alcoholic beverage each week?	Step 1:
C5:	I think at least 3 days a week.	Screening
S6:	On a typical drinking day, how many drinks do you have?	
C6:	I just drink... maybe a bottle of whisky.	
S7:	Sorry, I could not understand your answer, can you please repeat?	
C7:	I said one bottle of scotch.	
S8:	Ok, thanks for the information you have provided me about your drinking. Next I will try to determine some important effects of your drinking.	
S9:	Have you ever taken risks under the influence, such as drinking and driving, operating a motor vehicle, or swimming?	
C9:	No I have not.	
S10:	I see, so you are careful to avoid high-risk situations after or while having drinks, right?	
C10:	Yes, I try to be careful.	Step 2: Abuse
S11:	Have you continued to drink even though you knew it was causing you trouble with your family or friends?	Assessment
C11:	I think yes, I continue to drink while my family complains about my drinking.	
S12:	Thanks for the information you've provided. In the next step I will ask you questions about potential dependence-related aspects of your drinking. Is that okay?	
C12:	Yes I want to know, please go ahead.	
S13:	Have you had times when you ended up drinking more than you meant to? Or kept on drinking for longer than you intended?	
C13:	Not usually, but... yes I guess I did.	
S14:	Have you found that you have to drink much more than you once did in order to get the effect that you like?	
	Continued on next page	

Table 27.1 – continued from previous page

Turn	Utterance	Step in BI
C14:	I think my tolerance is increased.	
S15:	Sorry, I could not understand your answer. Do you need to drink a lot more sometimes to get the same effect?	
C15:	I meant yes, I need to drink more and more.	
S16:	Ok sorry but just to be sure: you cannot get the same effect with the same amount of alcohol. Is that right?	
C16:	Yes, that is correct.	
S17:	Have you more than once wanted to stop or cut down on your drinking? Or tried more than once to stop or cut down but found you couldn't?	
C17:	Well, I think I tried but I was not that serious about stopping or cutting down.	Step 2:
S18:	I see, so you really never attempted to stop or cut down. Is that right?	Dependence
C18:	No, it is wrong.	
S19:	Sorry for the misunderstanding, can you please repeat your answer? Have you more than once wanted to stop or cut down on your drinking but found you couldn't?	
C19:	Yes I did but not seriously.	
S20:	Ok, now, when the effects of alcohol are wearing off, have you had trouble sleeping, or found yourself shaking, nervous, nauseous, restless?	
C20:	I found myself sweating and my heart beating fast.	
S21:	Sorry I could not understand your answer. Can you please repeat it?	
C22:	I said I found myself sweating and my hard beating fast.	
S22:	I am sorry for asking again, can you repeat your answer please.	
C22:	I said I am sweating and my heart beating fast when I drink too much.	
S23:	Have you had a period when you spent a lot of time drinking? Or being sick or getting over the bad after effects of drinking?	
C23:	Yes several times.	
S24:	Thank you very much for all your answers. Now I'd like to just take one or two more minutes of your time. Is that okay?	
C24:	Yes, please go ahead.	
S25:	On a scale from 1 to 10, how ready are you to make a change?	
C25:	I think 7	Step 3:
	Continued on next page	

Table 27.1 – continued from previous page

Turn	Utterance	Step in BI
S26:	Great! Just for your information, men who drink more than 4 standard drinks in a day or more than 14 per week, and women who drink more than 3 drinks in a day or more than 7 drinks per week, are at increased risk of alcohol-related problems. Based on your answers, I recommend you stick with this limit or even abstain if you can. I also would like you to track your drinking, and I will send you a calendar for that. I'm also going to give you information about places near you where you can get help if you choose to. Finally, I would like to talk with you again 3 months later. Is it okay?	Disorder
S26:	Yes, it's okay.	
S27:	Thanks for talking with me. I hope you've learned something useful about your drinking pattern. Good bye and talk to you in 3 months.	

27.6   Conclusion

The goal of this chapter was to provide background information for important and novel topics in multimodal user interfaces including spoken dialog systems, dialog management methods, embodied conversational agents, and health dialog systems. In addition, brief alcohol interventions are introduced because it is the example problem of the next chapter which discusses design of dialog systems to deliver brief alcohol interventions.

Further Reading

The book titled *Reinforcement Learning for Adaptive Dialogue Systems* by Verena Rieser and Oliver Lemon is a good reference book for dialog management [Rieser et al. 11a]. Perception of embodied conversational agents in health-related dialogs is investigated deeply in [Lisetti et al. 13]. A comprehensive survey of health dialog systems is covered in [Bickmore and Giorgino 06].

28

Adaptive Dialog Systems for Health

Ugan Yasavur & Christine Lisetti

> Feeling my way through the darkness, guided by a
> beating heart, I can't tell where the journey will end,
> but I know where to start.
>
> —Aloe Blacc

This chapter describes how to develop end-to-end multimodal conversational systems using Markov decision processes (MDP) and reinforcement learning for dialog management. It also covers other required components to develop end-to-end systems.

28.1 Approach

The approach that we take is using MDPs and optimizing systems with reinforcement learning. An overview of the system architecture for the MDP-based system is shown in Figure 28.2, and explained in detail in Section 28.5. In short, we use a statistical dialog management method, combined with a 3D animated character who converses with the user with text-to-speech (TTS) utterances. The domain is a task-based spoken dialog to deliver brief alcohol interventions to people, and identify whether they are at-risk of health issues due to excessive alcohol consumption.

According to the clinician's guide that is introduced in a previous section for conducting brief interventions from the National Institute on Alcohol Abuse and Alcoholism (NIAAA) [on Alcohol Abuse and (U.S.) 07], a brief intervention for alcohol-related health problems can be delivered in three sequential steps:

- Step 1: *Asking* about Alcohol Use

- Step 2: *Assessing* for Alcohol Use Disorders

  – Assessment of Abuse

  – Assessment of Dependence

- Step 3: *Advising* and Assisting According to Degree of Alcohol Problem

  – At-Risk Drinkers

  – Drinkers with Alcohol Use Disorder

The details of brief intervention for alcohol is discussed in Section 27.5, but a very brief review is included in this section. The goal of the dialog system is to deliver alcohol screening and brief interventions based on this guide. Each step contains a set of questions.

In *Step 1*, there are 5 questions. The system asks these 5 questions, and if the user expresses that s/he is not consuming alcohol from time to time, the interaction is gracefully terminated by the system. Otherwise, the dialog manager continues to the second step.

In *Step 2*, in the assessment of abuse stage, there are 4 questions assessing alcohol abuse indicators. It is enough to find one indicator of alcohol abuse to move to the assessment of dependence stage. If the system cannot find any indicator of abuse with the 4 questions, it passes to the dependence stage. In the dependence stage, there are 7 questions.

It is enough to detect 3 dependence indicators to transit to *Step 3*, advice for drinkers with alcohol use *disorder*. If the system does not detects 3 dependence indicators, it transits to advice for *at-risk* drinkers. Therefore, the dialog branches into two separate steps in *Step 3*: **1)** one for *at-risk* drinkers, and **2)** one for drinkers with alcohol use *disorder*. In both branches, the system provides information related to the assessment of the system. If the system assesses that the user has an alcohol use disorder, it refers the user to treatment, asks the user if she or he is ready to change, and suggests a goal toward a change of drinking patterns, based on the user's readiness. If the user is an at-risk drinker, it gauges his or her readiness to change, and provides feedback and information about the person's drinking. Therefore in both stages, the system provides factual information about the person's drinking and suggested drinking limits, and asks what is the user's intention to change with a single question. In total there can be a maximum of 18 different questions in a single session.

A sample dialog between the system and the user is shown in Table 27.1. The dialog we presented in the table covers *Step 1* Screening about alcohol *use*, and *Step 2* Assessment of *abuse* completely. In *Step 2* Assessment of *dependence*, there are 7 questions, and then the system branches to Step 3. The system uses questions recommended by NIAAA. It uses simple reflections for confirmations

instead of explicit confirmations, and examples are shown in Table 27.1 with the
S4 and S10 system dialog turns.

28.2   Reinforcement Learning Background

The system design is based on leveraging reinforcement learning. *Reinforcement
Learning* (RL, henceforth) is a sequential decision-making algorithm, where the
RL agent interacts with its environment [Sutton and Barto 98]. The environment is
defined as: "anything that cannot be changed arbitrarily by the agent is considered
to be outside of it and thus part of its environment" [Sutton and Barto 98, p. 53].
Reinforcement learning treats the learning of dialog strategies as a sequential
optimization problem, leading to strategies which are globally optimal [Sutton and
Barto 98].

Within the RL framework for dialog development, dialog strategies are represented as mappings from states to actions within Markov decision processes
(MDPs) [Levin et al. 98]. In other words, a dialog strategy specifies, for each system state, what is the next action to be taken by the system [Levin et al. 98, Scheffler
and Young 02]. The MDP framework can be characterized by a 4-tuple (S,A,T,R),
where:

- S is a finite set of states

- A is a finite set of actions

- T is a state-transition function such that $T(s,\ a,\ s') = \mathbf{P}(s'|\ s,\ a)$ which
  describes how the probability of performing action **a** in state **s** will lead to
  state s'

- $\mathbf{R}(s, a, s')$ is a local reward function such that $R(s,a) = \sum_a \mathbf{P}(a|s)\mathbf{R}(s,a,s')$,
  and the objective of the SDS is to maximize the gained reward

28.3   Markov Decision Processes

To develop the system, It is required to represent the internal states of the system
using MDP formalization as described earlier. States, actions, and state transitions
need to be created. First, the state attributes are elicited. The most important dialog
attributes are identified to represent the dialog state concisely. To avoid the data
sparsity problem during training, it is possible to use smaller MDPs for subtasks.
In this design, it is possible to divide the whole system into 5 sections according
to the BI guide steps. Hence, there are 5 MDPs in the system. For each step, the
related state features are elicited.

For each state, there are 5 common **attributes**: Question, Confidence, Value, Grammar, and Aux (see Table 28.1 for the descriptions of each attribute). There is usually 1 extra attribute to represent the step-specific requirement at each step, e.g., Greet because in the first step the system needs to greet the user first and get consent of the user to start the dialog. The full list of state features for *Step 1* are listed in Table 28.1.

Then possible states are designed: for each question there are 34 possible states. Each state represents the state of the conversation. For example, dialog state *112101* indicates that the system has greeted the user (G=1), the first question has been asked (Q=1), the ASR confidence level is high (C=2), the value is obtained (V=1), the type of grammar is restrictive (Gr=0) and that the polarity of the alcohol usage indicator (i.e., positive or negative indicator such as consuming alcoholic beverages above limits is positive, below limits is negative) is positive (Ax=1). The Aux feature is set to 0 when it is not used. It is used for multiple purposes such as keeping track of the number of re-asked questions or of the polarity of the alcohol problem indicator.

The state representations are refined by eliminating the states that make no sense and manually checking each state. For example, state *040111* is a non-sensible state in *Step 1*. The system cannot be in that state because the system needs to greet the user *first*, before it can ask questions. It is not possible to ask question 4 in the first step without greeting or without asking prior questions. Excluding non-sensible states yielded a very large state-space reduction.

For *Step 1 Use*, *Step 2 Abuse*, *Step 2 Dependence*, *Step 3 At-risk*, and *Step 3*

Table 28.1: State Attributes and Values for Step 1: Asking about Alcohol Use.

Attribute	Values	Description
Greet (G)	0,1	Whether the system has greeted the user
Question (Q)	1,2,3,4	Which question is being asked
Confidence (C)	0,1,2,3, 4,5,6	0,1,2 for low, medium, and high confidence of speech recognizer. 3,4 for confirmed or not confirmed. 5 to indicate system is waiting for confirmation. 6 to indicate system transit to next question without confirmation
Value (V)	0,1	Is the value obtained for current question?
Grammar (Gr)	0,1	What type of ASR grammar used, restrictive or dictation (non-restrictive) grammar?
Aux (Ax)	0,1,2	Multiple purpose attribute. Use to indicate number of re-asks and semantic valence of the received answer. If it is 0, it indicates it is not used in that state.

Table 28.2: Dialog Actions for Step 1 Question1.

Dialog Action	System Utterances
S1-AskQ1Sys:	Do you sometimes drink beer, wine, or other alcoholic beverages?
S1-AskQ1User:	Can you briefly talk about your alcohol consumption?
S1-ReAskQ1Sys	Sorry, I could not understand your answer. Do you sometimes drink beer, wine, or other alcoholic beverages?
S1-RaAskQ1User:	Sorry, I could not understand your answer. Can you briefly talk about your alcohol consumption?
S1-ConfQ1Pos	So you like to have alcoholic beverages from time to time, is that right?
S1-ConfQ1Neg	So you are recently not having any alcoholic beverages, is that right?
S1-NoConf	—
S1-NotConfirmedQ1Sys	I am sorry for the misunderstanding. Do you sometimes drink beer, wine, or other alcoholic beverages?
S1-NotConfirmedQ1User	I am sorry for the misunderstanding. Can you briefly talk about your alcohol consumption?

Disorders, the number of states are 170, 136, 238, 68, and 68, respectively, i.e., 34 states multiplied by the number of questions in a step). Total number of states is 680.

Secondly the **dialog actions** are created for each question. The system uses 2 types of initiative dialog actions: system initiative, where the system asks close-ended questions (e.g., Do you sometimes drink beer, wine, or other alcoholic beverages?), and user initiative, where the system asks open-ended questions (e.g., Can you briefly talk about your alcohol consumption?). We refer to the system/user initiative terms in the same manner as they are widely referred to in the SDS community [Singh et al. 02, Singh et al. 00]. In the system initiative questions (where the expected answer is relatively restricted given the close-ended nature of the questions), the system uses a restrictive grammar for speech recognition (SR). In the user initiative, the system uses a non-restrictive SR grammar to handle the user's answer to open-ended questions.

There are 9 possible actions for each question, which are grouped under 4 categories: **1)** *Ask* actions are used when the system needs to ask a question of the user for the first time, which can be performed with the two types of initiatives; **2)** *re-ask* actions are used if the system cannot understand the user's speech, which can also be done with two types of initiatives; **3)** *confirmation* actions are used to

Table 28.3: Explaratory Policies for Step 1 Question 1.

States						Available Actions per State
G	Q	C	V	Gr	Ax	
1	1	0	0	0	0	S1-ReAskQ1Sys, S1-ReAskQ1User
1	1	0	0	1	0	S1-ReAskQ1Sys, S1-ReAskQ1User
1	1	0	0	0	1	S1-ReAskQ1Sys, S1-ReAskQ1User
1	1	0	0	0	2	S1-AskQ2Sys, S1-AskQ2User
1	1	0	0	1	1	S1-ReAskQ1Sys, S1-ReAskQ1User
1	1	0	0	1	2	S1-AskQ2Sys, S1-AskQ2User
1	1	0	1	0	1	S1-ConfQ1Pos, S1-NoConf
1	1	1	1	0	1	S1-ConfQ1Pos, S1-NoConf
1	1	2	1	0	1	S1-ConfQ1Pos, S1-NoConf
1	1	0	1	1	1	S1-ConfQ1Pos, S1-NoConf
1	1	1	1	1	1	S1-ConfQ1Pos, S1-NoConf
1	1	2	1	1	1	S1-ConfQ1Pos, S1-NoConf
1	1	0	1	0	2	S1-ConfQ1Neg, S1-NoConf
1	1	1	1	0	2	S1-ConfQ1Neg, S1-NoConf
1	1	2	1	0	2	S1-ConfQ1Neg, S1-NoConf
1	1	0	1	1	2	S1-ConfQ1Neg, S1-NoConf
1	1	1	1	1	2	S1-ConfQ1Neg, S1-NoConf
1	1	2	1	1	2	S1-ConfQ1Neg, S1-NoConf
1	1	6	1	1	1	S1-AskQ2Sys, S1-AskQ2User
1	1	6	1	1	2	S1-Q1End, S1-Q1End
1	1	6	1	0	1	S1-AskQ2Sys, S1-AskQ2User
1	1	6	1	0	2	S1-Q1End, S1-Q1End
1	1	3	1	0	1	S1-AskQ2Sys, S1-AskQ2User
1	1	3	1	1	1	S1-AskQ2Sys, S1-AskQ2User
1	1	3	1	0	2	S1-Q1End, S1-Q1End
1	1	3	1	1	2	S1-Q1End, S1-Q1End
1	1	4	1	0	1	S1-NotConfirmedQ1Sys,S1-NotConfirmedQ1User
1	1	4	1	1	1	S1-NotConfirmedQ1Sys,S1-NotConfirmedQ1User
1	1	4	1	0	2	S1-NotConfirmedQ1Sys,S1-NotConfirmedQ1User
1	1	4	1	1	2	S1-NotConfirmedQ1Sys,S1-NotConfirmedQ1User

ask for confirmation as to whether the system understood what the user said.

The confirmation actions are system initiative by default, and are of 3 types: positive, negative, and no confirmation. The positive type is used if the system receives an answer which reveals alcohol usage/abuse/dependence information. The negative type is used if the system receives an answer which indicates no drinking/abuse/dependence problem. The third type is no-confirmation, and it is used if the system decides to pass to the next question without confirmation (possible action at any question). *NotConfirmed* action is used if the user gives a negative answer to a confirmation action.

The available actions for the first question in *Step 1* Screening about Alcohol Use are shown in Table 28.2. The first column is the name of the dialog action, and the second column is the system utterance. The actual name of the dialog action starts with the step information (e.g., S1), then the type of dialog action (e.g., Ask), then the question being asked (Q1) and the initiative type (Sys). So S1-AskQ1Sys stands for *Step1* (S1), the question type is *Ask*, the question being queried is *question one* (Q1) and the initiative type is *system initiative* (Sys).

The number of available actions for each question is 9 (as for the first question shown in Table 28.2). Although the length of the dialog is not fixed, our system asks a maximum of 18 questions. There are 162 available actions (for asking questions, re-asking questions, and confirmations) for the system to select from in the longest dialog session (18 questions multiplied by the number of available actions). There are dialog actions which are used while transiting from one step to another step (e.g., from *Step 1* to *Step 2 Abuse*) and dialog actions for ending the conversation. There are 2 actions for giving feedback to at-risk drinkers and to drinkers with alcohol use disorder at the end of each session. The total number of the dialog actions is 169.

After creating the dialog actions, **dialog policies** are created. A dialog policy is a mapping of a state to sensible dialog actions. Each state is mapped to 2 possible dialog actions based on the initiative or confirmation type. Table 28.3 shows exploratory dialog policies for Question 1 in Step 1.

As has been mentioned earlier, for each question there are 34 states. State updates are performed based on the user's dialog actions or on systems dialog actions in each dialog turn. In Table 28.3, only 30 state-actions mappings that are updated by the system dialog actions or user dialog actions are shown. The remaining 4 states are only updated based on the user's dialog actions, which is why we did not include them in Table 28.3. The reason for this is that, if the system waits for the confirmation from the user (i.e., where C=5 as shown in Table 28.1), the system dialog actions cannot be used to update a state. In other words, the remaining 4 states need to be updated by the user's dialog actions. In Table 28.3, we only show the states that are updated by the system. However, the states in Table 28.3 are the result of the user's dialog actions since *Value Grammar, Confidence* and sometimes *Aux* are updated by the user's dialog actions in each dialog turn. For example, when the user speaks to the system, the speech recognizer *Confidence* level and *Value* attributes are updated based on the user's dialog action. The system aims to learn approximately optimal dialog strategies for the initiative style and the confirmation type selection.

28.4   Modeling World with Interconnected MDPs

To avoid the curse of the dimensionality problem, minimizing the number of system states is required. Since the BI dialog requires many dialog turns between the system and a user, the number of available dialog strategies is very large, and can make learning optimal policies infeasible with limited training data. To alleviate this problem, state space can be divided into separate MDPs for each phase.

In the system, each step or phase of the BI is represented with one MDP with local goals and reward functions. This approach divided the problem into 5 interconnected MDPs (shown in Figure 28.1) but, in any interaction with the system, we use a maximum 4 MDPs, i.e., 1) Step 1; 2) Abuse; 3) Dependence; and 4) one MDP from Step 3 based on Abuse or Dependence problem. This approach also reduced the number of required state features for each step, thus reducing the number of states required.

Since there are two phases in *Step 2* (one for querying alcohol abuse and one for querying alcohol dependence), I represent Step 2 with two distinct MDPs (as shown in Figure 28.1), which greatly reduces the number of exploratory policies (because it reduces the number of state features) without compromising fine-grained distinctions between dialog strategies. Because the two phases are independent from each other, representing each phase with a separate MDP is appropriate. It also provides advantages in terms of learning dialog strategies with less data.

There are two separate MDPs for representing the two different phases in *Step 3*. One is used for representing the model for "At-risk" drinkers who do not have alcohol use disorder problems (i.e., no abuse nor dependence). The second one is used to identify drinkers with alcohol use disorders.

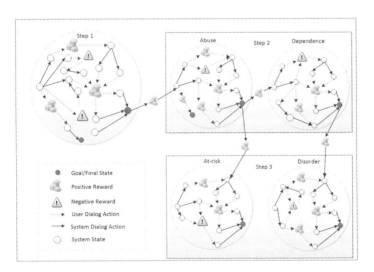

Figure 28.1: Representation of world model with MDPs.

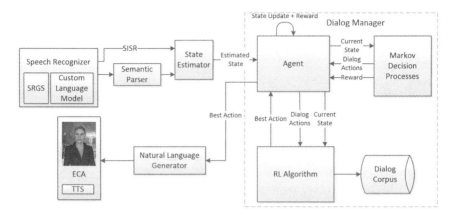

Figure 28.2: System architecture and dialog manager.

In conclusion, the system is modeled with 5 MDPs. In each MDP, there are multiple terminal states. Some terminal states terminate the Step (such as the consent state), and some terminal states provide transparent transitions to the start state (or start state distribution) of another MDP (see Figure 28.1). At the same time, the agent receives a positive reward. The agent also receives immediate positive/negative rewards as shown in Figure 28.1. For details on immediate rewards, please see Section 28.6. With this approach, learning the optimal dialog strategy for an entire dialog is reduced to learning optimal dialog strategy for each of the MDPs.

28.5   Agent and Dialog Strategy Learning

As shown in Figure 28.2, the *agent* component of the system operates as an interface between other main components of the system. If the system asks a system initiative question, the *Speech Recognizer* component operates by using *speech recognizer grammar specification (SRGS) grammars*,[1] and it outputs *semantic interpretation for speech recognition*[2] *(SISR)* tags. If the system uses non-restrictive grammar, it uses the *semantic parser* to parse the recognized speech. We use the Phoenix robust semantic parser [Ward 91], which requires us to write context-free grammar style recursive grammars to extract relevant information from the user utterances. An alternative natural language parser is Gemini [Dowding et al. 93] parser. Both parsers are available online for free. As an alternative to rule-based semantic parsers, a supervised open-source parser could be used such as [Jurcicek

---

[1] http://www.w3.org/TR/speech-grammar/
[2] http://www.w3.org/TR/semantic-interpretation/

et al. 09]. According to our experience, it is easy to create robust semantic parsing functionality with a Phoenix parser.

After semantic parsing, the *agent* component receives SISR tags (i.e., when the type of system dialog action is system initiative or closed questions), or Phoenix parser results (i.e., when the type of system dialog action is user initiative or open questions) according to the initiative type, as semantic interpretations. The agent updates the system *current state* and collects the *reward* according to the reward function (see Section 28.6 for the reward function). It then queries the corresponding *Markov decision process* with the current state, and receives *dialog actions* and *reward* information for the current state, and there might not be any associated rewards.

A reward is received only if the *current state* has an associated *reward*. For example, the final state of each MDP has associated rewards. The agent sends the received *dialog actions* from the MDP and the *current state* to the *RL algorithm*, and the RL algorithm selects the *best action — an action for which the agent received a maximum amount of reward in its prior experience* — based on the *dialog corpus* (see Section 28.8) which is collected from real user interactions.The dialog corpus contains information about gained rewards at each step and accumulated rewards for a whole dialog session. The best action is the one that leads the agent to collect the maximum amount of reward. If the system is running in exploration/unoptimized mode, it selects dialog actions randomly among available actions in that state. Therefore, the best action selection does not happen in the unoptimized version which is usually used to collect training data (exploration mode).

The *best action* is passed to the *natural language generator* component, which gives the final form of the system response and passes the text to the *text-to-speech (TTS)* engine. The embodied conversational agent *(ECA)* utters the response with lip synchronization. After each dialog turn, the *dialog corpus* is updated by the *agent* with the old dialog state, action, the new dialog state, and the reward information. Actually, the corpus contains more information about each turn but the RL algorithm uses reward signals to select the best dialog actions in each state.

At the inception of the project, usually there is not any data for optimizing the system for the domain of the system (the domain of alcohol use in this case). So the system can be first used with an algorithm which selects a dialog action randomly among the available ones. Since there are mappings between each state to sensible dialog actions, the system was able to deliver basic unoptimized functionality.

After having acquired the *dialog corpus* for the domain of alcohol abuse, it becomes possible to use the RL algorithm for learning optimized dialog policies and select the best action according to available data.

Based on each of the MDPs, the expected cumulative reward $Q(s, a)$ of taking *action a* from *state s* can be calculated in terms of Q-values of the next dialog states with the following equation [Sutton and Barto 98];

$$Q^*(s,a) = R(s,a) + \gamma \sum_{s'} P(s'|s,a) \max_{a'} Q^*(s',a') \qquad (28.1)$$

where $P(s'|s,a)$ is the transition model and R(s, a) is the local reward function. The γ $(0 \leq \gamma \leq 1)$ is the discount factor which is mainly used to indicate the importance of sooner versus later rewards.

The Q-values in Equation 28.1 can be easily computed with a desired threshold using the Q-value version of the standard *value iteration algorithm* [Sutton and Barto 98]. The algorithm updates iteratively the current value of Q(s, a) based on the current Q-values, and it stops when the update yields a difference that is below the threshold. Once the Value Iteration algorithm is completed, approximately optimal dialog strategies can be selected by the system, which are essentially dialog actions with the maximum Q-values. The optimized dialog strategy must collect the maximum amount of rewards from future users.

The biggest challenge of this approach is in collecting enough human–machine dialog data to learn an accurate model. To avoid the data sparsity problem, we used minimal state representations and approximated the true state of the system during the interaction. Since the length of the dialog is long, a large amount of data is required to optimize the system. We run the system in two modes, training/exploration and testing. Training mode is for data collection, and in testing mode, the system uses optimized dialog strategies based on the data collected in training. Therefore, Equation 28.1 is used only for testing mode.

28.6 Reward Function Design

The reward function is designed based on the amount of information collected and the cost of collecting each piece of information. For different dialog domains, new reward functions can be designed which are usually empirical, but compatible with the goal of the system. For example, for some systems the task-completion rate is the most important criteria, therefore the reward function can be a Boolean variable which indicates weather or not a task successfully completed. For some dialog systems, minimizing the length of dialog is more important, therefore they look at the number of turns in the dialog as a success metric. For our system both dialog length and task-completion rate are important.

The agent gets a reward in each question: if the value is obtained in the first attempt with the *ASK* type of action, it gets +10 reward; if on the other hand the value is not obtained, the agent gets no reward. For each *confirmation* action, if the obtained value is confirmed by the user, it gets +2, otherwise it gets -2. For each *ReAsk* action which could not result in obtaining the necessary information, the agent receives -3 reward, otherwise it receives +3 reward for the obtained value. If the obtained value is disapproved by the user, it deletes the previously gained reward. Therefore the agent gains a positive or negative reward for each question and dialog action. In addition to rewards gained per question, there are rewards in the MDPs which are associated with the final states. The system receives +15 reward if it is able to reach any of the final states in any MDP. For example, the successful completion of Step 1 gives the agent a +15 reward. In Figure 28.1, we depict the immediate rewards and the rewards that are received from the goal states for each MDP.

The described approach is used to perform strategy learning for each question. Since the system tries to obtain one piece of information in each question, learning the approximately optimal actions in each question is useful.

28.7   Speech Recognition and Language Model

In the system, the operation mode of the speech recognizer[3] can be adapted according to the dialog manager's action selection. If the dialog manager asks **system initiative** questions of the user, the system can use *speech recognizer grammar specification (SRGS) grammars*. Even though I refer to system initiative questions as closed questions, the SRGS grammar does not restrict the user to answer with short answers such as yes/no or a number. It can still understand unrestricted speech. If the system operates in system initiative mode, the Phoenix parser is not used. Instead *semantic interpretation for speech recognition (SISR)* tags are used. The SRGS grammar can be created by first authoring it in augmented Backus–Naur Form (ABNF), and then we converted it to SRGS by using the NuEcho[4] ABNF editor. The advantage of using ABNF is it is more readable and developer friendly than XML-based SRGS grammars.

The system uses the custom dictation grammar while it operates in **user initiative** mode. In user initiative mode, we load two types of grammars in the in-process speech recognizer. One is the SRGS grammar which is prepared for the system initiative version of the current question. If the speech recognition result is based on dictation grammar, we use the Phoenix parser; otherwise we use SISR tags. Since the standard dictation language model is comprehensive, it does not work well in specialized domains. To address this problem, a new language model is created by using Windows Vista Dictation Resource Kit software. It is a tool which enables the creation of custom speech recognition dictation language models.

Language models help a speech recognizer decide upon the likelihood of a word sequence. Hence it is useful independently of the acoustics of the word sequences. A language model lets the recognizer make the right guess when two different sentences sound similar. For example, both of the following sentences sound similar: "Because of alcohol, I had hard problems" and "Because of alcohol,

---

[3] Microsoft Speech Recognizer
[4] http://www.nuecho.com/en/

I had heart problems." With a language model on alcohol consumption, the recognizer knows that the first sentence is more likely to be what was said than the second one. Furthermore, a language model does not only give information about homonyms, it also gives statistical information about which word might appear after another, among other information. Therefore, if a language model consists of word sequences that are relevant in a specific context, it is very likely that it will operate better than a comprehensive language model for English.

To collect the data for the language model, a crowd sourcing service can be used such as the Mechanical Turk (MT) crowd sourcing website.[5] In the case of our dialog system we asked MT participants the same questions that the system in full mode would ask (after being built from the process described above and after we have acquired the language model). In the instructions, we requested them to role play a person who is having alcohol problems. The instructions were:

> "Imagine that you are recently having drinking problems and that you are talking with a health professional face-to-face about your drinking problems. The health practitioner asks you the questions on this page. Please answer as naturally as possible."

Because alcohol usage is a very common and universal social problem that everyone understands, MT users' answers were relevant. One can note that we would not necessarily have collected meaningful answers had we asked MT users, for example, to imagine having some complex disorder such as schizophrenia, because most people do not know what behaviors are associated with this condition. Consuming alcohol in different quantities however, is an experience that many people can relate to, and therefore the answers that we collected were very relevant.

Participants answered the 18 questions. The new domain-specific language model is created from the responses of 447 MT workers. The collected data is preprocessed (corrected spelling and grammar problems) before creating the language model. We improved the language model by adding sentences generated based on our SRGS grammars, and used this language model in our experiments. In the model, there are 7,599 utterances, the average length of an utterance is 11.82 words, there are 100,679 word tokens, and 5,423 distinct words.

The custom language model is used instead of the default dictation language model. The training data is collected from real user dialogs (described in Section 28.8) which includes sound files. Then we run the speech recognizer on the collected sound files and compared recognitions based on the two language models. We performed quantitative analysis to compare the Microsoft standard dictation language model with our custom language model. We found that when we use the custom language model, the word error rate is approximately 17% lower than the Microsoft standard dictation language model.

---

[5] https://www.mturk.com

28.8   Dialog Corpus

A very richly annotated XML-based dialog corpus is created from the test dialogs
in our implementation to optimize dialog policies. The corpus is organized turn by
turn. Each turn element contains: step and state information, questions asked by
the system, initiative type, best speech recognition, grammar type, semantic value
or result of the Phoenix parser, N-best recognitions with confidence score, reward
gained from the question, cumulative reward, and sound files. Each XML log file
contains sequences of dialog turns for one dialog session. This corpus provides
information to optimize dialog policies.

28.9   Conclusion

In this chapter, we provided implementation level details of a real-world conversational system for alcohol assessments. A dialog system is a pipeline, starting
from speech recognizer to text-to-speech generation. We reviewed all important
components, especially dialog management in this chapter.

Further reading

We used Markov decision processes in the design of the system. A more robust
approach to noisy speech recognition results is partially observable MDPs, but
they have serious scalability problems. The following two review papers discuss
recent advancements in these areas and provide good reviews of statistical dialog
management [Frampton and Lemon 09, Young et al. 13].

Exercises

1. It is possible to implement a dialogue system by using the mentioned tools
   and methods. All tools are freely available. Implement a dialogue system in
   domain of your choice for 3 slot dialogue.

2. Create a new language model for a specific domain and compare it with
   dictation language model. The data can be collected from crowd sourcing
   services. Other option is using existing dataset called ATIS[6] which contains
   transcribed speech.

3. Experiment with mentioned semantic parsers, write grammar or train according to your choice for the dialogue system you designed.

---

[6]https://catalog.ldc.upenn.edu/LDC95S26

Part V

Appendices

A

Displays

Jorge H. dos S. Chernicharo

The sky above the port was the color of television,
tuned to a dead channel.

—William Gibson

A.1 Fixed Displays

Research on fixed displays has been done for decades. Work in this area can be divided into two big groups: Work on single display systems, which deal mostly with effects of the size and position of the display; and work on multi-display environments, which explores effects of the number of displays, relative position between them, and comparison with single display setups. Many works also deal with the challenges of using multi-display environments, like the split-attention effect.

A.1.1 Single Display

Tan et al. [Tan et al. 03] discussed the effect of visual angles on small and large displays. They found that, for similar visual angles, although the size of the display didn't seem to affect reading comprehension, a large display did provide better spatial performance, as well as a greater sense of presence. Effects of screen size and viewing angle on user immersion were also studied by Hou et al. [Hou et al. 12]. Their results show that, when playing a virtual game, participants experienced a greater sense of physical and self-presence when using large displays. Also, players had a more favorable evaluation of the game characters when interacting in a large display. These results show the influence of the display size on emotional and behavioral responses in interactive media. Regarding input control, Wigdor et al. [Wigdor et al. 06] explored effects of display space location and control space orientation on interaction performance. Their experiment consisted of asking the users to perform several tasks in a monitor positioned in various positions around them. When asking for user preference, they found that, unsurprisingly, the users least preferred when the display is behind them. The results also showed that the most preferred interaction space was when the display was offset 45 degrees related to the input space, although the authors state that it may depend on the input device.

A.1.2   Multiple Displays

Many groups have studied how the combination of multiple displays affects user performance. Hutchings et al. [Hutchings et al. 04] found that people do use windows and other content differently between single display and multi-display environments, and also provided guidelines for measurement of user display space management activity. Colvin et al. [Colvin et al. 04] did very extensive research about the relation between productivity and the use of multi-screen displays. When comparing performance of simulated office work between groups using single screens and groups using multi-screens, they found that multi-screens scored significantly higher on measures like effectiveness, learning ease, time to productivity, and so on. The subjects using multi-screens also were able to finish the work faster and with fewer errors. Grudin [Grudin 01] found that when using dual displays, users tend to relegate second monitors to display secondary tasks, using the physical discontinuity between displays to separate two kinds of work, and thus focusing on the main task while still keeping an eye on others. Chang et al. [Chang et al. 11] compared cognitive loads and learning effects between groups using single- and dual-screen configurations to learn programming languages. Their results show that dual-screen configuration helped to significantly lower the cognitive load on the subjects.

However, while it is generally accepted that the use of multiple displays improves user performance, many groups were concerned with counter-effects of using such systems. For example, Rashid et al. [Rashid et al. 12] did a throughout review of the literature to understand the so-called split-attention effect. This effect happens when the amount of information spread across displays is overwhelming enough that windows management becomes frustrating and counterproductive. Visual separation [Tan and Czerwinski 03] also plays a role in the split attention effect, due to the fact that the users need to keep moving their focus of attention between displays, making it harder to keep track of multiple information simultaneously. Also it is known that the discontinuities caused by the physical separation of multiple displays also play a role on the split-attention effect. For example, Bi et. al. [Bi et al. 10] studied the effects of interior bezels of tiled-monitor large displays on user performance across various tasks. They found that, although interior bezels don't affect visual search time, error rate, or target selection, they are detrimental to search accuracy when objects are split across bezels, as well as to straight-tunnel steering. In fact, Bi et al. [Bi and Balakrishnan 09] found that users actually prefer to use a single high-definition wall-sized display than a dual display desktop configuration when doing daily work, since it actually minimizes the visual separation, and thus eases the split-attention effect. However, due to the relatively high cost of such high-definition large displays (and space restrictions), dual or multi-display environments are usually preferred over them.

Some groups have worked on systems that try to deal directly with the physical separation of the displays. Rekimoto et al. [Rekimoto and Saitoh 99] developed a spatially continuous workspace that allows users to smoothly interchange information among various devices. Using their proposed interaction technique, users can smoothly transfer information from one computer to another, by only knowing the physical relationship between them. Nacenta et al. [Nacenta et al. 07] go beyond Rekimoto's work, designing a seamlessly connected multi-display environment called E-conic. Using such techniques as perspective cursor [Nacenta et al. 06] and Halo [Baudisch and Rosenholtz 03], E-conic allows users to interact in the empty space between displays, allowing for a visually consistent inter-display interaction. E-conic will be treated in more detail later.

Finally, another point to be considered when using multi-display environments is that, as pointed out by Heider et al. [Heider and Kirste 07], the increase of the amount of real-state makes it increasingly hard to manage big amounts of information. In their paper, they propose computer-supported document display assignment on multi-display environments in order to improve the user experience. Biehl et. al. [Biehl and Bailey 04] also proposed a similar idea, using an interactive space window manager to enable richer collaboration among users in an interactive space. They provide an iconic map that allows the users to visually relocate information across screens of various sizes in arbitrary positions. Other groups were concerned not only with the positioning of information, but with the physical placement of the displays themselves. For example, Su et al. [Su and Bailey 05] provided some guidelines for optimal display arrangement. They suggest that displays should be separated in a horizontal plane by no more than a visual angle of 45 degrees; they should not be put behind a user (when necessary; they should be offset in relation to the user); and displays shouldn't be positioned orthogonally, but at a relative angle of 45 degrees between them.

Pointing on Multiple-Display Environments

Other groups have focused on the task of selecting and moving objects across multiple displays. As explained in a recent work by Hutchings [Hutchings 12], traditional formulations for Fitts' law equations [MacKenzie 92, MacKenzie and Buxton 92] do not accurately describe pointing tasks in multiple-display environments. He found that the difficulty of a given pointing task in a MDE is tied not only to the distance between targets and their sizes, but also to its position related to the gap between multiple displays, as well as the size of the gap itself. One of the reasons is that, differently from pointing in single-display environments, cross-display pointing does not benefit from "edge pointing" [Appert et al. 08], and as such, the traditional Fitts' law does not apply for targets near the edges between displays. Moreover, as cited by Tan et al. [Tan and Czerwinski 03] display stitching disrupts the consistency between visual movement (how far the cursor moves) and motor movement (how far the user actually moves the pointing device), further increasing the difficulty of pointing tasks.

As a result, many researchers have developed techniques aiming to facilitate cross-display pointing tasks. Benko et al. [Benko and Feiner 05] developed Multi-Monitor Mouse, that virtually simulates having multiple cursors across multiple displays, using a single pointing device. Their technique allows the user to "warp" the cursor to the same position on a different monitor, effectively reducing the travel distance compared with a traditional cursor. Baudisch et al. [Baudisch et al. 04] developed Mouse Ether, that takes into account the relative position and difference in sizes and resolutions between displays to allow the user to target across displayless space. It keeps the consistency between motor and visual space, eliminating warping effects, and allowing for increased performance of the users. Nacenta et al. [Nacenta et al. 06] improves this technique with Perspective Cursor, adding the user positional information to allow them to move the cursor through displayless space even when the relative position between the displays is not obvious, or when the user moves (and thus the perceived relative position between displays changes). Xiao et al. [Xiao et al. 11] further improves on both previous techniques, using a projector equipped with a hemispherical mirror to project the cursor when outside the displays, allowing for a direct visual feedback that improves over other techniques such as halo or stitching.

Some other groups studied not only the pointing task itself, but the effect of the pointing device used on multiple display environments. Pavlovych et al. [Pavlovych and Stuerzlinger 08] studied the effects of the input device and the screen configuration in a MDE. They performed an empirical study aiming to understand how technical restraints affect group performance in collaborative spaces, and found out that mice were slightly faster than laser pointers. They also discovered that interaction on wall displays was generally much faster than on tabletop surfaces, indicating that the position and angle of the displays play a very important role on task speed. And finally, Fukazawa et al. [Fukazawa et al. 10] compared multimodal interactions in perspective-corrected MDEs, using gestures, eye gaze, and head direction to move a cursor across multiple displays. They found out that task completion time for gesture-based interactions were the same as for perspective mouse, and that head direction offers a good alternative to reduce physical fatigue.

A.2 Portable Displays

On the other hand, advances in miniaturization technology have allowed devices to become increasingly small and powerful. As such, many groups have focused on interaction using portable devices. In particular, several research groups have explored possibilities of using handheld displays such as tablets and smartphones, and portable projectors.

A.2.1 Tablets and Smartphones

Tablet PCs (and more recently, smartphones) have traditionally been used as personal and independent devices. However, with the rapid popularization of such devices, many groups have become interested in exploring how such devices can work together, exchanging information between each other and integrating into existing workspaces. Rekimoto [Rekimoto 97] developed an early direct manipulation technique called pick-and-drop for the exchange of files between multiple portable devices. He used labeled pen devices to allow for intuitive and easy file exchange between devices. Fitzmaurice [Fitzmaurice 93] devised spatially aware palmtop computers where the position of the device was used to allow the mobile screen to show a part of a much larger workspace. This idea was further developed by Yee [Yee 03], and combined the spatially aware display with pen input, enabling two-handed interaction techniques. His idea not only expands the visual field of the device, but also the motor space, creating a much more efficient navigation method.

Multi-Display Environments with Portable Displays

By understanding the spatial relation between multiple portable displays, it is possible to set up a MDE composed only of such devices. Lyons et al. [Lyons et al. 09] used multiple tablet PCs connected over a wi-fi network to form a larger display. Over their user study, they found that the subjects enjoyed the extra real state, and were eager to engage in collaborative tasks. While Lyons' work was based on a pre-known spatial relation between devices, Schmitz et al. [Schmitz et al. 10] developed an ad-hoc mobile multi-display system that can be self calibrated. They used multiple smartphones that can be positioned in arbitrary, albeit coplanar, positions to form a MDE that support multi-touch and gestures.

A.2.2 Portable Projectors

While portable displays such as tablets and smartphones do provide a more flexible and dynamic experience compared with fixed displays, they also suffer from spatial restrictions. For example, the display in such devices is generally positioned close to the user (in handheld devices), or positioned on a surface. To overcome this limitation, many groups turned their attention to portable devices where the display can be positioned far from the user, namely portable projectors. Cauchard et al. [Cauchard et al. 11] surveyed a series of interaction designs using portable projectors. They divided the interaction techniques into two groups: interactions with the projected content, like gesture recognition or direct touch; and interactions with the projection space, which deals with the design and usage of the device itself.

About works related with interaction with the projected image, we can cite the work by Hosoi et al. [Hosoi et al. 07], who developed a "manipulation-by-projection" technique, where the users use a portable projector to navigate a robot in a game. They also developed techniques to correct the projections, as well as to stitch multiple projected images together. Song et al. [Song et al. 09] combined a mobile projector and a digital pen to allow dynamic visual overlay and manipulation of augmented content. In a later paper [Song et al. 10], they further developed the interaction with the augmented content, allowing for bi-manual interaction through the use of a mouse-shaped portable projector. This takes advantage of spatially aware independent input and output, enabling users to use simple remote commands like copy and paste. Forlines et al. [Forlines et al. 05] designed Zoom-and-Pick, a system comprised of a portable projector, a camera, and a trigger. This system allows users to zoom into the projected image, allowing for pixel-accurate pointing, which is usually very difficult on systems using portable projectors. Mistry et al. [Mistry et al. 09] developed a wearable projector-camera device, allowing for easy surface augmentation. Their system also uses color markers to allow in-the-air interaction with the projected content. Harrison et al. [Harrison et al. 11] combined a depth camera and a portable projector, allowing users to directly interact with contents projected onto their own body or other nearby surfaces.

Other groups researched how to use the portable projectors to interact with the workspace itself. Raskar et al. [Raskar et al. 04] used portable projectors to interact with the workspace via photosensitive wireless tags. When illuminated by the projector, tag data is shown to the user though direct projection, allowing for easy visualization and navigation. Molyneaux et al. [Molyneaux et al. 12] combined the use of Kinect [Zhang et al. 12] and portable projectors to allow users to interact in a spatially and geometrically aware workspace. In particular, they implemented an infrastructure-less sensing technique, allowing for a self-contained device that comprises both the sensing and the projection output.

Multi-Display Environments with Portable Projectors

Also, some groups focused on multi-device and multi-user interaction, using more than one portable projector. Cao et al. [Cao et al. 07] designed a series of interaction techniques for supporting co-located collaboration with multiple handheld projectors. They achieve this by using the flashlight metaphor, where the users can share the same workspace while still having individual control over parts of the overall virtual display. Also, Willis et al. [Willis et al. 11] designed a handheld camera-projector device that allows users to dynamically interact with each other in shared interactive spaces without the need of any external apparatus. They use hybrid/IR light projectors to track multiple independent images related to each other, allowing natural interaction between users.

A.3 Hybrid Systems

Other groups have tried to merge the benefits of both fixed and portable devices. By combining the flexibility and mobility of portable displays with the large real estate of physical displays these systems aim to create a more dynamic workspace. Researchers in this area can be divided into two groups: systems using handheld displays like smartphones and tablets, and systems using portable projectors.

A.3.1 Fixed Displays + Smartphones or Tablets

Handheld displays like smartphones and tablets provide a good method to visualize and interact with personal contents, but their reduced size is not suitable for information sharing. With this in mind, many groups developed interactive techniques to share information from portable devices into larger fixed displays. Rekimoto [Rekimoto 98] developed a multiple device approach for whiteboard based interactions. Giving handheld devices to multiple users, his technique allows them to select tools on their particular display to interact in a large workspace projected on a whiteboard. Doring et al. [Döring et al. 10] designed a digital poker table, integrating gesture based mobile phone interaction and a multi-touch surface. The mobile phones were used to show private information (such as the cards for each player), while the tabletop display was used to show shared information, such as cards and chips.

A.3.2 Fixed Displays + Portable Projectors

Finally, in recent years some groups have explored possibilities of using portable projectors on a fixed display environment. Weigel et al. [Weigel et al. 13] used the proxemic relations between portable projectors and a fixed display to create a dynamic focus+context interface. By moving the projector toward the fixed display, as the projected image gets smaller, its resolution increases, creating a high-resolution area (focus) within a lower resolution space on the fixed display (context). By moving away, as the resolution of the projected image gets lower, it becomes the context, while the image on the big display becomes the focus. Also, Chernicharo et al. [Chernicharo et al. 13] explored interaction using a portable projector on a multi-display environment. They found out that the introduction of a portable projector in a MDE can help to increase the seamlessness of the overall system, as well as to effectively and seamlessly extend the working area.

B

Creating Your Own Virtual Reality HeadSet

Karell Muller

> We are all created equal in the virtual world and we
> can use this equality to help address some of the soci-
> ological problems that society has yet to solve in the
> physical world.
>
> —Bill Gates

B.1 Introduction

Virtual reality headsets have become affordable commodity devices (e.g., Oculus Rift). Even the do-it-yourself (diy) community has developed easier ways to take your own existing phone and transform it into a stereoscopic headset. This has been helped in part by the introduction of the Oculus Rift VR developer edition. The announced Microsoft HoloLens, Durovis Dive, Razer OSVR, Samsung Galaxy VR, Archos VR, and many others now speckle the landscape. A few of the systems listed above require a specific smartphone(s). For instance the Samsung Galaxy VR requires a Samsung Galaxy Note (3 or 4) in order to work. Stereoscopic VR can now be found readily available and with several options to choose from.

When you compare VR headsets you find that the majority of the components are in fact just that — a device which has the following list of components: a gyroscope, accelerometer, a viewing screen with high-definition capabilities, a CPU, and GPU capable of rendering the appropriate frame rate, among other components. Therefore, current smartphones have most of the components listed. One of the components missing is a 45 degree focal lens, which will make the phone ready to become a VR headset. They also need the actual frame. With

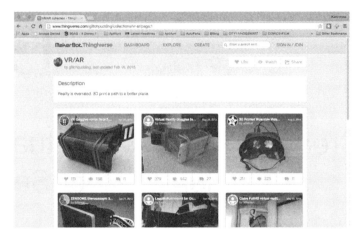

Figure B.1: MakerBot's Thingiverse.com.

the additional components, it makes sense to build a headset using a smartphone. Smartphones running iOS or Android, with at least a 5-inch screen, will be enough to make it a headset (assuming that the phone runs). While the instructions are very useful on the Internet, this chapter deals with the experience we had in our lab creating the headset.

B.2 Google Cardboard

One of the options is the Google Cardboard project is to get started by downloading the Kit from https://www.google.com/get/cardboard/downloads/cardboard_design_v1.1.zip. This package has all the needed instructions and parts lists. It is suggested that you read everything thoroughly before you begin, as working in paper craft can be a frustrating experience if the process is rush. Another option is to find digital designs for physical objects in http://www.thingiverse.com, as shown in Figure B.1.

Now when we sat down to make our own there were some things about using a material like cardboard that worried us, first of all it's basically hardened paper, it can bend and tear, and moisture and humidity are not friendly to cardboard, so it was decided that we should use something a little more resilient to the elements. The idea of using a laminated material seemed best, we struck out a quick foam board device and like the cardboard it began to tear and come apart with use. Luckily we had access to a 3D Printer, the Internet, time and patience. After a few minutes of searching online we found several candidates from which to choose. At first we decided to make a prototype Google Cardboard 3D file we found online at http://www.Thingiverse.com.

After a few minor settings corrections, we began to print our first headset. The components we could not print, we found online from Amazon.com (called *I AM CARDBOARD*[1]), which at the time retailed for approximately $15 (not including shipping of course). Next, we had to wait for the printing to finish and the parts to arrive. Having only one set of lenses, we decided that the initial printed device that resembled the folded cardboard model seen online, was found to be too flimsy, having cracked in several places and several times. Also, the placement of the lenses was fixed, which made it difficult to adjust the headset when worn. Hence we opted to go with another more rugged looking design, which turned out to be far sturdier and practical in its overall design, and most importantly the lenses where adjustable (which made a great difference). Next a few modifications were made to make the device even more practical, by fashioning a strap down system using key-rings and Velcro straps instead. This turned out to be lighter and kept the smartphone secured to the front of the goggles. This point was of paramount importance, while the headset cost just under $30 to build, the smartphone we were using cost over $500. The following is a step-by-step guide of how to build a headset, based on our experience, that can yield 3D:

What follows is a step-by-step guide for how and what we constructed using the resources available to us, w Starting after having located or creating a design to make with our 3D Printer:

1. Set up printer to output 3D object.

    (a) Connect your printer, turn it on and allow for extruders to heat up to the appropriate level. This depends on the material used. Our project used a black PLA 1.75 mm filament.

    (b) Load the Stereolithography (STL),[2], which contains the 3D model to be printed. Ensure that your file is correct; if you've downloaded the file from an online source, you may need to fix the STL file (to print correctly). It is possible to inspect the file on the NetFabb site https://netfabb.azurewebsites.net/ where there is an online tool that will fix and optimize the file for a better printing experience. Figures B.2 and B.3 show the rendering of the main headset component and accessories from an STL file.

2. Start print job.

    (a) All printers are not the same. Read the instructions for your device before beginning your print job. Additional steps may be required to ensure quality prints. We used a Rostock MAX 3D Printer, as shown in Figure B.4.

---

[1] http://goo.gl/AtNkOF.

[2] .stl file

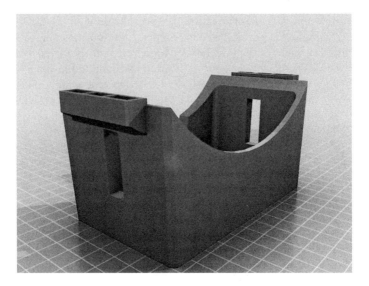

Figure B.2: Rendering of STL file (main headset component).

(b) Our printer required us to use a light fixative on the heat bed prior to beginning the process. For our particular project, we used a light with full strength hair spray to coat the heat bed. This was done in order to make the first couple of passes of the PLA filament stick to the bed and hold the initial print job in place during printing.

3. Prepare additional parts for assembly.

   (a) Since the print job took some 8+ hours, and we learned that 3D printing requires some supervision, especially when making large or complex objects (printer may fault or error).

   (b) Make use of that time to prepare the parts you will need to complete the accessories. In our case we used the time to measure out the elastic band, which would act as the head strap, and to prepare the Velcro straps for the front of the headset.

   (c) Ensure that you place the 45-degree focal lenses aside until the very end of the project (to protect them from damage).

4. Prepare tools and workbench for sanding and painting.

   (a) 3D Printers do not produce perfect objects. There is always some clean up that has to be done to the object prior to use. We recommend that you have access to tools for smoothing and polishing the object after it has finished printing.

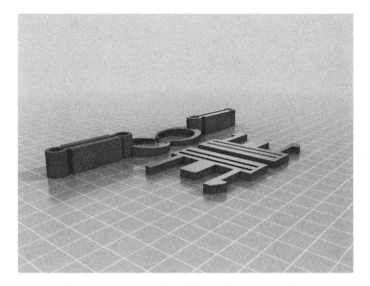

Figure B.3: Rendering of STL file (accessories).

(b) You may find the following items useful for this: fine grit sandpaper, course grit sandpaper, scissors or wire cutters, a utility knife or X-acto blade, a Dremel or other precision power tool for finishing, an epoxy or adhesive resin for touch ups or repairs.

5. Inspect freshly printed parts for flaws and defects once finished.

   (a) Avoid touching parts while on the print bed whenever possible to make sure that parts don't shift or misalign on the printer.

   (b) Once the printed parts are complete and before removal, all parts should be inspected to ensure that they are free of serious defects and warping.

6. Remove new parts from print bed.

   (a) Carefully remove the new parts from the printer. There will be several parts to collect. It is also important to allow some time for the printer to cool down between jobs.

   (b) Prepare the printer for the next part(s) to print and set the new parts aside for cleaning and sanding. Prior to assembly, make sure that all parts are done before assembling for best results.

7. Clean and sand new parts (carefully).

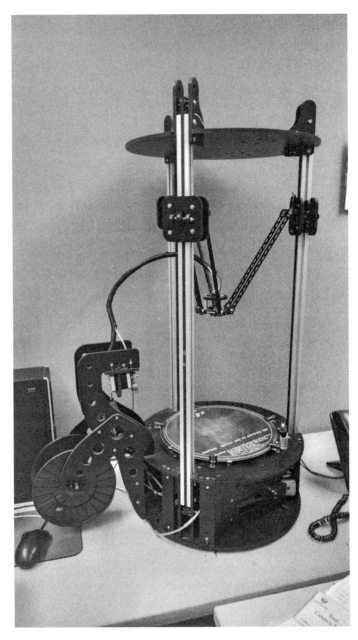

Figure B.4: Rostock MAX 3D printer.

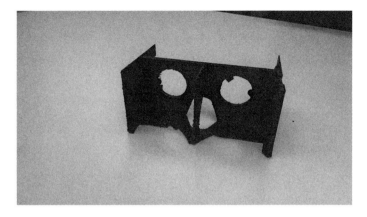

Figure B.5: Example of Bad HeadSet

(a) The parts required sometime to cool down and harden sufficiently after completion. Once the parts are ready, it is recommended to begin cleaning the excess material from the part.

(b) This stage should not be rushed. This ensures that you do not damage the printed parts, as some parts or edges may be thin and prone to crack, as shown in Figure B.5.

8. Test fit parts to ensure good fit where needed.

(a) Once you have printed all your parts and cleaned off any excess materials, you are ready to attach and insert parts as detailed in the instructions file (from the website from which you have downloaded your STL file). Figure B.6 shows some of the parts.

(b) Avoid over sanding on smaller parts, as they may end up being unusable.

(c) Make sure that the lenses fit into their respective spots correctly. Once this is confirmed, remove the lenses and store them for later use.

9. Paint parts as needed.

(a) If you decide to paint the headset, this step bears special attention. Follow all painting precautions. Ensure you are in a well-ventilated, dust-free area. Allow appropriate drying time once all parts have been painted.

(b) Please take note that all parts should be painted individually prior to assembly. Do not assemble the object and then paint it. This could ruin the object as it may have moving parts which will become fused.

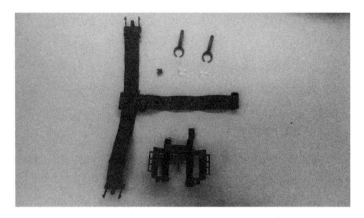

Figure B.6: Exploded View

(c) Under no circumstances should the lenses be left in the headset during the painting process.

(d) We chose to coat our headset with a rubberized spray paint. This spray acted as a sealant and gave the headset a smoother texture. This rubberized product, called "Plasti Dip" is available at most hardware stores.

(e) Allow the right amount of time between coats.

(f) Try not to use too many coats because this may cause problems with smaller parts and how they fit together.

10. Dry painted parts, clean up edges and corners of smaller parts.

(a) After the parts have been painted and allowed to dry, reassemble the device with care.

(b) Clean off any excess paint that may have pooled and dried on corners where parts will come together.

11. Assemble smaller parts first (ensure parts fit properly after painting).

12. Assemble larger components.

(a) Assemble any large parts and prepare to attach the smaller parts after the large parts fit together correctly.

(b) Pay attention to the position of parts; check to see if any parts fit oddly and adjust as necessary.

(c) Attach the head strap into the clips as per instructions. Make sure to leave excess or slack for adjustment later.

Figure B.7: Assemble headset without phone.

13. Fit headset to wearer (adjust and make sure it's comfortable and secure).

   (a) Before attaching the phone, adjust the headset to the wearer by putting it on and adjusting the straps while holding it over the face.

   (b) Adjust the lenses as needed to make sure they line up with the wearer's field of vision correctly. The lenses should not touch the user's face when adjusted correctly.

14. Insert phone into headset.

   (a) With the headset on, slide the phone onto the front of the device.

   (b) Attach the clip or strap onto one side and clinch into place.

   (c) Repeat with the second strap or clip. Make sure the phone is correctly spaced and the screen is positioned in the right orientation and distance from the edges.

   (d) Remove the entire headset and make sure the phone is in fact secured.

15. Sit down, put on headset, and enjoy the virtual world.

   Since the time of this build there have been a few recent developments to DIY VR headsets. Most recently there has been a new release by the developers at Leap Motion in integrating their motion controller into the VR headset to provide a more immersive VR experience, the Leap Motion controller when correctly attached to a VR headset allows users to see and control the virtual environment with their own hands. While this is not to say that the two work seamlessly out of the box, this new technology offers to make VR more in line with the expectations of VR systems since their inception. For additional information, please visit https://www.leapmotion.com/.

Figure B.8: Assemble headset with phone.

Finally, it is important to mention that there are 3D printing services:

- http://www.sculpteo.com/

- http://www.shapeways.com/

- http://materialise.com/

- http://www.ponoko.com/3d-printing

Bibliography

[3D 14] OGRE 3D. "Intermediate Tutorial 3 - Mouse Picking (3D Object Selection) and SceneQuery Masks (Part 2 of 2).", 2014. [Online; accessed 23-February-2015]. Available online (http://www.ogre3d.org/tikiwiki/tiki-index.php?page=Intermediate+Tutorial+3&structure=Tutorials).

[3M 13] 3M. "Touch Technology Brief : Projected Capacitive Technology." Technical Report 3M PCT TECH BRIEF-1013, 3M, 2013.

[5DT 14] 5DT. "5DT Data Glove 5 Ultra." 2014. [Online; accessed 5-January-2015]. Available online (http://www.5dt.com/products/pdataglove5u.html).

[Abadi and Gowen 04] R V Abadi and E Gowen. "Characteristics of saccadic intrusions." *Vision research* 44:23 (2004), 2675–2690.

[Abásolo and Della 07] María J Abásolo and José Mariano Della. "Magallanes: 3D navigation for everybody." In *Proceedings of the 5th International Conference on Computer Graphics and Interactive Techniques in Australia and Southeast Asia, GRAPHITE '07*, p. 135. ACM, 2007.

[Accot and Zhai 97] Johnny Accot and Shumin Zhai. "Beyond Fitts' law: models for trajectory-based HCI tasks." In *CHI '97: Proceedings of the ACM SIGCHI Conference on Human Factors in Computing Systems*, pp. 295–302. New York, New York, USA: ACM, 1997.

[Adafruit 10] Inc. Adafruit. "WE HAVE A WINNER - Open Kinect driver(s) released." 2010. [Online; accessed 22-February-2015]. Available online (http://goo.gl/H9o2bF).

[Akenine-Möller et al. 08] Tomas Akenine-Möller, Eric Haines, and Naty Hoffman. *Real-Time Rendering, Third*. A K Peters, Ltd., 2008.

[Allen et al. 06] James Allen, George Ferguson, Nate Blaylock, Donna Byron, Nathanael Chambers, Myroslava Dzikovska, Lucian Galescu, and Mary Swift. "Chester: towards a personal medication advisor." *J. of Biomedical Informatics* 39:5 (2006), 500–513. Available online (http://dx.doi.org/10.1016/j.jbi.2006.02.004).

[Andujar and Argelaguet 06] C Andujar and F Argelaguet. "Friction surfaces: scaled ray-casting manipulation for interacting with 2D GUIs." In *EGVE'06: Proceedings of the 12th Eurographics conference on Virtual Environments*. Eurographics Association, 2006.

[Anthony and Wobbrock 10] L Anthony and J Wobbrock. "A lightweight multistroke recognizer for user interface prototypes." In *Proceedings of Graphics Interface 2010, GI'10*. Toronto, ON, 2010.

[Anthony and Wobbrock 12] Lisa Anthony and Jacob O Wobbrock. "$N-protractor: a fast and accurate multistroke recognizer." In *Proceedings of Graphics Interface 2012, GI '12*. Canadian Information Processing Society, 2012.

[Anthony et al. 12] Lisa Anthony, Quincy Brown, Jaye Nias, Berthel Tate, and Shreya Mohan. "Interaction and recognition challenges in interpreting children's touch and gesture input on mobile devices." In *the 2012 ACM international conference*, p. 225. New York, New York, USA: ACM Press, 2012.

[Anthony et al. 13a] Lisa Anthony, Quincy Brown, Jaye Nias, and Berthel Tate. "Examining the need for visual feedback during gesture interaction on mobile touchscreen devices for kids." In *IDC '13: Proceedings of the 12th International Conference on Interaction Design and Children*, pp. 157–164. New York, New York, USA: ACM, 2013.

[Anthony et al. 13b] Lisa Anthony, Quincy Brown, Berthel Tate, Jaye Nias, Robin Brewer, and Germaine Irwin. "Designing smarter touch-based interfaces for educational contexts." *Personal and Ubiquitous Computing* 18:6 (2013), 1471–1483.

[Apostolellis et al. 12] P Apostolellis, B Laha, and Da Bowman. "A Gaming Interface Using Body Gestures for Collaborative Navigation." In *IEEE Symposium on 3D User Interfaces (3DUI), 2012, 3DUI '12*, 2012.

[Appert et al. 08] Caroline Appert, Olivier Chapuis, and Michel Beaudouin-Lafon. "Evaluation of Pointing Performance on Screen Edges." In *Proceedings of the Working Conference on Advanced Visual Interfaces, AVI '08*, pp. 119–126. New York, NY, USA: ACM, 2008. Available online (http://doi.acm.org/10.1145/1385569.1385590).

[Apple Inc., Elias, John, Greer, Haggerty, Myra, Mary, Westerman, Wayne, Carl 07] Apple Inc., Elias, John, Greer, Haggerty, Myra, Mary, Westerman, Wayne, Carl. "Multi-touch gesture dictionary." US Patent 7,840,912, 2007.

[Arduino 15a] Arduino. "Arduino AttachInterrupt.", 2015. [Online; accessed 25-February-2015]. Available online (http://www.arduino.cc/en/Reference/AttachInterrupt).

[Arduino 15b] Arduino. "Arduino Development Environment.", 2015. [Online; accessed 15-February-2015]. Available online (http://arduino.cc/en/Guide/Environment).

[Arduino 15c] Arduino. "Arduino Home Page.", 2015. [Online; accessed 12-February-2015]. Available online (http://arduino.cc).

[Arduino 15d] Arduino. "Arduino Uno.", 2015. [Online; accessed 13-February-2015]. Available online (http://arduino.cc/en/Main/ArduinoBoardUno).

[Arduino 15e] Arduino. "Getting Started with Arduino.", 2015. [Online; accessed 13-February-2015]. Available online (http://arduino.cc/en/Guide/HomePage).

[Arduino 15f] Arduino. "Language Reference.", 2015. [Online; accessed 15-February-2015]. Available online (http://arduino.cc/en/Reference/HomePage).

[Arduino 15g] Arduino. "Ping Ultrasonic Range Finder.", 2015. [Online; accessed 14-February-2015]. Available online (http://arduino.cc/en/Tutorial/ping).

[Arduino 15h] Arduino. "Serial Communication.", 2015. [Online; accessed 13-February-2015]. Available online (http://arduino.cc/en/Main/Products?from=Main.Hardware).

[Aretz and Wickens 92] Anthony J Aretz and Christopher D Wickens. "The Mental Rotation of Map Displays." *Human Performance* 5:4 (1992), 303–328.

[Argelaguet and Andujar 09a] F Argelaguet and C Andujar. "Efficient 3D Pointing Selection in Cluttered Virtual Environments." *Computer Graphics and Applications, IEEE* 29:6 (2009), 34–43.

[Argelaguet and Andújar 09b] Ferran Argelaguet and Carlos Andújar. "Visual feedback techniques for virtual pointing on stereoscopic displays." In *Proceedings of the 16th ACM Symposium on Virtual Reality Software and Technology - VRST '09*, p. 163. New York, New York, USA: ACM Press, 2009.

[Argelaguet and Andujar 13] F. Argelaguet and C. Andujar. "A survey of 3D object selection techniques for virtual environments." *Computers & Graphics* 37:3 (2013), 121 – 136.

[Arvo 94] James Arvo. *Graphics Gems II*. Morgan Kaufmann, 1994.

[Astur et al. 98] R S Astur, M L Ortiz, and R J Sutherland. "A characterization of performance by men and women in a virtual Morris water task: A large and reliable sex difference." *Behavioural brain research*.

[Aylett et al. 07] Ruth Aylett, Marco Vala, Pedro Sequeira, and Ana Paiva. "FearNot! An Emergent Narrative Approach to Virtual Dramas for Anti-Bullying Education." In *Virtual Storytelling. Using Virtual Reality Technologies for Storytelling*, LNCS 4871, edited by M Cavazza and S Donikian, LNCS 4871, pp. 202–205. Berlin Heidelberg: Springer-Verlag, 2007.

[Balaa et al. 14] E Balaa, M Raynal, Y B Issa, and E Dubois. "Classification of Interaction Techniques in the 3D Virtual Environment on Mobile Devices." *Virtual* 8525: Chapter 1 (2014), 3–13.

[Balakrishnan and Hinckley 99] Ravin Balakrishnan and Ken Hinckley. "The role of kinesthetic reference frames in two-handed input performance." In *UIST '99: Proceedings of the 12th Annual ACM Symposium on User Interface Software and Technology*, pp. 171–178. New York, New York, USA: ACM, 1999.

[Balakrishnan and Hinckley 00] Ravin Balakrishnan and Ken Hinckley. "Symmetric bimanual interaction." In *CHI '00: Proceedings of the SIGCHI Conference on Human Factors in Computing Systems*, pp. 33–40. New York, New York, USA: ACM, 2000.

[Balakrishnan and Patel 98] Ravin Balakrishnan and Pranay Patel. "The PadMouse: facilitating selection and spatial positioning for the non-dominant hand." In *CHI '98: Proceedings of the SIGCHI Conference on Human Factors in Computing Systems*, pp. 9–16. New York, New York, USA: ACM Press/Addison-Wesley Publishing Co., 1998.

[Balakrishnan et al. 97] Ravin Balakrishnan, Thomas Baudel, Gordon Kurtenbach, and George Fitzmaurice. *The Rockin'Mouse: integral 3D manipulation on a plane*. ACM, 1997.

[Balakrishnan et al. 99] Ravin Balakrishnan, George Fitzmaurice, Gordon Kurtenbach, and William Buxton. "Digital tape drawing." In *UIST '99: Proceedings of the 12th Annual ACM Symposium on User Interface Software and Technology*. ACM, 1999.

[Ball and Vardalas 94] Norman R Ball and John N Vardalas. *Ferranti-Packard*. Pioneers in Canadian Electrical Manufacturing, McGill-Queen's Press - MQUP, 1994.

[Banerjee et al. 11] Amartya Banerjee, Jesse Burstyn, Audrey Girouard, and Roel Verte-gaal. "Pointable: an in-air pointing technique to manipulate out-of-reach targets on tabletops." In *ITS '11: Proceedings of the ACM International Conference on Interactive Tabletops and Surfaces*, p. 11. New York, New York, USA: ACM, 2011.

[Barreto et al. 07a] Armando Barreto, Naphtali Rishe, J Zhai, and Ying Gao. "Potential of Pupil Diameter Monitoring for the Detection of Affective Changes in Human-Computer Interaction." In *LACCEI'2007: Fifth LACCEI International Latin American and Caribbean Conference for Engineering and Technology*, pp. 2B A1–A11. Tampico, México, 2007.

[Barreto et al. 07b] Armando Barreto, J Zhai, Naphtali Rishe, and Ying Gao. "Measure-ment of Pupil Diameter Variations as a Physiological Indicator of the Affective State in a Computer User." *Biomedical Sciences Instrumentation* 43 (2007), 146–151.

[Baudel and Beaudouin-Lafon 93] Thomas Baudel and Michel Beaudouin-Lafon. "Cha-rade: remote control of objects using free-hand gestures." *Communications of the ACM* 36:7 (1993), 28–35.

[Baudisch and Rosenholtz 03] Patrick Baudisch and Ruth Rosenholtz. "Halo: A Technique for Visualizing Off-Screen Objects." In *Proceedings of the SIGCHI Conference on Human Factors in Computing Systems, CHI '03*, pp. 481–488. New York, NY, USA: ACM, 2003. Available online (http://doi.acm.org/10.1145/642611.642695).

[Baudisch et al. 04] Patrick Baudisch, Edward Cutrell, Ken Hinckley, and Robert Gruen. "Mouse ether: accelerating the acquisition of targets across multi-monitor displays." In *CHI '04 Extended Abstracts on Human Factors in Computing Systems, CHI EA '04*, pp. 1379–1382. New York, NY, USA: ACM, 2004. Available online (http://doi.acm.org/10.1145/985921.986069).

[Beheshti et al. 12] Elham Beheshti, Anne Van Devender, and Michael Horn. "Touch, click, navigate: comparing tabletop and desktop interaction for map navigation tasks." In *Proceedings of the 2012 ACM international conference on Interactive tabletops and surfaces, ITS '12*, pp. 205–214. ACM, 2012.

[Benko and Feiner 05] Hrvoje Benko and Steven Feiner. "Multi-monitor mouse." In *CHI '05 Extended Abstracts on Human Factors in Computing Systems, CHI EA '05*, pp. 1208–1211. New York, NY, USA: ACM, 2005. Available online (http://doi.acm.org/10.1145/1056808.1056878).

[Benko and Feiner 07] H. Benko and S. Feiner. "Balloon Selection: A Multi-Finger Tech-nique for Accurate Low-Fatigue 3D Selection." In *Proceedings of the Symposium on 3D User Interfaces (3DUI)*, pp. 79–86, 2007.

[Benko and Wigdor 10] Hrvoje Benko and Daniel Wigdor. "Imprecision, Inaccuracy, and Frustration: The Tale of Touch Input." In *Tabletops - Horizontal Interactive Displays, Human-Computer Interaction Series*, edited by Christian Müller-Tomfelde, pp. 249–275. Springer London, 2010.

[Benko et al. 06] H Benko, AD Wilson, and P Baudisch. "Precise selection techniques for multi-touch screens." In *Proceedings of the SIGCHI Conference on Human Factors in Computing Systems, CHI '06*, pp. 1263–1272. ACM, 2006.

[Berg et al. 00] Mark Berg, Marc Kreveld, Mark Overmars, and Otfried Schwarzkopf. *Computational Geometry*, Second edition. Berlin, Heidelberg: Springer, 2000.

[Berthoz 00] Alain Berthoz. *The Brain's Sense of Movement*. Harvard University Press, 2000.

[Bhattacharyya et al. 13] S S Bhattacharyya, E F Deprettere, R Leupers, and J Takala. *Handbook of signal processing systems*. Springer New York, 2013.

[Bi and Balakrishnan 09] Xiaojun Bi and Ravin Balakrishnan. "Comparing usage of a large high-resolution display to single or dual desktop displays for daily work." In *Proceedings of the SIGCHI Conference on Human Factors in Computing Systems, CHI '09*, pp. 1005–1014. New York, NY, USA: ACM, 2009. Available online (http: //doi.acm.org/10.1145/1518701.1518855).

[Bi et al. 10] Xiaojun Bi, Seok-Hyung Bae, and Ravin Balakrishnan. "Effects of interior bezels of tiled-monitor large displays on visual search, tunnel steering, and target selection." In *Proceedings of the SIGCHI Conference on Human Factors in Computing Systems, CHI '10*, pp. 65–74. New York, NY, USA: ACM, 2010. Available online (http://doi.acm.org/10.1145/1753326.1753337).

[Bi et al. 13] Xiaojun Bi, Yang Li, and Shumin Zhai. "Fitts law: modeling finger touch with Fitts' law." In *CHI '13: Proceedings of the SIGCHI Conference on Human Factors in Computing Systems*. ACM, 2013.

[Bickmore and Giorgino 06] Timothy Bickmore and Toni Giorgino. "Health dialog systems for patients and consumers." *Journal of Biomedical Informatics* 39:5 (2006), 556–571.

[Bickmore and Gruber 10] Timothy Bickmore and Amanda Gruber. "Relational agents in clinical psychiatry." *Harvard review of psychiatry* 18:2 (2010), 119–30. Available online (http://www.ncbi.nlm.nih.gov/pubmed/20235777).

[Bickmore et al. 05] Timothy Bickmore, Amanda Gruber, and Rosalind Picard. "Establishing the computer – patient working alliance in automated health behavior change interventions." *Patient Education and Counseling* 59 (2005), 21–30.

[Bickmore et al. 09] Timothy Wallace Bickmore, Laura M Pfeifer, and Brian W Jack. "Taking the Time to Care : Empowering Low Health Literacy Hospital Patients with Virtual Nurse Agents." In *Proceedings of the 27th International ACM Conference on Human Factors in Computing Systems (CHI'09)*, pp. 1265–1274. New York: ACM, 2009.

[Bickmore et al. 10] Timothy W. Bickmore, Kathryn Puskar, Elizabeth a. Schlenk, Laura M. Pfeifer, and Susan M. Sereika. "Maintaining reality: Relational agents for antipsychotic medication adherence." *Interacting with Computers* 22:4 (2010), 276–288. Available online (http://linkinghub.elsevier.com/retrieve/pii/S095354381000010X).

[Bickmore et al. 11] Timothy W Bickmore, Daniel Schulman, and Candace L Sidner. "A reusable framework for health counseling dialogue systems based on a behavioral medicine ontology." *Journal of biomedical informatics* 44:2 (2011), 183–97. Available online (http://www.pubmedcentral.nih.gov/articlerender.fcgi?artid=3063319&tool= pmcentrez&rendertype=abstract).

[Bickmore 05] T.W. Bickmore. "Establishing and maintaining long-term human-computer relationships." *ACM Transactions on Computer-Human* 12:2 (2005), 293–327. Available online (http://dl.acm.org/citation.cfm?id=1067860.1067867).

[Biehl and Bailey 04] Jacob T. Biehl and Brian P. Bailey. "ARIS: an interface for application relocation in an interactive space." In *Proceedings of Graphics Interface 2004, GI '04*, pp. 107–116. School of Computer Science, University of Waterloo, Waterloo, Ontario, Canada: Canadian Human-Computer Communications Society, 2004. Available online (http://dl.acm.org/citation.cfm?id=1006058.1006072).

[Bier et al. 93] Eric A. Bier, Maureen C. Stone, Ken Pier, William Buxton, and Tony D. DeRose. "Toolglass and Magic Lenses: The See-through Interface." In *Proceedings of the 20th Annual Conference on Computer Graphics and Interactive Techniques, SIGGRAPH '93*, pp. 73–80. ACM, 1993.

[Binstead 07] Ronald Binstead. "A Brief History of Projected Capacitance Development by Binstead Designs.", 2007. [Online; accessed 5-February-2015]. Available online (http://binsteaddesigns.com/history1.html).

[Blackman 13] Sue Blackman. *Beginning 3D Game Development with Unity 4: All-in-one, multi-platform game development*, Second edition. Apress, 2013.

[Blanke and Metzinger 09] Olaf Blanke and Thomas Metzinger. "Full-body illusions and minimal phenomenal selfhood." *Trends in Cognitive Sciences* 13:1 (2009), 7–13.

[Blaskó and Feiner 04] Gábor Blaskó and Steven Feiner. "Single-handed interaction techniques for multiple pressure-sensitive strips." In *Extended Abstracts of the 2004 Conference on Human Factors and Computing Systems - CHI '04*, p. 1461. New York, New York, USA: ACM Press, 2004.

[Blumenstein et al. 03] M Blumenstein, B Verma, and H Basli. "A novel feature extraction technique for the recognition of segmented handwritten characters." In *Seventh International Conference Proceedings on Document Analysis and Recognition, 2003*, pp. 137–141. IEEE Computer Society, 2003.

[Blundell and Schwarz 00] Barry G Blundell and Adam J Schwarz. *Volumetric Three-dimensional Display Systems*. Wiley-IEEE Press, 2000.

[Boer et al. 03] W Boer, A Abileah, P Green, and T Larsson. "56.3: Active Matrix LCD with Integrated Optical Touch Screen - Boer - 2012 - SID Symposium Digest of Technical Papers - Wiley Online Library." *SID Symposium Digest of Technical Papers* 34 (2003), 1494–1497.

[Bohus and Rudnicky 09] Dan Bohus and Alexander I. Rudnicky. "The RavenClaw dialog management framework: Architecture and systems." *Computer Speech & Language* 23:3 (2009), 332 – 361. Available online (http://www.sciencedirect.com/science/article/pii/S0885230808000545).

[Bolt 80] Richard A Bolt. ""Put-that-there": Voice and gesture at the graphics interface." In *SIGGRAPH '80: Proceedings of the 7th Annual Conference on Computer Graphics and Interactive Techniques*, pp. 262–270. New York, New York, USA: ACM, 1980.

[Bono et al. 82] P R Bono, J L Encarnacao, F R A Hopgood, and P J W ten Hagen. "GKS The First Graphics Standard." *IEEE Computer Graphics and Applications* 2:5 (1982), 9–23.

[Bos et al. 03] J. Bos, E. Klein, O. Lemon, and T. Oka. "DIPPER: Description and formalisation of an information-state update dialogue system architecture." In *4th SIGdial Workshop on Discourse and Dialogue*, pp. 115–124, 2003.

[Botsch et al. 10] Mario Botsch, Leif Kobbelt, Mark Pauly, Pierre Alliez, and Bruno Levy. *Polygon Mesh Processing*. CRC Press, 2010.

[Boukricha and Becker-Asano 07] Hana Boukricha and Christian Becker-Asano. "Simulating empathy for the virtual human max." *on Emotion and Computing in conj.*

[Bowman and Hodges 97] Doug A Bowman and Larry F Hodges. "An evaluation of techniques for grabbing and manipulating remote objects in immersive virtual environments." In *I3D '97: Proceedings of the 1997 symposium on Interactive 3D graphics*. ACM, 1997.

[Bowman et al. 97] D A Bowman, D Koller, and L F Hodges. "Travel in immersive virtual environments: an evaluation of viewpoint motion control techniques." In *Virtual Reality Annual International Symposium, 1997*, pp. 45–52. IEEE Computer Society Press, 1997.

[Bowman et al. 98] D A Bowman, J Wineman, L F Hodges, and D Allison. "Designing animal habitats within an immersive VE." *Computer Graphics and Applications, IEEE* 18:5 (1998), 9–13.

[Bowman et al. 99a] Doug A Bowman, Elizabeth Thorpe Davis, Larry F Hodges, and Albert N Badre. "Maintaining Spatial Orientation during Travel in an Immersive Virtual Environment." *Presence* 8:6 (1999), 618–631.

[Bowman et al. 99b] Doug A Bowman, Donald B Johnson, and Larry F Hodges. "Testbed evaluation of virtual environment interaction techniques." In *Proceedings of the ACM Symposium on Virtual Reality Software and Technology, VRST '99*, pp. 26–33. ACM, 1999.

[Bowman et al. 01] D Bowman, C Wingrave, J Campbell, and V Ly. "Using Pinch Gloves™for both natural and abstract interaction techniques in virtual environments." In *Usability Evaluation and Interface Design: Cognitive Engineering, Intelligent Agents, and Virtual Reality*, edited by M.J. Smith, R.J. Koubek, G. Salvendy, and D. Harris, pp. 629–633. Taylor & Francis, 2001.

[Bowman et al. 04] D A Bowman, E Kruijff, J J LaViola, Jr, and I Poupyrev. *3D user interfaces: theory and practice*. Addison-Wesley Professional, 2004.

[Bowman et al. 06] DA Bowman, J Chen, CA Wingrave, A Ray, NF Polys, Q Li, Y Haciahmetoglu, and JS Kim. "New directions in 3D user interfaces." *International Journal of Virtual Reality* 5:2 (2006), 3–14.

[Bowman et al. 12] D A Bowman, R P McMahan, and E D Ragan. "Questioning naturalism in 3D user interfaces." *Communications of the ACM* 55:9 (2012), 78.

[Boxall] A. Boxall. "We learned how to control a Glass app with our mind (but it's kind of traumatic)." http://www.digitaltrends.com/mobile/mindrdr-controlling-google-glass-with-your-mind/. [Online; accessed on Mar. 04, 2015].

[Boyali and Kavakli 11] A Boyali and M Kavakli. "3D and 6 DOF user input platform for computer vision applications and virtual reality." In *Symposium on Innovations in Intelligent Systems and Applications (INISTA), 2011 International, INISTA '11*, pp. 258–263, 2011.

[Bradley and Lang 99] M M Bradley and P J Lang. "International Affective Digitized Sounds (AIDS): Stimuli, Instruction Manual and Affective Ratings." Technical report, University of Florida, 1999.

[Brandl et al. 08] Peter Brandl, Clifton Forlines, Daniel Wigdor, Michael Haller, and Chia Shen. "Combining and measuring the benefits of bimanual pen and direct-touch interaction on horizontal interfaces." In *AVI '08: Proceedings of the Working Conference on Advanced Visual Interfaces*. ACM, 2008.

[Bressloff and Wood 98] P Bressloff and C Wood. "Spontaneous oscillations in a nonlinear delayed-feedback shunting model of the pupil light reflex." *Physical review E* 58:3 (1998), 3597–3605.

[Brown and Anthony 12] Q Brown and L Anthony. "Toward comparing the touchscreen interaction patterns of kids and adults." In *CHI EIST*. ACM SIGCHI EIST Workshop 2012, 2012.

[Brown and Hwang 12] Robert Grover Brown and Patrick Y C Hwang. *Introduction to Random Signals and Applied Kalman Filtering with MATLAB Exercises, 4th Edition*. Wiley Global Education, 2012.

[Bruder et al. 12] G. Bruder, F. Steinicke, P. Wieland, and M. Lappe. "Tuning Self-Motion Perception in Virtual Reality with Visual Illusions." *Transactions on Visualization and Computer Graphics (TVCG)* 18:4.

[Brunner et al. 13] Clemens Brunner, G Andreoni, L Bianchi, Benjamin Blankertz, C. Breitwieser, S. Kanoh, C. A. Kothe, A. Lecuyer, S Makeig, J. Mellinger, P. Perego, Y. Renard, Gerwin Schalk, I.P. Susila, B Venthur, G.R. Mueller-Putz, B.Z. Allison, S. Dunne, R. Leeb, J. Del R. Millán, and A. Nijholt. *BCI Software Platforms*, Chapter 16, pp. 303–331. Biological and Medical Physics, 2013.

[Buchanan et al. 13] Sarah Buchanan, Bourke Floyd, Will Holderness, and Joseph J LaViola. "Towards user-defined multi-touch gestures for 3D objects." In *the 2013 ACM international conference*, pp. 231–240. New York, New York, USA: ACM Press, 2013.

[Burdea and Coiffet 03] Grigore C Burdea and Philippe Coiffet. *Virtual Reality Technology*. John Wiley & Sons, 2003.

[Burigat and Chittaro 07] Stefano Burigat and Luca Chittaro. "Navigation in 3D virtual environments: Effects of user experience and location-pointing navigation aids." *International Journal of Human-Computer Studies* 65:11.

[Bush 45] Vannevar Bush. "As we may think." *Atlantic Monthly*.

[Bush 96] Vannevar Bush. "As we may think." *Interactions* 3:2.

[Butler and Amant 04] Colin G Butler and Robert St Amant. "HabilisDraw DT: a bimanual tool-based direct manipulation drawing environment." *CHI EA '04: CHI '04 Extended Abstracts on Human Factors in Computing Systems*, p. 1301.

[Butler 92] R F Butler. *Paleomagnetism: magnetic domains to geologic terranes.* Blackwell Scientific Publications, 1992.

[Buxton and Myers 86] W Buxton and B Myers. "A study in two-handed input." In *Proceedings of the SIGCHI Conference on Human Factors in Computing Systems, CHI '86*, pp. 321–326. ACM, 1986.

[Buxton 68] W Buxton. "Human Input To Computer Systems: Theory, Techniques and Technology.", 1968. [Online; accessed 3-January-2015]. Available online (www.billbuxton.com/inputManuscript.html).

[Buxton 83] William Buxton. "Lexical and pragmatic considerations of input structures." *SIGGRAPH Computer Graphics* 17:1 (1983), 31–37.

[Buxton 90] W Buxton. "A three-state model of graphical input." *Human-computer interaction-INTERACT '90* 90 (1990), 449–456.

[Buxton 08] B Buxton. "The long nose of innovation." *Insight.*

[Buxton 10] B Buxton. *Sketching User Experiences: Getting the Design Right and the Right Design.* Focal Press, Morgan Kaufmann, 2010.

[Buxton 11] William Buxton. "Human Input to Computer Systems: Theories, Techniques and Technology.", 2011. Available online (http://www.billbuxton.com/inputManuscript.html).

[Buxton 13] Bill Buxton. "Video: Bill Buxton at TechFest2013: Designing for Ubiquitous Computing.", 2013. [Online; accessed 2-February-2015]. Available online (https://www.youtube.com/watch?v=ZQJIwjlaPCQ).

[Buxton 14] W Buxton. "Buxton Collection.", 2014. [Online; accessed 3-January-2015]. Available online (research.microsoft.com/en-us/um/people/bibuxton/buxtoncollection/).

[Calton and Taube 09] Jeffrey L Calton and Jeffrey S Taube. "Where am I and how will I get there from here? A role for posterior parietal cortex in the integration of spatial information and route planning." *Neurobiology of Learning and Memory* 91:2 (2009), 186–196.

[Camiciottoli et al. 98] R Camiciottoli, J M Corrifoni, A D Bimbo, E Vicario, and D Lucarella. "3D navigation of geographic data sets." *MultiMedia, IEEE* 5:2 (1998), 29–41.

[Campbell et al. 08] Bryan A Campbell, Katharine R O'Brien, Michael D Byrne, and Benjamin J Bachman. "Fitts' Law Predictions with an Alternative Pointing Device (Wiimote®)." *Proceedings of the Human Factors and Ergonomics Society Annual Meeting* 52:19 (2008), 1321–1325.

[Campbell 03] W H Campbell. *Introduction to geomagnetic fields.* Cambridge University Press, 2003.

[Cao et al. 07] Xiang Cao, Clifton Forlines, and Ravin Balakrishnan. "Multi-user interaction using handheld projectors." In *Proceedings of the 20th Annual ACM Symposium on User Interface Software and Technology, UIST '07*, pp. 43–52. New York, NY, USA: ACM, 2007. Available online (http://doi.acm.org/10.1145/1294211.1294220).

[Cao et al. 08] Xiang Cao, A.D Wilson, R Balakrishnan, K Hinckley, and S.E Hudson. "ShapeTouch: Leveraging contact shape on interactive surfaces." *Horizontal Interactive Human Computer Systems, 2008. 3rd IEEE International Workshop on TABLETOP 2008*, pp. 129–136.

[Card et al. 80] Stuart K Card, Thomas P Moran, and Allen Newell. "The keystroke-level model for user performance time with interactive systems." *Communications of the ACM* 23:7 (1980), 396–410.

[Card et al. 83] Stuart K Card, Allen Newell, and Thomas P Moran. *The Psychology of Human-Computer Interaction*. Mahwah, New Jersey: Lawrence Erlbaum Associates, Inc. and CRC Press, 1983.

[Card et al. 91] Stuart K Card, Jock D Mackinlay, and George G Robertson. "A morphological analysis of the design space of input devices." *Transactions on Information Systems (TOIS* 9:2.

[Carpenter 88] Roger H S Carpenter. *Movements of the eyes*. Pion Ltd, 1988.

[Carter et al. 13a] Tom Carter, Sue Ann Seah, Benjamin Long, Bruce Drinkwater, and Sriram Subramanian. "UltraHaptics: multi-point mid-air haptic feedback for touch surfaces." In *UIST '13: Proceedings of the 26th Annual ACM Symposium on User Interface Software and Technology*. ACM, 2013.

[Carter et al. 13b] Tom Carter, Sue Ann Seah, Benjamin Long, Bruce Drinkwater, and Sriram Subramanian. "UltraHaptics: Multi-point Mid-Air Haptic Feedback for Touch Surfaces." In *Proceedings of the Symposium on User Interface Software and Technology (UIST)*, pp. 505–514, 2013.

[Casalta et al. 99] Didier Casalta, Yves Guiard, and Michel Beaudouin-Lafon. "Evaluating two-handed input techniques: rectangle editing and navigation." *CHI EA '99: CHI '99 Extended Abstracts on Human Factors in Computing Systems*, pp. 236–237.

[Cashion et al. 12] J Cashion, C Wingrave, and J J LaViola. "Dense and Dynamic 3D Selection for Game-Based Virtual Environments." *Visualization and Computer Graphics, IEEE Transactions on* 18:4 (2012), 634–642.

[Cassell and Bickmore 03] Justine Cassell and Timothy Bickmore. "Negotiated Collusion : Modeling Social Language and its Relationship Effects in Intelligent Agents." *User Modeling and UserAdapted Interaction* 13:1-2 (2003), 89–132. Available online (http://www.springerlink.com/index/KT75146J03757124.pdf).

[Catizone et al. 08] Roberta Catizone, Alexiei Dingli, Hugo Pinto, and Yorick Wilks. "Information Extraction Tools and Methods for Understanding Dialogue in a Companion." In *LREC*, 2008.

[Catuhe 12] David Catuhe. *Programming with the Kinect for Windows Software Development Kit*. Microsoft Press, 2012.

[Cauchard et al. 11] Jessica R Cauchard, Mike Fraser, and Sriram Subramanian. "Designing mobile projectors to support interactivity." In *CHI 2011: Mobile and Personal Projection Workshop*, 2011. Other page information: - Conference Proceedings/Title of Journal: CHI 2011: Mobile and Personal Projection workshop Other identifier: 2001350.

[Chai and Jacobs 10] X J Chai and L F Jacobs. "Effects of cue types on sex differences in human spatial memory." *Behavioural brain research.*

[Chan et al. 10] Li-Wei Chan, Hui-Shan Kao, Mike Y. Chen, Ming-Sui Lee, Jane Hsu, and Yi-Ping Hung. "Touching the void: direct-touch interaction for intangible displays." In *Proceedings of the Conference on Human Factors in Computing Systems (CHI)*, pp. 2625–2634, 2010.

[Chang and Moura 10] H H Chang and JMF Moura. "Biomedical signal processing." *Biomedical Engineering and Design Handbook.*

[Chang et al. 11] Ting-Wen Chang, Jenq-Muh Hsu, and Pao-Ta Yu. "A Comparison of Single- and Dual-Screen Environment in Programming Language: Cognitive Loads and Learning Effects." *Educational Technology and Society* 14:2 (2011), 188–200. Available online (http://dblp.uni-trier.de/db/journals/ets/ets14.html#ChangHY11).

[Chang 11] L Chang. "A Nested Petri Net Framework for Modeling and Analyzing Multi-Agent Systems." Ph.D. thesis, Florida International University, 2011.

[Chassaing and Reay 11] Rulph Chassaing and Donald Reay. *Digital Signal Processing and Applications with the TMS320C6713 and TMS320C6416 DSK*, Second edition. Topics in Digital Signal Processing, Hoboken, NJ, USA: John Wiley & Sons, 2011.

[Chatty 94a] Stéphane Chatty. "Extending a graphical toolkit for two-handed interaction." In *UIST '94: Proceedings of the 7th Annual ACM Symposium on User Interface Software and Technology*, pp. 195–204. New York, New York, USA: ACM, 1994.

[Chatty 94b] Stéphane Chatty. "Issues and experience in designing two-handed interaction." In *CHI '94: Conference Companion on Human Factors in Computing Systems*, pp. 253–254. New York, New York, USA: ACM, 1994.

[Chen and Bowman 09] J Chen and D Bowman. "Domain-Specific Design of 3D Interaction Techniques: An Approach for Designing Useful Virtual Environment Applications." *Presence* 18:5 (2009), 370–386.

[Chen and Stanney 99] J Chen and K Stanney. "A Theoretical Model of Wayfinding in Virtual Environments: Proposed Strategies for Navigational Aiding." *Presence* 8:6 (1999), 671–685.

[Chen et al. 88] Michael Chen, S. Joy Mountford, and Abigail Sellen. "A Study in Interactive 3-D Rotation Using 2-D Control Devices." In *Proceedings of the 15th Annual Conference on Computer Graphics and Interactive Techniques*, SIGGRAPH '88, pp. 121–129. ACM, 1988.

[Chen et al. 07] J Y C Chen, E C Haas, and M J Barnes. "Human Performance Issues and User Interface Design for Teleoperated Robots." *Systems, Man, and Cybernetics, Part C: Applications and Reviews, IEEE Transactions on* 37:6 (2007), 1231–1245.

[Chen et al. 08] Yan-Rui Chen, Tao Wang, Xi Chen, and Xu Bai. "Research on Navigation Method in 3D Geographic Information System for Water Conservancy Projects of Large Basin." In *Education Technology and Training, 2008. and 2008 International Workshop on Geoscience and Remote Sensing. ETT and GRS 2008. International Workshop on*, 2, 2, pp. 521–524, 2008.

[Chen 00] C T Chen. *Digital signal processing: spectral computation and filter design.* Oxford University Press, Inc., 2000.

[Chernicharo et al. 13] Jorge H. dos S. Chernicharo, Kazuki Takashima, and Yoshifumi Kitamura. "Seamless interaction using a portable projector in perspective corrected multi display environments." In *Proceedings of the 1st Symposium on Spatial User Interaction, SUI '13*, pp. 25–32. New York, NY, USA: ACM, 2013. Available online (http://doi.acm.org/10.1145/2491367.2491375).

[Chin 06] Craig Anthony Chin. "Signal Processing and Information Fusing Algorithms for the Synthesis of an Alternative Electromyogram/Eye Gaze Tracking Computer Cursor Control System." Ph.D. thesis, Florida International University, Miami, FL, USA, 2006.

[Chittaro et al. 05] L Chittaro, V K Gatla, and S Venkataraman. "The Interactive 3D BreakAway Map: a navigation and examination aid for multi-floor 3D worlds." In *Cyberworlds, 2005. International Conference on*, pp. 8–66. IEEE, 2005.

[Chun et al. 04] Kwonsoo Chun, B Verplank, F Barbagli, and K Salisbury. "Evaluating haptics and 3D stereo displays using Fitts' law." In *Proceedings. Second International Conference on Creating, Connecting and Collaborating through Computing*, pp. 53–58. IEEE, 2004.

[Cockburn et al. 11] A Cockburn, P Quinn, C Gutwin, G Ramos, and J Looser. "Air pointing: Design and evaluation of spatial target acquisition with and without visual feedback." *International Journal of Human-Computer Studies* 69:6.

[Coffey et al. 12a] Dane Coffey, Nicholas Malbraaten, Trung Bao Le, Iman Borazjani, Fotis Sotiropoulos, A G Erdman, and Daniel F Keefe. "Interactive Slice WIM: Navigating and Interrogating Volume Data Sets Using a Multisurface, Multitouch VR Interface." *IEEE Transactions on Visualization and Computer Graphics* 18:10 (2012), 1614–1626.

[Coffey et al. 12b] Dane Coffey, Nicholas Malbraaten, Trung Bao Le, Iman Borazjani, Fotis Sotiropoulos, Arthur G Erdman, and Daniel F Keefe. "Interactive Slice WIM: Navigating and Interrogating Volume Data Sets Using a Multisurface, Multitouch VR Interface." *Visualization and Computer Graphics, IEEE Transactions on* 18:10 (2012), 1614–1626.

[Coffey et al. 12c] Dane Coffey, Nicholas Malbraaten, Trung Bao Le, Iman Borazjani, Fotis Sotiropoulos, Arthur G. Erdman, and Daniel F. Keefe. "Interactive Slice WIM: Navigating and Interrogating Volume Data Sets Using a Multisurface, Multitouch VR Interface." *IEEE Transactions on Visualization and Computer Graphics* 18:10 (2012), 1614–1626.

[Cohé and Hachet 12] Aurélie Cohé and Martin Hachet. "Understanding user gestures for manipulating 3D objects from touchscreen inputs." In *GI '12: Proceedings of Graphics Interface 2012*. Canadian Information Processing Society, 2012.

[Cohé et al. 11] Aurélie Cohé, Fabrice Dècle, and Martin Hachet. "tBox: A 3D Transformation Widget Designed for Touch-Screens." In *Proceedings of the Conference on Human Factors in Computing Systems (CHI)*, pp. 3005–3008, 2011.

[Cohen et al. 99] Jonathan M Cohen, Lee Markosian, Robert C Zeleznik, John F Hughes, and Ronen Barzel. "An interface for sketching 3D curves." In *I3D '99: Proceedings of the 1999 Symposium on Interactive 3D Graphics*, pp. 17–21. New York, New York, USA: ACM, 1999.

[Cohen et al. 00] Jonathan M Cohen, John F Hughes, and Robert C Zeleznik. "Harold: a world made of drawings." In *NPAR '00: Proceedings of the 1st International Symposium on Non-Photorealistic Animation and Rendering*, pp. 83–90. New York, New York, USA: ACM, 2000.

[Colle and Reid 98] Herbert A Colle and Gary B Reid. "The Room Effect: Metric Spatial Knowledge of Local and Separated Regions." *Presence: Teleoperators and Virtual Environments* 7:2 (1998), 116–128.

[Colvin et al. 04] J. Colvin, N. Tobler, and J.A. Anderson. "Productivity and multi-screen displays." In *Rocky Mountain Comm. Review*, pp. 31–53, 2004. Available online (http://www.ergotron.com/Portals/0/literature/whitePapers/english/Multi-Mon-Report.pdf).

[Connel and Baxeddale 11] J Connel and J Baxeddale. "Eyes Play a Focal Role in Research: Two unique techniques help characterize pharmacodynamic drug effects in healthy subjects." *Applied Clinical Trials*, pp. 37–41.

[Corbet et al. 05] Jonathan Corbet, Alessandro Rubini, and Greg Kroah-Hartman. *Linux Device Drivers*. O'Reilly, 2005.

[Cormen et al. 09] Thomas H Cormen, Charles E Leiserson, Ronald L Rivest, and Clifford Stein. *Introduction To Algorithms*, Third edition. MIT Press, 2009.

[Coyle and Doherty 09] David Coyle and Gavin Doherty. "Clinical evaluations and collaborative design: developing new technologies for mental healthcare interventions." In *Proceedings of the SIGCHI Conference on Human Factors in Computing Systems, CHI '09*, pp. 2051–2060. New York, NY, USA: ACM, 2009. Available online (http://doi.acm.org/10.1145/1518701.1519013).

[Coyle et al. 07] David Coyle, Gavin Doherty, Mark Matthews, and John Sharry. "Computers in talk-based mental health interventions." *Interact. Comput.* 19:4 (2007), 545–562. Available online (http://dx.doi.org/10.1016/j.intcom.2007.02.001).

[Cruz-Neira et al. 93] Carolina Cruz-Neira, Daniel J Sandin, and Thomas A DeFanti. "Surround-screen projection-based virtual reality: the design and implementation of the CAVE." *SIGGRAPH*, pp. 135–142.

[Cutler et al. 97] Lawrence D Cutler, Bernd Fröhlich, and Pat Hanrahan. "Two-handed direct manipulation on the responsive workbench." In *Proceedings of the 1997 symposium on Interactive 3D graphics, I3D '97*. ACM, 1997.

[Czerwinski et al. 02] Mary Czerwinski, Desney S Tan, and George G Robertson. "Women take a wider view." In *Proceedings of the SIGCHI Conference on Human Factors in Computing Systems, CHI '02*, pp. 195–202. New York, New York, USA: ACM, 2002.

[Daiber et al. 12a] Florian Daiber, Eric Falk, and Antonio Krüger. "Balloon Selection Revisited: Multi-Touch Selection Techniques for Stereoscopic Data." In *Proceedings of the International Working Conference on Advanced Visual Interfaces, AVI '12*, pp. 441–444. New York, NY, USA: ACM, 2012.

[Daiber et al. 12b] Florian Daiber, Dimitar Valkov, Frank Steinicke, Klaus H. Hinrichs, and Antonio Krüger. "Towards Object Prediction based on Hand Postures for Reach to Grasp Interaction." In *Proceedings of the Workshop on The 3rd Dimension of CHI: Touching and Designing 3D User Interfaces (3DCHI)*, 2012. Available online (http://viscg.uni-muenster.de/publications/2012/DVSHK12).

[Darken and Banker 98] R P Darken and W P Banker. "Navigating in natural environments: a virtual environment training transfer study." In *Proceedings on Virtual Reality Annual International Symposium*, pp. 12–19. IEEE Computer Society, 1998.

[Darken and Cevik 99] R P Darken and H Cevik. "Map usage in virtual environments: orientation issues." In *Virtual Reality, 1999. Proceedings., IEEE*, pp. 133–140, 1999.

[Darken and Peterson 15] Rudolph P Darken and Barry Peterson. "Spatial Orientation, Wayfinding, and Representation." In *Handbook of Virtual Environments*. CRC Press, 2015.

[Darken and Sibert 96] Rudolph P Darken and John L Sibert. "Wayfinding strategies and behaviors in large virtual worlds." In *Proceedings of the SIGCHI Conference on Human Factors in Computing Systems, CHI '96*, pp. 142–149. New York, New York, USA: ACM, 1996.

[Darken et al. 98] R Darken, T Allard, and L Achille. "Spatial Orientation and Wayfinding in Large-Scale Virtual Spaces: An Introduction." *Presence* 7:2 (1998), 101–107.

[Darken 93] Rudolph P Darken. "Navigation and Orientation in Virtual Space." Master's thesis, The University of Illinois at Chicago, Chicago, Illinois, 1993.

[Darken 96] Rudolph P Darken. "Wayfinding in Large-Scale Virtual Worlds." Ph.D. thesis, The University of Illinois at Chicago, Chicago, Illinois, 1996.

[David and Alla 10] René David and Hassane Alla. *Discrete, Continuous, and Hybrid Petri Nets*. Springer, 2010.

[Davidson and Han 08] Philip L Davidson and Jefferson Y Han. "Extending 2D object arrangement with pressure-sensitive layering cues." In *UIST '08: Proceedings of the 21st Annual ACM Symposium on User Interface Software and Technology*. ACM, 2008.

[Davis et al. 99] Elizabeth T Davis, Kevin Scott, Jarrell Pair, Larry F Hodges, and James Oliverio. "Can Audio Enhance Visual Perception and Performance in a Virtual Environment?" *Proceedings of the Human Factors and Ergonomics Society Annual Meeting* 43:22 (1999), 1197–1201.

[de Rosis et al. 06] Fiorella de Rosis, Nicole Novielli, Valeria Carofiglio, Addolorata Cavalluzzi, and Berardina De Carolis. "User modeling and adaptation in health promotion dialogs with an animated character.", 2006. Available online (http://www.ncbi.nlm.nih.gov/pubmed/16524784).

[DeLoura 01] Mark A DeLoura. *Game Programming Gems 2*. Cengage Learning, 2001.

[Dietz and Leigh 01] P Dietz and D Leigh. "DiamondTouch: a multi-user touch technology." *Proceedings of the 14th Annual ACM Symposium on User Interface Software and Technology*, p. 226.

[Dipietro et al. 08] L Dipietro, A M Sabatini, and P Dario. "A Survey of Glove-Based Systems and Their Applications." *IEEE Transactions on Systems, Man, and Cybernetics, Part C: Applications and Reviews* 38:4 (2008), 461–482.

[Dix et al. 04] Alan Dix, Janet Finlay, Gregory D Abowd, and Russell Beale. *Human-computer Interaction*. Pearson Education, 2004.

[Döring et al. 10] Tanja Döring, Alireza Sahami Shirazi, and Albrecht Schmidt. "Exploring gesture-based interaction techniques in multi-display environments with mobile phones and a multi-touch table." In *Proceedings of the International Conference on Advanced Visual Interfaces*, AVI '10, pp. 419–419. New York, NY, USA: ACM, 2010. Available online (http://doi.acm.org/10.1145/1842993.1843097).

[Dorobantu and Gerlach 04] R Dorobantu and C Gerlach. *Investigation of a navigation grade RLG SIMU type INAV-RQH*. IAPG, 2004.

[dos S Chernicharo et al. 13] Jorge H dos S Chernicharo, Kazuki Takashima, and Yoshifumi Kitamura. "Seamless interaction using a portable projector in perspective corrected multi display environments." In *SUI '13: Proceedings of the 1st Symposium on Spatial User Interaction*, p. 25. New York, New York, USA: ACM, 2013.

[Doulamis and Yiakoumettis 13] N Doulamis and C Yiakoumettis. "Personalised 3D Navigation and Understanding of Geo-Referenced Scenes." In *IEEE 14th International Symposium and Workshops on a World of Wireless, Mobile and Multimedia Networks (WoWMoM), 2013*, WowMoM '13, pp. 1–6, 2013.

[Dowding et al. 93] John Dowding, Jean Mark Gawron, Doug Appelt, John Bear, Lynn Cherny, Robert Moore, and Douglas Moran. "Gemini: A natural language system for spoken-language understanding." In *Proceedings of the 31st annual meeting on Association for Computational Linguistics*, pp. 54–61. Association for Computational Linguistics, 1993.

[Drewes 10] Heiko Drewes. "Only one Fitts' law formula please!" *CHI EA '10: CHI '10 Extended Abstracts on Human Factors in Computing Systems*, pp. 2813–2822.

[Drewes 15] H Drewes. "Eye Gaze Tracking." In *Interactive Displays*, edited by Achintya K Bhowmik. Chichester, UK: John Wiley & Sons, Ltd, 2015.

[Duchowski 07] Andrew Duchowski. *Eye Tracking Methodology: Theory and Practice*. London: Springer Science & Business Media, 2007.

[Dunn and Parberry 11] Fletcher Dunn and Ian Parberry. *3D Math Primer for Graphics and Game Development*, Second edition. A K Peters/CRC Press, 2011.

[Dvorkin et al. 07] A. Y. Dvorkin, R. V. Kenyon, and E. A. Keshner. "Reaching within a dynamic virtual environment." *Journal of NeuroEngineering and Rehabilitation* 4:23.

[Ebeling et al. 73] F A Ebeling, R L Johnson, and R S Goldhor. "Infrared Light Beam XY Position Encoder for Display Devices." US Patent 3,775,560, 1973.

[Eberly 05] David H Eberly. *3D Game Engine Architecture*. Engineering Real-Time Applications with Wild Magic, Elsevier, 2005.

[Eberly 07] David H Eberly. *3D Game Engine Design*. A Practical Approach to Real-Time Computer Graphics, Gulf Professional Publishing, 2007.

[Eberly 10] David H Eberly. *Game Physics*. Morgan Kaufmann, 2010.

[Eberly 14] David H Eberly. *GPGPU Programming for Games and Science*. CRC Press, 2014.

[Ebisawa and Satoh 93] Y Ebisawa and S i Satoh. "Effectiveness of pupil area detection technique using two light sources and image difference method." In *Engineering in Medicine and Biology Society, 1993. Proceedings of the 15th Annual International Conference of the IEEE*, pp. 1268–1269. IEEE, 1993.

[Ebisawa 98] Yoshinobu Ebisawa. "Improved video-based eye-gaze detection method." *IEEE T. Instrumentation and Measurement ()* 47:4 (1998), 948–955.

[Edelmann et al. 09] J Edelmann, A Schilling, and S Fleck. "The DabR - A multitouch system for intuitive 3D scene navigation." In *3DTV Conference: The True Vision - Capture, Transmission and Display of 3D Video, 2009*, pp. 1–4. IEEE, 2009.

[El Oraiby 04] Wael El Oraiby. "Scene Management." In *More OpenGL Game Programming*, edited by Dave Astle, pp. 565–605. Thomson Course Technology, 2004.

[El 08a] M El. "Calibration and stochastic modelling of inertial navigation sensor errors." *Journal of Global Positioning Systems.*

[El 08b] N El. "Analysis and modeling of inertial sensors using Allan variance." *Instrumentation and Measurement.*

[Engbert 06] Ralf Engbert. "Microsaccades: a microcosm for research on oculomotor control, attention, and visual perception." In *Visual Perception - Fundamentals of Vision: Low and Mid-Level Processes in Perception*, pp. 177–192. Elsevier, 2006.

[Engelbart and English 68a] D Engelbart and W K English. "The Mother Of All Demos.", 1968. [Online; accessed 3-January-2015]. Available online (www.dougengelbart.org/firsts/dougs-1968-demo.html).

[Engelbart and English 68b] Douglas C Engelbart and William K English. "A research center for augmenting human intellect." *AFIPS Fall Joint Computing Conference*, pp. 395–410.

[Engelhardt 08] L Engelhardt. "P-36: Native Dual Mode Digitizers: Supporting Pen, Touch and Multi-Touch Inputs in One Device on any LCD." *SID Symposium Digest of Technical Papers.*

[English et al. 67] W K English, Douglas C Engelbart, and M L Berman. "Display-Selection Techniques for Text Manipulation." *IEEE Transactions on Human Factors in Electronics* HFE-8:1 (1967), 5–15.

[Ericson 05] Christer Ericson. *Real-time Collision Detection.* Morgan Kaufmann, 2005.

[Evans] R. P. Evans. "The AI Architecture of Versu." https://versublog.files.wordpress.com/2014/05/ptai_evans.pdf. [Online; accessed on Mar. 04, 2015].

[Evans and Short] R. P. Evans and E. Short. "The AI Architecture of Versu." https://versublog.files.wordpress.com/2014/05/versu.pdf. [Online; accessed on Mar. 04, 2015].

[Fares et al. 13] Ribel Fares, Shaomin Fang, and Oleg Komogortsev. "Can we beat the mouse with MAGIC?" In *CHI '13: Proceedings of the SIGCHI Conference on Human Factors in Computing Systems.* ACM, 2013.

[Ferguson et al. 98] G. Ferguson, J.F. Allen, et al. "TRIPS: An integrated intelligent problem-solving assistant." In *Proceedings of the National Conference on Artificial Intelligence*, pp. 567–573. JOHN WILEY & SONS LTD, 1998.

[Ferguson et al. 10] G Ferguson, J Quinn, C Horwitz, M Swift, J Allen, and L Galescu. "Towards a Personal Health Management Assistant." *Journal of biomedical informatics* 43:5 Suppl (2010), S13–6. Available online (http://www.ncbi.nlm.nih.gov/pubmed/20937478).

[Field 09] Andy P Field. *Discovering Statistics Using SPSS for Windows*, Third edition. SAGE, 2009.

[Findlater et al. 12] Leah Findlater, Ben Lee, and Jacob Wobbrock. "Beyond QWERTY: augmenting touch screen keyboards with multi-touch gestures for non-alphanumeric input." In *CHI '12: Proceedings of the SIGCHI Conference on Human Factors in Computing Systems*, p. 2679. New York, New York, USA: ACM, 2012.

[Findlater et al. 13] Leah Findlater, Jon E Froehlich, Kays Fattal, Jacob O Wobbrock, and Tanya Dastyar. "Age-related differences in performance with touchscreens compared to traditional mouse input." In *CHI '13: Proceedings of the SIGCHI Conference on Human Factors in Computing Systems*. ACM, 2013.

[Fitts and Radford 66] Paul M Fitts and Barbara K Radford. "Information capacity of discrete motor responses under different cognitive sets." *Journal of Experimental Psychology* 71:4 (1966), 475.

[Fitts 54] Paul M Fitts. "The information capacity of the human motor system in controlling the amplitude of movement." *Journal of Experimental Psychology*.

[Fitts 64] Paul M Fitts. "Information capacity of discrete motor responses." *Journal of Experimental Psychology* 67:2 (1964), 103–112.

[Fitzmaurice et al. 95] George W Fitzmaurice, Hiroshi Ishii, and William A S Buxton. "Bricks: laying the foundations for graspable user interfaces." In *Proceedings of the SIGCHI Conference on Human Factors in Computing Systems, CHI '95*. ACM Press/Addison-Wesley Publishing Co., 1995.

[Fitzmaurice et al. 08] George Fitzmaurice, Justin Matejka, Igor Mordatch, Azam Khan, and Gordon Kurtenbach. *Safe 3D navigation*. Proceedings of the 2008 symposium on Interactive 3D graphics and games (I3D '08), 2008.

[Fitzmaurice 93] George W. Fitzmaurice. "Situated information spaces and spatially aware palmtop computers." *Commun. ACM* 36:7 (1993), 39–49. Available online (http: //doi.acm.org/10.1145/159544.159566).

[Foley and Wallace 74] J D Foley and V L Wallace. "The art of natural graphic man-machine conversation." *SIGGRAPH Computer Graphics* 8:3 (1974), 87–87.

[Foley et al. 84] J D Foley, V L Wallace, and P Chan. "The human factors of computer graphics interaction techniques." *Computer Graphics and Applications, IEEE* 4:11 (1984), 13–48.

[Foley et al. 96] James D Foley, Andries Van Dam, Steven K Feiner, and John F Hughes. *Computer Graphics: Principles & Practice In C*, Second edition. Pearson Education India, 1996.

[Forlines and Shen 05] Clifton Forlines and Chia Shen. "DTLens: multi-user tabletop spatial data exploration." In *UIST '05: Proceedings of the 18th Annual ACM Symposium on User Interface Software and Technology*. ACM, 2005.

[Forlines et al. 05] Clifton Forlines, Ravin Balakrishnan, Paul Beardsley, Jeroen van Baar, and Ramesh Raskar. "Zoom-and-pick: facilitating visual zooming and precision pointing with interactive handheld projectors." In *Proceedings of the 18th Annual ACM Symposium on User Interface Software and Technology, UIST '05*, pp. 73–82. New York, NY, USA: ACM, 2005. Available online (http://doi.acm.org/10.1145/1095034.1095046).

[Forsberg et al. 96] Andrew Forsberg, Kenneth Herndon, and Robert Zeleznik. "Aperture based selection for immersive virtual environments." In *UIST '96: Proceedings of the 9th annual ACM symposium on User interface software and technology*, pp. 95–96. New York, New York, USA: ACM, 1996.

[Foxlin 02] Eric Foxlin. "Chapter 7. Motion Tracking Requirements and Technologies." In *Handbook of Virtual Environments : Design, Implementation, and Applications.*, edited by Kay M Stanney, pp. 1–54. Lawrence Erlbaum Associates, 2002.

[Frampton and Lemon 09] Matthew Frampton and Oliver Lemon. "Recent research advances in reinforcement learning in spoken dialogue systems." *Knowledge Engineering Review* 24:4 (2009), 375–408.

[Frassinetti et al. 02] Francesca Frassinetti, Nadia Bolognini, and Elisabetta Làdavas. "Enhancement of visual perception by crossmodal visuo-auditory interaction." *Experimental Brain Research* 147:3 (2002), 332–343.

[FREAKS 15] ELEC FREAKS. "Ultrasonic Ranging Module HC - SR04 .", 2015. [Online; accessed 13-February-2015]. Available online (http://www.micropik.com/PDF/HCSR04.pdf).

[Frees et al. 07] Scott Frees, G Drew Kessler, and Edwin Kay. "PRISM interaction for enhancing control in immersive virtual environments." *Transactions on Computer-Human Interaction (TOCHI* 14:1.

[Frisch et al. 09] Mathias Frisch, Jens Heydekorn, and Raimund Dachselt. "Investigating multi-touch and pen gestures for diagram editing on interactive surfaces." In *ITS '09: Proceedings of the ACM International Conference on Interactive Tabletops and Surfaces.* ACM, 2009.

[Fröhlich et al. 05] Bernd Fröhlich, Roland Blach, Oliver Stefani, Jan Hochstrate, Jörg Hoffmann, Karsten Klüger, and Matthias Bues. "Implementing Multi-Viewer Stereo Displays." In *Proceedings of WSCG*, pp. 139–146, 2005.

[Fryberger and Johnson 72] D Fryberger and R G Johnson. "Touch actuable data input panel assembly." US Patent 3,673,327, 1972.

[Fu et al. 10] Chi-Wing Fu, Wooi Boon Goh, and Junxiang Allen Ng. "Multi-touch techniques for exploring large-scale 3D astrophysical simulations." In *Proceedings of the SIGCHI Conference on Human Factors in Computing Systems, CHI '10*, pp. 2213–2222. ACM, 2010.

[Fuchs and Hauser 09] R Fuchs and H Hauser. "Visualization of Multi-Variate Scientific Data." *Computer Graphics Forum* 28:6 (2009), 1670–1690.

[Fukazawa et al. 10] R. Fukazawa, K. Takashima, G. Shoemaker, Y. Kitamura, Y. Itoh, and F. Kishino. "Comparison of multimodal interactions in perspective-corrected multi-display environment." In *3D User Interfaces (3DUI), 2010 IEEE Symposium on*, pp. 103–110, 2010.

[Furness III and Kolin 92] T A Furness III and J S Kolin. "Virtual retinal display." US Patent 5,467,104, 1992.

[Gale et al. 90] N Gale, R G Golledge, and J W Pellegrino. "The acquisition and integration of route knowledge in an unfamiliar neighborhood." *Journal of Environmental Psychology* 10:1 (1990), 3–25.

[Gallo et al. 08] Luigi Gallo, Giuseppe De Pietro, and Ivana Marra. "3D Interaction with Volumetric Medical Data: Experiencing the WiiMote." In *Proceedings of the 1st International Conference on Ambient Media and Systems*, Ambi-Sys '08, pp. 14:1–14:6, 2008.

[Gamma et al. 94] Erich Gamma, Richard Helm, Ralph Johnson, and John Vlissides. *Design Patterns*. Elements of Reusable Object-Oriented Software, Pearson Education, 1994.

[Gan et al. 07] Guojun Gan, Chaoqun Ma, and Jianhong Wu. *Data Clustering: Theory, Algorithms, and Applications (ASA-SIAM Series on Statistics and Applied Probability)*. SIAM, Society for Industrial and Applied Mathematics, 2007.

[Gao et al. 09] Ying Gao, Armando Barreto, and Malek Adjouadi. "Detection of Sympathetic Activation through Measurement and Adaptive Processing of the Pupil Diameter for Affective Assessment of Computer Users." *American Journal of Biomedical Sciences*, pp. 283–294.

[Gao et al. 10] Ying Gao, Armando Barreto, and Malek Adjouadi. "An affective sensing approach through pupil diameter processing and SVM classification." *Biomedical Sciences Instrumentation* 46 (2010), 331–336.

[Garton et al. 09] M Garton, A Wutka, and A Leuzinger. "Local Magnetic Distortion Effects on 3-Axis Compassing." *PNI Sens Corp Tech Reports*.

[Genrich and Lautenbach 81] Hartmann J Genrich and Kurt Lautenbach. "System modelling with high-level Petri nets." *Theoretical computer science* 13:1 (1981), 109–135.

[Genrich 87] H J Genrich. "Predicate/transition nets." In *Advances in Petri nets 1986, part I on Petri nets: central models and their properties*, edited by W Brauer, W Reisig, and G Rozenberg. springer, 1987.

[Georgila et al. 10] Kallirroi Georgila, Maria K. Wolters, and Johanna D. Moore. "Learning Dialogue Strategies from Older and Younger Simulated Users." In *Proceedings of the 11th Annual Meeting of the Special Interest Group on Discourse and Dialogue*, SIG-DIAL '10, pp. 103–106. Stroudsburg, PA, USA: Association for Computational Linguistics, 2010. Available online (http://dl.acm.org/citation.cfm?id=1944506.1944527).

[Gerbert et al. 03] Barbara Gerbert, Steven Berg-Smith, Michelle Mancuso, Nona Caspers, Stephen McPhee, Daniel Null, and Judith Wofsy. "Using innovative video doctor technology in primary care to deliver brief smoking and alcohol intervention." *Health promotion practice* 4:3 (2003), 249–261.

[Gibbs 11] B P Gibbs. *Advanced Kalman filtering, least-squares and modeling: a practical handbook*. Wiley, 2011.

[Giesler et al. 14] Alexander Giesler, Dimitar Valkov, and Klaus H. Hinrichs. "Void Shadows: Multi-Touch Interaction with Stereoscopic Objects on the Tabletop." In *Proceedings of the 2nd Symposium on Spatial User Interaction (SUI 2014)*. ACM, 2014. Available online (http://viscg.uni-muenster.de/publications/2014/GVH14).

[Gillner and Mallot 98] S Gillner and H Mallot. "Navigation and Acquisition of Spatial Knowledge in a Virtual Maze." *Cognitive Neuroscience, Journal of* 10:4 (1998), 445–463.

[Glassner 93] Andrew S Glassner. *Graphics Gems*. Morgan Kaufmann, 1993.

[Gratch et al. 07a] Jonathan Gratch, Ning Wang, Jillian Gerten, and Edward Fast. "Creating rapport with virtual agents." *Intelligent Virtual Agents*. Available online (http://www. springerlink.com/index/X568357400058UM7.pdf).

[Gratch et al. 07b] Jonathan Gratch, Ning Wang, and Anna Okhmatovskaia. "Can virtual humans be more engaging than real ones?" In *12th International Conference on Human-Computer Interaction*. Springer, 2007. Available online (http://dl.acm.org/ citation.cfm?id=1769622).

[Grau et al. 14] Carles Grau, Romuald Ginhoux, Alejandro Riera, Thanh Lam Nguyen, Hubert Chauvat, Michel Berg, JuliÃ à L. Amengual, Alvaro Pascual-Leone, and Giulio Ruffini. "Conscious Brain-to-Brain Communication in Humans Using Non-Invasive Technologies." *PLoS ONE* 9:8 (2014), e105225.

[Greenberg and Boyle 02] Saul Greenberg and Michael Boyle. "Customizable physical interfaces for interacting with conventional applications." In *UIST '02: Proceedings of the 15th Annual ACM Symposium on User Interface Software and Technology*, pp. 31–40. New York, New York, USA: ACM, 2002.

[Greenberg and Buxton 08] Saul Greenberg and Bill Buxton. "Usability evaluation considered harmful (some of the time)." In *Proceedings of the SIGCHI Conference on Human Factors in Computing Systems, CHI '08*. ACM, 2008.

[Greenberg and Fitchett 01] Saul Greenberg and Chester Fitchett. "Phidgets: easy development of physical interfaces through physical widgets." In *UIST '01: Proceedings of the 14th Annual ACM Symposium on User Interface Software and Technology*. ACM, 2001.

[Gregoire et al. 11] Marc Gregoire, Nicholas A Solter, and Scott J Kleper. *Professional C++*. John Wiley & Sons, 2011.

[Gregory 14] Jason Gregory. *Game Engine Architecture, Second Edition*. CRC Press, 2014.

[Grewal and Andrews 11] M S Grewal and A P Andrews. *Kalman filtering: theory and practice using MATLAB*. Wiley, 2011.

[Grewal et al. 07] M S Grewal, L R Weill, and A P Andrews. *Global positioning systems, inertial navigation, and integration*. Wiley, 2007.

[Grijincu et al. 14] Daniela Grijincu, Miguel A Nacenta, and Per-Ola Kristensson. "User-Defined Interface Gestures: Dataset and Analysis." In *ITS '14: Proceedings of the Ninth ACM International Conference on Interactive Tabletops and Surfaces*. ACM, 2014.

[Grinblat and Peterson 12] Ilya Grinblat and Alex Peterson. *OGRE 3D 1.7 Application Development Cookbook*. Packt Publishing Ltd, 2012.

[Grossman and Balakrishnan 05] Tovi Grossman and Ravin Balakrishnan. "The bubble cursor." In *Proceedings of the SIGCHI Conference on Human Factors in Computing Systems - CHI '05*, p. 281. New York, New York, USA: ACM Press, 2005.

[Grossman and Balakrishnan 06] Tovi Grossman and Ravin Balakrishnan. "The design and evaluation of selection techniques for 3D volumetric displays." In *Proceedings of the 19th Annual ACM Symposium on User Interface Software and Technology - UIST '06*, p. 3. New York, New York, USA: ACM Press, 2006.

[Grossman and Wigdor 07] T. Grossman and D. Wigdor. "Going Deeper: a Taxonomy of 3D on the Tabletop." In *Proceedings of the Workshop on Horizontal Interactive Human Computer Systems (TABLETOP)*, pp. 137 – 144, 2007.

[Groves 13] P D Groves. *Principles of GNSS, inertial, and multisensor integrated navigation systems*. Artech House, 2013.

[Grudin 01] Jonathan Grudin. "Partitioning digital worlds: focal and peripheral awareness in multiple monitor use." In *Proceedings of the SIGCHI Conference on Human Factors in Computing Systems*, CHI '01, pp. 458–465. New York, NY, USA: ACM, 2001. Available online (http://doi.acm.org/10.1145/365024.365312).

[Guéniat et al. 13] Florimond Guéniat, Julien Christophe, Yoren Gaffary, Adrien Girard, and Mehdi Ammi. "Tangible windows for a free exploration of wide 3D virtual environment." In *Proceedings of the 19th ACM Symposium on Virtual Reality Software and Technology, VRST '13*, p. 115. New York, New York, USA: ACM, 2013.

[Guestrin and Eizenman 06] Elias Daniel Guestrin and Moshe Eizenman. "General theory of remote gaze estimation using the pupil center and corneal reflections." *Biomedical Engineering, IEEE Transactions on* 53:6 (2006), 1124–1133.

[Guiard 87] Yves Guiard. "Asymmetric division of labor in human skilled bimanual action: The kinematic chain as a model." *Journal of motor behavior* 19 (1987), 486–517.

[Guiard 09] Yves Guiard. "The problem of consistency in the design of Fitts' law experiments: consider either target distance and width or movement form and scale." In *CHI '09: Proceedings of the SIGCHI Conference on Human Factors in Computing Systems*, pp. 1809–1818. New York, New York, USA: ACM, 2009.

[Gunasekara and Wimalaratne 13] D Gunasekara and P Wimalaratne. "Towards Realism: Selection Techniques for Virtual Human Interaction." In *Computer Graphics, Imaging and Visualization (CGIV), 2013 10th International Conference*, pp. 116–119. IEEE Computer Society, 2013.

[Hachet et al. 06] Martin Hachet, Fabrice Decle, and Pascal Guitton. "Z-Goto for efficient navigation in 3D environments from discrete inputs." In *Proceedings of the ACM Symposium on Virtual Reality Software and Technology, VRST '06*, pp. 236–239. New York, New York, USA: ACM, 2006.

[Hachet et al. 09] Martin Hachet, Fabrice Decle, Sebastian Knödel, and Pascal Guitton. "Navidget for 3D interaction: Camera positioning and further uses." *International Journal of Human-Computer Studies* 67:3 (2009), 225–236.

[Hachet et al. 11] Martin Hachet, Benoit Bossavit, Aurélie Cohé, and Jean-Baptiste de la Rivière. "Toucheo: multitouch and stereo combined in a seamless workspace." In *Proceedings of the 24th Annual ACM Symposium on User Interface Software and Technology, UIST '11*, pp. 587–592. New York, New York, USA: ACM, 2011.

[Hagedorn and Döllner 08] Benjamin Hagedorn and Jürgen Döllner. "Sketch-Based Navigation in 3D Virtual Environments." In *Proceedings of the 9th International Symposium on Smart Graphics, SG '08*, edited by Andreas Butz, Brian Fisher, Patrick Olivier, and Marc Christie, pp. 239–246. Springer-Verlag, 2008.

[Haigron et al. 96] P Haigron, G Le Berre, and J L Coatrieux. "3D navigation in medicine." *Engineering in Medicine and Biology Magazine, IEEE* 15:2 (1996), 70–78.

[Hainich and Bimber 11] Rolf R Hainich and Oliver Bimber. *Displays.* Fundamentals and Applications, CRC Press, 2011.

[Hale and Stanney 02] Kelly S Hale and Kay M Stanney. *Handbook of Virtual Environments.* Design, Implementation, and Applications, CRC Press, 2002.

[Hamilton et al. 12] William Hamilton, Andruid Kerne, and Tom Robbins. "High-performance pen + touch modality interactions: a real-time strategy game eSports context." In *UIST '12: Proceedings of the 25th Annual ACM Symposium on User Interface Software and Technology*, pp. 309–318. New York, New York, USA: ACM, 2012.

[Hamon et al. 13] Arnaud Hamon, Philippe Palanque, José Luís Silva, Yannick Deleris, and Eric Barboni. "Formal description of multi-touch interactions." In *Proceedings of the 5th ACM SIGCHI symposium on Engineering interactive computing systems, EICS '13*, pp. 207–216. New York, New York, USA: ACM, 2013.

[Han 05] JY Han. "Low-cost multi-touch sensing through frustrated total internal reflection." *Proceedings of the 18th annual ACM symposium on User interface software and technology*, pp. 115–118.

[Han 11] Junghyun Han. *3D Graphics for Game Programming.* Chapman & Hall, 2011.

[Hancock et al. 07] M Hancock, S Carpendale, and A Cockburn. "Shallow-depth 3D Interaction: Design and Evaluation of One-, Two- and Three-Touch Techniques." In *Proceedings of the SIGCHI Conference on Human Factors in Computing Systems, CHI '07*, pp. 1147–1156. ACM, 2007.

[Hand 97] C Hand. "A survey of 3D interaction techniques." *Computer Graphics Forum* 16:5 (1997), 269–281.

[Hanson and Wernert 97] Andrew J. Hanson and Eric A. Wernert. "Constrained 3D Navigation with 2D Controllers." In *Proceedings of the 8th Conference on Visualization '97, VIS '97*, pp. 175–182. IEEE, 1997.

[Hanson 06] Andrew J Hanson. *Visualizing Quaternions.* Morgan Kaufmann, 2006.

[Harbour 10] Jonathan S Harbour. *Beginning Game Programming*, Third edition. Cengage Learning, 2010.

[Harris et al. 99] L Harris, M Jenkin, and D C Zikovitz. "Vestibular cues and virtual environments: choosing the magnitude of the vestibular cue." In *Virtual Reality, 1999. Proceedings., IEEE*, pp. 229–236, 1999.

[Harrison et al. 11] Chris Harrison, Hrvoje Benko, and Andrew D. Wilson. "OmniTouch: wearable multitouch interaction everywhere." In *Proceedings of the 24th Annual ACM Symposium on User Interface Software and Technology, UIST '11*, pp. 441–450. New York, NY, USA: ACM, 2011. Available online (http://doi.acm.org/10.1145/2047196.2047255).

[Harrison et al. 12] Chris Harrison, Munehiko Sato, and Ivan Poupyrev. "Capacitive fingerprinting: exploring user differentiation by sensing electrical properties of the human body." In *UIST '12: Proceedings of the 25th Annual ACM Symposium on User Interface Software and Technology*, p. 537. New York, New York, USA: ACM, 2012.

[Hasan et al. 12] Khalad Hasan, Xing-Dong Yang, Andrea Bunt, and Pourang Irani. "A-coord input: coordinating auxiliary input streams for augmenting contextual pen-based interactions." In *CHI '12: Proceedings of the SIGCHI Conference on Human Factors in Computing Systems*, pp. 805–814. New York, New York, USA: ACM, 2012.

[Hassabis et al. 13] Demis Hassabis, R. Nathan Spreng, Andrei A. Rusu, Clifford A. Robbins, Raymond A. Mar, and Daniel L. Schacter. "Imagine All the People: How the Brain Creates and Uses Personality Models to Predict Behavior." *Cerebral Cortex*.

[Haykin and Van Veen 07] S Haykin and B Van Veen. *Signals and systems*. Wiley India Pvt. Limited, 2007.

[He and Murata 05] X He and T Murata. "High-Level Petri Nets-Extensions, Analysis, and Applications." In *Electrical Engineering Handbook*, edited by W Chen, pp. 459–475. Elsevier Academic Press, 2005.

[Heap 63] B R Heap. "Permutations by interchanges." *The Computer Journal* 6:3 (1963), 293–298.

[Heckbert 94] Paul S Heckbert. *Graphics Gems IV*. Morgan Kaufmann, 1994.

[Heider and Kirste 07] Thomas Heider and Thomas Kirste. "Usable Multi-Display Environments: Concept and Evaluation." In *Universal Access in Human-Computer Interaction. Ambient Interaction*, Lecture Notes in Computer Science, 4555, edited by Constantine Stephanidis, Lecture Notes in Computer Science, 4555, pp. 93–102. Springer Berlin Heidelberg, 2007. Available online (http://dx.doi.org/10.1007/978-3-540-73281-5_10).

[Heilig 62] Morton L Heilig. "Sensorama simulator." US Patent 3,050,870 A, 1962.

[Henderson et al. 08] James Henderson, Oliver Lemon, and Kallirroi Georgila. "Hybrid reinforcement/supervised learning of dialogue policies from fixed data sets." *Computational Linguistics* 34:4 (2008), 487–511.

[Herlihy and Shavit 08] Maurice Herlihy and Nir Shavit. *The Art of Multiprocessor Programming*, First edition. Morgan Kaufmann, 2008.

[Herndon et al. 92] Kenneth P Herndon, Robert C Zeleznik, Daniel C Robbins, D Brookshire Conner, Scott S Snibbe, and Andries Van Dam. "Interactive shadows." In *Proceedings of the 5th Annual ACM Symposium on User Interface Software and Technology*, pp. 1–6. ACM, 1992.

[Hernoux and Christmann 15] Franck Hernoux and Olivier Christmann. "A seamless solution for 3D real-time interaction: design and evaluation." *Virtual Reality* 19:1.

[Herot and Weinzapfel 78] C F Herot and G Weinzapfel. "One-point touch input of vector information for computer displays." In *Proceedings of the 5th Annual Conference on Computer Graphics and Interactive Techniques*, SIGGRAPH '78, pp. 210–216. ACM, 1978.

[Hester et al. 05] Reid K Hester, Daniel D Squires, and Harold D Delaney. "The Drinker's Check-up: 12-month outcomes of a controlled clinical trial of a stand-alone software program for problem drinkers." *Journal of substance abuse treatment* 28:2 (2005), 159–69. Available online (http://www.ncbi.nlm.nih.gov/pubmed/15780546).

[Hick 52] William E Hick. "On the rate of gain of information." *Quarterly Journal of Experimental Psychology* 4:1 (1952), 11–26.

[Hilliges et al. 09] Otmar Hilliges, Shahram Izadi, Andrew D. Wilson, Steve Hodges, Armando Garcia-Mendoza, and Andreas Butz. "Interactions in the Air: Adding Further Depth to Interactive Tabletops." In *Proceedings of the Symposium on User Interface Software and Technology (UIST)*, pp. 139–148, 2009. Available online (http://doi.acm.org/10.1145/1622176.1622203).

[Hiltzik 09] Michael A Hiltzik. *Dealers of Lightning*. Xerox PARC and the Dawn of the Computer Age, HarperCollins, 2009.

[Hinckley and Widgor 12] Ken Hinckley and Daniel Widgor. "Input Technologies and Techniques." In *The Human-Computer Interaction*, edited by Julie A Jacko, pp. 95–132. CRC Press, 2012.

[Hinckley et al. 97] Ken Hinckley, Randy Pausch, Dennis Proffitt, James Patten, and Neal Kassell. "Cooperative bimanual action." In *CHI '97: Proceedings of the ACM SIGCHI Conference on Human factors in computing systems*, pp. 27–34. New York, New York, USA: ACM, 1997.

[Hinckley et al. 98] Ken Hinckley, Mary Czerwinski, and Mike Sinclair. "Interaction and Modeling Techniques for Desktop Two-Handed Input." *ACM Symposium on User Interface Software and Technology*, pp. 49–58.

[Hinckley et al. 06] Ken Hinckley, Francois Guimbretiere, Patrick Baudisch, Raman Sarin, Maneesh Agrawala, and Ed Cutrell. "The springboard: multiple modes in one spring-loaded control." In *CHI '06: Proceedings of the SIGCHI Conference on Human Factors in Computing Systems*, pp. 181–190. New York, New York, USA: ACM, 2006.

[Hinckley et al. 10a] K Hinckley, M Pahud, and B Buxton. "38.2: Direct Display Interaction via Simultaneous Pen+ Multi-touch Input." *Society for Information Display SID Symposium Digest of Technical Papers* 41 (2010), 537–540.

[Hinckley et al. 10b] Ken Hinckley, Koji Yatani, Michel Pahud, Nicole Coddington, Jenny Rodenhouse, Andy Wilson, Hrvoje Benko, and Bill Buxton. "Manual deskterity: an exploration of simultaneous pen + touch direct input." *CHI EA '10: CHI '10 Extended Abstracts on Human Factors in Computing Systems*, p. 2793.

[Hinckley et al. 10c] Ken Hinckley, Koji Yatani, Michel Pahud, Nicole Coddington, Jenny Rodenhouse, Andy Wilson, Hrvoje Benko, and Bill Buxton. "Pen + touch = new tools." In *Proceedings of the 23nd Annual ACM Symposium on User Interface Software and Technology*, UIST '10, p. 27. New York, New York, USA: ACM, 2010.

[Hinckley et al. 14] Ken Hinckley, Michel Pahud, Hrvoje Benko, Pourang Irani, Francois Guimbretiere, Marcel Gavriliu, Xiang Anthony' Chen, Fabrice Matulic, William Buxton, and Andrew Wilson. "Sensing techniques for tablet+stylus interaction." In *UIST '14: Proceedings of the 27th Annual ACM Symposium on User Interface Software and Technology*. ACM, 2014.

[Hinckley 08] Ken Hinckley. "Input Technologies and Techniques." In *Human-Computer Interaction*, edited by Andrew Sears and Julie A Jacko, pp. 161–176. New York: Newnes, 2008.

[Hochberg et al. 06] Leigh R. Hochberg, Mijail D. Serruya, Gerhard M. Friehs, Jon A. Mukand, Maryam Saleh, Abraham H. Caplan, Almut Branner, David Chen, Richard D.

Penn, and John P. Donoghue. "Imagine All the People: How the Brain Creates and Uses Personality Models to Predict Behavior." *Nature* 442 (2006), 164–171.

[Hoffmann 13] Errol R Hoffmann. "Which Version/Variation of Fitts' Law? A Critique of Information-Theory Models." *Journal of motor behavior* 45:3 (2013), 205–215.

[Hollerbach 02] John M Hollerbach. "Locomotion Interfaces." In *Handbook of Virtual Environments*, edited by Kelly S Hale and Kay M Stanney, pp. 239–254. CRC Press, 2002.

[Holz and Baudisch 10] Christian Holz and Patrick Baudisch. "The generalized perceived input point model and how to double touch accuracy by extracting fingerprints." In *CHI '10: Proceedings of the SIGCHI Conference on Human Factors in Computing Systems*, pp. 1165–1174. New York, New York, USA: ACM, 2010.

[Holz and Baudisch 11] Christian Holz and Patrick Baudisch. "Understanding touch." In *Proceedings of the Conference on Human Factors in Computing Systems (CHI)*, *CHI '11*, pp. 2501–2510. New York, NY, USA: ACM, 2011. Available online (http://doi.acm.org/10.1145/1978942.1979308).

[Holz and Baudisch 13] Christian Holz and Patrick Baudisch. "Fiberio: a touchscreen that senses fingerprints." In *UIST '13: Proceedings of the 26th Annual ACM Symposium on User Interface Software and Technology*. ACM, 2013.

[Holz 14] D. Holz. "Systems and methods for capturing motion in three-dimensional space." US Patent 8,638,989, 2014.

[Hong and Huang 00] P Hong and TS Huang. "Constructing finite state machines for fast gesture recognition." In *15th International Conference on Pattern Recognition*, ICPR'00, 3, ICPR'00, 3, 2000.

[Hong et al. 00] P Hong, TS Huang, and M Turk. "Gesture modeling and recognition using finite state machines." *IEEE Conference on Face and Gesture Recognition*.

[Hosoi et al. 07] Kazuhiro Hosoi, Vinh Ninh Dao, Akihiro Mori, and Masanori Sugimoto. "CoGAME: manipulation using a handheld projector." In *ACM SIGGRAPH 2007 emerging technologies*, *SIGGRAPH '07*. New York, NY, USA: ACM, 2007. Available online (http://doi.acm.org/10.1145/1278280.1278283).

[Hoste et al. 11] Lode Hoste, Bruno Dumas, and Beat Signer. "Mudra: a unified multimodal interaction framework." In *ICMI '11: Proceedings of the 13th international conference on multimodal interfaces*, p. 97. New York, New York, USA: ACM, 2011.

[Hou et al. 12] Jinghui Hou, Yujung Nam, Wei Peng, and Kwan Min Lee. "Effects of screen size, viewing angle, and players' immersion tendencies on game experience." *Comput. Hum. Behav.* 28:2 (2012), 617–623. Available online (http://dx.doi.org/10.1016/j.chb.2011.11.007).

[Huang et al. 11] Lixing Huang, Louis-philippe Morency, and Jonathan Gratch. "Virtual Rapport 2.0." In *International Conference on Intelligent Virtual Agents, Intelligence, Lecture Notes in Artificial Intelligence.*, pp. 68–79. Springer-Verlag Berlin Heidelberg, 2011.

[Hudlicka 03] Eva Hudlicka. "To feel or not to feel: The role of affect in human–computer interaction." *International Journal of Human-Computer Studies* 59:1-2 (2003), 1–32.

[Hugdahl 95] K Hugdahl. *Psychophysiology: the mind-body perspective, Harvard Uni.* Cambridge, MA: Hardvard University Press, 1995.

[Hughes et al. 13] John F Hughes, Andries Van Dam, Morgan McGuire, David F Sklar, James D Foley, Steven K Feiner, and Kurt Akeley. *Computer Graphics.* Principles and Practice, Addison-Wesley Professional, 2013.

[Hülsmann and Maicher 14] Adrian Hülsmann and Julian Maicher. "HOUDINI: Introducing Object Tracking and Pen Recognition for LLP Tabletops." In *Human-Computer Interaction. Advanced Interaction Modalities and Techniques*, pp. 234–244. Cham, Switzerland: Springer International Publishing, 2014.

[Hum 85] "Human engineering pioneer to be honored at WPAFB." *The Gazette MidWeek Daily, 1985.*

[Hutchings et al. 04] Dugald Ralph Hutchings, Greg Smith, Dugald Ralph, Hutchings Greg Smith, Brian Meyers, Mary Czerwinski, and George Robertson. "Display Space Usage and Window Management Operation Comparisons between Single Monitor and Multiple Monitor Users.", 2004.

[Hutchings 12] Dugald Hutchings. "An investigation of Fitts' law in a multiple-display environment." In *Proceedings of the SIGCHI Conference on Human Factors in Computing Systems, CHI '12*, pp. 3181–3184. New York, NY, USA: ACM, 2012. Available online (http://doi.acm.org/10.1145/2207676.2208736).

[Hutchinson et al. 89] T E Hutchinson, K P Jr White, Worthy N Martin, K C Reichert, and L A Frey. "Human-computer interaction using eye-gaze input." *Systems, Man and Cybernetics, IEEE Transactions on* 19:6 (1989), 1527–1534.

[Hyman 53] Ray Hyman. "Stimulus information as a determinant of reaction time." *Journal of experimental psychology* 45:3 (1953), 188.

[Ifeachor and Jervis 02] Emmanuel C Ifeachor and Barrie W Jervis. *Digital Signal Processing.* A Practical Approach, Pearson Education, 2002.

[Igarashi et al. 98] Takeo Igarashi, Rieko Kadobayashi, Kenji Mase, and Hidehiko Tanaka. "Path drawing for 3D walkthrough." In *UIST '98: Proceedings of the 11th Annual ACM Symposium on User Interface Software and Technology*, pp. 173–174. New York, New York, USA: ACM, 1998.

[Igarashi et al. 99] Takeo Igarashi, Satoshi Matsuoka, and Hidehiko Tanaka. "Teddy: a sketching interface for 3D freeform design." In *SIGGRAPH '99: Proceedings of the 26th Annual Conference on Computer Graphics and Interactive Techniques*, pp. 409–416. New York, New York, USA: ACM Press/Addison-Wesley Publishing Co., 1999.

[Insko et al. 01] B. Insko, M. Meehan, M. Whitton, and F. Brooks. "Passive Haptics Significantly Enhances Virtual Environments." In *Proceedings of 4th Annual Presence Workshop*, 2001.

[Insulander and Johlin-Dannfelt 03] P Insulander and A Johlin-Dannfelt. "Electrophysiologic effects of mental stress in healthy subjects: a comparison with epinephrine infusion." *Journal of Electrocardiology* 36:4 (2003), 301–309.

[International Organization for Standardization 00] International Organization for Standardization. "Ergonomic requirements for office work with visual display terminals (VDTs). Requirement for non-keyboard input devices." ISO Standards, 2000.

[International Organization for Standardization 07] International Organization for Standardization. "Ergonomics of human–system interaction – Part 400: Principles and requirements for physical input devices." ISO Standards, 2007.

[International Organization for Standardization 12] International Organization for Standardization. "Ergonomics of human-system interaction – Part 411: Evaluation methods for the design of physical input devices." ISO Standards, 2012.

[Ishii et al. 13] Masaki Ishii, Atsushi Minochi, Kimihiro Yamanaka, and Takanori Chihara. "Evaluation of Mental Workload Based on Pursuit Eye Movement." In *ICBAKE '13: Proceedings of the 2013 International Conference on Biometrics and Kansei Engineering*, pp. 121–124. IEEE Computer Society, 2013.

[Jacko 12] Julie A Jacko. *Human Computer Interaction Handbook*, Third edition. Fundamentals, Evolving Technologies, and Emerging Applications, CRC Press, 2012.

[Jackson et al. 12] Bret Jackson, David Schroeder, and Daniel F Keefe. "Nailing down multi-touch: anchored above the surface interaction for 3D modeling and navigation." In *Proceedings of Graphics Interface 2012, GI '12*. Canadian Information Processing Society, 2012.

[Jacob et al. 94] RJK Jacob, LE Sibert, DC McFarlane, and M Preston Mullen. "Integrality and separability of input devices." *ACM Transactions on Computer-Human Interaction (TOCHI)*.

[Jacob et al. 99] Robert J. K. Jacob, Leonidas Deligiannidis, and Stephen Morrison. "A Software Model and Specification Language for non-WIMP User Interfaces." *ACM Trans. Comput.-Hum. Interact.* 6:1 (1999), 1–46.

[Jacob et al. 08] RJK Jacob, A Girouard, LM Hirshfield, Michael S. Horn, Orit Shaer, Erin Treacy Solovey, and Jamie Zigelbaum. "Reality-based interaction: a framework for post-WIMP interfaces." In *Proceeding of the Twenty-Sixth Annual SIGCHI Conference on Human Factors in Computing Systems, CHI '08*, pp. 201–210. ACM, 2008.

[Jacob 90] Robert J K Jacob. "What you look at is what you get: eye movement-based interaction techniques." In *CHI '90: Proceedings of the SIGCHI Conference on Human Factors in Computing Systems*, pp. 11–18. New York, New York, USA: ACM, 1990.

[Jacob 91] Robert J K Jacob. "The use of eye movements in human-computer interaction techniques: what you look at is what you get." *Transactions on Information Systems (TOIS)* 9:2 (1991), 152–169.

[Jacob 93] R J K Jacob. "Hot topics-eye-gaze computer interfaces: what you look at is what you get." *Computer* 26:7 (1993), 65–66.

[Janarthanam and Lemon 10] Srinivasan Janarthanam and Oliver Lemon. "Adaptive referring expression generation in spoken dialogue systems: evaluation with real users." In *Proceedings of the 11th Annual Meeting of the Special Interest Group on Discourse and Dialogue, SIGDIAL '10*, pp. 124–131. Stroudsburg, PA, USA: Association for Computational Linguistics, 2010. Available online (http://dl.acm.org/citation.cfm?id= 1944506.1944530).

[Janwattanapong and Ratchatanantakit 12] P Janwattanapong and N Ratchatanantakit. "Design of the AU Self-Balancing Bicycle (AUSB)." *The ECTI Conference on journal Application Research and Development (CARD)*, pp. 21–22.

[Jensen and Kristensen 96] Kurt Jensen and Lars Kristensen. *Coloured Petri Nets*. Basic Concepts, Analysis Methods and Practical Use, Springer, 1996.

[Jensen and Rozenberg 91] Kurt Jensen and Grzegorz Rozenberg. "High-level petri nets." Springer-Verlag, 1991.

[Ji et al. 11] Li Ji, Zhang Qi, Chen Dixiang, Pan Mengchun, and Luo Feilu. "Integrated Compensation Method of Three-axis Magnetometer in Geomagnetic Navigation." In *Instrumentation, Measurement, Computer, Communication and Control, 2011 First International Conference on*, pp. 929–932, 2011.

[JIMB0 15] JIMB0. "Serial Communication.", 2015. [Online; accessed 12-February-2015]. Available online (https://learn.sparkfun.com/tutorials/serial-communication).

[Johnson et al. 09] G Johnson, MD Gross, and J Hong. "Computational support for sketching in design: a review." *Foundations and Trends in Human-Computer Interaction 2.*

[Jordan] Diana P. Jordan. "Sue Grafton's Advice for Writers: Put in the Time Writer's Digest." http://www.writersdigest.com/writing-articles/by-writing-goal/ improve-my-writing/sue-grafton-advice-for-writers. [Online; accessed on Mar. 04, 2015].

[Joshi and Barreto 07] V Joshi and Armando Barreto. "Design and Construction of a Head-Mounted System for the Real-Time Measurement of Pupil Diameter Variations." In *WMSCI 2007 Proceedings of the World Multi-Conference on Systemics, Cybernetics and Informatics*, pp. 36–40. Orlando, FL., 2007.

[Joshi and Barreto 08] V Joshi and Armando Barreto. "Real-Time Measurement of Pupil Diameter for Quantitative Monitoring of the Autonomic Nervous System." In *Biomerical Engineering - Recent Developments*, edited by H Nazeram, M Goldman, and Schoephoerster, pp. 47–50. Biomedical Engineering Recent Developments, 2008.

[Jota et al. 10] Ricardo Jota, Miguel A Nacenta, Joaquim A Jorge, Sheelagh Carpendale, and Saul Greenberg. "A comparison of ray pointing techniques for very large displays." In *GI '10: Proceedings of Graphics Interface 2010*. Canadian Information Processing Society, 2010.

[Ju 08] Wendy Ju. "The Mouse, the Demo, and the Big Idea." In *HCI Remixed*, edited by Thomas Erickson and David W McDonald, pp. 29–33. MIT Press, 2008.

[Jul and Furnas 97] S Jul and G W Furnas. "Navigation in electronic worlds: a CHI 97 workshop." *SIGCHI bulletin*.

[Junker 06] Gregory Junker. *Pro OGRE 3D Programming*. Apress, 2006.

[Jurcicek et al. 09] F Jurcicek, F Mairesse, M Gašic, S Keizer, B Thomson, K Yu, and S Young. "Transformation-Based Learning for Semantic parsing." In *Proceedings of INTERSPEECH*, pp. 2719–2722, 2009.

[Jurcicek et al. 10] Filip Jurcicek, Simon Keizer, François Mairesse, Kai Yu, Steve Young, Srinivanan Janarthanam, Helen Hastie, Xingkun Liu, and Oliver Lemon. "D5. 4:

Proof-of-concept CLASSIC Appointment Scheduling system ("System 2")." Technical report, Technical report, CLASSIC Project, 2010.

[Jurčíček et al. 12] Filip Jurčíček, Blaise Thomson, and Steve Young. "Reinforcement learning for parameter estimation in statistical spoken dialogue systems." *Computer Speech & Language* 26:3 (2012), 168–192.

[Kabbash et al. 93] Paul Kabbash, I. Scott MacKenzie, and William Buxton. "Human Performance Using Computer Input Devices in the Preferred and Non-Preferred Hands." In *Proceedings of the INTERACT '93 and CHI '93 Conference on Human Factors in Computing Systems*, CHI '93, pp. 474–481. IOS Press, 1993.

[Kabbash et al. 94] Paul Kabbash, William Buxton, and Abigail Sellen. "Two-handed input in a compound task." In *Proceedings of the SIGCHI Conference on Human Factors in Computing Systems*, CHI '94, pp. 417–423. ACM, 1994.

[Kaindl 10] Georg Kaindl. *Exploring multi-touch interaction: An overview of the history, HCI issues and sensor technology of multi-touch appliances.* Germany: VDM Verlag, 2010.

[Kalgaonkar and Raj 09] Kaustubh Kalgaonkar and Bhiksha Raj. "One-handed gesture recognition using ultrasonic Doppler sonar." *ICASSP*, pp. 1889–1892.

[Kalman 60] R E Kalman. "A new approach to linear filtering and prediction problems." *Journal of Fluids Engineering.*

[Kaltenbrunner et al. 05] M Kaltenbrunner, T Bovermann, and R Bencina. "TUIO: A protocol for table-top tangible user interfaces." In *Proceedings of the 6th International Workshop on Gesture in Human-Computer Interaction and Simulation*, GW 2005, 2005.

[Kaltenbrunner 09] Martin Kaltenbrunner. "reacTIVision and TUIO: a tangible tabletop toolkit." In *Proceedings of the ACM International Conference on Interactive Tabletops and Surfaces*, ITS '09, pp. 9–16. ACM, 2009.

[Kammer et al. 10] Dietrich Kammer, Jan Wojdziak, Mandy Keck, Rainer Groh, and Severin Taranko. "Towards a formalization of multi-touch gestures." In *International Conference on Interactive Tabletops and Surfaces*, ITS '10. ACM, 2010.

[Kara and Stahovich 05] LB Kara and T Stahovich. "An image-based, trainable symbol recognizer for hand-drawn sketches." *Computers & Graphics* 29:4 (2005), 501–517.

[Kato et al. 00] Hirokazu Kato, Mark Billinghurst, Ivan Poupyrev, Kenji Imamoto, and Keihachiro Tachibana. "Virtual object manipulation on a table-top AR environment." *ISAR*, pp. 111–119.

[Kay et al. 08] Kendrick N. Kay, Thomas Naselaris, Ryan J. Prenger, and Jack L. Gallant. "Imagine All the People: How the Brain Creates and Uses Personality Models to Predict Behavior." *Nature* 452 (2008), 352–355.

[KEIL 15] KEIL. "MDK-ARM Microcontroller Development Kit.", 2015. [Online; accessed 11-February-2015]. Available online (http://www.keil.com/arm/mdk.asp).

[Kelly] Morgan Kelly. "Word association: Princeton study matches brain scans with complex thought." http://www.princeton.edu/main/news/archive/S31/47/31I07/index.xml?section=topstories. [Online; accessed on Mar. 04, 2015].

[Kelso et al. 79] JA Scott Kelso, Dan L Southard, and David Goodman. "On the coordination of two-handed movements." *Journal of experimental psychology. Human perception and performance* 5:2 (1979), 229–238.

[Kennedy et al. 12] Catriona M Kennedy, John Powell, Thomas H Payne, John Ainsworth, Alan Boyd, and Iain Buchan. "Active assistance technology for health-related behavior change: an interdisciplinary review." *Journal of Medical Internet Research* 14:3.

[Kerger 10] Felix Kerger. *Ogre 3D 1.7 Beginner's Guide*. Packt Publishing Ltd, 2010.

[Kerrisk 10] Michael Kerrisk. *The Linux Programming Interface*. No Starch Press, 2010.

[Khan et al. 05] Azam Khan, Ben Komalo, Jos Stam, George W Fitzmaurice, and Gordon Kurtenbach. "HoverCam: interactive 3D navigation for proximal object inspection." In *Proceedings of the 2005 Symposium on Interactive 3D Graphics and Games, I3D '05*, pp. 73–80, 2005.

[Kim and Huh 11] Phil Kim and Lynn Huh. *Kalman Filter for Beginners With MATLAB® Examples*. CreateSpace, 2011.

[Kim et al. 13] Seung-Chan Kim, Ali Israr, and Ivan Poupyrev. "Tactile Rendering of 3D Features on Touch Surfaces." In *Proceedings of the Symposium on User Interface Software and Technology (UIST)*, pp. 531–538, 2013.

[Kin et al. 09] Kenrick Kin, Maneesh Agrawala, and Tony DeRose. "Determining the benefits of direct-touch, bimanual, and multifinger input on a multitouch workstation." In *Proceedings of Graphics Interface 2009, GI '09*, pp. 119–124. Canadian Information Processing Society, 2009.

[Kin et al. 12a] Kenrick Kin, Björn Hartmann, Tony DeRose, and Maneesh Agrawala. "Proton++: a customizable declarative multitouch framework." In *Proceedings of the 25th Annual ACM Symposium on User Interface Software and Technology, UIST '12*. ACM, 2012.

[Kin et al. 12b] Kenrick Kin, Björn Hartmann, Tony DeRose, and Maneesh Agrawala. "Proton: multitouch gestures as regular expressions." In *Proceedings of the SIGCHI Conference on Human Factors in Computing Systems, CHI '12*. ACM, 2012.

[King] Susan King. "SIDNEY SHELDON: The Plots Quicken." http://articles.latimes.com/1992-11-22/news/tv-1904_1_sidney-sheldon. [Online; accessed on Mar. 04, 2015].

[Kiriaty et al. 09] Yochay Kiriaty, Laurence Moroney, Sasha Goldshtein, and Alon Fliess. *Introducing Windows 7 for Developers*. Microsoft Press, 2009.

[Kirk 92] David Kirk. *Graphics Gems III*. Morgan Kaufmann, 1992.

[Kleinbauer 04] R Kleinbauer. "Kalman filtering implementation with Matlab.", 2004. Available online (http://elib.uni-stuttgart.de/opus/volltexte/2005/2183).

[Klochek and MacKenzie 06] Chris Klochek and I Scott MacKenzie. "Performance measures of game controllers in a three-dimensional environment." In *Proceedings of Graphics Interface*, pp. 73–79. Canadian Information Processing Society, 2006.

[Kluwer 11] T. Kluwer. "I like your shirt - Dialogue Acts for Enabling Social Talk in Conversational Agents." In *International Conference on Intelligent Virtual Agents,*

Intelligence, Lecture Notes in Artificial Intelligence., 6895, edited by H. Vihjalms-son, Stefan Kopp, Stacy Marsella, and K R Thorisson, Lecture Notes in Artificial Intelligence., 6895, pp. 14–27. Springer-Verlag Berlin Heidelberg, 2011.

[Knight 87] J L Knight. "Manual control and tracking." In *Handbook of Human Factors*, edited by Gavriel Salvendy. John Wiley & Sons, 1987.

[Kohli et al. 05] L. Kohli, E. Burns, D. Miller, and H. Fuchs. "Combining Passive Haptics with Redirected Walking." In *ACM Augmented Tele-Existence*, 157, 157, pp. 253 – 254, 2005.

[Konvalin 09] B C Konvalin. "Compensating for tilt, hard-iron and soft-iron effects.", 2009. Available online (http://www.sensorsmag.com/sensors/motion-velocity-displacement/compensating-tilt-hard-iron-and-soft-iron-effects-6475).

[Kopper et al. 11] R Kopper, F Bacim, and D A Bowman. "Rapid and accurate 3D selection by progressive refinement." *3D User Interfaces (3DUI), 2011 IEEE Symposium on*, pp. 67–74.

[Kosara et al. 03] R Kosara, H Hauser, and D L Gresh. "An interaction view on information visualization." *Proceedings EuroGraphics 2003: State-of-the-Art Report*.

[Kratz and Rohs 10] Sven Kratz and Michael Rohs. "A $3 gesture recognizer: simple gesture recognition for devices equipped with 3D acceleration sensors." In *Proceedings of the 15th International Conference on Intelligent User Interfaces, IUI '10*, pp. 341–344. New York, New York, USA: ACM, 2010.

[Kratz and Rohs 11] Sven Kratz and Michael Rohs. "Protractor3D: A Closed-form So-lution to Rotation-invariant 3D Gestures." In *Proceedings of the 16th International Conference on Intelligent User Interfaces, IUI '11*, pp. 371–374. ACM, 2011.

[Kristensson and Zhai 04] Per-Ola Kristensson and Shumin Zhai. "SHARK2: a large vocabulary shorthand writing system for pen-based computers." In *Proceedings of the 17th Annual ACM Symposium on User Interface Software and Technology, UIST '04*, p. 43. New York, New York, USA: ACM, 2004.

[Krueger et al. 85] Myron W Krueger, Thomas Gionfriddo, and Katrin Hinrichsen. "VIDEOPLACE—an artificial reality." In *Proceedings of the SIGCHI Conference on Human Factors in Computing Systems, CHI '85*, pp. 35–40. New York, New York, USA: ACM, 1985.

[Krueger 91] Myron W Krueger. *Artificial Reality II*. Addison-Wesley Professional, 1991.

[Kruger et al. 05] R Kruger, S Carpendale, SD Scott, and A Tang. "Fluid integration of rotation and translation." In *Proceedings of the SIGCHI Conference on Human Factors in Computing Systems, CHI '05*, pp. 601–610. ACM, 2005.

[Kruijff 06] Ernst Kruijff. "Unconventional 3D User Interfaces for Virtual Environments." Ph.D. thesis, Graz University of Technology, Graz University of Technology, 2006.

[Krumm 09] John Krumm. *Ubiquitous Computing Fundamentals*. CRC Press, 2009.

[Kuipers 99] J B Kuipers. *Quaternions and Rotation Sequences: A Primer with Appli-cations to Orbits, Aerospace, and Virtual Reality*. Princeton paperbacks, Prince-ton University Press, 1999. Available online (https://books.google.com/books?id=_2sS4mC0p-EC).

[Kulshreshth et al. 13] Arun Kulshreshth, Joseph J LaViola, and Jr. "Evaluating performance benefits of head tracking in modern video games." In *Proceedings of the 1st Symposium on Spatial User Interaction, SUI '13*, pp. 53–60. ACM, 2013.

[Kurtenbach and Buxton 91] Gordon Kurtenbach and William Buxton. "Issues in combining marking and direct manipulation techniques." In *UIST '91: Proceedings of the 4th Annual ACM Symposium on User Interface Software and Technology*, pp. 137–144. New York, New York, USA: ACM, 1991.

[LaFleur et al. 13] Karl LaFleur, Kaitlin Cassady, Alexander Doud, Kaleb Shades, Eitan Rogin, and Bin He. "Quadcopter control in three-dimensional space using a noninvasive motor imagery-based brain–computer interface." *Journal of Neural Engineering* 10:4 (2013), 046003.

[Lam 11] Pom Yuan Lam. "Gyroscopic stabilization of a kid-size bicycle." In *Cybernetics and Intelligent Systems (CIS), 2011 IEEE 5th International Conference on*, pp. 247–252, 2011.

[Lang et al. 10] Manuel Lang, Alexander Hornung, Oliver Wang, Steven Poulakos, Aljoscha Smolic, and Markus Gross. "Nonlinear disparity mapping for stereoscopic 3D." *SIGGRAPH '10: SIGGRAPH 2010 papers*.

[Langetepe and Zachmann 06] Elmar Langetepe and Gabriel Zachmann. *Geometric data structures for computer graphics.* A K Peters, Ltd., 2006.

[Lank and Saund 05] Edward Lank and Eric Saund. "Sloppy selection: Providing an accurate interpretation of imprecise selection gestures." *Computers & Graphics* 29:4.

[Lankford 00] Chris Lankford. "Effective eye-gaze input into Windows." In *ETRA '00: Proceedings of the 2000 Symposium on Eye Tracking Research & Applications*, pp. 23–27. New York, New York, USA: ACM, 2000.

[Lao et al. 09] Songyang Lao, Xiangan Heng, Guohua Zhang, Yunxiang Ling, and Peng Wang. "A gestural interaction design model for multi-touch displays." *Proceedings of the 23rd British HCI Group Annual Conference on People and Computers: Celebrating People and Technology (BCS-HCI '09)*, pp. 440–446.

[Lapointe et al. 11] J F Lapointe, P Savard, and N G Vinson. "A comparative study of four input devices for desktop virtual walkthroughs." *Computers in Human Behavior* 27:6 (2011), 2186–2191.

[Latulipe et al. 06] Celine Latulipe, Stephen Mann, Craig S Kaplan, and Charlie L A Clarke. "symSpline: symmetric two-handed spline manipulation." In *CHI '06: Proceedings of the SIGCHI Conference on Human Factors in Computing Systems*, pp. 349–358. New York, New York, USA: ACM, 2006.

[LaViola Jr. 99] Joseph J LaViola Jr. "Whole-Hand and Speech Input in Virtual Environments." Ph.D. thesis, Brown University, 1999.

[Lawrence 98] A Lawrence. *Modern inertial technology: navigation, guidance, and control*, 368. Springer, 1998.

[Lawton 94] C A Lawton. "Gender differences in way-finding strategies: Relationship to spatial ability and spatial anxiety." *Sex Roles*.

[Leap 14a] L. Leap. "Leap Motion official developer site.", 2014. [Online; accessed 23-January-2015]. Available online (https://www.developer.leapmotion.com).

[Leap 14b] L. Leap. "Leap Motion official site.", 2014. [Online; accessed 23-January-2015]. Available online (https://www.leapmotion.com/product).

[Leap 14c] L. Leap. "Leap Motion official VR site.", 2014. [Online; accessed 23-January-2015]. Available online (https://www.developer.leapmotion.com/vr).

[Lécuyer et al. 04] A Lécuyer, M Vidal, O Joly, C Megard, and A Berthoz. "Can haptic feedback improve the perception of self-motion in virtual reality?" In *Haptic Interfaces for Virtual Environment and Teleoperator Systems, 2004. HAPTICS '04. Proceedings. 12th International Symposium on*, pp. 208–215, 2004.

[Lee et al. 85] SK Lee, William Buxton, and K. C. Smith. "A Multi-Touch Three Dimensional Touch-sensitive Tablet." In *Proceedings of the SIGCHI Conference on Human Factors in Computing Systems, CHI '85*, pp. 21–25. New York, NY, USA: ACM, 1985. Available online (http://doi.acm.org/10.1145/317456.317461).

[Leganchuk et al. 98] Andrea Leganchuk, Shumin Zhai, and William Buxton. "Manual and cognitive benefits of two-handed input: an experimental study." *Transactions on Computer-Human Interaction (TOCHI* 5:4.

[Lemon and Konstas 09] Oliver Lemon and Ioannis Konstas. "User Simulations for Context-Sensitive Speech Recognition in Spoken Dialogue Systems." In *Proceedings of the 12th Conference of the European Chapter of the Association for Computational Linguistics, EACL '09*, pp. 505–513. Stroudsburg, PA, USA: Association for Computational Linguistics, 2009. Available online (http://dl.acm.org/citation.cfm?id=1609067.1609123).

[Lemon et al. 06] Oliver Lemon, Kallirroi Georgila, James Henderson, and Matthew Stuttle. "An ISU dialogue system exhibiting reinforcement learning of dialogue policies: generic slot-filling in the TALK in-car system." In *Proceedings of the Eleventh Conference of the European Chapter of the Association for Computational Linguistics: Posters & Demonstrations, EACL '06*, pp. 119–122. Stroudsburg, PA, USA: Association for Computational Linguistics, 2006. Available online (http://dl.acm.org/citation.cfm?id=1608974.1608986).

[Lemon et al. 07] Olivier Lemon, Olivier Pietquin, et al. "Machine learning for spoken dialogue systems." In *Proceedings of the European Conference on Speech Communication and Technologies (Interspeech'07)*, pp. 2685–2688, 2007.

[Lepinski et al. 10] G Julian Lepinski, Tovi Grossman, and George Fitzmaurice. "The design and evaluation of multitouch marking menus." In *CHI '10: Proceedings of the SIGCHI Conference on Human Factors in Computing Systems*, p. 2233. New York, New York, USA: ACM, 2010.

[Levin and Levin 06] Esther Levin and Alex Levin. "Evaluation of Spoken Dialogue Technology for Real-Time Health Data Collection." *J Med Internet Res* 8:4 (2006), e30. Available online (http://www.jmir.org/2006/4/e30/).

[Levin et al. 97] Esther Levin, Roberto Pieraccini, and Wieland Eckert. "Learning dialogue strategies within the Markov decision process framework." In *Automatic Speech Recognition and Understanding, 1997. Proceedings., 1997 IEEE Workshop on*, pp. 72–79. IEEE, 1997.

[Levin et al. 98] Esther Levin, Roberto Pieraccini, and Wieland Eckert. "Using Markov decision process for learning dialogue strategies." In *Acoustics, Speech and Signal Processing, 1998. Proceedings of the 1998 IEEE International Conference on*, 1, 1, pp. 201–204. IEEE, 1998.

[Levinew et al. 84] M Levinew, I Marchon, and G Hanley. "The Placement and Misplacement of You-Are-Here Maps." *Environment and Behavior* 16:2 (1984), 139–157.

[Levitin 12] Anany Levitin. *Introduction to the Design and Analysis of Algorithms*, Third edition. New Jersey: Pearson Higher Ed, 2012.

[Li et al. 13] William Li, Jim Glass, Nicholas Roy, and Seth Teller. "Probabilistic Dialogue Modeling for Speech-Enabled Assistive Technology." In *Proceedings of the Fourth Workshop on Speech and Language Processing for Assistive Technologies*, pp. 67–72. Grenoble, France: Association for Computational Linguistics, 2013. Available online (http://www.aclweb.org/anthology/W13-3912).

[Li 10] Y Li. "Protractor: a fast and accurate gesture recognizer." In *Proceedings of the 28th International Conference on Human Factors in Computing Systems, CHI '10*. ACM, 2010.

[Liang and Green 94] Jiandong Liang and Mark Green. "JDCAD: A highly interactive 3D modeling system." *Computers & Graphics* 18:4 (1994), 499–506.

[Liang et al. 91] Jiandong Liang, Chris Shaw, and Mark Green. "On temporal-spatial realism in the virtual reality environment." In *UIST '91: Proceedings of the 4th Annual ACM Symposium on User Interface Software and Technology*. ACM, 1991.

[Liang et al. 13] Hai-Ning Liang, Cary Williams, Myron Semegen, Wolfgang Stuerzlinger, and Pourang Irani. "an Investigation of Suitable Interactions for 3D Manipulation of Distant Objects Through a Mobile Device." *International Journal of Innovative Computing, Information and Control* 9 (2013), 4743–4752.

[Lisetti et al. 13] Christine Lisetti, Reza Amini, Ugan Yasavur, and Naphtali Rishe. "I Can Help You Change! An Empathic Virtual Agent Delivers Behavior Change Health Interventions." *ACM Transactions on Management Information Systems (TMIS)* 4:4 (2013), 19.

[Litman et al. 02] Diane Litman, Michael Kearns, and Marilyn Walker. "Optimizing Dialogue Management with Reinforcement Learning: Experiments with the NJFun System Satinder Singh tAvExA@ cs. coloRAdo. Edu Syntek Capital New York, NY 10019." *Journal of Artificial Intelligence Research* 16 (2002), 105–133.

[Liu and Räihä 10] Ying Liu and Kari-Jouko Räihä. "Predicting Chinese text entry speeds on mobile phones." In *CHI '10: Proceedings of the SIGCHI Conference on Human Factors in Computing Systems*, pp. 2183–2192. New York, New York, USA: ACM, 2010.

[Liu et al. 11] Su Liu, Reng Zeng, and Xudong He. "PIPE-A Modeling Tool for High Level Petri Nets." In *The 23rd International Conference on Software Engineering and Knowledge Engineering, Seke 2011*, 2011.

[Loguidice and Barton 14] Bill Loguidice and Matt Barton. *Vintage Game Consoles*. An Inside Look at Apple, Atari, Commodore, Nintendo, and the Greatest Gaming Platforms of All Time, CRC Press, 2014.

[Lowenstein 74] O E Lowenstein. "Comparative Morphology and Physiology." In *Vestibular System Part 1: Basic Mechanisms*, pp. 75–120. Berlin, Heidelberg: Springer Berlin Heidelberg, 1974.

[Lü and Li 12] Hao Lü and Yang Li. "Gesture coder: a tool for programming multi-touch gestures by demonstration." In *Proceedings of the SIGCHI Conference on Human Factors in Computing Systems*, CHI '12, pp. 2875–2884. ACM, 2012.

[Lu 13] Fei Lu. "System and Method for Providing Multi-Dimensional Touch Input Vector." US Patent 8,605,046, 2013.

[Lubos 14] Paul Lubos. "Touching the Third Dimension." In *ITS '14: Proceedings of the Ninth ACM International Conference on Interactive Tabletops and Surfaces*. ACM, 2014.

[Luna 11] Luna. *Introduction to 3D Game Programming With Directx 11*. Jones & Bartlett Publishers, 2011.

[Lundstrom et al. 11] C Lundstrom, T Rydell, C Forsell, A Persson, and A Ynnerman. "Multi-Touch Table System for Medical Visualization: Application to Orthopedic Surgery Planning." *IEEE Transactions on Visualization and Computer Graphics* 17:12 (2011), 1775–1784.

[Lynch 60] Kenneth Lynch. *The Image of the City*. MIT Press, 1960.

[Lynch 84] Kevin Lynch. "Reconsidering The Image of the City." In *Cities of the Mind*, pp. 151–161. Boston, MA: Springer US, 1984.

[Lyons et al. 09] Kent Lyons, Trevor Pering, Barbara Rosario, Shivani Sud, and Roy Want. "Multi-display Composition: Supporting Display Sharing for Collocated Mobile Devices." In *Proceedings of the 12th IFIP TC 13 International Conference on Human-Computer Interaction: Part I*, INTERACT '09, pp. 758–771. Berlin, Heidelberg: Springer-Verlag, 2009. Available online (http://dx.doi.org/10.1007/978-3-642-03655-2_83).

[M. et al. 07] Boly M., Coleman M. R., Davis M. H., Hampshire A., Bor D., Moonen G., Maquet P. A., Pickard J. D., Laureys S., and Owen A. M. "When Thoughts Become Action: an fMRI Paradigm to Study Volitional Brain Activity in Noncommunicative Brain Injured Patients." *Neuroimage* 36:3 (2007), 979–992.

[M. et al. 14] Proudfoot M., Woolrich M. W., Nobre A. C., and Turner M. R. "Magnetoencephalography." *Practical Neurology* 14:5 (2014), 336–343.

[MacGougan et al. 05] Glenn MacGougan, Per Ludvig Normark, and Christian Stahlberg. "Innovation-Satellite Navigation Evolution-The Software GNSS Receiver-A further evolution of the GNSS receiver–A receiver whose signal acquisition and processing is almost completely carried." *GPS World* 16:1 (2005), 48–55.

[MacKenzie and Buxton 92] I. Scott MacKenzie and William Buxton. "Extending Fitts' Law to Two-dimensional Tasks." In *Proceedings of the SIGCHI Conference on Human Factors in Computing Systems*, CHI '92, pp. 219–226. New York, NY, USA: ACM, 1992. Available online (http://doi.acm.org/10.1145/142750.142794).

[MacKenzie and Guiard 01] I Scott MacKenzie and Yves Guiard. "The two-handed desktop interface: are we there yet?" *CHI EA '01: CHI '01 Extended Abstracts on Human Factors in Computing Systems*, pp. 351–352.

[MacKenzie and Isokoski 08] I Scott MacKenzie and Poika Isokoski. "Fitts' throughput and the speed-accuracy tradeoff." In *CHI '08: Proceedings of the SIGCHI Conference on Human Factors in Computing Systems*, p. 1633. New York, New York, USA: ACM, 2008.

[MacKenzie and Teather 12] I Scott MacKenzie and Robert J Teather. "FittsTilt: the application of Fitts' law to tilt-based interaction." In *NordiCHI '12: Proceedings of the 7th Nordic Conference on Human-Computer Interaction: Making Sense Through Design*, p. 568. New York, New York, USA: ACM, 2012.

[MacKenzie and Ware 93] I Scott MacKenzie and Colin Ware. "Lag as a determinant of human performance in interactive systems." In *CHI '93: Proceedings of the INTERACT '93 and CHI '93 Conference on Human Factors in Computing Systems*, pp. 488–493. New York, New York, USA: ACM, 1993.

[MacKenzie et al. 01] I Scott MacKenzie, Hedy Kober, Derek Smith, Terry Jones, and Eugene Skepner. "LetterWise: prefix-based disambiguation for mobile text input." In *UIST '01: Proceedings of the 14th Annual ACM Symposium on User Interface Software and Technology*, pp. 111–120. New York, New York, USA: ACM, 2001.

[MacKenzie 89] I Scott MacKenzie. "A Note on the Information-Theoretic Basis for Fitts' Law." *Journal of motor behavior* 21:3 (1989), 323–330.

[MacKenzie 91] Ian Scott MacKenzie. "Fitts' Law As a Performance Model in Human-computer Interaction." Ph.D. thesis, University of Toronto, Toronto, Ont., Canada, Canada, 1991. UMI Order No. GAXNN-65985.

[MacKenzie 92] I Scott MacKenzie. "Fitts' law as a research and design tool in human-computer interaction." *Human–Computer Interaction* 7:1 (1992), 91–139.

[MacKenzie 12] I Scott MacKenzie. *Human-Computer Interaction: An Empirical Research Perspective*. Morgan Kaufmann;, 2012.

[MacKenzie 13] I S MacKenzie. "A Note on the Validity of the Shannon Formulation for Fitts' Index of Difficulty." *Open Journal of Applied Sciences*.

[Mackinlay et al. 90] J Mackinlay, SK Card, and GG Robertson. "A semantic analysis of the design space of input devices." *Human–Computer Interaction* 5:2 (1990), 145–190.

[MacLean and Labahn 10] S MacLean and G Labahn. "Elastic matching in linear time and constant space." In *International Workshop on Document Analysis Systems 2010*, *DAS '10*, 2010.

[Madgwick et al. 11] Sebastian OH Madgwick, Andrew JL Harrison, and Ravi Vaidyanathan. "Estimation of IMU and MARG orientation using a gradient descent algorithm." In *Rehabilitation Robotics (ICORR), 2011 IEEE International Conference on*, pp. 1–7. IEEE, 2011.

[Madgwick 10] Sebastian OH Madgwick. "An efficient orientation filter for inertial and inertial/magnetic sensor arrays." *Report x-io and University of Bristol (UK)*.

[Maenaka 08] K Maenaka. "MEMS inertial sensors and their applications." *Networked Sensing Systems*, pp. 71–73.

[Makofske et al. 04] David B Makofske, Michael J Donahoo, and Kenneth L Calvert. *TCP/IP Sockets in C#*. Practical Guide for Programmers, Morgan Kaufmann, 2004.

[Mapes and Moshell 95] Daniel P Mapes and J Michael Moshell. "A Two Handed Interface for Object Manipulation in Virtual Environments." *Presence* 4:4 (1995), 403–416.

[Margolis 11] Michael Margolis. *Arduino Cookbook.* "O'Reilly Media, Inc.", 2011.

[Marquardt et al. 11] N. Marquardt, R. Jota, S. Greenberg, and J. Jorge. "The Continuous Interaction Space: Interaction Techniques Unifying Touch and Gesture On and Above a Digital Surface." In *Proceedings of the 13th IFIP TCI3 Conference on Human Computer Interaction - INTERACT 2011*, p. 16 pages. Lisbon, Portugal, 2011. Earlier version with different author order as Report 2011-993-05 (January, 2011).

[Martinet et al. 10] A. Martinet, G. Casiez, and G. Grisoni. "The Design and Evaluation of 3D Positioning Techniques for Multi-touch Displays." In *Proceedings of the Symposium on 3D User Interfaces (3DUI)*, 2010.

[Martinez-Conde et al. 04] Susana Martinez-Conde, Stephen L Macknik, and David H Hubel. "The role of fixational eye movements in visual perception." *Nature Reviews Neuroscience* 5:3 (2004), 229–240.

[Martinez-Conde et al. 13] Susana Martinez-Conde, Jorge Otero-Millan, and Stephen L Macknik. "The impact of microsaccades on vision: towards a unified theory of saccadic function." *Nature Reviews Neuroscience* 14:2 (2013), 83–96.

[Martini et al. 01] Frederic H Martini, W C Ober, C W Garrison, K Welch, and R T Hutchings. *Fundamentals of Anatomy and Physiology*, Fifth edition. Upper Saddle River, NJ: Prentice Hall, 2001.

[Mateas and Stern 00] Michael Mateas and Andrew Stern. "Towards Integrating Plot and Character for Interactive Drama." In *Working notes of the Social Intelligent Agents: The Human in the Loop Symposium. AAAI Fall Symposium Series.*, pp. 113–118. AAAI Press, 2000.

[Matsushita et al. 00] Nobuyuki Matsushita, Yuji Ayatsuka, and Jun Rekimoto. "Dual touch: a two-handed interface for pen-based PDAs." In *UIST '00: Proceedings of the 13th Annual ACM Symposium on User Interface Software and Technology.* ACM, 2000.

[MATWORK 12] MATWORK. "Control Tutorial for MATLAB and Simulink.", 2012. Available online (http://ctms.engin.umich.edu/CTMS/index.php?example= InvertedPendulum&section=SystemModeling).

[Mauriello et al. 11] Leanne M. Mauriello, N. Simay Gökbayrak, Deborah F. Van Marter, Andrea L. Paiva, and Janice M. Prochaska. "An Internet-Based Computer-Tailored Intervention to Promote Responsible Drinking: Findings from a Pilot Test with Employed Adults." *Alcoholism Treatment* 30:1 (2011), 1–15. Available online (http://www.tandfonline.com/doi/abs/10.1080/07347324.2012.635528).

[McClellan et al. 98] James H McClellan, Ronald W Schafer, and Mark A Yoder. *DSP First.* A Multimedia Approach, Prentice-Hall, 1998.

[McCoy et al. 13] Joshua McCoy, Mike Treanor, Ben Samuel, Aaron A. Reed, Michael Mateas, and Noah Wardrip-Fruin. "Prom Week: Designing past the game/story dilemma." In *FDG 2013*, pp. 94–101, 2013.

[McCoy et al. 14] J. McCoy, M. Treanor, B. Samuel, A.A. Reed, M. Mateas, and N. Wardrip-Fruin. "Social Story Worlds With Comme il Faut." *Computational Intelligence and AI in Games, IEEE Transactions on* 6:2 (2014), 97–112.

[McCrae et al. 09] James McCrae, Igor Mordatch, Michael Glueck, and Azam Khan. "Multiscale 3D Navigation." In *Proceedings of the 2009 Symposium on Interactive 3D Graphics and Games, I3D '09*, pp. 7–14. ACM, 2009.

[McGahan 14] MIchael McGahan. "Perspective Switching in Virtual Environments." Ph.D. thesis, Columbia University, Columbia University, 2014.

[McGuffin and Balakrishnan 05] Michael J McGuffin and Ravin Balakrishnan. "Fitts' law and expanding targets: Experimental studies and designs for user interfaces." *Transactions on Computer-Human Interaction (TOCHI* 12:4 (2005), 388–422.

[McQuiggan and Lester 07] S. McQuiggan and J. Lester. "Modeling and evaluating empathy in embodied companion agents." *International Journal of Human-Computer Studies* 65 (2007), 348–360.

[McShaffry 13] Mike McShaffry. *Game Coding Complete, Fourth*, Fourth edition. Cengage Learning, 2013.

[McTear 02] Michael F. McTear. "Spoken dialogue technology: enabling the conversational user interface." *ACM Comput. Surv.* 34:1 (2002), 90–169. Available online (http://doi.acm.org/10.1145/505282.505285).

[McTear 11] Michael McTear. "Trends, Challenges and Opportunities in Spoken Dialogue Research." In *Spoken Dialogue Systems Technology and Design*, edited by Wolfgang Minker, Gary Geunbae Lee, Satoshi Nakamura, and Joseph Mariani, pp. 135–161. Springer New York, 2011. Available online (http://dx.doi.org/10.1007/978-1-4419-7934-6_6).

[Meng and Halle 04] Jeanette C Meng and Michael Halle. "Using a 2D colon to guide 3D navigation in virtual colonoscopy." In *Proceedings of the 1st Symposium on Applied Perception in Graphics and Visualization, APGV '04*, p. 179. New York, New York, USA: ACM, 2004.

[Messick 98] Paul Messick. *Maximum MIDI*. Music Applications in C++, Manning Publications, 1998.

[Meyer et al. 88] David E Meyer, Richard A Abrams, Sylvan Kornblum, Charles E Wright, and et al. "Optimality in human motor performance: Ideal control of rapid aimed movements." *Psychological Review* 95:3 (1988), 340–370.

[Meyer et al. 92] Kenneth Meyer, Hugh L. Applewhite, and Frank A. Biocca. "A Survey of Position Trackers." *Presence: Teleoper. Virtual Environ.* 1:2 (1992), 173–200. Available online (http://dl.acm.org/citation.cfm?id=196564.196568).

[Microchip 15] Microchip. "Development Tools Home Page." 2015. [Online; accessed 11-February-2015]. Available online (http://www.microchip.com/pagehandler/en-us/devtools/devtoolsmain/home.html).

[Microsoft 07] Microsoft. "Touch Technology." 2007. [Online; accessed 4-February-2015]. Available online (http://www.wacom-components.com/english/technology/index.html).

[Microsoft 09] Microsoft. "TOUCHINPUT structure." 2009. [Online; accessed 3-February-2015]. Available online (https://msdn.microsoft.com/en-us/library/windows/desktop/dd317334(v=vs.85).aspx).

[Microsoft 14a] Microsoft. "Coding4Fun.", 2014. [Online; accessed 23-January-2015]. Available online (http://channel9.msdn.com/coding4fun/kinect).

[Microsoft 14b] Microsoft. "Kinect Data Sources and Programming Model.", 2014. [Online; accessed 22-February-2015]. Available online (http://channel9.msdn.com/Series/ Programming-Kinect-for-Windows-v2/02).

[Microsoft 14c] Microsoft. "Kinect for Windows SDK 2.0.", 2014. [Online; accessed 22-February-2015]. Available online (http://www.microsoft.com/en-us/download/ details.aspx?id=44561).

[Microsoft 14d] Microsoft. "Kinect for Windows site.", 2014. [Online; accessed 23-January-2015]. Available online (https://www.kinectforwindows.com).

[Microsoft 14e] Microsoft. "Multi-Touch Systems that I Have Known and Loved.", 2014. [Online; accessed 5-February-2015]. Available online (http://www.billbuxton.com/ multitouchOverview.html).

[Microsoft 14f] Microsoft. "Programming for Kinect SDK 2.0.", 2014. [Online; accessed 22-February-2015]. Available online (http://www.microsoft.com/en-us/ kinectforwindows/develop/how-to-videos).

[Mine et al. 97] Mark R Mine, Frederick P Brooks, Jr, and Carlo H Sequin. "Moving objects in space: exploiting proprioception in virtual-environment interaction." In *SIGGRAPH '97: Proceedings of the 24th Annual Conference on Computer Graphics and Interactive Techniques*, pp. 19–26. New York, New York, USA: ACM Press/Addison-Wesley Publishing Co., 1997.

[Mine 95a] Mark R Mine. "ISAAC: A Virtual Environment Tool for the Interactive Construction of Virtual Worlds." Technical report, University of North Carolina Computer Science, Chapel Hill, NC, USA, 1995.

[Mine 95b] Mark R Mine. "Virtual Environment Interaction Techniques." Technical Report 95-018, University of North Carolina, 1995.

[Mine 97] Mark R Mine. "ISAAC: a meta-cad system for virtual environments." *Computer-Aided Design* 29:8 (1997), 547–553.

[Mine 98] Mark R Mine. "Exploiting proprioception in virtual-environment interaction." Ph.D. thesis, University of North Carolina at Chapel Hill, 1998.

[Mirick 24] C B Mirick. "Electrical distant-control system." US Patent 1,597,416, 1924.

[Mistry et al. 09] Pranav Mistry, Pattie Maes, and Liyan Chang. "WUW - wear Ur world: a wearable gestural interface." In *CHI '09 Extended Abstracts on Human Factors in Computing Systems*, *CHI EA '09*, pp. 4111–4116. New York, NY, USA: ACM, 2009. Available online (http://doi.acm.org/10.1145/1520340.1520626).

[Mitchell et al. 08] T. M. Mitchell, S. V. Shinkareva, A. Carlson, K. Chang, V. L. Malave, R. A. Mason, and M. A. Just. "Predicting Human Brain Activity Associated with the Meanings of Nouns." *Science* 320:5880 (2008), 1191–1195.

[Mitra and Kuo 06] S K Mitra and Y Kuo. *Digital signal processing: a computer-based approach*. Tata Mcgraw-Hill Publishing Company Limited, 2006. Available online (https://books.google.com/books?id=bHLXQQAACAAJ).

[Miyawaki et al. 08] Yoichi Miyawaki, Hajime Uchida, Okito Yamashita, Masa aki Sato, Yusuke Morito, Hiroki C. Tanabe, Norihiro Sadato, and Yukiyasu Kamitani. "Visual Image Reconstruction from Human Brain Activity using a Combination of Multiscale Local Image Decoders." *Neuron* 60:5 (2008), 915–929.

[Moeller and Kerne 12] Jon Moeller and Andruid Kerne. "ZeroTouch: an optical multi-touch and free-air interaction architecture." In *CHI '12: Proceedings of the SIGCHI Conference on Human Factors in Computing Systems*. ACM, 2012.

[Molyneaux et al. 12] David Molyneaux, Shahram Izadi, David Kim, Otmar Hilliges, Steve Hodges, Xiang Cao, Alex Butler, and Hans Gellersen. "Interactive environment-aware handheld projectors for pervasive computing spaces." In *Proceedings of the 10th International Conference on Pervasive Computing, Pervasive'12*, pp. 197–215. Berlin, Heidelberg: Springer-Verlag, 2012. Available online (http://dx.doi.org/10. 1007/978-3-642-31205-2_13).

[Monk 11] Simon Monk. *Programming Arduino Getting Started with Sketches*. McGraw Hill Professional, 2011.

[Monk 13] Simon Monk. *Programming Arduino Next Steps: Going Further with Sketches*. McGraw Hill Professional, 2013.

[Morbini et al. 12] Fabrizio Morbini, Eric Forbell, David DeVault, Kenji Sagae, David R. Traum, and Albert A. Rizzo. "A mixed-initiative conversational dialogue system for healthcare." In *Proceedings of the 13th Annual Meeting of the Special Interest Group on Discourse and Dialogue, SIGDIAL '12*, pp. 137–139. Stroudsburg, PA, USA: Association for Computational Linguistics, 2012. Available online (http://dl. acm.org/citation.cfm?id=2392800.2392825).

[Morris et al. 10] Meredith Ringel Morris, Jacob O Wobbrock, and Andrew D Wilson. "Understanding users' preferences for surface gestures." In *GI '10: Proceedings of Graphics Interface 2010*. Canadian Information Processing Society, 2010.

[Mortensen 01] Kjeld H Mortensen. "Efficient data-structures and algorithms for a coloured Petri nets simulator." In *In Proceedings of the 3rd Workshop and Tutorial on Practical Use of Coloured Petri Nets and the CPN Tools, DAIMI PB*, edited by Kurt Jensen, pp. 57–75. Department of Computer Science, Aarhus University, 2001.

[Mortenson 06] Michael E Mortenson. *Geometric modeling*, Third edition. New York: Industrial Press Inc., 2006.

[Moscovich and Hughes 06] Tomer Moscovich and John F Hughes. "Multi-finger cursor techniques." *Graphics Interface*, pp. 1–7.

[Moscovich and Hughes 08a] T Moscovich and J Hughes. "Indirect mappings of multi-touch input using one and two hands." In *Proceedings of the SIGCHI Conference on Human Factors in Computing Systems, CHI '08*, pp. 1275–1284. New York, NY, USA: ACM, 2008. Available online (http://doi.acm.org/10.1145/1357054.1357254).

[Moscovich and Hughes 08b] Tomer Moscovich and John F Hughes. "Indirect mappings of multi-touch input using one and two hands." In *Proceedings of the SIGCHI Conference on Human Factors in Computing Systems, CHI '08*, pp. 1275–1284. New York, New York, USA: ACM, 2008.

[Mossel et al. 13] Annette Mossel, Benjamin Venditti, and Hannes Kaufmann. "3DTouch and HOMER-S: intuitive manipulation techniques for one-handed handheld augmented reality." In *VRIC '13: Proceedings of the Virtual Reality International Conference: Laval Virtual*, p. 1. New York, New York, USA: ACM, 2013.

[Moyer et al. 02] Anne Moyer, John W. Finney, Carolyn E. Swearingen, and Pamela Vergun. "Brief interventions for alcohol problems: a meta-analytic review of controlled investigations in treatment-seeking and non-treatment-seeking populations." *Addiction* 97:3 (2002), 279–292. Available online (http://dx.doi.org/10.1046/j.1360-0443.2002.00018.x).

[Moyer et al. 04] Anne Moyer, John W Finney, et al. "Brief interventions for alcohol problems: Factors that facilitate implementation." *Alcohol Research and Health* 28:1 (2004), 44.

[Mukundan 12] Ramakrishnan Mukundan. *Advanced Methods in Computer Graphics. With Examples in OpenGL*, London: Springer Science & Business Media, 2012.

[Müller-Tomfelde et al. 10] Christian Müller-Tomfelde, Johannes Schöning, Jonathan Hook, Tom Bartindale, Dominik Schmidt, Patrick Oliver, Florian Echtler, Nima Motamedi, Peter Brandl, and Ulrich Zadow. "Building Interactive Multi-Touch Surfaces." In *Tabletops - Horizontal Interactive Displays, Human-Computer Interaction Series*, edited by Christian Müller-Tomfelde, pp. 27–49. Springer London, 2010.

[Müller-Tomfelde 10] C Müller-Tomfelde. "Tabletops: Horizontal Interactive Displays.", 2010.

[Munro et al. 14] Allen Munro, Jim Patrey, Elizabeth Biddle, and Meredith Carroll. "Cognitive Aspects of Virtual Environment Design." In *Handbook of Virtual Environments*, edited by Kelly S Hale and Kay M Stanney, pp. 391–410. CRC Press, 2014.

[Murata 89] Tadao Murata. "Petri nets: Properties, analysis and applications." *Proceedings of the IEEE* 77:4 (1989), 541–580.

[Murugappan et al. 12] Sundar Murugappan, Vinayak, Niklas Elmqvist, and Karthik Ramani. "Extended multitouch: recovering touch posture and differentiating users using a depth camera." In *UIST '12: Proceedings of the 25th Annual ACM Symposium on User Interface Software and Technology*, p. 487. New York, New York, USA: ACM, 2012.

[Myers et al. 00] Brad A Myers, Kin Pou Lie, and Bo-Chieh Yang. "Two-handed input using a PDA and a mouse." In *CHI '00: Proceedings of the SIGCHI conference on Human Factors in Computing Systems*, pp. 41–48. New York, New York, USA: ACM, 2000.

[Myers 90] Brad A Myers. "A new model for handling input." *ACM Transactions on Information Systems (TOIS)* 8:3 (1990), 289–320.

[Nacenta et al. 06] Miguel A. Nacenta, Samer Sallam, Bernard Champoux, Sriram Subramanian, and Carl Gutwin. "Perspective cursor: perspective-based interaction for multi-display environments." In *Proceedings of the SIGCHI Conference on Human Factors in Computing Systems, CHI '06*, pp. 289–298. New York, NY, USA: ACM, 2006. Available online (http://doi.acm.org/10.1145/1124772.1124817).

[Nacenta et al. 07] Miguel A. Nacenta, Satoshi Sakurai, Tokuo Yamaguchi, Yohei Miki, Yuichi Itoh, Yoshifumi Kitamura, Sriram Subramanian, and Carl Gutwin. "E-conic: a perspective-aware interface for multi-display environments." In *Proceedings of the 20th Annual ACM Symposium on User Interface Software and Technology, UIST '07*, pp. 279–288. New York, NY, USA: ACM, 2007. Available online (http://doi.acm.org/10.1145/1294211.1294260).

[Nacenta et al. 09] Miguel A Nacenta, Patrick Baudisch, Hrvoje Benko, and Andy Wilson. "Separability of spatial manipulations in multi-touch interfaces." In *Proceedings of Graphics Interface 2009, GI '09*. Canadian Information Processing Society, 2009.

[Nacenta et al. 13] Miguel A Nacenta, Yemliha Kamber, Yizhou Qiang, and Per Ola Kristensson. "Memorability of pre-designed and user-defined gesture sets." In *CHI '13: Proceedings of the SIGCHI Conference on Human Factors in Computing Systems*. ACM, 2013.

[Naci et al. 13] Lorina Naci, Rhodri Cusack, Vivian Z. Jia, and Adrian M. Owend. "The Brain's Silent Messenger: Using Selective Attention to Decode Human Thought for Brain-Based Communication." *The Journal of Neuroscience* 33:22 (2013), 9385–9393.

[Naef and Ferranti 11] M Naef and E Ferranti. "Multi-touch 3D navigation for a building energy management system." *IEEE Symposium on 3D User Interfaces (3DUI), 2011*, pp. 113–114.

[Nakatani and Rohrlich 83] Lloyd H Nakatani and John A Rohrlich. "Soft machines: A philosophy of user-computer interface design." In *Proceedings of the SIGCHI Conference on Human Factors in Computing Systems, CHI '83*, pp. 19–23. New York, New York, USA: ACM, 1983.

[Nam et al. 99] Yanghee Nam, Nwangyun Wohn, and Hyung Lee-Kwang. "Modeling and recognition of hand gesture using colored Petri nets." *IEEE Transactions on Systems, Man and Cybernetics, Part A: Systems and Humans* 29:5 (1999), 514–521.

[Naranjo and Hgskolan 08] Claudia C. Meruane Naranjo and Kungliga Tekniska Hgskolan. "Analysis and Modeling of MEMS Based Inertial Sensors. M.Sc. Thesis, School of Electrical Engineering Kungliga Tekniska HÃűgskolan.", 2008.

[Nelson] Graham Nelson. "Prompter: A Domain-Specific Language for Versu." https://versublog.files.wordpress.com/2014/05/graham_versu.pdfs. [Online; accessed on Mar. 04, 2015].

[Nets-Concepts 00] High-level Petri Nets-Concepts. "Definitions and Graphical Notation." *Final Draft International Standard ISO/IEC* 15909.

[Neuhauser and Kreps 11] L. Neuhauser and G.L Kreps. "Participatory design and artificial intelligence: Strategies to improve health communication for diverse audiences." In *Artificial Intelligence and Health Communication*, edited by D. (Eds.). Green, N., and Rubinelli, S., and Scott. Cambridge, MA: AAAI Press, 2011.

[Newell and Rosenbloom 80] A Newell and P S Rosenbloom. "Mechanisms of skill acquisition and the law of practice." In *Cognitive Skills and Their Acquisition*, edited by John Anderson. Hillsdale, New Jersey: MIT Press, 1980.

[Newell 94] Allen Newell. *Unified Theories of Cognition*. Harvard University Press, 1994.

[Newman 68] William M Newman. "A System for Interactive Graphical Programming." In *Proceedings of the April 30–May 2, 1968, Spring Joint Computer Conference, AFIPS '68 (Spring)*, pp. 47–54. New York, NY, USA: ACM, 1968. Available online (http://doi.acm.org/10.1145/1468075.1468083).

[Ni et al. 11] Tao Ni, Doug Bowman, and Chris North. "AirStroke: bringing unistroke text entry to freehand gesture interfaces." In *CHI '11: Proceedings of the SIGCHI Conference on Human Factors in Computing Systems*, p. 2473. New York, New York, USA: ACM, 2011.

[NIAAA 06] NIAAA. "NIAAA Alcohol Alert No. 66: Brief Interventions.", 2006. Available online (http://pubs.niaaa.nih.gov/publications/AA66/AA66.pdf).

[Nickel and Stiefelhagen 03] Kai Nickel and Rainer Stiefelhagen. "Pointing gesture recognition based on 3D-tracking of face, hands and head orientation." In *Proceedings of the Conference on Multimodal Interfaces (ICMI)*, pp. 140–146, 2003.

[Nielsen 94] Jakob Nielsen. *Usability Engineering*. Elsevier, 1994.

[Nielson and Olsen Jr 87] GM Nielson and DR Olsen Jr. "Direct manipulation techniques for 3D objects using 2D locator devices." *Proceedings of the 1986 workshop on Interactive 3D graphics*, pp. 175–182.

[Nikolic and Renaut 0] J Nikolic and F Renaut. "MEMS Inertial Sensors Technology." *students.asl.ethz.ch*.

[Norman 98] D. Norman. "The Design of Every-Day Things." Ph.D. thesis, MIT, 1998.

[Nurminen 08] Antti Nurminen. "Mobile 3D City Maps." *IEEE Computer Graphics and Applications* 28:4 (2008), 20–31.

[Ogata 09] Katsuhiko Ogata. *Modern Control Engineering* , Fifth edition. Modern Control Engineering, Prentice Hall, 2009.

[Oh and Stuerzlinger 05] Ji-Young Oh and Wolfgang Stuerzlinger. "Moving objects with 2D input devices in CAD systems and Desktop Virtual Environments." In *Graphics Interface 2005*, pp. 195–202, 2005.

[Olson 08] Gary M. Olson. "A Most Fitting Law." In *HCI Remixed*, edited by Thomas Erickson and David W McDonald, pp. 285–288. MIT Press, 2008.

[Olwal and Feiner 03] Alex Olwal and S Feiner. "The flexible pointer: An interaction technique for selection in augmented and virtual reality." In *UIST '03: Proceedings of the 16th Annual ACM Symposium on User Interface Software and Technology*, 2003.

[on Alcohol Abuse and (U.S.) 07] National Institute on Alcohol Abuse and Alcoholism (U.S.). *Helping Patients who Drink Too Much: A Clinician's Guide : Updated 2005 Edition*. NIH publication, U.S. Department of Health and Human Services, National Institutes of Health, National Institute on Alcohol Abuse and Alcoholism, 2007. Available online (https://books.google.com/books?id=LnMBD6Le_doC).

[Oostenveld and Praamstra 01] Robert Oostenveld and Peter Praamstra. "The five percent electrode system for high-resolution EEG and ERP measurements." *Clinical Neurophysiology* 112:4 (2001), 713–719.

[Orfanidis 98] S Orfanidis. *Introduction to Signal Processing*. Beijing: Tsinghua University Publishing House, 1998.

[Orland] Kyle Orland. "'Old Republic' writer discusses '60 man-years' of work." http://ingame-discuss.nbcnews.com/_news/2011/12/20/ 9569126-old-republic-writer-discusses-60-man-years-of-work. [Online; accessed on Mar. 04, 2015].

[Ortega et al. 13a] FR Ortega, A Barreto, N Rishe, M Adjouadi, and F Abyarjoo. "Poster: Real-Time Gesture Detection for Multi-Touch Devices." In *IEEE 8th Symposium on 3D User Interfaces, 3DUI '13*, pp. 167–168. IEEE, 2013.

[Ortega et al. 13b] Francisco R Ortega, Armando Barreto, and Naphtali Rishe. "Augmenting multi-touch with commodity devices." In *Proceedings of the 1st Symposium on Spatial User Interaction, SUI '13*, p. 95. New York, New York, USA: ACM, 2013.

[Ortega et al. 15] Francisco R Ortega, Armando Barreto, Naphtali Rishe, Nonnarit O-Larnnithipong, Fatemeh Abyarjoo, and Malek Adjouadi. "GyroTouch: Wrist gyroscope with a Multi-Touch Display." In *Human-Computer Interaction. Theories, Methods, and Tools*. Cham, Switzerland: Springer International Publishing, 2015.

[Orwick and Smith 07] Penny Orwick and Guy Smith. "Developing Drivers with the Windows Driver Foundation." Microsoft Press, 2007.

[Otsuki et al. 13] Mai Otsuki, Tsutomu Oshita, Asako Kimura, Fumihisa Shibata, and Hideyuki Tamura. "Touch & Detach: Ungrouping and observation methods for complex virtual objects using an elastic metaphor." In *2013 IEEE Symposium on 3D User Interfaces (3DUI)*, pp. 99–106. IEEE, 2013.

[Owen et al. 05] Russell N Owen, Gordon Kurtenbach, George W Fitzmaurice, Thomas Baudel, and William Buxton. "When it gets more difficult, use both hands: exploring bimanual curve manipulation." *Graphics Interface*, pp. 17–24.

[Packer and Jordan 02] Randall Packer and Ken Jordan. *Multimedia*. From Wagner to Virtual Reality, W. W. Norton & Company, 2002.

[Paek and Pieraccini 08] Tim Paek and Roberto Pieraccini. "Automating spoken dialogue management design using machine learning: An industry perspective." *Speech communication* 50:8 (2008), 716–729.

[Papadimitriou and Steiglitz 98] Christos H Papadimitriou and Kenneth Steiglitz. *Combinatorial Optimization*. Algorithms and Complexity, Courier Corporation, 1998.

[Parent 08] Rick Parent. *Computer Animation*, Second edition. Algorithms and Techniques, Newnes, 2008.

[Park and Han 10] Jae-Hee Park and Tackdon Han. "LLP+: multi-touch sensing using cross plane infrared laser light for interactive based displays." *SIGGRAPH 2010 Posters*, p. 1.

[Partala and Surakka 03] Timo Partala and Veikko Surakka. "Pupil size variation as an indication of affective processing." *International Journal of Human-Computer Studies*, pp. 185–198.

[Pavlovych and Stuerzlinger 08] Andriy Pavlovych and Wolfgang Stuerzlinger. "Effect of screen configuration and interaction devices in shared display groupware." In *Proceedings of the 3rd ACM International Workshop on Human-Centered Computing, HCC '08*, pp. 49–56. New York, NY, USA: ACM, 2008. Available online (http://doi.acm.org/10.1145/1462027.1462035).

[Pelachaud 09] Catherine Pelachaud. "Modelling multimodal expression of emotion in a virtual agent." *Philosophical Transactions of the Royal Society of London. Series B, Biological sciences* 364:1535 (2009), 3539–48. Available online (http://www.pubmedcentral.nih.gov/articlerender.fcgi?artid=2781894&tool=pmcentrez&rendertype=abstract).

[Pereira et al. 11] Francisco Pereira, Greg Detre, and Matthew Botvinick. "Generating Text from Functional Brain Images." *Frontiers in Human Neuroscience* 5:72.

[Perrault et al. 13] Simon T Perrault, Eric Lecolinet, James Eagan, and Yves Guiard. "Watchit: simple gestures and eyes-free interaction for wristwatches and bracelets." In *CHI '13: Proceedings of the SIGCHI Conference on Human Factors in Computing Systems*. ACM, 2013.

[Peruch et al. 86] Patrick Peruch, Jean Pailhous, and Christian Deutsch. "How do we locate ourselves on a map: A method for analyzing self-location processes." *Acta Psychologica* 61:1 (1986), 71–88.

[Péruch et al. 97] Patrick Péruch, Mark May, and Fredrik Wartenberg. "Homing in virtual environments: Effects of field of view and path layout." *Perception* 26:3 (1997), 301–311.

[Perumal 11] L Perumal. "Quaternion and its application in rotation using sets of regions." *International Journal of Engineering and Technology Innovation* 1:1 (2011), 35–52.

[Peters 81] Michael Peters. "Attentional asymmetries during concurrent bimanual performance." *The Quarterly Journal of Experimental Psychology Section A* 33:1 (1981), 95–103.

[Peterson 81] James Lyle Peterson. *Petri net theory and the modeling of systems*. Prentice Hall, 1981.

[Petzold 98] Charles Petzold. *Programming Windows*, Fifth edition. Microsoft Press, 1998.

[Petzold 13] Charles Petzold. *Programming Windows*, Sixth edition. Writing Windows 8 Apps With C# and XAML, Microsot Press, 2013.

[Pew and Baron 83] Richard W Pew and Sheldon Baron. "Perspectives on human performance modelling." *Automatica* 19:6 (1983), 663–676.

[Pfeiffer and Stuerzlinger 15] Max Pfeiffer and Wolfgang Stuerzlinger. "3D Virtual Hand Selection with EMS and Vibration Feedback." In *CHI EA '15: Proceedings of the 33rd Annual ACM Conference Extended Abstracts on Human Factors in Computing Systems*, pp. 1361–1366. New York, New York, USA: ACM, 2015.

[Pfeuffer et al. 14] Ken Pfeuffer, Jason Alexander, Ming Ki Chong, and Hans Gellersen. "Gaze-touch: combining gaze with multi-touch for interaction on the same surface." In *UIST '14: Proceedings of the 27th Annual ACM Symposium on User Interface Software and Technology*. ACM, 2014.

[Picard 97] Rosalind W Picard. *Affective Computing*. MIT Press, 1997.

[Picard 03] Rosalind W Picard. "Affective computing: challenges." *International Journal of Human-Computer Studies* 59:1-2 (2003), 55–64.

[Pick and Acredolo 83] Herbert Pick and Linda P Acredolo. *Spatial Orientation*. Theory, Research, and Application, Plenum Press, 1983.

[Pieraccini and Huerta 08] Roberto Pieraccini and Juan M. Huerta. "Where Do We Go from Here?" In *Recent Trends in Discourse and Dialogue*, Text, Speech and Language Technology, 39, edited by Laila DybkjÃẹr and Wolfgang Minker, Text, Speech and Language Technology, 39, pp. 1–24. Springer Netherlands, 2008. Available online (http://dx.doi.org/10.1007/978-1-4020-6821-8_1).

[Pierce and Pausch 02] Jeffrey S Pierce and Randy Pausch. "Comparing voodoo dolls and HOMER: exploring the importance of feedback in virtual environments." In *CHI '02: Proceedings of the SIGCHI Conference on Human Factors in Computing Systems*, pp. 105–112. New York, New York, USA: ACM, 2002.

[Pierce et al. 97] Jeffrey S Pierce, Andrew S Forsberg, Matthew J Conway, Seung Hong, Robert C Zeleznik, and Mark R Mine. "Image plane interaction techniques in 3D immersive environments." In *I3D '97: Proceedings of the 1997 Symposium on Interactive 3D Graphics*, pp. 39–ff. New York, New York, USA: ACM, 1997.

[Pierce et al. 99] Jeffrey S Pierce, Brian C Stearns, and Randy Pausch. "Voodoo dolls: seamless interaction at multiple scales in virtual environments." In *I3D '99: Proceedings of the 1999 symposium on Interactive 3D graphics*, pp. 141–145. New York, New York, USA: ACM, 1999.

[Pipho 03] Evan Pipho. *Focus on 3D Models*. Thomson Course Technology, 2003.

[Pittman 91] JA Pittman. "Recognizing handwritten text." In *Human Factors in Computing Systems: Reaching through Technology*, CHI '91, pp. 271–275. ACM, 1991.

[Plamondon and Srihari 00] R Plamondon and S N Srihari. "Online and off-line handwriting recognition: a comprehensive survey." *IEEE Transactions on Pattern Analysis and Machine Intelligence* 22:1 (2000), 63–84.

[Portnoy et al. 08] David B Portnoy, Lori a J Scott-Sheldon, Blair T Johnson, and Michael P Carey. "Computer-delivered interventions for health promotion and behavioral risk reduction: a meta-analysis of 75 randomized controlled trials, 1988-2007." *Preventive medicine* 47:1 (2008), 3–16. Available online (http://www.pubmedcentral.nih.gov/articlerender.fcgi?artid=2572996&tool=pmcentrez&rendertype=abstract).

[Poslad 11] Stefan Poslad. *Ubiquitous Computing*. Smart Devices, Environments and Interactions, John Wiley & Sons, 2011.

[Poupyrev et al. 96] Ivan Poupyrev, Mark Billinghurst, Suzanne Weghorst, and Tadao Ichikawa. "The Go-go Interaction Technique: Non-linear Mapping for Direct Manipulation in VR." In *Proceedings of the 9th Annual ACM Symposium on User Interface Software and Technology*, UIST '96, pp. 79–80. New York, NY, USA: ACM, 1996. Available online (http://doi.acm.org/10.1145/237091.237102).

[Poupyrev et al. 97] Ivan Poupyrev, Suzanne Weghorst, Mark Billinghurst, and Tadao Ichikawa. "A framework and testbed for studying manipulation techniques for immersive VR." In *Proceedings of the ACM Symposium on Virtual Reality Software and Technology - VRST '97*, pp. 21–28. New York, New York, USA: ACM Press, 1997.

[Poupyrev et al. 98] I Poupyrev, T Ichikawa, and S Weghorst. "Egocentric object manipulation in virtual environments: empirical evaluation of interaction techniques." *Computer Graphics Forum* 17:3 (1998), 41–52.

[Poupyrev et al. 99] Ivan Poupyrev, Suzanne Weghorst, Takahiro Otsuka, and Tadao Ichikawa. "Amplifying spatial rotations in 3D interfaces." In *CHI '99 Extended Abstracts on Human Factors in Computing Systems - CHI '99*, p. 256. New York, New York, USA: ACM Press, 1999.

[Poupyrev et al. 00] I Poupyrev, S Weghorst, and S Fels. "Non-isomorphic 3D rotational techniques." In *Proceedings of the SIGCHI Conference on Human Factors in Computing Systems*, CHI '00, pp. 540–547. ACM, 2000.

[Premaratne 14] Prashan Premaratne. *Human Computer Interaction Using Hand Gestures*. Cognitive Science and Technology, Singapore: Springer Science & Business Media, 2014.

[Prendinger and Ishizuka 05] Helmut Prendinger and M. Ishizuka. "The Empathic Companion - A Character-based Interface that Addresses Users' Affective States." *Applied Artificial Intelligence* 19:3-4 (2005), 267–286.

[Press et al. 07] W H Press, B P Flannery, S A Teukolsky, and W T Vetterling. *Numerical Recipes*, Third edition. The art of scientific computing, Hong Kong: Cambridge University Press, 2007.

[Priemer 91] R Priemer. *Introductory signal processing*. Advanced series in electrical and computer engineering, World Scientific, 1991. Available online (https://books.google.com/books?id=QBT7nP7zTLgC).

[Proakis 96] J G Proakis. *Digital signal processing: principles, algorithms, and application-3/E*. Prentice Hall, 1996. Available online (https://books.google.com/books?id=iuLTPQAACAAJ).

[Przybyla et al. 15] R J Przybyla, H Y Tang, A Guedes, S E Shelton, D A Horsley, and B E Boser. "3D Ultrasonic Rangefinder on a Chip." *Solid-State Circuits, IEEE Journal of* 50:1 (2015), 320–334.

[Putois et al. 10] Ghislain Putois, France Lannion, Romain Laroche, France Issy-les Moulineaux, and Philippe Bretier. "Enhanced monitoring tools and online dialogue optimisation merged into a new spoken dialogue system design experience." In *Proceedings of the SIGDIAL 2010 Conference*, pp. 185–192, 2010.

[Ramos and Balakrishnan 05] Gonzalo Ramos and Ravin Balakrishnan. "Zliding: Fluid Zooming and Sliding for High Precision Parameter Manipulation." In *Proceedings of the 18th Annual ACM Symposium on User Interface Software and Technology*, UIST '05, pp. 143–152. New York, NY, USA: ACM, 2005.

[Ramos and Balakrishnan 07] Gonzalo A. Ramos and Ravin Balakrishnan. "Pressure Marks." In *Proceedings of the SIGCHI Conference on Human Factors in Computing Systems*, CHI '07, pp. 1375–1384. New York, NY, USA: ACM, 2007.

[Ramos et al. 04] Gonzalo Ramos, Matthew Boulos, and Ravin Balakrishnan. *Pressure widgets*. New York, New York, USA: ACM, 2004.

[Rashid et al. 12] Umar Rashid, Miguel A. Nacenta, and Aaron Quigley. "Factors influencing visual attention switch in multi-display user interfaces: a survey." In *Proceedings of the 2012 International Symposium on Pervasive Displays*, PerDis '12, pp. 1:1–1:6. New York, NY, USA: ACM, 2012. Available online (http://doi.acm.org/10.1145/2307798.2307799).

[Raskar et al. 04] Ramesh Raskar, Paul Beardsley, Jeroen van Baar, Yao Wang, Paul Dietz, Johnny Lee, Darren Leigh, and Thomas Willwacher. "RFIG lamps: interacting with a self-describing world via photosensing wireless tags and projectors." In *ACM SIGGRAPH 2004 Papers*, *SIGGRAPH '04*, pp. 406–415. New York, NY, USA: ACM, 2004. Available online (http://doi.acm.org/10.1145/1186562.1015738).

[Ratliff and Riggs 50] Floyd Ratliff and Lorrin A Riggs. "Involuntary motions of the eye during monocular fixation." *Journal of Experimental Psychology* 40:6 (1950), 687–701.

[Razzaque 05] S. Razzaque. "Redirected Walking." Ph.D. thesis, University of North Carolina, Chapel Hill, 2005.

[Reddy 11] Martin Reddy. *API Design for C++*. Elsevier, 2011.

[Reeves and Nass 96] B. Reeves and C Nass. *The Media Equation: How People Treat Computers, Television, and New Media Like Real People and Places*. New York, NY: University of Chicago Press, 1996.

[Reisig 12] Wolfgang Reisig. *Understanding Petri Nets: Modelins Techniques, Analysis Methods, Case Studies*. Springer, 2012.

[Reisman et al. 09] JL Reisman, PL Davidson, and JY Han. "A screen-space formulation for 2D and 3D direct manipulation." In *Proceedings of the 22nd Annual ACM Symposium on User Interface Software and Technology*, *UIST '09*, pp. 69–78. ACM, 2009.

[Rekimoto and Saitoh 99] Jun Rekimoto and Masanori Saitoh. "Augmented surfaces: a spatially continuous work space for hybrid computing environments." In *Proceedings of the SIGCHI Conference on Human Factors in Computing Systems*, *CHI '99*, pp. 378–385. New York, NY, USA: ACM, 1999. Available online (http://doi.acm.org/10.1145/302979.303113).

[Rekimoto 97] Jun Rekimoto. "Pick-and-drop: a direct manipulation technique for multiple computer environments." In *Proceedings of the 10th Annual ACM Symposium on User Interface Software and Technology*, *UIST '97*, pp. 31–39. New York, NY, USA: ACM, 1997. Available online (http://doi.acm.org/10.1145/263407.263505).

[Rekimoto 98] Jun Rekimoto. "A multiple device approach for supporting whiteboard-based interactions." In *Proceedings of the SIGCHI Conference on Human Factors in Computing Systems*, *CHI '98*, pp. 344–351. New York, NY, USA: ACM Press/Addison-Wesley Publishing Co., 1998. Available online (http://dx.doi.org/10.1145/274644.274692).

[Rekimoto 13] Jun Rekimoto. "Traxion: A Tactile Interaction Device with Virtual Force Sensation." In *Proceedings of the Symposium on User Interface Software and Technology (UIST)*, pp. 427–432, 2013.

[Remazeilles et al. 06] A Remazeilles, F Chaumette, and P Gros. "3D navigation based on a visual memory." In *Proceedings 2006 IEEE International Conference on Robotics and Automation, 2006, ICRA 2006*, pp. 2719–2725. IEEE, 2006.

[Ren et al. 13] Peng Ren, Armando Barreto, Ying Gao, and Malek Adjouadi. "Affective Assessment by Digital Processing of the Pupil Diameter." *T. Affective Computing ()* 4:1 (2013), 2–14.

[Ren et al. 14] Peng Ren, Armando Barreto, Jian Huang, Ying Gao, Francisco R Ortega, and Malek Adjouadi. "Off-line and On-line Stress Detection Through Processing of the Pupil Diameter Signal." *Annals of Biomedical Engineering* 42:1 (2014), 162–176.

[Renaud and Blondin 97] Patrice Renaud and Jean-Pierre Blondin. "The stress of Stroop performance: physiological and emotional responses to color–word interference, task pacing, and pacing speed." *International Journal of Psychophysiology* 27:2 (1997), 87–97.

[Renaudin et al. 10] V Renaudin, M H Afzal, and G Lachapelle. "Complete triaxis magnetometer calibration in the magnetic domain." *Journal of sensors.*

[Rich et al. 01] Charles Rich, Ace L. Sidner, and Neal Lesh. "Collagen: Applying Collaborative Discourse Theory to Human-Computer Interaction." *AI Magazine* 22 (2001), 15–25.

[Richardson et al. 99] Anthony E Richardson, Daniel R Montello, and Mary Hegarty. "Spatial knowledge acquisition from maps and from navigation in real and virtual environments." *Memory & Cognition* 27:4 (1999), 741–750.

[Riege et al. 06] Kai Riege, Thorsten Holtkämper, Gerold Wesche, and Bernd Fröhlich. "The Bent Pick Ray: An Extended Pointing Technique for Multi-User Interaction." In *3DUI '06: Proceedings of the 3D User Interfaces (3DUI'06*, pp. 62–65. IEEE Computer Society, 2006.

[Rieser and Lemon 11] Verena Rieser and Oliver Lemon. *Reinforcement Learning for Adaptive Dialogue Systems: A Data-Driven Methodology for Dialogue Management and Natural Language Generation.* Theory and Applications of Natural Language Processing, Berlin, Heidelberg: Springer Berlin Heidelberg, 2011. Available online (http://www.springerlink.com/index/10.1007/978-3-642-24942-6).

[Rieser et al. 10] Verena Rieser, Oliver Lemon, and Xingkun Liu. "Optimising information presentation for spoken dialogue systems." In *Proceedings of the 48th Annual Meeting of the Association for Computational Linguistics, ACL '10*, pp. 1009–1018. Stroudsburg, PA, USA: Association for Computational Linguistics, 2010. Available online (http://dl.acm.org/citation.cfm?id=1858681.1858784).

[Rieser et al. 11a] Verena Rieser, Simon Keizer, Xingkun Liu, and Oliver Lemon. "Adaptive Information Presentation for Spoken Dialogue Systems: Evaluation with Human Subjects." In *Proceedings of the 13th European Workshop on Natural Language Generation (ENLG)*, 2011.

[Rieser et al. 11b] Verena Rieser, Simon Keizer, Xingkun Liu, and Oliver Lemon. "Adaptive information presentation for spoken dialogue systems: evaluation with human subjects." In *Proceedings of the 13th European Workshop on Natural Language Generation, ENLG '11*, pp. 102–109. Stroudsburg, PA, USA: Association for Computational Linguistics, 2011. Available online (http://dl.acm.org/citation.cfm?id=2187681.2187698).

[Rinck 14] P. A. Rinck. "Magnetic Resonance in Medicine. The Basic Textbook of the European Magnetic Resonance Forum. 8th edition.", 2014. Available online (http://www.magnetic-resonance.org/).

[Riva et al. 07] Giuseppe Riva, Fabrizia Mantovani, Claret Samantha Capideville, Alessandra Preziosa, Francesca Morganti, Daniela Villani, Andrea Gaggioli, Cristina Botella, and Mariano Alcañiz. "Affective Interactions Using Virtual Reality: The Link between Presence and Emotions." *CyberPsychology & Behavior* 10:1 (2007), 45–56.

[Robertson et al. 97] George Robertson, Mary Czerwinski, and Maarten van Dantzich. "Immersion in desktop virtual reality." In *Proceedings of the 10th Annual ACM Symposium on User Interface Software and Technology, UIST '97.* ACM, 1997.

[Rogers et al. 11] Yvonne Rogers, Helen Sharp, and Jenny Preece. *Interaction Design. Beyond Human - Computer Interaction*, John Wiley & Sons, 2011.

[Ropinski et al. 05] Timo Ropinski, Frank Steinicke, and Klaus Hinrichs. "A constrained road-based VR navigation technique for travelling in 3D city models." In *Proceedings of the 2005 International Conference on Augmented Tele-Existence, ICAT '05*, p. 228. ACM, 2005.

[Rossano and Warren 89] Matt J Rossano and David H Warren. "Misaligned maps lead to predictable errors." *Perception* 18:2 (1989), 215–229.

[Roth and Turner 09] Volker Roth and Thea Turner. "Bezel Swipe: Conflict-free Scrolling and Multiple Selection on Mobile Touch Screen Devices." In *Proceedings of the SIGCHI Conference on Human Factors in Computing Systems, CHI '09*, pp. 1523–1526. ACM, 2009.

[Rubine 91] Dean Rubine. "Specifying gestures by example." In *Proceedings of the 18th Annual Conference on Computer Graphics and Interactive Techniques, SIGGRAPH '91*, pp. 329–337. ACM, 1991.

[Ruddle and Jones 01] Roy A Ruddle and Dylan M Jones. "Movement in Cluttered Virtual Environments." *Presence* 10:5 (2001), 511–524.

[Ruddle and Lessels 06] R A Ruddle and S Lessels. "For efficient navigational search, humans require full physical movement, but not a rich visual scene." *Psychological Science* 17:6 (2006), 460–465.

[Ruddle and Lessels 09] Roy A Ruddle and Simon Lessels. "The benefits of using a walking interface to navigate virtual environments." *Transactions on Computer-Human Interaction (TOCHI* 16:1.

[Ruddle et al. 98] Roy A Ruddle, Stephen J Payne, and Dylan M Jones. "Navigating Large-Scale 'Desk-Top' Virtual Buildings: Effects of Orientation Aids and Familiarity." *Presence* 7:2 (1998), 179–192.

[Ruddle et al. 99] R A Ruddle, S J Payne, and D M Jones. "Navigating large-scale virtual environments: what differences occur between helmet-mounted and desk-top displays?" *Precense: Teleoperators and Virtual Environments* 8:2 (1999), 157–168.

[Ruddle 13] Roy A Ruddle. "The Effect of Translational and Rotational Body-Based Information on Navigation." Springer New York, New York, NY, 2013.

[Ruffieux et al. 13] Simon Ruffieux, Denis Lalanne, and Elena Mugellini. "ChAirGest: a challenge for multimodal mid-air gesture recognition for close HCI." In *ICMI '13: Proceedings of the 15th ACM on International Conference on Multimodal Interaction.* ACM, 2013.

[Ruiz et al. 11] Jaime Ruiz, Yang Li, and Edward Lank. "User-defined motion gestures for mobile interaction." In *CHI '11: Proceedings of the SIGCHI Conference on Human Factors in Computing Systems*, p. 197. New York, New York, USA: ACM, 2011.

[Rümelin et al. 11] Sonja Rümelin, Enrico Rukzio, and Robert Hardy. "NaviRadar: A Novel Tactile Information Display for Pedestrian Navigation." In *NaviRadar: A Novel Tactile Information Display for Pedestrian Navigation, UIST '11*, pp. 293–302. New York, NY, USA: ACM, 2011. Available online (http://doi.acm.org/10.1145/2047196. 2047234).

[Rumsey 94] Francis Rumsey. *MIDI Systems and Control*. Butterworth-Heinemann, 1994.

[Russell 80] James A Russell. "A circumplex model of affect." *Journal of Personality and Social Psychology* 39:6 (1980), 1161–1178.

[Russo dos Santos et al. 00] C Russo dos Santos, P Gros, P Abel, D Loisel, N Trichaud, and J P Paris. "Metaphor-aware 3D navigation." In *IEEE Symposium on Information Visualization, InfoVis 2000*, pp. 155–165, 2000.

[Säll and Merkel 11] J Säll and J Merkel. "Indoor Navigation Using Accelerometer and Magnetometer." Ph.D. thesis, Linköping University, Department of Electrical Engineering, 2011.

[Salvucci and Goldberg 00] Dario D Salvucci and Joseph H Goldberg. "Identifying fixations and saccades in eye-tracking protocols." In *ETRA '00: Proceedings of the 2000 Symposium on Eye Tracking Research & Applications*, pp. 71–78. New York, New York, USA: ACM, 2000.

[Samet 06] Hanan Samet. *Foundations of Multidimensional and Metric Data Structures*. Morgan Kaufmann, 2006.

[Sana 99] Pao Sana. "User Input Device For a Computer System." US Patent 5,914,709, 1999.

[Sanchez-Vives and Slater 05] M V Sanchez-Vives and M Slater. "From presence to consciousness through virtual reality." *Nature Reviews Neuroscience* 6:4 (2005), 332–339.

[Santello et al. 02] Marco Santello, Martha Flanders, and John F. Soechting. "Patterns of Hand Motion during Grasping and the Influence of Sensory Guidance." *J. Neurosci.* 22:4 (2002), 1426–1435. Available online (http://www.jneurosci.org/cgi/content/ abstract/22/4/1426).

[Santhanam et al. 06] Gopal Santhanam, Stephen I. Ryu, Byron M. Yu, Afsheen Afshar, and Krishna V. Shenoy. "A high-performance brain–computer interface." *Nature* 442 (2006), 195–198.

[Santos et al. 11] Selan Rodrigues Santos, Selan Rodrigues dos dos Santos, and Philip Michel Duarte. "Supporting Search Navigation by Controlled Camera Animation." *2011 XIII Symposium on Virtual Reality*, pp. 207–216.

[Saona-Vazquez et al. 99] C Saona-Vazquez, I Navazo, and P Brunet. "The visibility octree: a data structure for 3D navigation." *Computers & Graphics* 23:5 (1999), 635–643.

[Sato et al. 12] Munehiko Sato, Ivan Poupyrev, and Chris Harrison. "Touché: Enhancing Touch Interaction on Humans, Screens, Liquids, and Everyday Objects." In *Proceedings of the SIGCHI Conference on Human Factors in Computing Systems, CHI '12*, pp. 483–492. New York, NY, USA: ACM, 2012.

[Scheffler and Young 02] Konrad Scheffler and Steve Young. "Automatic learning of dia-logue strategy using dialogue simulation and reinforcement learning." In *Proceedings of the Second International Conference on Human Language Technology Research*, pp. 12–19. Morgan Kaufmann Publishers Inc., 2002.

[Schilbach et al. 06] Leonhard Schilbach, Afra M Wohlschlaeger, Nicole C Kraemer, Al-bert Newen, N Jon Shah, Gereon R Fink, and Kai Vogeley. "Being with virtual others: Neural correlates of social interaction." *Neuropsychologia* 44:5 (2006), 718–730.

[Schmalstieg et al. 99] D. Schmalstieg, L. Miguel Encarnação, and Zsolt Szalavári. "Us-ing transparent props for interaction with the virtual table." In *Proceedings of the Symposium on Interactive 3D Graphics and Games (I3D)*, pp. 147–153, 1999.

[Schmitz et al. 10] Arne Schmitz, Ming Li, Volker Schönefeld, and Leif Kobbelt. "Ad-Hoc Multi-Displays for Mobile Interactive Applications." In *Conference of the European Association for Computer Graphics, Eurographics '10*, pp. 45–52. The Eurographics Association, 2010.

[Scholliers et al. 11] Christophe Scholliers, Lode Hoste, Beat Signer, and Wolfgang De Meuter. "Midas: A Declarative Multi-touch Interaction Framework." In *Pro-ceedings of the Fifth International Conference on Tangible, Embedded, and Embodied Interaction, TEI '11*, pp. 49–56. New York, NY, USA: ACM, 2011. Available online (http://doi.acm.org/10.1145/1935701.1935712).

[Schomaker and Segers 99] L Schomaker and E Segers. "Finding features used in the human reading of cursive handwriting." *International Journal on Document Analysis* 2:1 (1999), 13–18.

[Schöning et al. 09] Johannes Schöning, Frank Steinicke, Dimitar Valkov, Anto-nio Krüger, and Klaus H. Hinrichs. "Bimanual Interaction with Interscopic Multi-Touch Surfaces." In *Proceedings of the IFIP TC13 Conference in Human-Computer Interaction (INTERACT)*, pp. 40–53, 2009. Avail-able online (http://viscg.uni-muenster.de/publications/2009/SSVKH09;http://www.dfki.de/web/forschung/publikationen/renameFileForDownload?filename=interactschoening2009.pdf&file_id=uploads_255).

[Schulman et al. 11] Daniel Schulman, Timothy W. Bickmore, and Candace L Sidner. "An Intelligent Conversational Agent for Promoting Long-Term Health Behavior Change using Motivational Interviewing." In *Association for the Advancement of Artificial Intelligence (AAAI) Spring Symposium Series*, pp. 61–64. Association for the Advancement of Artificial Intelligence (www.aaai.org), 2011.

[Schulz et al. 11] C M Schulz, E Schneider, L Fritz, J Vockeroth, A Hapfelmeier, M Was-maier, E F Kochs, and G Schneider. "Eye tracking for assessment of workload: a pilot study in an anaesthesia simulator environment." *British Journal of Anaesthesia* 106:1 (2011), 44–50.

[Schwarz et al. 10] Julia Schwarz, Scott Hudson, Jennifer Mankoff, and Andrew D Wil-son. "A framework for robust and flexible handling of inputs with uncertainty." In *Proceedings of the 23rd Annual ACM Symposium on User Interface Software and Technology, UIST '10*, pp. 47–56. New York, NY, USA: ACM, 2010. Available online (http://doi.acm.org/10.1145/1866029.1866039).

[Schwarz et al. 14] Julia Schwarz, Robert Xiao, Jennifer Mankoff, Scott E Hudson, and Chris Harrison. "Probabilistic palm rejection using spatiotemporal touch features and iterative classification." In *CHI '14: Proceedings of the SIGCHI Conference on Human Factors in Computing Systems.* ACM, 2014.

[Sellers et al. 13] Graham Sellers, Richard S Wright Jr, and Nicholas Haemel. *OpenGL SuperBible.* Comprehensive Tutorial and Reference, Pearson Education, 2013.

[Seow 08] Steven C Seow. *Designing and Engineering Time.* The Psychology of Time Perception in Software, Addison-Wesley Professional, 2008.

[Sezgin and Davis 05] TM Sezgin and R Davis. "HMM-based efficient sketch recognition." *Proceedings of the 10th International Conference on Intelligent User Interfaces (IUI '05).*

[Shaeffer 13] D K Shaeffer. "MEMS inertial sensors: A tutorial overview." *Communications Magazine, IEEE* 51:4 (2013), 100–109.

[Shannon 63] Claude Elwood Shannon. "The Mathematical Theory of Communication." University of Illinois Press, 1963.

[Shoemake 85] K Shoemake. "Animating rotation with quaternion curves." *ACM SIGGRAPH Computer Graphics.*

[Short] Emily Short. "Versu: Conversation Implementation." https://emshort.wordpress.com/2013/02/26/versu-conversation-implementation/. [Online; Posted on February 26, 2013].

[Shreiner and Group 13] Dave Shreiner and Bill The Khronos OpenGL ARB Working Group. *OpenGL Programming Guide.* The Official Guide to Learning OpenGL version 4.3, Pearson Education, 2013.

[Sibert and Jacob 00] Linda E Sibert and Robert J K Jacob. "Evaluation of eye gaze interaction." In *the SIGCHI Conference*, pp. 281–288. New York, New York, USA: ACM Press, 2000.

[Sibert et al. 01] Linda E Sibert, Robert J K Jacob, and J N Templeman. "Evaulation and Analysis of Eye Gaze Interaction." Technical report, Presented at NRL, Washington, DC., 2001.

[Siegel and White 75] Alexander W Siegel and Sheldon H White. "The Development of Spatial Representations of Large-Scale Environments." In *Advances in Child Development and Behavior Volume 10*, pp. 9–55. Elsevier, 1975.

[Signer et al. 07] B Signer, U Kurmann, and M C Norrie. "iGesture: A General Gesture Recognition Framework." In *Ninth International Conference on Document Analysis and Recognition, 2007, ICDAR 2007*, pp. 954–958. IEEE, 2007.

[Silfverberg et al. 00] Miika Silfverberg, I Scott MacKenzie, and Panu Korhonen. "Predicting text entry speed on mobile phones." In *CHI '00: Proceedings of the SIGCHI Conference on Human Factors in Computing Systems*, pp. 9–16. New York, New York, USA: ACM, 2000.

[Simeone and Gellersen 15] A.L. Simeone and H. Gellersen. "Comparing Direct and Indirect Touch in a Stereoscopic Interaction Task." In *3D User Interfaces (3DUI), 2015 IEEE Symposium on*, 2015.

[Simon 06] D Simon. *Optimal state estimation: Kalman, H infinity, and nonlinear approaches*. Wiley, 2006. Available online (https://books.google.com/books?id=UiMVoP_7TZkC).

[Simpson et al. 96] Rosemary Simpson, Allen Renear, Elli Mylonas, and Andries van Dam. "50 years after "As we may think": the Brown/MIT Vannevar Bush symposium." *interactions* 3:2 (1996), 47–67.

[Singh et al. 00] Satinder Singh, Michael Kearns, Diane J Litman, Marilyn A Walker, et al. "Empirical evaluation of a reinforcement learning spoken dialogue system." In *AAAI/IAAI*, pp. 645–651, 2000.

[Singh et al. 02] Satinder Singh, Diane Litman, Michael Kearns, and Marilyn Walker. "Optimizing Dialogue Management with Reinforcement Learning: Experiments with the NJFun System." *Journal of Artificial Intelligence Research* 16 (2002), 105–133.

[Singh 06] Amit Singh. *Mac OS X Internals. A Systems Approach*. Addison-Wesley Professional, 2006.

[Sipser 06] Michael Sipser. *Introduction to Theory of Computation*, Second edition. Cengage, 2006.

[Smith 97] S W Smith. *The scientist and engineer's guide to digital signal processing*. California Technical Pub., 1997. Available online (https://books.google.com/books?id=rp2VQgAACAAJ).

[Sommer et al. 99] O Sommer, A Dietz, and R Westermann. "An interactive visualization and navigation tool for medical volume data." *Computers & Graphics*.

[Song et al. 09] Hyunyoung Song, Tovi Grossman, George Fitzmaurice, François Guimbretiere, Azam Khan, Ramtin Attar, and Gordon Kurtenbach. "PenLight: Combining a Mobile Projector and a Digital Pen for Dynamic Visual Overlay." In *Proceedings of the SIGCHI Conference on Human Factors in Computing Systems, CHI '09*, pp. 143–152. New York, NY, USA: ACM, 2009. Available online (http://doi.acm.org/10.1145/1518701.1518726).

[Song et al. 10] Hyunyoung Song, Francois Guimbretiere, Tovi Grossman, and George Fitzmaurice. "MouseLight: bimanual interactions on digital paper using a pen and a spatially-aware mobile projector." In *Proceedings of the SIGCHI Conference on Human Factors in Computing Systems, CHI '10*, pp. 2451–2460. New York, NY, USA: ACM, 2010. Available online (http://doi.acm.org/10.1145/1753326.1753697).

[Song et al. 12] Peng Song, Wooi Boon Goh, William Hutama, Chi-Wing Fu, and Xiaopei Liu. "A Handle Bar Metaphor for Virtual Object Manipulation with Mid-Air Interaction." In *Proceedings of the Conference on Human Factors in Computing Systems (CHI)*, pp. 1297–1306, 2012.

[Sorenson 85] H W Sorenson. *Kalman filtering: theory and application*. IEEE Press selected reprint series, IEEE Press, 1985. Available online (https://books.google.com/books?id=2pgeAQAAIAAJ).

[Soukoreff and MacKenzie 04] R. William Soukoreff and I. Scott MacKenzie. "Towards a Standard for Pointing Device Evaluation, Perspectives on 27 Years of Fitts' Law Research in HCI." *Int. J. Hum.-Comput. Stud.* 61:6 (2004), 751–789. Available online (http://dx.doi.org/10.1016/j.ijhcs.2004.09.001).

[Sousa Santos et al. 08] Beatriz Sousa Santos, Paulo Dias, Angela Pimentel, Jan-Willem Baggerman, Carlos Ferreira, Samuel Silva, and Joaquim Madeira. "Head-mounted display versus desktop for 3D navigation in virtual reality: a user study." *Multimedia Tools and Applications* 41:1 (2008), 161–181.

[Sousa Santos et al. 10] Beatriz Sousa Santos, Bruno Prada, Hugo Ribeiro, Paulo Dias, Samuel Silva, and Carlos Ferreira. "Wiimote as an Input Device in Google Earth Visualization and Navigation: A User Study Comparing Two Alternatives." In *Information Visualisation (IV), 2010 14th International Conference, IV 2010*, pp. 473–478, 2010.

[Spano et al. 12] Lucio Davide Spano, Antonio Cisternino, and Fabio Paternò. "A compositional model for gesture definition." In *Proceedings of the 4th International Conference on Human-Centered Software Engineering, HCSE'12*, pp. 34–52. Berlin, Heidelberg: Springer-Verlag, 2012.

[Spano et al. 13] Lucio Davide Spano, Antonio Cisternino, Fabio Paternò, and Gianni Fenu. "GestIT: a declarative and compositional framework for multiplatform gesture definition." In *Proceedings of the 5th ACM SIGCHI Symposium on Engineering Interactive Computing Systems, EICS '13*, pp. 187–196. ACM, 2013.

[Spano 12] L D Spano. "Developing Touchless Interfaces with GestIT." *Ambient Intelligence*.

[Spence 99] Robert Spence. "A framework for navigation." *International Journal of Human-Computer Studies* 51:5 (1999), 919–945.

[Spindler et al. 10] Martin Spindler, Christian Tominski, Heidrun Schumann, and Raimund Dachselt. "Tangible views for information visualization." In *Proceedings of the Interactive Tabletops and Surfaces (ITS)*, pp. 157–166, 2010.

[Staal 14] Mark A. Staal Staal. "A descriptive history of military aviation psychology.", 2014. [Online; accessed 23-February-2015]. Available online (http://www.apadivisions.org/division-19/publications/newsletters/military/2014/04/aviation-psychology.aspx).

[Steed and Parker 05] A Steed and C Parker. "Evaluating Effectiveness of Interaction Techniques across Immersive Virtual Environmental Systems." *Presence* 14:5 (2005), 511–527.

[Steed 06] A Steed. "Towards a General Model for Selection in Virtual Environments." *3D User Interfaces, 2006. 3DUI 2006. IEEE Symposium on*, pp. 103–110.

[Steinhauer et al. 04] Stuart R Steinhauer, Greg J Siegle, Ruth Condray, and Misha Pless. "Sympathetic and parasympathetic innervation of pupillary dilation during sustained processing." *International Journal of Psychophysiology* 52:1 (2004), 77–86.

[Stellmach and Dachselt 12] S Stellmach and R Dachselt. "Designing gaze-based user interfaces for steering in virtual environments." In *Proceedings of the Symposium on Eye Tracking Research and Applications, ETRA '12*, pp. 131–138. ACM, 2012.

[Stern et al. 01] Robert Morris Stern, William J Ray, and Karen S Quigley. *Psychophysiological Recording*. Oxford University Press, 2001.

[Stevens and Coupe 78] A Stevens and P Coupe. "Distortions in judged spatial relations." *Cognitive psychology* 10:4 (1978), 422–437.

[Stevens et al. 04] W Richard Stevens, Bill Fenner, and Andrew M Rudoff. *UNIX Network Programming*. Addison-Wesley Professional, 2004.

[Stevenson and Lindberg 10] Angus Stevenson and Christine A Lindberg. *New Oxford American Dictionary, Third Edition*. Oxford, 2010.

[Stoakley et al. 95] Richard Stoakley, Matthew J Conway, and Randy Pausch. "Virtual reality on a WIM: interactive worlds in miniature." In *CHI '95: Proceedings of the SIGCHI Conference on Human Factors in Computing Systems*, pp. 265–272. New York, New York, USA: ACM Press/Addison-Wesley Publishing Co., 1995.

[Stoev et al. 01] Stanislav L Stoev, Dieter Schmalstieg, and Wolfgang Straßer. "Two-handed through-the-lens-techniques for navigation in virtual environments." In *Proceedings of the 7th Eurographics Conference on Virtual Environments & 5th Immersive Projection Technology, EGVE'01*. Eurographics Association, 2001.

[Stranneby 01] D Stranneby. *Digital Signal Processing: DSP and Applications: DSP and Applications*. Elsevier Science, 2001. Available online (https://books.google.com/books?id=1dHGdn2TYngC).

[Stroop 35] J R Stroop. "Studies of interference in serial verbal reactions." *Journal of Experimental Psychology* 18:6 (1935), 643.

[Strothoff et al. 11] Sven Strothoff, Dimitar Valkov, and Klaus H. Hinrichs. "Triangle Cursor: Interactions With Objects Above the Tabletop." In *Proceedings of the Interactive Tabletops and Surfaces (ITS)*, pp. 111–119, 2011. Available online (http://viscg.uni-muenster.de/publications/2011/SVH11).

[Strum and Kirk 88] R D Strum and D E Kirk. *First principles of discrete systems and digital signal processing*. Addison-Wesley series in electrical engineering : digital signal processing, Addison-Wesley, 1988. Available online (https://books.google.com/books?id=uABTAAAAMAAJ).

[Stuerzlinger and Teather 14] Wolfgang Stuerzlinger and Robert J Teather. "Considerations for targets in 3D pointing experiments." In *HCIK '15: Proceedings of HCI Korea*. Hanbit Media, Inc, 2014.

[Su and Bailey 05] Ramona E. Su and Brian P. Bailey. "Put them where? towards guidelines for positioning large displays in interactive workspaces." In *Proceedings of the 2005 IFIP TC13 International Conference on Human-Computer Interaction, INTERACT'05*, pp. 337–349. Berlin, Heidelberg: Springer-Verlag, 2005. Available online (http://dx.doi.org/10.1007/11555261_29).

[Suellentrop] Chris Suellentrop. "Text Games in a New Era of Stories." http://www.nytimes.com/2014/07/07/arts/video-games/text-games-in-a-new-era-of-stories.html?_r=0. [Online; Posted on July 6, 2014].

[Suh 10] Young Soo Suh. "Orientation estimation using a quaternion-based indirect Kalman filter with adaptive estimation of external acceleration." *Instrumentation and Measurement, IEEE Transactions on* 59:12 (2010), 3296–3305.

[Sultanum et al. 13] Nicole Sultanum, Emilio Vital Brazil, and Mario Costa Sousa. "Navigating and annotating 3D geological outcrops through multi-touch interaction." In *Proceedings of the 2013 ACM International Conference on Interactive Tabletops and Surfaces, ITS '13*. ACM, 2013.

[Suprapto 06] S Suprapto. "Development of a gyroscopic unmanned bicycle." *M. Eng. Thesis, Asian Institute of Technology, Thailand.*

[Sutherland 63] Ivan E Sutherland. "Sketchpad: a man-machine graphical communication system." In *AFIPS '63 (Spring): Proceedings of the May 21-23, 1963, Spring Joint Computer Conference.* ACM, 1963.

[Sutherland 65] I E Sutherland. "The Ultimate Display, invited lecture." In *IFIP Congress*, 1965.

[Sutter 84] Erich E Sutter. "The visual evoked response as a communication channel." In *Proceedings of the IEEE Symposium on Biosensor*, pp. 95–100, 1984.

[Sutton and Barto 98] Richard S Sutton and Andrew G Barto. *Reinforcement learning: An introduction.* Cambridge Univ Press, 1998.

[Sutton et al. 98] S. Sutton, R. Cole, J. De Villiers, J. Schalkwyk, P. Vermeulen, M. Macon, Y. Yan, E. Kaiser, B. Rundle, K. Shobaki, et al. "Universal speech tools: The CSLU toolkit." In *Proceedings of the International Conference on Spoken Language Processing (ICSLP)*, pp. 3221–3224. Sydney, Australia., 1998.

[Tan and Czerwinski 03] Desney S. Tan and Mary Czerwinski. "Effects of Visual Separation and Physical Discontinuities when Distributing Information across Multiple Displays." In *In Proceedings of Interact 2003*, pp. 252–255, 2003.

[Tan et al. 01] Desney S Tan, George G Robertson, and Mary Czerwinski. "Exploring 3D navigation: combining speed-coupled flying with orbiting." In *Proceedings of the SIGCHI Conference on Human Factors in Computing Systems, CHI '01*, pp. 418–425. ACM, 2001.

[Tan et al. 03] Desney S. Tan, Darren Gergle, Peter Scupelli, and Randy Pausch. "With similar visual angles, larger displays improve spatial performance." In *Proceedings of the SIGCHI Conference on Human Factors in Computing Systems, CHI '03*, pp. 217–224. New York, NY, USA: ACM, 2003. Available online (http://doi.acm.org/10.1145/642611.642650).

[Tappert et al. 90] C C Tappert, C Y Suen, and T Wakahara. "The state of the art in online handwriting recognition." *IEEE Transactions on Pattern Analysis and Machine Intelligence* 12:8 (1990), 787–808.

[Tappert 82] C. C. Tappert. "Cursive Script Recognition by Elastic Matching." *IBM J. Res. Dev.* 26:6 (1982), 765–771. Available online (http://dx.doi.org/10.1147/rd.266.0765).

[Taranta II et al. 15] Eugene M Taranta II, Thaddeus K Simons, Rahul Sukthankar, and Joseph J LaViola Jr. "Exploring the Benefits of Context in 3D Gesture Recognition for Game-Based Virtual Environments." *Transactions on Interactive Intelligent Systems (TiiS* 5:1.

[Teather and MacKenzie 14] Robert J Teather and I Scott MacKenzie. "Comparing Order of Control for Tilt and Touch Games." In *the 2014 Conference*, pp. 1–10. New York, New York, USA: ACM Press, 2014.

[Teather and Stuerzlinger 07] Robert J Teather and Wolfgang Stuerzlinger. "Guidelines for 3D positioning techniques." In *Future Play '07: Proceedings of the 2007 Conference on Future Play*, p. 61. New York, New York, USA: ACM, 2007.

[Teather and Stuerzlinger 11] R J Teather and W Stuerzlinger. "Pointing at 3D targets in a stereo head-tracked virtual environment." *3D User Interfaces (3DUI), 2011 IEEE Symposium on*, pp. 87–94.

[Teather and Stuerzlinger 14] Robert J Teather and Wolfgang Stuerzlinger. "Visual aids in 3D point selection experiments." In *SUI '14: Proceedings of the 2nd ACM symposium on Spatial user interaction*. ACM, 2014.

[Teplan 02] M. Teplan. "Fundamentals of EEG measurment." *Measurement Science Review* 2:2.

[Thanh and Parnichkun 08] B T Thanh and M Parnichkun. "Balancing control of bicyrobo by particle swarm optimization-based structure-specified mixed H2/H∞ control." *Journal of Advanced Robotic Systems*.

[Theoharis et al. 08] T Theoharis, Georgios Papaioannou, Nikolaos Platis, and Nicholas M Patrikalakis. *Graphics and Visualization*. Principles & Algorithms, CRC Press, 2008.

[Thompson et al. 13] William Thompson, Roland Fleming, Sarah Creem-Regehr, and Jeanine Kelly Stefanucci. *Visual Perception from a Computer Graphics Perspective*. CRC Press, 2013.

[Thomson and Young 10] Blaise Thomson and Steve Young. "Bayesian update of dialogue state: A POMDP framework for spoken dialogue systems." *Computer Speech & Language* 24:4 (2010), 562–588.

[Thorndyke and Goldin 83] Perry W Thorndyke and Sarah E Goldin. "Spatial Learning and Reasoning Skill." In *Spatial Orientation*, pp. 195–217. Boston, MA: Springer US, 1983.

[Thorndyke and Hayes-Roth 82] Perry W Thorndyke and Barbara Hayes-Roth. "Differences in spatial knowledge acquired from maps and navigation." *Cognitive psychology* 14:4 (1982), 560–589.

[Titterton and Weston 04] D Titterton and J L Weston. *Strapdown inertial navigation technology*. Electromagnetics and Radar Series, Institution of Engineering and Technology, 2004. Available online (https://books.google.com/books?id=WwrCrn54n5cC).

[Tobon 10] Ricardo Tobon. *The Mocap Book. A Practical Guide to the Art of Motion Capture*. Foris Force, 2010.

[Todor and Doane 78] John I Todor and Thomas Doane. "Handedness and Hemispheric Asymmetry in the Control Of Movements." *Journal of motor behavior* 10:4 (1978), 295–300.

[Tolman 48] Edward C Tolman. "Cognitive maps in rats and men." *Psychological Review* 55:4 (1948), 189–208.

[TouchSystems 09] ELO TouchSystems. "Elo TouchSystems IntelliTouch Plus Multi-touch & Windows 7 Communication Brief." 2009. [Online; accessed 6-February-2015]. Available online (http://www.elotouch.com/pdfs/faq_ip.pdf).

[Traum and Larsson 03] DavidR. Traum and Staffan Larsson. "The Information State Approach to Dialogue Management." In *Current and New Directions in Discourse and Dialogue*, Text, Speech and Language Technology, 22, edited by Jan van Kuppevelt and Ronnie W Smith, Text, Speech and Language Technology, 22, pp. 325–353. Springer

Netherlands, 2003. Available online (http://dx.doi.org/10.1007/978-94-010-0019-2_15).

[Trindade and Raposo 11] Daniel R Trindade and Alberto B Raposo. "Improving 3D navigation in multiscale environments using cubemap-based techniques." In *Proceedings of the 2011 ACM Symposium on Applied Computing, SAC '11*, p. 1215. New York, New York, USA: ACM, 2011.

[Tulen et al. 89] J H M Tulen, P Moleman, H G van Steenis, and F Boomsma. "Characterization of Stress Reactions to the Stroop Color Word Test." *Pharmacology Biochemistry and Behavior* 32:1 (1989), 9–15.

[Turunen et al. 11] Markku Turunen, Jaakko Hakulinen, Olov Ståhl, Björn Gambäck, Preben Hansen, Mari C Rodríguez Gancedo, Raúl Santos de la Cámara, Cameron Smith, Daniel Charlton, and Marc Cavazza. "Multimodal and mobile conversational health and fitness companions." *Computer Speech & Language* 25:2 (2011), 192–209.

[Ulinski et al. 07] A Ulinski, C Zanbaka, Z Wartell, P Goolkasian, and L F Hodges. "Two Handed Selection Techniques for Volumetric Data." *3D User Interfaces, 2007. 3DUI '07. IEEE Symposium on*.

[Ulinski et al. 09] A C Ulinski, Z Wartell, P Goolkasian, E A Suma, and L F Hodges. "Selection performance based on classes of bimanual actions." *3D User Interfaces, 2009. 3DUI 2009. IEEE Symposium on*, pp. 51–58.

[Ullmer and Ishii 97] Brygg Ullmer and Hiroshi Ishii. "The MetaDESK: Models and Prototypes for Tangible User Interfaces." *ACM Symposium on User Interface Software and Technology*, pp. 223–232.

[UNC 14] UNC. "Tracker.", 2014. [Online; accessed 23-January-2015]. Available online (http://cs.unc.edu/~tracker/).

[Unity 15a] Unity. "Prefabs.", 2015. [Online; accessed 15-March-2015]. Available online (http://docs.unity3d.com/Manual/Prefabs.html).

[Unity 15b] Unity. "Unity Script Reference.", 2015. [Online; accessed 30-March-2015]. Available online (http://docs.unity3d.com/ScriptReference/).

[UnityTechnologies 15] UnityTechnologies. "Unity System Requirements.", 2015. [Online; accessed 2-January-2015]. Available online (http://unity3d.com/unity/system-requirements).

[unsigned editorial 06] unsigned editorial. "Is this the bionic man?" *Nature* 7099:109.

[Usoh et al. 99] Martin Usoh, Kevin Arthur, Mary C. Whitton, Rui Bastos, Anthony Steed, Mel Slater, and Frederick P. Brooks, Jr. "Walking > Walking-in-place > Flying, in Virtual Environments." In *Proceedings of the 26th Annual Conference on Computer Graphics and Interactive Techniques, SIGGRAPH '99*, pp. 359–364. New York, NY, USA: ACM Press/Addison-Wesley Publishing Co., 1999. Available online (http://dx.doi.org/10.1145/311535.311589).

[Valdes et al. 14] Consuelo Valdes, Diana Eastman, Casey Grote, Shantanu Thatte, Orit Shaer, Ali Mazalek, Brygg Ullmer, and Miriam K Konkel. "Exploring the design space of gestural interaction with active tokens through user-defined gestures." In *the 32nd Annual ACM Conference*, pp. 4107–4116. New York, New York, USA: ACM Press, 2014.

[Valkov et al. 10] D Valkov, F Steinicke, G Bruder, and K Hinrichs. "A multi-touch enabled human-transporter metaphor for virtual 3D traveling." In *IEEE Symposium on 3D User Interfaces 2010, 3DUI '10*, pp. 79–82, 2010.

[Valkov et al. 11] Dimitar Valkov, Frank Steinicke, Gerd Bruder, and Klaus Hinrichs. "2D Touching of 3D Stereoscopic Objects." In *Proceedings of the Conference on Human Factors in Computing Systems (CHI)*, pp. 1353–1362, 2011. Available online (http://doi.acm.org/10.1145/1978942.1979142).

[Valkov et al. 12] Dimitar Valkov, Alexander Giesler, and Klaus H. Hinrichs. "Evaluation of Depth Perception for Touch Interaction with Stereoscopic Rendered Objects." In *Proceedings of the Interactive Tabletops and Surfaces (ITS)*, pp. 21–30, 2012. Available online (http://viscg.uni-muenster.de/publications/2012/VGH12a).

[Valkov et al. 14] Dimitar Valkov, Alexander Giesler, and Klaus Hinrichs. "Imperceptible Depth Shifts for Touch Interaction with Stereoscopic Objects." In *Proceedings of the 32nd annual ACM conference on Human factors in computing systems*, pp. 227–236. ACM, 2014.

[Vallance and Calder 01] S Vallance and P Calder. "Context in 3D planar navigation." In *In Proceedings User Interface Conference, 2001. Second Australasian, AUIC 2001*, pp. 93–99. IEEE Computer Society, 2001.

[van den Bergen 04] Gino van den Bergen. *Collision Detection in Interactive 3D Environments*. Morgan Kaufmann, 2004.

[Vaseghi 08] S V Vaseghi. *Advanced digital signal processing and noise reduction*. Wiley, 2008. Available online (https://books.google.com/books?id=vVgLv0ed3cgC).

[Vatavu et al. 12] R D Vatavu, L Anthony, and J O Wobbrock. "Gestures as point clouds: a $ P recognizer for user interface prototypes." In *Proceedings of the 14th ACM International Conference on Multimodal Interaction, ICMI '12*, pp. 2875–2884, 2012.

[Viscarola and Mason 99] Peter G Viscarola and W Anthony Mason. *Windows NT Device Driver Development*. New Riders Pub, 1999.

[Viviani and Flash 95] P Viviani and T Flash. "Minimum-jerk, two-thirds power law, and isochrony: converging approaches to movement planning." *Journal of Experimental Psychology: Human Perception and Performance* 21:1 (1995), 32–53.

[Viviani and Terzuolo 82] P Viviani and C Terzuolo. "Trajectory determines movement dynamics." *Neuroscience* 7:2 (1982), 431–437.

[Voelker et al. 13a] Simon Voelker, Kosuke Nakajima, Christian Thoresen, Yuichi Itoh, Kjell Ivar Øvergård, and Jan Borchers. "PUCs Demo: detecting transparent, passive untouched capacitive widgets on unmodified multi-touch displays." In *UIST '13 Adjunct: Proceedings of the Adjunct Publication of the 26th Annual ACM Symposium on User Interface Software and Technology*. ACM, 2013.

[Voelker et al. 13b] Simon Voelker, Kosuke Nakajima, Christian Thoresen, Yuichi Itoh, Kjell Ivar Øvergård, and Jan Borchers. "PUCs: detecting transparent, passive untouched capacitive widgets on unmodified multi-touch displays." In *ITS '13: Proceedings of the 2013 ACM International Conference on Interactive Tabletops and Surfaces*. ACM, 2013.

[Vogel and Balakrishnan 04] Daniel Vogel and Ravin Balakrishnan. "Interactive public ambient displays: transitioning from implicit to explicit, public to personal, interaction with multiple users." In *ACM Symposium on User Interface Software and Technology (UIST)*, pp. 137–146, 2004.

[Walker and Smelcer 90] Neff Walker and John B Smelcer. "A comparison of selection time from walking and pull-down menus." In *CHI Proceedings of the SIGCHI Conference on Human Factors in Computing Systems*, pp. 221–226. ACM, 1990.

[Walker et al. 91] Neff Walker, John B Smelcer, and Erik Nilsen. "Optimizing Speed and Accuracy of Menu Selection: A Comparison of Walking and Pull-Down Menus." *International Journal of Man-Machine Studies* 35:6 (1991), 871–890.

[Walker 14] Geoff Walker. "Touch Sensing." In *Interactive Displays*, edited by Achintya K Bhowmik. Chichester, UK: John Wiley & Sons, 2014.

[Walter et al. 13] Robert Walter, Gilles Bailly, and Jörg Müller. "StrikeAPose: Revealing Mid-air Gestures on Public Displays." In *Proceedings of the SIGCHI Conference on Human Factors in Computing Systems*, CHI '13, pp. 841–850. New York, NY, USA: ACM, 2013.

[Wander et al. 13] Jeremiah D. Wander, Timothy Blakely, Kai J. Miller, Kurt E. Weaver, Lise A. Johnson, Jared D. Olson, Eberhard E. Fetz, Rajesh P. N. Rao, and Jeffrey G. Ojemann. "Distributed cortical adaptation during learning of a brain-computer interface task." *Proceedings of the National Academy of Sciences* 110:26 (2013), 10818–10823.

[Wang and Blankenship 11] Tim Wang and Tim Blankenship. "Projected-Capacitive Touch Systems from the Controller Point of View." *Information Display*, pp. 8–11.

[Wang and Gratch 10] Ning Wang and Jonathan Gratch. "Don't just stare at me.pdf." In *CHI*, pp. 1241–1249. Atlanta, GA, USA, 2010.

[Wang and Ren 09] Feng Wang and Xiangshi Ren. "Empirical evaluation for finger input properties in multi-touch interaction." In *Proceedings of the SIGCHI Conference on Human Factors in Computing Systems*, CHI '09, pp. 1063–1072. New York, NY, USA: ACM, 2009. Available online (http://doi.acm.org/10.1145/1518701.1518864).

[Wang et al. 09] F Wang, X Cao, X Ren, and P Irani. "Detecting and leveraging finger orientation for interaction with direct-touch surfaces." In *Proceedings of the 22nd Annual ACM Symposium on User Interface Software and Technology*, UIST '09, pp. 23–32. ACM, 2009.

[Wang 11] Jia-Jun Wang. "Simulation studies of inverted pendulum based on PID controllers." *Simulation Modelling Practice and Theory* 19:1 (2011), 440–449.

[Ward 91] W. Ward. "Understanding spontaneous speech: the Phoenix system." In *Proceedings of the Acoustics, Speech, and Signal Processing, 1991. ICASSP-91., 1991 International Conference*, ICASSP '91, pp. 365–367. Washington, DC, USA: IEEE Computer Society, 1991. Available online (http://dl.acm.org/citation.cfm?id=1170742.1170864).

[Ware and Mikaelian 87] Colin Ware and Harutune H Mikaelian. "An evaluation of an eye tracker as a device for computer input2." In *CHI '87: Proceedings of the SIGCHI/GI Conference on Human Factors in Computing Systems and Graphics Interface*, pp. 183–188. New York, New York, USA: ACM, 1987.

[Ware and Osborne 90] Colin Ware and Steven Osborne. "Exploration and virtual camera control in virtual three dimensional environments." In *I3D '90: Proceedings of the 1990 Symposium on Interactive 3D Graphics*, pp. 175–183. New York, New York, USA: ACM, 1990.

[Warren 13] Tom Warren. "With an iWatch looming, Microsoft's Bill Buxton details the 37-year history of smartwatches." 2013. [Online; accessed 2-February-2015]. Available online (http://www.theverge.com/2013/3/6/4069812/ microsoft-bill-buxton-smartwatch-history).

[Watt and Policarpo 01] Alan H Watt and Fabio Policarpo. *3D Games*, Real-time rendering and Software Technology, 1. Addison-Wesley, 2001.

[Watt and Policarpo 03] Alan H Watt and Fabio Policarpo. *3D Games*, Animation and Advanced Real-Time Rendering, 2. Addison-Wesley, 2003.

[Weigel et al. 13] M. Weigel, S. Boring, N. Marquardt, J. Steimle, S. Greenberg, and A. Tang. "From Focus to Context and Back: Combining Mobile Projectors and Stationary Displays." In *Proceedings of the 4th Annual Digital Media Conference, GRAND '13*, 2013. Available online (http://hcitang.org/papers/ 2013-grand2013-from-focus-to-context-and-back.pdf).

[Weiser 91] M Weiser. "The computer for the 21st century." *Scientific American*, pp. 94–104.

[Weiss et al. 10] Malte Weiss, Simon Voelker, Christine Sutter, and Jan Borchers. "BendDesk: dragging across the curve." In *ITS '10: International Conference on Interactive Tabletops and Surfaces*, p. 1. New York, New York, USA: ACM, 2010.

[Welch and Bishop 97] Greg Welch and Gary Bishop. "SCAAT: incremental tracking with incomplete information." In *SIGGRAPH '97: Proceedings of the 24th Annual Conference on Computer Graphics and Interactive Techniques*. ACM Press/Addison-Wesley Publishing Co., 1997.

[Welch et al. 99] Greg Welch, Gary Bishop, Leandra Vicci, Stephen Brumback, Kurtis Keller, and D'nardo Colucci. "The HiBall Tracker: High-performance wide-area tracking for virtual and augmented environments." In *VRST '99: Proceedings of the ACM symposium on Virtual reality software and technology*, pp. 1–ff. New York, New York, USA: ACM, 1999.

[Welch et al. 01] G Welch, G Bishop, L Vicci, S Brumback, K Keller, and D Colucci. "High-Performance Wide-Area Optical Tracking: The HiBall Tracking System." *Presence* 10:1 (2001), 1–21.

[Welford 68] A T Welford. *Fundamentals of skill*. Methum and Co Ltd, 1968.

[Wellner 91] Pierre Wellner. "The DigitalDesk Calculator: Tangible Manipulation on a Desk Top Display." In *Proceedings of the 4th Annual ACM Symposium on User Interface Software and Technology, UIST '91*, pp. 27–33. ACM, 1991.

[Wheeler and Ikeuchi 95] M Wheeler and K Ikeuchi. "Iterative estimation of rotation and translation using the quaternion. School of Computer Science." Technical Report CMU-CS-95-215, Computer Science Department, Pittsburgh, PA, 1995.

[Widrow and Stearns 85] Bernard Widrow and S D Stearns. "Adaptive signal processing." *Englewood Cliffs, NJ, Prentice-Hall, Inc., 1985, 491 p. 1.*

[Wigdor and Wixon 11] Daniel Wigdor and Dennis Wixon. *Brave NUI World*. Designing Natural User Interfaces for Touch and Gesture, Elsevier, 2011.

[Wigdor et al. 06] Daniel Wigdor, Chia Shen, Clifton Forlines, and Ravin Balakrishnan. "Effects of display position and control space orientation on user preference and performance." In *Proceedings of the SIGCHI Conference on Human Factors in Computing Systems*, *CHI '06*, pp. 309–318. New York, NY, USA: ACM, 2006. Available online (http://doi.acm.org/10.1145/1124772.1124819).

[WIKI 14] WIKI. "Action Potential.", 2014. [Online; accessed 6-January-2015]. Available online (http://en.wikipedia.org/wiki/Action_potential).

[Wikipedia 14] Wikipedia. "UltraSound.", 2014. [Online; accessed 4-January-2015]. Available online (en.wikipedia.org/wiki/Ultrasound).

[Wikipedia 15a] Wikipedia. "Attitude and Heading Reference Systems.", 2015. [Online; accessed 30-March-2015]. Available online (http://en.wikipedia.org/wiki/AHRS).

[Wikipedia 15b] Wikipedia. "Heap's algorithm.", 2015. [Online; accessed 30-March-2015]. Available online (http://en.wikipedia.org/wiki/Heap's_algorithm).

[Wikipedia 15c] Wikipedia. "Infrared.", 2015. [Online; accessed 11-February-2015]. Available online (http://en.wikipedia.org/wiki/Infrared).

[Wikipedia 15d] Wikipedia. "Medical ultrasonography.", 2015. [Online; accessed 11-February-2015]. Available online (http://en.wikipedia.org/wiki/Medical_ultrasonography).

[Wikipedia 15e] Wikipedia. "Motion Capture.", 2015. [Online; accessed 30-March-2015]. Available online (http://en.wikipedia.org/wiki/Motion_capture).

[Wikipedia 15f] Wikipedia. "Oculus Rift.", 2015. [Online; accessed 23-February-2015]. Available online (http://en.wikipedia.org/wiki/Oculus_Rift).

[Wikipedia 15g] Wikipedia. "Paul M. Fitts.", 2015. [Online; accessed 23-February-2015]. Available online (http://en.wikipedia.org/wiki/Paul_Fitts).

[Wikipedia 15h] Wikipedia. "Piezoelectric Sensor.", 2015. [Online; accessed 6-February-2015]. Available online (http://en.wikipedia.org/wiki/Piezoelectric_sensory).

[Wikipedia 15i] Wikipedia. "Piezoelectric sensor.", 2015. [Online; accessed 12-February-2015]. Available online (http://en.wikipedia.org/wiki/Piezoelectric_sensor).

[Wikipedia 15j] Wikipedia. "Piezoelectricity.", 2015. [Online; accessed 6-February-2015]. Available online (http://en.wikipedia.org/wiki/Piezoelectricity).

[Wikipedia 15k] Wikipedia. "Polar coordinate system.", 2015. [Online; accessed 20-March-2015]. Available online (http://en.wikipedia.org/wiki/Polar_coordinate_system).

[Wikipedia 15l] Wikipedia. "Transducer.", 2015. [Online; accessed 11-February-2015]. Available online (http://en.wikipedia.org/wiki/Transducer).

[Wikipedia 15m] Wikipedia. "Vestibular System.", 2015. [Online; accessed 5-March-2015]. Available online (http://en.wikipedia.org/wiki/Vestibular_system).

[Wilcox 11] Rand Wilcox. *Modern Statistics for the Social and Behavioral Sciences*. A Practical Introduction, CRC Press, 2011.

[Williams and Young 07] Jason D Williams and Steve Young. "Partially observable Markov decision processes for spoken dialog systems." *Computer Speech & Language* 21:2 (2007), 393–422.

[Williams et al. 06] Betsy Williams, Gayathri Narasimham, Timothy P McNamara, Thomas H Carr, John J Rieser, and Bobby Bodenheimer. "Updating orientation in large virtual environments using scaled translational gain." *APGV*, pp. 21–28.

[Williams et al. 07] Betsy Williams, Gayathri Narasimham, Björn Rump, Timothy P Mc-Namara, Thomas H Carr, John J Rieser, and Bobby Bodenheimer. "Exploring large virtual environments with an HMD when physical space is limited." *APGV*, pp. 41–48.

[Williams 08] Jason D Williams. "The best of both worlds: unifying conventional dialog systems and POMDPs." In *INTERSPEECH*, pp. 1173–1176, 2008.

[Williams 12] Anthony Williams. *C++ Concurrency in Action: Practical Multithreading*, First edition. Manning Publications, 2012.

[Williamson et al. 10] B Williamson, C Wingrave, and J laviola. "Realnav: Exploring natural user interfaces for locomotion in video games." In *IEEE Symposium on 3D User Interfaces 2010, 3DUI '10*, 2010.

[Willis et al. 11] Karl D.D. Willis, Ivan Poupyrev, Scott E. Hudson, and Moshe Mahler. "SideBySide: ad-hoc multi-user interaction with handheld projectors." In *Proceedings of the 24th Annual ACM Symposium on User Interface Software and Technology, UIST '11*, pp. 431–440. New York, NY, USA: ACM, 2011. Available online (http://doi.acm.org/10.1145/2047196.2047254).

[Wilson and Benko 10a] Andrew D Wilson and Hrvoje Benko. "Combining multiple depth cameras and projectors for interactions on, above and between surfaces." In *UIST '10: Proceedings of the 23nd Annual ACM Symposium on User Interface Software and Technology*, p. 273. New York, New York, USA: ACM, 2010.

[Wilson and Benko 10b] Andrew D. Wilson and Hrvoje Benko. "Combining multiple depth cameras and projectors for interactions on, above and between surfaces." In *Proceedings of the Symposium on User Interface Software and Technology (UIST)*, pp. 273–282, 2010.

[Wilson et al. 08] AD Wilson, S Izadi, O Hilliges, A Garcia-Mendoza, and D Kirk. "Bringing physics to the surface." In *Proceedings of the 21st Annual ACM Symposium on User Interface Software and Technology, UIST '09*, pp. 67–76. ACM, 2008.

[Wilson 11] Pat Wilson. "Analog Input Processing.", 2011. [Online; accessed 2-January-2015]. Available online (franciscoraulortega.com/pwinput).

[Wilson 12] Andre Wilson. "Sensor- And Recognition-Based Input For Interaction." In *Human-Computer Interaction*, edited by Andrew Sears and Julie A Jacko, pp. 177–199. New York: CRC, 2012.

[Wilson 15] Clare Wilson. "Mind-reading goes portable." *New Scientist* 225:1230.

[Wing 82] Alan M Wing. "Timing and co-ordination of repetitive bimanual movements." *The Quarterly Journal of Experimental Psychology* 34:3 (1982), 339–348.

[Wing 90] J M Wing. "A specifier's introduction to formal methods." *Computer*.

[Witmer and Singer 98] Bob G Witmer and Michael J Singer. "Measuring Presence in Virtual Environments: A Presence Questionnaire." *Presence* 7:3 (1998), 225–240.

[Wloka and Greenfield 95] Matthias M Wloka and Eliot Greenfield. "The virtual tricorder: a uniform interface for virtual reality." In *UIST '95: Proceedings of the 8th Annual ACM Symposium on User Interface and Software Technology*. ACM, 1995.

[Wobbrock et al. 05] Jacob O Wobbrock, Htet Htet Aung, Brandon Rothrock, and Brad A Myers. "Maximizing the guessability of symbolic input." *CHI EA '05: CHI '05 Extended Abstracts on Human Factors in Computing Systems*, pp. 1869–1872.

[Wobbrock et al. 07] Jacob O Wobbrock, Andrew D Wilson, and Yang Li. "Gestures without libraries, toolkits or training: a $1 recognizer for user interface prototypes." In *Proceedings of the 20th Annual ACM Symposium on User Interface Software and Technology, UIST '07*. New York, New York, USA: ACM, 2007.

[Wobbrock et al. 09] J O Wobbrock, M R Morris, and A D Wilson. "User-defined gestures for surface computing." In *CHI '09: Proceedings of the SIGCHI Conference on Human Factors in Computing Systems*, 2009.

[Wobbrock et al. 11] Jacob O Wobbrock, Kristen Shinohara, and Alex Jansen. "The effects of task dimensionality, endpoint deviation, throughput calculation, and experiment design on pointing measures and models." In *CHI '11: Proceedings of the SIGCHI Conference on Human Factors in Computing Systems*, p. 1639. New York, New York, USA: ACM, 2011.

[Wolfeld 81] J A Wolfeld. "Real time control of a robot tacticle sensor." Ph.D. thesis, University of Pennsylvania, 1981.

[Wolter et al. 09] M Wolter, B Hentschel, I Tedjo-Palczynski, and T Kuhlen. "A direct manipulation interface for time navigation in scientific visualizations." In *Proceedings of the 2009 IEEE Symposium on 3D User Interfaces, 3DUI '09*, pp. 11–18, 2009.

[Woodman 07] O J Woodman. "An introduction to inertial navigation." *University of Cambridge*.

[Woodworth 99] R S Woodworth. "The Accuracy of Voluntary Movement." *The Journal of Nervous and Mental Disease* 26:12 (1899), 743–752.

[Wu et al. 06] Mike Wu, Chia Shen, Kathy Ryall, Clifton Forlines, and Ravin Balakrishnan. "Gesture Registration, Relaxation, and Reuse for Multi-Point Direct-Touch Surfaces." In *TABLETOP '06: Proceedings of the First IEEE International Workshop on Horizontal Interactive Human-Computer Systems*, pp. 185–192. IEEE Computer Society, 2006.

[Wu et al. 11] Andy Wu, Derek Reilly, Anthony Tang, and Ali Mazalek. "Tangible Navigation and Object Manipulation in Virtual Environments." In *Proceedings of the Fifth International Conference on Tangible, Embedded, and Embodied Interaction, TEI '11*, pp. 37–44. New York, NY, USA: ACM, 2011. Available online (http://doi.acm.org/10.1145/1935701.1935710).

[Xiao et al. 11] Robert Xiao, Miguel A. Nacenta, Regan L. Mandryk, Andy Cockburn, and Carl Gutwin. "Ubiquitous cursor: a comparison of direct and indirect pointing feedback in multi-display environments." In *Proceedings of Graphics Interface 2011, GI '11*, pp. 135–142. School of Computer Science, University of Waterloo,

Waterloo, Ontario, Canada: Canadian Human-Computer Communications Society, 2011. Available online (http://dl.acm.org/citation.cfm?id=1992917.1992939).

[Yarbus 67] Alfred L Yarbus. "Eye Movements and Vision." Plenuss Press, New York, 1967.

[Yasavur et al. 14] Ugan Yasavur, Christine Lisetti, and Naphtali Rishe. "Let's talk! speaking virtual counselor offers you a brief intervention." *Journal on Multimodal User Interfaces* 8:4 (2014), 381–398. Available online (http://dx.doi.org/10.1007/s12193-014-0169-9).

[Yatani et al. 08] Koji Yatani, Kurt Partridge, Marshall Bern, and Mark W Newman. "Escape: a target selection technique using visually-cued gestures." In *CHI '08: Proceedings of the SIGCHI Conference on Human Factors in Computing Systems*, p. 285. New York, New York, USA: ACM, 2008.

[Yee 03] Ka-Ping Yee. "Peephole displays: pen interaction on spatially aware handheld computers." In *Proceedings of the SIGCHI Conference on Human Factors in Computing Systems, CHI '03*, pp. 1–8. New York, NY, USA: ACM, 2003. Available online (http://doi.acm.org/10.1145/642611.642613).

[Yee 04] K P Yee. "Two-handed interaction on a tablet display." *CHI'04 Extended Abstracts on Human Factors in Computing Systems*.

[YEI 15a] YEI. "YEI 3-Space Mocap Studio.", 2015. [Online; accessed 30-March-2015]. Available online (http://www.yeitechnology.com/yei-3-space-mocap-studio).

[YEI 15b] YEI. "YEI 3-Space Sensor.", 2015. [Online; accessed 30-March-2015]. Available online (http://www.yeitechnology.com/yei-3-space-sensor).

[YEI 15c] YEI. "YEI 3-Space Sensor Family Tech Brief. Space Sensor Family Technical Brief.", 2015. [Online; accessed 30-March-2015]. Available online (http://www.yeitechnology.com/sites/default/files/TSS_Family_Tech_Brief_v1.0.4b.pdf).

[YEI 15d] YEI. "YEI PrioVR Motion Sensing Suit. Prio Suit Information.", 2015. [Online; accessed 30-March-2015]. Available online (http://priovr.com/).

[Young et al. 10] Steve Young, Milica Gašić, Simon Keizer, François Mairesse, Jost Schatzmann, Blaise Thomson, and Kai Yu. "The hidden information state model: A practical framework for POMDP-based spoken dialogue management." *Computer Speech & Language* 24:2 (2010), 150–174.

[Young et al. 13] Steve Young, M Gašić, Blaise Thomson, and JD Williams. "POMDP-Based Statistical Spoken Dialog Systems: A Review." *Proceedings of the IEEE* 101:5 (2013), 1160–1179.

[Yu et al. 10] Lingyun Yu, P. Svetachov, P. Isenberg, M. H. Everts, and T. Isenberg. "FI3D: Direct-Touch Interaction for the Exploration of 3D Scientific Visualization Spaces." *IEEE Transactions on Visualization and Computer Graphics* 16:6 (2010), 1613–1622.

[Yu et al. 12] Lingyun Yu, K Efstathiou, P Isenberg, and T Isenberg. "Efficient Structure-Aware Selection Techniques for 3D Point Cloud Visualizations with 2DOF Input." *IEEE Transactions on Visualization and Computer Graphics* 18:12 (2012), 2245–2254.

[Yun and Bachmann 06] X Yun and E R Bachmann. "Design, Implementation, and Experimental Results of a Quaternion-Based Kalman Filter for Human Body Motion Tracking." *Robotics, IEEE Transactions on* 22:6 (2006), 1216–1227.

[Yun et al. 03] Xiaoping Yun, Mariano Lizarraga, Eric R Bachmann, and Robert B McGhee. "An improved quaternion-based Kalman filter for real-time tracking of rigid body orientation." In *Intelligent Robots and Systems, 2003.(IROS 2003). Proceedings. 2003 IEEE/RSJ International Conference on*, 2, 2, pp. 1074–1079. IEEE, 2003.

[Yury 09] Yury. "ellipsoid-fit.", 2009. [zip file]. Available online (http://www.mathworks.com/matlabcentral/fileexchange/24693-ellipsoid-fit).

[Zander 07] T E Zander. *Applied low-cost inertial sensor systems and efficient measurement data processing*. MEMS technology and engineering, Andere Verlag, 2007. Available online (https://books.google.com/books?id=-B6ttgAACAAJ).

[Zarchman and Musoff 09] Paul Zarchman and Howard Musoff. *Fundamentals of Kalman Filtering: A Practical Approach*, Third edition. AIAA, 2009.

[Zeagler et al. 14] Clint Zeagler, Scott Gilliland, Larry Freil, Thad Starner, and Melody Jackson. "Going to the dogs: towards an interactive touchscreen interface for working dogs." In *UIST '14: Proceedings of the 27th Annual ACM Symposium on User Interface Software and Technology*. ACM, 2014.

[Zeleznik et al. 02] R C Zeleznik, J J LaViola, D Acevedo Feliz, and Daniel F Keefe. "Pop through button devices for VE navigation and interaction." In *Virtual Reality, 2002. Proceedings. IEEE*, pp. 127–134. IEEE Comput. Soc, 2002.

[Zeleznik et al. 10] Robert Zeleznik, Andrew Bragdon, Ferdi Adeputra, and Hsu-Sheng Ko. "Hands-on math: a page-based multi-touch and pen desktop for technical work and problem solving." In *UIST '10: Proceedings of the 23nd Annual ACM Symposium on User Interface Software and Technology*, p. 17. New York, New York, USA: ACM, 2010.

[Zhai and Barreto 06] Jing Zhai and Armando Barreto. "Stress Detection in Computer Users Based on Digital Signal Processing of Noninvasive Physiological Variables." In *2006 International Conference of the IEEE Engineering in Medicine and Biology Society*, pp. 1355–1358. IEEE, 2006.

[Zhai and Milgram 93] Shumin Zhai and Paul Milgram. "Human performance evaluation of manipulation schemes in virtual environments." *Virtual Reality Annual International Symposium, 1993, 1993 IEEE*, pp. 155–161.

[Zhai et al. 94] Shumin Zhai, William Buxton, and Paul Milgram. "The "Silk Cursor": investigating transparency for 3D target acquisition." In *CHI '94: Proceedings of the SIGCHI Conference on Human Factors in Computing Systems*, pp. 459–464. New York, New York, USA: ACM, 1994.

[Zhai et al. 96] Shumin Zhai, Paul Milgram, and William Buxton. "The influence of muscle groups on performance of multiple degree-of-freedom input." In *CHI '96: Proceedings of the SIGCHI Conference on Human Factors in Computing Systems*. ACM, 1996.

[Zhai et al. 04] Shumin Zhai, Jing Kong, and Xiangshi Ren. "Speed-accuracy tradeoff in Fitts' law tasks: on the equivalence of actual and nominal pointing precision." *International Journal of Human-Computer Studies* 61:6 (2004), 832–856.

[Zhai 95] S Zhai. "Human Performance in Six Degree of Freedom Input Control." Ph.D. thesis, University of Toronto, 1995.

[Zhang et al. 12] Xinyong Zhang, Hongbin Zha, and Wenxin Feng. "Extending Fitts' law to account for the effects of movement direction on 2D pointing." In *Proceedings of the SIGCHI Conference on Human Factors in Computing Systems, CHI '12*, pp. 3185–3194. New York, NY, USA: ACM, 2012. Available online (http://doi.acm.org/10.1145/2207676.2208737).

[Zölzer 08] Udo Zölzer. *Digital Audio Signal Processing*. Chichester, UK: John Wiley & Sons, 2008.

[Zurawski and Zhou 94] R Zurawski and M Zhou. "Petri nets and industrial applications: A tutorial." *IEEE Transactions on Industrial Electronics* 41:6 (1994), 567–583.

Index

Symbols

2D 248
    data points 262
    position 211, 217
    space 315
    visuializations 229
3-Space Sensor . . . . *see* YEI
3D . . . . *see also* 3D Rotations, Coordinates,
    Computer Graphics,Interactions,
    Manipulation, Navigation,
    Stereoscopic Touch, Techniques,
    Transformations, Vectors,
    Virtual Enviroments, 207, 329,
    340
    applications 28, 269
    axes 329
    axis angle rotations 341–342
    input
        applications 342
    objects 121, 511
    position 208, 211, 216–218, 243
    space 88, 211, 373
3D Interaction . . . . *see* Interactions
3D Models . . . . *see* Computer Graphics
3D Navigation . . . . *see* Navigation
3D Printer 653
3D Rotations . . *see also* Aircraft Principal
    Axes, Frames, 216, 341, 342,
    373, 378, 414
    airplanes 373
    angle 383
    cartesian 373
        orthogonal 374
        right-handed 374
    objects 373

orthogonal
    axes 373
    perpendicular 373
    reference frames 374
    sequences 377, 384
3D Touch . . . . *see* Stereoscopic Touch
3D Travel . . . . *see* Travel
3D User Interfaces . . . . *see* User Interfaces
3DConnexion 570, 571
3DS Max 77, 570
3DUI . . . . *see* User Interfaces
3M 24, 163
    multi-touch display 271, 586
    Touch Systems . . . . *see also*
        Multi-Touch, 171
3rdTech 117
5DT . . . . *see* Input Devices

A

A Behavior Language . . . . *see* ABL
A Brave NUI World 265
A Computer Animated Hand Film 128
ABL 320
ABNF editor 638
Accelerometers . . . . *see* Inertial Sensors
Accesibility
    click . . . . *see also* Input Devices, 301
Active Desk 163
Active Devices . . . . *see* Input Devices
AdaFruit 521
Adaptive Signal Processing . . . . . . *see* DSP
ADC . . . . *see* DSP
Adler, Robert
    clicker 163
    surface acoustic wave 163
Affective Computing 303

affect modeling
    machine 301
    user 301
affective shift 302
circumplex model of affect 303
emotional stimuli 301
frustration 304
interaction 301
parasympathetic 303
recognition 301
relaxed 303
sensing 301
state 301
stress 303, 304
sympathetic 303
AI 301, 320
Aircraft Principal Axes . . . *see also* Euler
    Angles, Quaternions,
    Transformations, 439
    bank 80
    elevation 80
    heading 80
    pitch 80, 216, 218, 373, 413, 570
    roll 80, 216, 373, 413, 570
    angle 453
    rotation 218
    yaw 80, 218, 373, 413, 570
Algorithms
    Big O 264
    linear 265
    complexity 365
    EGT 299
    gradient descent 418
    greedy 264
    heap permute . . *see also* Recognition,
    263
    minimum spanning trees 299
    NP-complete . . *see also* Recognition,
    264
    optimization 417
    Gauss–Newton 417
    gradient descent 417
    Petri Nets
    picking 288
    probabilistics 432
    QUEST 424
    sensor fusion 435

Analog Signals . . . *see also* DSP, 348, 392,
    538
    notations 348
    transducer 538
Android 652
ANS . . . . . *see* Autonomic Nervous System
API 177, 567
    gestures . . *see also* Multi-Touch, 175
    multi-touch 176
Apple
    iOS 652
    iPad 161, 586
    iPhone 161, 164, 165, 586
    expectations 166
    projected capacitive . . . . . . *see also*
    Multi-Touch, 165
    Mac OS X 183, 440, 483, 513
    Macintosh 5, 12
    Macintosh II 191
    Magic Mouse 31
    Objective-C 586
Archos
    VR 651
Arduino 535
    connecting 543
    sensors 544
    hands-on project
    ultrasonic proximity 540–552
    Pins 540
    serial communication 539
    UART 539
    serial monitor 551
    Sketch 541, 545–550
    uploading 549–550
    UNO R3 540
    software 541
Artificial Intelligence . . . . *see* AI
As We May Think . . . . *see* Bush, Vannevar
ASCII 438, 441, 442
Asimove, Isaac
    Pebble in the Sky 313
Atari
    joystick . . *see also* Input Devices, 32,
    580
    paddles 580
Atmel . . . . . *see also* Multi-Touch, 170, 535
Augmented Reality 103, 124

AutoCad 570
Autonomic Nervous System ...... *see also*
    Affective Computing, 302, 310
    flight or fight 302
    housekeeping 302
    innervate organs 303
    parasympathetic 302, 303
    rest and repose 302
    sympathetic 302, 303
Autostereoscopic Displays ... *see* Displays
AWSD .... *see* Navigation

B

BCI 314, 317, 319, 325
    constructing images 318–319
    constructing text 318–319
    controlling a cursor 314
        vertical 314
    controlling a prosthetic hand ....
        314–315
    controlling a robotic arm ... 314–315
    electrode arrays
        implanted 315
    electrodes
        implanted 314
    invasive 314–315
    neuroprostheses 314
    neuroscience 314
    recordings.................... 314
    selecting keys 315
    system 319
BeagleBone 535
Bi-manual .... *see* Interactions, Models,
    Multi-Touch, Techniques
Bicycle
    autonomous self-balancing 555
        data processing 557, 559–560
        implementation 561–564
        mechanical structure 557–558
Big O .... *see* Algorithms
Binary 441, 443, 444
Blender 77
Bluetooth 438
Brain .... *see also* EEG
    cortex
        dorsal premotor 315
        occipital 315

scans 316, 318
signal capture 321
signals 315
systems
    signal-based 319
Transcranial magnetic stimulation
    biphasic 315
Brain-Computer Interfaces .... *see* BCI
Braun, Ferdinand
    CRT 66
Bush, Vannevar 4
    As We May Think 4, 5
    Memex 4
Buxton, Bill 11, 27, 29, 48, 255
    a three-state model .. *see also* Models,
        24, 156, 255, 279
    chess player's syndrome .... *see also*
        Multi-Touch, 175
    collection 10, 27
    Cracker Jacker 48
    input structure 49
    multi-touch 161

C

C++ 288, 290, 467, 519, 541, 592, 600
C:D .... *see* Input Devices
Calibration 469
    bias 343
    cross-axis effect and rotation 344
    filters
        average.................... 345
        low-pass filter.............. 345
        median 345
        running average 345
    misalignment matrix 390
    oversampling 345
    process 390
    rotation 344
    scale 343–344
    smoothing.................... 344
    three-axis sensors 342–345
Camera ... *see* Computer Graphics, Input
    Devices, Recognition, 119, 511
    color......................... 44
    computer vision 118
    depth 432
    depth sensor 44, 521

infrared 132, 166, 172, 293, 511
   camera 293, 294
   emitter 44
   illumination 295
   image 296
   LED 296, 511
   receiver 44
   sensor 538
   vision-based 44
   midAir 166, 212, 511
parallexes
   position 215
RGB 521
Capacitive . . . . see Multi-Touch
Cathode Ray Tube . . . . see Displays
CAVE . . . . see Virtual Reality
CG . . . . see Computer Graphics
Cognitive Process of Navigation . . . . . . see
   Wayfinding
Collision Detection . . . . see Computer
   Graphics
Communication Channel . . see also Models
Compass . . . . see Inertial Sensors
Computer Graphics 75, 129
   3D
      limited depth 206
      models 82, 570, 627
      camera 75–77
      first person 75
      first-person shooter 76
      third person 76, 120
   camera componets
      at 77
      eye 77
      up 77
   collision detection 84, 594
      bouding boxes 84
      bounding volume 84
      boxes 84
      physics engines 84
      spheres 84
   engine 592
   FBX 472
   geometric modeling 82
      bi-cubic 82
      constructive solid geometry 82
      half-edge 82

hierarchical representation 82
implicit surface representation . . . .
   82
polygon representation 82
skeletal animation 82
spatial representation 82
GPU and GPGPU 80
interactive 75
models 472
monoscopic rendering . . . . . . see also
   Stereoscopic Touch, 206
non-realistic rendering
   shadow 224
pipeline 76
scene managers 82–84
   bsp 84
   culling 83
   dynamic 84
   instancing 83
   octree 83
   Ogre3D 83
   quadtree 84
   scene graph 82, 83
   static 84
   types 82
shallow depth . . . . see also
   Stereoscopic, 208
space camera 76
   local 76
   world 76, 77
stereoscopic
   projection 217
view frustum 77
   fovy 77
virtual ray 208
z-order . . . . see also Stereoscopic
   Touch, 248
Computer Keyboard . . . . see Input Devices
Connexion 567
   Space Navigator 40
Context-free grammar 279
Control Systems 555
Control-Display Ratio . . see Input Devices
Conversions
   Quaternions to Euler Angles 425
Coordinates
   3D 329

conventions 329
axes 373
left-handed 330
polar 101
right-handed 330
right-handed system 215
systems 330, 374–376
   air and sea vehicles 330
   axes 439
   DirectX 330
   land vehicles 330
   OpenGL 330
   reference frame 342
   Unreal Engine 330
   user-centered 101
CRT . . . . *see* Displays
Cruise, Tom 430
Cursor . . . . *see also* Input Devices, Models,
   Techniques, 299, 314
Cypress . . . . *see also* Multi-Touch, 170

D

Dürer, Albrecht . . . . *see* Displays
Da Vinci, Leonardo . . . . *see* Displays
Data Gloves . . . . *see* Input Devices
Definitions 15
   Input Device 16
Degress of Freedom . . . . . . *see* Interactions
Depth Cues . . . . *see* Visual Displays
Depth-sensing . . . . *see* Input Devices
Descriptive Models . . . . *see* Models
Design Patterns 567
   observer 567
Device Clutching . . *see also* Manipulations,
   93
DFT . . . . *see* Fourier Analysis
Diamond-Touch . . . . *see also* Multi-Touch,
   164
Diffused Surface Illumination . . . . *see also*
   Multi-Touch, 174
Digital Games . . . . *see* Video Games
Digital Pen . . . . *see* Input Devices
Digital Signal Processing . . . . *see* DSP
Direct3D . . . . *see* Microsoft
DirectX . . . . *see* Microsoft
Display cursor . . . . *see* Cursor

Displays . . *see also* HMD, User Interfaces,
   Multi-Touch, Stereoscopic,
   Stereoscopic Touch, Visual
   Displays, 67–73, 229, 293
arm-mounted displays 68
autostereoscopic displays 68
bezel 234
conventional monitor 67
desktop 131
field of view 69, 70
fixed 643–646
   multiple 644–645
   single 643–644
head-mounted displays 67
hemispherical displays 68
history 66
   Braun, Ferdinand 66
   CRT 66
   Dürer, Albrecht 66
   Da Vinci, Leonardo 66
   Gurney 66
   Huygens 66
   Kirchner 66
   LCD 66
   light reflection 66
   limelight effect 66
   magic lantern 66
   Nipkow disk 66
   OLED 66
   projected drawing 66
hybrid 649
   fixed and projectors 649
   fixed and smartphones 649
interactive
   directions 206
large 183
   public 231
   vertical 231
LCD 540
monitor 67
   crt 67
   lcd 67
multi-touch
   capacitive 286
   vision-based 286
near-eye 69–70
   augmented-reality 69

field of view 69
fighther-jet pilots 69
high-resolution 69
optical see-through displays ... 70
semicovering displays......... 69
technology 69–72
view-covering displays........ 69
optical head-mounted display 67
portable 647–649
multiple 647
projectors 647–649
tablets and smartphones 647
stereoscopic 237, 503
projection 217
surfaces 208, 210, 211, 248
2D........................ 206
2D input................... 207
surround-screen 67, 68
tabletops 231
below the interactive surface .. 223
large 199
three-dimensional 70–73
3D TV 73
cinema 73
considerations 71
corrective lenses............. 73
depth perception.............. 72
distance 72
orientation 71
perspective 73
puppet-theater............... 73
tilt........................... 241
touch
sensing precision 205
touch surfaces
on-surface target 213
touch-sensitive 208
tunnel vision 131
vertical...................... 231
large 241
virtual retina Display
Google Glasses............... 67
virtual retina display............. 67
workbenches 68
Distributed Computing .... *see* Parallel
Programming
DIY 651

Do-it-yourself .... *see* DIY
DOF................... *see* Interactions
Dollar Family .... *see* Recognition
Domain-driven ...... *see* Domain-specific
Domain-specific
application 183
language 283
travel .... *see also* Travel, 118
DSL................ *see* Domain-specific
DSP .... *see also* Analog Signals, Signals,
44, 190, 347, 350, 371, 392
adaptive...................... 307
ADC 536, 557, 560
aliasing 361
amplitute..................... 348
applications 350
classification.............. 349–350
convolution 368–371
high sampling frequency........ 361
low sampling frequency 361
noise 351–352, 390–394, 403
color...................... 352
impulsive.................. 352
narrow-band 352
random.................... 391
sources.................... 352
transient pulses............. 352
white 352, 422, 425
notations..................... 348
Nyquist–Shannon theorem..........
360–361
power spectra 392
quantization 361–362
sampling rate......... *see also* Input
Devices, 21
sampling theorem 357–360
signal 347–349
system....................... 347
time......................... 348
toolbox 351
z-Transform
definitions 366–368
discrete-time............... 366
region of convergence 368
single-sided transform 366
z-plane.................... 368
z-Transofrm.................. 365

discrete 365
   inverse 365
Durovis
   Dive 651
DYI 659
Dynamic Programming 255
Dynamo Effect . . . . *see also* Earth, 395

E

Earth 375, 415–417
   axes 375
      magnet 396
      orthogonal 375
      rotational 396
   equator 375
   frame 414, 415, 418, 419
   geography
      north 396
      south 396
   gravitational
      direction 417
      vector 420
   gravity 376, 388
   layers 395
   magnetic
      declination 396
      field 395, 417
      vector 419, 420
   pole
      geographical 396
      magnetic 396
   temperatures 395
ECA 607, 617, 627
   dialog 627
   corpus 640
   dynamic 611
   finite state-based 609
   health 613–614
   plan-based 609
   reinforcement 611–613
   statgey learning 635
   statistical approach 610
   supervised vs reinforcement . . . . . .
      610–611
   task-based 615–616
   end-to-end dialog
      system architecture 608

in-depth 616–617
information state 609
EEG . . . . *see also* Input Devices, 298, 315,
      317, 321, 323, 324, 350
   controlling a quadcopter 315
   devices 321–323
   neuroheadsets 321–323
   noninvasive 315
   recognition 323–324
   recognizing brain regions 325
   research survey 322
   telekinetic headband 323
   transferring bits 315
EEPROM 536
EGT 293, 299, 301, 310
   3D vector
      direction 293
   adaptive interference canceller
      example 308
   adaptive signal processing 307
   affective sensing 300–310
   binocular 297
   blips 299
   calibration 296
   cornea
      center of reflection 293
   corneal reflection 293
      high intensity 293
      landmark 294
      white 293
   direction of gaze 296
      intersection 296
   display cursor 299, 300
   eye saccades 304
   fixation 298, 309
      gaze 299
      identification algorithm 299
   fixational eye movements . . 304, 309
      microsaccades 309
      saccadic intrusions 309
      tremors 309
   glint 293
   high-speed 304
   illumination changes 307
   infrared
      camera 296
      off-axis 296

on-axis 296
instrument 308
isolation of pupil 294
modern 304
optical axis of the eye 293
real-time analysis 293
point-of-gaze 293, 301
geometric considerations 293
post-processing 298–299
processed modified pupil diameter . . .
308
pupil 293
black 294
bright 294, 295
centroid 294
dark 294, 295
dark circle 294
difference image 295
ellipse 294
low intensity 294
size variations 307
pupil diameter 308
monitoring 304
variations 304
red eye 294
remote gaze estimation theory . . . 296
saccades 298
definition 310
transient 299
sympathetic activation detection . . . . .
303
system
camera 296
tracking
early attempts 298
visual evoked potential 298
Elastic Matching . . . . *see also* Recognition,
257
Electroencephalogram . . . . *see* EEG
ELO TouchSystems . . . . *see also*
Multi-Touch, 172
Embodied Conversational Agents . . . . . *see*
ECA
Emotiv . . . . *see also* EEG, 324
EPOC 322, 323
EPOC+ 322
headsets 322

Insight 323
Engelbart, Douglas 3, 5, 27
bi-manual system 28
Mouse 8, 27
mouse . . . . . *see also* Input Devices, 3
The Mother of All Demos 6, 28
Epilepsy 314
Equations
are gestures natural? 183
dollar algorithms
$P 264
Fitts' law 138, 140
alternate effective width 142
Mackenzie . . *see also* Models, 139
movement time 138
gaze . . . . *see also* Travel, 118
Hick-Hyman law . . . *see also* Models,
146
information 147
Kalman filters
gain 408
prediction 408
Keystroke-level 148
map-based
target . . . . *see also* Travel, 121
pointing . . . . *see also* Travel, 119
pinch 119
Shannon . . . . . *see also* Theorem, 139
stereoscopic
shifted scene position 237
stereoscopic touch
generalized scaled shift 243
touching parallexes 215
triangle cursor
quadratic function 217
Euclidean . . . . *see also* Coordinates,
Transformations
distances 263, 264
space 258, 376
Euler Angles . . . . *see also* Matrices,
Quaternions, Transformations,
Vectors, 79–81, 376–379, 425,
439, 464, 470
angle differences
axes 465
gimbal lock 81, 378
quaternions 380

pitch........................... 80
roll............................ 80
rotation matrices 376–378
   combinations 376
   orientation.................. 376
rotations
   3 DOF 377
   theorem...................... 376
     rotational 376
   yaw.......................... 80
Experiment Module
   implementation 600–604
Extended Kalman Filters......... *see also*
   Kalman Filters
Eye Dominance..... *see also* Stereoscopic
   Touch
   left-eye
     negative camera offset 215
   right-eye
     positive camera offset........ 215
Eye Gaze Tracking .... *see* EGT
Eyes .... *see also* EGT, 315
   cornea 293
   fixation................... 298, 309
     jittery motions 298
   fixational eye movements .. 298, 309
   fixations 298
   gaze
     target 309
   microsaccades 298
   movements.................... 309
   optical axis................... 293
   photography.................. 294
   pupil 294, 305
     dark....................... 296
     size variations............... 307
   red 294
   saccades 298
     suppression 298
   slow drifts................... 298
   subject....................... 293
   tremors 298

F

Facebook........................... 67
Facial Expressions 607
Fast Fourier Transform .... *see* FFT

Fat Fingers .... *see* Multi-Touch
Feature-based classifiers .. *see* Recognition
FFT .. *see also* DSP, Fourier Analisys, 365
Field Of View .... *see* Displays
Filters ...... *see also* Calibration, Kalman
   Filters, 403, 436
   average 345
   linear adaptive................ 403
   low-pass 345
   median 345
Fingers 209, 217, 229, 235, 243, 247,
   274
   detection..................... 286
   index 217
   Leap Motion 511
   motion....................... 210
   occlusion..................... 217
   relative depth motion........... 243
   rotation.... *see also* Transformations
   size.......................... 205
   surface....................... 217
   thumb 217
Finite State Machine............ *see* FSM
Firmware 190
Fitts' law.................... *see* Models
Fitts, Paul .... *see also* Models, 139
   about.................... 158–159
fMRI
   connecting images......... 316–317
   generating text................ 316
   locating personality models ....
     317–318
   nonivasive 315–318
   recognizing yes-no answers 317
   systems 318
Fourier Analysis .. *see also* DSP, 362–363
   discrete................... 363–364
     finite...................... 363
     inverse transform............ 365
   discrete time 363
   transform................. 363, 365
Fourier, Joseph 362
Frames .... *see also* 3D Rotations
   body-fixed 376
     orthogonal.................. 376
     perpendicular 376
   inertial...................... 375

FSM 255, 265, 268, 284
FTIR . . . . *see also* Multi-Touch, 207

G

G.Techonology
   g.Nautilus 325
Galvin Skin Response . . . . *see* GSR
GamePad . . . . *see* Input Devices
Games . . . . *see* Video Games
Gauss, Karl 404
Geographic Information System . . *see* GIS
Geometric Modeling . . . . *see* Computer
   Graphics
Geometry
   object 224
Gestures 175
Gestures . . . . *see also* Multi-Touch,
   Stereoscopic Touch, 255, 257,
   265, 286, 313, 518, 607
   1D 257
   2D 257
   circle 516, 518
   detection 256
   interactive recognition 257
   key tap 516
   kinect
      built-in 523
   memorability . . *see also* Multi-Touch,
      188–189
   midAir 212
   multi-touch 207, 279
      definition: FETouch++ 274
   one hand . . *see also* Multi-Touch, 183
   orientation-invariant 262
   orientation-sensitive 262
   pan 222
   pinch 222, 268, 273
   pre-design 188
   random touches 215
   RegEx 265, 284
   rotate 222, 268, 273
   scale 217, 265
      objects 222
   screen tap 516
   swipe . . 268, 273, 287, 289, 514, 516,
      518
   touch 247

two fingers 290
two hands . . . . . *see also* Multi-Touch,
   183
user-design 188
zoom 268, 273, 287, 289, 570
   camera 222
gG.Techonology . . . . *see also* EEG
Gimbal . . . . *see also* Euler Angles, 378
Gimbal Lock . . . . *see* Euler angles
GIS . . . . *see also* Stereoscopic Touch
GKS 49
Global Navigation Satellite System . . . 350
Golder Section Search . . . . *see* Recognition
Google . . . . *see also* Displays
   Cardboard 4, 652
   Earth 132
   Glass 67, 69, 125, 323
GPGPU . . . . *see* Computer Graphics
GPS 350, 540
GPU . . . . *see* Computer Graphics
Graphical User Interface . . . . *see* GUI
Graspable . . . . *see* TUI
GSR . . . . *see also* Input Devices
GUI . . . . *see also* Models, 3, 12–13, 22, 29,
   301, 501
   radial menu 122
   widgets 122
Guidelines . . . . *see* Interactions, Input
   Devices, Manipulation,
   Navigation
Gyroscopes . . . . *see* Inertial Sensors

H

Hamilton, William 379
Hand-motion tracking . . . . *see also*
   Recognition, 413, 414
   correction step 417
   orientation 420
   prediction step 415–416
Hands 206, 217, 235, 511, 607
   dominant 217
   frame 414
   motion 210
   palm
      contact 229
   size
      differences 218

Haptic . . . . *see also* Stereoscopic Touch
 feedback 241, 247
 passive 229
 stimuli 229
HCI . . . 4–14, 137–139, 144–146, 154, 185,
 293, 300, 303, 310, 511, 521
 experiments 185
 input methodology 299
Head-Mounted Display . . . . *see* HMD
Head-worn systems . . . *see also* HMD, 296
Heap Permute . . . . *see* Algorithms
Hemispherical Displays . . . . . *see* Displays
Hewlett-Packard . . . . *see* HP
HiBall . . . . *see* Input Devices
Hick-Hyman law . . . . *see* Models
Hidden Markov model . . . . *see* HMM
High-Level Petri Nets . . . . . . *see* Petri Nets
HLPN . . . . *see* Petri Nets
HMD . . . *see also* Displays, Oculus Rift, 4,
 67, 131, 229, 455, 456, 459, 484,
 503, 651
 environments 229
 Oculus Rift 67, 116
HMM 255, 256, 299
HoloLens . . . . *see* Displays, Microsoft
Homing . . . . *see* Input Devices
HP
 9-inch CRT touch model 172
 Envy 360 Touchsmart 23
 multi-touch
  infrared 162
Human Interface 429
 full-body motion 430
Human Motor System . . . . *see also* Models
Human Performance 148
Human Visual System . . . . . . *see also* User
 Interfaces, Visual Displays,
 61–62
 human vision 61
 optical schema 61
 properties 61–62
Human-Computer Interaction . . . . *see* HCI
Humans
 movements 431

I

Ideum

Gesture Works 279, 586
GML . . . . . *see also* Recognition, 279
Open Exhibits 279
Immersive . . . . . . *see* Virtual Environments
Immersive Environments . . . . *see* HMD,
 Interactions, Navigation, Virtual
 Environments, Virtual Reality
IMU . . . . *see* Inertial Sensors
In-air . . . . *see* Camera
Inertial Measurement Unit . . . . *see* Inertial
 Sensors
Inertial Sensors . . *see also* Input Devices,
 177, 376, 387–390, 403, 420,
 430, 504
 3-axis 43, 342
 9-axis 44, 435
 data 417, 436
 orientation 436
 accelerometers 43, 342, 387–389,
  413, 417, 419, 420, 437
  axes 388
  linear 388
  tri-axis 388
 advantages and disadvantages . . . 435
 angular 388
 applications 437
  types 388
 data 420
  filtered 439
  normalized 439
  raw 439
 drift-free orientation 451
 error accumulation 44
 errors 436
 examples 448
  general 437–438
  head tracking 455–461
  human body input 462–466
  multiple sensors 461–466
  navigation and compassing . . . .
   448–451
  pointing 451–455
  PrioVR with Unity 471–478
 forces 387
  external motion 387
 frame 415–417
 full-body configuration 437

gyroscopes... 43, 342, 387–390, 413, 417, 424, 437, 504, 556
  angle...................... 558
  angular.................... 389
  angular momentum.......... 556
  angular rate............... 415
  drift................. 413, 435
  fiber optic................ 390
  mechanical................ 389
  MEMS..................... 390
  optical................... 390
  orientation................ 389
  ring laser................. 390
  rotation................... 389
  Sagnac effect.............. 390
  spinning wheel............. 390
  tri-axis data.............. 415
  velocity.................. 389
implementation............... 575
IMU................. 387, 388, 436
magnetometers........ 43, 342, 387, 395–397, 413, 417, 420, 437
  3-axis.................... 435
  description............. 396–397
  measurement vector......... 419
  tri-axis.................. 396
MEMS....................... 43
  Accelerometers............ 389
  Coriolis acceleration......... 390
  Coriolis effect.............. 390
  vibrating wheel............. 390
MEMS errors.... 390–394, 397–401
  accuracy.................. 391
  angle random walk.......... 391
  bias...................... 392
  cross-coupling.............. 393
  dead zone................. 394
  deterministic............... 391
  flicker noise............... 392
  hard iron compensation.. 397–401
  hard iron disturbance........ 397
  misalignment............... 393
  non-linear................. 393
  random.................... 391
  rate random walk............ 391
  scale..................... 392
  sign asymmetry............. 392

sinusoidal noise............. 392
soft iron compensation.. 397–401
soft iron disturbance........ 397
stochastic.................. 391
systematic................. 391
temperature effect........... 394
motion
  translation.................. 387
motion sensing............... 430
multiple sensors
  configuration............... 437
orientation................ 417, 462
  tared...................... 455
  untared................ 457, 462
position...................... 436
raw data..................... 390
sampling..................... 344
single sensor configuration.......... 436–437
systems................. 434–435
tare
  orientation................. 451
  torque...................... 556
Information Theory...... *see also* Models
Infrared Camera.................... 540
Input Devices... *see also* EEG, Microsoft, Multi-Touch, Muscle Group, Nintendo, Speech Recognition, Stereoscopic Touch, USB, 19, 26, 48, 54, 95, 190, 255, 279, 282, 329, 429, 451, 535, 555, 567, 592, 600
  3D.......................... 26
  active devices............... 27
  degrees of freedom........... 26
  frequency of data............. 27
  passive devices............... 27
  3D characteristics............ 26–27
  audio..................... 42–43
  speech recognition........... 42
  ultrasound... *see also* Interactions, 43
  common properties.......... 20–21
  control-display ratio..... 21, 34, 101
  display.................... 34
  gain....................... 34
  Mac OS X example........... 34

cycling 117
data gloves 44–45, 93
  5DT 44
  active 44
  bend-sensing 44
  fiber optic 44
  flexible tubes 44
  pinch 44
  resitive ink 44
  Sayre 44
digital pen . . . . *see also* Multi-Touch,
    24, 166, 177, 189, 193, 196, 258
  active 24
  draw 193
  electromagnetic 166
  inductive coupling 24
  palm - false inputs 193
  passive 190
  pressure 192
  strokes 196
direct 23–24, 46, 430
  questions 23–24
drivers 535, 567
force sensing 22
GamePad 31–40, 118, 580–581
  analog 33
  buttons 118
  digital 34
  dpad 34
  implementation 581–585
  squaring the circle 38
  thumbstick 32, 38
  thumnstick 36
  Xbox One 34
haptic gloves 241
HiBall . . *see also* Navigation, Travel,
    117
  inside-out 117
  outside-in 117
HID 429
home-brew 540
Homing Time 21
indirect 95, 431
input technologies 19–21
joypad 581
joystick 29, 31–40, 46, 429, 580
  airplanes 31

analog 33
digital 34
isometric 38–40
isotonic 38–40
keyboard 22, 27, 28, 120, 154
  chord 28
  homing 21
  implementation 578–580
  Microwriter 29
  typewriter 27
  Writehander 29
Leap Motion 25, 44, 284
microphone 521
mouse . . . 3, 8–10, 22, 24, 26, 29–31,
    94, 120, 122, 182, 301, 523
  3D 40–42, 47, 567, 570, 571
  3D User-Worn 40–42
  control to display ratio 21
  Engelbart, Douglas 3
  Finger Sleeve 42
  implementatin 578–580
  optical tracking 30
  potentiometers 29
  Ring 42
  rollers 29
  Space Navigator 40
  SpaceMouse Pro 41
  track pad 30
  trackball 30
  weighted ball 29
multi-modal . . . . *see also* Interactions
normalization 37
  scaling 37
paddles 580
phantoms 241
physical 94
physiological sensing
  BVP 307, 308
  GSR 45, 307, 308
  skin tempetature 307
pinch glove 119
properties
  device acquisition time 21
  gain 21
  indirect versus direct devices . . 20
  number of dimensions 20
  performance metrics 21

property sensed 20
sampling rate 21
state sensed 21
prototype 535
psychophysiological sensing 45
EEG 45
galanic skin response 45
pupil 45
recognition 47
common issues 47
rotations 570
states 24–25
stylus 121, 163
conductive 167
pressure sensitive 191
tip 194
wacom 191
tangibles 24
taxonomies 47, 49
connection composition 55
design of input devices 50–56
input domain 50
input structure . . . *see also* Buxton,
Bill, 49
layout 55
manipulator operator 50
merge composition 55
orient 49
output domain 50
path 49
position 49
production rules 50
quantify 49
resolution function 50
select 49
state 50
task oriented 49
text 49
the dead zone 35–38
tracking 42, 45, 119, 435
acoustic 42
eye-gazed . . . *see also* EGT, Travel,
118, 293
head 118, 248
jitter 99
large areas 117
optical 173

transfer functions 22, 25, 101
additional mappings 22
appropiate mapping 22
relative-mapping 34
self centering devices 22
translations 570
treadmills 45–46, 117
using Windows API 571–575
virtual 47–48, 131
arcball 48
button 49
hand 95
locator 49
pick 49
rolling ball 48
sphere 48, 122
trackball 48
triad mouse 47
valuator 49
Virtual Motion Controller 119
vision-based 44
monochromatic cameras 44
systems 113
watches . . . . *see also* Interactions,
Orient, Smart Watches, 29
LG 29
WiiMote 43, 44, 118, 131, 594
Balanced Board 117
Motion Plus 21, 44
wiimote 132
Input Taxonomies . . . . . . *see* Input Devices
Intel 165
Interactions . . . . . . *see also* Input Devices,
Manipulations, Multi-Touch,
Techniques, 25, 137, 197, 205,
247, 265, 283, 286, 313, 607
2D 32, 212, 246
3D 31, 87, 129, 131, 198, 240
pure 248
space 248
bi-manual . . . *see also* Manipulations,
28, 40, 104, 163, 197, 218
asymmetry 191
input 96
computer 87
control-to-display ratio 105, 106
degrees of freedom 31–33

four 31, 33
six 25, 26, 40, 42, 93, 95, 102,
   105, 218, 570
digital pen 255
direct . . . . *see also* Input Devices,
   Manipulations, Navigation,
   Stereoscopic Touch, Travel, 22,
   105
guidelines 25–26
Immersive 31
input 255
isomorphic 101
keyboard 28
multi-modal . . . *see also* Multi-Touch,
   166, 189, 193, 196
   touch and pen comparison 192
multi-user 161
non-isomorphic rotations . . . 108–109
pointing 94–230
   cursor 94
   delay 95
   dense 95
   mouse's button 94
   noise 95
   Put-That-There 94
   ray-casting 95
   two-handed 96
   virtual 96
   virtual hands 96
ray-casting selection 95
rotation 87
selection 87, 191
stereo touch
   input modality 212
stereoscopic touch
   fine level of control 218
   Norman's cycle 231
   space 217
tabletop
   shallow area 217
touch 229, 230
   stereoscopic 230
transfer functions . . . . . *see also* Input
   Devices
translation 87
travel task 112
ultrasound

gestures 43
virtual hand
   infinite ray 95
watch
   double tap 29
   seealsoInput Devices 29
   single tap 29
InteraXon . . . . *see also* EEG
Muse 323
Intuitive . . . . *see also* Multi-Touch, 182
Isomorphic Manipulations . . . . *see*
   Manipulations
IVA . . . . *see* ECA

J

JavaScript 519
Joints . . . . *see also* Manipulations
   angles 433
Joysticks . . . . *see* Input Devices

K

Kalman Filters . . . 403, 405, 408, 413, *see*
   also Quaternions, 437
   applications 403, 405
   assumptions 406
   correction component 409
   correction step 405, 408, 417
      observation vector 417
   discrete 405–409
      linear systems 405
   equations
      gain 408
      prediction 408
   estimates
      posteiori 408
      priori 408
   extended 410–411, 422–425
      angular rate 422
      correction step 411
      derivation 411
      non-linear 423
      non-linear navigation equations . . .
         410
      observation model 410
      prediction step 411
      recursive predictor 411
      state model 410

state vector 422
transformation to linear 423
finding Q and R matrices 407
gain 408
Gaussian 408
normal distribution 408
implementation 409
linear quadratic estimation 405
measurement equation 417
measurement noise
covariance matrix 425
measurement process 424–425
linear measurement 424
noise 407
covariance matrix 416
Gaussian 408
noise covariance matrix process . . . . .
424–425
non-linear 410, 417
observation vector 417, 420, 424
gauss–newton method . . . 420–422
gradient descent optimization . . . . .
418–420
optimization
orientation 418
prediction 408
prediction step 405, 415–416
normalization 416
orientation 416
recursive 405
recursive estimator 405
state-space representation 406
system
model 406
state 405
time update 408
update
error covariance 409
weight factor 409
Kalman, Rudolf 405
Keyboard . . . . *see* Input Devices
keystroke-level model . . . . . *see* Interaction,
Models, Techniques
Kinect . . . . *see* Microsoft
KLM . . . . *see* Models

L

LCD . . . . *see* Displays
Leap Motion . . . *see also* Input Devices, 25,
44, 166, 284, 511, 514
data 517–518
firmware
windows 513
frame 517
hands-on project 513–519
installation 512–513
Linux 513
Mac OS X 513
Windows 513
Least Square Estimators . . . . *see* LSQ
LED . . . . *see also* Camera
Legendre, Andien-Marie 404
LG
smart watch 29
light-emitting diode . . . . *see* Camera
Linear Regression Model . . . . . *see* Models
Linux 440
Ubuntu 513
Liquid Crystal Displays . . . . . *see* Displays
LSQ . . . . *see also* Kalman Filters, 403–405
linear adaptive filters 403
non-linear 420

M

Machine Learning . . . . *see* Recognition
MacKenzie, Scott
Fitts law . . . . . . *see also* Models, 139
Magic Lantern . . . . *see* Displays
Magnetometers . . . . *see* Inertial Sensors
Manipulations . . . . *see also* Models,
Interactions, Stereoscopic Touch,
Techniques, Transformations, 87,
183, 243
2D 87
interfaces 87
target acquisition 88
3D 88
acquisition 88
bi-manual
baloon selection 96
camera 229
canonical 88
orientation 88

positioning 88
selection 88
classification 91–93
  decomposition of tasks 91
  egocentric 91
  exocentric 91
device clutching 93
direct 101
guidelines 91
  2D 91
  performance metrics 91
isomorphic 94
muscle groups 25, 93–94
  larger 93
  precision grasp 93
  smaller 93
non-isomorphic 94
non-isomorphic rotations . . . *see also*
  Interactions, 108–109
  definitions 109
  joints 108
  magic 109
  scale factor 108
orientation . . . . *see also* Euler angles,
  Transformations, 89
performance metrics 90
positioning 88
ray-casting
  very large displays 100
scene 240
selection 87, 88
  additional literature 101
  bi-manual 96
  bounding volume 88
  bubble cursor 88
  cubic silk cursor 88
  direction to target 88
  distance to target 88
  flashlight 96
  image-plane 97
  methaphor 88
  object picking 88
  properties 88
  ray intersection with cylinder . . 88
  ray query 88
  selection count 88
  target acquisition 88

  target occlusion 88
  target size 88
shadow 224
spatial rigid object 87
stereoscopic 212
stereoscopic touch 241
testbed evaluation 91
translation 88
uni-manual 218
Mapping 102
  function 102
  scale 103
  touch and object . . . . *see also*
  Stereoscopic Touch, 213
Maps . . . . *see* Navigation
Markov . . . . . *see* HMM, Markov Decision
  Process
Markov Decision Process . . 611, 615, 627,
  629–633, 640
  partially observable 615
MATLAB 351, 401
Matrices . . . . *see also* Euler Angles,
  Quaternions, Transformations,
  335–341, 404
  addition 336
  cofactor 339
  column vector 339
  covariance 407, 408
  determinant 338–339
  diagonal 408
  Eigenvalues 340–341
  Eigenvectors 340–341
  finding
    Kalman Q and R 407
  identity 338
  Jacobian 419, 421
  minor 339
  multiplication 337–338
  non-diagonal elements 408
  reflection 340
  rotation 90, 384, 464, 470
    angle 340
    clockwise 340
    counter-clockwise 340
  rotations 415
  row vector 339
  scalar multiplication 336

trace 336
transformations 339–340
transposition 335
Maya 77, 570
Memex . . . . *see* Bush, Vannevar
MEMS . . . . . *see also* Inertial Sensors, 387,
      413
   magnetometers 397
Methaphors . . . *see* Models, *see* Techniques
Microchip
   dsPIC30F4011 557
Microcontrollers 536, 540, 555, 556
   analog sensors 538
   board 535
   chip 536
      components 536
   interrupts 536
   ioport 536
   pulse width modulation 536, 537,
      555, 557, 560, 563
   serial ports 537
   software environment 538
   transmition ports 536
Microsoft 116, 166, 639
   C# 271, 456, 500, 519, 586
      Tasks 274
   Direct3D 77
   DirectX 77, 330
   flight . . . . *see also* Video Games, 132
   HoloLens 70, 116, 651
   IntelliMouse . . . . *see also* Input
      Devices, 156
   Kinect . . . *see also* Input Devices, 44,
      521, 538
      drivers update 524
      frame sources 525
      frame types 525
      hands-on project 523–533
      implementation 576–578
      installation 523
      near and far modes 522
      requirements 523
      SDK 523
      version 1 . . . . 521, 575–576
      version 2 521–523
      version 2 improvements 522
   kinect 432

PixelSense . . . . *see also* Multi-Touch,
      24, 183
speech recognizer 638
surface 132
tablet
   surface pro 183
tabletop
   Surface 161, 164, 183
   Surface 2.0 164
Visual Studio 271, 523
Windows 12, 183, 441, 483, 513,
      523
Windows 7 . . 161, 176, 268, 271, 287,
      571, 586
Windows 8 . . . . . . 161, 176, 268, 522
Windows API 24, 176, 271, 287,
      567, 576, 593
Windows Vista
   dictation 638
Winows API 571
Xbox 360 521
   GamePad 38, 581
Xbox One 523
   GamePad 34, 581
Microstrain
   3DM-GX1 557
MicroTouch Systems . . . . *see* Multi-Touch,
      163
Mid-Air . . *see also* Camera, Input Devices
Midas Framework
   CLIPS . . . . *see also* Recognition, 279
MIDI 535
Minority Report 430
Mocap Systems . . . . . . *see* Inertial Sensors,
      Motion Capture
Models . . . . *see also* Input Devices,
      Interactions, Manipulations,
      Petri Nets, Stereoscopic Touch,
      Techniques, 137, 639
   a Three-State Model of Graphical
      Input . . . . *see also* Buxton, Bill,
      24, 25, 156–157, 255
   acquisition time 148
   bi-manual 137, 154–156, 189
      asymmetric 155
      coordination 154
      dominant hand 154

example 155
Guiard's action model 155
indirect mapping 156
kinematic movements 154
multi-touch 156
repetitive tasks 154
roles 155
signle unit 154
synchronized 154
definition 137
descriptive 154
a three-state-model 156
bi-manual 154
definition 137
predictive 137
Fitts' law 137–146, 191
2D 145
3D 145
3D - PC Mouse and GamePad . . . .
    see also Input Devices, 145
3D selection by pointing 145
3D stereoscopic and haptics . . 145
adjustment of accuracy 140
amplitude 139
binary index of performance . . 140
discussion 143
effective target width 140
findings 138–139
finger touch 145
index difficulty with adjustment . . .
    140
index of difficulty 140
index of performance 139
Mackenzie 139
movement time 140
percentage of error 140
recommendations 142–143
standard deviation 140
target acquisition 139
throughput 140
width 139
Fitts' law and Woodworth
    guidelines 144
GOMS 148
Hick-Hyman law 138, 146–148
choice reaction time 147
definition 146
information 147
prediction 146
reaction time 146
input devices 255
sketchpad . . . . *see also* Sutherland,
    Ivan, 255
input interaction 255
Kalman
system models 406
Keystroke-Level model 138,
    148–151
assumptions 148
execution time 148
modern use 151
operators and encoding methods . .
    149
predictive 148
type of users 148
linear regression model 138, 152
mathematical 280
mental
fake shadows 224
model human behavior 138
others 152–154
Petri Nets 280
Power law 153
predictive 138–154
psychological processes 138
bits noise 138
channels 138
probability 138
redundancy 138
state diagram 255
Steering law 152
stereoscopic touch
precise selection 205
user perception 205
Woodworth 144
Monitor . . . . *see* Displays
Monkeys 315
Monoscopic . . . . *see* Stereoscopic, 212
Motion Capture 431
Motion Sensing . . *see also* Inertial Sensors,
    430
inertial systems 434–435
magentic 434
orthogonal sensor coils 434

mechanical 433–434
    exoskeleton 433
optical systems
    marker 431–432
    marker-less 432–433
Mouse .... *see* Input Devices
MRI 316
Multi-Touch
gestures 175
taxonomy
    surface gestures 180
Multi-Touch .. *see also* Fingers, Gestures,
    Input Devices, Interactions,
    Manipulation, Models, Petri
    Nets, Recognition, Stereoscopic
    Touch, Strokes, Techniques, 23,
    24, 55, 122, 161, 189, 197, 258,
    271, 279, 283, 284, 286
2D 205
    surfaces 230
3D touch .... *see* Stereoscopic Touch
accesibility 256
are gestures natural? 182–188
    agreement value 183
    gesture set 184
    lessons 187–188
    winning gesture 183
ballon selection methaphor 206
basics 175–176
bi-manual 156
    dual finger stretch 156
capacitive 23, 164
chess player's syndrome ... 175, 193
children 256
clustering 268
considerations 197
contact area 24
contact points 24
coordinates 167
data structure 176
    contact size 176
    id 268
    identification number 176
    timestamp 176, 268
    trace 267
diffused illumination 174
diffused surface illumination 174

displays 119, 161, 197, 198
dollar family .... *see* Recognition
electromagnetic pen-digitizers ... 166
events 175, 272
    touch down 268, 272
    touch move 268, 272
    touch up 268, 272
false contact points 193
false-positive 166
fat fingers 265, 267
    avoiding the problem 267
    iceberg targets 267
fatigue 23
fingers 23, 177, 193, 195
    two 196
frustrated total internal reflection ....
    173–174
FTIR 164
GestIT .... *see also* Recognition, 265
gesture
    definition 177
    design questions 177
Gesture Coder .... *see also*
    Recognition, 265
gesture memorability .... *see also*
    Gestures
gestures ..... *see also* Gestures, 154,
    176–177, 257
guidelines .. *see also* Interactions, 25
hard-touch 23
hardware 164–175
history 161
holdovers 256
homing ... *see also* Input Devices, 21
iceberg targets 267
implementation 586–591
integral tasks 197
integrated cameras 175
interaction 265
interfaces 205
laser light plane 174–175
Midas problem 193
multi-modal 189–196
    touch and pen 189–196
multi-user 161
mutual-capacitance 168–171
    components 170–171

diamond pattern 170
electrodes 168
ghost points 169
grip suppression 170
palm rejection 170
rows and columns 170
trasnparent dual layer 170
trasnparent single layer 170
vendors 170
native dual mode 190
optical touch surfaces 172–173
ELO 172
FlatFrog - Baanto ShadowSense . .
173
FlatFrog - Planar Scatter Detection
173
HP 1983 172
PLATO IV 172
PQ Labs 172
problems 173
palm rejection 190, 194
Pen + Touch = New Tools . . 193–196
bezel menu 195
bezel-crossing gesture 195
brushing 194
carbon copy 194
cross-screen pinch 196
dual-view mode 196
flipping 196
more 196
novice-to-expert 195
post-it note 196
ruler 194
stapler 193
tape curve 194
X-acto knife 193
pervasive 161
points 175, 211, 265
pressure sensing 23
pressure-sensing
piezoelectronics 166
projective capacitive 165–167
air-traffic control 165
detection 166
mutual-capacitance 166, 167
origins? 165
self-capacitance 167

properties 177
beyond the display 178
finger 179
hand postures and shape-based
input 178
latency 179
parallax 179
pressure and contact area 177
touch versus multi-touch 177
Proton++ . . . . see Recognition
public spaces 161
raw 176
raw data 272, 586
Rotate N Translate
friction 198
self-capacitance 167–168
dual layer 168
ghost points 168
multi-pad 167
row and column 168
single layer 167
simultaneous
rotation and translation 197
simultaneous contact points
thirty two 172
soft-touch 23
stereo vision 161
surface 118
surface capacitive 171–172
conductive coating 172
highly senstive 172
tabletop displays 161
figures 199
taxonomy 180–182
surface gestures 180
techniques 197–198
technology 268
timeline 161–164
Apple iPhone 164
bi-manual input 163
bidirectional displays 163
camera-based 162
capacive CRT 162
Diamond-Touch 164
Digital Desk Calculator 163
Dynapro Thin Films 163
Flexible Machine Interface . . . 162

FTIR 164
graspable computing 163
Houdini LLP 164
infrared touch 162
metaDESK 164
Microsoft Surface tabletop . . . 164
Microsoft Surface tabletop 2.0 . . . .
  164
MicroTouch Systems 163
NXT PLC - dispersive signal
  technology 164
Plannar 164
PLATO IV Touch Screen Terminal
  162
Sensitive bending-wave touch . . . .
  164
sensor frame 163
Simon 163
Single Touch 162
Soft Machines 162
SoundTouch 164
tablet 163
tactile array sensor 162
tangile for capacitive 164
Vector Touch 162
Video Place - Video Desk 162
Wacom Tablet 163
Wacom TouchKO 164
waveguide infrared touch 164
Zenith 163
Zyntronic self-capacitive 164
traces 175, 265, 269, 286
transformations
  combination 198
typing 318
vertical displays 161
vision-based optical 173
zoom 196
Muscle Groups . . . . *see* Manipulations
Mutual-Capacitance . . . . . *see* Multi-Touch

N

N-trig
DuoSense . . . . . *see also* Multi-Touch,
  190
Natural Language
  Backus–Naur Form 638

generation 608
grammar
  SRGS 638
Natural User Interfaces . . . . *see* NUI
Nature journal 314
Navigation . . *see also* Interactions, Travel,
  Wayfinding, 25, 111, 118, 119,
  123, 124, 191, 448, 568
3D . . . 76, 87, 111, 129, 576, 579, 581
Apollo Project 410
applications 448
compass 395
  north 395
cues
  vestubular 116
degrees of freedom
  four 129
  six 129
direction 120
execution 120
geological 129
keyboard 28
  awsd 28
knowledge 112
maps 120
  2D 120
  3D 120
negotiation 122
path 120
planning 120
terminology 129
video games 132
Neural Networks 255, 256
Neuroheadsets . . . . *see also* EEG, 321–323
Neuroscience . . . . *see also* BCI, 319
NeuroSky . . . . *see also* EEG, 323
  MindRDR 323
  MindWave 323
Newman, William
  A System for Interactive Graphical
    Programming 255
Nintendo . . . . . . *see also* Input Devices, 76
  NES 34, 581
  Wii 43, 117
  wiiMote 594
Nipkow disk . . . . *see* Displays
NLS 28

NP-complete . . . . *see* Algorithms
NuEcho 638
NUI . . . . *see also* Multi-Touch, 182

O
Oculus Rift . . . . . . *see also* Displays, HMD,
    116, 118, 484, 519, 651
    integration with unity 503–508
Ogre3D 82, 88, 592
    implementation 592–600
    mesh
        binary 82
        xml 82
    MyGui 594
    OgreMax 592
    scene controller 592
    scene manager 83
    version 2.1 592
OLED . . . . *see* Displays
Omni . . . . *see* Virtuix
oN-Line System . . . . *see* NLS
OpenGL 77, 215, 330
Optical Head-Mounted Display . . . . *see*
    Displays
Organic Light Emitting diodes . . . . *see*
    Displays
Orient
    Touchtron 29

P
Palm rejection . . . . *see* Multi-Touch
Palo Alto Research Center . . . . . *see* Xerox
Paradigms . . . . *see* Models, Techniques
Parallax . . . . *see* Stereocopic, Stereoscopic
    Touch
Parallel Programming . . *see also* Computer
    Graphics, 284
    atomic 283
    SIMD 80
PARC . . . . *see* Xerox
Passive Devices . . . . *see* Input Devices
PC Mouse . . *see* Engelbart, Douglas, Input
    Devices
PCAP - Projected Capacitive . . . . *see*
    Multi-Touch
Pen . . . . *see* Input Devices
PERQ Systes Corp.

PERQ 1 190
Petri Nets 255, 284
    arcs 281
    colour 288
    developers 283
    GestIT 284
    gesture detection 279–280
    high-level 280, 283, 284
        algebraic notation 285
        formal definition 281–282
        function 288
        function calling 285
        graphical representation 281
        picking 288
        post-condition 288
        pre-condition 287
        predicate transition net 280
        tokens 288
        variations 280
    low-level 265, 283, 284
        definition 280
        definitoin 280
        gesture detection 280
    PeNTa 282–292
        arc expressions 287–288
        data structure 288
        definition 285–286
        example 289–290
        generic call backs 288
        multi-touch 286–287
        places 288
        priority function 288
        simulation and execution . . . .
        290–292
        structure 289
        target audience 283
        tokens 288–289
        tour 289–290
        update function 288
    places 281
    tokens 265
    transitions 281
        cold 289, 290, 292
        hot 289
Petri, Carl . . . . *see also* Petri Nets, 280
Phoenix parser 640

Physco-physiological .... *see also* EGT,
    Physiological, 309
Physics
    force 388
       external 388
       inertia 388
       Newton's second law of motion .. 388
       springs 388
Physiological .. *see also* Input Devices, 302
    measurements 303
       sympathetic 303
       sympathetic activation 303
Picard, Rosalind
    Affective Computing 301
Piezoelectronics .... *see also* Multi-Touch,
    166
    effect 167
    sensor 167
    sensors 539
PixelSense ... *see* Microsoft, *see* Microsoft
Planer .... *see* Multi-Touch
Point of Sale .... *see* POS
Pointing .... *see* Interactions
POS 166
PQ Labs .... *see also* Multi-Touch, 172
Praxis 321
Precision Grasp .... *see* Manipulations
Predicate Transition Net .... *see* Petri Nets
Predictive Models .... *see* Models
Probability .... *see* Statistics
Project Capacitive .... *see* Multi-Touch
Prompter 321
Proportional-Derivative Controller ... 555,
    557, 561, 563
Props
    tangible 241
Protractor .... *see* Recognition
PrT Net .... *see* Petri Nets
Psychophysiological Sensing .... *see* Input
    Devices
Purely Passive Devices .. *see* Input Devices

Q

Qt framework 586
Quaternions .. *see also* Conversions, Euler
    Angles, Kalman Filters,
    Transformations, 79, 81, 108,

    342, 379–384, 413–415, 417,
    422, 439, 457, 470
    algorithms
       QUEST 424
    complex numbers 379
       imaginary 379
    compound 415
    conjugate 382–384
    difference 464
    equality 381
    gimbal lock
       avoiding 380
    inverse 383
    Kalman extended filters 422–425
    Kalman filters 414–422
    multiplication 381–382
       commutative 382
    norm 383
    normalized 383
    notations 379
    orientation 415, 463
    product 415
    rotations 379, 384, 415
       angle 415
    tared 455
    unit 383
QWERTY .... *see also* Input Devices,
    Typewriter, 28

R

Raspberry Pi 535
Razer OSVR 651
ReactiVision 586
Real-Time 431, 433, 437
    motion 466
Recognition ... *see also* Gestures, Models,
    Multi-Touch, Strokes,
    Techniques, 523
    acoustic pulse 164
    automatic 257
       gestures 1D 257
       gestures 2D 257
    classifiers 194, 255
    cloud of points 257, 264
    context-free grammar 279
    digital pen ... *see also* Input Devices,
    255

dollar algorithms 256–265
  $1 . . . . 256–258, 262, 264
  $1 RotateBy 259
  $1 UniStroke Recognizer 258
  $1 complexity 258
  $1 distance from the candidate to a
    template 259
  $1 limitations 258
  $1 recognizer 258
  $1 resampling 258
  $1 with protractor 262
  $N 257, 262–263
  $N contributions 262
  $N example 263
  $N limitations 263
  $P 257, 258, 264–265
  $P match 264
  bounding box 257
  candidate symbol 263
  centroid 257
  cheat sheet 265
  cloud of points 264
  combinatorial explosion 263
  comparison table 265
  complexity explosion 264
  goals 257
  heap permute 263
  indicative angle 257, 259, 261
  linear 265
  linear versus constant 262
  multiple strokes 258, 262, 263,
    265
  nearest neighbor approach 257
  orientation-invariant 262
  orientation-sensitive 262
  permutations 263–265
  protractor gesture recognizer . . 257
  re-scaling 257
  resampling 257
  rotation invariance discrimination
    257
  scaling 261
  shape 261
  single strokes 257
  translation 257, 261
  uni-strokes 265
dynamic programming 255

EEG 323–324
Elastic Matching 257
facial expressions 521
feature-based classifiers 255
features 258
FETouch 267
  algorithm 269–270
  angle rotation 269
  features 274
  grip 269
  queue 268
  real-time 269
  selecting correct gesture 274
  spread 269
  thread-safe 268
  trace 269
  trace vector 269
  traces 269
FETouch+ 270–274
  algorithm 272–274
  events 272
  multi-thread 271
  noise removal 273
  real-time 270
  trace 272
  trace point 272
  window size 272
FETouch++
  finger count 274
  implementation 274–277
  split function 274
FETouch: Feature Extraction Touch . .
  267–277
FSM 255
GestIT 265, 284
Gesture Coder 265, 279, 284
gestures 255, 256, 430
golden section search 257
  algorithm 261
  golden ratio 261
handwritting 255
hill-climbing approach 261
HMM 255
interactive graphical programming . . .
  255
Machine Learning 301
machine learning 610

advantages.................. 610
reinforcement 610, 615, 627,
    629
supervised 610, 611
temporal................... 610
motion....................... 388
motion detection.............. 387
multi-touch...... 255, 258, 279, 284
neural networks................ 255
oblique position............ *see also*
    Multi-Touch, 258
PeNTa 283, 284
Proton.................... 265, 279
Proton++ 265, 279, 284
    RegEx 265
reviews 255
Rubine algorithm 256
SHARK2 257
    proportial shape............. 264
speech 521, 608
state-diagrams................. 279
strokes....................... 257
template matching 255
templates................. 257, 258
    sub-set 257
training.................. 256, 284
training set 257, 265
Recursive Least Squares .... *see* RSQ
RegEx 265, 279, 284
Regular Expressions .... *see* RegEx
Roll-Pitch-Yaw ..... *see* Aircraft Principal
    Axes
Rotations .... *see* 3D Rotations,
    Transformations
RS232........................... 438
RSQ.... *see also* Kalman Filters, 403–405
Rubine Algorithm.................. 256
Rubine algorithm ... *see also* Recognition,
    258

S

Samsung.......................... 118
    Galaxy VR 651
Scaling .... *see* Transformations
Scene Managers .. *see* Computer Graphics
Schmidt, Stanley.................. 410
Screen cursor................ *see* Cursor

Sensomora Simulator................ 128
Sensor fusion...................... 413
    measurement noise
        covariance matrix 425
    measurement process 424–425
    noise covariance matrix process .....
        424–425
Set Theory 283
Shannon-Hartley Theorem .... *see also*
    Models, 139
SHARK2 ...... *see also* Recognition, 257
Signals ...... *see also* DSP, 365, 392, 555
    continuous 349
    deterministic 349
    discrete 349
    elementary 353
    energy 352–353
    even.......................... 349
    exponential function 355
    Gaussian function.............. 357
        bell shaped 357
    impulse function............... 353
    non-periodic.................. 349
    odd.......................... 349
    periodic...................... 349
    power.................... 352–353
    ramp function 355
    random 349
    the cosine function 354–355
    the sine function 354–355
    unit step function.......... 353–354
Sketchpad .. *see also* Sutherland, Ivan, 3, 5,
    8
Smart watches .. *see also* Input Devices, 29
Smartphone 67
SmartPhones 651
Smartphones............... 44, 161, 301
    projected capacitive .... *see also*
        Multi-Touch, 165
    samsung 118
    Simon
        single-touch 163
Space Navigator .... *see* Connexion, Input
    Devices
SpaceMouse Pro .... *see* Input Devices
Spaceship.......................... 120
Spatial .... *see also* Navigation

awareness 121
criteria 299
EGT
    area-based 299
    dispersion-based 299
    velocity-based 299
location 224
misaligned . . . . *see also* Stereoscopic, 208
separability . . . *see also* Multi-Touch, 198
understanding 123, 124
Speech 313, 318, 607
recognition 608, 639
spoken dialog systems 617
spoken language understanding . . 608
text-to-speech engine 608
SPI 438
Statistics . . . . *see also* Kalman Filters, 610, 639
brief review 407–408
covariance 407
    matrix 407, 408
expected value 407
probabilty 407
random variable 407
Stereo Touch . . . . . *see* Stereoscopic Touch
Stereoscopic Touch . . . . *see also* Multi-Touch, 217, 231
accomodation-convergence 209
anaglyph 207
apex 217
application space 241
ballistic 214, 242, 243
    phase 228, 235
balloon selection 218–219
benefits 207
binocular
    disparity cues 208
brute-force interface 206
convergence
    3D Position 208
correction phase 215, 235
cues 247
depth discrimination 246–248
    misaligments 247
design paradigms 210–212

direct 207
    interaction with stereoscopically . . 207
disparity cues 208, 209
dominant hand 216
extraretinal cues 237
    proprioception 237
    vestibular 237
fish tank 223
haptic feedback 207, 208
hardware
    mechanical actuators 229
    ultrasound actuators 229
imperceptible shift 235
indirect 208
innacuracies
    users 245
intended touch position 205
    examples 205
inter-ocular distance 234
interaction 241
interface design space 205
interfaces 206
manipulation 241–242
manipulation techniques . . . 233–236
    illusion paradigm 233
    spatial parameters 234–236
    visualization parameters 233–234
micro-cycles 232
misalignment 207
    range 208
motion cues 242
move the surface paradigm 210–211
    3D volume 210
    direct 211
    eye accomodation 211
    large disparity 211
    top projection 211
    transparent 210
move the touches paradigm 211–212
object attraction shift 248
object shifts during touch . . . 240–241
occlusion 209
occlusion cues 208, 209

parallax 207
parallax plane
    zero 217
parallax problem 207–210
    constraints 207
    different visual impressions . . . 207
    half-spaces 207
    major challenge 208
    negative 207, 208
    positive 207, 208
    strong positive 208
    zero 207, 224, 233
passive polarization-based 207
perceptual detection threshold . . . 239
perceptual illusions 229–252
perceptual illusions paradigm . . . 212
physical movement 237
precise selection 205
precision 213
problems 206–207
    adequate visual feedback 205
    missing hover 205
    occlusion 205
    precision 205
projection 209
scene shifts 236–241
    depth 237
semi-transparent 224
sensitive 207
separate
    interactive surface and screen . . . . .
        207
shadow hand 226–227
shadow hand versus void shadows . . .
        227–228
shallow depth 208
spherical cursor 217, 218
states
    interaction 240
    specification 240
tabletop 216–223
techniques
    balloon selection 212
    fishnet methaphor 212
    generalized scaled shift . . 242–246
    triangle cursor 212

third-order polynomial interpolation
        238
tonic 232
touch 212
touch gesture 208
touching parallaxes 212–216
    dominant eye 213
    intended object 212
    middle eye projection 212
    non-dominant eye 213
    object selection 212
    shadow 213
    touch point 212
traceable features 205
transparents props 211
triangle cursor 216–218
    3-DOF 217
    4-DOF 216
    conflict with other gestures . . . 222
    degrees of freedom 217
    design considerations . . . 221–223
    different height mappings . . . .
        222–223
    indirect 217
    multiple users 221–222
    scale 217
    widget versus tool 221
Triangle versus Balloon 219–221
user interaction states 231–232
    execution 232
    observation 231
    real 232
    specification 231
user perception 205
visual depth 207
visually pereceived
    motion 237
void shadows 224–226
Strokes . . . . *see also* Multi-Touch, 177, *see
        also* Recognition, 257, 265
    1D 263
    2D 120, 263
    multi-stroke 262
    multiple 258
    detection 286
    order 264
    shape 261

single 257, 258
Stroop Color-Word Interference Test . . *see also* EGT, User Studies, 305
   congruent 305
   incongruent 305
   limitations 307
Stylus . . . . *see* Input Devices
Support Vector Machine . . . . *see* SVM
Surround-Screen Displays . . . *see* Displays
Sutherland, Ivan . . . . *see also* Sketchpad, 3, 129
SVM 308
Synamptics . . . . *see also* Multi-Touch, 170

T

Tablets 44, 55, 161, 301, 586
   iPad 161
   projected capacitive . . . . *see also* Multi-Touch, 165
Tangible . . . . *see* TUI
Tangible User Interfaces . . . . *see* TUI
Taxonomies . . . . *see also* Interactions, Manipulations, Multi-Touch, Navigation, Travel, Techniques
   egocentric
      virtual hand metaphors 93
      virtual pointer metaphors 93
   EGT
      fixation tasks 299
   exocentric
      automatic scaling 92
      world-in-miniature 92
   interactive surfaces . . . . *see also* Multi-Touch
   points-of-view 92
   selection . . . . *see also* Manipulations, 91
   travel tasks 115
      decomposition 115
      decomposition 115
      flying carpet 115
      methaphor 115
      spaceship travel 115
Techniques . . . . *see also* Interactions, Manipulations, Models, Multi-Touch, Stereoscopic Touch, Taxonomies, 610

2D 207
balloon selection 96
bi-manual 104
bubble cursor 88
direct
   go-go 101
   virtual hand 101
dollar family 256
flashlight 96
   aperture 97
   illumination 96
free-hand 217
hybrid 103
   aggregation 103
   HOMER 103
   integration 103
   PRISM 105
   scale-world-grab 104
   Voodoo Dolls 104
image-plane 97
   arm fatigue 99
   framing hands 98
   guidelines 98
   head crusher 97
   lifting palm 98
   occlusion 99
   stereo rendering 99
   sticky finger 98
magic paradigm 248
   3D Interaction 248
pointing 101
PRISM
   axis independent scaling 107
   offset recovery 106
ray-casting for large displays
   parallax 100
ray-casting selection
   bent pick ray 95
silk cursor 88
   semi-transparency 88
spotlight 96
SQUAD 99
   cone-casting 99
   progressive refinement 99
   sphere-casting 99
stereoscopic
   shadow hand 224

void shadows 224
stereoscopic touch
    trackball methaphor 218
    usable 230
    trackball methaphor 216
virtual reality
    redirected walking 229
    void shadows methaphor 224
    World-in-Miniature 94, 103
Temporal
    criteria 299
The Dead Zone . . . . *see* Input Devices
The Image of a City 124
The Mother of All Demos . . *see* Engelbart,
    Douglas
The Psychology of Human-Computer
    Interaction 5, 145, 148
Thumbstick . . . . . *see* Input Devices, Video
    Games
Touch . . . . *see* Input Devices, Multi-Touch
Touch Konnection Oasis . . . . *see also*
    Multi-Touch, 172
Trackball . . . . *see* Input Devices
Transfer Functions . . . . . *see* Input Devices
Transformations . . . . *see also* Aircraft
    Principal Axes, Euler Angles,
    Matrices, Stereocopic Touch,
    Quaternions, Vectors, 77
    angular displacement 79
    direction 78
    euler angles
        angular displacement 79
        order 79
    matrices 339
    orientation 78, 224, 455
    rotations 47, 216, 218
        3D 47, 77–79
        angular difference 342
    scaling 47
    stereoscopic
        translation shift 237
    translations 47, 242, 243
        3D 77–79
Translations . . . . *see* Transformations
Travel . . *see also* Interactions, Navigation,
    Wayfinding, 112, 118, 122
    3D 111, 112, 129

3D tasks 112–113
    naïve search 112, 130
    constraint 112
    exploration 112
    maneuvering 112
    primed search 112, 130
    search 112
    travel-by-scaling 113
3D tasks characteristics 113
engine 111
locomotion 116
    virtual 118
    walking 116
    walking in place 117
maps 120
    2D 120
    3D 120
motion 122
non-isomorphic rotations 122
path 120
physical 116–117
    locomotion 116, 118
    realistic 118
planning strategies
    drawing a path 120
    points along a path 120
    user representation 120
presence
    association 117
ray-casting 121
route-planing techniques
    target-based 120
search 112
target-based techniques
    manual entry 122
    map-based 121
    menu-based 122
    object selection 122
    placing target object 122
    wim-based 121
    zoom-based 121
task decomposition 114–115
    sub-tasks 114
    taxonomy 115
techniques 114
    active 114
    grabbing the air 122

passive 114
physical 114
semi-automated 114
virtual 114
testbed 130
naïve search 130
primed search 130
selection 130
viewing direction 118
virtual techniques 118–122
camera-in-hand 119
eye-gazed tracking 118
gaze-directed steering 118
head tracking 118
pointing 119
route planning 119, 120
semiautomated steering 119
steering 118
torso-directed steering 119
Triangles
isosceles 217
position 217
TUI . . *see also* Input Devices, Multi-Touch,
24, 163, 164, 177, 210
multi-touch 173
TUIO . . . . *see also* Multi-Touch, 586
Tunnel Vision . . . . *see* Displays
Typewriter
Sholes–Glidden 28

U
UART 438
UI . . . . *see* User Interfaces
Ultrasonic . . . . *see also* Camera, Input
Devices
sensors 538, 541–543
input and output 543
sonar 539
ultrasonography 539
UNC 117
United Kingdom
air traffic control . . . . *see also*
Multi-Touch, 165
Unity Game Engine . . . 455, 456, 471, 483,
592
camera 493
character 493

collision detection 84
directional light 494
game material 496
game object 495
game scene 486–492
GUI 501–503
material to object 499
mouse 488
new project 486
script 500–501
sky 494
texture 498
user interface 484–486
version 4 483
version 5 483
Unity Technology . . . . *see* Unity Game
Engine
University of North Carolina . . . . *see* UNC
Unreal Game Engine 330
Usability 6
USB . . . . *see also* Input Devices, 438
port 440
User Interfaces . . . *see also* Input Devices,
26, 29, 49, 131, 191, 248, 318
2D 87, 94
3D 4, 13–14, 26–27, 61, 87, 94,
103, 112, 247
system 26
BCI
dictation systems 318
brain 318
designer 94, 194
GKS
string 49
stroke 49
illusions 229
input 26
motion sensing 430
multimodal 607
Tangibles 163
text 301
User Studies
3D astrophysical simulations 131
are gestures natural? . . . . *see also*
Multi-Touch, *see also*
Multi-Touch, 183–185
bias 183

commands 183
follow up 185–186
observations 185
others 186–188
bi-manual 96, 155
adapting Guiard's model 155
cognitive benefits of bi-manual
input 191
cooperative 191
others 191–192
symmetry 192
toolglass 191
direct 102
Display Selection Techniques for Text
Manipulation 10–12, 29
ECA
alcohol 618–625
EEG
quadcopter 315
transferring bits 315
EGT
Affective Computing 307
algorithms comparison 299
fixation identification task 299
fixational eye movements 309
isolation of pupil 294
others 305–306
pupil affective stimulation 305
pupil monitoring 307
experiment
implementation . . . *see* Experiment
module
eye tracking
psycho-physiological 310
Fitts' law . . . . *see also* Models
first study: 1954 139
research impact 139, 142–143
second study:1964 140
fMRI
connecting images 316
generating text 316
recognizing yes-no answers . . 317
gaze-directed steering 118
gesture memorability . . . . *see also*
Gestures, 188
head tracking 132
interactive surfaces

review 206
large-scale environments 131
multi-modal
findings 196
multi-touch
3D manipulations 182
contact shape and physics 197
gestures for 3D objects 182
mobile interaction 182
one-hand versus two-hand 197
orientation for oblique touches . . . .
197
others 197–198
Rotate N Translate 198
taxonomy . . *see also* Multi-Touch,
180
transformation better separate or
combined? 197
User-Defined Gestures for Surface
Computing 180
navigation 128–134
4-DOF comparision 132
more 133–134
others 131–134
search 130
non-stereo display versus hmd . . . 131
Pen + Touch = New Tools 190
findings 196
perceptual detection threshold
2-Alternatives-Forced-Choice . . . .
239
pointing comparison 95
pupil diameter monitoring 307
ray-casting
very-large-displays 100
scene shifts
large 238
selection
SQUAD 99
shallow-depth . . . . *see also*
Stereoscopic Touch241
stereoscopic touch
ballistic arm 212
depth discrimination . . . . . *see also*
Stereoscopic Touch
hand shaping and the object . . 206
others 248

touching parallaxes 215
steresocopic touch
   triangle versus balloon 219
touch 133
   seven degrees of freedom 133
travel testbed .... *see also* Travel
   flags 130
   gaze-directed 130
   go-go 130
   painted circle 130
   pointing 130
visualization
   medicine 134

V

Vectors ... *see also* 3D, Matrices, 330–335,
   373, 384, 404, 415
3D 293, 383
addition 332
   commutative 332
basis 333–334
cross product 342
   3D 335
direction 330
distance 330
dot product 334
equality 332
magnitude 334
negation 333
normalization 334
orthogonal 342
perpendicular 335
rotation 452
scalar multiplication 333
substraction 333
two-vector orientation 342
   example 342
unit 334
Video Games
Doom 75
Mario Bros 76
Quake 75
Video Games .... *see also* Computer
   Graphics, Input Devices,
   Navigation, 43, 112, 132, 388,
   471, 568
accelerator 119

Arma II 132
awsd ..... *see also* Input Devices, 28
camera
   first-person 455
developers 321
development 38, 483
   multi-platform 483
Dirt2 132
engine 592
environment 504
Façade 319
   dialog 320
joysticks .. *see also* Input Devices, 31
   plane simulator 32
Marble Blast Ultra
   transfer function 38
Microsoft Flight 132
personality models 319–321
players 321
   casual 132
   experienced 132
Prom Night 320
social simulation 319, 320
Star Wars: The Old Republic
   dialog 320
steering wheel .. *see also* Travel, 119
thought controlled 323
Versu 320
   Blood and Laurels 321
Wii 43
Wings of Prey 132
Virtual Devices .... *see* Input Devices
Virtual Environments .. *see also* Computer
   Graphics, 82, 88, 91, 94, 103,
   118–120, 122–124, 145, 600
3D 111, 118, 120, 123, 246, 503
camera 234, 237, 243
helicoper 315
immersive 116, 117, 503
objects 229
   augmenting 230
   shifts 230
props ... *see also* Stereoscopic Touch,
   211
   opaque 211
   physical 229
   transparent 211, 229

right-hand system .... *see also*
    Computer Graphics
scene 224, 230, 233, 241
world 455
    scene 237
world space 77
Virtual Humans .... *see* ECA
Virtual Reality 455, 503, 519, 651
    CAVE 236
    fish tank ...... *see also* Stereoscopic
      Touch, 223
    headset 651
    redirected walking 229
Virtual Retina Displays ...... *see* Displays
Virtual Scene ... *see* Virtual Environments
Virtual Worlds .. *see* Virtual Environments
Virtuix
    Omni 116–118
Vision-based .. *see* Camera, Input Devices
Visual Displays .... *see also* Displays
    binocular cues 64
      disparity 64
      stereopsis 64
    characteristics 63–65
      dots per inch 63
      ergonomics 63
      field of regard 63
      field of view 63
      light transfer 63
      refresh rate 63
      screen geometries 63
      spatial resolution 63
    depth 65
    depth cues 63
      blur 65
      categories 63
      color 65
      human perception 63
      more 65
    how to convey depth 64
    monocular cues 64
      pictorial cue 64
    motion parallax 65
      perspective 65
    oculomotor cues 65
      accommodation 65
      convergence 65

      divergence 65
      muscle tension 65
Visualizations
    3D volumetric .... *see also* Computer
      Graphics
    medical .... *see also* Stereoscopic
      Touch, 241
Voltage
    DC 536, 537

W
Wacom 163, 164, 166, 172
    stylus
      SD42x 191
Walking .... *see* Travel
Watch .... *see* Input Devices
Wayfinding .. *see also* Navigation, Spatial,
    Stereoscopic Touch, Travel, 111,
    122–128
    categories
      applications 123
      complex environments 123
      transfer spatial knowledge 123
    cognitive map 123, 126, 234
      hierarchical model 126
      landmark, route, survey model ....
      126
    cognitive process 111, 122
    cues
      artificial 127
    direct environmental exposure ... 124
      districts 124
      edges 124
      landmarks 124
      nodes 124
      paths 124
      routes 124
    egocentric 125
    exocentric 125, 126
    large-scale virtual enviroments .. 126
    mental map 111, 123
    mental model 126
    navigation model 126
    procedural knowledge 125
    reference frames 125
    route knowledge 126
    spatial comprenhension 123

spatial knowledge 124
   landmark 124
   procedural 124
   survey 124
spatial understanding 124
   images 124
   maps 124
   sound 124
   speech 124
   video 124
   virtual environments 124
strategies 126, 128
   environment-centered 127
   real-wolrd 127
   user-centered 127
transfer spatial understanding . . . 123
virtual mazes 126
Weiser, Mark 182
Widget 208, 221, 222, 241, 248
WiiMote . . . . *see* Input Devices
WIMP . . . *see also* GUI, Models, 3, 12–13, 22, 24, 29, 301
WinAPI . . . . *see* Microsoft
Windows API . . . . *see* Microsoft
Windows-Icons-Menus-Pointers . . . . . . *see* WIMP
Wireless . . . . . . *see also* Input Devices, 433, 438, 466
Workbenches . . . . *see* Displays
World-in-Miniature . . *see also* Techniques, 120

X

X-acto knife . . . *see also* Multi-Touch, 193
Xbox . . . . *see* Microsoft
Xerox
   PARC 12, 163
   Star System 5, 12
   Star Workstation 10
XML 279, 640

Y

YEI 430
   3-Space Sensor 430, 435, 437
      data 439
      installing 439
      Mac OS X 440

using 438–439
Windows 441
3-Space Sensors
   commands 439
   Linux 440
   tare 451
3-Space-Sensor
   API 447–448
   communication 441
   connection 442
   disconnect 444–445
   examples 466
   receiving ASCII command 442–443
   receiving binary command . . . 444
   sending ASCII command 442
   sending binary command 443–444
   streaming communication 445–447
   streaming example 446–447
Prio VR 430
   calibration 469
   examples 466–478
   motion 478
Skeletal 467
   API 470
YEI 3-Space Mocap Studio 478
YEI MotionBuilder Plug-in 478–479

Z

Zenith 163